America Reads

Projection in Literature

Counterpoint in Literature

Outlooks through Literature

Exploring Life through Literature

The United States in Literature
ALL MY SONS EDITION

The United States in Literature
THE GLASS MENAGERIE EDITION

England in Literature
MACBETH EDITION

England in Literature
THE TAMING OF THE SHREW EDITION

EDYTHE DANIEL
Associate Professor of Education, Supervisor of Off-Campus Student Teaching of Secondary English and Speech, Wisconsin State University, Platteville. Formerly teacher of English and Speech, Lincoln Junior High School, Kenosha, Wisconsin

EDMUND J. FARRELL
Assistant Executive Secretary, National Council of Teachers of English. Formerly Supervisor of Secondary English, University of California, Berkeley; formerly English Department Chairman, James Lick High School, San Jose, California

ALFRED H. GROMMON
Professor of Education and English, Stanford University, Formerly teacher of English and department head, Ithaca High School, Ithaca, New York, Editor, The Education of Teachers of English for American Schools and Colleges, *National Council of Teachers of English*

OLIVE STAFFORD NILES
Consultant in Reading, State Department of Education, Hartford, Connecticut; Lecturer, American International College, Springfield, Massachusetts; formerly Director of Reading, Public Schools of Springfield

ROBERT C. POOLEY
Formerly Professor of English, University of Wisconsin; and Director, Wisconsin English-Language Arts Curriculum Project. First Chairman of the Board of Trustees of the Research Foundation of the National Council of Teachers of English. First Recipient of the W. Wilbur Hatfield Award for extraordinary contributions to the teaching of English

PROJECTION
in literature

SCOTT, FORESMAN AND COMPANY ● Glenview, Illinois

Dallas, Tex. ● Oakland, N.J. ● Palo Alto, Cal. ● Tucker, Ga. ● Brighton, England

PROJECTION
in literature

ROBERT C. POOLEY
EDYTHE DANIEL
EDMUND J. FARRELL
ALFRED H. GROMMON
OLIVE STAFFORD NILES

ILLUSTRATIONS by Franz Altschuler, 130, 229, 233, 249; Robert Amft, 527; Robert Blechman, 267; Ralph Creasman, 68–69, 193, 216–217, 222. 225, 274; Herb Danska, 71, 78–79, 83, 197; Joe De-Velasco, 191; Pat Doyle, 515, 518, 519, 525. 531, 533, 535; John Everds, 336–337, 347, 530, 537: Bill Gregg, 242; Cynthia Hellyer, 372–373; Elmer Jacobs, 368–369; Zbigniew Jastrzebski, 277; Herb Kane, 209; Ken Kenniston, 284–285, 295; Carl Kock, 4, 11, 14, 121, 126, 445; Joan Landis, 380, 381: Sally Linn, 415; Warren Linn, 97; Charles Mikolaycak, 495,501; Tak Murikami, 257; Ralph Pinto, 455; Wade Ray, 314–315; Phil Renaud, 35, 39; Leslie Robin, 433, 436, 479; George Roth, 139, 143, 151; Hy Roth, 465, 472, 516–517, 520; Fred Steffen, 323, 329; Arno Sternglass, 488; George Suyeoka, 43, 109, 181, 352; Phero Thomas, 54, 57, 303, 307; Tomi Ungerer, 528 PHOTOGRAPHY by Peter Amft, 24, 378; Robert Amft, 19, 179, 272–273, 374, 383, 452; James Ballard, 400, 539; George Olexy, 168–169, 172

PICTURE CREDITS: Courtesy of The Field Museum of Natural History, 393, 395, 399, 401, 402, 405, 406, 408, 409, 410, 411, 418, 419, 429 (photography by James Ballard); courtesy of Barbara Frankel, 427 (photography by James Ballard); Stef Leinwohl, 513; Courtesy of Nigerian Antiquities Service, 421 (photography by James Ballard); courtesy of The University of Pennsylvania Museum, 413

COVER   Squeeze by Sven Lukin, 1968, courtesy of the artist, photo by Al Mozell, NY

ISBN: 0-673-10218-1

2345678910-VHJ-858483828180797877

The authors and editors of *Projection in Literature* wish to acknowledge the important contributions to this anthology made by a group of wise and dedicated teachers and administrators. They suggested areas of study appropriate to students at this age level; they tried out materials in classrooms; they assessed the effect of various selections on students; and they sent us thoughtful analyses of why a given piece was, or was not, suitable for inclusion in a junior-high-school anthology. The students also helped in commenting with candor and perception on the selections they were asked to read.

Miss Mary Jo Cannizzaro, Governor Mifflin Junior High School,
    Shillington, Pennsylvania
Mr. William E. Dunkum, Garfield Junior High School,
    Berkeley, California
Miss Caroline Flad, Alexander Hamilton Junior High School,
    Cleveland, Ohio
Sister Maureen Francis SCN, St. Agnes School,
    Louisville, Kentucky
Mrs. Dorothy Johnson, Northlawn School,
    Streator, Illinois
Mrs. Lorraine Kapell, Walnut Hills High School,
    Cincinnati, Ohio
Mr. Fred Kinkin, Lincoln School,
    Spring Valley, Illinois
Mrs. Naomi Madgett, Northwestern High School,
    Detroit, Michigan
Mrs. Florence Meaghan, Franklin Junior High School,
    Cedar Rapids, Iowa
Mrs. Mary Ellen Murphy, Monroe Junior High School,
    Mason City, Iowa
Mrs. Lena Sawtelle, Thomas Williams Junior High School,
    Cheltenham Township Schools, Elkins Park, Pennsylvania
Mr. Glenn Scharfenorth, McClure Junior High School,
    Western Springs, Illinois
Mrs. Elizabeth Spirduso, Oakland Park School,
    Streator, Illinois

CONTENTS

UNIT **1** | *Standpoint*

INTRODUCTION PAGE 2

4 **THE DUBBING OF GENERAL GARBAGE** | Herman Wouk
NOVEL EXCERPT

16 **SPEED ADJUSTMENTS** | John Ciardi
POETRY

18 **THANKSGIVING HUNTER** | Jesse Stuart
SHORT STORY

24 **STRAWBERRY ICE CREAM SODA** | Irwin Shaw
SHORT STORY

34 **BEAUTY IS TRUTH** | Anna Guest
SHORT STORY

42 **THE LESSON** | Jessamyn West
SHORT STORY

54 **DEATH BY DROWNING** | Richard Eberhart
POETRY

56 **THE PHEASANT HUNTER** | William Saroyan
SHORT STORY

68 **OLD AGE STICKS** | E. E. Cummings
POETRY

70 **THE GIFT** | John Steinbeck
SHORT STORY

UNIT 2 | *A Gallery of Heroes*

INTRODUCTION PAGE 94

96 **SWINGER** | Paul Darcy Boles

SHORT STORY

106 **SPEAKING: THE HERO** | Felix Pollak

POETRY

108 **THE RESCUE** | Max Steele

SHORT STORY

116 **THE COMPANION** | Yevgeny Yevtushenko

POETRY

119 **THE TWO HOAXERS** | Stratis Myrivilis

SHORT STORY

129 *from* **HARRIET TUBMAN** | Ann Petry

BIOGRAPHY

138 **THE PHARMACIST'S MATE** | Budd Schulberg

TELEVISION PLAY

165 **A TIME OF GREATNESS** | Dorothy Johnson

SHORT STORY

178 **ADVICE TO A KNIGHT** | T. H. Jones

POETRY

180 **THE CAMPERS AT KITTY HAWK** | John Dos Passos

ESSAY

Poetry I

INTRODUCTION PAGE 189

190   **SIMULTANEOUSLY** | David Ignatow

192   **THE DEMON OF THE GIBBET** | Fitz-James O'Brien

194   **RAIN** | Ross Parmenter

195   **ONE A.M.** | X. J. Kennedy

197   **THE PASTURE** | Robert Frost

198   **GOOD-BY AND KEEP COLD** | Robert Frost

200   **THE CIRCUS; OR ONE VIEW OF IT** | Theodore Spencer

203   **THE CONTRAPTION** | May Swenson

205   **CRYSTAL MOMENT** | Robert P. Tristram Coffin

UNIT **3** *The Outsider*

INTRODUCTION PAGE 206

208 **FIRST PRINCIPAL** | A. B. Guthrie
SHORT STORY

216 **THE NEW KID** | Murray Heyert
SHORT STORY

228 **NANCY** | Elizabeth Enright
SHORT STORY

241 **I'M NOBODY** | Emily Dickinson
POETRY

242 **WIN OR LOSE** | Brian Glanville
SHORT STORY

249 **SLED** | Thomas E. Adams
SHORT STORY

256 **THE BAROQUE MARBLE** | E. A. Proulx
SHORT STORY

265 **A LOUD SNEER FOR OUR FEATHERED FRIENDS** | Ruth McKenney
ESSAY

271 **THE BOY WHO LAUGHED AT SANTA CLAUS** | Ogden Nash
POETRY

274 **THE SKUNK** | Robert P. Tristram Coffin
POETRY

275 **HUNGER** | Richard Wright
AUTOBIOGRAPHY

UNIT 4 | *Yesterday and Tomorrow*

INTRODUCTION **PAGE 282**

284   **THE MONSTERS ARE DUE ON MAPLE STREET** | Rod Serling
      TELEVISION PLAY

299   **RIKKI-TIKKI-TAVI** | Rudyard Kipling
      SHORT STORY

312   **MACAVITY: THE MYSTERY CAT** | T. S. Eliot
      POETRY

314   **THE STORYTELLER** | Saki (H. H. Munro)
      SHORT STORY

320   **JABBERWOCKY** | Lewis Carroll (Charles Lutwidge Dodgson)
      POETRY

322   **RIP VAN WINKLE** | Washington Irving
      SHORT STORY

336   **THE UGLY DUCKLING** | A. A. Milne
      DRAMA

352   **VIRTUOSO** | Herbert Goldstone
      SHORT STORY

358   **METROPOLITAN NIGHTMARE** | Stephen Vincent Benét
      POETRY

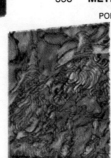

Poetry II

INTRODUCTION PAGE 363

364 **THE BUILDERS** | Sara Henderson Hay

365 **THE FOX AND THE GRAPES** | Marianne Moore

366 **REQUIEM FOR A MODERN CROESUS** | Lew Sarett

367 **TO A DEAD GOLDFISH** | O. B. Hardison, Jr.

368 **ARTIFACT** | Sheila Pritchard

372 **TIME OUT** | John Montague

374 **WHO KNOWS IF THE MOON'S** | E. E. Cummings

376 **AT THE AQUARIUM** | Max Eastman

377 **THOUGHTS IN A ZOO** | Countee Cullen

378 **STREET WINDOW** | Carl Sandburg

379 **PRIMER LESSON** | Carl Sandburg

380 **THE FORECAST** | Dan Jaffe

381 **HELD BACK** | Laurie Abrams

UNIT 5 | *In the Beginning...*

INTRODUCTION PAGE 382 | Susan Taubes

388   **THE STORYTELLING STONE**

394   **THE BLACKFOOT GENESIS**

400   **HOW THE LAME BOY BROUGHT FIRE FROM HEAVEN**

402   **HOW RAVEN HELPED THE ANCIENT PEOPLE**

403   **MAN CHOOSES DEATH**

403   **THE ORIGIN OF DEATH**

404   **WHY THE SUN AND THE MOON LIVE IN THE SKY**

405   **THE MAN WHO ACTED AS THE SUN**

411   **HOW THE ANIMALS GOT THEIR COLOR**

411   **HOW THE ANIMALS GOT THEIR TAILS**

412   **WHY THERE ARE CRACKS IN TORTOISE'S SHELL**

414   **WHY THE WOODPECKER HAS A LONG BEAK**

415   **THE DOG, THE SNAKE, AND THE CURE OF HEADACHE**

416   **WHY THE STORK HAS NO TAIL**

419   **THE LEFTOVER EYE**

420   **THE TWO STRANGERS**

422   **A TUG-OF-WAR**

425   **THE SEPARATION OF GOD FROM MAN**

431   **THE FLYING SHIP**

438   **FISH IN THE FOREST**

UNIT 6 | *Parallels*

INTRODUCTION PAGE 442

444 **MY FATHER AND THE HIPPOPOTAMUS** | Leon Hugo
SHORT STORY

452 **MAMA IS A SUNRISE** | Evelyn Tooley Hunt
POETRY

454 **THE JAR** | Luigi Pirandello
SHORT STORY

463 **ON HEARING FRENCH CHILDREN SPEAK FRENCH** | Irwin Edman
POETRY

464 **FORTUNATA WRITES A LETTER** | Theodore Apstein
DRAMA

476 **THE BATTLE OF BLENHEIM** | Robert Southey
POETRY

478 **THE GRAVEYARD** | Lysander Kemp
SHORT STORY

487 **A RIDE THROUGH SPAIN** | Truman Capote
ESSAY

492 **THE RIVER MERCHANT'S WIFE: A LETTER** | Li T'ai-Po
POETRY (translated by Ezra Pound)

494 **MISERY** | Anton Chekhov
SHORT STORY

500 **THE OLD DEMON** | Pearl Buck
SHORT STORY

Supplementary Articles

55 **QUESTIONS PUT TO A POET** | Richard Eberhart

164 **EMERGENCY AT SEA** | George Weller

196 **IT SAYS A LOT IN A LITTLE**

298 **QUESTIONS PUT TO A PLAYWRIGHT** | Rod Serling

321 **GLOSSARY OF JABBERWOCKY TERMS**

370 **IT DOESN'T HAVE TO RHYME**

408 **THE ART OF THE PRIMITIVES**

424 **THE ORIGIN OF SPEECH**

Handbook of Literary Terms

514 **BIOGRAPHY**

516 **CHARACTERIZATION**
I Methods of Characterization
II Motivation

518 **CONFLICT**

519 **CONTRAST**

520 **ENDINGS**

521 **FANTASY**

522 **FIGURATIVE LANGUAGE**

524 **IMAGERY**

526 **INFERENCES**

528 **IRONY**
I Irony of Situation
II Ironic Tone

529 **NARRATOR**

531 **PLOT**

532 **SATIRE**

533 **SETTING**

534 **SUSPENSE**

534 **SYMBOL**

536 **THEME**

537 **TONE**

Composition Guide

INTRODUCTION PAGE 538

540 Lesson One: Persuasion

540 Lesson Two: Description

541 Lesson Three: Character Sketch

541 Lesson Four: Opinion

542 Lesson Five: Character Sketch

543 Lesson Six: Explanation

543 Lesson Seven: Interview

544 Lesson Eight: Opinion

544 Lesson Nine: News Story

545 Lesson Ten: Description

545 Lesson Eleven: Interpretation

545 Lesson Twelve: Persuasion

546 Lesson Thirteen: Comparison and Contrast

547 Lesson Fourteen: Narration

547 Lesson Fifteen: Narration

548 Lesson Sixteen: Opinion

548 Lesson Seventeen: Character Sketch

549 Lesson Eighteen: Explanation

549 Lesson Nineteen: News Story

550 Lesson Twenty: Character Sketch

550 Lesson Twenty-One: Opinion

551 Lesson Twenty-Two: Interpretation

551 Lesson Twenty-Three: Narration

552 Lesson Twenty-Four: Opinion

552 Lesson Twenty-Five: Explanation

553 Lesson Twenty-Six: Description

553 Lesson Twenty-Seven: Opinion

553 Lesson Twenty-Eight: Comparison and Contrast

554 Lesson Twenty-Nine: Reviews

554 Lesson Thirty: Explanation

555 Lesson Thirty-One: Character Sketch

555 Lesson Thirty-Two: Evaluation

556 **GLOSSARY**

591 **INDEX OF LITERARY TYPES**

592 **INDEX OF AUTHORS AND TITLES**

594 **INDEX OF SKILLS**

Interpretative Skills

Vocabulary Skills

1

Being young means meeting challenges,

making decisions, facing difficulties—growing up.

Discover how youth

> *—finds beauty in the dirt and poverty of a slum*
>
> *—doubts the opinion of a respected uncle*
>
> *—tries to save face on a hunting trip*
>
> *—faces the sale of a favorite pet*
>
> *—suffers in raising a red pony*
>
> *—confronts a conceited bully*
>
> *—handles a prudent brother.*

Eddie, Jeanie, John Thomas—all encounter life

from youth's . . .

STANDPOINT

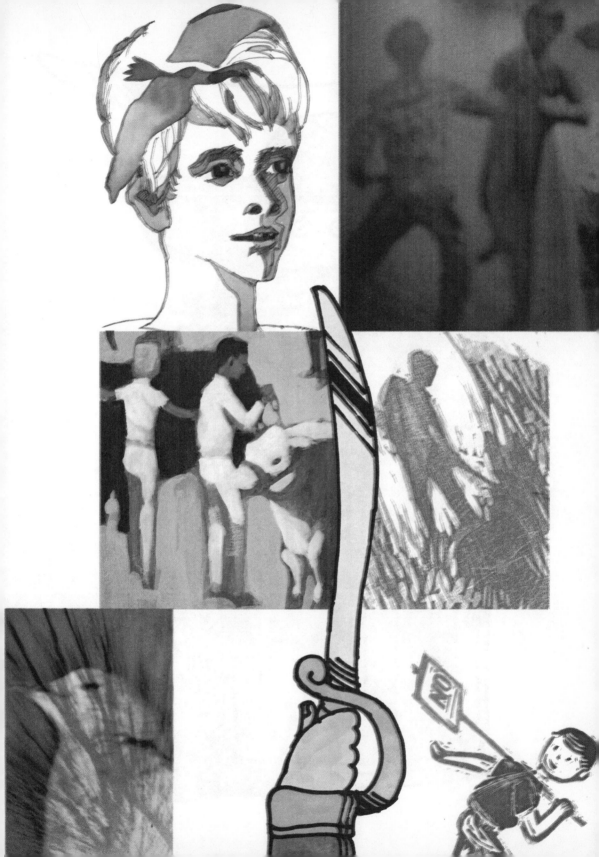

*Herbie acquires the name
"General Garbage," but he emerges,
in the end, smelling like a rose.*

The Dubbing of General Garbage

HERMAN WOUK

CONCRETE pressed roughly against one's nose is not enjoyable at best, and when the concrete is part of a schoolyard and has been baking in a May sun, it is hot and dirty enough to be positively unpleasant. So Herbie decided, as Lennie Krieger sat on his back twisting his left arm up behind him with one hand, thrusting his head against the ground with the other, and requesting the utterance of the word "uncle" before changing this state of things. With Lucille Glass standing a foot away looking on, this was not easy to do. "Uncle" is a code word understood by all children to mean "You're a better man than I am." However, Lennie was much heavier and stronger; the lunch period had twenty minutes to go; and the concrete was very hard, hot, and dusty. So Herbie said, "Uncle," adding under his breath, "in a pig's eye," and the two boys rose, brushing themselves.

Lucille bent a lively glance at Lennie and said, "I think you're awful, picking on someone smaller than you."

"Let him not be so smart, then," said Lennie, carelessly tucking his flapping shirt back into his trousers.

It was the Thursday after the museum meeting.[1] Herbie, not finding Lucille at the accustomed landing, had wandered around the school and finally come upon her eating lunch with Lennie in a shady corner of the boys' yard. He had cheerfully joined the conversation, hiding his jealous pangs. The topic had been Lennie's boastful plans for playing football in high school.

"What'll *you* do in high school?"

From THE CITY BOY by Herman Wouk. Copyright 1948, 1952 by Herman Wouk. Reprinted by permission of The Harold Matson Company, Inc.

1. *museum meeting.* In an earlier chapter of *The City Boy,* Herbie contrives to meet Lucille and her mother at an art museum.

he said to Herbie derisively. "Try out for the tiddlywinks[2] team?"

Herbie looked foolish and was silent. Lennie went on, "I bet I play halfback in my first year. Maybe even fullback."

"Maybe even left back," chirped Herbie.

It was a good shot. Lennie had been left back twice in his school career. Lucille choked over a bite of her sandwich, coughed it out, and shrieked with merriment. A short scuffle between the boys followed, ending in the nose-to-concrete situation described above.

"Look out, Lucille," said Herbie as he got up, ruefully rubbing the dirt off his nose and forehead. "He'll beat you up next. He's real brave."

Instantly Lennie had him by his shirt front and tie, grasped in an up-thrusting fist. "What's the matter, you want more?" he said, and when Herbie answered nothing he beat the fat boy's chest lightly with his other fist, in time to this chant:

Three, six, nine,
A bottle of wine,
I can fight you any old time.

This was a challenge which a Bronx[3] boy was supposed to take up even if it meant getting all his bones broken. But Herbie had had enough pounding of his ribs and concrete in his face for one day, so he let it pass. A code that required him to take two successive lickings from the same bigger boy seemed to have a flaw in it somewhere. He did not miss the flicker of disappointment in Lucille's eyes as Lennie released him with a contemptuous little push.

"O.K., Herbie darling," he said, "You can play jacks with Lucille now. So long." He strode off.

A vendor of water ices pushed his wooden cart past them on the other side of the steel webbing of the school fence. "How about ices, Lucille? I got four cents," said Herbie humbly.

"No, thanks." Then impulsively, "I'll be glad when I'm transferred to the Mosholu Parkway Public School next term. I hate Lennie and I hate you!" She stamped her foot at him and ran to the girls' yard.

It is a sad thing to be beaten and humiliated in the presence of one's lady fair. Herbie moped around the yard without aim, and was so poor in spirits that it actually made him happy to hear the gong summoning him back to class. He pinned on his yellow armband, and took his privileged way up the stairs[4] ahead of the other pupils, lonely and chopfallen. Even his imagination was chilled by Lucille's frostiness. It refused to produce the usual comforting pictures of Lennie in beggar's rags at the age of twenty-one, pleading with a prosperous, glittering Herbie for a small loan. The fat boy was indeed brought low.

The depression lessened when he came back to Mrs. Gorkin's classroom. There, lying on his desk, was his costume for the assembly play: an army general's cap, a long overcoat with brass buttons, and, most wonderful of all, an honest-to-goodness cigar. In honor of Decoration Day he was to play General Ulysses S. Grant in *The Surrender at Appomattox.*[5]

Mrs. Gorkin had spent a year at dramatic school before abandoning her dreams and becoming a schoolteacher. She was therefore the official theatrical manager of Public School 50. Her class benefited by the excite-

---

2. *tiddlywinks,* a game in which the player snaps small discs from a flat surface into a cup or basket.
3. *Bronx,* a borough in New York City.
4. *took . . . stairs.* Herbie is captain of the Social Service Squad, whose members are responsible for maintaining cleanliness in the school building.
5. *General Ulysses S. Grant . . . Appomattox.* Grant was the leader of the Union army which defeated the Confederate forces commanded by General Robert E. Lee in the Civil War. Lee officially surrendered to Grant at Appomattox, Virginia, April 9, 1865.

ment of rehearsals, irregular hours, release from homework, and other privileges of a troupe of actors. She rarely troubled to go outside her own classroom for talent; it made control more difficult. Herbie, quick-witted and something of a show-off, was the natural choice for the long part of Grant. The casting of Robert E. Lee was harder. In the end Mrs. Gorkin had reluctantly given the role to Lennie Krieger, despite his low marks and truculent manner, because he was taller than any other boy and had the handsome figure required for General Lee—whom Mrs. Gorkin, with many historians, regarded as the hero of the scene.

When it was too late she regretted the choice a dozen times. Lennie's entrances, exits, and warlike gestures were things of spread-eagle beauty, but he couldn't remember lines, and those he did recall he mumbled jerkily out of the side of his mouth. He obviously believed that clear speech would compromise his manliness. Coaching, threats, and pleas by Mrs. Gorkin induced him to say a few speeches correctly at a rehearsal; next day, Robert E. Lee once more sounded like a bad boy reciting, "I must not throw erasers, I must not throw erasers." But the mistake was past remedy. Mrs. Gorkin instructed Herbie to memorize Lee's lines as well as Grant's, and to prompt Lennie whenever necessary.

Class 7B-1 lined up in front of the room and marched gaily to assembly hall for dress rehearsal. Eight of the boys carried costumes and props hired by Mrs. Gorkin from a downtown shop. Only Grant and Lee had complete outfits. The minor military figures were represented by a cap here, a jacket there, a pistol elsewhere. In the interest of economy two uniforms were furnishing out two

chiefs of staff, four orderlies, and several miscellaneous generals. The rest of the class were coming along to watch the fun, freed from the drone of study by Mrs. Gorkin's theatrical duties.

In a tiny dressing room on one side of the assembly-hall platform the boys put on their costumes. Lennie soon became a dignified, glittering man of war, with a noble white beard that looped over his ears with elastic threads. By contrast, Herbie made a shabby Grant. The brass-buttoned overcoat slumped and lost its military aspect on his narrow shoulders and chubby body. The braided cap flopped down over his ears. He looked like the son of a doorman wearing his father's castoffs. Worst of all, the item of whiskers had apparently been overlooked in his case. Out of all his ludicrously oversized attire there peeped a round, clean pink face with a cigar in it. When Mrs. Gorkin came into the dressing room, she was greeted by a wail from the victor of Richmond.[6] "Gosh, Mrs. Gorkin, where's my beard?"

"You have a beard."

"I have not."

"It's in your overcoat pocket."

"Oh." Herbie reached into the pockets and brought out a square piece of greasy black felt. *"This?"* he said in horror.

"Yes, *that*," said Mrs. Gorkin. She took it out of his hand and affixed it to the bottom of his hat with two snap fasteners. "There, you look fine," she said heartily.

Herbie hurried to a mirror, took one look, and almost burst into tears. The black felt looked exactly like what it was: a piece of black felt. It no more resembled a beard than it did an American flag. He tried putting the

---

6. *victor of Richmond.* Grant won a decisive battle at Richmond, Virginia, shortly before Lee's surrender.

cigar in his mouth. That gorgeous effect was also ruined. He had to raise the beard like a curtain, and it hung over the cigar on either side, leaving his mouth and chin bare. It was a fraud, a monstrosity.

"What the heck is that thing on your face?" The voice of Lennie Krieger spoke out of a resplendent form fairly resembling the Robert E. Lee of history books.

"A beard," Herbie faltered.

"A beard!" Lennie emitted a hoot and called, "Hey, guys, look what Herbie calls a beard!"

The wolves descended, baying with laughter.

"Haw! It looks like a shoeshine rag."

"It looks like a Mohammedan veil."[7]

"It looks like something out of a garbage can."

"It is."

"He looks like he's playin' cops and robbers."

"Is that a hat or a soup pot?"

"Is that an overcoat or a laundry sack?"

"Hooray for General Garbage!"

The last was Lennie's contribution. The boys took it up with whoops. "General Garbage! General Garbage!" They danced in front of Herbie with mock bows and salutes. Mrs. Gorkin came charging to the rescue, and silenced the din with a yell of "What's going on here?"

The teacher was wild of eye and mussed of hair. Calm, controlled at all other times, she became a jumpy artist when staging an assembly-hall show. She had once thrown a memorable fit of hysterics just before curtain time at the Gorkin production of *Pinafore*.[8] Glaring at the cowed boys, she snapped, "Another whisper out of any of you, and there'll be no show," and went out. Lennie drew his sword and brandished it at her retreating back in a highly impolite gesture. The other actors covered their mouths and snickered.

Dress rehearsal had just started when one of the rear doors of the hall opened and Mr. Gauss walked down the center aisle in lone majesty. Mrs. Gorkin was seen to shudder. She rose, stopped the rehearsal with a wave of her hand, and said, "Class, stand." The children came to attention at their seats while the actors froze in their attitudes. Mr. Gauss strolled alongside the teacher and sat placidly in the front row beside her. "Class, sit," said Mrs. Gorkin.

"Boys, go right on with your play as though I weren't here," said Mr. Gauss.

The actors resumed their roles. Lennie, scared by the principal's presence, barked out his lines so that the hall echoed, to the teacher's great surprise and pleasure. Herbie, however, could not be understood no matter how hard he shouted. The black felt over his mouth worked as well as a Maxim silencer.[9] His roars were reduced to murmers.

"I remember you well from the Mexican War, General Lee," he howled.

"*A rumble you bell your Max can whoa*," was what reached the front row.

"What on earth is that thing over Grant's mouth?" whispered the principal.

"That," said Mrs. Gorkin, clenching and unclenching her fists, "is a beard."

"It looks like a flap of black felt," said the principal.

---

7. Mohammedan veil. Moslem women who follow the teachings of the prophet Mohammed traditionally wear veils over the lower half of their faces.

8. Pinafore, a popular comic opera, written in 1878 by W. S. Gilbert and Arthur Sullivan.

9. Maxim silencer, a device invented by H. P. Maxim for suppressing the sound of a gunshot.

"Herbert, speak louder!" cried the teacher.

Herbert screamed so that his ears rang. "I regret we meet again in such melancholy circumstances."

"*Rugger meegin smellnek shirtshtan,*" Mr. Gauss dimly heard.

"Really," he said to the teacher, "the boy must take that thing off."

"And have Grant look like a fat boy of eleven?"

"Yes, rather than have him sound gagged."

So Herbert's beard came off, to his relief. But Mrs. Gorkin steamed. Things went smoothly after that, however, and she was beginning to simmer down, when Lee drew his sword to hand it over in surrender.

"One moment," called the principal. Action was suspended.

"Wherever did you get this playlet, Mrs. Gorkin?" said Mr. Gauss.

"I wrote it myself."

"Surely you are aware, my dear, that the legend of Lee's surrender of his sword is spurious?"

"Yes," said the teacher. "But it's a famous legend and has a good moral."

"Nothing that is false has a good moral. I think we will cut out this part."

Mrs. Gorkin gasped and trembled. "There's no point to the play without it. The curtain line is what General Grant says as he returns the sword: 'General Lee, I have not defeated an enemy; I have found a lost brother.'"

"A very nice line, my dear. But we can't go on planting these silly stories in children's minds."

"There's no drama, no entertainment whatever without the sword," shrilled the red-haired teacher.

The invisible fingers pushed the ends of Mr. Gauss' mouth up in his well-known smile.

"We are not here to entertain, but to instruct," he said with satisfaction.

Mrs. Gorkin threw her head back and screamed into her handkerchief.

The children were aghast and delighted. Mr. Gauss was stupefied. The silence of the huge hall was rent by a second muffled shriek. The principal rose, patted Mrs. Gorkin's arm, and said, "Please, please, collect yourself, my dear. [*Shriek*] I had no idea you felt so strongly. [*Shriek*] Please, we'll *leave* the scene as it is."

Two or three short sobs, and Mrs. Gorkin emerged from the handkerchief, bright-eyed and happy. "Thank you, Mr. Gauss," she said. "On with the rehearsal, boys. All right, Lennie. 'Sir, in yielding this sword——'"

Lennie, who had been staring open-mouthed at her, quickly drew the sword once more and held it high.

"Sir, in yielding this weapon I give you the sword of the South, but not its soul," he said.

"One moment," said Mr. Gauss.

Mrs. Gorkin jumped as though a spider had walked on her.

"May I merely suggest," said the principal, "that etiquette would require him to unbuckle his belt and hand over sword, scabbard, and all?"

"Mr. Gauss," said the teacher, her voice like the plucking of an overtightened banjo string, "it is more dramatic to see the sword drawn." She took her handkerchief from her cuff again.

"Merely a suggestion," said Mr. Gauss hurriedly. "I withdraw it."

But at this moment the gong rang, summoning the school to assembly, and the dress rehearsal had to be adjourned. Children lugging violins, cellos, trumpets, and trombones began straggling in through the rear doors. Mr. Meng, the slight, dark teacher who played the piano and led

the school orchestra, appeared with three boys staggering under piles of folding chairs which they dropped at the piano and began setting up with much scraping and banging. Mrs. Gorkin left her acting troupe in the dressing room with a terrifying final warning, spoken with hands shaking and eyeballs showing white, all around the pupils, and then led her class out of the hall.

Mr. Gauss took his place in the large ornate armchair at the center of the platform. The assistant principal, Mrs. Corn, large, yellow-haired, and ferocious, sat on one side of him; on the other was a stout lady from the Board of Education. The school gong clanged once more. Mr. Meng, at the piano, lifted one hand in the air and looked at Mr. Gauss. The principal nodded. Down came the hand, yowl went the wind instruments, squeal went the string instruments, slam went the percussion instruments and an obscure, muddy fog of sound arose, through which the piano could vaguely be heard, pounding out "The Stars and Stripes Forever," double fortissimo.[10] A line of boys began marching in from one side, a line of girls from the other. Mrs. Gorkin, whatever her trials as a theatrical manager, had this unique blessing: her productions never failed to play to a full house.

Soon the hall was full. Heads, eyes, and arms of the standing children were motionless. Mrs. Corn stepped forward and shouted like a drill sergeant, "Color guard, forward—MARCH!" Three well-combed-and-washed honor boys from the eighth grade came down the center aisle, the middle one carrying a flag on a staff. The drum and cymbal speeded them on their way, dying off uncertainly as the flag reached the platform. Mrs. Corn snapped her right arm to her forehead; all the children did likewise. From a thousand young throats came a chant: "I pledge allegiance to the flag . . ."

The eye of Mrs. Corn swept the hall, looking for a wavering hand, a straying eye, a dirty shirt, or a neckerchief of the wrong color. At the end of the pledge two piano chords sounded, and all the heads sank at once as the children sat. Mrs. Corn came down the steps of the platform and silently glared a girl (who had yawned during the pledge) out of her seat, up the aisle, and into her office to await doom. As she returned to her armchair Mr. Gauss rose and read from a Bible on a stand the Psalm beginning, *"Lord, how numerous are my persecutors,"* but if the children caught the appropriateness, there were no grins to show it.

Meantime, the actors stranded in the dressing room were very gay. Few things are so sweet in this world as seeing your fellows go through a foolish rigmarole while you are free from it yourself (this is the secret of the popularity of all parades and military reviews). A hot game of "tickets" was going on, organized and dominated by Lennie. It was a sort of poker, evolved in the gutters of New York like scores of other games, played with small villainously colored pictures of baseball players which sold in strips of ten for a cent. Herbie, having no tickets, was out of the game, and was curiously examining General Lee's sword, which lay in a corner. Finally he buckled it on, and drew and brandished it a few times, yearning over it.

"Take off that sword, General Garbage, or I'll push your face in," growled Lennie, looking up from the game. The other boys laughed.

---

10. *double fortissimo* (fôr tis′ə mō), extremely loud.

Herbie, his face burning, obeyed. As he was putting the sword back in the corner he noticed a little black button on the hilt. He pressed it. With some difficulty it yielded, and the sword settled another inch into the scabbard. He tried to pull the sword out again, but it remained locked in place until he pressed the catch, whereupon it slid out easily. This was a feature of the weapon which Lennie had clearly overlooked. In his boastful flourishing he had pointed out every detail he had noticed to the envious boys. Herbie glanced over his shoulder at General Lee, intent on heavy betting of tickets, his beard pushed up on his forehead. The small

stout boy reviewed several incidents of the day in his mind: concrete against his nose, jeers at his black felt beard, "General Garbage," and the recent threat to render his face concave. Then he softly pressed the catch, locked the sword in its scabbard, leaned it against the wall, and strolled away to watch the assembly through the crack of the dressing-room door.

A tall girl with lank black hair and heavily rimmed glasses was standing in the center of the platform, reciting "In Flanders fields the poppies blow." The rows of rigid children sat listening with eyes dulled by an overdose of poppies, for this was the third rendition of the poem in ten minutes. The fifth, sixth, and eighth grades had each been asked to furnish one recitation, and had each sent its best English student to the stage primed with the same Decoration Day warhorse. Nothing could stop the repetitions. An assembly, once started, ticked itself off like an infernal machine. For the third time the children heard the performer make the daring turn around the elocutionary corner in the last verse:

> Take up our quarrel with the foe:
> To you from failing hands we
> throw THE TORCH;
> Be yours to hold it high.

instead of the usual

> Take up our quarrel with the foe:
> To you from failing hands we
> throw
> The torch; be yours to hold it high.

This was considered original and very fine by each of the three teachers who had coached the reciters. It was sad to find that the others had all had the same inspiration. The unlucky girl reached the last line and sneaked off the platform to feeble applause.

Now Mr. Gauss introduced the stout lady from the Board of Education, Mrs. Moonvess. He stated that a great musical treat was in store for the children, as she was going to teach them a song of her own composition. Mrs. Moonvess stood, adjusted her pince-nez,[11] produced a conductor's baton, and came forward, coughing nervously.

"Boys and girls of P.S. 50, I have set to music a piece which is very appropriate to this holiday. I shall now sing for you with the aid of my good friend, Mr. Meng, the first stanza of my song—a musical setting of 'In Flanders Fields.'"

By the laws of nature there should not be any such thing as a silent groan, but a sound describable in no other terms swelled through the hall. Mrs. Corn glared around, but all the children were sitting with faces of stone. The silent groan went unpunished, and Mrs. Moonvess caroled the first stanza of "In Flanders Fields." During the next fifteen minutes she tried to browbeat the children into learning it. They had no trouble with the words, which by now they knew almost from memory, but Mrs. Moonvess' bizarre time was beyond them. At the last, when she drove them through it mercilessly with her baton from beginning to end, the effect was strange and dismal, like a hymn chanted by Chinese monks. Mr. Gauss jumped up as she seemed to be rallying herself for another try, and thanked her for her beautiful contribution to the holiday. Loud applause ensued as she backed unwillingly into her seat.

Mrs. Gorkin now sidled up the platform steps. Herbie whispered, "Chickie!" The card game broke up

11. *pince-nez* (pans nā'), eyeglasses clipped to the nose.

and the tickets all disappeared in a twinkling. The actors were standing around virtuously when the teacher came in. Lennie had just finished buckling on the sword, but in his haste he forgot to pull the white beard down from his forehead, incurring a tongue lashing. Mrs. Gorkin faithfully promised to put him back to 7A if he spoiled her show in any way. Lennie was hangdog and mute.

Introducing the playlet, Mr. Gauss reviewed the whole Civil War from Fort Sumter to Richmond. He paused at Gettysburg long enough to quote Lincoln's address, verbatim. He painstakingly explained that the surrender of Lee's sword, which they were about to see, never really happened, so they need not pay attention to that part of the play. At this, Mrs. Gorkin, who had been wringing a handkerchief between her perspiring hands, ripped it in half.

"And now," said Mr. Gauss to the drooping audience, "Mrs. Gorkin's play, *The Surrender at Appomattox.*"

The principal sat. Mrs. Gorkin gave Herbie a push, and he walked out on the stage, followed by a general and an orderly. As instructed, he strode to the center, faced the audience, and was about to bellow his first line when lo, he beheld in the second girls' row the face of Lucille Glass, turned up to him with eager eyes. The speech vanished from his memory. He became aware of a thousand faces staring at him in a dead silence. His knees shook. His mouth hung open. Panic gripped him.

A hoarse whisper from Mrs. Gorkin floated to him. "What can be keeping General Lee? *What can be keeping General Lee?*"

"What can be keeping General Lee?" he declaimed. The sound of his own voice filling the hall gave him new life, and he ranted on with zest.

"True, as my senior by sixteen years he is entitled to keep me waiting. Ha, ha." He thrust the cigar vigorously into his mouth, causing shocked chuckles in the audience. From then onward his performance was in the best tradition of that approach to the stage art known as "chewing the scenery."[12] The absence of a black beard went quite unnoticed in the fireworks of his style.

General Robert E. Lee looked so dashing when he came on the stage that he received an ovation.

"I trust I am not unduly tardy, General Grant," he said, in a murmur that barely reached Mr. Gauss, sitting five feet from him. Lennie was not frightened. He simply balked at speaking clear, correct English before all the boys he knew, and casting an everlasting shadow on his virility. No vengeance Mrs. Gorkin could take was worse than that. He loved the uniform and the sword, and was happy of the chance to be showing them off before the school. That was enough for him, and would have to do for Mrs. Gorkin.

The scene proceeded, General Grant shaking the windows with his lines and General Lee confiding his answers to the orderly at his right (away from the audience) because it was his practice to speak out of the right side of his mouth. To the audience, the effect was to make Robert E. Lee out as bashful and deaf, an unexpected characterization. Mrs. Gorkin had revised the lines so that the audience could follow the scene merely from what Grant said, but the alternation of shouts and murmurs was decidedly queer. Mr. Gauss finally intervened.

"Speak up, General Lee, nobody

---

12. *chewing the scenery,* acting in an overly emotional manner.

can hear you," he said, and a wave of giggles went through the girls.

Stung, Lennie blared out, "Sir, in yielding this weapon I give you the sword of the South, but not its soul." He clapped his hand to the hilt, gave a vicious tug, and spun himself clear around. The sword remained fast in the scabbard.

He was astounded. Once more he wrenched at the weapon; it would not budge. The audience was tittering. He took a deep breath. "Sir, in yielding you this weapon," he yelled, "I give you the sword of the South, but not its soul." With both hands on the hilt he heaved at it and pulled the belt halfway up his chest, hauling up his jacket and shirt so that his naked chest showed. But the sword did not come out.

"Never mind your soul," said Herbie in a flash of inspiration. "I'll settle for the sword."

There was a deluge of laughter. Mrs. Gorkin was almost shouting from the dressing room: "Unbuckle the belt! Unbuckle the belt!" Lennie lost his head, tugged and tugged at the sword, and began to swear. Mr. Gauss rose to take action. Herbie, emboldened by success, suddenly held up his hand and bawled, "One moment, General."

The laughter stopped and Lennie looked at him wonderingly. Herbie reached over to General Lee's side, seized the hilt, and drew out the sword as easily as if it had been greased. The audience gasped in astonishment. Herbie turned to his orderly and blandly said, "Give General Lee a cup of coffee. He seems to be weak from hunger."

Amid the roars and handclapping which followed this coup, Mr. Gauss stepped forward and shook his hand. The play was over, and was acknowledged a great hit.

Lennie lay in ambush near 1075 Homer Avenue from four until seven-thirty that evening, waiting for Herbie to come home. The only result was that he missed his dinner. Herbie came home at six, via the basement of 1042 Tennyson Avenue and a connecting passageway to his own cellar. General Garbage outmaneuvered General Lee to the end.

✦ ✦ ✦ ✦

DISCUSSION

1. (a) What has caused the predicament in which Herbie finds himself at the beginning of this selection? **(b)** What results from this situation?

2. (a) What does Herbie look like? **(b)** Why does Mrs. Gorkin choose him to play General Grant? **(c)** How does he win the name "General Garbage"?

3. (a) Why is Lennie chosen to play Lee? **(b)** Describe Lennie's acting technique.

4. (a) In what way does Herbie improve the end of the play? **(b)** How does the situation at the end of the play contrast with the situation on the playground?

5. (a) Why does Mr. Gauss object to the play? **(b)** How does Mrs. Gorkin handle his objection? **(c)** How does Mr. Gauss make his point eventually despite Mrs. Gorkin?

6. Point out the humor in different parts of the assembly program.

THE AUTHOR

"I was a fat boy like Herbie," writes Herman Wouk, "but alas, I never had a beautiful if difficult sweetheart like Lucille; and thank Heaven, I was never dubbed General Garbage." Herbie is the hero of Wouk's *The City Boy,* an amusing novel about life in New York's crowded Bronx, where the author grew up. Wouk draws on past experience for the background of his novels, and many details in *The City Boy* are taken from his own life. *The Caine Mutiny,* his most popular work, grew out of his navy service in the South Pacific during World War II.

Are you ever a two-speed person like John?

Speed Adjustments / *JOHN CIARDI*

A man stopped by and he wanted to know
Why my son John had become so slow.

I looked out the window and there was John
Running so fast he had been and gone
Before I saw him. "Look at him go!"   5
I said to the man. "Do you call *that* slow?"

"He seems to be fast when he wants to be,"
The man said. "He appears to be
One of those two-speed boys. You know—
Sometimes fast, and sometimes slow,   10
He can run a mile in nothing flat.
He can run right out from under his hat
When there's nowhere, really, to go. And yet
That very same boy that's as fast as a jet
Will take all day—and sometimes two—   15
To get to school. I'm sure that you
Send him to school. But yesterday
He didn't arrive. And all he would say
Was, yes, he started at half-past eight
But it took so long he got there late."   20

"How late?" said I.
              Said the man, "A day."

"I see," said I, "and I think I can say
He won't be late again. He needs
A little adjustment of his speeds,
And I'm sure I know the place to adjust."   25

"Well, then," said he, "that's that, and I must
Be on my way."
              "Thank you," said I.
"If you see John as you go by
Would you be so good as to send him in?

There is never a better time to begin   30
A speed adjustment than right away."

"Agreed, and I will," said the man. "Good day."

And just a few minutes after that
In came John and down he sat:
"You wanted to see me, I understand?"   35

"I did and I do. But you'll have to stand—
At least at first—for what I need.
I'm going to have to adjust your speed.
And when I'm through adjusting it,
I think you won't much care to sit.   40
Do you know what I mean?"
                    "Oh, oh," said he,
"I'm afraid I do. Is it going to be
Terribly long before you're through?"

"Why, not at all," said I. "Like you,
I can be speedy sometimes, too."   45

And soon after that his speed was adjusted.
And also the seat of his pants was dusted.
It was busy work, but it didn't take long,
Though I double-checked as I went along
Just to make sure there was nothing wrong.   50
And whatever *was* wrong, I set it straight,
For since that time he hasn't been late.

DISCUSSION

1. When is John fast and when is he slow?
2. How does his father adjust his speed?
3. (a) Do you think his father's method is the best one? Explain. (b) How are your own speed problems adjusted?

THE AUTHOR

The truant officer didn't really come by to check on John Ciardi's son. Instead, Ciardi says that he began "Speed Adjustments" " . . . as a joke about him, and probably to remind him that he is fast about what he likes to do and slow about what I want him to do, and that I intend to speed him up a bit about what I want him to do."

The Boston-born poet served as a gunner on Air Force B-29's in World War II. He was poetry editor and a weekly columnist for *Saturday Review* magazine for more than a decade. A nationally popular lecturer on poets and poetry, he writes poems for both children and adults.

See
CONFLICT
Handbook
of Literary
Terms
page 518

*He wanted to do what was
expected of him, but certain feelings
kept preventing him from acting. What
were the forces that compelled the
Thanksgiving hunter first in
one direction, then in another?*

THANKSGIVING HUNTER

JESSE STUART

"HOLD YOUR RIFLE like this," Uncle Wash said, changing the position of my rifle. "When I throw this marble into the air, follow it with your bead[1]; at the right time gently squeeze the trigger!"

Uncle Wash threw the marble high into the air and I lined my sights with the tiny moving marble, gently squeezing the trigger, timing the speed of my object until it slowed in the air ready to drop to earth again. Just as it reached its height, my rifle cracked and the marble was broken into tiny pieces.

Uncle Wash was a tall man with a hard leathery face, dark discolored teeth and blue eyes that had a far-away look in them. He hunted the year round; he violated all the hunting laws. He knew every path, creek, river and rock cliff within a radius of ten miles. Since he was a great hunter, he wanted to make a great hunter out of me. And tomorrow, Thanksgiving Day, would be the day

1. bead, bit of metal at the front end of a gun used for sighting.

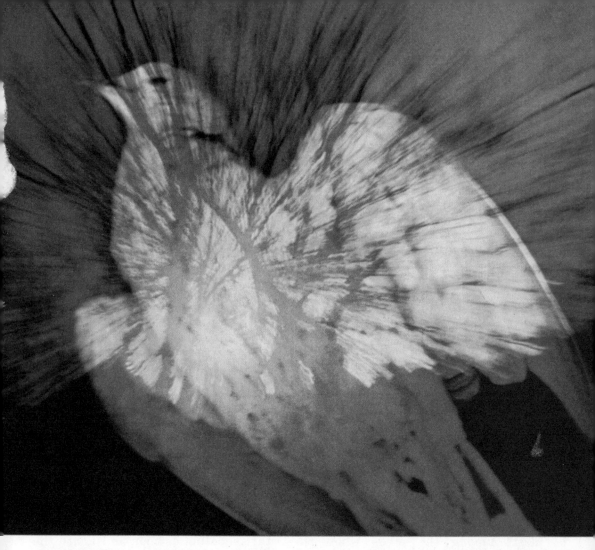

for Uncle Wash to take me on my first hunt.

Uncle Wash woke me long before daylight.

"Oil your double-barrel,"[2] he said. "Oil it just like I've showed you."

I had to clean the barrels with an oily rag tied to a long string with a knot in the end. I dropped the heavy knot down the barrel and pulled the oily rag through the barrel. I did this many times to each barrel. Then I rubbed a meat-rind over both barrels and shined them with a dry rag. After this was done I polished the gunstock.[3]

"Love the feel of your gun," Uncle Wash had often told me. "There's nothing like the feel of a gun. Know how far it will shoot. Know your gun better than you know your own self; know it and love it."

Before the sun had melted the frost from the multicolored trees and from the fields of stubble and dead grasses, we had cleaned our guns, had eaten our breakfasts and were on our way. Uncle Wash, Dave Pratt, Steve

---

2. *double-barrel,* gun with two barrels or metal tubes.
3. *gunstock,* wooden handle to which the barrel of a gun is fastened.

Blake walked ahead of me along the path and talked about the great hunts they had taken and the game they had killed. And while they talked, words that Uncle Wash had told me about loving the feel of a gun kept going through my head. Maybe it is because Uncle Wash speaks of a gun like it was a living person is why he is such a good marksman, I thought.

"This is the dove country," Uncle Wash said soon as we had reached the cattle barn on the west side of our farm. "Doves are feeding here. They nest in these pines and feed around this barn fall and winter. Plenty of wheat grains, rye grains, and timothy seed here for doves."

Uncle Wash is right about the doves, I thought. I had seen them fly in pairs all summer long into the pine grove that covered the knoll east of our barn. I had heard their mournful songs. I had seen them in early April carrying straws in their bills to build their nests; I had seen them flying through the blue spring air after each other; I had seen them in the summer carrying food in their bills for their tiny young. I had heard their young ones crying for more food from the nests among the pines when the winds didn't sough among the pine boughs to drown their sounds. And when the leaves started turning brown I had seen whole flocks of doves, young and old ones, fly down from the tall pines to our barnyard to pick up the wasted grain. I had seen them often and been so close to them that they were no longer afraid of me.

"Doves are fat now," Uncle Wash said to Dave Pratt.

"Doves are wonderful to eat," Dave said.

And then I remembered when I had watched them in the spring and summer, I had never thought about killing and eating them. I had thought of them as birds that lived in the tops of pine trees and that hunted their food from the earth. I remembered their mournful songs that had often made me feel lonely when I worked in the cornfield near the barn. I had thought of them as flying over the deep hollows in pairs in the bright sunlight air chasing each other as they flew toward their nests in pines.

"Now we must get good shooting into this flock of doves," Uncle Wash said to us, "before they get wild. They've not been shot among this season."

Then Uncle Wash, to show his skill in hunting, sent us in different directions so that when the doves flew up from our barn lot, they would have to fly over one of our guns. He gave us orders to close in toward the barn and when the doves saw us, they would take to the air and we would do our shooting.

"And if they get away," Uncle Wash said, "follow them up and talk to them in their own language."

Each of us went his separate way. I walked toward the pine grove, carrying my gun just as Uncle Wash had instructed me. I was ready to start shooting as soon as I heard the flutter of dove wings. I walked over the frosted white grass and the wheat stubble until I came to the fringe of pine woods. And when I walked slowly over the needles of pines that covered the autumn earth, I heard the flutter of many wings and the barking of guns. The doves didn't come my way. I saw many fall from the bright autumn air to the brown crabgrass-colored earth.

I saw these hunters pick up the doves they had killed and cram their limp, lifeless, bleeding bodies with tousled feathers into their brown hunting coats. They picked them up

as fast as they could, trying to watch the way the doves went.

"Which way did they go, Wash?" Dave asked soon as he had picked up his kill.

"That way," Uncle Wash pointed to the low hill on the west.

"Let's be after 'em, men," Steve said.

The seasoned hunters hurried after their prey while I stood under a tall pine and kicked the toe of my brogan shoe against the brown pine needles that had carpeted the ground. I saw these men hurry over the hill, cross the ravine and climb the hill over which the doves had flown.

I watched them reach the summit of the hill, stop and call to the doves in tones not unlike the doves' own calling. I saw them with guns poised against the sky. Soon they had disappeared the way the doves had gone.

I sat down on the edge of a lichened rock that emerged from the rugged hill. I laid my double-barrel down beside me, and sunlight fingered through the pine boughs above me in pencil-sized streaks of light. And when one of these shifting pencil-sized streaks of light touched my gun barrels, they shone brightly in the light. My gun was cleaned and oiled and the little pine needles stuck to its meat-rind-greased barrels. Over my head the wind soughed lonely among the pine needles. And from under these pines I could see the vast open fields where the corn stubble stood knee-high, where the wheat stubble would have shown plainly had it not been for the great growth of crabgrass after we had cut the wheat; crabgrass that had been blighted by autumn frost and shone brilliantly brown in the sun.

Even the air was cool to breathe into the lungs; I could feel it deep down when I breathed and it tasted of the green pine boughs that flavored it as it seethed through their thick tops. This was a clean cool autumn earth that both men and birds loved. And as I sat on the lichened rock with pine needles at my feet, with the soughing pine boughs above me, I thought the doves had chosen a fine place to find food, to nest and raise their young. But while I sat looking at the earth about me, I heard the thunder of the seasoned hunters' guns beyond the low ridge. I knew that they had talked to the doves until they had got close enough to shoot again.

As I sat on the rock, listening to the guns in the distance, I thought Uncle Wash might be right after all. It was better to shoot and kill with a gun than to kill with one's hands or with a club. I remembered the time I went over the hill to see how our young corn was growing after we had plowed it the last time. And while I stood looking over the corn whose long ears were in tender blisters, I watched a ground hog come from the edge of the woods, ride down a stalk of corn, and start eating a blister-ear. I found a dead sassafras stick near me, tiptoed quietly behind the ground hog and hit him over the head. I didn't finish him with that lick. It took many licks.

When I left the corn field, I left the ground hog dead beside his ear of corn. I couldn't forget killing the ground hog over an ear of corn and leaving him dead, his gray-furred clean body to waste on the lonely hill.

I can't disappoint Uncle Wash, I thought. He has trained me to shoot. He says that I will make a great hunter. He wants me to hunt like my father, cousins and uncles. He says that I will be the greatest marksman among them.

I thought about the way my people had hunted and how they had

loved their guns. I thought about how Uncle Wash had taken care of his gun, how he had treated it like a living thing and how he had told me to love the feel of it. And now my gun lay beside me with pine needles sticking to it. If Uncle Wash were near he would make me pick the gun up, brush away the pine needles and wipe the gun barrels with my handkerchief. If I had lost my handkerchief, as I had seen Uncle Wash often do, he would make me pull out my shirttail to wipe my gun with it. Uncle Wash didn't object to wearing dirty clothes or to wiping his face with a dirty bandanna; he didn't mind living in a dirty house—but never, never would he allow a speck of rust or dirt on his gun.

It was comfortable to sit on the rock since the sun was directly above me. It warmed me with a glow of autumn. I felt the sun's rays against my face and the sun was good to feel. But the good fresh autumn air was no longer cool as the frost that covered the autumn grass that morning, nor could I feel it go deep into my lungs; the autumn air was warmer and it was flavored more with the scent of pines.

Now that the shooting had long been over near our cattle barn, I heard the lazy murmur of the woodcock in the pine woods near by. Uncle Wash said woodcocks were game birds and he killed them wherever he found them. Once I thought I would follow the sound and kill the woodcock. I picked up my gun but laid it aside again. I wanted to kill something to show Uncle Wash. I didn't want him to be disappointed in me.

Instead of trying to find a rabbit sitting behind a broom-sedge cluster or in a brier thicket as Uncle Wash had trained me to do, I felt relaxed and lazy in the autumn sun that had now penetrated the pine boughs from directly overhead. I looked over the brown vast autumn earth about me where I had worked when everything was green and growing, where birds sang in the spring air as they built their nests. I looked at the tops of barren trees and thought how a few months ago they were waving clouds of green. And now it was a sad world, a dying world. There was so much death in the world that I had known: flowers were dead, leaves were dead, and the frosted grass was lifeless in the wind. Everything was dead and dying but a few wild birds and rabbits. I had almost grown to the rock where I sat but I didn't want to stir. I wanted to glimpse the life about me before it all was covered with winter snows. I hated to think of killing in this autumn world. When I picked up my gun, I didn't feel life in it—I felt death.

I didn't hear the old hunters' guns now but I knew that, wherever they were, they were hunting for something to shoot. I thought they would return to the barn if the doves came back, as they surely would, for the pine grove where I sat was one place in this autumn world that was a home to the doves. And while I sat on the rock, I thought I would practice the dove whistle that Uncle Wash had taught me. I thought a dove would come close and I would shoot the dove so that I could go home with something in my hunting coat.

As I sat whistling a dove call, I heard the distant thunder of their guns beyond the low ridge. Then I knew they were coming back toward the cattle barn.

And, as I sat whistling my dove calls, I heard a dove answer me. I called gently to the dove. Again it answered. This time it was closer to me. I picked up my gun from the rock and gently brushed the pine needles from

its stock and barrels. And as I did this, I called pensively to the dove and it answered plaintively.

I aimed my gun soon as I saw the dove walking toward me. When it walked toward my gun so unafraid, I thought it was a pet dove. I lowered my gun; laid it across my lap. Never had a dove come this close to me. When I called again, it answered at my feet. Then it fanned its wings and flew upon the rock beside me trying to reach the sound of my voice. It called, but I didn't answer. I looked at the dove when it turned its head to one side to try to see me. Its eye was gone, with the mark of a shot across its face. Then it turned the other side of its head toward me to try to see. The other eye was gone.

As I looked at the dove the shooting grew louder; the old hunters were getting closer. I heard the fanning of dove wings above the pines. And I heard doves batting their wings against the pine boughs. And the dove beside me called to them. It knew the sounds of their wings. Maybe it knows each dove by the sound of his wings, I thought. And then the dove spoke beside me. I was afraid to answer. I could have reached out my hand and picked this dove up from the rock. Though it was blind, I couldn't kill it, and yet I knew it would have a hard time to live.

When the dove beside me called again, I heard an answer from a pine bough nearby. The dove beside me spoke and the dove in the pine bough answered. Soon they were talking to each other as the guns grew louder. Suddenly, the blind dove fluttered through the treetops, chirruping its plaintive melancholy notes, toward the sound of its mate's voice. I heard its wings batting the wind-shaken pine boughs as it ascended, struggling, toward the beckoning voice.

DISCUSSION

1. (**a**) Why is Uncle Wash considered a great hunter? (**b**) What are the boy's feelings toward him?
2. (**a**) When does the boy first realize that it will be difficult for him to shoot the doves? (**b**) What conflict does this realization cause? (**c**) Trace the development of the conflict from the time the boy becomes aware of it until the time he settles it.
3. (**a**) Why does the boy finally decide to let the blind dove live? (**b**) Explain why the decision was so difficult to make. (**c**) In what other way could he have resolved his conflict?
4. (**a**) What explanation do you think the boy will give Uncle Wash for not shooting any doves? (**b**) Would he have been more, or less, courageous if he'd shot the bird? Explain.

THE AUTHOR

Jesse Stuart was born in a one-room shack in Kentucky to an illiterate father and a mother with a second-grade education. Fifteen years later, he made an important decision. While running a concrete mixer for a street paving crew, he watched students filing in and out of the high school and made up his mind to join them.

After working his way through high school and college, Jesse went back home to teach fourteen pupils in a converted barn. Three years later, however, the Depression forced him to become a farmer. As he plowed, ideas for poems poured through his mind. He scribbled them down and sent several to magazine editors. To his delight, they were accepted. Soon an entire volume of poems, *Man with a Bull-Tongue Plow*, was published and widely acclaimed. Next, he wrote short stories which proved equally popular. Success came quickly then.

Jesse Stuart now lives on a large farm in his native Kentucky hills, where he continues to add to his long list of published works. "Thanksgiving Hunter" is a story he particularly likes, since it shows his distaste for hunting.

Strawberry Ice Cream Soda

IRWIN SHAW

What leads Eddie to shout, "Yella!
Yella as a flower. My own brother . . ."?
And how does Lawrence feel as he hears it?

EDDIE BARNES looked at the huge Adirondack hills,[1] browning in the strong summer afternoon sun. He listened to his brother Lawrence practice finger-exercises on the piano inside the house, onetwothreefour*five*, onetwothreefour*five*, and longed for New York. He lay on his stomach in the long grass of the front lawn and delicately peeled his sunburned nose. Morosely he regarded a grasshopper, stupid with sun, wavering on a bleached blade of grass in front of his nose. Without interest he put out his hand and captured it.

"Give honey," he said, listlessly. "Give honey or I'll kill yuh . . ."

But the grasshopper crouched unmoving, unresponsive, oblivious to Life or Death.

Disgusted, Eddie tossed the grasshopper away. It flew uncertainly, wheeled, darted back to its blade of grass, alighted and hung there dreamily, shaking a little in the breeze in front of Eddie's nose. Eddie turned over on his back and looked at the high blue sky.

The country! Why anybody ever went to the country . . . What things must be doing in New York now, what rash, beautiful deeds on the steaming, rich streets, what expeditions, what joy, what daring sweaty adventure among the trucks, the trolley cars, the baby carriages! What cries, hoarse and humorous, what light laughter outside the red-painted shop where lemon ice was sold at three cents the double scoop, true nourishment for a man at fifteen.

Eddie looked around him, at the silent, eternal, granite-streaked hills. Trees and birds, that's all. He sighed,

torn with thoughts of distant pleasure, stood up, went over to the window behind which Lawrence seriously hammered at the piano, onetwothreefour*five*.

"Lawrrrence," Eddie called, the rrr's rolling with horrible gentility in his nose, "Lawrrrence, you stink."

Lawrence didn't even look up. His thirteen-year-old fingers, still pudgy and babyish, went onetwothreefour*five*, with unswerving precision. He was talented and he was dedicated to his talent and someday they would wheel a huge piano out onto the stage of Carnegie Hall[2] and he would come out and bow politely to the thunder of applause and sit down, flipping his coat-tails back, and play, and men and women would laugh and cry and remember their first loves as they listened to him. So now his fingers went up and down, up and down, taking strength against the great day.

Eddie looked through the window a moment more, watching his brother, sighed and walked around to the side of the house, where a crow was sleepily eating the radish seeds that Eddie had planted three days ago in a fit of boredom. Eddie threw a stone at the crow and the crow silently flew up to the branch of an oak and waited for Eddie to go away. Eddie threw another stone at the crow. The crow moved to another branch. Eddie

1. *Adirondack* (ad'ə ron'dak) *hills,* a mountain range in northeastern New York State. The Adirondacks are a part of the Appalachian mountain chain.
2. *Carnegie Hall,* large concert auditorium in New York City.

STRAWBERRY ICE CREAM SODA 25

wound up and threw a curve, but the crow disdained it. Eddie picked his foot up the way he'd seen Carl Hubbell[3] do and sizzled one across not more than three feet from the crow. Without nervousness the crow walked six inches up the branch. In the style now of Dizzy Dean, with terrifying speed, Eddie delivered his fast one. It was wild and the crow didn't even cock his head. You had to expect to be a little wild with such speed. Eddie found a good round stone and rubbed it professionally on his back pocket. He looked over his shoulder to hold the runner close to the bag, watched for the signal. Eddie Hubbell Dean Mungo Feller Ferrell Warnecke Gomez Barnes picked up his foot and let go his high hard one. The crow slowly got off his branch and regretfully sailed away.

Eddie went over, kicked away the loose dirt, and looked at his radish seeds. Nothing was happening to them. They just lay there, baked and inactive, just as he had placed them. No green, no roots, no radishes, no anything. He was sorry he'd ever gone in for farming. The package of seeds had cost him a dime, and the only thing that happened to them was that they were eaten by crows. And now he could use that dime. Tonight he had a date.

"I got a date," he said aloud, savoring the words. He went to the shade of the grape arbor to think about it. He sat down on the bench under the cool flat leaves, and thought about it. He'd never had a date before in his life. He had thirty-five cents. Thirty-five cents ought to be enough for any girl, but if he hadn't bought the radish seeds, he'd have had forty-five cents, really prepared for any eventuality. "Darn crow," he said, thinking of the evil black head feeding on his dime.

Many times he'd wondered how you managed to get a date. Now he knew. It happened all of a sudden. You went up to a girl where she was lying on the raft in a lake and you looked at her, chubby in a blue bathing suit, and she looked seriously at you out of serious blue eyes where you stood dripping with lake water, with no hair on your chest, and suddenly you said, "I don't s'pose yuh're not doing anything t'morra night, are yuh?" You didn't know quite what you meant, but she did, and she said, "Why, no, Eddie. Say about eight o'clock?" And you nodded and dived back into the lake and there you were.

Still, those radish seeds, that crow food, that extra dime . . .

Lawrence came out, flexing his fingers, very neat in clean khaki shorts and a white blouse. He sat down next to Eddie in the grape arbor.

"I would like a strawberry ice cream soda," he said.

"Got any money?" Eddie asked, hopefully.

Lawrence shook his head.

"No strawberry ice cream soda," Eddie said.

Lawrence nodded seriously. "You got any money?" he asked.

"Some," Eddie said carefully. He pulled down a grape leaf and cracked it between his hands, held up the two parts and looked at them critically.

Lawrence didn't say anything, but Eddie sensed a feeling developing in the grape arbor, like a growth. "I gotta save my money," Eddie said harshly. "I got a date. I got thirty-five cents. How do I know she won't want a banana split tonight?"

Lawrence nodded again, indicating that he understood, but sorrow washed up in his face like a high tide.

---

3. *Carl Hubbell,* a famous baseball pitcher of the 1930's. Dean, Mungo, Feller, Ferrell, Warnecke, and Gomez were also pitchers.

They sat in silence, uncomfortably, listening to the rustle of the grape leaves.

"All the time I was practicing," Lawrence said, finally, "I kept thinking, 'I would like a strawberry ice cream soda, I would like a strawberry ice cream soda . . .'"

Eddie stood up abruptly. "Aaah, let's get outa here. Let's go down to the lake. Maybe something's doing down the lake."

They walked together through the fields to the lake, not saying anything, Lawrence flexing his fingers mechanically.

"Why don't yuh stop that fer once?" Eddie asked, with distaste. "Just fer once?"

"This is good for my fingers. It keeps them loose."

"Yuh give me a pain."

"All right," Lawrence said, "I won't do it now."

They walked on again, Lawrence barely up to Eddie's chin, frailer, cleaner, his hair mahogany dark and smooth on his high, pink, baby brow. Lawrence whistled. Eddie listened with disguised respect.

"That's not so bad," Eddie said. "You don't whistle half bad."

"That's from the Brahms second piano concerto."[4] Lawrence stopped whistling for a moment. "It's easy to whistle."

"Yuh give me a pain," Eddie said, mechanically, "a real pain."

When they got to the lake, there was nobody there. Flat and unruffled it stretched across, like a filled blue cup, to the woods on the other side.

"Nobody here," Eddie said, staring at the raft, unmoving and dry in the still water. "That's good. Too many people here all the time." His eyes roamed the lake, to the farthest corner, to the deepest cove.

"How would yuh like to go rowing in a boat out in that old lake?" Eddie asked.

"We haven't got a boat," Lawrence answered reasonably.

"I didn't ask yuh that. I asked, 'How'd yuh like to go rowing?'"

"I'd like to go rowing if we had a . . ."

"Shut up!" Eddie took Lawrence's arm, led him through tall grass to the water's edge, where a flat-bottomed old boat was drawn up, the water just lapping at the stern, high, an old red color, faded by sun and storm. A pair of heavy oars lay along the bottom of the boat.

"Jump in," Eddie said, "when I tell yuh to."

"But it doesn't belong to us."

"Yuh want to go rowing, don't yuh?"

"Yes, but . . ."

"Then jump in when I give yuh the word."

Lawrence neatly took off his shoes and socks while Eddie hauled the boat into the water.

"Jump in!" Eddie called.

Lawrence jumped. The boat glided out across the still lake. Eddie rowed industriously once they got out of the marsh grass.

"This isn't half bad, is it?" He leaned back on his oars for a moment.

"It's nice," Lawrence said. "It's very peaceful."

"Aaah," said Eddie, "yuh even talk like a pianist." And he rowed. After a while he got tired and let the boat go with the wind. He lay back and thought of the night to come, dabbling his fingers in the water, happy. "They oughta see me now, back on a Hunnerd and Seventy-

---

4. **Brahms** (brämz) **second piano concerto** (kən cher'tō). Johannes Brahms was a German composer of music; his second piano concerto is a long musical composition for the piano, accompanied by an orchestra.

third Street," he said. "They oughta see me handle this old boat."

"Everything would be perfect," Lawrence agreed, picking his feet up out of the puddle that was collecting on the bottom of the boat, "if we only knew that when we got out of this boat, we were going to get a strawberry ice cream soda."

"Why don't yuh think of somethin' else? Always thinkin' of one thing! Don't yuh get tired?"

"No," Lawrence said, after thinking it over.

"Here!" Eddie pushed the oars toward his brother. "Row! That'll give yuh somethin' else t' think about."

Lawrence took the oars gingerly. "This is bad for my hands," he explained as he pulled dutifully on the oars. "It stiffens the fingers."

"Look where yuh're goin'!" Eddie cried impatiently. "In circles! What's the sense in goin' in circles?"

"That's the way the boat goes," Lawrence said, pulling hard. "I can't help it if that's the way the boat goes."

"A pianist. A regular pianist. That's all yuh are. Gimme those oars."

Gratefully Lawrence yielded the oars up.

"It's not my fault if the boat goes in circles. That's the way it's made," he persisted quietly.

"Aaah, shut up!" Eddie pulled savagely on the oars. The boat surged forward, foam at the prow.

"Hey, out there in the boat! Hey!" A man's voice called over the water.

"Eddie," Lawrence said, "there's a man yelling at us."

"Come on in here, before I beat your pants off!" the man called. "Get out of my boat!"

"He wants us to get out of his boat," Lawrence interpreted. "This must be his boat."

"You don't mean it," Eddie snorted with deep sarcasm. He turned around to shout at the man on the shore, who was waving his arms now. "All right," Eddie called. "All right. We'll give yuh yer old boat. Keep your shirt on."

The man jumped up and down. "I'll beat yer heads off," he shouted.

Lawrence wiped his nose nervously. "Eddie," he said, "why don't we row over to the other side and walk home from there?"

Eddie looked at his brother contemptuously. "What're yuh—afraid?"

"No," Lawrence said, after a pause. "But why should we get into an argument?"

For answer Eddie pulled all the harder on the oars. The boat flew through the water. Lawrence squinted to look at the rapidly nearing figure of the man on the bank.

"He's a great big man, Eddie," Lawrence reported. "You never saw such a big man. And he looks awfully sore. Maybe we shouldn't've gone out in this boat. Maybe he doesn't like people to go out in his boat. Eddie, are you listening to me?"

With a final heroic pull, Eddie drove the boat into the shore. It grated with a horrible noise on the pebbles of the lake bottom.

"That," the man said, "is the end of that boat."

"That doesn't really hurt it, mister," Lawrence said. "It makes a lot of noise, but it doesn't do any damage."

The man reached over and grabbed Lawrence by the back of his neck with one hand and placed him on solid ground. He was a very big man, with tough bristles that grew all over his double chin and farmer's muscles in his arms that were quivering with passion now under a mat of hair.

There was a boy of about thirteen with him, obviously, from his look, his son, and the son was angry, too.

"Hit 'im, Pop," the son kept calling. "Wallop 'im!"

The man shook Lawrence again and again. He was almost too overcome with anger to speak. "No damage, eh? Only noise, eh!" he shouted into Lawrence's paling face. "I'll show you damage. I'll show you noise."

Eddie spoke up. Eddie was out of the boat now, an oar gripped in his hand, ready for the worst. "That's not fair," he said. "Look how much bigger yuh are than him. Why'n't yuh pick on somebody yuh size?"

The farmer's boy jumped up and down in passion, exactly as his father had done. "I'll fight him, Pop! I'll fight 'im! I'm his size! Come on, kid, put yer hands up!"

The farmer looked at his son, looked at Lawrence. Slowly he released Lawrence. "O.K.," he said. "Show him, Nathan."

Nathan pushed Lawrence. "Come into the woods, kid," he said belligerently. "We cin settle it there."

"One in the eye," Eddie whispered out of the corner of his mouth. "Give 'im one in the eye, Larry!"

But Lawrence stood with eyes lowered, regarding his hands.

"Well?" the farmer asked.

Lawrence still looked at his hands, opening and closing them slowly.

"He don't wanna fight," Nathan taunted Eddie. "He just wants t' row in our boat, he don't wanna fight."

"He wants to fight, all right," Eddie said stanchly, and under his breath, "Come on, Larry, in the kisser, a fast one in the puss . . ."

But Larry stood still, calmly, seeming to be thinking of Brahms and Beethoven,[5] of distant concert halls.

"He's yella, that's what's the matter with him," Nathan roared. "He's a coward, all city kids're cowards!"

"He's no coward," Eddie insisted, knowing in his deepest heart that his brother was a coward. With his knees he nudged Lawrence. "Bring up yuh left! Please, Larry, bring up yuh left!"

Deaf to all pleas, Lawrence kept his hands at his sides.

"Yella! Yella! Yella!" Nathan screamed loudly.

"Well," the farmer wanted to know, "is he goin' to fight or not?"

"Larry!" Fifteen years of desperation was in Eddie's voice, but it made no mark on Lawrence. Eddie turned slowly toward home. "He's not goin' to fight," he said flatly. And then, as one throws a bone to a neighbor's noisy dog, "Come on, you . . ."

Slowly Lawrence bent over, picked up his shoes and socks, took a step after his brother.

"Wait a minute, you!" the farmer called. He went after Eddie, turned him around. "I want to talk to ye."

"Yeah?" Eddie said sadly, with little defiance. "What do yuh wanna say?"

"See that house over there?" the farmer asked, pointing.

"Yeah," Eddie said. "What about it?"

"That's my house," the farmer said. "You stay away from it. See?"

"O.K. O.K.," Eddie said wearily, all pride gone.

"See that boat there?" the farmer asked, pointing at the source of all the trouble.

"I see it," Eddie said.

"That's my boat. Stay away from it or I'll beat ye. See?"

---

5. **Beethoven** (bā'tō vən), Ludwig van Beethoven, a German musical composer.

"Yeah, yeah, I see," Eddie said. "I won't touch yer lousy boat." And once more, to Lawrence, "Come on, you . . ."

"Yella! Yella! Yella!" Nathan kept roaring, jumping up and down, until they passed out of earshot, across the pleasant fields, ripe with the soft sweet smell of clover in the late summer afternoon. Eddie walked before Lawrence, his face grimly contracted, his mouth curled in shame and bitterness. He stepped on the clover blossoms fiercely, as though he hated them, wanted to destroy them, the roots under them, the very ground they grew in.

Holding his shoes in his hands, his head bent on his chest, his hair still mahogany smooth and mahogany dark, Lawrence followed ten feet back in the footsteps, plainly marked in the clover, of his brother.

"Yella," Eddie was muttering, loud enough for the villain behind him to hear clearly. "Yella! Yella as a flower. My own brother," he marveled. "If it was me I'da been glad to get killed before I let anybody call me that. I would let 'em cut my heart out first. My own brother. Yella as a flower. Just one in the eye! Just *one!* Just to show 'im . . . But he stands there, takin' guff from a kid with holes in his pants. A pianist. Lawrrrrence! They knew what they were doin' when they called yuh Lawrrrrence! Don't talk to me! I don't want yuh ever to talk to me again as long as yuh live! Lawrrrrence!"

In sorrow too deep for tears, the two brothers reached home, ten feet, ten million miles apart.

Without looking around, Eddie went to the grape arbor, stretched out on the bench. Lawrence looked after him, his face pale and still, then went into the house.

Face downward on the bench, close to the rich black earth of the arbor, Eddie bit his fingers to keep the tears back. But he could not bite hard enough, and the tears came, a bitter tide, running down his face, dropping on the black soft earth in which the grapes were rooted.

"Eddie!"

Eddie scrambled around, pushing the tears away with iron hands. Lawrence was standing there, carefully pulling on doeskin gloves over his small hands. "Eddie," Lawrence was saying, stonily disregarding the tears, "I want you to come with me."

Silently, but with singing in his heart so deep it called new tears to his wet eyes, Eddie got up, blew his nose, and followed after his brother, caught up with him, walked side by side with him across the field of clover, so lightly that the red and purple blossoms barely bent in their path.

Eddie knocked sternly at the door of the farmhouse, three knocks, solid, vigorous, the song of trumpets caught in them.

Nathan opened the door. "What do ye want?" he asked suspiciously.

"A little while ago," Eddie said formally, "yuh offered to fight my brother. He's ready now."

Nathan looked at Lawrence, standing there, straight, his head up, his baby lips compressed into a thin tight line, his gloved hands creased in solid fists. He started to close the door. "He had his chance," Nathan said.

Eddie kept the door open firmly. "Yuh offered, remember that," he reminded Nathan politely.

"He shoulda fought then," Nathan said stubbornly. "He had his chance."

"Come on," Eddie almost begged. "Yuh wanted to fight before."

"That was before. Lemme close the door."

"Yuh can't do this!" Eddie was shouting desperately. "Yuh offered!"

Nathan's father, the farmer, appeared in the doorway. He looked bleakly out. "What's goin' on here?" he asked.

"A little while ago," Eddie spoke very fast, "this man here offered to fight this man here." His eloquent hand indicated first Nathan, then Lawrence. "Now we've come to take the offer."

The farmer looked at his son. "Well?"

"He had his chance," Nathan grumbled sullenly.

"Nathan don't want t' fight," the farmer said to Eddie. "Get outa here."

Lawrence stepped up, over to Nathan. He looked Nathan squarely in the eye. "Yella," he said to Nathan.

The farmer pushed his son outside the door. "Go fight him," he ordered.

"We can settle it in the woods," Lawrence said.

"Wipe him up, Larry!" Eddie called as Lawrence and Nathan set out for the woods, abreast, but a polite five yards apart. Eddie watched them disappear behind trees, in silence.

The farmer sat down heavily on the porch, leaned back against a pillar, stretched comfortably.

"Sit down," the farmer said, "ye cin never tell how long kids'll fight."

In silence they both looked across the field to the woods that shielded the battlefield. The tops of the trees waved a little in the wind and the afternoon was collecting in deep blue shadows among the thick brown tree trunks where they gripped the ground. A chicken hawk floated lazily over the field, banking and slipping with the wind. The farmer regarded the chicken hawk without malice.

"Someday," the farmer said, "I'm going to get that son of a gun."

"What is it?" Eddie asked.

"Chicken hawk. You're from the city, ain't ye?"

"Yeah."

"Like it in the city?"

"Nothing like it."

The farmer puffed reflectively. "Someday I'm goin' to live in the city. No sense in livin' in the country these days."

"Oh, I don't know," Eddie said. "The country's very nice. There's a lot to be said for the country."

The farmer nodded, weighing the matter in his own mind. "Say," he said, "do you think your brother'll damage my kid?"

"It's possible," Eddie said. "He's very tough, my brother. He has dozens a' fights, every month. Every kid back home's scared stiff a' him. Why," said Eddie, sailing full into fancy, "I remember one day Larry fought three kids all in a row. In a half a hour. He busted all their noses. In a half a hour! He's got a terrific left jab—one, two, bang! like this—and it gets 'em in the nose."

"Well, he can't do Nathan's nose any harm." The farmer laughed. "No matter what you did to a nose like that it'd be a improvement."

"He's got a lot of talent, my brother," Eddie said, proud of the warrior in the woods. "He plays the piano. He's a very good piano player. You ought to hear him."

"A little kid like that," the farmer marveled. "Nathan can't do nothing."

Off in the distance, in the gloom under the trees, two figures appeared, close together, walked slowly out into the sunlight of the field. Eddie and the farmer stood up. Wearily the two fighters approached, together, their arms dangling at their sides.

Eddie looked first at Nathan. Nathan's mouth had been bleeding and there was a lump on his forehead and his ear was red. Eddie smiled with satisfaction. Nathan had been in a fight. Eddie walked slowly toward Lawrence. Lawrence approached with head high. But it was a sadly battered head. The hair was tangled, an eye was closed, the nose was bruised and still bled. Lawrence sucked in the blood from his nose from time to time with his tongue. His collar was torn, his pants covered with forest loam, with his bare knees skinned and raw. But in the one eye that still could be seen shone a clear light, honorable, indomitable.

"Ready to go home now, Eddie?" Lawrence asked.

"Sure." Eddie started to pat Lawrence on the back, pulled his hand back. He turned and waved to the farmer. "So long."

"So long," the farmer called. "Any time you want to use the boat, just step into it."

"Thanks." Eddie waited while Lawrence shook hands gravely with Nathan.

"Good night," Lawrence said. "It was a good fight."

"Yeah," Nathan said.

The two brothers walked away, close together, across the field of clover, fragrant in the long shadows. Half the way they walked in silence, the silence of equals, strong men communicating in a language more eloquent than words, the only sound the thin jingle of the thirty-five cents in Eddie's pocket.

Suddenly Eddie stopped Lawrence. "Let's go this way," he said, pointing off to the right.

"But home's this way, Eddie."

"I know. Let's go into town. Let's get ice cream sodas," Eddie said; "let's get strawberry ice cream sodas." END

1. (a) What is Lawrence's aim in life? (b) What are Eddie's chief interests? (c) What problems do their differing interests cause between the brothers? (d) In what way do their very different physical characteristics intensify their problems?

2. (a) For what reasons does Lawrence refuse to fight? (b) How does Eddie then feel towards his brother? (c) Why does Lawrence finally agree to fight Nathan?

3. (a) Why does the farmer offer the boys the use of his boat after the fight? (b) What attitudes does Eddie share with the farmer?

4. (a) After the fight, why does Eddie decide not to pat Lawrence on the back? (b) What is Eddie really telling Lawrence in his offer of a soda? (c) Is "Strawberry Ice Cream Soda" a good title for this story? Why or why not?

5. What is the most important conflict in this story?

6. Read the biographical sketch of Irwin Shaw (page 33). (a) By making Lawrence a piano player does Shaw make his unwillingness to fight more believable? Why or why not? (b) Are there boys who might not want to fight for other reasons? Explain.

WORD STUDY

A. Does the word *wound* rhyme with *sound* or *tuned*? Does it mean "injury" or is it a form of the verb "wind"? How could you be sure that the meaning and pronunciation you've given *wound* are correct?

He inflicted the *wound* upon himself while he *wound* the mechanical train.

Which of the italicized words in the above sentence means "injury"? What is the meaning of the other italicized word? Which context clues helped you determine the correct meaning and pronunciation in each case? *Context* is the setting in which a word appears. It is made up of the other words or

ideas in a sentence, paragraph, or selection. The context in which a word is set often provides helpful clues to its meaning.

When a word has more than one definition or pronunciation, the context in which it appears usually indicates which definition or pronunciation is intended.

B. Conrad is a *pusillanimous* boy.

Does the above sentence give you enough clues to the meaning of *pusillanimous*? How can you find out what it means?

Unlike Henry, who is brave, Conrad is *pusillanimous*.

According to the above sentence, does *pusillanimous* mean (**a**) fat; (**b**) cowardly; (**c**) near-sighted? Which two words in the sentence are the best clues to its meaning? Turn to the Glossary to find out how to pronounce *pusillanimous*.

The context in which an unfamiliar word appears often provides clues to its meaning.

C. For the past week, my sister and I have been having *spats* even before I'm *wide-awake*.

What are *spats*? What does *wide awake* mean?

The old gentleman wore *spats* to cover his ankles and a *wide-awake* to cover his head.

What clue to a new meaning for *spats* is given in the above sentence? According to the above sentence, what purpose does a *wide-awake* serve? To give precise definitions of *spats* and *wide-awake* as used in this context, what other information would you need and where could you find it?

The context in which a word appears sometimes reveals an unfamiliar definition for a familiar word.

D. In four of the five sentences below you should be able to figure out the meaning of the italicized word from context clues. Read each sentence and complete the statement that follows. In which sentence is there no helpful clue?

1. Eddie lay on the grass trying to think of something to do, but none of his ideas seemed interesting enough to be put into action; the heat had robbed Eddie of his energy and imagination, making him bored and *listless*.

Listless means (**a**) mean; (**b**) interested in things; (**c**) too tired to care about anything.

2. Lawrence, who was afraid of hurting his hands, handled the oars *gingerly*.

Gingerly means (**a**) easily; (**b**) roughly; (**c**) with extreme caution.

3. He seemed *oblivious* of his surroundings.

Oblivious means (**a**) cautious; (**b**) context clues are inadequate; (**c**) unaware.

4. Lawrence seemed to *disdain* the names Eddie called him; he seemed to be unaffected by his brother's anger and hurt pride; but his later actions proved that Eddie's words had moved him deeply.

Disdain means (**a**) scorn; (**b**) consider; (**c**) enjoy.

5. Eddie knocked sternly at the door of the farmhouse—three knocks, solid and *vigorous*.

Vigorous means (**a**) timid; (**b**) forceful; (**c**) context clues are inadequate.

THE AUTHOR

Dick Tracy started Irwin Shaw writing professionally. After graduating from college, Shaw spent two years writing scripts for weekly radio shows featuring the comic strip character. He left Dick Tracy in 1936; since then, he has devoted himself to writing plays, novels, and short stories.

Shaw claims a "particularly friendly feeling" for "Strawberry Ice Cream Soda," because it was one of his first published works. Of the story, he says " . . . its subject was suggested to me by a friend who described an incident somewhat like the one I used, which had happened to him and his brother when they were boys. Neither of the brothers in the actual incident was a pianist, so that part of the story was pure invention designed to make the younger boy's disinclination to fight more comprehensible."

See
SETTING
*Handbook
of Literary
Terms
page 533*

*While Miss Lowy talked about beauty and truth and
skylarks, Jeanie wished she could see some sky.
How is Jeanie's attitude toward the world
she lives in changed by Miss Lowy's words?*

BEAUTY is TRUTH

ANNA GUEST

AT 125TH STREET, they all got off, Jeanie and her friend, Barbara, and a crowd of other boys and girls who went to the same downtown high school. Through the train window, Jeanie thought she saw the remaining passengers look at them with relief and disdain. Around her, the boys and girls pressed forward with noisy gaiety. They were all friends now. They were home again in Harlem.[1]

A tall boy detached himself from a group, bowed low and swept his cap before him in a courtly salute.

"Greetings, Lady Jeanie. Greetings, Barbara."

Jeanie bit her lip. Frowning, she pulled her coat closer and shrugged. Barbara smiled and dimpled, pleased for her friend.

"I told you he likes you," she whispered. "Look, he's waiting. Want me to go on ahead?"

Jeanie really was wasting an opportunity. Norman was keen. She saw Jeanie's head, slightly bowed and thrust forward. It was no use. She was an odd girl, but Barbara liked her anyway. The boy swung gracefully back to his group.

"Coming to the show tonight?" Barbara asked.

"No, I can't. I'm so far behind in my homework, I'd better try to do some before they decide to throw me out." Jeanie still frowned.

"Beauty is Truth" by Anna Guest from STORIES FROM SEVENTEEN.
1. *Harlem*, a largely black community in New York City.

"Want a Coke or something?" asked Barbara as they passed the big ice-cream parlor window, cluttered with candy boxes and ornate with curly lettering. They could see the juke box near the door and some boys and girls sitting down at a table. It looked warm and friendly.

Jeanie shook her head, one brief shake.

"I think I'll stop in. I'm awful thirsty," said Barbara.

Jeanie shrugged.

"So long then."

"So long."

She walked along the busy street, aimlessly looking in the store windows, turned the corner, and walked the few blocks to her house. Though it was chilly, each brownstone or gray stoop had its cluster of people clinging to the iron railings. Some children on skates played a desperate game of hockey with sticks that were not hockey sticks.

When a car approached, they did not interrupt their game until it was almost too late. Amid shouts from the driver and wild jeers from the children, the car passed, and the game was resumed in all its concentrated intensity.

Her little brother Billy was playing in front of the stoop with three or four other kids. They were bending over something on the sidewalk, in a closed circle. Pitching pennies again, she thought with repugnance. She was going to pass them, and started up the three stone steps to the doorway. A window on the ground floor opened, and Fat Mary leaned out, dressed only in a slip and a worn, brown sweater.

"Now you're going to catch it, Billy Boy. Your sister's going to tell your mama you been pitching pennies again."

Jeanie did not pause.

Billy sprang up, "Hi, Jeanie. Jeanie, gimme a nickel. I need a nickel. A nickel, a nickel. I gotta have a nickel."

The other little boys took up the chant. "A nickel, a nickel. Billy needs a nickel."

She threw them a furious glance and went in. Two little girls sat on the second landing, playing house. They had a set of toy dishes spread out on the top stair, and held dolls in their laps. She stepped over them, careful not to disturb their arrangements.

The kitchen smelled dank and unused, and the opening of the door dislodged a flake of green-painted plaster. It fell into the sink, with a dry powdering. A black dress someone had given her mother lay over the chair before the sewing machine. It reminded her that her sleeve had torn half out, dressing after gym. She really should sew it, but the sight of the black dress waiting to be made over made her dislike the thought of sewing. She would just have to wear her coat in school tomorrow. Lots of kids did.

She hung her coat on a hook in the room she shared with her mother, and stood irresolute. Her mother would be coming in soon, and would expect to find the potatoes peeled and the table laid. She caught sight of a comic book and, unwillingly attracted by the garish colors, read one side. "Ah!" she thought in disgust. "Billy!" She thought of her homework. She was so far behind in social studies that she could probably never make it up. It was hardly worth trying. Mercantilism. The rise of the merchant class. She would probably fail. And gym, all those cuts in gym. Miss Fisher, her grade adviser, had called her down yesterday and warned her. "Ah!" she said again. Miss Fisher was all right. She had even been encour-

aging. "I know you can do it," she had said.

She sat down on the bed and opened her looseleaf notebook at random. A page fell out. She was about to jam it back in, when the freshly inked writing caught her eye. Today's English. Some poem about a vase, and youths and maidens. Miss Lowy had brought in some pictures of vases with people on them, dressed in togas or whatever they were, spinning and reading from scrolls. Why did everybody get so excited about the Greeks? It was so long ago. "Wonderful! Wonderful!" Miss Lowy had exclaimed. How could anybody get so stirred up over a poem? She meant it too. You could tell from her expression.

"Listen, boys and girls. Listen." A lifted arm enjoined them.

> *Beauty is truth, truth beauty,—*
> *that is all*
> *Ye know on earth, and all ye need*
> *to know.*[2]

There it was, copied into her notebook. Caught by something in the lines, she tried to find the poem in her tattered anthology, not bothering about the index, but riffling the pages to and fro. John Keats, at last—"On First Looking into Chapman's Homer." More Greeks. Here it was—"Ode on a Grecian Urn." The poem, all squeezed together in the middle of the page, looked dry and dusty, withered and far away, at the bottom of a dry well. She saw, not so much words, as an uninteresting, meandering pattern. The big THOU at the opening repelled her. She turned the page to find that the poem went on. Recognizing the last lines, she heard them again, falling so roundly, so perfectly, from the lips of Miss Lowy. She turned back to the beginning. Why "Grecian," why not "Greek"? With an effort, she began to

dig the poem out of its constricted print.

"*Thou foster child of silence and slow time,*" its soft susurrus carried her on. She read the poem through to the end, trying to remember her teacher's cadences.

"Write about beauty and truth. Write about life," Miss Lowy had said.

She tore a page out of her notebook and opened her pen. Pulling over a chair, she rested her book on the sooty window sill. She stared out at the dusk falling sadly, sadly, thickening into darkness over the coal yards.

A crash of the kitchen door caused a reverberation in the window sill. The notebook slipped out of her hands.

"Where'd you get that bottle of pop?" she heard her mother's voice, hard and sounding more Southern than usual.

A high-pitched, wordless sniveling came in reply. "I asked you. Where'd you get that pop? You better tell me."

"A lady gave me a nickel. A lady came down the street and ask me——"

"You lying. I know where you got that money. Gambling, that's what you was doing."

"I was only pitching pennies, Ma. It's only a game, Ma."

"Gambling and stealing and associating with bad friends. I told you to stay away from them boys. Didn't I? Didn't I?" Her mother's voice rose. "I'm going to give you a beating you ain't going to forget."

Billy wailed on a long descending note.

Jeanie could hear each impact of the strap and her mother's heavy breathing.

---

2. **Beauty . . . know,** the concluding lines of "Ode on a Grecian Urn," by the English poet John Keats (1795–1821). The poem explores the ideas inspired by pictures of men and women which decorate an ancient vase.

"I want you to grow up good, not lying and gambling and stealing," her mother gasped, "and I'm going to make you good. You ain't never going to forget this." When it had been going on forever, it stopped. A final slap of the strap. "And you ain't going to get any supper either. You can go now. You can go to bed and reflect on what I told you."

He stumbled past her, whimpering, fists grinding into eyes, and into the dark little alcove which was his room. Jeanie heard the groan of the bed as he threw himself on it. She felt a pain in her fingers and saw them still pressed tightly around the pen.

Her mother appeared in the doorway. She wore her hat and coat.

"Come help me get supper, Jeanie. You should have got things started." Her voice was tired and tremulous, and held no reproach.

"I don't want any supper, Ma."

Her mother came in and sat down heavily on the bed, taking off her hat, and letting her coat fall open.

"I had a hard day. I worked hard every minute," she said. "I brought you something extra nice for dessert. I stood in line to get some of them tarts from Sutter's."

Jeanie rose and silently put her mother's hat on the shelf. She held out her hand for her mother's coat, and hung it up.

Together they opened the paper bags on the kitchen table. She set the water to boil.

As they ate in silence, the three tarts shone like subtle jewels on a plate, at one end of the chipped porcelain table. Her mother looked tired and stern.

"You better fix your brother up a plate," she said, still stern. "Put it on a tray. Here, take this." And she put on the tray the most luscious, the most perfect of the tarts. "Wait." She went heavily over to her swollen black handbag, took out a small clasp purse, opened it, and carefully, seriously, deliberately, picked out a coin, rejected it, and took out another. "Give him this." It was a quarter.

After the dishes were washed, Jeanie brought her books into the kitchen and spread them out under the glaring overhead light. Billy had been asleep, huddled in his clothes. Tears had left dusty streaks on his face.

Her mother sat in the armchair, ripping out the sides of the black dress. Her spectacles made her look strange.

"*Beauty is truth,*" Jeanie read in her notebook. Hastily, carelessly, defiantly disregarding margins and doubtful spellings, letting her pen dig into the paper, she began to write: "Last night my brother Billy got a terrible beating. . . ."

Scramble to borrow the social studies homework from a girl in her homeroom, say hello to Barbara, undress for gym, dress again, the torn sleeve, bookkeeping—a blot, get another piece of ledger paper. "This is the third I've given you. You might say thank you." Get to English early. Slip her composition in under the others, sit in the last seat. Don't bother me. I am in a bad mood. Rows and rows of seats. Rows and rows of windows opposite. She could even read the writing on some of the blackboards, but who cared? A boy leaned far out of the window before closing it. Other heads turning. Would he fall? No, he was safe. Heads turned back. A poem about a skylark. From where she sat, she could see about a square foot of sky, drained of all color by the looming school walls. Miss Lowy read clearly, standing all alone at the front of the room in her clean

white blouse and with her smooth blonde hair.

Miss Lowy, maybe you see skylarks. Me, I'd be glad to see some sky, she thought and nearly uttered it. Around her, students were writing in their notebooks. Miss Lowy was about to speak to her. Better start writing something. Sullen, Mr. MacIver had called her last week. She felt about for her notebook and pen. It had been a mistake to write as she had done about her brother's beating. They would laugh if they knew. Shirley, who was the class secretary, and Saul, with the prominent forehead. No, he would not laugh. He was always writing about space ships and the end of the world. No danger, though, that her story would be read. Only the best manuscripts were read. She remembered keenly the blotched appearance of the paper, the lines crossed out, and the words whose spelling she could never be sure of. Oh, well, she didn't care. Only one more period and then the weekend. "Lady Jeanie's too proud to come to our party. Jeanie, what are you waiting for? Jeanie's waiting for a Prince Charming with a red Cadillac to come

and take her away." If Barbara asked her again, she would go with her, maybe. There was going to be a party at Norma's Saturday night, with Cokes and sandwiches and records and dancing, everybody chipping in. "Jeanie, I need a nickel. Mama, I need a dollar. I need, I need."

The bell rang, and the pens dropped, the books were closed with a clatter. She slipped out ahead of the pushing, jostling boys and girls.

Monday, Miss Lowy had on still another perfect white blouse. She stood facing the class, holding a sheaf of papers in her hand. Most of the students looked at her expectantly. Marion, who nearly always got ninety, whispered to her neighbor. Michael, who had but recently come from Greece—ah, but that was a different Greece—grumbled and shifted in his seat. He would have to do his composition over. He always did.

"I spent a very enjoyable time this weekend, reading your work," said Miss Lowy, waiting for the class to smile.

"Seriously, though, many of your pieces were most interesting, even though they were a trifle unconven-

tional about spelling and punctuation." A smile was obviously indicated here too, and the class obeyed. She paused. "Sometimes, however, a piece of writing is so honest and human, that you have to forgive the technical weaknesses. Not that they aren't important," she said hastily, "but what the writer has to say is more significant."

The three best students in the class looked confused. It was their pride not to have technical errors.

"When you hear this," Miss Lowy continued, "I think you'll agree with me. I know it brought tears to my eyes." The class looked incredulous.

"It's called 'Evening Comes to 128th Street.'" Her face took on that rapt look.

Jeanie's heart beat painfully. She picked up a pencil, but dropped it, so unsteady were her fingers. Even the back of Shirley's head was listening. Even the classes in the other wing of the building, across the courtyard, seemed fixed, row on row, in an attitude of listening. Miss Lowy read on. It was all there, the coal yards and Fat Mary, the stoop and the tarts from Sutter's, Billy asleep with tears dried on his face, the clasp purse and the quarter.

" 'The funny part of it was, when I woke him, Billy wasn't mad. He was glad about the quarter, and ate his supper, dessert and all, but Mama never did eat her tart, so I put it away.' "

A poignancy of remembrance swept over Jeanie, then shame and regret. It was no business of theirs, these strange white people.

No one spoke. The silence was unbearable. Finally Marion, the incomparable Marion, raised her hand.

"It was so real," she said, "you felt you were right there in that kitchen."

"You didn't know who to feel sorry for," said another student. "You wanted to cry with the mother and you wanted to cry with Billy."

"With the girl too," said another. Several heads nodded.

"You see," said Miss Lowy. "It's literature. It's life. It's pain and truth and beauty."

Jeanie's heart beat so, it made a mist come before her eyes. Through the blur she heard Miss Lowy say it was good enough to be sent in to *Scholastic*.[3] It showed talent, it showed promise. She heard her name called and shrank from the eyes turned upon her.

After school, she hurried out and caught the first train that you could catch only if you left immediately and did not stroll or stop the least little bit to talk to someone. She did not want to meet anyone, not even Barbara.

Was that Billy among the kids on the stoop?

"Billy," she called, "Billy."

What would she say to him? Beauty is truth, truth beauty?

"Billy," she called again urgently.

Billy lifted his head, and seeing who it was, tore himself reluctantly away from his friends, and took a step toward her.   THE END

---

3. *Scholastic,* literary magazine for high schools which periodically publishes student compositions.

1. (a) Describe the community in which Jeanie lives. **(b)** What kind of home life does she have? **(c)** Compare Jeanie's home life with the sort of things she learns at school. **(d)** How does her life at home affect her feelings toward school?

2. What influence does the community have on Billy and on Jeanie's mother?

3. (a) How is Jeanie different from her friends? **(b)** What causes this difference?

4. (a) What things does Jeanie write about? **(b)** Why does she emphasize the tarts and the quarter in her composition? **(c)** What does Miss Lowy mean when she says that literature is "pain and truth and beauty"?

5. (a) What is Jeanie's mood as she starts writing the essay? **(b)** What are her feelings while Miss Lowy reads the essay aloud? **(c)** What has Jeanie learned from this experience? **(d)** How does this knowledge help her to resolve her conflict?

6. Why doesn't Jeanie want to meet anyone after school following the reading of her composition?

WORD STUDY

A large number of difficult-looking words are really simple words with syllables added to them. Recognizing the various parts in a word can often help you understand its meaning. Many words are made up of three kinds of parts:

1. A root word such as *bake, born, late, write, claim* or *move.* Root words give you clues to the meaning of the longer word.

2. Prefixes—syllables such as *un-, re-, pre-, dis-* and *ex-.* Prefixes are placed in front of the root word and often change its meaning (*un*moved, *pre*bake, *re*born). A word may have more than one prefix, as in *unre*moved.

3. Suffixes—meaningful parts added to the ends of words, as in late*ness*, writ*er*, claim*ant.* Suffixes usually determine the way a word can be used in a sentence and also affect its meaning. (Karen is the *happiest* person I

know. *Happiness* is Karen's chief characteristic.) A word may have more than one suffix, as in care*lessness.* (The term *affix* is used to indicate both prefixes and suffixes.)

Analyze the italicized word in each sentence below. What is the root word in each? What are its affixes? How does each affix add to the meaning or change the use of the word in the sentence? What does the total word mean?

1. Jeanie walked along the busy street, *aimlessly* looking in the store windows.

Was Jeanie looking for something special? How do you know?

2. The opening of the door *dislodged* a flake of green-painted plaster.

Did the plaster come loose or stay in place? What affix helps you answer this question?

3. Miss Fisher had even been *encouraging.*

Was Jeanie more likely to have been cheered or depressed by Miss Fisher's words? Explain.

4. To Jeanie, the silence was *unbearable.*

Is Jeanie comfortable? Which affix helps you understand her state of mind?

5. Jeanie dropped a pencil from her *unsteady* fingers.

Was Jeanie nervous or calm? How do you know?

See
CHARACTERIZATION: *Methods of*
Handbook
of Literary
Terms
page 516

Johnny Hobhouse doesn't realize how the day
would change his life—but his family does.
What kind of people would act as
the Hobhouses do?

The Lesson

JESSAMYN WEST

JOHN THOMAS had awakened thinking of Curly—or, rather, when he woke up, he did not stop thinking of Curly, for all night he had been with the young steer, encouraging him, patting him on his curling forelock, leading him before the admiring judges. The boy was wide awake now, yet Curly's image was still as strongly with him as in the dream—the heavy shoulders, the great barrel, the short legs, the red coat shining with health and with the many brushings John Thomas had given it. And Curly's face! The boy's own face crinkled happily as he thought of it, and then turned scornful as he thought of the people who said one baby beef[1] was just like another. Curly looked at you with intelligence. His eyes weren't just hairless spots on his head, like the eyes of most baby beeves. They showed that Curly knew when eating time had come and that he understood the difference between being told he was a lazy old cuss and a prize-winning baby beef. You had only to say to him, "You poor old steer," and he put his head down and looked at you as much as to say he knew it

was true and not to kid him about it. John Thomas remembered a hundred humors and shrewdnesses of Curly's, and lay in bed smiling about them—the way he had of getting the last bite of mash out of his feed pail, and his cleverness in evading the vet, and how he would lunge at Wolf when the collie barked at him.

"This is the day!" John Thomas said aloud. "This is the day!"

Across the hall came a girl's sleepy voice. "Johnny, you promised to be quiet."

John Thomas didn't answer. No use arguing with Jo when she was sleepy. He sat up and slipped his arms into the sleeves of his bathrobe, and then stepped onto the floor boards, which were so much cooler than the air, and walked slowly, because he wanted so much to walk fast, to the window.

---

1. *baby beef*, a beef calf from one year to twenty months old. The term is usually applied to an animal fattened for butchering.

There Curly was, standing with his nose over the corral fence looking up toward John Thomas' window. Curly acts as if he knows, the boy thought. I bet he does know.

"Hey, Curly!" he called softly. "How you feel this morning? Feel like a prize baby beef? Feel like the best steer in California? First prize for Curly?" Curly swished his tail. "Don't you worry, Curly. You *are* the best."

John Thomas knew he was going to have to go in and talk to Jo, even though she'd be mad at being waked so early. If he stood another minute looking at Curly—so beautiful in his clean corral, with the long blue early-morning shadows of the eucalyptus falling across it—and listening to the meadow larks off in the alfalfa and remembering that this was the day, he'd give a whoop, and that would make both Jo and Pop mad. He tiptoed across the hall, opened his sister's door, and looked at her room with distaste. Grown-up girls like Jo, almost twenty, ought to be neater. All girls ought to be neater. The clothes Jo had taken off before she went to sleep made a path from her door to her bed, starting with her shoes and hat and ending with her underwear. Curly's corral's neater, he thought, and said, "It's time to get up, Jo!"

Jo rolled over on her face and groaned. John Thomas stepped over Jo's clothes and sat down on the edge of the bed.

Jo groaned again. "Please don't wake me up yet, Johnny," she said.

"You're already awake. You're talking."

"I'm talking in my sleep."

"I don't care if you don't wake up, if you'll talk. I've seen Curly already. He looks pretty good. He looks like he knows it's the day."

"He's dead wrong, then. It's still the night."

John Thomas laughed. If he got Jo to arguing, she'd wake up. "It's six o'clock," he said.

Jo, still face down, raised herself on one elbow and looked at her wristwatch. Then she whirled onto her back, stuck one leg out from under the sheet, and gave her brother a kick that set him down on the floor with a thud. "Why, John Thomas Hobhouse!" she said indignantly. "It's only five-fifteen and Nicky didn't get me home until two. You're so kind to that old steer of yours, but you don't care whether your own sister gets any sleep or not."

John Thomas bounced back onto the bed. Jo looked at him sharply and he knew what was to come.

"What have you got on under that bathrobe, John Thomas Hobhouse?" she demanded. "Did you sleep in your underwear last night?"

"I slept in my shorts."

"That's a filthy thing to do."

"You say it's filthy if I don't wear them in the daytime and filthy if I do wear them at night. What's daylight or dark got to do with it? Now, if I—"

"Look, Johnny, let's not get started on that. There are some things you're going to have to do that aren't reasonable. Once school starts, you'll be spending some nights with the other boys, and their mothers will be saying I don't look after you, and let you sleep in your underwear."

"I don't do it away from home, Jo, but it was so hot last night. You tell Mrs. Henny to do my ducks up special for today? Boy, wait till you see me and Curly go by the grandstand! Wait till you see us in the ring when Curly wins!"

"When Curly wins! Maybe he won't win, Johnny."

"Maybe the judges *won't* see he's best—but they will if they're any good."

John Thomas lay on his stomach, hanging his head over the edge of the bed until his long pompadour spread out on the floor like a dust mop and his face was out of Jo's sight. "I prayed about today," he said.

"Did you, Johnny?"

"Yep, but I didn't think it was fair to pray for Curly to win." He heaved himself up and down, so that his hair flicked back and forth, across the floor. "A lot of kids probably did pray they'd win, though."

Jo regarded him with tenderness and amazement. "I never would have thought most of the kids who go to the fair had ever heard of praying," she said.

"Oh, sure, they all heard of it," Johnny said, "and when it comes to something important like this, they all think you ought to try everything. But I didn't ask for Curly to win. I just prayed the judges would be good and know their stuff. If they do, Curly will get the blue ribbon, all right. With everyone else asking to win, I thought maybe that would kind of make an impression on God."

It made an impression on Jo. Lord, she thought, I'm a heathen. "What do you care whether or not Curly wins, if you know he's best?" she asked.

John Thomas heaved his head and shoulders up onto the bed and lay on his stomach with his face near Jo's. "How can you wear those tin things in your hair?" he asked. Then he answered her question. "I know for sure Curly's best, but *he* don't. He knows he's good, but he don't know he's that good. I want him to win so he can have the blue ribbon on his halter and walk up in front of the people while all the other baby beeves watch him."

"You going to walk with him, kid?" Jo asked.

"Yep, I got to."

"Kinda nice to have the other kids watch, too?"

This slyness tickled John Thomas and he laughed. No use trying to fool Jo about anything. "Anyway, it's mostly Curly," he said.

Jo started taking the curlers out of her hair. She tucked them, one by one, into Johnny's bush of hair as she took them out. "Remember when Curly got bloated?" she asked. "You weren't much help then. You cried and didn't want the vet to stick him."

"Yeah, but, Jo, it looked so awful. To take a knife and stick it inside him. And Curly was so darned scared." He spoke dreamily, with the satisfaction and relief of dangers past. "He looked like he was going to have a calf, didn't he? And I guess it hurt more."

"Yep, Johnny. A cow's made to have a calf, but a steer isn't made to have gas. Hand me my comb. Top left-hand drawer."

John Thomas got up and stood looking at himself in the mirror. His hair was thick enough to keep the curlers from dropping out.

"You look like an African Bushman,"[2] Jo said. "Come on, get that comb."

When John Thomas handed it to her, she began loosening her sausagelike curls. He watched her turn the fat little sausages into big frankfurters.

"Time to get dressed, kid," she said. "Jump into your ducks. They're all done up fresh and hanging in your closet."

"Do you think I've been giving him too much mash, Jo?" Johnny asked. "Does he look kind of soft to you? Too fat?"

"He looks just right to me. But

---

2. *African Bushman*, a member of a roving South African tribe.

it's all over now. No use worrying any more. This time tomorrow, he'll be someone else's problem."

John Thomas sat down on the window sill and looked out at the tank house. The sunlight lay on it in a slab as heavy and yellow as a bar of naphtha soap. There was already a dance of heat out across the alfalfa fields. White clouds were boiling up from behind purple Tahquitz. The morning-glories were beginning to shut themselves against the sun. This was the day all right, but he could not think ahead until tomorrow, when Curly would have been sold.

The boy made the width of the room in three jack-rabbit hops, and banged the door behind him.

Jo swung herself out of her bed and stood before her mirror. I guess it's bad to be thirteen and not have a mother, and to love a steer that's going to be beefsteak in forty-eight hours, she thought somberly. I ought to take better care of Johnny, and Dad ought to wake up from remembering Mother. He's been that way ever since she died.

The sound of Johnny's leaps down the stairs—four house-shuddering thuds—and his cracked voice calling out to Mrs. Henny made her look at her watch. Almost six. Jo grabbed fresh underwear from the drawer and ran for the bathroom.

When Jo came downstairs, ten minutes later, all dressed except for putting on the scarf and belt that were hanging over her shoulders, she saw her father, seated at the table on the screened porch where they ate breakfast in summer and reading the morning paper. She was fond of her father, but in one respect he was unsatisfactory: She didn't like his appearance. He didn't look fatherly to her. There wasn't any gray in his black hair or any stoop to his shoulders.

He called to her now, "Tell Mrs. Henny we're ready to eat."

Jo went through the porch door into the sunny kitchen, where Mrs. Henny was slicing peaches for breakfast. She was already dressed for the fair, in a lavender dotted swiss with a lavender ribbon through her bobbed gray hair. "Hello, Mrs. Henny," Jo said. "Dad says let's eat. Gee, you look swell!"

"I thought I'd better wear something light," Mrs. Henny said. "It's going to be hot as a little red wagon today. Take these peaches out with you. Time you've finished them, everything else will be ready."

Jo stopped to buckle on her belt and tie her scarf. Then she took the peaches out to the porch. Her father put the Los Angeles *Times* under his chair and took his dish of peaches out of her hand. "Well, Josephine," he said, "considering you only had three hours' sleep last night, you don't look so bad."

"You hear me come in?"

"Nope, but I heard that fellow drive away. He ran into everything loose and bangable on the place. What's wrong with him?"

"Blind with love, I guess," Jo said lightly.

Her father held his third spoonful of sugar poised over his peaches. "I take it that you have no impairment in your eyesight," he said.

"Things look a little rosy, but the outline's still plain, I think."

Mrs. Henny came in with the eggs and bacon and muffins. "I don't want to hurry you," she said, pausing, on her way out, at the kitchen door, "but it's not getting any earlier."

"Where did Johnny go?" Jo asked. "He ought to be eating. He'll be sick this afternoon if he doesn't eat." She

took two muffins, buttered them, and put them on Johnny's plate.

"He's out talking to Curly. You'd better call him."

"Dad, what's Johnny going to do about not having Curly any more after today?" Jo asked. "You know he acts as if Curly were a dog—or a brother."

"Oh, Johnny's all right. He knows what the score is," her father said, with his mouth full of muffin and scrambled eggs. "But call him, call him. We've less than an hour to eat and load the steer. I ought to have taken him down last night, but John Thomas was afraid Curly would look peaked today if he spent a night away from home."

"Remember John Thomas' kitten?"

"Kitten?" said her father grumpily. "He's had a dozen."

"This was the one he had when he broke his leg. Don't you remember? He said, 'Let's never let her see herself in a mirror, and then she'll think she's just like us, only smaller.' He's that way about Curly now, you know. He never lets Curly know there's any other difference than size between them."

"Doesn't he know where Curly'll be tomorrow?"

"He *must* know it, but he hasn't felt it yet."

"Well, call him, call him," her father said. He got up from the table and stood with his back to her. "He can't learn to say good-by any earlier."

He's thinking of Mama, Jo thought, and walked slowly out through the screen door and down the steps into the sunshine, eating a muffin-and-bacon sandwich as she went. She stopped at the foot of the steps to pick up the cat, and balanced him, heavy and purring, on her shoulder, and let him lick the last of the muffin crumbs from her fingers. "Oh, Nicky, Nicky," she murmured, pressing her face close against the cat's soft, furry side. Then she saw Johnny, sitting hunched up on the top rail of the corral, looking at Curly. "Well, bud," she called out, "he looks like silk!"

"He's kind of rough on the left flank," Johnny said as she came and stood beside him. "Been rubbing against something. Can you notice it? I been working on it."

"Can't see a thing," Jo said. "Now, look here, John Thomas, you're going to make him nervous, sitting there staring at him—give him the jitters before he ever gets to the fair. You'll spoil his morale. Dad let you keep him here till this morning when he didn't want to, so don't you gum things up now."

John Thomas slid to the ground. "So long, Curly," he said. "I got to eat now." And he ran for the house.

A little before eight, they all drove in to Verdant, the county seat—Mr. Hobhouse and Mrs. Henny and Jo and Johnny in the car, and Curly in the trailer behind them. "Awnings up early this morning," said Mr. Hobhouse as they moved slowly forward in the already long line of cars. "Going to be a scorcher, I guess. Flags look dead when there isn't any wind, don't they?"

Jo, who was riding beside her father in the front seat, nodded, but nothing looked dead to her. She loved the beginning-again look of a town in the morning—the sidewalks sluiced down, the vegetables fresh and shining, the storekeepers in clean shirts, the feeling that nothing that had been spilled or broken or hurt or wronged the day before need be carried over into the new day. The heat made her sleepy, and because she

wouldn't be seeing Nicky until evening, the day seemed dreamlike, unimportant. She would move through it, be kind to Johnny, and wait for evening and Nicky again. Her father swerved sharply to avoid hitting a car that had swung, without signaling, out of the line of cars heading for the fair.

"Hey, Pop, take it easy!" John Thomas yelled anxiously from the back seat, where he sat with Mrs. Henny. "You almost busted Curly's ribs then."

"John Thomas ought to be riding back there with that steer," declared Mrs. Henny. "Or else I wish I could have rid in the trailer and the steer could have set here with John Thomas. The boy hasn't done a thing since we started but put his feet in my lunch basket and squirm, till I've got a rash watching him."

"Hold out five minutes longer, both of you, and we'll be there," Mr. Hobhouse said.

Jo roused herself, lifted her eyelids, which seemed weighed down with the heat, and turned around. "Hi ya, Johnny," she murmured.

As soon as they were well inside the fairgrounds, her father maneuvered out of the line of cars and stopped. "Jo, you and Mrs. Henny had better get out here," he said. "It'll take me and Johnny some time to get Curly unloaded."

As Jo climbed out, John Thomas touched her arm. "You'll sure be there, won't you, Sis?" he asked.

"Where?"

"In the grandstand for the parade at ten-thirty. All the baby beeves."

"Johnny, where'd you think I'd be then? Looking at the pickle exhibit, maybe? Of course I'll be there. Just you and Curly listen when you go by the stand. You'll hear me roar."

"Hurry up, you two," said her father. "It's getting late."

"When's the judging, Johnny?" Jo asked.

"Two-thirty. Front of the Agriculture Pavilion," he replied.

"I'll see you then. Don't worry. I think the judges are going to know their business." She poked a finger through the trailer's bars and touched Curly. "So long, Curly. You do your stuff!"

Her father edged the car and trailer back into the line of traffic. Mrs. Henny lumbered off, with a campstool on one arm and the lunch basket on the other, and Jo was left alone. The day was already blistering and she was glad. She took no pleasure in a moderately warm day, but a record breaker, one that challenged her ability to survive, elated her. She went into one of the exhibition buildings and walked through acres of handiwork, wondering if she would ever find life so empty that she would need to fill it with the making of such ugly and useless articles. Children whimpered as mothers jerked them doggedly through the heat. Oh, Nicky, I promise you never to be like them, Jo thought.

She was in the grandstand at ten-thirty when a voice from the loudspeaker announced, "Ladies and gentlemen! The Future Farmers of Riverbank County and their baby beeves will now pass in front of the grandstand for your inspection. At two-thirty, the final judging will take place in front of the Agriculture Pavilion, and after that the steers will be auctioned to the highest bidders. I'm proud to announce that there isn't a first-rate hotel in Los Angeles that hasn't a representative here to bid in one or more of these famous Riverbank beeves. There they come now, ladies and gentlemen, through

the west gate. Let's give them a big hand—the Future Farmers of Riverbank County!"

Jo craned forward to watch the long line of steers and boys move proudly in review before the grandstand. The steers were mostly Herefords, shining like bright-russet leather in the blazing sun. Jo had not realized how thoroughly John Thomas had convinced her of Curly's superiority. She looked down the long line, expecting Curly, by some virtue of size or spirit, to be distinct from all the others.

A woman leaned heavily against her to nudge a friend in the row below them. "There they are!" she said excitedly.

Jo followed their glances before it occurred to her that they were not talking about John Thomas and Curly. Finally, she saw them, well along toward the end of the line, the steer like the other red steers, the boy like the other white-clothed boys. But unlike, too, for surely no other boy walked with the sensitive, loving pride of her brother. Then she saw that Johnny was the only boy who did not lead his animal by a halter or a rope. He walked beside Curly, with only a hand on his neck. Idiot, thought Jo, he's put something over on somebody; he ought not to be doing that.

She stood up and, to fulfill her promise, shouted, over and over, "Hi, Johnny! Hi, Curly!" until a man behind her jerked her skirt and said, "Sit down, Sis, you're not made of cellophane."

After the boys and the steers had circled the grandstand and passed through the west gate again and out of sight, Jo closed her eyes and half slept, hearing as in a dream the announcement of the next event. She fully awakened, though, when someone wedged himself into the narrow space that separated her from the stair railing on her right.

"Dad! Where did you come from?" she exclaimed.

"I was up above you," her father said. "Well, the boy's having his day. You're half asleep, Jo."

"More than half. Where's the car? I think I'll go and sleep in it until the judging. I've seen all the Yo-Yo pillows[3] and canned apricots I can take in one day."

"I don't know whether you can find the car or not," her father said. "It's over in the first nine or ten rows of cars back of the dining tents. Here's the key, and don't forget to lock it when you leave."

Jo slept for a long time, doubled up on the back seat of the car, and then awakened with a sudden sick start. She seemed to be drowning in heat, and the velours of the seat she was sleeping on was a quicksand that held her down. She looked at her watch and saw with consternation that it was after four o'clock.

She had a long way to go to reach the Agriculture Pavilion, and because she was so angry with herself and still so sleepy, she ran clumsily, bumping into people. I'm so full of fair promises, she accused herself bitterly, and now I've let poor Johnny down. She wanted to hurt herself running—punish herself—and she finally reached the Pavilion with a sick, cutting pain in her side and a taste of sulfur in her throat. A deep circle of onlookers stood around the judging ring, laughing and talking quietly. At last, she saw Johnny and her father in the front line of the circle, a little to her left. Paying no heed to the sour looks she got, she pushed her way to them. John Thomas saw what she had

3. **Yo-Yo pillows,** fancy handmade pillows.

done and frowned. "You oughtn't to do that, Jo," he said. "People'll think we can get away with anything just because we own the winner."

"Has Curly won already?" Jo asked.

"No, not yet," Johnny said. "Couldn't you see the judging from where you were?"

"Not very well," Jo said. "No, I couldn't see a thing."

She looked now at the animals that were still in the ring, and saw that Curly was there with three other Herefords and an enormous black Angus. He was wearing a halter now, and one of the judge's assistants was leading him. Unless one of the five steers had a cast in his eye or a tick in his ear, Jo did not see how any man living could say that one was an iota better than another. She knew the points in judging as well as Johnny himself; she had stood by the corral many half-hours after breakfast while Johnny recounted them for her, but while she knew them well, her eye could not limn them out in the living beasts.

"Why're you so sure Curly will win?" she asked Johnny.

"Higgins said he would."

"Who's Higgins?"

Johnny shook his head, too absorbed to answer her question. The judge, an old, bowlegged fellow in a pale-blue sweater, had stopped examining the animals and was reading over some notes he had taken on the back of a dirty envelope. He walked over for another look at the Angus. Seemingly satisfied by what he saw, he took off his gray felt hat and, with the back of his hand, wiped away the sweat that had accumulated under the sweatband. He set his hat on the back of his head, stuffed his envelope in a hip pocket, stepped to the edge of the ring, and began to speak.

"Ladies and gentlemen, it gives me great pleasure to be able to announce to you the winner of the Eighteenth Annual Riverbank Baby Beef Contest."

There was a hush as the spectators stopped talking, and Jo tried to find in her father's face some hint of what he thought the decision would be. She saw nothing there but concern. Johnny, though, had a broad and assured smile. His eyes were sparkling; the hour of Curly's recognition had come.

"And I may say," continued the judge, enjoying the suspense he was creating, "that in a lifetime of cattle judging I have never seen an animal that compares with today's winner."

The fool, thought Jo, the fool orator! What's got into him? They never do this. Why can't he speak out?

But Johnny looked as if he enjoyed it, as if he knew whose name would be announced when people's ears had become so strained to hear it that it would seem to be articulated not by another's lips but by their own heartbeats.

"The winner, ladies and gentlemen, is that very fine animal, John Thomas Hobhouse's Hereford, Curly!" said the judge.

There was a lot of good-natured hand clapping. A few boys yelled "Nerts!" but the choice was popular with the crowd, most of whom knew and liked the Hobhouses. The judge went on to name the second-and third-prize winners and the honorable mentions. Then he called out, "I would like to present to you Curly's owner, John Thomas Hobhouse himself. Come take a bow, Johnny!"

Jo was proud of the easy, happy way Johnny ran over to his side. The judge put out a hand intended for the boy's shoulder, but before it could settle there, Johnny was pressing his

cheek against Curly's big, fat jowl. The steer seemed actually to lower his head for the caress and to move his cheek against Johnny's in loving recognition. This delighted the spectators, who laughed and cheered again.

"Now, ladies and gentlemen, the show's almost over," said the judge. "Only one thing left—the auctioning of these animals—and, believe you me, the enjoyment you've had here is nothing to the enjoyment you're going to have when you bite into one of these big, juicy baby-beef steaks. Now if you'll all just clear the ring. Ladies and gentlemen, may I present that silver-tongued Irish auctioneer, Terence O'Flynn."

The non-prize winners were disposed of first and in short order. They fetched fancy prices, but nothing like what would be paid for the prize winners. The big Los Angeles hotels and the Riverbank Inn liked to be able to advertise "Steaks from Riverbank's Prize Baby Beeves." Jo felt sick at her stomach during the auction. This talk of club steaks and top sirloins seemed indecent to her, in front of animals of whom these cuts were still integral parts. But Johnny seemed unaffected by the auction. "Bet you Curly will get more than that," he said whenever a high price was bid.

"He'll fetch top price," his father answered him shortly. "You'll have a big check tonight, besides your blue ribbon, Johnny." The prize winners were auctioned last. All of them except Curly went to Los Angeles hotels, but the Riverbank Inn, determined not to let outside counties get all the prize winners, bid Curly in for itself.

"I'm not a Riverbank citizen," boomed O'Flynn, "but I don't mind admitting, folks, that I'm going to come back the day my good friend Chef Rossi of the Riverbank Inn serves steak from Curly. I know that baby beef is going to yield juices that haven't been equaled since Abel[4] broiled the first steak. If I was young Hobhouse, I'd never sell that animal. I'd barbecue it and pick its bones myself."

Most of the animals had already been led into slaughter house vans and trucks, and the rest were being quickly loaded. A van belonging to Mack's Market, the Riverbank Inn's butchers, backed up to the ring, which now held only Curly and the Angus. As O'Flynn finished speaking, two young fellows in jumpers marked "Mack's" leaped out and came over to give Curly a congratulatory pat before sending him up the runway.

"Well, kid," one said pleasantly to John Thomas, "you got a fine animal."

Johnny didn't hear him. He was looking at O'Flynn, hearing those last words of his.

Now it's come, thought Jo. Now he's really taken in what he's been preparing Curly for. Now he knows for the first time. Don't look that way, Johnny, she pleaded silently. Oh, Johnny, you *must* know you can't keep Curly—you can't keep a fat pet steer.

But Johnny didn't smile. He walked over and stood with one arm about Curly's neck, staring incredulously at O'Flynn. "Nobody's going to pick Curly's bones," he said to the auctioneer. Then he turned to the steer, "Don't you worry, Curly. That guy hasn't got anything to do with you."

There was a sympathetic murmur among the bystanders. "The poor kid's made a pet of him," one man said. "Too bad. Well, he can't learn any earlier."

---

4. *Abel* (ā′bəl), in the Bible, the second son of Adam and Eve.

The men from Mack's Market tried to take the matter lightly. "Look here, bud," said one of them. "Get yourself a canary. This steer don't want to be nobody's pet. He wants to be beefsteaks." And he put a hand on Curly's halter.

Johnny struck it down. "Don't touch Curly!" he shouted. "He's going home, where he belongs! He's won the prize! That's all he came here to do!"

The circle of onlookers came closer, augmented by passers-by whose ears had caught in Johnny's voice the sound of passion and hurt. The buzzards, Jo thought. She saw Johnny press himself still more closely against Curly, keeping his eyes all the time on O'Flynn. She gripped her father's arm. "Dad, do something!" she cried. "Let Johnny take Curly home. There's plenty of food and room. Johnny wouldn't feel this way about him except for you and me. It's our fault!" She was half crying.

"Yes, this nonsense can't go on," her father agreed, and went quickly over to Johnny.

Jo couldn't hear what he said or see his face, for he stood with his back to her, but she could see Johnny's face, and its anguish and disbelief. At last, the boy turned and threw both arms around Curly's neck and buried his face against the steer's heavy muscles. Jo saw his thin shoulder blades shaking.

When her father turned and came toward her, eyes to the ground, she found she could not say to him any of the bitter things that had been on her tongue's tip.

"Dad," she said, and put her hand out to him.

"There's no use, Jo."

"But he loves Curly so."

"Oh, love!" her father said, and then added more quietly, "It's better to learn to say good-by early than late, Jo."

"I'm going to the car," Jo said, and she turned and ran blindly through the crowd. Because Dad's had to learn, why must Johnny, she thought bitterly.

She got into the front seat and leaned across the wheel, without any attempt to stop crying. Then, as the sobs let up, she pounded the wheel. "No, sir!" she said aloud. "I *won't* learn! I refuse to learn! I'll be an exception!"

✦　　✦　　✦　　✦

DISCUSSION

1. (a) Describe Johnny's feelings at the beginning of the story. (b) Why does Johnny's mood worry Jo? (c) Does Mr. Hobhouse share Jo's concern for Johnny? Explain. (d) Why isn't Johnny worried?

2. (a) What lesson does Mr. Hobhouse feel Johnny must learn? (b) What facts in his own life make him want to teach this lesson to Johnny at an early age? (c) What does Mr. Hobhouse tell his son when Johnny finally realizes what is to become of Curly? (d) Should he have found some other way to teach Johnny this lesson?

3. (a) What is Jo's feeling about her father's attitude? (b) What in her own life might account for her feeling? (c) Which lines in the story reveal the most important conflict between Jo and Mr. Hobhouse?

4. (a) What do you learn about the characters from what the author tells you? **(b)** What do you learn about them from what they say and do? **(c)** What do their thoughts reveal about them? **(d)** What do their feelings toward each other reveal?

5. (a) What evidence exists that Johnny has not actually known what to expect at the end of the day? **(b)** Is Johnny believable —that is, is it possible that a young boy could close his mind to the thought of losing a pet?

6. (a) Would this story have been more believable if Mr. Hobhouse had allowed Johnny to keep Curly? Why or why not? **(b)** Could Jo have persuaded her father to change his mind if she'd tried a little harder? Explain.

WORD STUDY

"Help! I've been shot full of *upas!*" What is *upas*? How is the word pronounced? How is a person shot full of *upas*? Is it harmful, or merely painful? In what part of the world is one most apt to be shot full of *upas*? To answer these questions, you'll probably have to consult the dictionary.

My brother has one *idiosyncrasy*; he eats nothing but *guava* on *pumpernickel*.

Does context supply enough clues for you to determine the meanings of any of the unfamiliar words above? Can you analyze the structure of any of the words? What does *guava* on *pumpernickel* taste like? What's an *idiosyncrasy*? Do you have one? If you can't figure out the meanings and pronunciations of the unfamiliar words, use the dictionary.

Use either a dictionary or the Glossary to answer the following questions:

1. Johnny's *pompadour* spread out on the floor.

Describe Johnny's hair. How did the pompadour get its name?

2. Lord, thought Jo, I'm a *heathen*.

What is the most common definition of *heathen*? Which of the definitions given best explains what Jo means?

3. Mothers jerked children *doggedly* through the heat.

What are some substitutes for *doggedly*?

4. Jo's eyes could not *limn* them out in the living beasts.

How is *limn* pronounced? What does it mean in this sentence?

5. I present that *silver-tongued* Irish auctioneer.

What kind of speaker is the auctioneer?

PHOTO COURTESY OF
THE BANCROFT LIBRARY, UNIVERSITY OF CALIFORNIA

THE AUTHOR

Jessamyn West writes with a warm, sympathetic understanding of the problems of youth. *Cress Delahanty,* one of her longer works, describes the fun and the troubles of a California girl who seems every bit as real as John Thomas Hobhouse. Miss West drew on her Quaker background (both her grandmothers were Quaker preachers) and childhood years in Indiana for her famous book *The Friendly Persuasion,* which was later made into a popular movie.

A woman of many ideas, she declares that she has more projects in mind than she has time for. She is a steady contributor to a number of magazines, has written several movie scripts, and frequently lectures at writing conferences throughout the country.

THE LESSON **53**

Death by Drowning

RICHARD EBERHART

His guitar was found in the canoe on the river
But cold grappling hooks brought his body up from the deeps.
He was a young man introduced to death by a gust.
They were upset by the nature wildness keeps.

Unbelievable, fierce, eternal, high wind in clear air   5
Tossed three youths; the boat escaped downstream.
One met the brutal grip of the cold, hands of ice
Pulled him down; the others barely made it to life's dream.

His guitar was found in the canoe on the river,
O unbelievable! May all the gay songs of youth   10
Assuage, if they can, the brutal indifference of fate.
His companions live to ponder on death's truth.

From THE QUARRY by Richard Eberhart. Copyright © 1964 by Richard Eberhart. Reprinted
by permission of Oxford University Press, Inc. and Chatto and Windus Ltd.

1. (a) What did the rescuers find in the canoe? (b) How was the youth's body recovered? (c) What caused the boy to drown?
2. (a) From the following list of words, choose those that best describe the view of nature in the poem: *soothing; calm; wild; dull; dangerous.* (b) What is the poet describing in the phrases "grip of the cold" and "hands of ice"?
3. (a) How do you know that the poet is impressed by the connection between the guitar and death? (b) Which of the following emotions are usually associated with a guitar: *boredom; gaiety; sorrow; light-hearted-ness?* (c) Why is the guitar such an effective contrast to the drowning?
4. (a) What does the poet call on music to do for the survivors? (b) Does he believe that music will actually be able to do this? Find evidence in the poem to support your answer. (c) What is the truth of death that friends are left to ponder?
5. Read *Questions put to a poet,* page 55. (a) On what facts did Eberhart base "Death by Drowning"? (b) What do you think the critic who said the last line was "too obvious, even sentimental" meant? (c) Do you agree with him? Why or why not?

Questions put to a poet

QUESTION: *Would you tell us something about your background?*
MR. EBERHART: I was born in Austin, Minnesota and I studied in both England and the United States. I've spent a great deal of my life teaching — mostly at the university level. But during one year in the early thirties I was tutor to the son of King Prajadhipok of Siam. My wife, Helen, and I have two children — Rick and Gretchen. We live in Hanover, New Hampshire, in a house on the Connecticut River.

QUESTION: *Where do you get ideas for your poetry?*
MR. EBERHART: Poetry, with me, often comes considerably after any event or series of events. A poem may come from the spur of memory, unexpectedly, and be fashioned in a short time of writing when the mind is somehow — I don't know how — able to hold all the meanings together and project them onto paper. But then, after getting it on paper, there are revisions and more revisions.

QUESTION: *What prompted you to write "Death by Drowning"?*
MR. EBERHART: Up the river — I think it was two years ago — three boys were turned over in a canoe by the river winds, unexpectedly gusty. As I recall, one got to shore. One tried to save another but he went down and this boy had a hard time getting to shore.

It was touching that there was a guitar. The appalling death of the drowned boy occasioned the poem which was written shortly after I heard the dreadful news.

QUESTION: *What feelings did you want to express in the poem?*
MR. EBERHART: "Death by Drowning" could not have been more costly, for its price was a life. It was written in an access of recognition — sympathy, concern. The poem is a simple song of grief. Some critic took the last line to task because he felt it was too obvious, even sentimental from his view of art. I see that the critic has a point. But the poem is the way I felt when I wrote it.

Mayo is "a perfectly normal boy,"
says the author. Mayo is an
"arrogant ignoramus," thinks the town.
Which opinion is the right one?

The Pheasant Hunter

WILLIAM SAROYAN

MAYO MALONEY at eleven was a little runt of a fellow who was not rude so much as he was rudeness itself, for he couldn't even step inside a church, for instance, without giving everybody who happened to see him an uncomfortable feeling that he, Mayo, despised the place and its purpose.

It was much the same everywhere else that Mayo went: school, library, theater, home. Only his mother felt that Mayo was not a rude boy, but his father frequently asked Mayo to get down off his high horse and act like everybody else. By this, Michael Maloney meant that Mayo ought to take things easy and stop finding so much fault with everything.

Mayo was the most self-confident boy in the world, and he found fault with everything, or so at least it seemed. He found fault with his mother's church activities. He found fault with his father's interest in Shakespeare and Mozart.[1] He found fault with the public-school system, the Government, the United Nations, the entire population of the world. And he did all this fault-finding without so much as going into detail about anything. He did it by being alive, by being on hand at all. He did it by being nervous, irritable, swift, wise and bored. In short, he was a perfectly normal boy. He had contempt for everything and everybody, and he couldn't help it. His contempt was unspoken but unmistakable. He was slight of body, dark of face and hair, and he went at everything in a hurry because everything was slow and stupid and weak.

The only thing that didn't bore him was the idea of hunting, but his father wouldn't buy him a gun, not even a .22-caliber single-shot rifle. Michael Maloney told Mayo that as soon as he was sure that Mayo had calmed down a little, he would think about buying him a gun. Mayo tried to calm down a little, so he could have his gun, but he gave it up after a day and a half.

"O.K.," his father said, "if you don't want your gun, you don't have to try to earn it."

From THE ASSYRIAN AND OTHER STORIES by William Saroyan. Reprinted by permission of the author and Laurence Pollinger Limited.

1. **Shakespeare and Mozart,** William Shakespeare, (1564–1616), England's greatest poet and dramatist, and Wolfgang Amadeus Mozart (1756–1791), Austrian music composer. The works of both men are considered classics.

"I did try to earn it," Mayo said.

"When?"

"Yesterday and today."

"I had in mind," his father said, "a trial covering a period of at least a month."

"A month?" Mayo said. "How do you expect a fellow to stay calm all through October with pheasant to shoot in the country?"

"I don't know how," Mike Maloney said, "but if you want a gun, you've got to calm down enough so I can believe you won't shoot the neighbors with it. Do you think my father so much as let me sit down to my dinner if I hadn't done something to earn it? He didn't invite me to earn any gun to shoot pheasant with. He told me to earn my food, and he didn't wait until I was eleven, either. I started earning it when I was no more than eight. The whole trouble with you is you're too pent-up from not doing any kind of work at all for your food or shelter or clothing to be decently tired and ordinary like everybody else. You're not human, almost. Nobody's human who doesn't know how hard it is to earn his food and the other basic things. It's the fault of your mother and father that you're such a sarcastic and fault-finding man instead of a calm, handsome one. Everybody in this whole town is talking about how your mother and father have turned you into an arrogant ignoramus of a man by not making you earn your right to judge things."

Mr. Maloney spoke as much to the boy's mother as to the boy himself, and he spoke as well to the boy's younger brother and younger sister, for he had left his office at half-past four, as he did once a week, to sit down with the whole family for early supper, and it was his intention to make these mid-week gatherings at the table memorable to everyone, including himself.

"Now, Mike," Mrs. Maloney said. "Mayo's not as bad as all that. He just wants a gun to hunt pheasant with."

Mike Maloney laid down his fork that was loaded with macaroni baked with tomatoes and cheese, and he stared at his wife a long time, rejecting one by one two dozen angry remarks he knew would do no one present any good at all to hear, and only make the gathering *unpleasantly* memorable.

At last he said, "I suppose you think I ought to get him a gun, just like that?"

"Mayo isn't really rude or anything like that," the boy's mother said. "It's just that he's restless, the way every human being's got to be once in his lifetime for a while."

Mayo didn't receive this defense of himself with anything like gratitude. If anything, it appeared as if he were sick and tired of having so much made of a simple little matter like furnishing him with an inexpensive .22-caliber single-shot rifle.

"Now don't you go to work and try to speak up for him," Mike Maloney said to his wife, "because, as you can see for yourself, he doesn't like it. He doesn't enjoy being spoken up for, not even by his mother, poor woman, and you can see how much he thinks of what his father's saying this minute."

"What did I say?" Mayo asked.

"You didn't say anything," his father said. "You didn't need to." He turned to Mrs. Maloney. "Is it a gun I must buy for him now?" he said.

Mrs. Maloney didn't quite know how to say that it was. She remained silent and tried not to look at either her husband or her son.

"O.K.," Mike Maloney said to both

his wife and his son. "I have to go back to the office a minute, so if you'll come along with me I'll drop into Archie Cannon's and buy you a gun."

He got up from the table and turned to Mrs. Maloney.

"Provided, of course," he said, "that that meets with your approval."

"Aren't you going to finish your food?" Mrs. Maloney said.

"No, I'm not," Mike Maloney said. "And I'll tell you why, too. I don't want him to be denied anything he wants or anything his mother wants him to have, without earning it, for one unnecessary moment, and as you can see, his cap's on his head, he's at the door, and every moment I stand here explaining is unnecessary."

"Couldn't you both finish your food first?" Mrs. Maloney said.

"Who wants to waste time eating," Mike Maloney said, "when it's time to buy a gun?"

"Well," Mrs. Maloney said, "perhaps you'll have something after you buy the gun."

"We should have been poor," Mike Maloney said. "Being poor would have helped us in this problem."

Mike Maloney went to the door where his nervous son was standing waiting for him to shut up and get going.

He turned to his wife and said, "I won't be able to account for him after I turn the gun over to him, but I'll be gone no more than an hour. If we'd been poor and couldn't afford it, he'd know the sinfulness of provoking me into this sort of bitter kindness."

When he stepped out of the house onto the front porch, he saw that his son was at the corner, trying his best not to run. He moved quickly and caught up with him, and then he moved along as swiftly as his son did.

At last he said, "Now, I'm willing to walk the half mile to Archie Cannon's, but I'm not going to run, so if you've got to run, go ahead, and I'll meet you outside the place as soon as I get there."

He saw the boy break loose and disappear far down the street. When he got to Archie Cannon's, the boy was waiting for him. They went in and Mike Maloney asked Archie to show him the guns.

"What kind of a gun do you want, Mike?" Archie said. "I didn't know you were interested in hunting."

"It's not for myself," Mike Maloney said. "It's for Mayo here, and it ought to be suitable for pheasant shooting."

"That would be a shotgun," Archie said.

"Would that be what it would be?" Mike Maloney asked his son, and although the boy hadn't expected anything so precisely suitable for pheasant shooting, he said that a shotgun would be what it would be.

"O.K., Archie," Mike said. "A shotgun."

"Well, Mike," Archie said, "I wouldn't like to think a shotgun would be the proper gun to turn over to a boy."

"Careful," Mike Maloney said. "He's right here with us, you know. Let's not take any unnecessary liberties. I believe he indicated the gun ought to be a shotgun."

"Well, anyway," Archie said, "it's going to have a powerful kick."

"A powerful kick," Mike Maloney repeated, addressing the three words to his son, who received them with disdain.

"That is no matter to him," Mike Maloney said to Archie Cannon.

"Well, then," Archie Cannon said, "this here's a fine double-barrel twelve-gauge shotgun and it's just about the best bargain in the store."

"You shouldn't have said that,

Archie," Mike Maloney said. "This man's not interested in bargains. What he wants is the best shotgun you've got that's suitable for pheasant shooting."

"That would be this twelve-gauge repeater," Archie Cannon said, "that sells for ninety-eight fifty, plus tax, of course. It's the best gun of its kind."

"Anybody can see it's a better gun," Mike Maloney said. "No need to waste time with inferior firearms."

He handed the gun to Mayo Maloney, who held it barrel down, resting over his right arm, precisely as a gun, loaded or not, ought to be held.

"I'll show you how it works," Archie Cannon made the mistake of saying to Mayo Maloney. The boy glanced at Archie in a way that encouraged him to say quickly, "Anything else, then? Fishing tackle, hooks, boxing gloves, rowing machines, tennis rackets?"

"Anything else?" Mike Maloney said to his son, who said nothing, but with such irritation that Mike quickly said to Archie Cannon, "Shells, of course. What good is a shotgun without shells?"

Archie Cannon jumped to get three boxes of his best shotgun shells, and as he turned them over to Mike Maloney, who turned them over to Mayo, Archie said, "A hunting coat in which to carry the shells? A red hunting cap?"

Mayo Maloney was gone, however.

"He didn't want those things," Mike Maloney said.

"Some hunters go to a lot of trouble about costume," Archie Cannon said.

"He doesn't," Mike Maloney said. "What do I owe you?"

"One hundred and five dollars and sixty-nine cents, including tax," Archie said. "Has he got a license?"

"To hunt?" Mike Maloney said. "He hasn't got a license to eat, but damned if I don't halfway admire him sometimes. He must know something to be so sure of himself and so contemptuous of everybody else."

"To tell you the truth," Archie Cannon said, "I thought you were kidding, Mike. I thought you were kidding the way you sometimes do in court when you're helping a small man fight a big company. I didn't expect you to actually buy a gun and turn it over to an eleven-year-old boy. Are you sure it's all right?"

"Of course it's all right," Mike Maloney said. "You saw for yourself the way he held the gun." He began to write a check. "Now, what did you say it came to?"

"A hundred and five sixty-nine," Archie Cannon said. "I hope you know there's no pheasant to speak of anywhere near here. The Sacramento Valley[2] is where the pheasant shooting is."

"Where you going to be around ten o'clock tonight?" Mike Maloney said.

"Home, most likely," Archie Cannon said. "Why?"

"Will you be up?"

"Oh, yes," Archie said. "I never get to bed before midnight. Why?"

"Would you like to drop over to my house for a couple of bottles of beer around ten?" Mike said.

"I'd like that very much," Archie said. "Why?"

"Well," Mike said, "the way I figure is this: It's a quarter after five now. It'll take him about three minutes to hitch a ride with somebody going out to Riverdale, which is about twenty-five miles from here. That would take an average driver forty or forty-five minutes to make, but he'll

---

2. **Sacramento Valley,** a valley in north central California.

get the driver, whoever he is, or she is, for that matter, to make it in about half an hour or a little under. He'll do it by being excited, not by saying anything. He'll get the driver to go out of his or her way to let him off where the hunting is, too, so he'll start hunting right away, or a little before six. He'll hunt until after dark, walking a lot in the meantime. He won't get lost or anything like that, but he'll have to walk back to a road with a little traffic. He'll hitch a ride back, and he'll be home a little before or a little after ten."

"How do you know?" Archie said. "How do you even know he's going hunting at all tonight? He just got the gun, and he may not even know how to work it."

"You saw him take off, didn't you?" Mike Maloney said. "He took off to go hunting. And you can be sure he either knows how to work the gun or will find out by himself in a few minutes."

"Well," Archie said, "I certainly would like to drop by for some beer, Mike, if you're serious."

"Of course I'm serious," Mike said.

"I suppose you want to have somebody to share your amusement with when he gets back with nothing shot and his body all sore from the powerful kick of the gun," Archie said.

"Yes," Mike said. "I want to have somebody to share my amusement with but not for those reasons. He may be a little sore from the powerful kick of the gun, but I think he'll come back with something."

"I've never heard of anybody shooting any pheasant around River-dale," Archie said. "There's a little duck shooting out there in season, and jack rabbits, of course."

"He said pheasants," Mike Ma-loney said. "Here's my check. Better make it a little before ten, just in case."

"I thought you were only kidding about the gun," Archie said. "Are you sure you did the right thing? I mean, considering he's only eleven years old, hasn't got a hunting license and the pheasant-shooting season doesn't open for almost a month?"

"That's one of the reasons why I want you to come by for some beer," Mike said.

"I don't get it," Archie said.

"You're game warden of this area, aren't you?"

"I am."

"Okay," Mike said. "If it turns out that he's broken the law, I want you to know it."

"Well," Archie said, "I wouldn't want to bother about a small boy shooting a few days out of season without a license."

"I'll pay his fine," Mike Maloney said.

"I don't think he'll get anything," Archie said, "so of course there won't be any fine to be paid."

"I'll see you a little before ten, then," Mike Maloney said.

He spent a half-hour at his office, then walked home slowly, to find the house quiet and peaceful, the kids in bed and his wife doing the dishes. He took the dish towel and began to dry and put the clean dishes into the cupboard.

"I bought him the best shotgun Archie Cannon had for pheasant shooting," he said.

"I hope he didn't make you too angry," Mrs. Maloney said.

"He did for a while," Mike said, "but all of a sudden he didn't, if you know what I mean."

"I don't know what you mean," Mrs. Maloney said.

"I mean," Mike said, "it's all right not being poor."

"What's being poor got to do with it?" Mrs. Maloney said.

"I mean it's all right, that's all," Mike said.

"Well, that's fine," Mrs. Maloney said. "But where is he?"

"Hunting of course," Mike said. "You don't think he wanted a gun to look at."

"I don't know what I think now," Mrs. Maloney said. "You've had so much trouble with him all along, and now all of a sudden you buy him an expensive gun and believe it's perfectly all right for him to go off hunting in the middle of the night on the third day of October. Why?"

"Well," Mike Maloney said, "it's because while I was preaching to him at the table, something began to happen. It was as if my own father were preaching to me thirty years ago when I was Mayo's age. Oh, I did earn my food, as I said, and I wanted a gun, too, just as he's been wanting one. Well, my father preached to me, and I didn't get the gun. I mean, I didn't get it until almost five years later, when it didn't mean very much to me any more. Well, while I was preaching to him this afternoon I remembered that when my father preached to me I was sure he was mistaken to belittle me so, and I even believed that some-how—somehow or other, perhaps because we were so poor, if that makes sense—he would suddenly stop preaching and take me along without any fuss of any kind and buy me a gun. But of course he didn't. And I *remembered* that he didn't, and I decided that perhaps I'd do for my son what my father had not done for me, if you know what I mean."

"Do you mean you and Mayo are alike?" Mrs. Maloney said.

"I do," Mike said. "I do indeed."

"Very much alike?"

"Almost precisely," Mike said.

"Oh, he'll not be the great man he is now for long, and I don't want to be the one to cheat him out of a single moment of his greatness."

"You must be joking," Mrs. Maloney said.

"I couldn't be more serious," Mike said. "Archie Cannon thought I was joking, too, but why would I be joking? I bought him the gun and shells, and off he went to hunt, didn't he?"

"Well, I hope he doesn't hurt himself," Mrs. Maloney said.

"We'll never know if he does," Mike said. "I've asked Archie to come by around ten for some beer because I figured he'll be back by then."

"Is Mrs. Cannon coming with Archie?"

"I don't think so," Mike said. "Her name wasn't mentioned."

"Then I suppose you don't want me to sit up with you," Mrs. Maloney said.

"I don't know why not, if you want to," Mike said.

But Mrs. Maloney knew it wouldn't do to sit up, so she said, "No, I'll be getting to bed long before ten."

Mike Maloney went out on the front porch with his wife, and they sat and talked about their son Mayo and their other kids until a little after nine, and then Mrs. Maloney went inside to see if the beer was in the icebox and to put some stuff out on the kitchen table, to go with the beer. Then she went to bed.

Around a quarter to ten Archie Cannon came walking up the street and sat down in the rocker on the front porch.

"I've been thinking about what you did," he said, "and I still don't know if you did right."

"I did right all right," Mike Maloney said. "Let's go inside and have some beer. He'll be along pretty soon."

They went inside and sat down at the kitchen table. Mike lifted the caps off two bottles of cold beer, filled two tall glasses, and they began to drink. There was a plate loaded with cold roast beef, ham, bologna and sliced store cheese, and another plate with rye bread on it, already buttered.

When it was almost twelve and Mayo Maloney hadn't come home, Archie Cannon wondered if he shouldn't offer to get up and go home or maybe even offer to get his car and go looking for the boy, but he decided he'd better not. Mike Maloney seemed excited and angry at himself for having done such a foolish thing, and he might not like Archie to rub it in. They stopped talking about Mayo Maloney around eleven, and Archie knew Mike wanted the situation to remain that way indefinitely.

A little before one in the morning, after they had finished a half-dozen bottles of beer apiece and all the food Mrs. Maloney had set out for them, and talked about everything in the world excepting Mayo Maloney, they heard footsteps on the back stairs, and then on the porch, and after a moment he came into the kitchen.

He was a tired man. His face was dirty and flushed, and his clothes were dusty and covered with prickly burs of several kinds. His hands were scratched and almost black with dirt. His gun was slung over his right arm, and nested in his left arm were two beautiful pheasants.

He set the birds on the kitchen table, and then broke his gun up for cleaning. He wrapped a dry dish towel around the pieces and put the bundle in the drawer in which he kept his junk. He then brought six unused shells out of his pockets and placed them in the drawer, too, locked the drawer with his key and put the key back into his pocket. Then he went to the kitchen sink and rolled up his sleeves and washed his hands and arms and face and neck, and after he'd dried himself, he looked into the refrigerator and brought out some bologna wrapped in butcher paper, and began to eat it without bread while he fetched bread and butter and a chair. He sat down and began to put three thick slices of bologna between two slices of buttered bread. Mike Maloney had never before seen him eat so heartily.

He didn't look restless and mean any more, either.

Mike Maloney got up with Archie Cannon, and they left the house by the back door in order not to disturb Mrs. Maloney and the sleeping kids.

When they were in the back yard, Archie Cannon said, "Well, aren't you going to ask him where he got them?"

"He's not ready to talk about it just yet," Mike said. "What's the fine?"

"Well," Archie said, "there won't be any fine because there's not supposed to be any pheasants in the whole area of which I'm game warden. I didn't believe he'd get anything, let alone pheasants, and both of them cocks, too. Damned if I don't admire him a little myself."

"I'll walk you home," Mike said.

In the kitchen, the boy finished his sandwich, drank a glass of milk and rubbed his shoulder.

The whole evening and night had been unbelievable. Suddenly at the table, when his father had been preaching to him, he'd begun to understand his father a little better, and himself, too, but he'd known he couldn't immediately stop being the way he had been for so long, the way that was making everybody so uncomfortable. He'd known he'd have to go on for a while longer and see the thing through. He'd have to go along with

his father. He'd known all this very clearly, because his father had suddenly stopped being a certain way—the way everybody believed a father ought to be—and Mayo had known it was going to be necessary for him to stop being a certain way, too—the way he had believed he had to be. But he'd known he couldn't stop until he'd seen the thing through.

In the kitchen, almost asleep from weariness, he decided he'd tell his father exactly what he'd done, but he'd wait awhile first, maybe ten years.

He'd had a devil of a time finding out how the gun worked, and he hadn't been able to hitch a ride at all, so he'd walked and run six miles to the countryside around Clovis, and there he'd loaded the gun and aimed it at a blackbird in a tree leaning over Clovis Creek, and pressed the trigger.

The kick had knocked him down and he had missed the bird by a mile. He'd had to walk a long way through tall dry grass and shrubs for something else to shoot at, but all it was was another blackbird, and again the kick had knocked him down and he'd missed it by a mile.

It was getting dark fast by then and there didn't seem to be anything alive around at all, so he began to shoot the gun just to get used to it. Pretty soon he could shoot it and not get knocked down. He kept shooting and walking, and finally it was dark and it seemed he was lost. He stumbled over a big rock and fell and shot the gun by accident and got a lot of dirt in his eyes. He got up and almost cried, but he managed not to, and then he found a road, but he had no idea where it went to or which direction to take. He was scratched and sore all over, and not very happy about the way he'd shot the gun by accident. That should never have happened. He was scared, too, and he said a prayer a minute and meant every word of what he said. And he understood for the first time in his life why people liked to go to church.

"Please don't let me make a fool of myself," he prayed. "Please let me start walking in the right direction on this road."

He started walking down the road, hoping he was getting nearer home, or at least to a house with a light in it, or a store or something that would be open. He felt a lot of alive things in the dark that he knew must be imaginary, and he said, "Please don't let me get so scared." And pretty soon he felt so tired and small and lost and hopeless and foolish that he could barely keep from crying, and he said, "Please don't let me cry."

He walked a long time, and then far down the road he saw a small light, and he began to walk faster. It was a country store with a gasoline pump out front and a new pickup truck beside the pump. Inside the store was the driver of the truck and the storekeeper, and he saw that it was twenty minutes to twelve. The storekeeper was an old man with a thick white mustache who was sitting on a box talking to the driver of the truck, who was about as old as the boy's father.

He saw the younger man wink at the older one, and he thanked God for both of them, and for the wink, because he didn't think people who could wink could be unfriendly.

He told them exactly what he had done, and why, and the men looked at him and at each other until he was all through talking. They both examined the brand-new gun, too. Then the storekeeper handed the gun back to the boy and said to the younger man,

"I'll be much obliged to you, Ed, if you'll get this man home in our truck."

They were a father and a son, too, apparently, and good friends, besides. Mayo Maloney admired them very much, and on account of them, he began to like people in general, too.

"Not at all," the younger man said.

"And I'd like to think we might rustle up a couple of pheasant for him to take home, too."

"That might not be easy to do this hour of the night," the younger man said, "but we could try."

"Isn't there an all-night Chinese restaurant in town that serves pheasant in and out of season?" the old man said. "Commercial pheasant, that is?"

"I don't know," the younger man said, "but we could phone and find out."

"No," the older man said. "No use phoning. They wouldn't be apt to understand what we were talking about. Better just drive up to it and go on in and find out. It's on Kern Street between F and G, but I forget the name. Anyhow, it's open all night, and I've heard you can get pheasant there any time you like."

"It certainly is worth looking into," the younger man said.

The younger man got up, and Mayo Maloney, speechless with amazement, got up, too. He tried to say something courteous to the older man, but nothing seemed to want to come out of his dry mouth. He picked up his gun and went out to the truck and got in beside the younger man, and they went off. He saw the older man standing in the doorway of the store, watching.

The younger man drove all the way to town in silence, and when the boy saw familiar places, he thought in prayer again, saying, *I certainly don't*

deserve this, and I'm never going to forget it.

The truck crossed the Southern Pacific tracks to Chinatown,[3] and the driver parked in front of Willie Fong's, which was in fact open, although nobody was inside eating. The driver stepped out of the truck and went into the restaurant, and the boy saw him talking to a waiter. The waiter disappeared and soon came back with a man in a business suit. This man and the driver of the truck talked a few minutes, and then they both disappeared into the back of the restaurant, and after a few minutes the driver of the truck came back, and he was holding something that was wrapped in newspaper. He came out of the restaurant and got back into the truck, and they drove off again.

"How's your father?" the man said suddenly.

"He's fine," Mayo managed to say.

"I mean," the man said, "you *are* Mike Maloney's boy, aren't you?"

"Yes, I am," Mayo Maloney said.

"I thought you were," the man said. "You look alike and have a lot in common. You don't have to tell me where you live. I know where it is. And I know you want to know who I am, but don't you think it would be better if I didn't tell you? I've had dealings with your father, and he lent me some money when I needed it badly and we both weren't sure I'd ever be able to pay him back. So it's all right. I mean, nobody's going to know anything about this from me."

"Did they have any pheasants?" the boy said.

"Oh, yes," the man said. "I'm sorry I forgot to tell you. They're in that newspaper. Just throw the paper out the window."

The boy removed the paper from

3. **Chinatown,** the section of a city where Chinese live.

around the birds and looked at them. They were just about the most wonderful-looking things in the whole world.

"Do they have any shot in them?" he asked. "Because they ought to."

"No, I'm afraid they don't," the driver said, "but we'll drive out here a little where it's quiet and we won't disturb too many sleeping farmers, and between the two of us we'll get some shot into them. You can do the shooting, if you like."

"I might spoil them," the boy said.

"I'll be glad to attend to it, then," the driver said.

They drove along in silence a few minutes, and then the truck turned into a lonely road and stopped. The driver got out and placed the two birds on some grass by the side of the road in the light of the truck's lights about twenty yards off. Then he took the gun, examined it, aimed, fired once, unloaded the gun, fetched the birds, got back into the truck and they drove off again.

"They're just right now," he said.

"Thanks," the boy said.

When the truck got into his neighborhood Mayo said, "Could I get off a couple of blocks from my house, so nobody will see this truck accidentally?"

"Yes, that's a good idea," the driver said.

The truck stopped. The boy carefully nested the two birds in his left arm, then got out, and the driver helped him get the gun slung over his right arm.

"I never expected anything like this to happen," the boy said.

"No, I suppose not," the man said. "I never expected to find a man like your father when I needed him, either, but I guess things like that happen just the same. Well, good night."

"Good night," the boy said.

The man got into the truck and drove off, and the boy hurried home and into the house.

When Mike Maloney got back from walking Archie Cannon home, he was surprised to find the boy asleep on his folded arms on the kitchen table. He shook the boy gently, and Mayo Maloney sat up with a start, his eyes bloodshot and his ears red.

"You better get to bed," Mike said.

"I didn't want to go," the boy said, "until you got back, so I could thank you for the gun."

"That wasn't necessary," the man said. "That wasn't necessary at all."

The boy got up and barely managed to drag himself out of the room without falling.

Alone in the kitchen, the father picked up the birds and examined them, smiling because he knew whatever was behind their presence in the house, it was certainly something as handsome as the birds themselves.

✦   ✦   ✦   ✦

DISCUSSION

1. (a) What are some things with which Mayo finds fault? **(b)** Why does he scorn them?

2. (a) When does Saroyan first let you see how Mayo himself feels about things? **(b)** Does this look into Mayo's mind alter your impression of him? Explain.

3. Refer to the paragraph on page 63 that begins "The whole evening and night had been unbelievable." **(a)** In what "certain way" has Mayo felt he has to behave? **(b)** Why do you think he feels he must act that way? **(c)** Why does he believe he must change, but not immediately?

4. (a) How do Mayo and Ed make it look as though Mayo has actually had a successful hunting trip? **(b)** Why does Mayo feel he has to hide the truth from his father? **(c)** What will enable him to tell the truth in ten years or so?

5. Reread paragraph 6, column 1, page 62. **(a)** How does Mike Maloney account for his sudden change in attitude toward Mayo? **(b)** What does he mean when he says, "It's all right not being poor"? **(c)** What does he mean when he says that Mayo will "not be the great man he is now for long, and I don't want to be the one to cheat him out of a single moment of his greatness"? **(d)** Has Mayo, at the end of the story, stopped being "great"? Explain.

6. What does the last sentence of the story mean to you?

7. Do you agree with Saroyan's statement that Mayo was "a perfectly normal boy"? Why or why not?

8. (a) Describe the setting of the story. **(b)** Does it influence the action or reveal character in any way? Explain.

9. (a) Describe the inner conflict in "The Pheasant Hunter." **(b)** Is there also a conflict between Mayo and his father? If so, what kind of conflict is it?

UPI PHOTO

THE AUTHOR

"Kids are best," says William Saroyan, quoting his son. And Saroyan agrees that kids *are* best, "because they are essentially what the human race just might be, at its best."

Saroyan was born in California to Armenian parents. His writing reflects his delight in people, young and old, and his eager zest for living. One of his books, *The Human Comedy,* is a brief, warm novel about the family and friends of young Homer Macauley, who bicycles joyfully and painfully down the road to maturity as a telegraph messenger during World War II. In *My Name Is Aram,* Saroyan relates the adventures of a boy growing up in California. *The Time of Your Life,* a play which is considered one of his best works, won him special acclaim.

And the eternal battle
between generations goes on . . . .

old age sticks

E. E. CUMMINGS

old age sticks
up Keep
Off
signs)&

youth yanks them   5
down(old
age
cries No

Tres)&(pas)
youth laughs   10
(sing
old age

scolds Forbid
den Stop
Must   15
n't Don't

&)youth goes
right on
gr
owing old

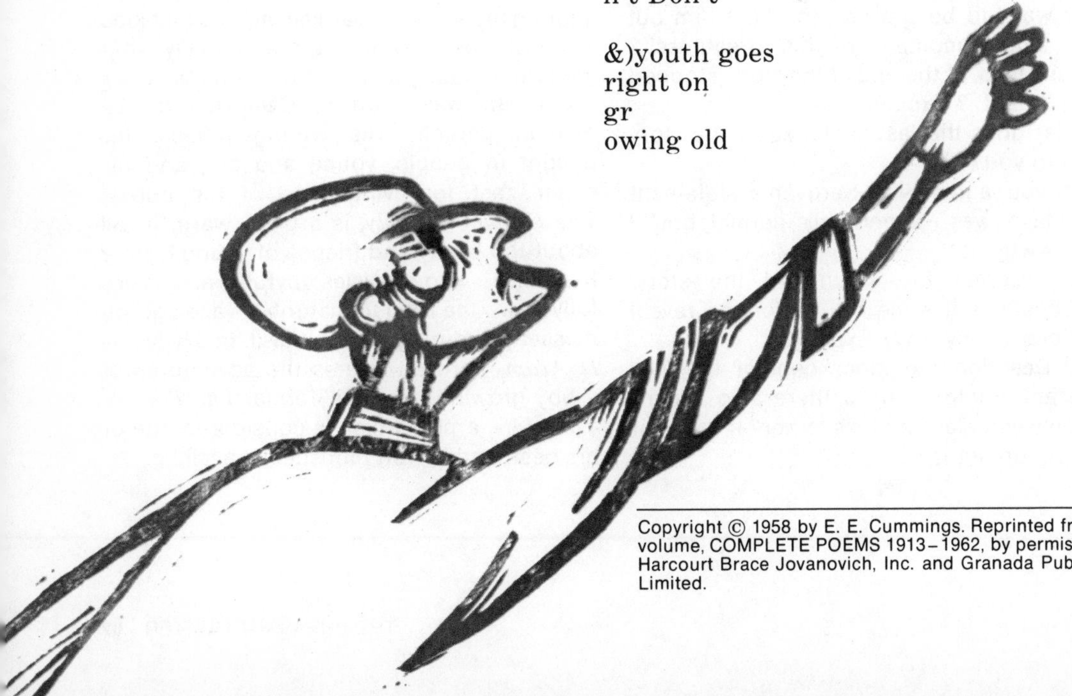

1. (a) What, in general, are adults always saying to young people? (b) How do young people react to their elders' advice? (c) What then, is the basic difference between the attitudes of youth and age?
2. (a) What is suggested by the lines

> youth goes
> right on
> gr
> owing old

(b) Is a change in outlook an inevitable part of aging? Why or why not?

3. (a) What are some unusual features in the form of this poem? (b) Why do you think the poet chose such a form? (c) What effect does the form have on you?

4. In what way is the conflict described in this poem similar to the conflict between Mayo and Mike in "The Pheasant Hunter"?

THE AUTHOR

E. E. Cummings (1894–1962) drove an ambulance for the French during World War I. But through a series of misunderstandings, he was mistakenly accused of treason and thrown into a French prison. He didn't stay in prison long, but his experiences were the basis for a book called *The Enormous Room.*

A daring experimenter in both art and poetry, Cummings searched for new ways to convey sounds and movement in verse. He often ignored conventional spacing and punctuation. Sometimes he ran words together to suggest speed, or separated them, one to a line, for a slower pace. His poems are sprightly and forceful in their originality, not because they "look different," but because he succeeded in making the form of his poems fit the particular ideas and feelings he wished to express.

See
CHARACTERIZATION: *motivation*
*Handbook
of Literary
Terms
page 516*

*Jody isn't a talkative boy, but you can find out
a lot about him and his feelings for a red pony
by thinking about the things he does
and why he does them.*

THE GIFT

JOHN STEINBECK

AT DAYBREAK Billy Buck emerged from the bunkhouse and stood for a moment on the porch looking up at the sky. He was a broad, bandy-legged little man with a walrus mustache, with square hands, puffed and muscled on the palms. His eyes were a contemplative, watery gray and the hair which protruded from under his Stetson hat was spiky and weathered. Billy was still stuffing his shirt into his blue jeans as he stood on the porch. He unbuckled his belt and tightened it again. The belt showed, by the worn shiny places opposite each hole, the gradual increase of Billy's middle over a period of years. When he had seen to the weather, Billy cleared each nostril by holding its mate closed with his forefinger and blowing fiercely. Then he walked down to the barn, rubbing his hands together. He curried and brushed two saddle horses in the stalls, talking quietly to them all the time; and he had hardly finished when the iron triangle started ringing at the ranch house. Billy stuck the brush and currycomb together and laid them on the rail, and went up to breakfast. His action had been so deliberate and yet so wasteless of time that he came to the house while Mrs. Tiflin was still ringing the triangle. She nodded her gray head to him and withdrew into the kitchen. Billy Buck sat down on the steps, because he was a cow hand, and it wouldn't be fitting that he should go first into the dining room. He heard Mr. Tiflin in the house, stamping his feet into his boots.

The high jangling note of the triangle put the boy Jody in motion. He was only a little boy, ten years old, with hair like dusty yellow grass, and with shy polite gray eyes, and with a mouth that worked when he thought. The triangle picked him up out of sleep. It didn't occur to him to disobey

the harsh note. He never had: no one he knew ever had. He brushed the tangled hair out of his eyes and skinned his nightgown off. In a moment he was dressed—blue chambray shirt and overalls. It was late in the summer, so of course there were no shoes to bother with. In the kitchen he waited until his mother got from in front of the sink and went back to the stove. Then he washed himself and brushed back his wet hair with his fingers. His mother turned sharply on him as he left the sink. Jody looked shyly away.

"I've got to cut your hair before long," his mother said. "Breakfast's on the table. Go on in, so Billy can come."

Jody sat at the long table which was covered with white oilcloth washed through to the fabric in some places. The fried eggs lay in rows on their platter. Jody took three eggs on his plate and followed with three thick slices of crisp bacon. He carefully scraped a spot of blood from one of the egg yolks.

Billy Buck clumped in. "That won't hurt you," Billy explained. "That's only a sign the rooster leaves."

Jody's tall stern father came in then and Jody knew from the noise on the floor that he was wearing boots, but he looked under the table anyway, to make sure. His father turned off the oil lamp over the table, for plenty of morning light now came through the windows.

Jody did not ask where his father and Billy Buck were riding that day, but he wished he might go along. His father was a disciplinarian. Jody obeyed him in everything without questions of any kind. Now, Carl Tiflin sat down and reached for the egg platter.

"Got the cows ready to go, Billy?" he asked.

"In the lower corral," Billy said. "I could just as well take them in alone."

"Sure you could. But a man needs company. Besides your throat gets pretty dry." Carl Tiflin was jovial this morning.

Jody's mother put her head in the door. "What time do you think to be back, Carl?"

"I can't tell. I've got to see some men in Salinas.[1] Might be gone till dark."

The eggs and coffee and big biscuits disappeared rapidly. Jody followed the two men out of the house. He watched them mount their horses and drive six old milk cows out of the corral and start over the hill toward Salinas. They were going to sell the old cows to the butcher.

When they had disappeared over the crown of the ridge Jody walked up the hill in back of the house. The dogs trotted around the house corner hunching their shoulders and grinning horribly with pleasure. Jody patted their heads—Doubletree Mutt with the big thick tail and yellow eyes, and Smasher, the shepherd, who had killed a coyote and lost an ear in doing it. Smasher's one good ear stood up higher than a collie's ear should. Billy Buck said that always happened. After the frenzied greeting the dogs lowered their noses to the ground in a businesslike way and went ahead, looking back now and then to make sure that the boy was coming. They walked up through the chicken yard and saw the quail eating with the chickens. Smasher chased the chickens a little to keep in practice in case there should ever be sheep to herd. Jody continued on

---

1. *Salinas* (sə lē′nəs), city in west central California.

through the large vegetable patch where the green corn was higher than his head. The cow pumpkins were green and small yet. He went on to the sagebrush line where the cold spring ran out of its pipe and fell into a round wooden tub. He leaned over and drank close to the green mossy wood where the water tasted best. Then he turned and looked back on the ranch, on the low, whitewashed house girded with red geraniums, and on the long bunkhouse by the cypress tree where Billy Buck lived alone. Jody could see the great black kettle under the cypress tree. That was where the pigs were scalded. The sun was coming over the ridge now, glaring on the whitewash of the houses and barns, making the wet grass blaze softly. Behind him, in the tall sagebrush, the birds were scampering on the ground, making a great noise among the dry leaves; the squirrels piped shrilly on the side hills. Jody looked along at the far buildings. He felt an uncertainty in the air, a feeling of change and of loss and of the gain of new and unfamiliar things. Over the hillside two big black buzzards sailed low to the ground and their shadows slipped smoothly and quickly ahead of them. Some animal had died in the vicinity. Jody knew it. It might be a cow or it might be the remains of a rabbit. The buzzards overlooked nothing. Jody hated them as all decent things hate them, but they could not be hurt because they made away with carrion.

After a while the boy sauntered down hill again. The dogs had long ago given him up and gone into the brush to do things in their own way. Back through the vegetable garden he went, and he paused for a moment to smash a green muskmelon with his heel, but he was not happy about it. It was a bad thing to do, he knew per-

fectly well. He kicked dirt over the ruined melon to conceal it.

Back at the house his mother bent over his rough hands, inspecting his fingers and nails. It did little good to start him clean to school, for too many things could happen on the way. She sighed over the black cracks on his fingers, and then gave him his books and his lunch and started him on the mile walk to school. She noticed that his mouth was working a good deal this morning.

Jody started his journey. He filled his pockets with little pieces of white quartz that lay in the road, and every so often he took a shot at a bird or at some rabbit that had stayed sunning itself in the road too long. At the crossroads over the bridge he met two friends and the three of them walked to school together, making ridiculous strides and being rather silly. School had just opened two weeks before. There was still a spirit of revolt among the pupils.

It was four o'clock in the afternoon when Jody topped the hill and looked down on the ranch again. He looked for the saddle horses, but the corral was empty. His father was not back yet. He went slowly, then, toward the afternoon chores. At the ranch house, he found his mother sitting on the porch, mending socks.

"There's two doughnuts in the kitchen for you," she said. Jody slid to the kitchen, and returned with half of one of the doughnuts already eaten and his mouth full. His mother asked him what he had learned in school that day, but she didn't listen to his doughnut-muffled answer. She interrupted, "Jody, tonight see you fill the woodbox clear full. Last night you crossed the sticks and it wasn't only about half full. Lay the sticks flat tonight. And Jody, some of the hens are hiding eggs, or else the dogs are eat-

ing them. Look about in the grass and see if you can find any nests."

Jody, still eating, went out and did his chores. He saw the quail come down to eat with the chickens when he threw out the grain. For some reason his father was proud to have them come. He never allowed any shooting near the house for fear the quail might go away.

When the woodbox was full, Jody took his twenty-two rifle up to the cold spring at the brush line. He drank again and then aimed the gun at all manner of things, at rocks, at birds on the wing, at the big black pig kettle under the cypress tree, but he didn't shoot, for he had no cartridges and wouldn't have until he was twelve. If his father had seen him aim the rifle in the direction of the house he would have put the cartridges off another year. Jody remembered this and did not point the rifle down the hill again. Two years was enough to wait for cartridges. Nearly all of his father's presents were given with reservations which hampered their value somewhat. It was good discipline.

The supper waited until dark for his father to return. When at last he came in with Billy Buck, Jody could smell the delicious brandy on their breaths. Inwardly he rejoiced, for his father sometimes talked to him when he smelled of brandy, sometimes even told things he had done in the wild days when he was a boy.

After supper, Jody sat by the fireplace and his shy polite eyes sought the room corners, and he waited for his father to tell what it was he contained, for Jody knew he had news of some sort. But he was disappointed. His father pointed a stern finger at him.

"You'd better go to bed, Jody. I'm going to need you in the morning."

That wasn't so bad. Jody liked to do things he had to do as long as they weren't routine things. He looked at the floor and his mouth worked out a question before he spoke it. "What are we going to do in the morning, kill a pig?" he asked softly.

"Never you mind. You better get to bed."

When the door was closed behind him, Jody heard his father and Billy Buck chuckling and he knew it was a joke of some kind. And later, when he lay in bed, trying to make words out of the murmurs in the other room, he heard his father protest, "But, Ruth, I didn't give much for him."

Jody heard the hoot owls hunting mice down by the barn, and he heard a fruit tree limb tap-tapping against the house. A cow was lowing when he went to sleep.

When the triangle sounded in the morning, Jody dressed more quickly even than usual. In the kitchen, while he washed his face and combed back his hair, his mother addressed him irritably. "Don't you go out until you get a good breakfast in you."

He went into the dining room and sat at the long white table. He took a steaming hot cake from the platter, arranged two fried eggs on it, covered them with another hot cake and squashed the whole thing with his fork.

His father and Billy Buck came in. Jody knew from the sound on the floor that both of them were wearing flat-heeled shoes, but he peered under the table to make sure. His father turned off the oil lamp, for the day had arrived, and he looked stern and disciplinary, but Billy Buck didn't look at Jody at all. He avoided the shy questioning eyes of the boy and soaked a whole piece of toast in his coffee.

Carl Tiflin said crossly, "You come with us after breakfast!"

Jody had trouble with his food then, for he felt a kind of doom in the air. After Billy had tilted his saucer and drained the coffee which had slopped into it, and had wiped his hands on his jeans, the two men stood up from the table and went out into the morning light together, and Jody respectfully followed a little behind them. He tried to keep his mind from running ahead, tried to keep it absolutely motionless.

His mother called, "Carl! Don't you let it keep him from school."

They marched past the cypress, where a single-tree hung from a limb to butcher the pigs on, and past the black iron kettle, so it was not a pig killing. The sun shone over the hill and threw long, dark shadows of the trees and buildings. They crossed a stubble field to short-cut to the barn. Jody's father unhooked the door and they went in. They had been walking toward the sun on the way down. The barn was black as night in contrast and warm from the hay and from the beasts. Jody's father moved over toward the one box stall. "Come here!" he ordered. Jody could begin to see things now. He looked into the box stall and then stepped back quickly.

A red pony colt was looking at him out of the stall. Its tense ears were forward and a light of disobedience was in its eyes. Its coat was rough and thick as an airedale's fur and its mane was long and tangled. Jody's throat collapsed in on itself and cut his breath short.

"He needs a good currying," his father said, "and if I ever hear of you not feeding him or leaving his stall dirty, I'll sell him off in a minute."

Jody couldn't bear to look at the pony's eyes any more. He gazed down at his hands for a moment, and he asked very shyly, "Mine?" No one answered him. He put his hand out toward the pony. Its gray nose came close, sniffing loudly, and then the lips drew back and the strong teeth closed on Jody's fingers. The pony shook its head up and down and seemed to laugh with amusement. Jody regarded his bruised fingers. "Well," he said with pride—"Well, I guess he can bite all right." The two men laughed, somewhat in relief. Carl Tiflin went out of the barn and walked up a side hill to be by himself, for he was embarrassed, but Billy Buck stayed. It was easier to talk to Billy Buck. Jody asked again—"Mine?"

Billy became professional in tone. "Sure! That is, if you look out for him and break him right. I'll show you how. He's just a colt. You can't ride him for some time."

Jody put out his bruised hand again, and this time the red pony let his nose be rubbed. "I ought to have a carrot," Jody said. "Where'd we get him, Billy?"

"Bought him at a sheriff's auction," Billy explained. "A show went broke in Salinas and had debts. The sheriff was selling off their stuff."

The pony stretched out his nose and shook the forelock from his wild eyes. Jody stroked the nose a little. He said softly, "There isn't a—saddle?"

Billy Buck laughed. "I'd forgot. Come along."

In the harness room he lifted down a little saddle of red morocco leather. "It's just a show saddle," Billy Buck said disparagingly. "It isn't practical for the brush, but it was cheap at the sale."

Jody couldn't trust himself to look at the saddle either, and he couldn't speak at all. He brushed the shining red leather with his finger tips, and

after a long time he said, "It'll look pretty on him though." He thought of the grandest and prettiest things he knew. "If he hasn't a name already, I think I'll call him Gabilan Mountains," he said.

Billy Buck knew how he felt. "It's a pretty long name. Why don't you just call him Gabilan? That means hawk. That would be a fine name for him." Billy felt glad. "If you will collect tail hair, I might be able to make a hair rope for you sometime. You could use it for a hackamore."

Jody wanted to go back to the box stall. "Could I lead him to school, do you think—to show the kids?"

But Billy shook his head. "He's not even halter-broke yet. We had a time getting him here. Had to almost drag him. You better be starting for school though."

"I'll bring the kids to see him here this afternoon," Jody said.

Six boys came over the hill half an hour early that afternoon, running hard, their heads down, their forearms working, their breath whistling. They swept by the house and cut across the stubble field to the barn. And then they stood self-consciously before the pony, and then they looked at Jody with eyes in which there was a new admiration and a new respect. Before today Jody had been a boy, dressed in overalls and a blue shirt—quieter than most, even suspected of being a little cowardly. And now he was different. Out of a thousand centuries they drew the ancient admiration of the footman for the horseman. They knew instinctively that a man on a horse is spiritually as well as physically bigger than a man on foot. They knew that Jody had been miraculously lifted out of equality with them, and had been placed over them. Gabilan put his head out of the stall and sniffed them.

"Why'n't you ride him?" the boys cried. "Why'n't you braid his tail with ribbons like in the fair?" "When you going to ride him?"

Jody's courage was up. He too felt the superiority of the horseman. "He's not old enough. Nobody can ride him for a long time. I'm going to train him on the long halter. Billy Buck is going to show me how."

"Well, can't we even lead him around a little?"

"He isn't even halter-broke," Jody said. He wanted to be completely alone when he took the pony out the first time. "Come and see the saddle."

They were speechless at the red morocco saddle, completely shocked out of comment. "It isn't much use in the brush," Jody explained. "It'll look pretty on him though. Maybe I'll ride bareback when I go into the brush."

"How you going to rope a cow without a saddle horn?"

"Maybe I'll get another saddle for every day. My father might want me to help him with the stock." He let them feel the red saddle, and showed them the brass chain throatlatch on the bridle and the big brass buttons at each temple where the headstall and brow band crossed. The whole thing was too wonderful. They had to go away after a little while, and each boy, in his mind, searched among his possessions for a bribe worthy of offering in return for a ride on the red pony when the time should come.

Jody was glad when they had gone. He took brush and currycomb from the wall, took down the barrier of the box stall and stepped cautiously in. The pony's eyes glittered, and he edged around into kicking position. But Jody touched him on the shoulder and rubbed his high arched neck as he had always seen Billy Buck do, and he crooned, "So-o-o boy," in a deep voice. The pony gradually relaxed his

tenseness. Jody curried and brushed until a pile of dead hair lay in the stall and until the pony's coat had taken on a deep red shine. Each time he finished he thought it might have been done better. He braided the mane into a dozen little pigtails, and he braided the forelock, and then he undid them and brushed the hair out straight again.

Jody did not hear his mother enter the barn. She was angry when she came, but when she looked in at the pony and at Jody working over him, she felt a curious pride rise up in her. "Have you forgot the woodbox?" she asked gently. "It's not far off from dark and there's not a stick of wood in the house, and the chickens aren't fed."

Jody quickly put up his tools. "I forgot, ma'am."

"Well, after this do your chores first. Then you won't forget. I expect you'll forget lots of things now if I don't keep an eye on you."

"Can I have carrots from the garden for him, ma'am?"

She had to think about that. "Oh—I guess so, if you only take the big tough ones."

"Carrots keep the coat good," he said, and again she felt the curious rush of pride.

Jody never waited for the triangle to get him out of bed after the coming of the pony. It became his habit to creep out of bed even before his mother was awake, to slip into his clothes and to go quietly down to the barn to see Gabilan. In the gray quiet mornings when the land and the brush and the houses and the trees were silver-gray and black like a photograph negative, he stole toward the barn, past the sleeping stones and the sleeping cypress tree. The turkeys, roosting in the tree out of coyotes' reach, clicked drowsily. The fields glowed with a gray frostlike light and in the dew the tracks of rabbits and of field mice stood out sharply. The good dogs came stiffly out of their little houses, hackles up and deep growls in their throats. Then they caught Jody's scent, and their stiff tails rose up and waved a greeting—Doubletree Mutt with the big thick tail, and Smasher, the incipient shepherd— then went lazily back to their warm beds.

It was a strange time and a mysterious journey to Jody—an extension of a dream. When he first had the pony he liked to torture himself during the trip by thinking Gabilan would not be in his stall, and worse, would never have been there. And he had other delicious little self-induced pains. He thought how the rats had gnawed ragged holes in the red saddle, and how the mice had nibbled Gabilan's tail until it was stringy and thin. He usually ran the last little way to the barn. He unlatched the rusty hasp of the barn door and stepped in, and no matter how quietly he opened the door, Gabilan was always looking at him over the barrier of the box stall and Gabilan whinnied softly and stamped his front foot, and his eyes had big sparks of red fire in them like oakwood embers.

Sometimes, if the work horses were to be used that day, Jody found Billy Buck in the barn harnessing and currying. Billy stood with him and looked long at Gabilan and he told Jody a great many things about horses. He explained that they were terribly afraid for their feet, so that one must make a practice of lifting the legs and patting the hoofs and ankles to remove their terror. He told Jody how horses love conversation. He must talk to the pony all the time, and tell him the reasons for everything. Billy wasn't sure a horse could

understand everything that was said to him, but it was impossible to say how much was understood. A horse never kicked up a fuss if someone he liked explained things to him. Billy could give examples, too. He had known, for instance, a horse nearly dead-beat with fatigue to perk up when told it was only a little farther to his destination. And he had known a horse paralyzed with fright to come out of it when his rider told him what it was that was frightening him. While he talked in the mornings, Billy Buck cut twenty or thirty straws into neat three-inch lengths and stuck them into his hatband. Then during the whole day, if he wanted to pick his teeth or merely to chew on something, he had only to reach up for one of them.

Jody listened carefully, for he knew and the whole country knew that Billy Buck was a fine hand with horses. Billy's own horse was a stringy cayuse with a hammerhead,[2] but he nearly always won the first prizes at the stock trials. Billy could rope a steer, take a double half-hitch about the horn with his riata, and dismount, and his horse would play the steer as an angler plays a fish, keeping a tight rope until the steer was down or beaten.

Every morning, after Jody had curried and brushed the pony, he let down the barrier of the stall, and Gabilan thrust past him and raced down the barn and into the corral. Around and around he galloped, and sometimes he jumped forward and landed on stiff legs. He stood quivering, stiff ears forward, eyes rolling so that the whites showed, pretending to be frightened. At last he walked snorting to the water trough and buried his nose in the water up to the nostrils. Jody was proud then, for he knew that was the way to judge a horse. Poor horses only touched their lips to the water, but a fine spirited beast put his whole nose and mouth under, and only left room to breathe.

Then Jody stood and watched the pony, and he saw things he had never noticed about any other horse, the sleek, sliding flank muscles and the cords of the buttocks, which flexed like a closing fist, and the shine the sun put on the red coat. Having seen horses all his life, Jody had never looked at them very closely before. But now he noticed the moving ears which gave expression and even inflection of expression to the face. The

---

2. **cayuse** (kī ūs′) **with a hammerhead,** an Indian pony with a head shaped like a double-headed hammer.

pony talked with his ears. You could tell exactly how he felt about everything by the way his ears pointed. Sometimes they were stiff and upright and sometimes lax and sagging. They went back when he was angry or fearful, and forward when he was anxious and curious and pleased; and their exact position indicated which emotion he had.

Billy Buck kept his word. In the early fall the training began. First there was the halter-breaking, and that was the hardest because it was the first thing. Jody held a carrot and coaxed and promised and pulled on the rope. The pony set his feet like a burro when he felt the strain. But before long he learned. Jody walked all over the ranch leading him. Gradually he took to dropping the rope until the pony followed him unled wherever he went.

And then came the training on the long halter. That was slower work. Jody stood in the middle of a circle, holding the long halter. He clucked with his tongue and the pony started to walk in a big circle, held in by the long rope. He clucked again to make the pony trot, and again to make him gallop. Around and around Gabilan went thundering and enjoy-

ing it immensely. Then he called, "Whoa," and the pony stopped. It was not long until Gabilan was perfect at it. But in many ways he was a bad pony. He bit Jody in the pants and stomped on Jody's feet. Now and then his ears went back and he aimed a tremendous kick at the boy. Every time he did one of these bad things, Gabilan settled back and seemed to laugh to himself.

Billy Buck worked at the hair rope in the evenings before the fireplace. Jody collected tail hair in a bag, and he sat and watched Billy slowly constructing the rope, twisting a few hairs to make a string and rolling two strings together for a cord, and then braiding a number of cords to make the rope. Billy rolled the finished rope on the floor under his foot to make it round and hard.

The long halter work rapidly approached perfection. Jody's father, watching the pony stop and start and trot and gallop, was a little bothered by it.

"He's getting to be almost a trick pony," he complained. "I don't like trick horses. It takes all the—dignity out of a horse to make him do tricks. Why, a trick horse is kind of like an actor—no dignity, no character of his own." And his father said, "I guess

you better be getting him used to the saddle pretty soon."

Jody rushed for the harness room. For some time he had been riding the saddle on a sawhorse. He changed the stirrup length over and over, and could never get it just right. Sometimes, mounted on the sawhorse in the harness room, with collars and hames and tugs hung all about him, Jody rode out beyond the room. He carried his rifle across the pommel. He saw fields go flying by; and he heard the beat of the galloping hoofs.

It was a ticklish job, saddling the pony the first time. Gabilan hunched and reared and threw the saddle off before the cinch could be tightened. It had to be replaced again and again until at last the pony let it stay. And the cinching was difficult, too. Day by day Jody tightened the girth a little more until at last the pony didn't mind the saddle at all.

Then there was the bridle. Billy explained how to use a stick of licorice for a bit until Gabilan was used to having something in his mouth. Billy explained, "Of course we could force-break him to everything, but he wouldn't be as good a horse if we did. He'd always be a little bit afraid, and he wouldn't mind because he wanted to."

The first time the pony wore the bridle he whipped his head about and worked his tongue against the bit until the blood oozed from the corners of his mouth. He tried to rub the headstall off on the manger. His ears pivoted about and his eyes turned red with fear and with general rambunctiousness. Jody rejoiced, for he knew that only a mean-souled horse does not resent training.

And Jody trembled when he thought of the time when he would first sit in the saddle. The pony would probably throw him off. There was no disgrace in that. The disgrace would come if he did not get right up and mount again. Sometimes he dreamed that he lay in the dirt and cried and couldn't make himself mount again. The shame of the dream lasted until the middle of the day.

Gabilan was growing fast. Already he had lost the long-leggedness of the colt; his mane was getting longer and blacker. Under the constant currying and brushing his coat lay as smooth and gleaming as orange-red lacquer. Jody oiled the hoofs and kept them carefully trimmed so they would not crack.

The hair rope was nearly finished. Jody's father gave him an old pair of spurs and bent in the side bars and cut down the strap and took up the chainlets until they fitted. And then one day Carl Tiflin said:

"The pony's growing faster than I thought. I guess you can ride him by Thanksgiving. Think you can stick on?"

"I don't know," Jody said shyly. Thanksgiving was only three weeks off. He hoped it wouldn't rain, for rain would spot the red saddle.

Gabilan knew and liked Jody by now. He nickered when Jody came across the stubble field, and in the pasture he came running when his master whistled for him. There was always a carrot for him every time.

Billy Buck gave him riding instructions over and over. "Now when you get up there, just grab tight with your knees and keep your hands away from the saddle, and if you get throwed, don't let that stop you. No matter how good a man is, there's always some horse can pitch him. You just climb up again before he gets to feeling smart about it. Pretty soon, he won't throw you no more, and pretty soon he *can't* throw you no more. That's the way to do it."

"I hope it don't rain before," Jody said.

"Why not? Don't want to get throwed in the mud?"

That was partly it, and also he was afraid that in the flurry of bucking Gabilan might slip and fall on him and break his leg or his hip. He had seen that happen to men before, had seen how they writhed on the ground like squashed bugs, and he was afraid of it.

He practiced on the sawhorse how he would hold the reins in his left hand and a hat in his right hand. If he kept his hands thus busy, he couldn't grab the horn if he felt himself going off. He didn't like to think of what would happen if he did grab the horn. Perhaps his father and Billy Buck would never speak to him again, they would be so ashamed. The news would get about and his mother would be ashamed too. And in the school yard—it was too awful to contemplate.

He began putting his weight in a stirrup when Gabilan was saddled, but he didn't throw his leg over the pony's back. That was forbidden until Thanksgiving.

Every afternoon he put the red saddle on the pony and cinched it tight. The pony was learning already to fill his stomach out unnaturally large while the cinching was going on, and then to let it down when the straps were fixed. Sometimes Jody led him up to the brush line and let him drink from the round green tub, and sometimes he led him up through the stubble field to the hilltop from which it was possible to see the white town of Salinas and the geometric fields of the great valley, and the oak trees clipped by the sheep. Now and then they broke through the brush and came to little cleared circles so hedged in that the world was gone and only the sky and the circle of brush were left from the old life. Gabilan liked these trips and showed it by keeping his head very high and by quivering his nostrils with interest. When the two came back from an expedition they smelled of the sweet sage they had forced through.

Time dragged on toward Thanksgiving, but winter came fast. The clouds swept down and hung all day over the land and brushed the hilltops, and the winds blew shrilly at night. All day the dry oak leaves drifted down from the trees until they covered the ground, and yet the trees were unchanged.

Jody had wished it might not rain before Thanksgiving, but it did. The brown earth turned dark and the trees glistened. The cut ends of the stubble turned black with mildew; the haystacks grayed from exposure to the damp, and on the roofs the moss, which had been all summer as gray as lizards, turned a brilliant yellow-green. During the week of rain, Jody kept the pony in the box stall out of the dampness, except for a little time after school when he took him out for exercise and to drink at the water trough in the upper corral. Not once did Gabilan get wet.

The wet weather continued until little new grass appeared. Jody walked to school dressed in a slicker and short rubber boots. At length one morning the sun came out brightly. Jody, at his work in the box stall, said to Billy Buck, "Maybe I'll leave Gabilan in the corral when I go to school today."

"Be good for him to be out in the sun," Billy assured him. "No animal likes to be cooped up too long. Your father and me are going back on the hill to clean the leaves out of the spring." Billy nodded and picked his teeth with one of his little straws.

"If the rain comes, though—" Jody suggested.

"Not likely to rain today. She's rained herself out." Billy pulled up his sleeves and snapped his arm bands. "If it comes on to rain—why a little rain don't hurt a horse."

"Well, if it does come on to rain, you put him in, will you, Billy? I'm scared he might get cold so I couldn't ride him when the time comes."

"Oh sure! I'll watch out for him if we get back in time. But it won't rain today."

And so Jody, when he went to school, left Gabilan standing out in the corral.

Billy Buck wasn't wrong about many things. He couldn't be. But he was wrong about the weather that day, for a little after noon the clouds pushed over the hills and the rain began to pour down. Jody heard it start on the schoolhouse roof. He considered holding up one finger for permission to go to the outhouse and, once outside, running for home to put the pony in. Punishment would be prompt both at school and at home. He gave it up and took ease from Billy's assurance that rain couldn't hurt a horse. When school was finally out, he hurried home through the dark rain. The banks at the sides of the road spouted little jets of muddy water. The rain slanted and swirled under a cold and gusty wind. Jody dog-trotted home, slopping through the gravelly mud of the road.

From the top of the ridge he could see Gabilan standing miserably in the corral. The red coat was almost black, and streaked with water. He stood head down with his rump to the rain and wind. Jody arrived running and threw open the barn door and led the wet pony in by his forelock. Then he found a gunny sack and rubbed the soaked hair and rubbed the legs and ankles. Gabilan stood patiently, but he trembled in gusts like the wind.

When he had dried the pony as well as he could, Jody went up to the house and brought hot water down to the barn and soaked the grain in it. Gabilan was not very hungry. He nibbled at the hot mash, but he was not very much interested in it, and he still shivered now and then. A little steam rose from his damp back.

It was almost dark when Billy Buck and Carl Tiflin came home. "When the rain started we put up at Ben Herche's place, and the rain never let up all afternoon," Carl Tiflin explained. Jody looked reproachfully at Billy Buck and Billy felt guilty.

"You said it wouldn't rain," Jody accused him.

Billy looked away. "It's hard to tell, this time of year," he said, but his excuse was lame. He had no right to be fallible, and he knew it.

"The pony got wet, got soaked through."

"Did you dry him off?"

"I rubbed him with a sack and I gave him hot grain."

Billy nodded in agreement.

"Do you think he'll take cold, Billy?"

"A little rain never hurt anything," Billy assured him.

Jody's father joined the conversation then and lectured the boy a little. "A horse," he said, "isn't any lap-dog kind of thing." Carl Tiflin hated weakness and sickness, and he held a violent contempt for helplessness.

Jody's mother put a platter of steaks on the table and boiled potatoes and boiled squash, which clouded the room with their steam. They sat down to eat. Carl Tiflin still grumbled about weakness put into animals and men by too much coddling.

Billy Buck felt bad about his mistake. "Did you blanket him?" he asked.

"No. I couldn't find any blanket. I laid some sacks over his back."

"We'll go down and cover him up after we eat, then." Billy felt better about it then. When Jody's father had gone in to the fire and his mother was washing dishes, Billy found and lighted a lantern. He and Jody walked through the mud to the barn. The barn was dark and warm and sweet. The horses still munched their evening hay. "You hold the lantern!" Billy ordered. And he felt the pony's legs and tested the heat of the flanks. He put his cheek against the pony's gray muzzle and then he rolled up the eyelids to look at the eyeballs and he lifted the lips to see the gums, and he put his fingers inside the ears. "He don't seem so chipper," Billy said. "I'll give him a rubdown."

Then Billy found a sack and rubbed the pony's legs violently and he rubbed the chest and the withers. Gabilan was strangely spiritless. He submitted patiently to the rubbing. At last Billy brought an old cotton comforter from the saddle room, and threw it over the pony's back and tied it at neck and chest with string.

"Now he'll be all right in the morning," Billy said.

Jody's mother looked up when he got back to the house. "You're late up from bed," she said. She held his chin in her hand and brushed the tangled hair out of his eyes and she said, "Don't worry about the pony. He'll be all right. Billy's as good as any horse doctor in the country."

Jody hadn't known she could see his worry. He pulled gently away from her and knelt down in front of the fireplace until it burned his stomach. He scorched himself through and then went in to bed, but it was a hard thing to go to sleep. He awakened after what seemed a long time. The room was dark but there was a grayness in the window like that which precedes the dawn. He got up and found his overalls and searched for the legs, and then the clock in the other room struck two. He laid his clothes down and got back into bed. It was broad daylight when he awakened again. For the first time he had slept through the ringing of the triangle. He leaped up, flung on his clothes and went out of the door still buttoning his shirt. His mother looked after him for a moment and then went quietly back to her work. Her eyes were brooding and kind. Now and then her mouth smiled a little but without changing her eyes at all.

Jody ran on toward the barn. Halfway there he heard the sound he dreaded, the hollow rasping cough of a horse. He broke into a sprint then. In the barn he found Billy Buck with the pony. Billy was rubbing its legs with his strong thick hands. He looked up and smiled gaily. "He just took a little cold," Billy said. "We'll have him out of it in a couple of days."

Jody looked at the pony's face. The eyes were half closed and the lids thick and dry. In the eye corners a crust of hard mucus stuck. Gabilan's ears hung loosely sideways and his head was low. Jody put out his hand, but the pony did not move close to it. He coughed again and his whole body constricted with the effort. A little stream of fluid ran from his nostrils.

Jody looked back at Billy Buck. "He's awful sick, Billy."

"Just a little cold, like I said," Billy insisted. "You go get some breakfast and then go back to school. I'll take care of him."

"But you might have to do something else. You might leave him."

"No, I won't. I won't leave him at all. Tomorrow's Saturday. Then you can stay with him all day." Billy had failed again, and he felt bad about it. He had to cure the pony now.

Jody walked up to the house and took his place listlessly at the table. The eggs and bacon were cold and greasy, but he didn't notice it. He ate his usual amount. He didn't even ask to stay home from school. His mother pushed his hair back when she took his plate. "Billy'll take care of the pony," she assured him.

He moped through the whole day at school. He couldn't answer any questions nor read any words. He couldn't even tell anyone the pony was sick, for that might make him sicker. And when school was finally out he started home in dread. He walked slowly and let the other boys leave him. He wished he might continue walking and never arrive at the ranch.

Billy was in the barn, as he had promised, and the pony was worse. His eyes were almost closed now, and his breath whistled shrilly past an obstruction in his nose. A film covered that part of the eyes that was visible at all. It was doubtful whether the pony could see any more. Now and then he snorted, to clear his nose, and by the action seemed to plug it tighter. Jody looked dispiritedly at the pony's coat. The hair lay rough and unkempt and seemed to have lost all of its old luster. Billy stood quietly beside the stall. Jody hated to ask, but he had to know.

"Billy, is he—is he going to get well?"

Billy put his fingers between the bars under the pony's jaw and felt about. "Feel here," he said and he guided Jody's fingers to a large lump under the jaw. "When that gets bigger, I'll open it up and then he'll get better."

Jody looked quickly away, for he had heard about that lump. "What is the matter with him?"

Billy didn't want to answer, but he had to. He couldn't be wrong three times. "Strangles," he said shortly, "but don't you worry about that. I'll pull him out of it. I've seen them get well when they were worse than Gabilan is. I'm going to steam him now. You can help."

"Yes," Jody said miserably. He followed Billy into the grain room and watched him make the steaming bag ready. It was a long canvas nose bag with straps to go over a horse's ears. Billy filled it one-third full of bran and then he added a couple of handfuls of dried hops. On top of the dry substance he poured a little carbolic acid and a little turpentine.

"I'll be mixing it all up while you run to the house for a kettle of boiling water," Billy said.

When Jody came back with the steaming kettle, Billy buckled the straps over Gabilan's head and fitted the bag tightly around his nose. Then through a little hole in the side of the bag he poured the boiling water on the mixture. The pony started away as a cloud of strong steam rose up, but then the soothing fumes crept through his nose and into his lungs, and the sharp steam began to clear out the nasal passages. He breathed loudly. His legs trembled in an ague, and his eyes closed against the biting cloud. Billy poured in more water and kept the steam rising for fifteen minutes. At last he set down the kettle and took the bag from Gabilan's nose. The pony looked better. He breathed freely, and his eyes were open wider than they had been.

"See how good it makes him feel," Billy said. "Now we'll wrap him up in the blanket again. Maybe he'll be nearly well by morning."

"I'll stay with him tonight," Jody suggested.

"No. Don't you do it. I'll bring my blankets down here and put them in the hay. You can stay tomorrow and steam him if he needs it."

The evening was falling when they went to the house for their supper. Jody didn't even realize that someone else had fed the chickens and filled the woodbox. He walked up past the house to the dark brush line and took a drink of water from the tub. The spring water was so cold that it stung his mouth and drove a shiver through him. The sky above the hills was still light. He saw a hawk flying so high that it caught the sun on its breast and shone like a spark. Two blackbirds were driving him down the sky, glittering as they attacked their enemy. In the west, the clouds were moving in to rain again.

Jody's father didn't speak at all while the family ate supper, but after Billy Buck had taken his blankets and gone to sleep in the barn, Carl Tiflin built a high fire in the fireplace and told stories. He told about the wild man who ran naked through the country and had a tail and ears like a horse, and he told about the rabbit-cats of Moro Cojo that hopped into the trees for birds. He revived the famous Maxwell brothers who found a vein of gold and hid the traces of it so carefully that they could never find it again.

Jody sat with his chin in his hands; his mouth worked nervously and his father gradually became aware that he wasn't listening very carefully. "Isn't that funny?" he asked.

Jody laughed politely and said, "Yes, sir." His father was angry and hurt, then. He didn't tell any more stories. After a while, Jody took a lantern and went down to the barn. Billy Buck was asleep in the hay, and, except that his breath rasped a little in his lungs, the pony seemed to be much better. Jody stayed a little while, running his fingers over the red rough coat, and then he took up the lantern and went back to the house. When he was in bed, his mother came into the room.

"Have you enough covers on? It's getting winter."

"Yes, ma'am."

"Well, get some rest tonight." She hesitated to go out, stood uncertainly. "The pony will be all right," she said.

Jody was tired. He went to sleep quickly and didn't awaken until dawn. The triangle sounded, and Billy Buck came up from the barn before Jody could get out of the house.

"How is he?" Jody demanded.

Billy always wolfed his breakfast. "Pretty good. I'm going to open that lump this morning. Then he'll be better maybe."

After breakfast, Billy got out his best knife, one with a needle point. He whetted the shining blade a long time on a little carborundum stone. He tried the point and the blade again and again on his calloused thumb ball, and at last he tried it on his upper lip.

On the way to the barn, Jody noticed how the young grass was up and how the stubble was melting day by day into the new green crop of volunteer. It was a cold sunny morning.

As soon as he saw the pony, Jody knew he was worse. His eyes were closed and sealed shut with dried mucus. His head hung so low that his nose almost touched the straw of his bed. There was a little groan in each breath, a deep-seated, patient groan.

Billy lifted the weak head and made a quick slash with the knife. Jody saw the yellow pus run out. He held up the head while Billy swabbed out the wound with weak carbolic acid salve.

"Now he'll feel better," Billy assured him. "That yellow poison is what makes him sick."

Jody looked unbelieving at Billy Buck. "He's awful sick."

Billy thought a long time what to say. He nearly tossed off a careless assurance, but he saved himself in time. "Yes, he's pretty sick," he said at last. "I've seen worse ones get well. If he doesn't get pneumonia, we'll pull him through. You stay with him. If he gets worse, you can come and get me."

For a long time after Billy went away, Jody stood beside the pony, stroking him behind the ears. The pony didn't flip his head the way he had done when he was well. The groaning in his breathing was becoming more hollow.

Doubletree Mutt looked into the barn, his big tail waving provocatively, and Jody was so incensed at his health that he found a hard black clod on the floor and deliberately threw it. Doubletree Mutt went yelping away to nurse a bruised paw.

In the middle of the morning, Billy Buck came back and made another steam bag. Jody watched to see whether the pony improved this time as he had before. His breathing eased a little, but he did not raise his head.

The Saturday dragged on. Late in the afternoon Jody went to the house and brought his bedding down and made up a place to sleep in the hay. He didn't ask permission. He knew from the way his mother looked at him that she would let him do almost anything. That night he left a lantern burning on a wire over the box stall.

Billy had told him to rub the pony's legs every little while.

At nine o'clock the wind sprang up and howled around the barn. And in spite of his worry, Jody grew sleepy. He got into his blankets and went to sleep, but the breathy groans of the pony sounded in his dreams. And in his sleep he heard a crashing noise which went on and on until it awakened him. The wind was rushing through the barn. He sprang up and looked down the lane of stalls. The barn door had blown open, and the pony was gone.

He caught the lantern and ran outside into the gale, and he saw Gabilan weakly shambling away into the darkness, head down, legs working slowly and mechanically. When Jody ran up and caught him by the forelock, he allowed himself to be led back and put into his stall. His groans were louder, and a fierce whistling came from his nose. Jody didn't sleep any more then. The hissing of the pony's breath grew louder and sharper.

He was glad when Billy Buck came in at dawn. Billy looked for a time at the pony as though he had never seen him before. He felt the ears and flanks. "Jody," he said, "I've got to do something you won't want to see. You run up to the house for a while."

Jody grabbed him fiercely by the forearm. "You're not going to shoot him?"

Billy patted his hand. "No. I'm going to open a little hole in his windpipe so he can breathe. His nose is filled up. When he gets well, we'll put a brass button in the hole for him to breathe through."

Jody couldn't have gone away if he had wanted to. It was awful to see the red hide cut, but infinitely more terrible to know it was being cut and

not to see it. "I'll stay right here," he said bitterly. "You sure you got to?"

"Yes. I'm sure. If you stay, you can hold his head. If it doesn't make you sick, that is."

The fine knife came out again and was whetted again just as carefully as it had been the first time. Jody held the pony's head up and the throat taut, while Billy felt up and down for the right place. Jody sobbed once as the bright knife point disappeared into the throat. The pony plunged weakly away and then stood still, trembling violently. The blood ran thickly out and up the knife and across Billy's hand and into his shirt sleeve. The sure square hand sawed out a round hole in the flesh, and the breath came bursting out of the hole, throwing a fine spray of blood. With the rush of oxygen, the pony took a sudden strength. He lashed out with his hind feet and tried to rear, but Jody held his head down while Billy mopped the new wound with carbolic salve. It was a good job. The blood stopped flowing and the air puffed out the hole and sucked it in regularly with a little bubbling noise.

The rain brought in by the night wind began to fall on the barn roof. Then the triangle rang for breakfast. "You go up and eat while I wait," Billy said. "We've got to keep this hole from plugging up."

Jody walked slowly out of the barn. He was too dispirited to tell Billy how the barn door had blown open and let the pony out. He emerged into the wet gray morning and sloshed up to the house, taking a perverse pleasure in splashing through all the puddles. His mother fed him and put dry clothes on. She didn't question him. She seemed to know he couldn't answer questions. But when he was ready to go back to the barn she brought him a pan of steaming meal. "Give him this," she said.

But Jody did not take the pan. He said, "He won't eat anything," and ran out of the house. At the barn, Billy showed him how to fix a ball of cotton on a stick, with which to swab out the breathing hole when it became clogged with mucus.

Jody's father walked into the barn and stood with them in front of the stall. At length he turned to the boy. "Hadn't you better come with me? I'm going to drive over the hill." Jody shook his head. "You better come on, out of this," his father insisted.

Billy turned on him angrily. "Let him alone. It's his pony, isn't it?"

Carl Tiflin walked away without saying another word. His feelings were badly hurt.

All morning Jody kept the wound open and the air passing in and out freely. At noon the pony lay wearily down on his side and stretched his nose out.

Billy came back. "If you're going to stay with him tonight, you better take a little nap," he said. Jody went absently out of the barn. The sky had cleared to a hard thin blue. Everywhere the birds were busy with worms that had come to the damp surface of the ground.

Jody walked to the brush line and sat on the edge of the mossy tub. He looked down at the house and at the old bunkhouse and at the dark cypress tree. The place was familiar, but curiously changed. It wasn't itself any more, but a frame for things that were happening. A cold wind blew out of the east now, signifying that the rain was over for a little while. At his feet Jody could see the little arms of new weeds spreading out over the ground. In the mud about the spring were thousands of quail tracks.

Doubletree Mutt came sideways and embarrassed up through the vegetable patch, and Jody, remembering how he had thrown the clod, put his arm about the dog's neck and kissed him on his wide black nose. Doubletree Mutt sat still, as though he knew some solemn thing was happening. His big tail slapped the ground gravely. Jody pulled a swollen tick out of Mutt's neck and popped it dead between his thumbnails. It was a nasty thing. He washed his hands in the cold spring water.

Except for the steady swish of the wind, the farm was very quiet. Jody knew his mother wouldn't mind if he didn't go in to eat his lunch. After a little while he went slowly back to the barn. Mutt crept into his own little house and whined softly to himself for a long time.

Billy Buck stood up from the box and surrendered the cotton swab. The pony still lay on his side and the wound in his throat bellowsed in and out. When Jody saw how dry and dead the hair looked, he knew at last that there was no hope for the pony. He had seen the dead hair before on dogs and cows, and it was a sure sign. He sat heavily on the box and let down the barrier of the box stall. For a long time he kept his eyes on the moving wound, and at last he dozed, and the afternoon passed quickly. Just before dark his mother brought a deep dish of stew and left it for him and went away. Jody ate a little of it, and, when it was dark, he set the lantern on the floor by the pony's head so he could watch the wound and keep it open. And he dozed again until the night chill awakened him. The wind was blowing fiercely, bringing the north cold with it. Jody brought a blanket from his bed in the hay and wrapped himself in it. Gabilan's breathing was quiet at last; the hole in his throat moved gently. The owls flew through the hayloft, shrieking and looking for mice. Jody put his hands down on his head and slept. In his sleep he was aware that the wind had increased. He heard it slamming about the barn.

It was daylight when he awakened. The barn door had swung open. The pony was gone. He sprang up and ran out into the morning light.

The pony's tracks were plain enough, dragging through the frost-like dew on the young grass, tired tracks with little lines between them where the hoofs had dragged. They headed for the brush line halfway up the ridge. Jody broke into a run and followed them. The sun shone on the sharp white quartz that stuck through the ground here and there. As he followed the plain trail, a shadow cut across in front of him. He looked up and saw a high circle of black buzzards, and the slowly revolving circle dropped lower and lower. The solemn birds soon disappeared over the ridge. Jody ran faster then, forced on by panic and rage. The trail entered the brush at last and followed a winding route among the tall sage bushes.

At the top of the ridge Jody was winded. He paused, puffing noisily. The blood pounded in his ears. Then he saw what he was looking for. Below, in one of the little clearings in the brush, lay the red pony. In the distance, Jody could see the legs moving slowly and convulsively. And in a circle around him stood the buzzards, waiting for the moment of death they know so well.

Jody leaped forward and plunged down the hill. The wet ground muffled his steps and the brush hid him. When he arrived, it was all over. The first buzzard sat on the pony's head and its beak had just risen dripping

with dark eye fluid. Jody plunged into the circle like a cat. The black brotherhood arose in a cloud, but the big one on the pony's head was too late. As it hopped along to take off, Jody caught its wing tip and pulled it down. It was nearly as big as he was. The free wing crashed into his face with the force of a club, but he hung on. The claws fastened on his leg and the wing elbows battered his head on either side. Jody groped blindly with his free hand. His fingers found the neck of the struggling bird. The red eyes looked into his face, calm and fearless and fierce; the naked head turned from side to side. Then the beak opened and vomited a stream of putrefied fluid. Jody brought up his knee and fell on the great bird. He held the neck to the ground with one hand while his other found a piece of sharp white quartz. The first blow broke the beak sideways and black blood spurted from the twisted, leath-ery mouth corners. He struck again and missed. The red fearless eyes still looked at him, impersonal and unafraid and detached. He struck again and again, until the buzzard lay dead, until its head was a red pulp. He was still beating the dead bird when Billy Buck pulled him off and held him tightly to calm his shaking.

Carl Tiflin wiped the blood from the boy's face with a red bandana. Jody was limp and quiet now. His father moved the buzzard with his toe. "Jody," he explained, "the buzzard didn't kill the pony. Don't you know that?"

"I know it," Jody said wearily.

It was Billy Buck who was angry. He had lifted Jody in his arms, and had turned to carry him home. But he turned back on Carl Tiflin. "'Course he knows it," Billy said furiously, "Good Lord! man, can't you see how he'd feel about it?"   THE END

DISCUSSION

1. (a) Describe Jody's physical appearance. (b) Which of his mannerisms reveals most about him? (c) Which of the following character traits does Jody possess: *obedience; belligerence; forcefulness; patience; shyness; responsibility*? Find evidence in the story to support your answers.
2. What does Jody reveal about his feelings for the red pony when he names it Gabilan Mountains?
3. (a) What ideas about discipline does Carl Tiflin have? (b) How does he demonstrate his ideas in giving Jody the twenty-two? (c) What restrictions does he put upon Jody's use of the pony? (d) Describe the relationship between Jody and his father.
4. (a) What bond exists between Jody and Billy Buck? (b) Why is there no such bond between Jody and his father?
5. (a) What in Jody's nature prevents him from leaving school when it starts to rain? (b) How much blame for the pony's death does Billy Buck take upon himself? (c) Is Jody in part responsible for Gabilan's death? Explain.
6. (a) How does Jody's mother express her sympathy during the pony's illness? (b) How does Carl Tiflin show his sympathy? (c) How

do you think Steinbeck wants you to feel toward Carl Tiflin? Cite evidence to support your answer.

7. (a) Find the first mention of buzzards in the story. **(b)** At this point, what attitude does Jody display toward the birds? **(c)** If Gabilan hadn't died, would Jody ever have attacked a buzzard? How do you know? **(d)** What motivates him to do so? **(e)** Why is he able to kill a bird almost as large as he is?

8. (a) As the story ends, why is Billy Buck so angry at Carl Tiflin? **(b)** What is the meaning of Billy's final exclamation?

9. Characters in good fiction are often described as being "alive." **(a)** What does this statement mean? **(b)** Which character in "The Gift" seemed particularly lifelike to you? **(c)** Find details in the story which make that character seem real.

10. (a) When is the setting of "The Gift" Jody's enemy? **(b)** Is it ever his friend? Explain.

11. Does Jody mature through his experience with the red pony? Explain.

WORD STUDY

What would you do with a sentence such as the following?

Hardy was the only member of the group who was *unspent* by the mountain-climbing expedition.

If you take the word *unspent* apart, you'll find that it means "not spent." But this definition probably won't help you understand the sentence. To find a meaning suitable to the context, you'll have to look up the word *spent* in a dictionary. (Words beginning with common prefixes such as *un-* are often unlisted in dictionaries.) Since the dictionary gives two definitions for *spent*, you have to decide which one is better suited to the context.

In the preceding vocabulary exercises, you learned the three aids a good reader uses to determine the meanings and pronunciations of unfamiliar words. They are:

Context-	The setting in which a word appears; the other words or ideas in the sentence, paragraph or selection.
Structure-	The arrangement of meaning parts (root words and affixes) in a word.
Dictionary-	If the meaning can't be determined by using context or structure clues, consult the dictionary. Use the dictionary when you need help with pronunciation.

Read each sentence below. Then, answer the questions that follow by using context clues, structure clues, and the Glossary.

1. Billy Buck's eyes were a *contemplative*, watery gray, reflecting an intense and thoughtful nature.

What does *contemplative* mean? What context clues helped you determine its meaning? How is it pronounced?

2. Jody *sauntered* down the walk. He had no place to go, and he was in no hurry.

How was Jody walking? How do you know? Give some synonyms for *saunter*.

3. Jody could hear a cow *low* in the background.

Which definition of *low* is suited to this context? Which word in the sentence is the best clue to the definition that should be used? How does a *low* sound?

4. Jody rejoiced at Gabilan's *rambunctiousness*, for he knew that only a mean-souled horse does not resent training.

Rambunctious means: **(a)** wild and disorderly; **(b)** calm and well-behaved; **(c)** careful and cautious.

5. Jody looked *dispiritedly* at the pony's coat.

What is the root word in *dispiritedly*? What does the root word mean? How does the addition of the prefix *di-* alter the meaning of the word? When saying the word, which syllable should you accent? *Continued*

The Gift *continued*

UPI PHOTO

THE AUTHOR

Ranch hands, fruit pickers, grocers, or simple drifters were the kinds of men about whom John Steinbeck (1902–1968) most often wrote. In his early career he was at one time or another a ranch hand, fruit picker, and bricklayer, but his determination to write eventually earned him the Nobel Prize in Literature, the highest honor an author can receive. The Swedish Academy which gave him the prize in 1962 explained that in Steinbeck ". . . we find the American temperament . . . expressed, in his great feeling for nature, for the tilled soil, the wasteland, the mountains, and the ocean coasts. . . ."

California's Salinas valley, where he was born and where he spent much of his life, is the setting of many of his works, including *The Red Pony*, from which "The Gift" is taken. All America forms the background of *Travels with Charley*, the account of his journeys with a discriminating friend, Charley the French poodle.

UNIT **1** *Review*

1. All the main characters in the stories in this unit face a problem. Whose problem seems most difficult to you? Why do you think so? Who learns the most from the way in which he handles his problem? Explain.

2. What characteristics does Herbie ("The Dubbing of General Garbage") share with Lawrence ("Strawberry Ice Cream Soda")? What problem do they have in common? What do Lennie and Eddie add to the boys' problem? Which boy do you think comes up with the better solution? Explain.

3. Both "Thanksgiving Hunter" and "Strawberry Ice Cream Soda" present boys undergoing conflicts. In what way is Lawrence's conflict similar to the Thanksgiving Hunter's? How is Eddie's influence on Lawrence similar to Uncle Wash's influence on the hunter? Which boy displays the greater courage and maturity in settling his conflict?

4. In what ways is Jeanie's relationship with Billy ("Beauty is Truth") like Jo's relationship with Johnny ("The Lesson")? Jo, in her outlook on life, is much happier than Jeanie. Why is this so? If Jo were put in Jeanie's place, would she accept life as Jeanie does? Why or why not?

5. What problem does John Thomas ("The Lesson") share with Jody ("The Gift")? Compare Jo's attitude toward John Thomas with Billy Buck's attitude toward Jody. Defend or criticize the following statement: Both Carl Tiflin and Mr. Hobhouse are hard, practical men who object strongly to their sons' sensitive attitudes toward things.

SUGGESTED READING

ALCOTT, LOUISA MAY, *Little Women*. (World *Penguin) This story of four sisters, as popular today as when it was written over a hundred years ago, is based on the author's youth: Miss Alcott is the fiery and quick-tempered Jo, who longs for the freedom of a boy's life.

ANNIXTER, PAUL, *Swiftwater*. (Hill & Wang) A boy is called upon to do a man's job in an exciting story set in the north woods of Maine.

BELL, MARGARET ELIZABETH, *The Totem Casts a Shadow*. (Morrow) A wilderness home in Alaska is the setting for a moving story of a young girl's struggle to be brave.

CAVANNA, BETTY, *Going on Sixteen*. (Westminster) Though she initially feels that dogs are better companions than people, Judy gradually learns that friendship with high-school boys and girls may offer rich rewards.

CLEMENS, SAMUEL L., *Adventures of Tom Sawyer*. (Harper *Washington Square) Rich humor, high suspense, and shrewd observation of character make this one of the greatest boys' books ever written. Characters range from the beautiful Becky Thatcher to the notorious Injun Joe. And always there is Tom.

FELSEN, HENRY GREGOR, *Street Rod*. (Random) Crazy about hot rods, headstrong Ricky Madison is ready for trouble — and trouble is ready for Ricky.

GIPSON, FRED, *Old Yeller*. (*Harper) A young boy and an old yellow dog are the main characters in a powerful novel of life on the Texas frontier.

KJELGAARD, JIM, *Double Challenge*. (Dodd) Two very different ambitions cause a conflict in the life of a boy from the Pennsylvania mountains.

MONTGOMERY, L.M., *Anne of Green Gables*. (**Grosset) Anne, the orphan girl who brings happiness and love to her foster parents, is one of the best-loved heroines of juvenile literature.

NEVILLE, EMILY, *It's Like This, Cat*. (Harper) The many problems facing every teen-age boy are captured in this realistic novel of modern city life.

SAROYAN, WILLIAM, *The Human Comedy*. (Harcourt) The author says much about the forces of love and hate in this touching story of a California family.

SAROYAN, WILLIAM, *My Name is Aram*. (Harcourt) Saroyan relates his boyhood adventures in a very funny book that appeals to both boys and girls.

SCHAEFER, JACK, *Shane*. (Houghton) When Shane, a drifter, joins the Starrett household, he makes an impact on Starrett's fourteen-year-old son by helping the Starretts in their fight against the man who is trying to force them off their land.

SPEARE, ELIZABETH GEORGE, *The Witch of Blackbird Pond*. (Houghton) In colonial Connecticut, a young girl is forced to fight against prejudice and bigotry because she chooses to be friendly with a woman who has been labeled a witch.

STREET, JAMES, *Goodbye, My Lady*. (Lippincott) Mississippi swamp country forms the background for a heartwarming story about a boy and an unusual dog.

STUART, JESSE, *Hie to the Hunters*. (McGraw) Didway Hargis, a city boy, runs away from home to the hill country of Kentucky. There he lives a strange, exciting life with a large family in a one-room cabin.

WEST, JESSAMYN, *Cress Delahanty*. (Harcourt *Washington Square) Cress has problems — the sort of problems that beset every teen-age girl. How she solves them and how she grows in understanding make a warmly human, amusing novel.

WOUK, HERMAN, *The City Boy*. (Doubleday *Dell) You'll find the rest of Herbie's adventures as funny as those recounted in "The Dubbing of General Garbage."

*paperback
**paperback and hardcover

UNIT 2

Heroes are often set above and apart in history and legend

by their bravery and boldness,

by their skill and intelligence,

by their worthiness and will.

But do those we call heroes always act

totally without fear?

deliberately and without hesitation?

with a worthy goal in mind?

How different from the rest of us are those we call heroes?

Why do we admire them?

What qualities do the persons in these stories

and poems have that qualify them for . . .

A GALLERY OF HEROES?

What qualities separate heroism from reckless foolishness?
What causes a person to do something that common sense,
feelings of fear, and even friends warn him not to do?

SWINGER

PAUL DARCY BOLES

INTO THE NIGHT, green as an olive, green as mint, they drove. They'd all graduated from high school the week before; summer lay ahead with giant promise. The cool wind promised enormous surprises. The stars seen through flying foliage promised even more, and winked about it.

They were four—one driving, the others watching the stars and the night as it flowed by: Hal was driving, Jim and Carla and Cricket were observing. The dashboard clock in the convertible, still new enough so that the clock worked, pointed to fourteen past eleven.

There wasn't much traffic along the bluff road; sometimes a truck ambled along and pulled sharp right to let their car zoom by on the gravel; sometimes there was a staid, dusty-looking car like a plodding turtle. But for the most part, there was only the road curling around the bluffs and sweeping them with it in a hint of surprises ahead.

"Look." Carla gripped Jim's arm. "Raccoon. See its eyes?" Carla was blond. She and Jim had gone together since junior year.

"That was quartz," Jim said. He was tall, loose-hung, fair-haired, sardonic. And an excellent athlete. "Quartz in the rocks."

"What's quartz doing sitting up in the bushes and wrinkling its nose then?"

"It was a badger," said Cricket. She sat in the front beside Hal. It was Hal's car; he'd worked nights in a

laundry for two years to get the money for it. It was just a convertible, nothing special, but it was pleasant and he took good care of it and drove well, slowing before the curves, coming out of them in full control with a sizzling of gravel under the tires but no spooky action. "Raccoons have masks, black masks. They're not as muscular as that thing was."

"Cricket, the natural history expert," Jim said. "Hal, what was it?"

"I didn't see it," Hal said. "I'm driving, hadn't you noticed?"

"I thought somebody was," Jim said, and they all laughed a little. So Jim improved on it. He did that sometimes; he could be a little mean when he had an edge. Not nasty mean, only laboring a point because it gave him more edge. "I figured we were *moving*," Jim went on, leaning forward and wetting a finger and holding it up to feel the airslip. "Not very fast, but, you know, moving along. You have a governor[1] put on this hack when you bought it?"

"Sure," Hal said. "I figured to use it for a taxi later this summer. Taxicabs require governors in this county."

"Yeah," Jim said. "That explains it." Carla, her blond hair lifting slightly in the slipstream of air over the back seat, was smiling with some appreciation. Jim said, "Forty," squinting forward over the front seat at the speedometer. "That's about the top, huh?"

"Forty-one, in a tail wind," Hal said easily.

Cricket said nothing, and Hal wished she would say something. He wished she would say something about his driving, how he wasn't silly or childish enough to take big risks. To drive much faster than forty on this road, with its curves and its unbanked gravel loose on the curves, you would have to be out of your head. Jim knew

it and Carla knew it and Cricket knew it, but nobody mentioned it. Hal wished Cricket would say something soothing and right. He hadn't gone with her long, but he felt he knew her to some extent, knew what her real reactions were, knew what she'd say in a thunderstorm, how she felt about the world and the people in it.

He glanced at Cricket out of the corner of his eye; she was looking ahead, but she wasn't smiling. She was small, dark, poised, with very large black eyes. He liked the way her short hair lifted a trifle in the wind. He liked her tanned arms against the dark green blouse. She looked over at him as he glanced that way, and she didn't wink, didn't even smile, but there was something there: an understanding. Jim settled back again and began singing the theme song from the movie they'd seen over in West Fentriss. It had been one of those big movies, very epic, with a lot of sand and camels and shooting in it. Jim couldn't do real justice to the twenty-five trumpets and sixteen trombones of the sound track, but you got the idea.

Carla said, over Jim's voice, "Sand, sand, *sand!* I was never so thirsty in my life."

"You drank four oranges," Jim said.

"I had to. I would've withered otherwise. I still feel as though there's sand all over me."

"When we get to the quarry, you'll feel better," Cricket said. "That's the coolest place in the world. Absolutely the coolest."

"It's the way the wind funnels up," Hal said. "Makes a thermal[2] right there near the top."

---

1. *governor,* automatic device which controls or limits the speed of an engine.
2. *thermal,* rising current of warm air.

Jim was sitting forward again. "I wish we'd brought some suits. We could swim."

"Come *on*," Carla said. "You couldn't swim in there. Too many rocks."

"Not so sure," Jim said. "I think I could. You can see where most of the rocks are, the water's so clear from up-top. Anyhow—" He leaned farther and tapped Hal gently on the right shoulder. "Anyhow, we can swing across on the vine, huh, old buddy?"

Hal took his time about answering. Jim said again, "We can swing over and back, right?" This time Hal said, trying to make it light and simple, "Oh, I dunno. I may, and then again I may not."

He could hear the satisfaction, the edge, coming back in Jim's voice. He didn't have to look at Jim. Jim said, "Well, well. I thought you got over the fear of heights two years ago."

"That hasn't got anything to do with it," Hal said, but this time, try as he might, he didn't say it with much lightness. He tried again. "Maybe I will," he said. "Maybe I'll swing over. I just don't know yet. Okay?"

"Okay," Jim murmured, but dubiously. *Show me*, his tone said. Then, for a little while, there was no sound but the gravel under the tires and the smooth purring voice of the engine. Hal reached and flipped on the radio. While the music was going Hal looked very quickly at Cricket and then away. This time she wasn't looking at him.

She couldn't know about the way he had felt a couple of years ago on a summer afternoon when he and Jim and a couple of other guys had been at the quarry. She couldn't be expected to know. He remembered, though. While the music went lilting along, he thought of that hot, dry, mid-August day, and the great, green shape of the quarry, silent at midday, still and

waiting in the depths of the green water. On the other side, across from this bluff-peak, the few houses of the people who lived year-round above the quarry seemed small and remote. Jim and the other guys were saying to him urgently, "You've got to try it now. Just take hold of the vine hard, get a good grip, and hook around it with your legs. Get back and then swing out! It'll carry you all the way across. You can stand on the other side for a second! It'll swing you back, too. Look how high it is! Look how tough it is!"

Now, staring straight ahead, taking another curve gently, he could still feel the sun on his eyes as he stared up at the giant vine which hung from the trees arching the bluff. It was a very old vine, almost tortoise-old. It was twisted into many, many strands; it was a cable of strength and it looked capable of supporting a lot of weight. But there was something else about the situation, something threatening, waiting. Dry-mouthed, staring up to where the top of the vine vanished among polished, deep-green leaves, he couldn't explain to Jim and the others what he felt; he couldn't explain it even now. He couldn't explain that when, one by one, they had gripped the vine and clung to it with their knees and the insides of their ankles and let the vine swing them out as though they were on a pendulum across the dark waiting water, he'd had to shut his eyes; each time a wave of sickness had come over him and crammed up in his throat. It wasn't until the swinger on the vine had come all the way back and stood safe and solid on the bluff-top that he'd been able to smile at all.

He supposed he was afflicted with vertigo, or whatever you were supposed to call it, pretty badly. He'd had the same feeling a couple of times before that day on the bluff. Once, with

his parents and his aunt and uncle, he'd visited the top of a tall building. The guide had asked everyone to come near the edge and look out. He had been the only one to stay back, gritting his teeth.

Another time had been when he was about thirteen. A bunch of other kids had climbed the water tower in the suburb where he lived. He'd barely made it. Sometimes, when he let his mind go back to it, he could still remember the painful process of inching down, of making his fingers come free, one by one, from the rungs of the ladder, of finally standing on the beautiful ground below and thinking with wonder, "I was up there. I never want to climb up there again."

He wasn't afraid to fly. It wasn't that at all. It was something else which he'd forgotten until this moment, or, if he hadn't forgotten, had managed to stuff away in the corners of his memory. And now the thing was very close, looming ahead of him. He wondered, for a second, why he was driving toward the quarry right now. Was it because everybody wanted to?

But it wouldn't have been bad if Jim hadn't brought up the vine. He should have known Jim wouldn't forget.

Cricket said, over the music, "There's the road." Hal slowed and turned. The quarry road led straight into rich, thick oaks and gumwood and pine. When he slowed the car, there was a sudden feeling of quiet. Leaves, hanging low, brushed lightly over the windshield, and Jim reached up. He grabbed a handful, stripped them off and let them tumble behind like confetti. Hal drove slowly over the ruts; even above the radio you could hear the night birds singing as the car cut into the silence of leaves. Then they were at the foot of the bluff and the path was just visible in the headlights.

It wound around like a mountain road; it took quite a bit of climbing to get to the top. Hal wondered if by the time they got there, Jim would have forgotten about the vine. Or maybe the vine had disintegrated over the years. . . .

Hal cut the ignition, and as everybody got out, Jim stretched and hoisted his belt up a trifle. Standing arrow-straight, in his white shirt and white pants in the moonlight, he said, "I bet that vine's still there."

"Could be," Hal said.

Carla, trying to smooth her hair down, said, "What's this about a vine you keep gabbing about? Ouch I've got a snarl."

"Here," Cricket said, "I'll comb it out for you." She stood beside the slightly taller Carla, tugging a comb through the long light hair. Head bent, Carla said, "Do we have to shinny up some stupid vine after we've climbed this terrible thing here?"

Hal said, and it sounded loud in the moonlight, "We don't *have* to. It's—it's sort of optional."

"You don't shinny up the vine," Jim said. He was looking at Hal. "You just take hold of it. Right, Hal?"

"That's right," Hal said. He wasn't very loud. "I've done it."

"Co-rrect," Jim said. He stretched again, amiably. "I'll go first, this trip. Women and children don't have to."

Cricket tossed the comb back in the car. "When did all this happen?" she asked. "When did you and Hal last go on this wonderful trip?"

"Few years ago," Jim said. "Really no danger, kids. No sweat. You just let the vine do the work. You can touch toes to the other side. Puts you right in front of one of those houses over there. Then you swing back." He went on, ruminatively, starting toward the path, "Remember, Hal? We had to call you chicken before you'd go. Took a lot of hollering."

"I remember," Hal said.

"Then, when you got there, it was easy, wasn't it?"

Jim moved on, and part of his shirt was swallowed up and shadowed by boughs. Carla had stepped in behind him. Cricket moved in front of Hal as he waited. Jim was now a short way up the path, long-striding, sure. "Nothing to it, was there?" came Jim's voice.

Oh, yes, there was, there was a lot to it, Hal thought. He, too, was a little way up the path now. The heat of the day was still held in the leaves and the grass. He could see bits and glints of Cricket's blouse ahead; a slice of moonlight played on her dark hair like satin. There was a smell of crushed mint, of pink long-stemmed clover, of magic in the dark. There was something else, not magic at all, in the dark on the other side of the bluff above the quarry. They were moving up toward it. He wished Cricket would turn around and look at him, but she didn't.

After they had come out in the blaze of clear moonlight on top of the bluff and were standing around getting their wind back, it didn't, for a few seconds, seem so bad. The vine was still there. It hung heavy and dark from the trees which rose seventy and eighty feet above it. It was too heavy to swing in the cool wind. The draft came streaming up from the base of this side of the bluff, from the cold green water. Across the quarry, above the sheer rock bluff on the other side, the houses had warm yellow lights. No, Hal told himself, it doesn't seem so bad. It really doesn't.

"It is, it *is*," Carla said, looking like a Valkyrie[3] as she faced the quarry. "It's the coolest place on earth. Somebody ought to build a house on this side."

"Be a little hard to get up to," Hal said. "On the other side, the road's level with the properties."

Cricket wasn't saying much. Sometimes, in a sideward look, Hal caught her watching him. He grinned a trifle, but there wasn't any real answer. Her voice was light and casual as she knelt at the bluff-lip. "Some violets. I thought it was too late for them," she said. "They're tucked under here in a little pocket." Reaching down, staying well back from the edge, she picked a few violets and held them carefully.

As she got up, brushing off her knees, Hal said, flatly, "I'm not going to swing over."

"No?" Jim said.

"Nope," Hal said. As he said it, one part of him felt miserable, but the other part felt quiet and firm and complete. "Nope. Not tonight or any other time. I'm chicken."

"I didn't say it," Jim said softly. "I don't believe I said a thing about that."

"Okay," Hal said. "Let's leave it there, shall we?"

"Fine with me," Jim said as softly as he'd said it before. "Anybody else care to try it after I do?"

"Don't be utterly idiotic," Carla said.

Cricket shook her head.

Jim was moving toward the vine. He took hold of it, tugged on it a little, then gripped it with his full weight, drawing his feet up. The vine made no sound, but the trees above gave a creak. A few leaves, left over from last fall, came fluttering down slowly, aimless as lost boats on a river of moonlight. One fell at Cricket's feet. Eyes bright and rather wide, Carla watched Jim as he swung in a small circle above the ground, hunched over close to the vine.

---

3. *Valkyrie*, goddess in Scandinavian mythology.

Out in the quarry frogs were croaking. It was a noise you noticed very much at first, then the din became part of the air and turned into a kind of singing that went along with everything else. You could hear anything above that hum, even your own breath.

"The thing is," Jim was saying as he swung lightly, his shadow clumped beneath him, "it's so simple. Shooting fish in a barrel. Slow fish."

You could even hear your own heart above the noise of the frogs.

"Listen," Hal said. He spoke plainly and without special expression in his voice. "Listen, it's two years since we — since you did this trick. The branch, or the branches up there that hold that crazy vine — those babies could rot in two years."

"Sure they could," Jim said. His words came now louder, now softer, as he swung in the gentle circle. The vine hung straight, only its strands seeming to turn, the bulk of it like a dark, frazzled ship's hawser. "But if they'd done that, wouldn't they have busted by now?" He thrust down a toe suddenly, pushed with it, and shinnied farther up. There was no protest from above and, this time, no more leaves floating down.

Cricket had been looking at the ground near Jim's slightly turning shadow. She looked up. "It's your life," she said. "But I think it's up to us to try to talk you into keeping it a little longer. You know, since we're here, it makes us sort of responsible."

Carla nodded. "That's right. Enough of this Tarzan jazz. Everybody out of the pool!"

Jim laughed. It wasn't loud. "Look." His words kept coming louder or softer, depending on where you were standing, as the vine turned. "I don't happen to be chicken. All right? Somebody here has to hold up his head. This is something I want to do . . ." His voice trailed off, and he only swung there.

Cricket had taken a step toward him. "Why? What do you want to prove?"

He didn't answer that, and Carla said, "Seriously, now. Seriously, Jim!"

As his face came turning around toward Hal in the bright light, Jim said, "I'm serious enough. Thanks for your mutual warnings. It's fun, that's all. Look out." Still gripping the vine with his hands, he let his feet drop and was swiftly, very swiftly, running back toward the path behind them. Shadows swallowed him for an instant, then Hal could see Jim's legs rise as, at the apex of the back swing, he gripped the vine tight. Carla moved forward, Hal with her, but the forward swing was already coming, and there was a rush of air as Jim went by them.

Carla started to make a noise, then made no noise at all. Nobody did. Out, out over the quarry went Jim. This time Hal didn't shut his eyes. He realized he wasn't able to shut them as he had two years ago. Jim was growing smaller, tinier, toward the opposite lip of the quarry. He would be very near that center house now, with its warm lights shining.

Above, the boughs which supported the vine were creaking like ancient stairs. More leaves were dislodged, spraying through the white light, new summer-green leaves among them. Several fell in Carla's hair, in Cricket's, in Hal's. Nobody brushed them off. The green, smooth quiet water of the quarry held Jim's stark shadow and that of the stretching vine over its full length. Then Jim had touched on the other side and was coming back.

Coming back, Hal thought, was better. It wasn't much of an improvement but you knew you'd make it, because this was where the vine started

from. He felt his muscles relax. The whole thing had taken just a few seconds. He was still feeling tense and angry, though. He couldn't quite place the punishment. On top of the anger was the wish to have Jim here, back on the land, brought safely home.

The rushing shadow over the water grew. The vine came whipping back, and more leaves spun off. Then Jim, with a great, happy sigh, was dropping from the vine into the brushy shadows. He came out dusting his hands.

"Boy! There's nothing like it. Nothing." Face mildly flushed, breath coming a little short, he stood there, alive, triumphant. "Sure you won't try it, old buddy?"

"No," Hal said. He was looking directly at Jim. He couldn't help it. Jim didn't say "Chicken" or anything like it. He didn't have to. He only kept on looking and after a few seconds, he nodded. Everything about him—face, eyes, the way he stood—said, "Now the men are separated from the boys. You know it. I know it. That's exactly the way it is."

Carla had a hand on Jim's arm. "Let's get away from this grotty place, shall we, all of us?"

Still looking at Jim as Jim turned away, Hal saw that there was a glow around Jim and that there might always be. A glow of some kind of daring, maybe heroism, maybe just rank foolishness. It was directed toward *him;* it was something no amount of common sense could cover. You could use words like "maturity" for people like Hal, and "recklessness" for people like Jim, but that wasn't accurate either. He felt his anger rise higher against everything Jim had stood for as he swung out over the water. The anger was also against himself, burning and hot.

Cricket still wasn't talking. She'd already turned to be the first one back down the path. It was then that the scream came. It was a knifing, very young, terrified scream. It sounded above the croaking of the frogs with urgent appeal and need. Cricket, on the path, jerked around. Carla stopped and spun, her mouth open. Jim said, "It's one of those houses—" And again the noise came, a child's cry. For one second with the cool breath of the water and the air rising from the water around him, Hal waited.

Then he was running back toward the vine. It had stopped spinning, stopped trembling. It hung there, still and waiting. When he took hold of it and started a run back before hoisting himself up, its texture, grainy and rough to the palms, felt exactly as it had two years ago on a hot afternoon. But he didn't think about that now. There wasn't time. As he ran back with it, lifted his feet and started the swing out, he felt nothing: no fear, no danger. Only that he had to make it. The child's voice— from the center house, he figured—sounded again when he was halfway over the quarry, and he grunted to himself, without quite saying it, "Hold on. I'll be right there."

Dropping from the vine to the lawn on the other side, he nearly fell backward and down the bluff. But there wasn't time to notice that, either. He was spurting toward the pale amber light of the center house. The screaming had stopped, but as he approached the front door, there was a sobbing from inside. He took hold of the knob, turned it, found himself in a small front parlor. A girl of about five, eyes aghast and staring, stood in the center of the room holding her chubby right hand in her left. The right hand was bleeding. Hal could see where she had

climbed to the fireplace mantel, and realized what had happened; she'd fallen off, after placing all those footstools and chairs so she could get up there, and, in falling, she'd knocked over a lamp. The lamp was in pieces.

He knelt beside her. She was very grubby, very frail; she made him think for some stupid reason of a young bird caught in a hailstorm. He took her hand and, looking at the gash—not so deep as the blood made it seem—managed with his free hand to snake a handkerchief out of his pocket.

"All right," he said. "It's not so bad. Didn't cut an artery. We'll wind this thing around it, okay? Wind it tight until we can get some antiseptic in that or maybe take a couple of stitches."

She was still frightened, but she was only snuffling, running down like an out-of-gas engine. She watched with more and more trust as he made the rough-and-ready bandage and knotted it. By that time, a woman had come in, racing and out of breath. He told her what had happened. She was a dark, large woman with deerlike eyes; she too knelt beside the girl and stroked the child's hair, murmuring. "I'm Mrs. Marsden. I just went out for a few minutes, down to the end house. . . . There, there, honey, we'll pop you in the car and go see the doctor, shall we?" It wasn't until she and her daughter were in the car, out under the fine moon again, that she suddenly said, with wonder, "But where did you *come* from? How? Did you come from the road?"

Hal said, "I took a shortcut." It was no use explaining right now; he could see Carla and Jim and Cricket coming around the flank of the house, from the road. They'd gone all the way down the bluff-path on the other side and come up again. He was sorry they'd had such a long hike. They couldn't have driven because he had the car keys in his pocket.

The three came running. He introduced them quickly to Mrs. Marsden; she wanted to get the little girl, Mary, to the doctor. When she had gone off with Mary in their car everything was very quiet again—except, of course, for the frogs.

Hal breathed out in a sigh. He looked at Cricket. Then he looked at Carla. Then at Jim.

He said, "You could've come over the same way I did."

Jim was shaking his head. His face was just a trifle pale, which was strange, because he'd had a good run all the way around the quarry, and he wasn't the kind to pale at just anything. Yet you could see a few freckles standing out. Jim said, "Take a look, old buddy."

Hal turned around to where Jim was pointing back across the quarry.

At first he couldn't see much because of the moon on the water, but then his eyes got accustomed to it and he saw, in the light on the bluff-top on the other side, a couple of big branches in a tangle—and something that looked like a grayish, very dried-up snake looping around the boughs.

"Snapped," Jim said. "Couple of the branches. They just fell after the vine swung back into place." Jim wasn't exactly stammering, but Hal would have hated to see him try a professional debate at the moment.

"Well," Hal said. "That's very interesting. That's a very interesting development." He marveled for a second, then he turned to Cricket and really smiled. And she answered, with all her good smile and her understanding look, every bit of it. He took her arm and said, "Let's get back to my car, shall we, before owls roost in it or something?" And they all headed out toward the road which

would take them back to the foot of the bluff.

When they got back, no owl had roosted in the convertible, and not even a raccoon or a piece of quartz or a badger had picked it for a hideout, so they just drove home. Hal drove very well, at no special speed; the difference was that now he felt fine, with no split forces inside him, with no anger at himself at all—or, for that matter, at Jim.

Into the night, green as an olive, green as mint, green as a go-light ahead, they drove.

✦　✦　✦　✦

THE AUTHOR

Paul Darcy Boles has said that a short story is a swift and living bridge from writer to reader, a passage that carries the reader to a new, and enlightening vision of the world. Over the years he has published a great many of his stories in many major magazines.

A former vice-president of an advertising agency in Atlanta, Boles has extended his talents to the art of the novel, and, most recently, has undertaken the writing and direction of a documentary movie. But his major interest lies in literature and the written word which he feels is still a more powerful and persuasive medium of communication than any other, and likely to remain so.

Speaking: The Hero

FELIX POLLAK

I did not want to go.
They inducted me.

I did not want to die.
They called me yellow.

I tried to run away.   5
They court-martialed me.

I did not shoot.
They said I had no guts.

They ordered the attack.
A shrapnel tore my guts.   10

I cried in pain.
They carried me to safety.

In safety I died.
They blew taps over me.

They crossed out my name
and buried me under a cross.   15

They made a speech in my hometown
I was unable to call them liars.

OFFICIAL COAST GUARD PHOTO

"Speaking: The Hero" by Felix Pollak.
Reprinted by permission.

They said I gave my life.
I had struggled to keep it. 20

They said I set an example.
I had tried to run.

They said they were proud of me.
I had been ashamed of them.

They said my mother should also be proud. 25
My mother cried.

I wanted to live.
They called me a coward.

I died a coward.
They call me a hero. 30

DISCUSSION

1. (a) What is the difference between what "the hero" says he did, and what the people ("they") say he did? (b) Is either party in the right? Why?
2. (a) Point out three instances of irony in this poem, and explain why they are ironic. (b) Which do you find the most significant irony? Explain your point of view briefly.
3. Discuss the poem in terms of this statement: "There is no such thing as a fearless hero."

THE AUTHOR

Felix Pollak was born in Vienna, Austria, in 1909, became a lawyer there, studied stage directing, and only then decided on a life in America. After service in World War II in the U.S. Army, he became curator of rare books and the Sukov Collection of Little Magazines at the University of Wisconsin library.

Pollak's poetry appears most often in small, literary magazines like the ones under his charge as librarian, magazines in which many famous poets have made their start. This particular poem, "Speaking: The Hero," can also be found in a book called *Where is Vietnam?*, a collection that grew out of the American experience in Southeast Asia in the 1960's.

What is the similarity between a small boy's sympathy for an
animal and the type of heroism the world admires and rewards?
To understand you will have to see the world
through this boy's eyes.

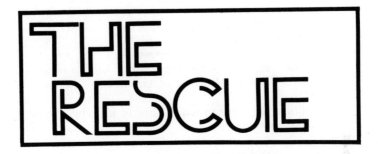

THE RESCUE

MAX STEELE

HE WAS IDLING down Piedmont Street, stepping on every line in the sidewalk. If he missed one, didn't step on it, he'd die before he got to the corner.

At the corner he was still alive, and so he paused for a moment, stuck his big toe in the soft tar that filled the crack between the asphalt street and the concrete curb, then ran across.

"I'll count every line on this block." It was just lately he'd started talking to himself, like Crazy Mattie, the vegetable woman who stopped in the middle of the street sometimes to talk to herself, and to dead people, and to God. "I'm not crazy. I just haven't got anybody to talk to . . . four, five, six . . ." One day, about a week after the Fourth of July, he'd counted sixty-three lines, and that was a lot for a boy who just weighed forty-eight

pounds. He could have counted more, but old Miss Hallie Thompson who was as deaf as a giraffe had hollered from her porch, "How's your grandmother? How's your grandmother? How's your grandmother?" He couldn't tell whether she heard his answer or not. She just nodded and went back to reading her newspaper. It looked like an ordinary newspaper to him, but everybody said she read Lips.

He lost count again this afternoon, thinking about Miss Hallie reading Lips. He took out of his pocket the black carbon stick from a flashlight battery and drew a long thin lip on the sidewalk. Then he turned sideways

and drew another, smaller, fatter lip in the other direction. It looked like a T but not very much like one. Then he spelled out, in regular letters, his name — Ted — the way Miss Clark, his first-grade teacher, who had a one-legged canary at home, had taught him.

He stood up and hopped on one leg to the top of the hill on Piedmont Street. He jumped up on a wall under an oak tree and sat down to cool between two roots that made a regular little nest. When he had caught his breath he jumped up and began clucking like a hen: "Oh, cluck cluck cluck, look what *I* did. Cluck cluck cluck . . ." He couldn't cluck like Red Andrews, but he could crow better. He let out a healthy crow for the city rooster, then cupped his hands over his mouth and crowed again for the country rooster who was answering from way off.

Down at the bottom of the hill, across from the lumber yard where he was headed to play in the sawdust pile, and next to the filling station where Jake, the Purple-Heart[1] man, worked, a trailer was parked. It hadn't been there yesterday, and now all of a sudden here it was. Just like that. Ted ran down the street and coasted, with a screeching of brakes, to a stop across the street from the trailer.

Three men were out in front, two of them seated on boxes, watching the third one placing bottles on shelves at the end of the trailer. A faded sign above the trailer door said in red letters: "DR. BROWN'S BIGWORD BIGWORD TONIC!"

Warily Ted crossed over, pretending he was going to the filling station. But then when the men didn't notice him, he edged up closer to the group (one of them was Jake) and looked at the bottles. There were flat ones filled with red-brown stuff, and then there were big fruit jars with look-like strips of dough swimming in them.

"What's those things?" His shyness was no match for his curiosity.

"Worms," Jake said. "Out of little boys like you."

Ted looked quickly away so that he wouldn't have a bad dream about them tonight and be fussed at in the morning.

"And this is Worm Medicine," the man with the bottle said. "Dr. Brown's Invigorating Resuscitating Tonic. Finest of its kind."

"Do they like it?" He was fascinated by the idea and planned immediately to watch the worms take the medicine even if it gave him bad dreams.

"Certainly. Sold three bottles to the mayor yesterday."

Ted looked back at the bottles. The big one in the bottle by itself must be the mayor. "What's his name?"

The two seated men laughed. The other, the red-faced ugly man, put the last bottle on the shelf. "Do you think I'm lying to you?" He glared at Ted. "You think I remember the names of all my customers? From the looks of those skinny legs I'd say you need some of this tonic. Tell your mother and father."

"Look behind you, boy!" Jake hollered.

Ted jumped around. There was no lion behind him, only a box covered with a screen.

"Nothing but a box," he said.

"Yeah, but look in the box."

He hesitated, then cautiously approached. He looked down into the box. The late-afternoon light coming through the screened top and one screened side was dim, so he dropped down on his knees to see in. There,

---

1. *Purple-Heart,* United States military medal for wounds received as a result of enemy action.

near a saucer of water, in the one crack of sunlight, a toad sat blinking.

"What d'ya see?"

"A little ole frog."

"What else?" Jake asked.

"Nothing. A saucer and water."

Jake walked over to the box and squinted. He took the boy's head firmly in his big fingertips and turned it toward the opposite corner. "Over there."

"Oh," the boy whispered when he saw the snake. Without moving he was in a deep forest, and there were no men around, no trailer, and no screen between himself and the snake that was looking right at him.

"Two-foot rattler with three rattles," the medicine man said, but his voice did not reach into the deep forest where the child knelt motionless staring at the snake. Sometimes the snake faded into the trees, and the boy would have to squint his eyes to bring it back into view. The sandy swish of car tires passing on the street filtered through the trees and became running water in the forest stream. The snake would brighten until every dark band on his back glowed, then slowly fade again into the darkness. The voices of the men talking were not loud enough to come through the murmuring of the wind in the trees, and the boy would have stayed in the forest forever if the toad had not jumped against the screen.

Ted looked up at the men who were no longer watching him. "Do they like each other?" He didn't see how anybody could like the snake.

"Just like you like ice cream," Jake answered.

"He's going to eat him?" There was an anxious note in the boy's high thin voice.

"Certainly," the medicine man said. "That's what I put him in there for."

The toad jumped again.

"He wants out."

The men went on talking to each other, and no one answered. The boy looked at the box, hoping there was some little hole or little secret door the frog could hop through when the snake wasn't looking. The only way out was through the top, at one corner where the screen had not been tacked down but was merely fastened over the edge with a bent nail.

The toad sat next to the screen now, blinking, his soft underside, chin and stomach heaving in and out like the vacuum cleaner when it's cut on and off real fast.

"Froggy. Froggy." Ted's voice was so high it was almost a whisper. "You're afraid, aren't you, froggy?"

The toad didn't answer, not so you could hear; but the boy could see by its expression, the way its mouth turned down like a pipe smoker's, the way it wouldn't look at the snake, the way it was panting—in all these ways the boy could see that it was scared.

"Let's get him out!" He had to say it three times before the men quit talking. "Let's get the frog out!"

"How?" the medicine man asked.

"He's afraid. Get him out!"

"How?" the man asked in a flat tone.

"*You* get him out!"

"Not me. Not with that snake in there. *You* get him out!"

The two men laughed, and Jake smiled.

"Can I have him if I get him out?"

"Sure. Sure." The medicine man winked at Jake. "Tell you what. I'll get the frog out for you if you'll help me."

"All right." the boy said, excitement rising in his voice. He stood up and walked toward the medicine man.

"All you have to do is hold the snake back while I get the frog."

"Noooo." Ted stopped. He hadn't

noticed before that the sun was gone and only the sunset glow remained in the sky.

"Why not?"

"'Cause. I got to go home." He started toward the street. "I'll be back tomorrow."

He ran up the hill, turning his head every few seconds to watch his dim shadow slanting across the street and racing with him against darkness. Already the sidewalk was losing its heat, and he ran faster. "Lickety-split. Lickety-split all the way home."

He stopped in the side yard, pushed back the tiger lilies (that didn't look like tigers after all of his waiting for them to bloom) and washed his hands at the garden spigot. He dried them on his pants as he slipped across the side porch and into the lighted dining room where his grandmother, aunts, and uncles were already seated at the table.

After supper, after his bath, alone upstairs in bed, he had a thousand ways of going to sleep. Usually he thought about something sad, like the thing he had learned this summer: that everyone in the house, all his aunts and uncles, were more kin to his grandmother than he was; that they were all more kin to each other than they were to him. Or he thought about Jake with a belly full of lead waiting for them to come along with a stretcher, and a red cross, and a Purple Heart. When he thought of things like that he wanted to go to sleep and would not fight the growing heaviness in his eyelids. Tonight he thought about the frog that was kin to nobody in the world.

It was sitting behind the saucer with one eye open watching the snake. It wanted to close both eyes and go to sleep but was afraid to. He held his head behind the pillow and peeped with one eye at the gray square light

of window. He let both eyes shut and saw the snake crawling up the stairs. It made a dry, scraping noise as it crawled. The noise was the pecan tree brushing against the window screen, but it was also the snake crawling.

He opened his eyes now and blinked. He drew his knees up against his chest and waited. He was breathing slow and deep like the vacuum cleaner as the snake crawled down the hall and into the room. He raised his head from behind the pillow. The pecan tree was no longer scraping; only the sound of the snake filled the room with its rattling and hissing that was not close or far but all around him. The snake was crawling around under the bed looking for him. Then he heard — his body tense for there was no mistake — the snake wrapping itself around the leg of the bed. Through the dark, through the pillow and mattress he could see its head sliding up the post.

If he screamed for help the snake would strike. He slid down in his bed farther and farther, pulling the sheet up over him as he moved. He stopped to listen. Once more he pushed his foot down to move farther away when it struck the cold, round body of the snake.

"Granny! Granny! Granny!" He screamed it again and again, not hearing the footsteps on the stairs and in the hall. When he opened his eyes, the light was on and his grandmother was pulling the sheet from over him. The iron bedrail was still there. The snake was gone.

"You play too hard, and you get too tired. That's why you have all these bad dreams. Today you're to get all your playing done before noon, and after lunch you're not to go out of this yard."

They were on the north side of the

house. His grandmother was cutting tiger lilies for the dining-room table, and Ted was between the row of lilies and the house, where thick moss grew in the dampness from the leaking water spigot.

With the handle of a tablespoon he was cutting the moss in squares, prying it up and patting it into place on the mud frog-house he had dug and molded on the bank of the drain. As he washed the mud from his hands, he noticed that the water made a river right past the door of the frog-house. The frog would like that.

"Can I have a frog?" He was drying his hands on the seat of his pants.

His grandmother was looking for a lily without too many buds.

"Frogs don't chase chickens. And they don't bark at the garbage man."

"I suppose so. Where're you going to get one?"

"The medicine man," he hollered back as he ran down the drive, his arms churning back and forth like the piston shaft of a train wheel. "The medicine man, medicine-man, medicineman, mediceman, messman, messman, yesmam, yessum, yessm, essm." He blew the whistle, and the train was full steam ahead. "Essm, essm." As he turned up Piedmont Street, the train stopped, to give him time to get his breath and to move the patients to the ambulance. "Arrrunh, arrrrruuunh." On two wheels he turned into Jake's filling station just in time to save the patients, a young couple, from bleeding to death.

"How much?" Jake asked.

"Filler up," Ted answered, pulling up the emergency brakes with a grinding of gears.

"You already owe me two thousand dollars."

"Pay you tomorrow!"

He backed out of the filling station in small, quick steps, circled once and stopped in front of the trailer. The medicine man was sitting on the edge of the unmade bunk, his head between his hands, a whiskey bottle between his feet.

"Good morning," the boy said quietly. The man did not hear so he said in an even softer voice, "I've come after the frog." That done, he went over and lifted the flour sack that was spread over the box.

Sunlight made the cage look larger inside, and the snake smaller. During the night the snake had moved over to the corner behind the saucer of water, away from the opening in the top. The frog was gone.

"He's jumped out." But then Ted saw that the screen was still fastened with the sharp end of the nail that had been driven from the inside of the box. He dropped to his knees and shaded his eyes from the sun glare. In the little triangle between the snake and the corner of the box, the frog was sitting, still blinking, still breathing, in and out, in and out. "Uh, oh!" Ted spoke with his mouth still open in amazement.

He looked about for a stick long enough to reach in and make the frog jump away from the snake, but thin enough to go between the wires of the screen. Wild onion shoots were not long enough; peach switches were too big around. He scooped up a handful of sand and let it funnel through his tight-clasped fist onto the frog. The frog moved a few inches away but did not hop; then it sat motionless. Ted picked up another handful and threw it with stinging force through the screen. Both the snake and the frog moved.

The frog hopped twice and landed in the middle of the cage. The snake moved only its head, sliding it along the sandy floor until it touched the

saucer. It lifted its tail and shook the rattles in a short, angry warning. It lifted its head from behind the saucer and darted its tongue in and out.

Ted poured another handful of sand in a steady stream onto the frog. It jumped once more so that it was now almost under the opening in the top of the cage. The snake's flat head weaved back and forth, and the rattles now hummed steadily, like a katydid on the first cool nights of autumn when school has started and the circus is coming to town.

The boy was on his knees now before the box. The distances, he figured, were in his favor. He twisted the bent nail and slipped the screen wire loose. He bent the wire back and held his hand poised in the opening, watching the snake, the frog, his hand, the snake — and breathing not at all. Quickly he thrust his hand into the box. He grabbed the frog. He had it and was pulling out his hand when the snake struck, and missed.

He didn't hear himself scream, nor feel the bent nail point as it tore his skin from elbow to wrist. He only felt the wet frog struggling to be free and saw the snake, crawling and coiling, in sudden curves.

"My God, boy! Get away from there!" The medicine man was holding on to the door of the trailer and was the color of the pale worms that floated in the bottles on each side. "Get away! You wanta be killed?"

Ted stood up. His knees were trembling; he'd been stooping so long. He turned and started toward the street, holding the frog in the palms of his cupped hands. If Jake hadn't called at that moment, he would have been sick.

Jake was running toward him. "Did it bite you? Let's see your arm there. Hold up, Ted."

He turned and started back toward Jake. The sun was so hot and white that he was dazed. Jake led him into the filling station. "Did the snake do that? Did the snake do that?"

"No. I did it on that old nail."

"No. I don't suppose a snake could do all that." Jake laughed his forced laugh, now that he knew. "Better put something on it anyway." He was getting out a flat tin box with a red cross on it. Outside the medicine man was trying to fasten the screen on the box without bending over. He was mumbling to himself.

"Now where're we going to put the frog while we fix your arm? Let's see now," Jake said, looking on the shelf, where he kept the Purple Heart, for an empty cigar box.

"I don't want him any more." Ted spoke gravely.

"Don't want him any more?" Jake was still laughing each time he spoke and searching the boy's face for tears. "Why, you'll want him soon as we get that old arm of yours all doctored up."

"No. Let's turn him free."

"All right," Jake said. He studied the boy's face. "If that's what you want. It's yours."

They walked out to the side of the filling station away from the snake cage. There, in the shadow of a stone back of the air pump, Ted set the frog on the ground. As Jake spread the iodine up and down the long scratch on his arm, the boy watched the frog jump across the wire grass and into the wild strawberries growing in the shade of the oak. Each time it jumped, the boy wanted to laugh and cry at the same time, but he could not because he was not alone.

He turned and watched Jake's large hand dip the glass rod back into the bottle, and watched the wrinkles deepen on Jake's face.

"Jake," he asked, "how much kin am I to you?"

1. (a) How old is Ted? What details of his thought, speech, or actions indicate this? (b) Are there any details that suggest that he is sensitive and imaginative for his age? (c) What aspects of Ted's character or behavior seem most realistic in terms of what you know about children his age?

2. (a) How does Jake treat Ted? (b) What in Jake's past seems to have made the greatest impression on Ted? (c) How does the medicine man treat Ted? (d) What type of men do Jake and the medicine man seem to be, judging from their actions?

3. (a) How does Ted first react to the sight of the frog in the cage with the snake? (b) What are the reactions of the two men at this time? (c) In what context does Ted think of the frog before he falls asleep? (d) What might be the cause of Ted's bad dream, other than what his grandmother says? (e) Why does Ted build a house for the frog, do you suppose? (f) Why does he finally let the frog go?

4. What does the question that Ted asks Jake at the end of the story have to do with: (a) Ted's feelings of kinship? (b) Ted's courage?

5. Would you say that Ted was courageous or stupid in trying to rescue the frog as he did? Explain.

COURTESY OF THE AUTHOR

THE AUTHOR

Critics have noted that Max Steele seems to be at his best when writing of childhood and the relationships between young people and adults. Many of his stories are recollections of his early years in the South, where he was born in 1922. Reviewers have called "The Rescue" a sensitive and beautifully written account of the joy and nightmare that lie beneath the surface of a young boy's life.

But there is a more cosmopolitan side to Max Steele. He studied in Paris at the Sorbonne and he holds a professorship at the University of North Carolina where he is the director of the creative writing program.

The Companion

YEVGENY YEVTUSHENKO

She was sitting on the rough embankment,
her cape too big for her tied on slapdash
over an odd little hat with a bobble on it,
her eyes brimming with tears of hopelessness.
An occasional butterfly floated down   5
fluttering warm wings onto the rails.
The clinkers underfoot were deep lilac.
We got cut off from our grandmothers
while the Germans were dive-bombing the train.
Katya was her name. She was nine.   10
I'd no idea what I could do about her,
but doubt quickly dissolved to certainty:
I'd have to take this thing under my wing;
—girls were in some sense of the word human,

a human being couldn't just be left.   15
The droning in the air and the explosions
receded farther into the distance,
I touched the little girl on her elbow.
"Come on. Do you hear? What are you waiting for?"
The world was big and we were not big,   20
and it was tough for us to walk across it.
She had galoshes on and felt boots,
I had a pair of second-hand boots.
We forded streams and tramped across the forest;
each of my feet at every step it took   25
taking a smaller step inside the boot.
The child was feeble, I was certain of it,
"Boo-hoo," she'd say. "I'm tired," she'd say.
She'd tire in no time I was certain of it,
but as things turned out it was me who tired.   30
I growled I wasn't going any further
and sat down suddenly beside the fence.
"What's the matter with you?" she said.
"Don't be so stupid! Put grass in your boots.
Do you want to eat something? Why don't you talk?   35
Hold this tin, this is crab.
We'll have refreshments. You small boys,
you're always pretending to be brave."
Then out I went across the prickly stubble
marching beside her in a few minutes.   40
Masculine pride was muttering in my mind:
I scraped together strength and I held out
for fear of what she'd say. I even whistled.
Grass was sticking out from my tattered boots.
So on and on   45
we walked without thinking of rest
passing craters, passing fire,
under the rocking sky of '41
tottering crazy on its smoking columns.

1. (**a**) Briefly describe in your own words the setting in which the speaker meets Katya. (**b**) When did the events described in the poem take place? (**c**) How is Katya dressed? (**d**) Does the speaker seem younger or older than, or the same age as Katya? Explain.

2. (**a**) What is the speaker's attitude toward Katya in the first half of the poem? What does he expect of her? What particular words or phrases indicate this? (**b**) Does Katya act as the speaker expects? Explain.

3. (**a**) What kind of trouble does the speaker have? (**b**) How does Katya react to his problem? (**c**) What emotions is the speaker describing in lines 41–43?

4. (**a**) Do you feel that the poet has honestly described an encounter between two young people? (**b**) Do you feel there is any indication in the poem that a similar episode happened to him? Explain.

THE AUTHOR

SOVFOTO

It seems a long way from the soccer field to the pages of a poem, but for Yevgeny Yevtushenko the trip was a short one. It was in 1949, while preparing to become a professional soccer player, that sixteen-year-old Yevtushenko had his first poem published. Since that time he has risen to become the spokesman for the new generation of Soviet writers who are able to mix their praise of Russian life with a critical, questioning examination of the faults and injustices of a bureaucratic society.

Yevtushenko was born in the remote village of Zima, a small stop on the Trans-Siberian Railway, in 1933. Less than thirty years later he was to find himself an international figure, reading his poetry to audiences in Western Europe and the United States.

A great many of Yevtushenko's poems, like the one presented here, are notable for their emphasis on personal emotions and strong feelings of human sympathy. It is this aspect of his poetry that seems to have the most appeal to his foreign readers.

See
PLOT
*Handbook
of Literary
Terms
page 531*

Is it possible to be heroic in spite of oneself?
What series of events allows the two crafty characters in
this story to outwit both the "bad guys" and each other?

The Two Hoaxers

STRATIS MYRIVILIS

ONCE UPON A TIME—in the old days—there were two famous hoaxers on the island of Mytilene:[1] Crooked-Thodoros of Hora, and Foxy-Manolis of Skamnia. Everybody suffered from their wiles and knavery. As their fame spread throughout the hundred villages of the island, it occurred to each of them simultaneously to go and get acquainted with the other, in order to establish his own cleverness and become the unrivaled champion in duplicity.

So Foxy-Manolis went down to the seashore and gathered two bags of seaweed. He packed the bags well, sewed the tops together, and loaded them on his mule with himself between them.

"Good-by," he said to his wife.

"I'm off to Hora to find Crooked-Thodoros. I must outwit him at any cost, for it annoys me to hear his name coupled with mine."

"And how will you do it?" asked his wife.

"I will palm this load of seaweed off on him for silk. If I fail, I am finished."

And off he went, on his little mule toward Hora, for there were no highways and automobiles in those days.

Crooked-Thodoros, on the other side of the island, went to a valley full

---

Translated by Abbott Rick from *The Charioteer* (Vol. 1, No. 1, Summer 1960). Reprinted by permission of *The Charioteer* and Parnassos, Greek Cultural Society.

1. **Mytilene** (mitə'lē'nē), a Greek island in the Aegean Sea.

of fragrant osiers[2]—for it was summer. There he picked and winnowed two bags of osier seeds. He sewed the tops of the bags together, loaded them on his mule, and set out for Skamnia.

"I'll be away for a few days," he said to his wife. "I'm going to meet this Foxy-Manolis, whose reputation has reached Hora and makes me ashamed to show myself in public. I'm going to get acquainted with him, outwit him, and make him realize who Crooked-Thodoros is."

"How do you intend to outwit him?" asked his wife.

"Do you see this load?" replied Crooked-Thodoros. "It is worthless osier seeds. May I be called Simple Simon if I don't palm them off on him for pepper."

The next day, in the heat of noon, the two hoaxers met without recognizing each other under a plane tree near a spring, where mule drivers were in the habit of stopping to rest and water their animals, eat their salt meat and moisten their hard-baked barley loaf in the bubbling water of the spring.

"Where to, countryman?" Foxy-Manolis asked Crooked-Thodoros.

"I had a grocery shop," replied the latter, "and I sold out. This load of pepper is all that is left, and I have come to get rid of it in some village around here. What have you got on your animal?"

"I have a load of silk," said Foxy-Manolis. "It is a matter of some hundred and fifty skeins, and I'm going to get rid of it in a lump."

Each one, hearing the other speak so frankly and so convincingly, took him for an honest man and thought to himself:

"Let me try to swindle this simpleton that heaven has sent my way today. As for the other one, it is no matter. I'll have time later on to deal with him even better than now."

So Crooked-Thodoros rolled a fat cigarette and offered his tobacco pouch to the other. Then striking his flint, he lighted up and said to Foxy-Manolis:

"I've got an idea, comrade . . . by the way, what is your name please?"

"Kyriákos."

"I've got an idea, friend Kyriákos . . . ah, yes, my name is Theophánis . . ."

"I'm listening," said the other very calmly.

"I suggest, friend Kyriákos, now that we are acquainted that we make a deal. . . ."

"What kind of a deal?" asked Foxy-Manolis, affecting ignorance.

"Let's trade loads. . . . I'll give you my pepper and you give me your silk."

Foxy-Manolis almost jumped for joy. "It's worked out just right!" he said to himself. "Who can find fault with this scheme? Like a lured bird, he has put his head in the noose." In order not to show how great was his joy and thus arouse the other's suspicion, he said, after pretending to be calculating in his mind for a long time:

"Well, friend, I confess that your suggestion doesn't seem bad to me. But since the silk is more costly, how about giving me a piece of silver to boot?"

Crooked-Thodoros thought, "Done! I have beaten the blockhead. I have unloaded the osier seed on him and taken his silk." So he assumed a thoughtful manner and said:

"A piece of silver! You're a hard bargainer, friend. But I don't want to spoil the deal. There. Take your piece of silver and shake hands."

They got up promptly and exchanged their loads with incredible

---

2. **osiers** (ō'zhərz), willows with tough, flexible shoots or branches.

speed. Each cast furtive, sidelong glances at the other, and both hearts were pounding anxiously lest the "victim" should open the bags to look at the contents. When they had completed the exchange, they got on their animals, and whipping them with a switch, they rode off toward their respective homes, each one afraid that the other might discover the fraud.

About dawn next morning, exhausted by their all-night ride, they knocked on the door of their homes.

"Oh, husband," said Dame Foxy-Manolis, rubbing her eyes drowsily. "Why have you returned so soon, and why are you and your animal in such a state?"

Foxy-Manolis put his hands proudly on his hips and replied with a smile:

"Now see what a husband you have. While I was on my way to Hora to meet this Crooked-Thodoros, fate threw a goose into my clutches, a mule driver with a load of pepper. I palmed my seaweed off on him for silk and he gave me these bags of pepper and a piece of silver to boot. As for Crooked-Thodoros, I'll go and meet him some other day. How does this strike you, eh? Now you will put pepper even in my beans, as the saying goes!"

"You fool! You dolt! Let me pepper you to keep you from smelling!" shrieked Dame Foxy-Manolis in a rage, who in the meantime had opened the bags and discovered the osier seeds. "You have been cheated, cuckoo! You have been outwitted like a child. Look at your pepper!" And she shook her fist in his face.

Foxy-Manolis was furious and suspected that the bogus peddler was none other than Crooked-Thodoros himself, but when he recalled that he still had the piece of silver, he was comforted and said to his wife:

"Nothing can be done about it,

wife. I traded the silk with him for the pepper. The important thing is that he gave me a piece of silver to boot. And this means that it is he who has been outwitted and I am the winner, even though it is only a piece of silver. It's the principle that counts!"

The same thing took place at the home of Crooked-Thodoros when he arrived in Hora, worn out from riding, to brag to his wife that on the way to Skamnia he had outwitted a stupid peasant and bought from him a whole load of silk for the osier seeds and a piece of silver!

But when he saw that the silk which he had told her to make into scarves and breeches and kerchiefs and sheets was mere seaweed, he was furious at the other man for having outwitted him and taken his piece of silver, and he could not sleep for nights out of chagrin. He reflected that as long as another man could show this piece of silver to the world, he must sink into the bowels of the earth and not dare to whisper about being the champion hoaxer. For he suspected that the man who had tricked him was none other than Foxy-Manolis.

"Confound the knave," he thought, throwing down his fez,[3] "and now what will become of me!"

At last, in desperation, he got up and went straight to Skamnia. It was late afternoon when he arrived. Entering the village coffeehouse, he saw Foxy-Manolis in a corner, smoking a water pipe. He pretended that he did not see him and went to the other side and ordered a drink. But Foxy-Manolis had seen him the moment he entered and recognized him. He understood why he had come. So he let the mouthpiece of the pipe fall to the floor

---

3. *fez*, brimless felt cap with a flat top.

and left discreetly by the other door of the coffeehouse.

He went straight home and told his wife that he had seen the man who sold him the pepper enter the coffeehouse.

"The knave has surely come for his piece of silver, wife!"

"What shall we do now?" she asked him.

"You will do what I tell you and ask no questions. I am going to die now. Say that I have died."

"Heaven help us!" she said to him and struck her wooden stool three times for good luck. "May the hour that heard you be harmless, husband!"

"Stop that and listen to what I tell you. I will pretend to be dead. You will undo your hair and drop your headcloth over your face and scream. You will lay me out and hold my funeral. The church bells will toll. Everything will be done according to custom. Only, you will tell the elders that lest you do violence to yourself out of grief they must carry me to the cemetery tonight, and since a corpse is not buried at night, let them leave me in the cemetery chapel so that they can bury me in the morning. Crooked-Thodoros will be satisfied and go away. In the morning I will get up and come home, saying that I had a fainting fit."

Everything was done as the hoaxer ordained. Presently Crooked-Thodoros heard the church bells tolling a dirge. "Who's dead?" "Foxy-Manolis." "But he was here just now." "My, my, my, what a thing is man!" "And what was the matter with the poor fellow?" "He had a stroke." "His widow is about to lose her mind!" "They say they are going to take him to the cemetery chapel this evening lest the poor woman kill herself!"

Crooked-Thodoros listened to the villagers' conversation and slapped his hands against his thighs. "There's something fishy here," he thought. "This 'stroke' is just a little too pat."

So he got up with the others and followed Foxy-Manolis' funeral procession to the cemetery, which was outside the village at the foot of the mountainside. All the way, the widow tore her hair and beat her breast. Her shrieks moved even the stones.

"Ooooh, my husband! My beloved husband! My dear protector and provider!"

When Crooked-Thodoros learned that the burial would not take place till next day, he became suspicious.

"The rascal has something up his sleeve," he thought. "The rascal has something up his sleeve!"

While the last rites were being chanted and everybody was going up to kiss the corpse, Crooked-Thodoros pretended to leave and hid behind a pile of crutches which had been heaped in a corner of the chapel. In those days there were no pews in the churches. Instead, the elders and the infirm leaned on these crutches while the liturgy was being performed.

There were some seventy pairs of walnut crutches lying there in the corner. Crooked-Thodoros hid underneath them in one of the hollow spaces.

"My clever fellow," he said to himself, "I will keep watch here till morning to see whether you will move or not."

But the other hoaxer had not been caught off guard. Not for an instant had he lost sight of Crooked-Thodoros from between his eyelids. He saw him in the procession, he saw him in the chapel, he felt his mustache on his forehead when he gave the last kiss, and finally he saw and made note of where he was hiding under the crutches.

"Take care, Foxy-Manolis!"

thought Crooked-Thodoros. "One move and you are lost! Your silver piece will be gone and so will your self-respect!"

But Foxy-Manolis, the dog, didn't so much as shift his position. He even bit his tongue lest lying there on the bier he should be overtaken by sleep and begin to snore as he always did, or forget and turn over on his side.

In this way, time passed. Night fell and the securely locked chapel was illuminated only by the sputtering lamps. In the silence, a mouse was heard trying to get at the can of oil which was kept covered with a flat stone in the sanctuary, and there was the patient crunching of insects chewing the old icons[4] and the walnut screen.

Suddenly, in the middle of the night, a strange disturbance was heard outside the chapel. The two hoaxers, the dead one and the hidden one strained their ears anxiously.

There was the sound of many feet, talking and general commotion. Someone tried to force open the door but was unable to do it, because the door was strong and double-locked. Then there was a clatter against the walls. Men or demons, they were climbing up on the roof. The church was covered by a flat, earthen terrace; the ceiling boards had been laid, then a layer of seaweed and on that a layer of well-trodden earth which was rolled with a marble cylinder.

In a little while, the two hoaxers realized that somebody was digging through the roof. Soon the points of two swords penetrated the ceiling. Then strong hands opened a large hole, dropping the earth and pieces of wood down on the floor. When the hole was large enough, a man's bulk slipped through and landed on the floor with a clatter which made the church ring like a hollow jar.

Then a second, a third, a fourth — until twenty young strapping fellows had dropped through the hole. They were all sun-bronzed lads with black beards and mustaches. Their eyes shone and their chests were crossed with broad gold-plated bandoleers. At their waists they all had leather belts stuffed with pistols and double-edged daggers, and at their sides hung large curved swords with silver-wrought scabbards. Through the hole in the ceiling they had dropped a half score of bags which clashed metallically on the floor.

They were a gang of bandits who raided towns and villages along the coast of the island, pillaged mansions and villas of the aristocrats, and stripped churches and chapels of their valuables. They had entered this isolated cemetery chapel to divide their spoils, certain that nowhere else could they have found so remote and safe a refuge.

First they all crossed themselves, fez in hand, and kissed the icon of the Archangel Michael. Then they sat down on the floor in a circle to begin the distribution. Since they were all uneducated lads, they conducted the business in a very primitive manner. The captain's fez was to be filled and emptied in front of each bandit in turn.

With beating heart the two hoaxers, one through his eyelids and the other from among the crutches, watched the bandits grasping handfuls of diamonds, solid gold plate, gold coins, which gleamed under the lamps, an incalculable treasure.

"My brothers, we have labored for years," said the captain. "We have labored honorably and loyally. Now that the time has come for us to dis-

---

4. **icons,** sacred religious pictures, usually painted on wood or ivory.

band, let us divide justly the wealth we have earned."

With these words, he filled his fez with jewels and emptied it in front of each man. When the captain's fez had gone around two or three times in this way, one fezful was found left over. A loud argument arose as to how this remaining share should be justly disposed of.

At last the captain stood up and said to them:

"Lads, we have labored so many years like brothers and we have never quarreled. Always when your talk reached the quarreling point, you obediently followed my advice. Now that we are going to separate forever, it is necessary that we separate in a friendly manner. Will you agree for the last time to what I have to say?"

"We agree, Captain!" they all shouted. "Your word is law!"

"Very well," said the captain. "Do you see that dead man in his coffin over there?" (Foxy-Manolis felt a pang in his vitals, but he did not move.) "Well, then. Draw your swords." (With a clash, they all drew their swords from their scabbards.) "Now all of us will test our metal and our strength on this corpse. Whoever can with one stroke cleave the dead man's carcass and the coffin clear to the floor, he will get the remaining jewels and he will deserve them!"

"Agreed!" cried the bandits. "You try first, Captain!"

The captain went to the bier and was about to raise his sword. But before he could bring it down, a terrible crash roared through the chapel, as if the whole world had collapsed and was falling about their ears. And a deep, terrifying voice seemed to come from the earth:

"Arise, ye dead, and let us devour the living!"

It was Crooked-Thodoros, who had thought up this trick when he saw the sword over Foxy-Manolis, whom he wanted alive in order to get his silver piece again. He had given a sudden kick at the crutches, causing them to fall with a fearful crash, while he bellowed out a call to the dead. Foxy-Manolis, who was beside himself with terror in the coffin when he realized that they were going to slice him in two like a cucumber, understood that the call to the dead was meant for him, leaped up in his shroud, kicked against the coffin and howled as if demented:

"Arise! Up and at them, all ye dead!"

The bandits, seeing and hearing these horrible apparitions, were convinced that all the dead had risen from the cemetery to devour them, and with hair standing on end, they fought to see which could be the first to escape from the hell which was opening around them to engulf them, by leaping like rabbits through the hole in the ceiling.

Left alone in the church, Crooked-Thodoros and Foxy-Manolis stared at each other.

"How did you like my idea?" asked Crooked-Thodoros.

"Not bad at all," said Foxy-Manolis. "You rescued me in the nick of time."

"And now?"

"Now that we are acquainted so well, let's sit down and divide like good friends the treasure that the living in their flight have left behind for us dead."

So they sat down and separated the jewels into two piles with the understanding that each was to take whichever share he wished. In this way, they were sure that neither of them would be cheated by so much as a needle. Then each one put his share into a bag and tied it.

"We have done a good night's

work," said Foxy-Manolis. "Shall we go now?"

"With your indulgence, my friend," said Crooked-Thodoros, "we have still a small account to settle. You got a silver piece from me when you palmed off the seaweed on me for silk. I want it!"

"In the name of all that's holy!" cried the other. "You have all this wealth now, and you talk to me about a piece of silver, three of which wouldn't be worth a shilling!"

Crooked-Thodoros would listen neither to persuasion nor to threats.

"I don't care what you say. I want my silver piece. I'm not leaving till you give me my silver piece!"

Meanwhile, the bandits, leaping from the chapel roof, had taken to their heels in silence and stumbled through the fields down to the beach of Skamnia, where in a sheltered cove they had anchored their boat.

When they became weary from running in the darkness and jumping the walls between the olive groves, taking every boulder that rolled after them for the pursuing horde of the dead, they finally stopped to get their breath by a little fountain.

"My brave lads," said the captain, "what has happened has happened, and we have got out of it cheap. All these years, we have demonstrated clearly that our hearts are sound and that we can take on any man. But who can face the dead? They are air. Neither sword nor lead wounds them. But I would like to know what is going on now in the chapel and what the dead are doing with so much treasure and the labor of years. Has any of you the courage—not to go in, just to look through the hole in the roof—to learn what is taking place there?"

No one answered the captain, except the bravest of them, who said:

"Let us speak no more of this matter, Captain! Set us to grapple with monsters and dragons! But with the dead? I confess that I don't have the courage even to look at them again, may God have mercy on me!"

The captain was stubborn.

"Very well," he said. "Since none of you has enough courage, I'll go alone. Wait here for me."

He got up and made straight for the cemetery. He leaped cautiously over the wall. Then—on tiptoe—he approached the church and without making a sound climbed up on the roof. Creeping with his heart in his mouth, he drew near the hole in the ceiling and thrust his head down to see what was going on inside. At that moment Crooked-Thodoros was shouting angrily, "I want my silver piece! I want my silver piece! I want my silver piece!" Foxy-Manolis stood under the hole with his sack in his arms, about to burst with vexation.

When he saw the captain's head appear through the hole, he lost no time. He reached up and snatched the fez from the bandit's head (who drew back and made off half dead with fresh terror) and gave it to Crooked-Thodoros, saying:

"You are driving me wild with your piece of silver. Here. Take this fez, which is worth more than a piece of silver, and call it square!"

When the captain reached his companions, who were anxiously waiting for him, he fell swooning at their feet. With great effort, they revived him and begged him to tell what he had seen and suffered.

"Cursed be the hour that I went back there!" he said when he had recovered a little and had got his breath. "My brave lads, imagine how many dead must have gathered there! After they divided up the thousands of piasters of wealth we left behind, there were so many of them that to

each fell only a piece of silver. And even that wasn't enough for them all. One of them was left without his piece of silver. When I looked in, he was making an uproar over not getting his share. 'I want my silver piece! I want my silver piece! I want my silver piece!' And their captain seized my fez and gave it to him for his share!''

+ + + +

DISCUSSION

1. (a) What irony do you find in the circumstances of the two hoaxers' first meeting? **(b)** What irony is there in what each hoaxer thinks and expects? **(c)** What actions previous to this meeting contribute to the irony? **(d)** Who gets the better of the trade? Or are both hoaxers fooled? Explain.

2. (a) Why does Crooked-Thodoros go looking for Foxy-Manolis? **(b)** What trick does Foxy-Manolis employ to throw Crooked-Thodoros off his track? **(c)** Does this trick work? Why or why not?

3. (a) How does Crooked-Thodoros save Foxy-Manolis's life? **(b)** What irony do you find in this event?

4. (a) Do you find Crooked-Thodoros's insistence on having his silver piece, even after the treasure has been divided, logical or ridiculous? Explain. **(b)** What unintended effect does the hoaxers' argument have?

5. Would you say that this story was written for entertainment or with some more serious purpose in mind? Explain.

WORD STUDY

When the bandits' Captain asks, "Has any of you the *courage* . . . to look through the hole in the roof . . .," he is using a word that came from the Old French *corage*. This French word has much the same meaning as the English word *courage*. The French derived *corage* from the Latin *cor*, which means

"heart." What does the English expression "take heart" mean? What is the relationship between the English *courage* and the Latin *cor?*

Each of the three sentences below is followed by a brief history of the italicized word. Read both the sentence and the history following it. Then, explain its present meaning, showing its relationship to the original.

1. "Foxy-Manolis . . . kicked against the coffin and howled as if *demented* . . ." (Demented was taken into English from the Latin word *dementare* which was derived from the word *demens* meaning "mad" which was formed from the two Latin elements demeaning "out" and *mentem* meaning "mind.")

2. ". . . nowhere else could they have found so remote and safe a *refuge*." (Refuge comes from the Latin *refugium* which was formed by combining *re-* meaning "back" with a form of *fugere* meaning "flee.")

3. "The church was covered by a flat, earthen *terrace* . . ." (Terrace comes from the French word *terrain* which came from the Latin word *terra* meaning "earth.")

THE AUTHOR

Stratis Myrivilis (1892–1969) was himself a product of the Greek island of Mytilene, the scene for his story of the two hoaxers. Born there in 1892, Myrivilis went on to study philosophy and law at the University of Athens, and later extended his career to include journalism, publishing, and the Greek national radio. In World War II he helped organize the Greek resistance movement and from these experiences came one of his finest novels, *Life in the Grave*. Today he is considered by his countrymen to be one of the finest of modern Greek writers.

See
BIOGRAPHY
Handbook
of Literary
Terms
page 514

When they heard the whisper "Moses is back again,"
the daring handful of slaves tied up some ashcake and salt herring
in their bandannas and waited for the signal.
Who was Moses and what role did she play in American history?

from Harriet Tubman

ANN PETRY

ALONG THE EASTERN SHORE of Maryland, in Dorchester County, in Caroline County, the masters kept hearing whispers about the man named Moses, who was running off slaves. At first they did not believe in his existence. The stories about him were fantastic, unbelievable. Yet they watched for him. They offered rewards for his capture.

They never saw him. Now and then they heard whispered rumors to the effect that he was in the neighborhood. The woods were searched. The roads were watched. There was never anything to indicate his whereabouts. But a few days afterward, a goodly number of slaves would be gone from the plantation. Neither the master nor the overseer had heard or seen anything unusual in the quarter. Sometimes one or the other would vaguely remember having heard a whippoorwill call somewhere in the woods, close by, late at night. Though it was the wrong season for whippoorwills.

Sometimes the masters thought they had heard the cry of a hoot owl, repeated, and would remember having thought that the intervals between the low moaning cry were wrong, that it had been repeated four times in succession instead of three. There was never anything more than that to suggest that all was not well in the quarter. Yet when morning came, they invariably discovered that a group of the finest slaves had taken to their heels.

Unfortunately, the discovery was almost always made on a Sunday. Thus a whole day was lost before the machinery of pursuit could be set in motion. The posters offering rewards for the fugitives could not be printed until Monday. The men who made a living hunting for runaway slaves were out of reach, off in the woods with their dogs and their guns, in pursuit of four-footed game, or they

were in camp meetings saying their prayers with their wives and families beside them.

Harriet Tubman could have told them that there was far more involved in this matter of running off slaves than signaling the would-be runaways by imitating the call of a whippoorwill, or a hoot owl, far more involved than a matter of waiting for a clear night when the North Star was visible.

In December, 1851, when she started out with the band of fugitives that she planned to take to Canada, she had been in the vicinity of the plantation for days, planning the trip, carefully selecting the slaves that she would take with her.

She had announced her arrival in the quarter by singing the forbidden spiritual—"Go down, Moses, 'way down to Egypt Land"—singing it softly outside the door of a slave cabin, late at night. The husky voice was beautiful even when it was barely more than a murmur borne on the wind.

Once she had made her presence known, word of her coming spread from cabin to cabin. The slaves whispered to each other, ear to mouth, mouth to ear, "Moses is here." "Moses has come." "Get ready. Moses is back again." The ones who had agreed to go North with her put ashcake and salt herring in an old bandanna, hastily tied it into a bundle, and then waited patiently for the signal that meant it was time to start.

There were eleven in this party, including one of her brothers and his wife. It was the largest group that she had ever conducted, but she was determined that more and more slaves should know what freedom was like.

She had to take them all the way to Canada. The Fugitive Slave Law[1]

was no longer a great many incomprehensible words written down on the country's lawbooks. The new law had become a reality. It was Thomas Sims, a boy, picked up on the streets of Boston at night and shipped back to Georgia. It was Jerry and Shadrach, arrested and jailed with no warning.

She had never been in Canada. The route beyond Philadelphia was strange to her. But she could not let the runaways who accompanied her know this. As they walked along she told them stories of her own first flight, she kept painting vivid word pictures of what it would be like to be free.

But there were so many of them this time. She knew moments of doubt when she was half-afraid, and kept looking back over her shoulder, imagining that she heard the sound of pursuit. They would certainly be pursued. Eleven of them. Eleven thousand dollars' worth of flesh and bone and muscle that belonged to Maryland planters. If they were caught, the eleven runaways would be whipped and sold South, but she—she would probably be hanged.

They tried to sleep during the day but they never could wholly relax into sleep. She could tell by the positions they assumed, by their restless movements. And they walked at night. Their progress was slow. It took them three nights of walking to reach the first stop. She had told them about the place where they would stay, promising warmth and good food, holding these things out to them as an incentive to keep going.

When she knocked on the door of

---

1. *Fugitive Slave Law.* Between 1793 and 1850, Congress enacted several laws to provide for the return of escaped slaves. The Underground Railroad was largely a result of public distaste for these laws. Among other harsh measures, the law of 1850 imposed severe penalties upon anyone who helped a slave in his escape.

a farmhouse, a place where she and her parties of runaways had always been welcome, always been given shelter and plenty to eat, there was no answer. She knocked again, softly. A voice from within said, "Who is it?" There was fear in the voice.

She knew instantly from the sound of the voice that there was something wrong. She said, "A friend with friends," the password on the Underground Railroad.

The door opened, slowly. The man who stood in the doorway looked at her coldly, looked with unconcealed astonishment and fear at the eleven disheveled runaways who were standing near her. Then he shouted, "Too many, too many. It's not safe. My place was searched last week. It's not safe!" and slammed the door in her face.

She turned away from the house, frowning. She had promised her passengers food and rest and warmth, and instead of that, there would be hunger and cold and more walking over the frozen ground. Somehow she would have to instill courage into these eleven people, most of them strangers, would have to feed them on hope and bright dreams of freedom instead of the fried pork and corn bread and milk she had promised them.

They stumbled along behind her, half-dead for sleep, and she urged them on, though she was as tired and as discouraged as they were. She had never been in Canada but she kept painting wondrous word pictures of what it would be like. She managed to dispel their fear of pursuit, so that they would not become hysterical, panic-stricken. Then she had to bring some of the fear back, so that they would stay awake and keep walking though they drooped with sleep.

Yet during the day, when they lay down deep in a thicket, they never really slept, because if a twig snapped or the wind sighed in the branches of a pine tree, they jumped to their feet, afraid of their own shadows, shivering and shaking. It was very cold, but they dared not make fires because someone would see the smoke and wonder about it.

She kept thinking, eleven of them. Eleven thousand dollars' worth of slaves. And she had to take them all the way to Canada. Sometimes she told them about Thomas Garrett, in Wilmington. She said he was their friend even though he did not know them. He was the friend of all fugitives. He called them God's poor. He was a Quaker[2] and his speech was a little different from that of other people. His clothing was different, too. He wore the wide-brimmed hat that the Quakers wear.

She said that he had thick white hair, soft, almost like a baby's, and the kindest eyes she had ever seen. He was a big man and strong, but he had never used his strength to harm anyone, always to help people. He would give all of them a new pair of shoes. Everybody. He always did. Once they reached his house in Wilmington, they would be safe. He would see to it that they were.

She described the house where he lived, told them about the store where he sold shoes. She said he kept a pail of milk and a loaf of bread in the drawer of his desk so that he would have food ready at hand for any of God's poor who should suddenly appear before him, fainting with hunger. There was a hidden room in the store. A whole wall swung open, and behind it was a room where he could

2. **Quaker,** a member of a Christian group called the Society of Friends. The Quakers participated actively in the anti-slavery effort.

hide fugitives. On the wall there were shelves filled with small boxes—boxes of shoes—so that you would never guess that the wall actually opened.

While she talked, she kept watching them. They did not believe her. She could tell by their expressions. They were thinking, New shoes, Thomas Garrett, Quaker, Wilmington—what foolishness was this? Who knew if she told the truth? Where was she taking them anyway?

That night they reached the next stop—a farm that belonged to a German. She made the runaways take shelter behind trees at the edge of the fields before she knocked at the door. She hesitated before she approached the door, thinking, suppose that he, too, should refuse shelter, suppose— Then she thought, Lord, I'm going to hold steady on to You and You've got to see me through—and knocked softly.

She heard the familiar guttural voice say, "Who's there?"

She answered quickly, "A friend with friends."

He opened the door and greeted her warmly. "How many this time?" he asked.

"Eleven," she said and waited, doubting, wondering.

He said, "Good. Bring them in."

He and his wife fed them in the lamplit kitchen, their faces glowing, as they offered food and more food, urging them to eat, saying there was plenty for everybody, have more milk, have more bread, have more meat.

They spent the night in the warm kitchen. They really slept, all that night and until dusk the next day. When they left, it was with reluctance. They had all been warm and safe and well-fed. It was hard to exchange the security offered by that clean warm kitchen for the darkness and the cold of a December night. . . .

Harriet had found it hard to leave the warmth and friendliness, too. But she urged them on. For a while, as they walked, they seemed to carry in them a measure of contentment; some of the serenity and the cleanliness of that big warm kitchen lingered on inside them. But as they walked farther and farther away from the warmth and the light, the cold and the darkness entered into them. They fell silent, sullen, suspicious. She waited for the moment when some one of them would turn mutinous. It did not happen that night.

Two nights later she was aware that the feet behind her were moving slower and slower. She heard the irritability in their voices, knew that soon someone would refuse to go on.

She started talking about William Still and the Philadelphia Vigilance Committee.[3] No one commented. No one asked any questions. She told them the story of William and Ellen Craft and how they escaped from Georgia. Ellen was so fair that she looked as though she were white, and so she dressed up in a man's clothing and she looked like a wealthy young planter. Her husband, William, who was dark, played the role of her slave. Thus they traveled from Macon, Georgia, to Philadelphia, riding on the trains, staying at the finest hotels. Ellen pretended to be very ill—her right arm was in a sling, and her right hand was bandaged, because she was supposed to have rheumatism. Thus she avoided having to sign the register at the hotels for she could not read or write. They finally arrived safely in Philadelphia, and then went on to Boston.

No one said anything. Not one of them seemed to have heard her.

3. *Philadelphia Vigilance Committee,* a group of citizens who guided slaves and helped pay their way to Canada.

She told them about Frederick Douglass,[4] the most famous of the escaped slaves, of his eloquence, of his magnificent appearance. Then she told them of her own first vain effort at running away, evoking the memory of that miserable life she had led as a child, reliving it for a moment in the telling.

But they had been tired too long, hungry too long, afraid too long, footsore too long. One of them suddenly cried out in despair, "Let me go back. It is better to be a slave than to suffer like this in order to be free."

She carried a gun with her on these trips. She had never used it— except as a threat. Now as she aimed it, she experienced a feeling of guilt, remembering that time, years ago, when she had prayed for the death of Edward Brodas, the Master, and then not too long afterward had heard that great wailing cry that came from the throats of the field hands, and knew from the sound that the Master was dead.

One of the runaways said, again, "Let me go back. Let me go back," and stood still, and then turned around and said, over his shoulder, "I am going back."

She lifted the gun, aimed it at the despairing slave. She said, "Go on with us or die." The husky low-pitched voice was grim.

He hesitated for a moment and then he joined the others. They started walking again. She tried to explain to them why none of them could go back to the plantation. If a runaway returned, he would turn traitor, the master and the overseer would force him to turn traitor. The returned slave would disclose the stopping places, the hiding places, the cornstacks they had used with the full knowledge of the owner of the farm, the name of the German farmer who

had fed them and sheltered them. These people who had risked their own security to help runaways would be ruined, fined, imprisoned.

She said, "We got to go free or die. And freedom's not bought with dust."

This time she told them about the long agony of the Middle Passage[5] on the old slave ships, about the black horror of the holds, about the chains and the whips. They too knew these stories. But she wanted to remind them of the long hard way they had come, about the long hard way they had yet to go. She told them about Thomas Sims, the boy picked up on the streets of Boston and sent back to Georgia. She said when they got him back to Savannah, got him in prison there, they whipped him until a doctor who was standing by watching said, "You will kill him if you strike him again!" His master said, "Let him die!"

Thus she forced them to go on. Sometimes she thought she had become nothing but a voice speaking in the darkness, cajoling, urging, threatening. Sometimes she told them things to make them laugh, sometimes she sang to them, and heard the eleven voices behind her blending softly with hers, and then she knew that for the moment all was well with them.

She gave the impression of being a short, muscular, indomitable woman who could never be defeated. Yet at any moment she was liable to be seized by one of those curious fits of sleep, which might last for a few minutes or for hours.[6]

Even on this trip, she suddenly

---

4. *Frederick Douglass* (1817–1895), an ex-slave who became a leading figure in the anti-slavery movement through his eloquent lectures and abolitionist newspaper.
5. *Middle Passage,* the slaves' journey from Africa to America over the Atlantic Ocean.
6. *curious . . . hours.* At thirteen, Harriet nearly died from an accidental blow on her head. The resulting brain damage caused periodic sleeping seizures that troubled her throughout her life.

fell asleep in the woods. The runaways, ragged, dirty, hungry, cold, did not steal the gun as they might have, and set off by themselves, or turn back. They sat on the ground near her and waited patiently until she awakened. They had come to trust her implicitly, totally. They, too, had come to believe her repeated statement, "We got to go free or die." She was leading them into freedom, and so they waited until she was ready to go on.

Finally, they reached Thomas Garrett's house in Wilmington, Delaware. Just as Harriet had promised, Garrett gave them all new shoes, and provided carriages to take them on to the next stop.

By slow stages they reached Philadelphia, where William Still hastily recorded their names, and the plantations whence they had come, and something of the life they had led in slavery. Then he carefully hid what he had written, for fear it might be discovered. In 1872 he published this record in book form and called it *The Underground Railroad*. In the foreword to his book he said: "While I knew the danger of keeping strict records, and while I did not then dream that in my day slavery would be blotted out, or that the time would come when I could publish these records, it used to afford me great satisfaction to take them down, fresh from the lips of fugitives on the way to freedom, and to preserve them as they had given them."

William Still, who was familiar with all the station stops on the Underground Railroad, supplied Harriet with money and sent her and her eleven fugitives on to Burlington, New Jersey.

Harriet felt safer now, though there were danger spots ahead. But the biggest part of her job was over.

As they went farther and farther north, it grew colder; she was aware of the wind on the Jersey ferry and aware of the cold damp in New York. From New York they went on to Syracuse, where the temperature was even lower.

In Syracuse she met the Reverend J. W. Loguen, known as "Jarm" Loguen. This was the beginning of a lifelong friendship. Both Harriet and Jarm Loguen were to become friends and supporters of Old John Brown.[7]

From Syracuse they went north again, into a colder, snowier city— Rochester. Here they almost certainly stayed with Frederick Douglass, for he wrote in his autobiography:

"On one occasion I had eleven fugitives at the same time under my roof, and it was necessary for them to remain with me until I could collect sufficient money to get them to Canada. It was the largest number I ever had at any one time, and I had some difficulty in providing so many with food and shelter, but, as may well be imagined, they were not very fastidious in either direction, and were well content with very plain food, and a strip of carpet on the floor for a bed, or a place on the straw in the barn-loft."

Late in December, 1851, Harriet arrived in St. Catharines, Canada West (now Ontario), with the eleven fugitives. It had taken almost a month to complete this journey; most of the time had been spent getting out of Maryland.

That first winter in St. Catharines was a terrible one. Canada was a strange frozen land, snow everywhere, ice everywhere, and a bone-biting cold the like of which

---

7. **Old John Brown** (1800–1859), a devoted abolitionist who tried to stir up a rebellion among the slaves. He was captured at Harpers Ferry, a town in West Virginia, when he attempted to raid a government arsenal there in 1859.

none of them had ever experienced before. Harriet rented a small frame house in the town and set to work to make a home. The fugitives boarded with her. They worked in the forests, felling trees, and so did she. Sometimes she took other jobs, cooking or cleaning house for people in the town. She cheered on these newly arrived fugitives, working herself, finding work for them, finding food for them, praying for them, sometimes begging for them.

Often she found herself thinking of the beauty of Maryland, the mellowness of the soil, the richness of the plant life there. The climate itself made for an ease of living that could never be duplicated in this bleak, barren countryside.

In spite of the severe cold, the hard work, she came to love St. Catharines, and the other towns and cities in Canada where black men lived. She discovered that freedom meant more than the right to change jobs at will, more than the right to keep the money that one earned. It was the right to vote and to sit on juries. It was the right to be elected to office. In Canada there were black men who were county officials and members of school boards. St. Catharines had a large colony of ex-slaves, and they owned their own homes, kept them neat and clean and in good repair. They lived in whatever part of town they chose and sent their children to the schools.

When spring came she decided that she would make this small Canadian city her home—as much as any place could be said to be home to a woman who traveled from Canada to the Eastern Shore of Maryland as often as she did.

In the spring of 1852, she went back to Cape May, New Jersey. She spent the summer there, cooking in a hotel. That fall she returned, as usual, to Dorchester County, and brought out nine more slaves, conducting them all the way to St. Catharines, in Canada West, to the bone-biting cold, the snow-covered forests —and freedom.

She continued to live in this fashion, spending the winter in Canada, and the spring and summer working in Cape May, New Jersey, or in Philadelphia. She made two trips a year into slave territory, one in the fall and another in the spring. She now had a definite crystallized purpose, and in carrying it out, her life fell into a pattern which remained unchanged for the next six years.

✦ ✦ ✦ ✦

DISCUSSION

1. (a) What exactly were the "station stops" of the Underground Railroad? (b) Why was "Underground Railroad" an appropriate term for the system?
2. (a) Why was "Moses" a good code name for Harriet Tubman? (b) Why was the spiritual "Go Down, Moses" forbidden?
3. (a) In what different ways did Harriet help the slaves find the will and courage to keep on? (b) Why couldn't she let a runaway return?
4. (a) What aspects of Harriet's personality does the biographer stress in the selection? (b) Of these aspects, which reveal heroic qualities in Harriet? (c) In your opinion, should anyone else in the selection be called a hero or heroine? Why or why not?
5. Reread the scene dealing with the Germans who gave shelter to the slaves (page 133).

(a) What details about the characters' thoughts and actions has the author added to increase interest? (b) Find other scenes that contain imaginary details. (c) What paragraphs present purely factual material? 6. (a) What did Harriet Tubman mean when she said "Freedom's not bought with dust"? (b) Do these words have application in the world today? Explain.

WORD STUDY

In the sentences below you should be able to determine from context clues the meaning of the italicized words. Read each sentence; then choose from the words that follow the one closest in meaning to the italicized word.

1. The man looked scornfully at the eleven ragged and *disheveled* runaways before him; for after nights of walking, days of fitful sleeping on the cold ground and hiding in thickets, their clothes were naturally mussed, their faces unwashed, and their hair sprinkled with pine needles.

Disheveled means (a) exhausted; (b) fresh; (c) untidy.

2. Harriet had told them about the place where they would stay, promising warmth, comfortable beds, and good food, holding these things out as an *incentive* to keep on.

Incentive means (a) motive; (b) warning; (c) agreement.

3. Harriet gave the impression of being an *indomitable* woman, who would always be victorious despite hardship and difficulty.

Indomitable means (a) uneducated; (b) undefeatable; (c) understanding.

4. The runaways were not very *fastidious* about the quality of meals and shelter they received from Douglass, since they were used to sleeping on the ground and eating whatever they could find.

Fastidious means (a) grateful; (b) critical; (c) hasty.

5. Sometimes Harriet thought she had become nothing but a persuasive voice in the darkness, *cajoling*, encouraging, pleading.

Cajoling means (a) singing; (b) coaxing; (c) menacing.

FROM THE AUTHOR

It seems to me that I have always been fascinated by American history—especially the period which encompasses the African slave trade, the ever increasing use of slaves in the South, the growing outcry for the abolition of slavery and ends with the Civil War and the period of reconstruction.

Slowly, over the years, I have become convinced that the most dramatic material available to the writer in this country is that which deals with the Negro, and his history in the United States. This material is rich, varied, and comparatively untouched, reaching back as it does to the seventeenth-century freedman or runaway slave or plantation hand, early ancestor of the mid-twentieth-century doctor or lawyer or schoolteacher.

As for Harriet Tubman—I think she is the ideal heroine. When she is first seen, she is defenseless and much abused and slowly develops into a courageous woman with an impelling desire for freedom.

See
SUSPENSE
*Handbook
of Literary
Terms
page 534*

*Somewhere off the coast of Australia
the submarine's routine was disrupted. . . .
This television play concerns real people and real events.
Note how the playwright handles facts to
build suspense.*

The Pharmacist's Mate

BUDD SCHULBERG

CHARACTERS

JIMMY BRUCE, *Pharmacist's Mate. Jimmy is the seaman in
complete charge of the sick bay, or the place on the ship used as
a hospital.*

LT. COMMANDER MILLER, *Skipper. Miller is the Captain of the
ship; his word is the final authority.*

FLOYD HUDSON, *Executive Officer. Hudson ranks just below
Miller and is his representative at all times.*

APPRENTICE SEAMAN TOMMY FORD, *patient.*

ENSIGN RIGGS, *Diving Officer. Riggs is the officer in charge of controlling the depth of the submarine.*

Other Members of the Crew

FANELLI, *Seaman.*

GOODMAN, *Seaman.*

O'BRIEN, *Seaman.*

SONARMAN, *the sound operator. He is
in charge of using the apparatus for
detecting enemy ships when the submarine is submerged.*

YOUNG PETTY OFFICER, *a noncommis-
sioned officer.*

LEROY JOHNSON, *mess boy.*

RADIOMAN, *the ship's radio operator.*

SWEDE, *ship's cook.*

LT. DAVISON

QUARTERMASTER WILLIAMS

HELMSMAN

MESSENGER

FIRST ACEY-DEUCY PLAYER

SECOND ACEY-DEUCY PLAYER, *partici-
pants in a game in which both cards
and dice are used.*

"The Pharmacist's Mate," a TV play by Budd Schulberg is adapted from EMERGENCY AT SEA
by George Weller, originally published in *The Chicago Daily News.* Reprinted by permission
of Ad Schulberg and Harold Ober Associates, Inc.

[*Fade in*[1] *on view of the sea as seen in an enlarged circle through a submarine periscope. The sea is disturbed, boiling up. Dissolve to*[2] *interior view of conning tower. Present are the* EXECUTIVE OFFICER *at the periscope, the* QUARTERMASTER, *working the periscope for him, the* HELMSMAN *and, off to the starboard side, the* SONARMAN. *The* EXECUTIVE OFFICER, LT. FLOYD HUDSON, *is in his late twenties, goodlooking, tight-lipped, serious to the point of being disagreeable. He is walking the periscope around.*[3]]

HUDSON (*turning from the periscope and addressing the* QUARTERMASTER). Down periscope, Williams.

WILLIAMS. Aye, aye, sir.

[HUDSON *goes to the squawk box*[4] *near the wheel. Close shot of* HUDSON.]

HUDSON (*into the squawk box*). Lt. Hudson in the conning tower. Lt. Hudson in the conning tower. Are you listening, Skipper?

VOICE OF SKIPPER (*on squawk box*). Go ahead, Hudson.

HUDSON. Still all clear. Nothing in sight. And it's all clear from the sonarman, too.

VOICE OF SKIPPER. Very well. Come up for a look every twenty minutes. And don't bother reporting again until you sight something.

HUDSON. Aye, aye, sir. (*Pause.*) Ensign Riggs. Ensign Riggs, run at 90 feet until 1350 and then come back to periscope depth.[5]

[*Cut to*[6] *control room, below the conning tower. Present are the diving officer, young, sandy-haired* ENSIGN RIGGS; *the two planesmen, who operate the wheels that affect the angle and depth and control of the boat; men on the trim and air manifolds*[7]; *a chief of the watch*[8]; *and stand-by men and messengers.*]

RIGGS (*getting his order from the squawk box*). Aye, aye, Hudson.

[*He turns to check the enormous depth-control gauge and addresses the planesmen.*]

RIGGS. Five-degree down angle. Level off at 90.

[*One planesman nods and the giant wheel begins to turn. The depth-gauge needle drops. Cut back to conning tower.*]

WILLIAMS (*standing near and addressing the youthful* HELMSMAN). Man, this is one night I wouldn't mind a little shore duty. Christmas Eve in Pearl.[9] (*Sighs.*) Oughta be quite a brawl.

[LT. HUDSON, *behind him, overhears.*]

HUDSON. They didn't send us here to go to Christmas parties, Williams; they sent us to——

WILLIAMS (*rather tolerantly, with an old, wrinkled smile*). I know, I know, Lieutenant. If we can spot the enemy troopships and get a report back on their course, the islands fall into our hands like ripe apples. But Christmas Eve—a guy can dream, can't he?

HUDSON (*sharply, humorlessly*). Not when he's on watch. We can't slack off up here. We're out here to find them. They must be somewhere.

WILLIAMS (*dead-pan*). I'm sure they are, sir.

[*New camera angle:* HUDSON *turns to consult with* SONARMAN *in the background. In the foreground are* WILLIAMS *and the* HELMSMAN.]

---

1. *Fade in,* bring slowly into sight.
2. *Dissolve to,* change picture gradually.
3. *walking the periscope around,* making a complete turn of the periscope to search for enemy ships or airplanes.
4. *squawk box,* intercommunication system of ship.
5. *run at 90 feet . . . periscope depth,* keep the submarine 90 feet below the surface until 1:50 P.M. and then come up to the depth at which the periscope can be used for observation. Naval time is reckoned from midnight through for twenty-four hours; thus 1350 is 1:50 P.M.
6. *Cut to,* change picture to view of.
7. *the trim and air manifolds.* The trim manifold shifts water from some tanks to others to keep the boat level; the air manifold blows water from tanks into the sea to level the boat when surfacing.
8. *chief of the watch,* man responsible for the men on duty during a four-hour period.
9. *Pearl,* Pearl Harbor, the United States naval base in the Hawaiian Islands.

HELMSMAN (in a mumble). Pretty serious fella—that new Exec.

WILLIAMS. Aw, he's just a little Academy-happy.[10] The Old Man[11] will straighten him out.

[Fade to corridor leading to galley, etc. The "Old Man" appears. He is in his early thirties, not as good-looking in a conventional way as the EXECUTIVE OFFICER. Also in contrast to LT. HUDSON, he is relaxed, and underlying his control of every situation there is a current of good humor. He looks into the galley. SWEDE, the cook, big and easygoing, turns around with a wide grin. He looks much too rough to be an expert on fancy pastry; but just the same, he is. He works in shorts and he is bare to the waist, exhibiting some fancy tattooing.]

SWEDE (respectfully, but familiarly). Cap'n.

MILLER. What've you got tonight, Swede?

SWEDE. Well, seein' it's Christmas, I thought I'd break out some steaks.

MILLER. And a cake?

SWEDE. Wait'll you see it. It's gonna have red and green lights that pop up and spell Merry Christmas.

MILLER (grinning). Good boy. You know what they say on a sub, Swede. Good chow is the skipper's secret weapon. What else is there to do on a pigboat but hunt and hide—and sleep and eat?

SWEDE. You can say that again, Cap'n. This is gonna be a rum cake that'll make 'em forget all about home cooking.

MILLER (suddenly more serious). I doubt that, Swede—even though you are the best cook I ever had aboard. (Picking up something to munch on.) You know, when you get to be as old as I am, you learn something—to pick your cooks even more carefully than your gunnery officers.

[During the above conversation SWEDE is not idle. He is kneading dough, checking his oven, etc. Now he takes some fried potatoes off the griddle.]

SWEDE. Thanks, Cap'n. But if I had a little more room, I could really show you something.

MILLER (picking up a potato slice). That's how we all feel. But on a pigboat, you make do. Good luck with the cake, Swede. You better plan to serve it pretty early. I doubt if we'll have much time for celebration after sundown.

SWEDE. Aye, aye, sir.

[COM. MILLER goes on down the corridor toward the bow. SWEDE grins, picks up a plate of French fries, and turns toward the dinette next door. Cut to dinette. SWEDE enters, sets the plate down.]

SWEDE. Free sample, fellers. Wrap your molars around these.

[He exits. Half a dozen men are crowded into this dinette. A couple of petty officers are playing acey-deucy; another, a first-class gunner's mate[12]—squat, husky, tough-looking veteran submariner O'BRIEN—is kibitzing. FANELLI, a dark-haired young seaman, is trying to read a pocketbook while an apprentice seaman, TOMMY FORD, who hardly looks old enough to be away from home, is trying, in the midst of all this relaxed confusion, to write a letter.]

FIRST ACEY-DEUCY PLAYER. Boy, I'll bet that girl of yours will be pining for you tonight——

SECOND ACEY-DEUCY PLAYER. Come on, play your cards. You haven't even got a girl.

FIRST PLAYER (winking to the others).

---

10. *Academy-happy.* Williams means that Hudson, a recent graduate of the Naval Academy at Annapolis, is overproud of his training and commission as an officer in the regular Navy.
11. *The Old Man,* the commander of the ship.
12. *first-class gunner's mate,* a seaman having charge of munitions.

Why should I? I c'n always take yours.

FANELLI. All right, knock it off, you guys. I'm trying to read.

O'BRIEN (in a false soprano). I'm trying to read.

[Everyone except the letter writer laughs.]

FANELLI (putting the book down). Christmas. At least on a CV[13] they'd have a tree . . . maybe a regular party with a band . . . and look at us . . . the only way we know it's Christmas is by short wave.

[Camera centers on TOMMY FORD trying to write his letter. As he writes, he looks off meditatively, not hearing the adlib cracks, his mind thousands of miles away. While he goes on writing, we peek at his letter in an insert.]

Dear Mom and Pop. Sure seems funny to be away from you for the first time on Christmas Eve. . . .

[The pen pauses.]

SECOND ACEY-DEUCY PLAYER. A year ago I was home-sweet-home, eating hot mince pie and then my girl came in and gave me this watch and when I turned it over it said——

EVERYONE (except TOMMY who continues to write). To my dearest from his Bibsey.

SECOND ACEY-DEUCY PLAYER (disgusted). Aw, nothing's sacred around you guys.

O'BRIEN. That home-baked hot mince pie and a good ten-cent cigar after the turkey and your arm around the old lady's waist. (Sighs.) Last Christmas I got so bloomin' sentimental about it I went down and got this little art job.

[He rolls up his sleeve to show his powerful forearm. Close-up of tattoo on forearm showing "Mike" and "Kate" in a Christmas wreath. As he flexes his muscle, their heads go back and forth as in a kiss. Camera cuts back to group laughing.]

ADLIB. What a man! (Etc.)

[Close-up of TOMMY ignoring the banter. Insert of letter.]

Tonight I can just see the tree by the fireplace, and the kids and Mary Lou. . . .

O'BRIEN (out of camera range). You had him, if you'da rolled a six.

SECOND ACEY-DEUCY PLAYER (out of camera range). I know what they keep you around for, Obie—in case they run out of high-pressure air they've always got you.

O'BRIEN (out of camera range, flaring up). Listen, Jackson, I was wearin' Dolphins[14] when you——

[In a wider camera angle TOMMY FORD looks up, still oblivious of the group around him. The memory his words evoke makes it difficult for him to go on.]

FANELLI (looking up from his book again). Slow it down to two knots, you guys. You're racing your motors.

[TOMMY tries to go on writing, then stops as his hand goes to his right side; a small sound of pain escapes him. The others look up.]

O'BRIEN (sympathetically). Whatsa matter, Tommy?

TOMMY. I dunno. I had a gut ache all night. Feels like a knife in there.

FIRST ACEY-DEUCY PLAYER. It's those biscuits we had last night. I tell ya that Swede is trying to poison us. It's sabotage, that's what it is.

O'BRIEN. Why don't you see the quack[15]; let him put you on the binnacle list.[16]

TOMMY (talking with effort but trying

---

13. **CV,** aircraft carrier.
14. **Dolphins,** insignia worn by officers and enlisted men on a submarine. A man wins his Dolphin only after finishing school and qualifying—or demonstrating that he knows the complete operation of the boat—on his first submarine.
15. **the quack,** a joking reference to the pharmacist's mate.
16. **binnacle list,** sick list, so called because it is posted near the binnacle, a case containing a ship's compass and a lamp for night use.

to *minimize the pain).* Aw, I guess I'll be all right. Maybe I did wolf too many of those biscuits down last night.

SECOND ACEY-DEUCY PLAYER. Whatta ya wanna bet the Swede worked in a cement factory before he got this job?

[TOMMY *rubs his right side, obviously in distress, yet trying not to make too much of it.*]

O'BRIEN. No kidding, boy, I'd do something about that.

TOMMY. I did. I took some tablets the Chief[17] gave me this morning.

FIRST ACEY-DUECY PLAYER. Oh, great. Just because the Chief knows how to doctor a Diesel,[18] he thinks he's a great medical man.

SECOND ACEY-DEUCY PLAYER. Well, he can't kill you any quicker than the quack—that's for sure.

[*A* MESSENGER *enters.*]

MESSENGER. Fanelli, Ford, O'Brien —five minutes and you're on watch, fellows.

[*The* MESSENGER *exits. The three he alerted rise and start toward the door.*]

FANELLI. Back to the salt mines, Tommy.

TOMMY *(trying to grin).* Right, Joe.

[O'BRIEN, *the veteran submariner, gunner's mate first-class, older than the others, puts his hand on* TOMMY'S *shoulder.*]

O'BRIEN. That's a tough job on the planes,[19] kid. I wouldn't stand watch if I looked the way you do.

TOMMY. Aw, if I was back at the base I guess I'd see the doc. But out here, with something liable to happen any second—well, I c'n take it for four hours, and then I'll hit the sack.

O'BRIEN *(easily).* Know what I always say, lad? "Do what you're man enough to do."

[*Cut to control room. In the background we can see* TOMMY *and* FA-

NELLI *relieving the planesmen. In the foreground are* COM. MILLER, ENSIGN RIGGS, *and* LT. DAVISON, *a hulking, affable young Southerner.*]

MILLER. I'll be in the wardroom if you need me for anything, Riggs.

RIGGS. Yes, sir.

MILLER *(to* DAVISON*).* Come on, Jeff. I'll give you another chess lesson.

DAVISON. Chess? When we're practically up on the enemy beach?

MILLER *(smiling).* That's the time for chess.

[*They start off toward the forward compartments. As they do so, they pass* PHARMACIST'S MATE JIMMY BRUCE, *on his way aft.* MILLER *says, "Jimmy," and gives him an offhand salute, a habitual gesture.* JIMMY *grins, mumbles a respectful "Cap'n," and we follow him as he continues on toward the rear compartments. Cut back to dinette as* JIMMY BRUCE *enters. He is a blond, wiry kid from Arkansas, about twenty-two years old. He has unruly hair and is cocky in an unobjectionable way, quick to grin. As soon as they see him, the* ACEY-DEUCY PLAYERS *set up a cross fire of banter that is apparently a stylized bit of by-play on the sub.*]

FIRST ACEY-DEUCY PLAYER. Hi ya, ducky.

BRUCE. Waddya mean, ducky?

FIRST ACEY-DEUCY PLAYER. The quack, quack, quack. *(They laugh.)*

SECOND ACEY-DEUCY PLAYER. How's everything back in Ar-*kansas?*

BRUCE. It's not Ar-*kansas,* it's—*(then realizing it is a rib)*—aw, why don't you guys get a new joke?

[*He sits down and pulls out a comic book.*]

FIRST ACEY-DEUCY PLAYER. Hey,

---

17. *the Chief,* the chief petty officer, the highest rating among enlisted men.
18. *Diesel* (dē′zəl or dē′səl), the oil-burning engine used to run the submarine.
19. *the planes,* the wheels that affect the angle, depth, and control of the submarine. Tommy is to serve as planesman for this watch.

quack, I got a hangnail that's painin' me somethin' awful.

SECOND ACEY-DEUCY PLAYER. Put 'im on the binnacle list so you c'n gold-brick[20] together.

BRUCE *(jovially)*. Keep on callin' me quack and I'll cut that hangnail off — right up to here. *(He indicates the player's neck.)*

SECOND ACEY-DEUCY PLAYER. No kiddin', Brucie, how come you rate this soft job? The only noncombatant on the whole darn boat. Nothin' to do but sit around readin' comics.

BRUCE. Oh, sure. All I've got to do is stand regular watches like the rest of you, and doctor up you goof-offs on the side.

FIRST ACEY-DEUCY PLAYER. Listen to the boy. He never had it so good.

BRUCE *(grinning)*. Sure, it's a breeze — as long as everyone stays in one piece around here.

[He settles down comfortably with his comic book; the ACEY-DEUCY PLAYERS chatter up a little adlib on their game. Dissolve to periscope cutting through the rough sea. Then dissolve to conning tower. EXECUTIVE OFFICER HUDSON appears up the ladder from the control room, takes over the periscope lookout from the Chief, and peers intently at the sea and the sky. Cut to interior of control room. TOMMY on the bow plane is perspiring from the effort to overcome his pain.]

RIGGS. Mind your bubble,[21] Ford. Hold her to a half-degree down angle.

TOMMY *(through his teeth)*. Aye, aye, sir.

[Shot of depth indicator. It is fluctuating, showing that the boat is in danger of broaching.[22] Close shot of RIGGS.]

RIGGS *(observing the indicator)*. Flood auxiliary from sea — one thousand pounds.

[Close shot of O'BRIEN at trim manifold. He is opening the valve, and watching the gauge.]

YOUNG PETTY OFFICER. Auxiliaries are flooding, sir.

[Close shot of air manifold.]

O'BRIEN. One thousand pounds flooded in auxiliary. Trim manifold secure.

[Wider angle shot of control room angled toward planes. ENSIGN RIGGS comes up and looks over TOMMY'S shoulder critically.]

RIGGS. You've got a two-degree down angle. Come on, Ford, stay awake.

[TOMMY wipes the sweat from his forehead and, operating the plane automatically, adjusts the angle of the boat. Cut to wardroom. COM. MILLER has sat down to his game of chess with LT. DAVISON. To one side are charts which MILLER has been working on.]

DAVISON *(in his slow drawl)*. Chess. Sure never thought I'd learn to play a brainy game like chess.

MILLER *(with a slight smile, as he takes two of DAVISON'S pawns with his knight)*. What makes you think you've learned, Jeff?

DAVISON. Sure beats me how you figured that out, Skipper. I thought I had you trapped.

MILLER *(studying the board)*. If you hope to skipper one of these boats some day, Jeff, this game can give you some pointers. A sub is like this king. Everything on the board is hunting you. And you can't use it to strike without fatally exposing yourself. *(He makes another move on the board and DAVISON winces.)* To stay alive, you always have to be at least two or three jumps ahead.

[Over the squawk box in the corner we hear:]

SQUAWK BOX. Wardroom, this is the conning tower, Lt. Hudson. Is the Captain there?

---

20. **goldbrick,** get out of work.
21. **bubble.** Above each plane is an instrument called a level; it is filled with a fluid in which a bubble rides. When the submarine is level, the bubble is dead center. It moves to indicate whether the boat is pointing up or down.
22. **broaching,** coming to the surface.

MILLER (operating the squawk box). What's the story, Floyd?

SQUAWK BOX. We've sighted smoke, sir. Maybe fifteen miles. Bearing 0–2–7.[23]

MILLER. Very well.

[He rises and pushes the chessboard back, moving as quickly as possible in the cramped quarters.]

DAVISON (over the squawk box). Okay, Hudson. The Skipper's on his way up.

[Cut to conning tower. HUDSON is peering through the periscope again. The rough sea makes it difficult to maintain depth control.]

WILLIAMS (over the squawk box). Mr. Hudson wants you to run at 55 feet.

SQUAWK BOX (RIGGS' voice). I need more speed.

[HUDSON goes to the squawk box.]

HUDSON. All right. But slow her down as soon as you can maintain trim at one-third speed.

SQUAWK BOX. Aye, aye, sir.

HUDSON. Down periscope.

[QUARTERMASTER WILLIAMS begins to comply. Cut to control room, ENSIGN RIGGS at the squawk box.]

RIGGS. All ahead two-thirds.

[Cut to engine room: the engineman responds. Dissolve to exterior of submarine moving through water. Cut to conning tower as COM. MILLER appears up the ladder from the control room.]

HUDSON. I think I have a destroyer bearing 0–3–5. And it looks like another one off our port bow. Hull down.[24]

MILLER. Very well. Let me have a look as soon as we get back to one-third.

[After a pause, we hear over the squawk box:]

RIGGS' VOICE. I can hold her at 55.

MILLER. Very well. Up periscope.

[WILLIAMS raises the periscope. Meanwhile MILLER turns to the SONARMAN.]

MILLER. Do you have the target bearing 0–3–5?

SONARMAN. Still all clear for me, sir.

MILLER. Keep searching in that quadrant. Let me know as soon as you pick them up. (He turns and peers intently into the periscope. After a moment's study he speaks with quiet satisfaction.) That looks like our little friends, all right. (Studies them further.) We'll continue to close and track them at periscope depth until sundown. (To QUARTERMASTER WILLIAMS.) What time is it, Williams?

WILLIAMS. 1317 hours, sir.

MILLER. Very well. Keep tracking their course and speed and at 1330 we'll surface to get off our report.

HUDSON. Aye, aye, sir. (After a pause.) Sure wish we could take a crack at them now, Captain.

MILLER. So do I. But if our report brings our striking force[25] over in time to intercept them, that will more than make up for having to wait. (MILLER returns to the periscope.) Let's be very careful on these observations. We don't want some zoomy[26] to pick us up before we can accomplish this mission.

[The boat pitches upward, almost throwing them off balance.]

HUDSON (on squawk box). What's the matter down there? Can't you hold her at 55?

[Cut to control room. ENSIGN RIGGS checks the depth gauge, which records 48, and then turns on TOMMY FORD who has been fighting collapse.]

RIGGS (angrily). Come on, Ford. Watch that bubble.

FORD (weakly). Aye . . . aye, sir.

---

23. **Bearing 0–2–7.** Numbers are used to indicate the angle from which a ship is approaching.
24. **Hull down,** a submariner's expression meaning "Only the mast and stacks are visible; the hull is invisible."
25. **our striking force,** nearby surface vessels to attack the enemy destroyers.
26. **zoomy,** enemy aircraft.

RIGGS. What's the matter with you today?

FORD. Sir, I'm not feeling well . . . there's something wrong. I . . .

RIGGS. Why didn't you say something right away so I could get you relieved?

FORD. Well, I—I thought I'd be all right, and . . . (*He clutches his side.*)

RIGGS (*turning to a stand-by planesman*). Goodman, relieve the stern planes. Depth 55. One-degree down angle. And don't let the waves suck you up.

[SEAMAN GOODMAN *moves in to take* FORD'S *place. As* FORD *rises he is suddenly seized with excruciating pain and slumps to the deck.* ENSIGN RIGGS *and a stand-by messenger kneel beside him.* ENSIGN RIGGS *looks up at the chief of the watch.*]

RIGGS. Get Bruce. Have him report here right away.

[TOMMY, *unconscious, writhes and groans.* RIGGS *rises and addresses the messenger and another stand-by.*]

RIGGS. Carry him in to my bunk.

[RIGGS *turns back to check the depth gauge. Cut to dinette.* JIMMY BRUCE *is reading his comic book. The acey-deucy game goes on.*]

SQUAWK BOX. Pharmacist's Mate Bruce. Pharmacist's Mate Bruce. Report to control room at once.

BRUCE (*pushing his comic book away reluctantly and rising*). Yeah, I got a cinch. All I have to do is sit down and one of you clumsy jokers is sure to bump his head on a hatchway. (*He folds his comic book into his pocket.*) I've been trying to finish "Li'l Abner" for three days!

FIRST ACEY-DEUCY PLAYER (*as* BRUCE *exits*). Don't worry, boy, you got lots of time. At the rate we're going, we'll still be out here next Christmas.

SECOND ACEY-DEUCY PLAYER (*calling after* BRUCE *in a mimicking voice*). Calling Dr. Kildare.[27] Calling Dr. Kildare. Emergency case of hiccoughs in the control room.

[*The two men are laughing together at their wit as* JIMMY BRUCE *hurries out. Cut to Chief's room.* JIMMY BRUCE *enters.* TOMMY *is lying on the bunk, conscious but in terrible pain.*]

BRUCE. Hello, Tommy. Let's have a look at you. (*He kneels at the bunk, feels* TOMMY'S *head and sticks a thermometer in his mouth.* TOMMY *screws his face up against the pain.* BRUCE *takes a hypodermic needle from his kit.*) This'll make you ride a little more comfortable. (*He shoots the morphine. Then he sits on the edge of the bunk and feels* TOMMY'S *pulse. There is a tense silence. The water can be heard sloshing against the boat's sides.* TOMMY *rolls his head as another spasm of pain seizes him.* JIMMY *seems worried by the pulse.*)

BRUCE. How long has this been going on? (TOMMY *tries to answer with the thermometer in his mouth.*) Hold it a second. I c'n never remember not to ask questions when I got that thing in their mouths. (*He removes the thermometer.*)

TOMMY (*speaking with great effort*). Since . . . yesterday.

[JIMMY *studies the thermometer.*]

BRUCE. Why didn't you tell me right away?

TOMMY. I . . . I thought . . .

BRUCE. I'm the closest thing to a doctor they got on board, chum. Sometimes you fellas seem to forget that. (*Looks at the thermometer.*) A hundred an'——(*He shakes his head.*)

[JIMMY *returns to the bunk and presses his hand on* TOMMY'S *abdomen.*]

BRUCE. Hurt there?

---

27. **Dr. Kildare,** an imaginary doctor, made famous by fiction, movies, and, more recently, by television.

[TOMMY *shakes his head.* JIMMY *moves his hand and presses again.*]

BRUCE. There?

[TOMMY *shakes his head.* JIMMY *now presses the right lower abdomen.* TOMMY *gives a tense cry of pain.* JIMMY *maintains the pressure . . . and then suddenly releases it. The reaction on* TOMMY *is even greater than it was before.*]

BRUCE. Mmmmmm-hmmmm. Mmmm-hmmmm. *(Then suddenly.)* Take it easy a minute, kid. I better see the Skipper. *(He exits quickly.)*

[*Cut to control room.* COM. MILLER *is just coming down the ladder from the conning tower when* JIMMY BRUCE *appears.*]

BRUCE. Captain, c'n I talk to you a minute?

MILLER. Sure thing, son.

BRUCE. I just examined Tommy — Seaman Apprentice Ford. Looks to me like appendicitis — maybe acute.

MILLER. Any chance of holding out until we get back to port?

BRUCE. I don't see how, sir.

MILLER. Then what do you suggest, Jimmy?

BRUCE. Well, everything points to an immediate operation — if we had a surgeon on board.

MILLER. We never carry any *ifs* aboard these boats. *(Suddenly.)* Don't suppose you were ever called upon to perform an appendectomy?

BRUCE *(taken aback).* Are you kidding? *(Catching himself.)* I mean . . . no, sir. At Pearl, before I won my Dolphins, all the training I had was as a cardiographer.[28]

MILLER. Ever seen this operation performed?

BRUCE. Well, I . . . I wheeled a fellow in for one once. That's about as close as I ever came.

MILLER. Think you can do it?

BRUCE. I . . . I . . . well, I'd hate to say "yes" for sure and then foul it up.

MILLER. Jimmy, there's nothing in the book says a pharmacist's mate has to perform any duty for which he hasn't been specifically trained. So I'm not going to order you to do this. I'm going to ask you to think it over for five minutes. *(Close on* BRUCE, *listening, as* MILLER *continues.)* If you say "yes" we'll give you all the coöperation possible. If you say "no," we'll give up our mission and see if we can't make it back to the tender[29] before —

BRUCE. Yes, sir, I understand.

[*Medium shot, holding the two.* JIMMY *starts to turn away, obviously troubled.*]

MILLER. And Jimmy . . .

BRUCE *(turning around).* Yes, sir.

MILLER. Before we left the States, I had the opportunity of picking out every one of you men individually. For every one of you aboard there are at least ten others — almost as good. I didn't pick you for my pharmacist's mate because you happened to have a high rating as a technician — but because you impressed me as the kind of a man who could come through in emergencies.

[COM. MILLER'S *words seem to increase* JIMMY'S *confidence.*]

BRUCE. Yes, sir.

[COM. MILLER *turns and starts toward the ladder, passing* ENSIGN RIGGS.]

MILLER. How's she behaving, Bill?

RIGGS. This dirty weather's making her tough to handle. We nearly broached there a minute ago. *(He keeps his eye on the depth gauge while he is talking. Now, noticing that it is pointing a little too high, he*

---

28. cardiographer (kär′di og′rə fər), a technician who operates a machine which registers the movements of the heart and interprets the results.

29. tender, submarine tender, a boat having aboard all supplies to replenish fuel, food, etc.

acts promptly.) Plane her down another five feet. . . .

[COM. MILLER *has started up to the conning tower. Cut to conning tower. As* MILLER *appears,* LT. HUDSON *is studying the chart.*]

HUDSON. Two more destroyers approximately twelve miles off the bow. Looks like the screen for the main force all right!

MILLER. That's fine. I—hope we don't have to lose 'em.

HUDSON. Lose 'em? Why should we if we keep closing in?

MILLER. That's the hitch. One of our seamen—young Ford—has appendicitis. Needs an operation pronto, according to Bruce. If he thinks he can do it, and I agree to let him go ahead, we'd have to get down for at least an hour.

HUDSON. An hour! They'll be out of sight by then. We may never pick up their trail again.

MILLER. I know. I know, Floyd. I suppose you're right . . . from a military standpoint. *(Close shot of the two men, favoring* MILLER.*)* But, Floyd, one of these days you'll have your own command. Then you'll know a little more than you do now about the human side of this job. What makes these boats run? It's not the Diesels—they can always be replaced. It's the men—they aren't interchangeable. Not even young apprentice seamen like Tommy Ford.

[*Close-up* MILLER.]

MILLER. It didn't take just months and months to train them and work them in as a team. It took years—all their lives—to develop into the kind of men who can stand the gaff of living on top of each other for fifty days at a time under constant danger without getting on each other's nerves.

[*Medium shot favoring* MILLER.]

MILLER. No, Floyd, the life—even an outside chance to save the life—of one of my men still means more to me than the course and disposition of the whole enemy fleet.

HUDSON. In an hour or two we could crack the secret of a major enemy movement—

MILLER. In another hour or two a nice kid from Chautauqua, Kansas, may be dead because his Skipper was afraid to take a chance.

HUDSON. But this kid, Bruce, if you don't mind my saying so, still seems pretty wet behind the ears. I can't see him performing any miracles.

MILLER. Floyd, I've seen my share of miracles aboard these boats. I've seen the big brave fellows cave in and I've seen panicky, half-grown kids suddenly find out they're men. Keep tracking 'em to the last possible moment. I'll send word up as soon as I decide.

[*He starts down the ladder. Quick dissolve to corridor outside the Chief's room. As* COM. MILLER *appears, coming forward from the control room,* JIMMY BRUCE *enters the corridor from the Chief's room, where the body of* TOMMY FORD *can be seen in the background.*]

MILLER. What's the story, Jimmy?

BRUCE. I'll take a crack at it.

MILLER. Good boy. Only now, for the record, I'm ordering you to do it. So, just in case we're unlucky and a bunch of second-guessing, top-brass medics[30] decide we could've waited, at a court martial three stripes on your arm look better than the crow.[31] *(*MILLER *forces a grin.)* Only I wouldn't have put this up to you if I wasn't dead sure you had it in you.

---

30. *top-brass medics,* doctors who hold high officer rank.
31. *at a court-martial . . . the crow,* if the matter comes before a Navy court, my three stripes as a lieutenant commander will carry more weight than your insignia as an enlisted man (the crow).

BRUCE (a little shaky). Thanks, Skipper. I just wish I was as sure as you are.

MILLER (placing his hand on JIMMY'S shoulder). Better go in and see your patient. Put it up to him the same way I did you. This is a volunteer service. I want everybody to go in with his eyes open.

BRUCE (his respect for the Skipper is obvious despite his conventional response). Aye, aye, sir.

[He turns toward the Chief's room. Cut to Chief's room. As BRUCE enters, TOMMY looks up and forces a weak grin.]

BRUCE. Tommy, there's no sense giving you a snow job.[32] I'm gonna be level with you.

TOMMY. Okay, Jim.

BRUCE. If I just sit here picking my teeth and feeding you pills, I think you've had it.[33]

TOMMY (in a whisper). Yeah, I know.

BRUCE. So the Skipper's giving me the green light to operate. It's a heck of a thing to tell you, but somehow I feel I've gotta say it — I'm not sure I know how. There's a chance that — (He looks at TOMMY, almost begging.) Well, it's plenty rugged either way. But I've gotta know if you think I should.

TOMMY. Whatever you say, Doc.

[JIMMY straightens up.]

BRUCE. That's the first time anybody on this boat ever called me anything but quack. (He rises.) Rest easy, kid. It's a tough point but we're gonna get lucky and make it.

[TOMMY, wincing, but forcing back any sound, makes a feeble but definite circle of approval with his thumb and forefinger. Dissolve to control room. COM. MILLER talking into the general address system:]

MILLER. Attention, all hands. We've got an emergency on our hands that calls for teamwork, and I want you all to know exactly what we're up against. We're going deeper so that Pharmacist's Mate Bruce can perform an appendectomy on Apprentice Seaman Ford.

[Wider angle of room as all listen intently.]

MILLER. I don't have to tell you what a ticklish job this is going to be. We'll have to keep her awful steady down there. Just a little better trim than we ever had before.

[Quick flashes of men in torpedo room, engine room, pump room, etc., listening.]

MILLER. Every one of you, wherever you're standing watch — the planesmen, you on the manifolds, you back there in the engine rooms — is going to be part of this thing. We've been in tough spots before and we've come through because each one of you knew that. So I've got a hunch you're all going to deliver this Christmas Eve for Tommy Ford and Jimmy Bruce. That is all. (MILLER turns to ENSIGN RIGGS.) Better check the pressure we've got in the boat. We'll need all the good air we can get because that ether's going to smell things up. Take her to a hundred feet. (He turns away as RIGGS gives him an "Aye, aye, sir.")

[Exterior of submarine as it noses down into the sea. Dissolve to the control room, discovering JIMMY BRUCE, nervous but controlled; COM. MILLER; LT. HUDSON; LT. DAVISON. At the planes are FANELLI and GOODMAN. Keeping an eye on the bubble, the depth gauge, the Christmas tree[34] etc., is the diving officer, ENSIGN RIGGS. At one of the manifolds is the chunky, tattooed veteran O'BRIEN.]

---

32. *giving you a snow job,* not telling you the truth.
33. *you've had it,* it's the end for you.
34. *the Christmas tree,* the board with red and green lights that controls the hydraulic system for the hull openings.

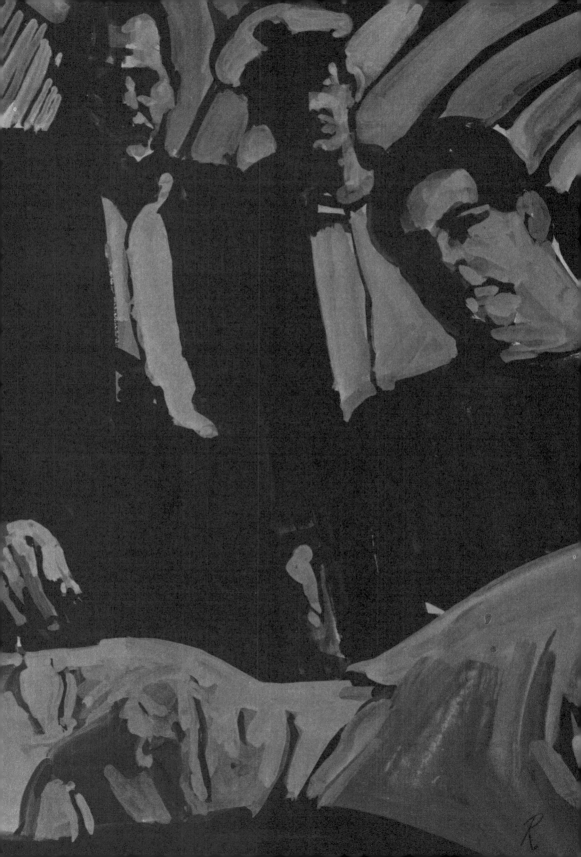

MILLER. Now, Jimmy, there's nothing in the book to cover this kind of deal. So we're going to stow rank and Navy regs.[35] From this point until the end of the operation, you're the boss. You pick your staff from any level you want—you tell us where you want us and what you want us to do.

[JIMMY BRUCE *still seems uncertain about his authority. During this period he should seem to be groping his way toward the confidence and strength he will eventually assert.*]

BRUCE. Aye, aye, sir. Can we have Tommy moved to the wardroom? See that he's made as comfortable as possible. And tell him I'll be with him as soon as I get everything squared away.

MILLER (*to* DAVISON). Get a detail and take care of that, Jeff.

BRUCE. Now for my chief assistant . . . (*He looks around.*) I don't want you to think I'm giving you the business, Skipper, but I think I'd pick you even if you were an apprentice striker.[36]

MILLER. Thanks, Jimmy. I wanted to be in on every step of this thing. His life's in your hands, but I want there to be no doubt about the responsibility's being mine.

BRUCE. Now, I'm not sure exactly where to use him yet, but I'd like to have the Swede. He's one of those fellows who c'n do a little bit of everything, and also he's the luckiest gambler on the boat.

HUDSON. Sir, if I can butt in, don't you think it's a little more proper if all those in attendance were officers? After all——

MILLER (*rather sharply*). Hudson, a good officer knows when to pull rank, and when to stow it. And, I don't want to disillusion you, but the best men in the Navy aren't always the ones with the gold on their sleeves. Now send a messenger for Swede Engstrum.

HUDSON (*silenced but obviously not convinced*). Yes, sir.

BRUCE. Now for my nurse. (*Looks around again.*) Lemme see, I'd like to have O'Brien.

[COM. MILLER *crosses to* RIGGS.]

MILLER. Have a stand-by take over the trim manifold. We want to use O'Brien.

RIGGS. Aye, aye, sir.

[*He goes to* O'BRIEN, *taps him on the shoulder and points to the group around* BRUCE. O'BRIEN—*balding, bare-chested, and perspiring—joins the group.*]

BRUCE. Obie, you're going to be a nurse.

O'BRIEN. A nurse!

BRUCE. Yeah. I won't say you're the prettiest nurse I ever saw— (O'BRIEN'S *face wrinkles into a hard, likable grin*)—but you're another guy I'd like to have around if things really get tough.

O'BRIEN (*not at all maliciously*). Okay, kid. If you c'n be a surgeon, I guess I c'n be a nurse.

BRUCE. Good deal, Pop. Now, let's see—an anesthetist. I want someone who's a real cool customer, and won't lose his head. (*He nods to* LT. HUDSON.) Lt. Hudson, I guess you'll fill the bill. I'll show you what I want when we get in there. Meanwhile, go check on the ether supply.

[LT. HUDSON *hesitates, resenting being ordered around by a mere pharmacist's mate.*]

BRUCE. Then I'd like Leroy Johnson——

HUDSON (*stopping just as he's turning away*). Johnson—the mess boy?

BRUCE. I know, Lieutenant, but his

---

35. *we're going to stow rank and Navy regs,* we're going to disregard a man's rank and Navy regulations governing relationships between ranks.
36. *an apprentice striker,* a sailor learning new and specific duties to get a petty officer's rating.

old man happens to be a doctor, and I figure . . .

MILLER (*severely*). That's all right, Jimmy. A surgeon doesn't need to know the rank or pedigree of his assistants. You're not handing out invitations to the Officers' Ball. You're picking *men*.

HUDSON (*rebuked again, leaving*). I'll check on that ether, Skipper.

BRUCE. Now lessee—we'll need a recorder—someone to make sure that everything that goes in, comes out.

[*At this point* LT. DAVISON *has returned.* SWEDE *enters from left.*]

BRUCE. I guess that'll be your job, Mr. Davison.

DAVISON. Aye, aye, Doc.

BRUCE. I've got a list of all the stuff we're going to need and, brother, it's rough. No ether cone, no antiseptic powder, no scalpel—in fact, no surgical instruments of any kind. (*Shakes his head.*) They say one way to tell a submariner is the way he c'n open a bottle of beer with a fifty-cent piece. That's what we all gotta do now—get our noggins workin' on how t' make do.

SWEDE. I got some fine tea strainers in the galley. How about tryin' one of them for an ether cone?

BRUCE. I think ya got something there, Swede. Get on it. (*As* SWEDE *starts off.*) Oh, and while you're there, we're gonna need something for muscular retractors—that's to hold the wound open after I make the incision. I think maybe we c'n use some of your tablespoons, if we double 'em all the way back.

SWEDE (*heading back toward the control room*). Back in a flash, Doc.

BRUCE. Antiseptic powder. Well, why don't we just grind up some sulfanilamide tablets? Leroy, find as many as you can in the medicine chest and powderize 'em for me.

LEROY. Right, Jimmy. (*He starts off.*)

BRUCE. Then we'll need something to sterilize the instruments.

O'BRIEN. We could use the alcohol in the torpedoes.

BRUCE. Good deal.

[O'BRIEN *hurries off.*]

BRUCE. Then there's lights. We'll need a lot more'n we got in there. Maybe we can string some floods from the overhead.[37]

DAVISON. I'll get Chief Childs to put a couple of his electricians on that.

BRUCE. Check. Let's see, that takes care of just about everything except—except the scalpel. All I could find was an old scalpel blade without a handle.

MILLER. Could you hold it with a pair of pliers?

BRUCE. Kinda clumsy, Skipper. Wait a minute; I think I've got it—those hemostats we use for pinching blood vessels. Maybe one of the machinists could rig that up for me.

MILLER. Okay, I'll get somebody on it. You better go in and have a look at your patient.

BRUCE. Yes, Commander.

[COM. MILLER *puts his hand on* JIMMY'S *shoulder.*]

MILLER. And remember what I told you, Jimmy. This deal is going to depend on you giving the orders. Until you get it all battened down, you're in command.

BRUCE (*suddenly*). Do you believe in God, sir?

MILLER (*seriously*). I certainly do, Jimmy. And I still believe He watches over all of us on earth.

BRUCE (*literally, with a deep sigh as he turns to enter the wardroom*). Boy, I just hope He doesn't have any trouble getting down here twenty fathoms below the surface.

[*Close shot of* LEROY JOHNSON *pounding tablets to powder. Close shot of*

---

37. **the overhead**, the ceiling.

SWEDE *stretching gauze over a strainer to form a homemade ether cone. Close shot of* O'BRIEN *draining alcohol from a torpedo. Close shot of machinist rigging the scalpel with a hemostat. Close shot of electricians in wardroom rigging overhead lights. Close shot of* COM. MILLER *bending the Monel-metal spoons into retractors. Close shot of* JIMMY *in a corner of the wardroom, studying his handbook with a pencil in his hand. Cut to control room. Angle toward* FANELLI *and depth gauge, which is fluctuating.* RIGGS *enters to* FANELLI.]

RIGGS. Watch that bubble, Fanelli. Hold her to one-half degree.

FANELLI. It's rough holding her against the swells, sir.

RIGGS. I know it. Do the best you can. [*Cut to conning tower. Close on* SO-NARMAN, *listening intently with earphones on. He turns to* QUARTERMAS-TER WILLIAMS.]

SONARMAN. All clear on sound.

[*Interior of wardroom. Close on clock showing time to be five minutes after two. Camera pans down*[38] *to full shot around table. Ready with the ether cans, behind* TOMMY'S *head, is* LT. HUDSON. *Near him is* SWEDE, *who holds the improvised ether cone. At the side of the table facing the camera are* JIMMY BRUCE *and* COM. MILLER. *At the foot of the table is* O'BRIEN, *and sitting near him,* LT. DAVISON, *with medical books open and paper and pencil to record the movements of the operation. All these men wear white reversed pajama coats and their faces are covered by gauze masks, all except their eyes, which express tenseness and anxiety. In the taut silence we can hear, over the sound of the water washing the hull, the ticking of the clock.*

Cut to the pantry. Here LEROY JOHN-SON *is stationed. He is placing the bent-double spoons into a pot of boiling water and is ready to pass them through the small sliding panel that leads directly into the wardroom. Cut to wardroom.*]

BRUCE (*his voice tight in his throat, the tone belying his attempts at confident words and manners*). Well, Tommy, I guess we're all set. In a minute or two we're gonna start feeding you the ether. You're not gonna feel a thing.

TOMMY (*in a hoarse whisper*). Listen, Jimmy, I don't wantcha to think I'm chicken or anything, but just in case, you know, if something goes wrong, I wantcha to go see my folks. Tell 'em . . . Tell 'em . . .

BRUCE (*embarrassed*). Aw, knock it off. You're gonna see your own folks. Pretty lucky guy, prob'ly get a fat sixty-day leave outa this deal.

TOMMY. Okay, Doc. But, just in case . . .

BRUCE. Sure . . . sure. . . . Now quit gabbin'. Think about something cheerful.

TOMMY (*to himself in a whisper*). I'll think about bein' home . . . Christmas Eve . . . Mary Lou . . .

[NOTE: *Through the above the trim of the submarine has been far from perfect. The boat has been pitching, not violently, but enough to be disturbing.* SWEDE, *at* TOMMY'S *head,* O'BRIEN, *at his feet, have been holding the patient in place on the table. Suddenly the submarine lurches upward.* TOMMY *groans.*]

BRUCE (*on edge*). Whatsa matter with those guys? Don't they know what they're doin'?

[COM. MILLER'S *manner, in contrast to* JIMMY'S, *is controlled and quieting.*]

MILLER. Easy, Jimmy. Let me see if I can straighten them out.

[*He exits quickly. Cut to control room. The depth-gauge needle swings between 100 and 95. The planesmen are*

---

38. pans down, gradually moves downward to cover a large area.

working the electrical. ENSIGN RIGGS *hovers over them.* COM. MILLER *enters.*]

MILLER. What's the trouble, Bill?

RIGGS. It's so rough down here that it's hard to maintain depth control. The two best men I've got are having trouble.

MILLER. Okay. Let's ease her down another fifty feet and see if it's any better. We'll never get this job done without perfect depth control.

RIGGS. Aye, aye, sir. We'll do the best we can. *(Slight smile.)* And then we'll try to do even a little better than that.

[COM. MILLER *slaps* RIGGS *on the shoulder and turns back toward the wardroom.* RIGGS *turns to his men to give an order. Exterior of submarine as the boat noses down into a quieter layer. Interior of wardroom as the table becomes level at last. Everyone leaning in slightly toward* TOMMY, *all faces washed out in the glare of the overhanging flood lights.*]

BRUCE *(in a strange, quiet voice).* That's better. Now if they can just hold like that. *(Pause.)* Gloves.

[O'BRIEN *comes forward and holds them for* JIMMY *while he sterilizes his hands in a ready bowl of alcohol. The fingers of the gloves are too long for* JIMMY'S *small hands and the rubber ends are ludicrously limp.*]

O'BRIEN. You look like Mickey Mouse, Doc.

[JIMMY *grins a little through his gauze, then turns back to the table and addresses* SWEDE.]

BRUCE. Okay, Swede. I guess we're ready for your strainer. (SWEDE *starts to lower it over* TOMMY'S *mouth.* JIMMY *turns to* HUDSON.) Now, just like I told you, drop a little . . . easy . . . onto the strainer. (HUDSON *appears to pour the ether too freely.)* I said *easy.* We've only got five pounds. And when you figure all this pressure —

[COM. MILLER *turns to the squawk box.*]

MILLER. See if the pressure's built up again. If so, pump it back to one-tenth.

[*Almost simultaneously,* HUDSON *has turned on* BRUCE.]

HUDSON. Look, Bruce, I'm doing what I —

BRUCE *(with a curt gesture).* Pipe down. Watch him close. And remember — another drop — another — until the eyes begin to dilate. *(To* TOMMY *softly.)* Now relax, Tommy — like you're sacking in[39] after a tough watch. Breathe deep. *(Takes a deep breath with him.)* Attaboy.

[*Close on* TOMMY *breathing deeply, his eyes going vague. Angle on faces peering down at him slowly going out of focus. The ticking of the clock can be heard. Dissolve to control room. The gauge now shows nearly 150 feet.* FANELLI *and* GOODMAN, *the two planesmen, are obviously on edge to keep the boat steady.*]

RIGGS. That's it, fellows. Now, try to hold to a maximum of a half-degree down angle.

[*Dissolve to wardroom.* TOMMY *is now unconscious. The clock on the wall shows twelve minutes after two.* JIMMY *bends over his patient and studies his face. The silence is oppressive.* JIMMY'S *face has begun to shine with perspiration under the lights.*]

BRUCE *(sounding jittery).* Well, I guess it's my move. *(He reaches out his hand.)* Scalpel.

[JOHNSON *removes scalpel from the improvised sterilizer and passes it through the panel to* O'BRIEN; O'BRIEN *takes the scalpel from* JOHNSON *and hands it across to* JIMMY. JIMMY *stares at it almost as if afraid of it. His hesitation is noticeable. He nods at* LT. DAVISON.]

BRUCE. Davison, before I make the

39. *sacking in,* going to bed.

incision, maybe you better check me out again to make sure. Read that page I got turned down.

DAVISON (opening the handbook). "When a hospital corpsman on duty on a ship that has no medical officer is confronted with a case of acute appendicitis, his judgment is put perhaps to its supreme test. . . ."

BRUCE (impatiently). Brother, you c'n say that again! But I mean further down where it's marked.

DAVISON. "In the case of appendectomies, it is the rare pharmacist's mate whose chances of proper diagnosis and successful operation are at all good. . . ."

BRUCE (reacting angrily). Hey, you pinhead, you're in the wrong book—the other big red one—General Surgery.

[DAVISON picks up the other volume, already opened to the right page.]

DAVISON. "The incision begins above a line between the anterior superior iliac spine and the umbilicus, about four centimeters medial to the anterior spine."

[Close on BRUCE straining to understand.]

DAVISON (out of camera range). "It extends downward and inward parallel to the fibers of the external oblique muscle and fascia. . . ."

[Now the sweat is really standing out on JIMMY'S face. He places his little finger on TOMMY'S hip, the thumb on his umbilicus.]

BRUCE (muttering to himself in intense concentration). Downward and inward . . . between the anterior superior iliac. . . .

[Camera pans up and holds on clock ticking industriously. The minute hand moving slowly but at abnormal speed. We hear only JIMMY'S staccato demands:]

BRUCE. A spoon. . . .

DAVISON'S VOICE. One spoon.

BRUCE. Little more ether. . . .

[Camera shoots through panel as JOHNSON'S hand, encased in white glove, passes instruments through to wardroom.]

BRUCE. Those tweezers . . . sponge . . . scalpel . . . all right, quick—another spoon. . . .

[Close on DAVISON recording insertion.]

DAVISON. Spoon two.

BRUCE'S VOICE. Hemostat. . . .

[Cut to control room medium close on FANELLI and GOODMAN.]

FANELLI. Wonder how it's going?

[GOODMAN turns to ENSIGN RIGGS.]

GOODMAN. Any news yet, sir?

RIGGS (shaking his head). He's still hunting around. (Checks gauge and bubble.) Nice work, boys. Hold her right there.

[Back to wardroom. JIMMY'S strained face reflects frustration and the dreadful possibility of failure.]

BRUCE. Gee . . . this . . . oughta be the right place . . . but I . . . can't seem to find it.

[Close on HUDSON.]

HUDSON (to MILLER in undertone). What did I tell you? (His eyes betray his lack of confidence in BRUCE. He looks at the clock.)

MILLER (with a firm warning gesture). Shhh. . . .

[Close on clock showing that twenty minutes have passed. Back to full shot of wardroom.]

BRUCE. Sometimes these things aren't where they oughta be. Guess I'll hafta try the other side of the caecum. (Pause.) Better widen the incision. (He reaches his hand out.) Scalpel.

[COM. MILLER doesn't pass it quite quickly enough for JIMMY. He snaps his fingers impatiently, his nerves in danger of cracking.]

BRUCE. Come on, snap it up. I said the scalpel.

MILLER (*very quietly as he passes the scalpel to* BRUCE). Take it easy, son. You'll get there.

[COM. MILLER'S *manner seems to quiet* JIMMY. *When he addresses* DAVISON *now, he sounds as though he has pulled himself together.*]

BRUCE. Hey, Davison, hold that picture up for me again.

[DAVISON *holds the open book up, right over* TOMMY'S *prostrate figure.* JIMMY *reads from it while he holds the scalpel poised over* TOMMY'S *body, hidden from us by the sheet.*]

BRUCE (*reading slowly*). "To retract the muscle medially, the anterior and posterior sheaths are—" (TOMMY *groans feebly.* JIMMY *looks up at* LT. HUDSON. *Curtly.*) Come on—more ether.

HUDSON (*hesitating*). How long do you think this will take?

BRUCE (*flaring up*). How should I know? Y'think I do 'em every day?

HUDSON. But we have only four pounds left. If it takes you—

BRUCE. I don't want back talk. I want ether.

HUDSON. Back talk? What do you think you're—

MILLER (*breaking in*). Come on, Floyd, leave it up to the doc. Follow instructions.

HUDSON (*sullenly*). Yes, sir. (*He pours more ether onto the strainer* SWEDE *is holding.*)

BRUCE (*to* MILLER). Now, have a spoon ready, and I mean *ready*.

MILLER (*soothingly*). Okay, Doc. Okay.

[*Cut to control room. The men are silently, tensely doing their jobs.* RIGGS *glances at the clock. It shows half an hour has passed. Cut to conning tower. The* HELMSMAN *is sweating it out, too. He turns to check the time. Cut to dinette. The two* ACEY-DEUCY PLAYERS *are also involved, though the game still goes on.*]

FIRST PLAYER. It's taking a long time.

SECOND PLAYER. Come on, roll those bones.

FIRST PLAYER (*taking a deep breath*). Get a load of that ether. What they tryin' t' do with it—asphyxiate all of us?

[*Back to wardroom. Somewhat drugged by the ether,* JIMMY *runs his hand over his face.* COM. MILLER *watches him solicitously.*]

MILLER. Is the ether getting you, Doc?

BRUCE (*impatiently*). Nah, come on, let's get on with it. What's the next line, Davison?

DAVISON (*reading from the surgery book*). "Injury to the ilio . . . ilio. . . ."

BRUCE (*brusquely*). Ilioinguinal nerve.

DAVISON (*continuing*). "May result in paralysis. . . ."

[*Close on* DAVISON *reacting. Close on* BRUCE.]

BRUCE (*abruptly*). Okay, okay. On your toes everybody. Another spoon ready.

[*We feel from* BRUCE'S *eyes and the strain of his face the fearful pressure of this critical moment. Close shot of* SWEDE. *Close shot of* O'BRIEN. *Close shot of* JOHNSON. *All are watching tensely. Close on* BRUCE *who is sweating profusely, straining, then suddenly relieved.*]

BRUCE. Got around the nerve okay. (*He probes further. We can hear the ticking of the clock. Suddenly he looks up in triumph.*) I see it! No wonder I couldn't find it. All covered with adhesions and the tip is gangrenous.

[*Group shot showing the response—relief—a momentary breather. Close on* BRUCE.]

BRUCE (*all business now, and with more confidence*). All right now, fast. Catgut. Hemostat. Another retractor—

DAVISON. Catgut for first suture.

[DAVISON *looks up at clock. Close on*

clock showing two minutes before half past two. Dissolve. Close on clock, now showing nearly five past three. Camera pans down to full show of wardroom. The room is full of foul ether vapors and JIMMY *shows signs of nervous exhaustion.*]

BRUCE *(to* MILLER*).* Come on . . . clamps . . . hold it open so I c'n. . . .

[TOMMY *groans. Close on* TOMMY.]

TOMMY *(stirring and groping up toward the surface of consciousness, hardly audible).* Oh . . .

[*Close group shot at table.*]

BRUCE *(anxiously).* More ether. He's coming out!

HUDSON. How much more do you think it's going to take?

BRUCE *(flaring up).* How many times must you ask me that? I'm trying my best. I——

HUDSON *(glancing at clock).* It's over an hour already. I just want to be sure we don't run out of ether before——

BRUCE *(facing him angrily).* If we do, Hudson, it'll be your fault and I'll—— *(He seems almost ready to strike* HUDSON *who cuts in sharply.)*

HUDSON. Listen, Bruce, I don't care what you're doing. You're still an enlisted man and——

[COM. MILLER *takes control at this point in his authoritative, but very quiet, way.*]

MILLER. I think it's time to clear the air a little bit, fellows. Getting pretty foul in here. *(Looks across at* SWEDE.*)* Better get the blowers working, Swede.

[HUDSON *and* BRUCE *relax.* JIMMY *goes back to work.*]

BRUCE *(snapping his fingers).* More catgut. Hemostat. Alcohol——

[*Cut to dinette. The* MESSENGER *who was seen previously kneeling over the fallen body of* TOMMY *appears in the entrance way.*]

FIRST ACEY-DEUCY PLAYER. How's it going?

MESSENGER *(looking up).* They say he's got hold of a whole mess of appendix.

SECOND PLAYER. That's the *mesoappendix*—the little knob near the base.

FIRST PLAYER. Listen to the man—another quack!

[*Cut to conning tower, angling toward* HELMSMAN *and* WILLIAMS.]

HELMSMAN *(glancing up at clock).* What's taking so long?

WILLIAMS. What's the diff, long as he makes it?

[*Medium close of* SONARMAN, *listening intently as he moves his dial.*]

HELMSMAN. That stinkin' ether'll put us all under before he's through.

[*Suddenly the* SONARMAN *cocks his head, moves his dial slowly back and holds it. He listens more eagerly and signals* WILLIAMS.]

SONARMAN. Tell the Skipper I think I hear screws[40] bearing 0-3-9.

[*Dissolve to wardroom. Close of* BRUCE. *He has reached a delicate phase of the operation—the purse-string suture.*]

BRUCE *(hoarsely).* Okay. What's the next step?

DAVISON *(reading).* "The ends of the tied purse-string suture are again tied over the stump of the mesoappendix. . . ."

BRUCE *(gritting his teeth).* The ends of the——

[*Suddenly they are interrupted by the squawk box.*]

SQUAWK BOX *(voice of* QUARTERMASTER WILLIAMS*).* Sound reports screws bearing 0-3-9, Skipper.

[*Close on* COM. MILLER, *reacting to this report of the presence of an enemy vessel. Wider angle of wardroom. The others also react to this new danger. They hesitate for a moment.*]

40. screws, the propellers of a subchaser.

BRUCE (to O'BRIEN). All right . . . more alcohol. . . . Let the Skipper worry about that.

[COM. MILLER goes to the squawk box.]

MILLER (to squawk box). Let me know if they're closing. And get a turn count.[41]

[He turns back to the table and looks at BRUCE questioningly.]

BRUCE (to himself). Oh, brother! If I make a mistake now.

SQUAWK BOX (voice of QUARTERMASTER WILLIAMS). The screws are highspeed, Skipper. Still closing. Bearing 0–3–6.

[MILLER looks at JIMMY.]

BRUCE. Go ahead, Skipper. I'll get Swede to relieve you. Better go fight your ship.

MILLER (turns back to the squawk box). I'm on my way up to take charge of evasive action. Rig for silent running. Change course—right fifteen degrees rudder. (He turns back to JIMMY, puts his hand on his shoulder.) Back as soon as I can shake this baby, Jimmy.

BRUCE (so intent on what he is doing that he merely nods and goes on with his labors). Vaseline gauze. More catgut. . . .

[COM. MILLER exits. Cut to control room angled toward plane wheels. ENSIGN RIGGS comes over to the planesmen.]

RIGGS. Shift the bow and stern planes to hand power.

FANELLI and GOODMAN. Aye, aye, sir.

[While they attend to this, RIGGS crosses back and gets on the squawk box.]

RIGGS. Secure the I.C. motor generators.[42] Secure the blower and air conditioning.

[As COM. MILLER appears on his way to the conning tower, the motors go off and the sudden quiet permits us to hear the water sloshing against the hull. Close on FANELLI and GOODMAN. Having to hold the planes with their own muscle power is a tremendous strain. Their arms tremble with the effort.]

RIGGS. Hold her with everything you've got!

[FANELLI and GOODMAN can only nod as they put their strength against the wheels. Cut to interior of wardroom. The lights go out because of the cutting off of the generators.]

BRUCE. Now what's the matter?

HUDSON. They've cut off the generators.

BRUCE (cracking for a moment). Oh, brother, what a SNAFU![43] (Then he takes hold again.)

[There is a quick look between HUDSON and BRUCE, nothing more.]

HUDSON. We can finish up with the emergency lanterns.

BRUCE. Right. Break 'em out. No stinkin' subchaser's gonna foul up this operation.

[HUDSON stares at him a moment, impressed, then sets to work with the others. And DAVISON, SWEDE, O'BRIEN, and HUDSON grab the lanterns and rapidly set them up so that they throw a strange but adequate light on the operating table.]

BRUCE (going back to his work). Okay. We've almost got it now.

[Cut to conning tower. COM. MILLER approaches the SONARMAN. The latter switches on the loud-speaker so MILLER and the audience can hear the sound of the approaching screws.]

SONARMAN. Closing fast. Bearing 0–2–3.

MILLER (to WILLIAMS). We'll keep turning away from them—left rudder another ten degrees.

---

41. **a turn count,** a count of the rate of speed at which the propellers of the approaching ship are turning, to determine the speed of the vessel.
42. **Secure the I.C. motor generators,** shut off the intercommunication motor generators.
43. **SNAFU,** snarled-up situation. The word *snafu* is derived from the initial letters of "situation normal—all fouled up." It is Army and Navy slang.

WILLIAMS. Aye, aye, sir.

SONARMAN (calling out over the sound of the sonar). Still closing, sir. Bearing 0–2–1.

MILLER. Very well.

[Cut to control room. FANELLI and GOODMAN show perspiration on their faces as they strain to hold the boat steady. Cut to interior of dinette. The two ACEY-DEUCY PLAYERS are now silently sweating it out. One of them rattles the dice listlessly over and over. Cut to wardroom. With the ventilation system off, the effect of the ether fumes is overpowering. JIMMY pauses and holds his head, seemingly overcome for a moment.]

JIMMY. Oh, this ether.

[HUDSON'S reaction is surprisingly sympathetic.]

HUDSON. With those ventilators off, it's rough, kid. But at least it solves one thing for us—(indicates the unconscious form of TOMMY FORD)—it keeps him under. (To O'BRIEN.) Try holding a little alcohol under his nose. That'll pep him up.

BRUCE (looking at HUDSON warmly for the first time). Thanks. (Goes on with his work.)

[Cut to conning tower. Medium close at sonar table. The sound of the oncoming screws is considerably louder.]

SONARMAN. Seem to be coming right for us, Skipper. Bearing 1–8–8.

MILLER (to WILLIAMS, wearing earphones for silent running). Right fifteen degrees rudder. We'll try to get on their course in the opposite direction.

[Close on sonar apparatus as the sound of the screws grows louder. Cut to control room. FANELLI and GOODMAN, who can hear the approaching subchaser now, exchange a look of apprehension. Cut to dinette. The ACEY-DEUCY PLAYERS can hear it. They look at each other meaningfully. Back to wardroom.]

BRUCE (in a hoarse whisper). Another drain. Alcohol. Have the needle ready.

[The men in the wardroom too can hear the sound of the approaching enemy screws, but—except for a quick glance in the direction of the sound—all keep at their jobs. Cut to conning tower, close at sonar system. The sound of the enemy vessel is exceedingly loud now.]

SONARMAN. Closing, closing. Gonna pass right over us.

MILLER (in whisper to QUARTERMASTER WILLIAMS). All stop.

[Cut to control room. Now with all motors off, FANELLI and GOODMAN must strain harder than ever to hold the boat level. Their muscles stand out against the pressure of it.]

RIGGS (quietly). Hang on! Hang on!

[Cut to conning tower. The rumbling grows louder as the subchaser begins to pass over them. It sounds like an elevated railway. They all look up instinctively. Cut back to wardroom. The subchaser is passing over with a subway roar. Even JIMMY is interrupted by the terrible proximity of the enemy. He looks up with anxious eyes. Then he takes hold again.]

BRUCE. Okay, let's keep going. Every second counts now.

[Reaction from HUDSON—increasingly impressed. Dissolve to interior of conning tower, close at sonar system. The sound indicates that the subchaser is now going away.]

SONARMAN (suppressing a tendency to smile). Screws now opening on one-eighty.[44]

MILLER (relieved, turning to WILLIAMS). All right. Make 50 R.P.M.'s[45] again. At 1540, if screws continue to open, return to normal running.

---

44. Screws now opening on one-eighty, the propellers of the subchaser are now going away from the stern.

45. 50 R.P.M.'S, fifty revolutions per minute. The R.P.M.'S determine the speed of the motors.

WILLIAMS (also showing relief). Aye, aye, sir.

MILLER (to SONARMAN). Report to me when it's all clear. (He starts down the hatchway.)

[Exterior of submarine underway, submerged. Dissolve to wardroom. Close on clock showing the time as 3:40.]

BRUCE'S VOICE. Ready . . . scalpel.

[Camera pulls back to full shot of everyone including COM. MILLER, waiting tensely while JIMMY goes in with scalpel off scene. He bends down over the body and probes with his other gloved hand. Close on BRUCE so that you cannot see what he is holding.]

BRUCE (triumphantly). Well, there it is. Funny that a little thing like that c'n cause all this fuss. (He snaps back into his job, clicking with efficiency and confidence now.) All right now, let's get this thing battened down—sew Tommy back in one piece.

[Close shot favoring HUDSON. He looks at MILLER.]

HUDSON (recalling MILLER'S words at the beginning; muttering them to himself). "Panicky, half-grown kids suddenly find out they're men."

[MILLER just manages to overhear him and smiles.]

BRUCE (to HUDSON). What was that?

HUDSON. Nothing, Doc. Just talking to myself. Anything else you want me to do?

BRUCE. Just keep watching his eyes. We don't want him to come out of this too soon.

HUDSON (under his breath). Aye, aye.

SQUAWK BOX. Conning tower reporting on sound. All clear. All clear.

[MILLER grins. Goes to squawk box.]

MILLER. Return to normal running. Get the ventilators going. And bleed oxygen into the boat[46] so we can purify the air.

SQUAWK BOX. Aye, aye, sir. Oh, and Skipper, how's it going down there?

MILLER (cheerfully). Operation appendix is just about secured.

[He returns to the table. In a moment the lights come on. The ventilator starts. The men breathe in with relief. Cut to control room.]

RIGGS. Return bow and stern planes to normal power.

[SEAMEN FANELLI and GOODMAN grin and heave deep sighs of relief. Cut to interior of conning tower. Close on HELMSMAN, grinning. Cut to dinette. Close on ACEY-DEUCY PLAYERS, also grinning. Wardroom again.]

BRUCE (briskly). Okay, before this final suture—one last check to make sure we haven't left anything inside of Tommy.

DAVISON (checking his list). Hemostats—eight.

MILLER (counting the ones removed). Er . . . eight . . . check.

DAVISON. Gauze drains—five.

MILLER. Check.

DAVISON. Retractors, that is, spoons —three.

MILLER (counting them). Three. Check.

VOICE OF LEROY JOHNSON. Wait a minute! (They turn toward his voice in the pantry. Cut to pantry. JOHNSON bends down to talk through sliding door.) I handed out four spoons, and I want every one of my spoons back!

[Cut to wardroom. BRUCE reaches in out of the scene.]

BRUCE. Leroy, you're really on the ball. Here's your spoon!

[Everyone laughs and the tension is released.]

MILLER. Okay, Doc, soon as you give us the all clear, we'll surface and air out the boat, and see if we can't

---

46. **bleed oxygen into the boat,** open the compressed-oxygen flasks in each compartment to get fresh oxygen into the boat.

reëstablish contact with our little friends.

[*They turn back to finish the job. Dissolve to exterior of submarine surfacing. Then to interior of conning tower. Present, waiting with bursting lungs for the hatch to open, are all the principals at the operation.* WILLIAMS *throws open the hatch to the bridge.* COM. MILLER, JIMMY BRUCE, SWEDE, O'BRIEN, LTS. HUDSON *and* DAVISON, *and* LEROY JOHNSON *raise their faces to the open air, breathing luxuriously.* HUDSON *turns around and smiles at* JIMMY. *We should have a feeling, without hitting it too hard, that this experience has mellowed him and brought him closer to the men.*]

HUDSON (*quietly*). Nice work, Jimmy. I'm sorry I blew.

BRUCE. Aw, forget it, Mr. Hudson. You're a good man to have around.

HUDSON. Thanks, Jimmy. I feel the same way about you. (HUDSON *relaxes slightly.*)

SWEDE (*suddenly lets out a wail of dismay*). Oh, what I forgot!

O'BRIEN. Not another spoon?

SWEDE. My cake! My Christmas cake! It's been in the oven all this time! (*He shoots down through the hatchway to the control room. Dissolve to galley.*)

SWEDE (*runs in, throws the oven door open and draws out his cake. It is burnt to ash. Half bitterly, half with humor*). Serves me right for trying to get fancy on a pigboat. It happens every time.

[*Back to conning tower with hatch to bridge open.*]

MILLER. Well, Jimmy, I think you've got a Christmas present coming. I could have orders cut to send you home to college — pre-med. If ever I saw a great natural surgeon —

BRUCE. Me a surgeon? Are you kidding? I never want to go through anything like that again as long as I live. (MILLER, HUDSON, O'BRIEN, *and the others grin.*)

[*The* RADIOMAN *enters.*]

RADIOMAN. I got the report off, sir. Oh, and everybody back at the base is wishing us a Merry Christmas.

MILLER. That reminds me, men — we've been a little busy around here today or I would have said it sooner: Merry Christmas to all of you.

ADLIBS. Thanks, Skipper. Merry Christmas, sir.

[*There is a general exchange of handshakes.* BRUCE *and* HUDSON *shake, too, but casually, like the others.*]

MILLER (*all business again*). All right, men. Let's pull the plug[47] and get on with the job.

[*Fade out.*]

---

47. *pull the plug*, dive.

DISCUSSION

1. (a) What is the most important conflict in "The Pharmacist's Mate"? (b) What larger conflict is taking place outside the submarine? (c) Does the background conflict increase the suspense of the main conflict? Explain.

2. (a) What is the purpose of the conversation on the squawk box between Hudson and the Skipper (page 140)? (b) What functions does the scene in the dinette serve (pages 141–145)? (c) Are both these incidents necessary to the plot of the play? Why or why not?

3. Read "Emergency at Sea" (page 164), the edited newspaper story on which this television play is based. What does the playwright emphasize by changing the name to "The Pharmacist's Mate"?

4. (a) Explain how the fourth paragraph of the newspaper article was expanded to add suspense to the play. (b) What important character was developed to create an additional conflict? (c) What is the purpose of this additional conflict?

5. (a) Compare the roles of each of the following in the two versions of the story: the cook; ether; rubber gloves; spoons. **(b)** Which details in the play were the author's inventions?

6. In your opinion, what is the point of greatest suspense in the play? In the newspaper article?

7. (a) Is there any humor in the newspaper article? **(b)** Find evidences of humor in the play. **(c)** Why are these humorous touches desirable in a drama of this type?

8. In most plays, you learn about a character through dialogue and actions. **(a)** What sort of person is Jimmy Bruce when you first meet him? **(b)** Cite dialogue and actions that give you your first clues to his character. **(c)** Trace Bruce's development from the time he settles down with a comic book to his successful completion of the operation. **(d)** In what ways does he bear out the Skipper's statement, "I've seen panicky, half-grown kids suddenly find out they're men"?

9. (a) What are Commander Miller's outstanding qualities? **(b)** How are these qualities demonstrated?

10. (a) What was your first impression of Hudson? **(b)** What created this impression? **(c)** Do you think Hudson will ever make a good commander? Why or why not?

11. (a) Show how the courage of Jimmy, Tommy, and the Skipper is tested in the play. **(b)** Which character do you consider most heroic? Why?

12. (a) Does either Harriet Tubman or Jimmy Bruce derive any personal rewards from his heroic acts? Explain. **(b)** What do you think motivates Harriet and Jimmy to act as they do? **(c)** In your opinion, who is more heroic —the person who acts courageously for his own benefit, or the one who acts in behalf of others? Why?

THE AUTHOR

People in the television industry often look back on the 1950's as the medium's "golden years." During that decade television viewers were presented with truly creative, thought-provoking drama. There were, in the industry, a few writers who consistently produced works of both quality and originality. Budd Schulberg was one of them.

Schulberg's best-known television drama is *What Makes Sammy Run?* the story of a ruthless young man who achieves his goals only to find they are not enough to fill his life. The drama was such a critical and popular success that it was later produced on the Broadway stage.

But Schulberg's successes have not been limited to television. His movie script for the motion picture *On the Waterfront* won the Academy Award for the best screenplay of 1954. He has also received recognition as a novelist.

WIDE WORLD PHOTOS

EMERGENCY AT SEA

GEORGE WELLER

"They're giving him ether now," they said in the torpedo room.

"They've made the first cut. They're feeling around for it."

"They" were a group of anxious-faced men with their arms thrust into reversed white pajama coats. Gauze bandages hid all their expressions except the tensity in their eyes.

"It" was an acute appendix inside Dean Rector. The pains had become unendurable the day before, Rector's first birthday at sea. He was nineteen years old.

They were below the sea's surface. Above them were enemy waters crossed and recrossed by Japanese destroyers and transports.

The nearest surgeon competent to operate on Rector was thousands of miles away. There was just one way to prevent the appendix from bursting, and that was for the crew to operate.

And that's what they did.

The chief surgeon was a twenty-three-year-old pharmacist's mate. His name was Wheeler B. Lipes. He was classified as an electrocardiographer, but he'd seen Navy doctors take out one or two appendixes and thought he could do it.

There was difficulty about the ether. The crew did not know how long it would take to find the appendix. They didn't want the patient waking before they finished.

They decided to operate on the table in the officers' wardroom. The room was just long enough so that the patient's head and feet reached the two ends without hanging over.

First they got out a medical book and read up on the appendix. Everyone knew his role.

The cook provided the ether mask. It was an inverted tea-strainer, covered with gauze.

The "surgeon" had, as his staff, all men his senior in age and rank.

Before they carried Rector to the wardroom, the submarine captain asked Lipes to talk with the patient.

"Look, Dean, I never did anything like this before," Lipes said. "You don't have much chance to pull through anyhow. What do you say?"

"I know how it is, Doc."

It was the first time anybody had called Lipes "Doc." But there was in him, added to the steadiness that goes with a submariner's profession, a new calmness.

The tools were laid out. They were far from perfect or complete for a major problem. The scalpel had no handle.

But submariners are used to "rigging" things. The machinist "rigged" a handle for the scalpel from a hemostat.

For an antiseptic agent, they ground sulfanilamide tablets into powder. In the cook's galley they found tablespoons. They bent these at right angles and made retractors with which to hold open the wound. Sterilizers? They milked alcohol from the torpedo mechanism and used it as well as boiling water.

The light in the wardroom was insufficient. They brought one of the big floods used for night loading and rigged it inside the wardroom's ceiling.

Rubber gloves were drawn upon the "Doc's" hands. The fingers were too long. The ends dribbled limply.

Rector wet his lips, glancing a side look at the tea-strainer ether mask. It was put down over his face. They waited for his pupils to dilate.

Lipes found the point where he intended to cut. It took him nearly twenty minutes to find the appendix.

Bulletins seeped back into the engine room and they kept the sub steady below a stormy sea.

The patient's face began to grimace.

"More ether," ordered the Doc.

There was hardly three-quarters of one can from the original five pounds left, but once again the tea-strainer was soaked in ether. The fumes made the operating staff giddy.

Suddenly came the moment when the Doc reached out his hand, pointing toward the needle threaded with catgut.

One by one the tablespoons were withdrawn and returned to the galley. It was the Skipper who noticed one spoon was missing. Lipes reached into the incision for the last time and withdrew the spoon and closed the incision.

At that moment the last can of ether went dry. It had taken the amateurs two and a half hours to perform a forty-five minute operation.

"It wasn't one of those 'snappy valve' appendixes," Lipes apologized as he felt the first handclasps upon his shoulder.

Reprinted with permission from the *Chicago Daily News*.

See
ENDINGS
*Handbook
of Literary
Terms
page 520*

*There is a certain kind of hero
that progress strips of glory. Cal Crawford
was such a man. Is the ending
to his story appropriate?*

A Time
of
Greatness

DOROTHY JOHNSON

I WAS TEN years old the summer I worked for old Cal Crawford. For years afterward I remembered it as a time of terror. I was grown up before I understood it had been a time of greatness, too.

Cal Crawford did not hire me and probably did not know I was working for him. He never remembered my name—he called me "Boy" when he noticed me at all—and at the end, he got the idea that through some misfortune he had to look after me, instead of the other way around.

But I was hired to look after him, because he was blind and very old. If my father hadn't needed the money desperately, he would not have let me go to the Crawford place. Old Cal's daughter, who hired me, was half-Indian. White people didn't work for Indians. It was unthinkable.

She looked immensely old, older than Cal Crawford himself, for he was tall and straight, while she was short and stooped. I never knew her name but got around it by calling her "Missus." What most people called her was "Monkeyface."

She wore her purple silk dress the day she came to our place. My sister Geraldine saw her through the window and said, "The old squaw's coming this way. Aren't we being honored, though! And all dressed up in silk. *I* haven't got a silk dress."

Geraldine snickered at the sight. She had little enough to make her laugh those days. Her young man had gone West without her, because she had to stay home and look after Pa.

She didn't think she would ever see her man again.

I laughed, too, at the old Indian woman, and was sorry later. If I hadn't laughed at Monkeyface, then maybe I wouldn't have had to go away with her that day. Maybe it was a punishment. But she did look ridiculous in the purple silk dress, astride an old white horse and slumped like a sack of meal. Her gray hair hung in frowzy braids from under a red kerchief. When she got close enough, you saw the dress was grease-spotted and dull with dirt.

Monkeyface had little English, but she kept saying, "Mistah? Mistah?" and making the Indian sign for "man."

"She wants to see Pa," I explained to Geraldine. I answered the old woman with the sign for "sick," and added, "He's got a broken leg."

She still wanted to see him, so Geraldine took her into the bedroom. Any visitor broke the monotony.

Pa and Monkeyface had quite a talk, in her mangled English and sign language, and I shivered because she kept motioning toward me.

A boy of ten does not expect his own father will give him away, but that was how it looked. And dreadful things not expected had happened lately in our cabin, like the way my sister cried at night because she had to stay home instead of go West with her man. It wasn't Pa that made her stay, though. It was her conscience.

"You want a summer job, Buck?" my father asked.

I took heart. "Sure." Herding cows, maybe. I wasn't big enough for much else.

"She wants you to look after her father," Pa explained. "Cal Crawford, the old mountain man."

"Look after him how?" I demanded, getting suspicious. I had few skills and little ability, nothing to be proud of. If I had been big enough to amount to anything, I could have been taking care of Pa so Geraldine wouldn't have had to stay home. She sometimes told me so.

"Just see he don't stray off," Pa explained. "He's blind, and he wanders. She don't want him to get hurt or lost." He added, "They'll give you your keep and a dollar a month wages."

I had no choice, really. It was a big thing to relieve the folks of feeding me, and a bigger one to earn that much money.

So I went to Cal Crawford's place, twenty miles away, on a pinto pony, trailing behind Cal's half-Indian daughter. I was scared all the way, and all summer.

That was before he became a legend, and after he had stopped being one, you might say. He was like a deposed god. He had gloried and drunk deep with his peers, had dared much and suffered much, had gained and lost. But all his peers were dead. Conestoga wagons had swayed westward along trails he had unwittingly helped mark, and as the frontier crept forward, settlements nestled where his campfires had starred the vast and silent night.

After he had gone, historians resurrected the legends and found most of them were true. He had trapped beaver and traded furs with the Indians, had lived with Indians and fought against them. He had traveled the wild Missouri and the Roche Jaune, or Yellowstone, had seen a mountain of black glass and the place where hell broke through the earth's surface to spout boiling water toward the sky. He had sat in council with chiefs, had taken scalps and never lost his own. But when I worked for him, nobody was left who had known

him when he was young and strong and in his glory.

In that last summer of his life, he was only a blind old man, looked after by his Indian daughter.

She never gave me any orders. She showed me a pallet on the floor by his bunk and signed, "You sleep there." The cabin had two rooms. She slept in the other one, the kitchen.

Cal Crawford rode into the yard on a tired old white horse, herded by a tired old black dog. Monkeyface made a gesture toward him as if to say, This is what you are here for, to help the horse and the dog keep him from getting lost.

So I went outside and stood around while he dismounted. I cleared my throat and asked, "Want me to take the saddle off, Mr. Crawford?"

He looked over my head with his blazing blue blind eyes, scowling, his defiant chin held high, and said, "No!" He didn't want me there, and if I had to be there, he didn't care to be reminded.

There was no conversation at supper. Monkeyface had changed from her silk dress to a faded gray one, such as any farm woman might wear. She cut up his meat and murmured to him, but he didn't answer.

He would not stay in the house or near it, and rain didn't matter, except that he would turn his face up to catch it. And sometimes he would get off his horse and kneel down in a field, reaching with his hands to see how high the grain had grown.

Uncounted miles of tipped mountains and rolling prairie had passed beneath his moccasin-clad feet when he was young and had his sight. He had been at home in tepees and brush shelters, and fifteen years had passed in one stretch without his ever setting foot in a house. When he was old,

he did not like houses but wandered on horseback, with the old dog to herd him home.

When he was not riding, he walked around the yard, prodding ahead with a long stick. I kept quiet and out of his way, and when he saddled his old horse, I scrambled bareback onto the pinto.

Cal knew I was there, but he acted as if I had never been born. Once or twice he asked irritably, "Boy, you there?" but most of the time he preferred to forget me.

Once, when he was walking to the house, he prodded me with his pole by accident—I hadn't jumped fast enough when he turned around—but he wasn't sorry. He challenged, "Well?" while I rubbed my shin.

I said apologetically, "Sorry I got in the way, Mr. Crawford," and was mad at myself for being such a ninny.

Then came the morning when he whistled as usual for the dog but the dog did not come stiffly out of the shed. He whistled again, scowling, and seemed lost in his darkness. For the first time, I was sorry enough for him to forget being scared.

"I'll get him," I offered.

The dog was too tired to get up. I went out of the shed and reported, "Dog's sick, Mr. Crawford."

The old man prodded in with his stick and was not grateful when I touched his arm and said, "He's to your right."

He hunkered down and the dog inched himself over and put his head on the old man's groping hand, wagging his tail feebly. After a while, Cal Crawford stopped petting him and grumbled, "Well, he's dead."

When Monkeyface found out, she handed me a shovel and I dug a grave for the dog. Cal didn't pay any attention except that he was impatient be-

cause his daughter wouldn't let him ride anywhere while I was busy.

When the dog was gone, I felt more useful, but I never bossed old Cal. I followed him and warned when he came to a fence or a creek.

I was desperately lonesome and homesick, with nobody to tell about it. The Indian woman never talked to me, and the tall, stiff-jointed mountain man usually would not admit I was there. I suppose each of them was lonely, too. The old man looked blindly through me or over my head, and Monkeyface sometimes glanced at me with no expression—wondering, I think now, whether this boy who was her last hope would stay while she needed him.

Back home, my sister would be crying for her lost love or shouting angrily at my father, and he would be helpless and melancholy, as dependent as Cal Crawford but lacking his defense of arrogance. Nevertheless, it was home, and I wanted to be there.

Homesickness was bad enough, but something worse happened. One day, old Cal began to talk to people I could not see. We were riding along beside a grove. I was watching so as to warn him when he came to a creek with a steep bank. Suddenly he chuckled.

He pointed ahead and said, "Good beaver there last year. Plenty Blackfeet, too. Waugh!"

"Did you want to go back now, Mr. Crawford?" I asked.

He swung around, scowling, and said something in a language that was not English. Then he ignored the interruption and went on talking loudly in some tongue unknown to me, gesturing, telling a story. Along with the spoken language he used the sign talk of the prairie tribes, but more gracefully, more swiftly, than I had ever seen it. I got a few of the

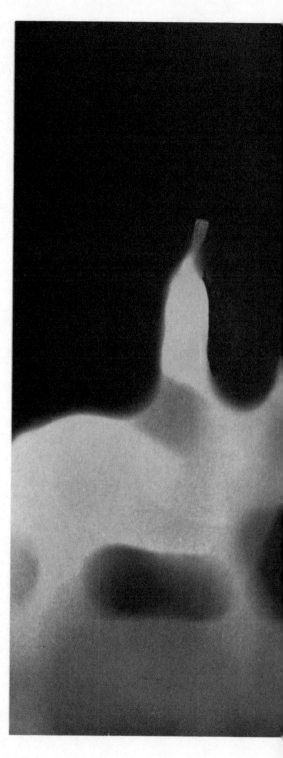

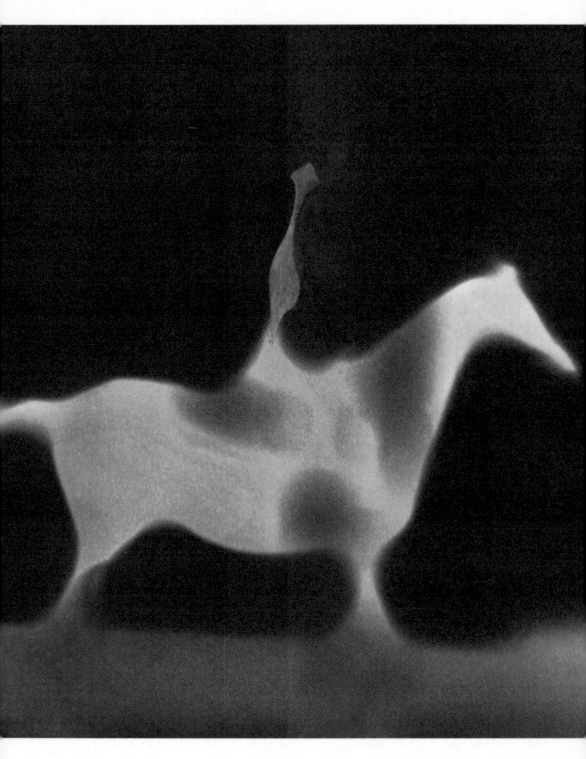

signs—men riding, an evil person, somebody dead. To the rider on his left he spoke, and to the rider on his right. I was on his right, but it was not to me he told his story. It was to someone I could not see, someone who wasn't there.

And the comrades of long ago must have answered, because once in a while he laughed. He pointed off toward the place where prairie met sky, and kicked his horse into a faster walk.

I was afraid to warn him of the creek. He sat easy in his battered saddle as his horse slid down the bank, waded across, and lunged up the other side. I kept behind him, shivering.

Long afterward, when historians revived the legend of Cal Crawford, I knew in what company I had ridden that day. The ghosts were bearded trappers in fringed buckskin, long-haired men with shapeless headgear of fur, moccasined men who rode like wary kings, who had forgotten fear but not caution. And Indians, too, rode with us, half-naked, curious, cruel, with paint stripes on their dark faces and hair in long black locks like snakes.

It was I who was invisible. Cal Crawford was young again in a time long years before I was born.

I did not guide him home that day. His horse turned and headed back to the cabin with him. But I did not desert him. I rode with him all the way, and did not know when we lost those other riders only he could see and hear.

I was going to tell his daughter at first, but what was the use? There comes a time when you have to look out for yourself, and I figured it had come. I decided to leave that night, sneak out of the cabin and walk the twenty miles back home.

But he slept poorly. He mumbled and tossed, and when he groaned, how could I leave?

He cried out, "Arrowhead under my shoulder, boy. Dig it out! Dig it out!"

With some hazy conviction that it would be cowardly for me to leave him wounded, I went over to him and said firmly, "It's all right, Mr. Crawford. Everything's all right."

He turned toward me and threw out his hand, groping, and I took hold of it.

"Don't leave me, boy," he whispered. He was not speaking to those lost, unseen comrades. I was the one he called "Boy."

"I won't leave you," I promised.

The next morning he pretended as usual that I wasn't there. He may not have remembered my promise, but I did. It worried me. How could I stay there, being scared all the time? Well, I hadn't said I would never leave him. Any day I was free to go, I thought. That was how I endured staying, just one day at a time, always knowing I could go.

One day he told me a story—or maybe he told it to someone else, but I could hear it, and he talked in English.

"My little girl," he said, chuckling. "Right smart young one, she is. I got her at a mission school, where they can bring her up right. Wouldn't have been there if I hadn't went to a lot of trouble. Her mother died, you know."

I made a sound indicating I was listening.

"Shoshone woman, her mother was. Died when we was camped on Little Muddy. If I'd knowed how sick she was, I'd have gotten her back to her people some way, but we was all alone. And the baby only three months old.

"Well, now, how was I going to feed the baby? No other woman around to give her to. Had to get out to someplace there'd be milk. But we was five hundred miles from a settlement. So I rode for buffalo country.

"I fed the young one on juice from chewed-up meat, but she cried all the time, getting weaker so she sounded like a sick kitten. First buffalo I seen was a dry cow, didn't do me no good. Then I come on a little herd of 'em, and there was milk to be had."

He laughed, remembering.

"You can't make no buffalo cow stand still to be milked. I had to shoot 'em. A dead cow you can get milk from. I fixed up a buckskin sack to nurse her with, and you should have seen her light into that milk! Every time she yelled for dinner and the sack was dry, I'd kill another buffalo cow.

"And did I ride! The last two days she got awful hungry, because the closer I came to the settlement, the scarcer the buffaloes was. But we made it through. I saved her. The Sisters at the mission took her.

"That girl baby was more darned trouble! I got me boys, too—Cheyenne, Sioux, Crow, Nez Percé—lots of boys, but darned if I know what become of 'em. They wasn't no trouble to me, and I wasn't no trouble to them. It's that little girl that was all the trouble."

He went back into silence, and after a while he talked to someone not present.

Seldom did anyone come to the Crawford place. A distant neighbor sometimes, looking for strayed stock, would ride in and stare with curiosity, nodding a brief greeting at Monkeyface and perhaps shouting, "Hello there, Cal, how are you?"

The old man might answer angrily,

"Think I'm deaf as well as blind?" or he might stare with those blazing blue eyes and not answer at all.

The few visitors were curious about me, but beyond asking whether I was any relation, they seldom bothered to speak. A lordly boy of fifteen or so did condescend to conversation. He asked, grinning, "The old man been fighting any Injuns lately?"

Cal's wandering mind was known to him, apparently, but a burst of loyalty prevented me from admitting anything.

I said stiffly, "You crazy? No Injun fighting around here."

"The old squaw's man been around this summer?" he asked. "Long-hair Injun, comes to see her once in a long while."

"Nobody's been here. I don't know who you mean."

"He's her man. Wants her to go back to the tribe, but she stays with her pa," the boy explained. "She's waiting to inherit all his property. She don't want to live with the savages anyhow, not when she can have everything good like white folks, silk dress and all."

"She's got it good here, all right," I agreed, jumping to the conclusion that anything white was bound to be better than anything Indian.

He rode on after a while. He was the only boy I saw all that summer, and I used to wish he would come again.

The tax collector came one day when Cal and I had just got back from riding and the old man was lying on his bunk, tired out. I was in the yard, throwing chips at the chickens, when a rig turned in from the road. I went to tell Monkeyface, and she seemed disturbed. She woke up her father, and he was angry.

He shouted at her and groped out with his long stick to face the enemy.

Monkeyface scowled at me and ordered, "You stay!"—the only time she ever gave me a direct order. This was private business, humiliating, not for me to know.

But even in the house I could hear the conversation, because the tax collector was one of the people who took it for granted that Cal Crawford, being blind, must be deaf as well.

"This ain't no place for you, Cal," he pleaded. "Come winter, what you going to do? We got a county farm. You'd be well took care of there, wouldn't have to worry about nothing."

"I got nothing to worry about now," Cal roared.

"But this place is going to be sold for taxes, I tell you. You could keep it, did you have the tax money."

Monkeyface snatched the purple silk dress from its nail by the door and put it on over her other dress and walked out to stand by her father, glaring at the visitor.

I saw a thing then that struck me with pity, young as I was and lacking in understanding. Cal put out his hand and touched the silk of the dress and took new strength from it. He expected it to be there, and it was.

"I look after my own," he boasted. "Bought my daughter a nice white-woman dress. You think I ain't got money? I can pay them taxes any time I please to!"

"Then pay me now, Cal, and save trouble," the tax collector pleaded. "It's not that anybody wants to put you off. But you don't need this place. You'd be better took care of on the county farm."

"Hundred and sixty acres," muttered Cal Crawford. "And he says I don't need all that." He stared blindly at the man in the rig and said with pride, "Young feller, once I owned

half the continent. Me and a few others, we shared it and all that was in it. I ain't got much room to spread out in any more, but what I got, I need. And I'm going to keep it till I go under."

The man in the rig looked as if he might cry. "It's only what I'm supposed to do," he defended.

Cal lifted his stick in a vast, threatening gesture. "I'm going to keep what I got as long as I need it," he said, spacing the words. "I'll kill the man that tries to put me off."

The tax collector swatted his team with the whip and drove out fast.

At that moment, I loved old Cal. For the ring of truth was in his voice. *I'll kill him, that's what I'll do.* When other men said that, the threat was a crutch for weakness. But old Cal had killed, he could kill. If necessary, he would.

He turned toward the house, probing out ahead with his stick. Walking behind him, I straightened my shoulders. I was still afraid of him, but I was not lonely any more.

Cal lay down in his bunk again, one arm across his eyes. I hunkered on the floor, willing to wait as long as need be. Where was he then? In that Kansas cabin, maybe, thinking about the tax collector. Or maybe he was behind the log walls of a trading post far to the westward, planning defense against painted savages.

Wherever he was, he knew I was there, too. Because after a while he said, "Bring my gun."

I was honored to be so commanded, but I didn't know which gun he wanted. He had four, hanging on the wall of the kitchen. I had not touched them but had admired them from a distance. I was ignorant, but how could I confess it? Guns belonged to men, so a man naturally knew all about guns. But only one of Cal's looked like the rifle we had at home.

Cal Crawford's life had spanned two great developments in firearms. Flintlocks had been his weapons in his younger days. As civilization crept westward, he had used percussion arms. Before his sight went dim, metal cartridges and breech-loading rifles were available. So he had three kinds on the wall. One of them was a flintlock with the stock scarred and set with brass-headed tacks.

I climbed on a chair and reached for the flintlock because it was the strongest. Monkeyface objected, "Uh! Uh!" and I told her, "He wants his gun."

She did not try again to stop me. I carried the strange, long old rifle carefully to the other room and put it in Cal's hands.

He knew it by touch and smiled. "Not that one, boy." He fondled it. "I took that off Bull Back in forty-three, lost it twice, and got it again. See this here, boy?" He fingered a bit of long black hair on a scrap of leather, attached to the trigger guard. "That there is Bull Back's scalp lock."

Shrinking, I touched it and thought, Now I have touched an Indian scalp, and I know the man who took it.

"Bring me the rest, boy. And the ammunition."

I carried the guns in one at a time, with more journeys for the dirty beaded and quill-worked bags for lead balls and percussion caps, two powder horns so thin you could see light through them, a couple of metal powder containers, and a box of cartridges.

"Lay 'em down here," Cal Crawford ordered. "And git out."

When I came back, half an hour later, I was disappointed. The old man was sleeping, and Monkeyface had

put the weapons back where they belonged.

After that day, Cal never went riding any more. He stayed to defend the last vestige of his empire, the little hundred and sixty acres. And for the first time, he fretted. A couple of times he whistled for the dog, and I was afraid to remind him the dog couldn't answer his signal any more. He stayed in the cabin for hours at a time, going over the logs with his hands, measuring the windows, getting his bearings.

His Indian daughter fretted, too, but silently. Sometimes she stood looking to the west, always looking west, as if waiting for somebody. Cal Crawford was waiting, too, but not for the same person.

But someone came for me before anyone came for either of them. A man from town, on his way out to our home place with a wagon load of lumber, drove in to say, "Your pa said I might's well pick you up and carry you home, Buck, seeing's I'm going right by there."

He got down from the wagon and walked around, loosening up his muscles, looking things over. Monkeyface came out, but she didn't say anything. She only looked at me.

"This here's a friend of Pa's," I explained. "Pa says I'm to come home now."

She didn't answer. She turned to the house to get the pay I had coming, the three silver dollars.

"I'll get my stuff," I told the driver. "Be with you in a minute."

Getting my possessions didn't take long. But my extra shirt was in the room where Cal lay on his bunk, and it was only decent to tell him I was going.

"G'by, Mr. Crawford," I said politely. "A man's come for me, going to give me a lift home."

He was silent for a while, with one arm over his eyes. Then he said bitterly, "All right. You don't need to stay. I'll stand 'em off."

So something was going to happen, and if I went home then, I might never get the straight of it. That wasn't the important thing, though. What mattered was that I mattered to Cal Crawford.

"Shucks, I needn't go yet," I told him. "There's no hurry. I'll tell him I'm going to stay around a while more."

"Whatever you want to do," Cal Crawford answered. He would not beg. He gave me pride I had never had before. I could afford to stay.

When I explained to the driver, he thought I was crazy and said so.

Neither Cal nor Monkeyface said anything about how I was a good boy and thank you. They just went on waiting.

One morning before dawn, the way Cal was fighting for breath woke me out of a sound sleep, or maybe it was his daughter's presence that woke me. She held an oil lamp high and was looking at Cal, speaking to him in her own language. She put a gnarled brown hand on his forehead and he shook it off angrily.

She looked at me with pleading. When she went outside, I saw in the dim light that she had a rope to catch up a horse with, so I guessed she was going for a doctor. I was more afraid than ever before in my life. I guessed what was coming for Cal Crawford.

He had faced it often before, stared it down, fought it off, conquered it, got away. Now he was going to fight it again, or maybe he thought it was some other enemy.

"Get my gun, boy," he gasped. "Help me sit up."

The breech-loading cartridge rifle was the one he had preferred be-

fore, so I brought that, but he disdained it.

"What's this thing?" he demanded. "Give me one a man can shoot with! And see the flint's sharp and the powder's dry."

So I got the old long flintlock with the bit of Bull Back's scalp dangling from the trigger guard. His hands claimed and caressed it.

"'Tain't Old Fury," he muttered, "but it'll do. Look around the rocks, boy, and tell me what you see. Keep your head down."

My voice wasn't above a whisper. "Nothing coming yet, Mr. Crawford."

"Stay clear and give me room, that's all I ask," he said. His breathing was full and fast by then. "And listen, boy, if I go under, you run and hide. Don't worry none. If they take you, likely they'll raise you like one of their own." He managed a grating chuckle. "There's worse ways to live than like an Injun."

I wanted to run, not from the Indians but from Cal Crawford and the enemy. I had not reckoned on staying alone with him while Monkeyface rode for a doctor. I still wonder why she did it. Probably because she was proud he maintained her in the style of a white woman and she wanted to go on to the end doing, for his sake, what a white woman would try to do.

Cal loaded the battered old flintlock. He didn't need to see. He put the lead ball in his cupped hand and spilled powder so the ball was almost covered. Getting the right amount of powder into the pan was harder, and he spilled some.

When he had the charge rammed home, he was tired out. He lay back, commanding, "Watch for 'em, boy, and let me know when they come up over the hill."

I never saw them come, and he never spoke again.

It was near noon when Monkeyface came with the doctor. I was crouching in a corner with my face turned away from the bunk. But I had not retreated.

Maybe it was not an enemy who came for Cal Crawford. Maybe it was the mountain men, riding in to guide him on a journey through a country of wonders even he had never glimpsed.

His daughter let me go home that day on the pinto pony.

It was good to be home, better than if I had gone scared and retreating. I went as one who had earned the right because the job was finished and the duty done. I didn't tell them much, only that the old man was dead.

Pa was better, he could walk with a cane. Geraldine went around with a look on her face as if she had seen angels. She had a letter from her man, the first one since he went West without her. She wouldn't let us read it. But she hummed at her work and her steps were light.

About a week after I went home, Geraldine said, "Some old Injun is riding in with a squaw following. Now, what would they want?"

The Indian man stayed mounted, but when the squaw got down, I saw it was Cal's daughter. She was not wearing the purple silk dress. She had a striped shawl over an old cotton dress, and a kerchief on her head, squaw-fashion.

"It's Monkeyface," I said. "And that must be her husband, come to take her back to the tribe."

"She waited long enough," Geraldine said, "to get what old Cal left her. She earned it."

I suddenly understood something. "That wasn't why she stayed with him. She ain't got much of a pack on that horse. He didn't have anything

to leave. She was just looking after her old pa because he needed her."

"Faithful," Geraldine whispered softly. "Faithful. That's what John says I am. He said it in the letter." She began to cry in a happy, sparkling way, and ran out to make a fuss over Monkeyface.

They had come for the pinto, so I went out and roped it. And Monkeyface gave me something for a remembrance of her pa.

Then they rode on, the man ahead and Cal Crawford's daughter following, leading the pinto, going home, wherever that was. Somewhere west, in the direction she used to look.

"There *is* faith and trust," my sister said softly. "She knew her man would wait till she could leave her pa. I wonder what she did with her purple dress."

We heard later. She left it hanging on a nail in the cabin. She left almost everything there. She had no use for anything white women treasured.

I don't know what happened to Cal Crawford's things, except that his daughter brought me the flintlock rifle he had held when he made his last stand.

✦   ✦   ✦   ✦

DISCUSSION

1. In the first paragraph the boy says: "For years afterward I remembered it as a time of terror. I was grown up before I understood it had been a time of greatness, too." **(a)** For whom was it "a time of terror"? **(b)** For whom had it been "a time of greatness"?
2. The boy says that he went to work for Cal "before he became a legend, and after he had stopped being one." What does he mean by this statement?
3. Which of the following might explain why Cal lives in the past? Be sure you can defend your answers with logical arguments based on evidence that is either stated or suggested in the story. **(a)** He is lonely and longs for the company of men like himself. **(b)** He is afraid to admit he is old and defeated. **(c)** He fears death, and living in the past helps him to dismiss thoughts of it from his mind. **(d)** He is rebelling against civilization. **(e)** He finds the past more glorious than the present.
4. (a) What inner conflict does the boy undergo throughout most of his stay at the Crawford place? **(b)** At what point does he definitely settle this conflict? **(c)** What does he mean when he says Cal "gave me pride I never had before. I could afford to stay"?
5. (a) What effect does the tax collector's visit have on Cal? **(b)** While talking to the collector, Cal touches his daughter's dress. What strength does he find in this action? **(c)** What does the collector represent to Cal? **(d)** Why does Cal's encounter with the collector cause the boy to love the old man?
6. What was Cal fighting during his last stand?
7. (a) While at the Crawfords, how does Buck feel about Monkeyface? **(b)** What does he finally come to understand about her? **(c)** Why does Monkeyface bring Buck her father's flintlock rifle?
8. Read the biography of Dorothy Johnson, page 177. Miss Johnson is quoted as saying, "I don't care to write about people I don't admire for at least one quality. I admire the people in this story because of their loyalty to one another." If you admired the charac-

ters in the story, what qualities in each did you admire most?

9. (a) Explain the importance of the story's setting in Cal's life. **(b)** How are the other characters affected by the setting?

10. (a) Were you prepared for the ending of the story? **(b)** Find details that suggested it might end this way. **(c)** Is the ending happy, unhappy, or indeterminate? Explain. **(d)** Is it appropriate? Why or why not?

11. Cal Crawford represents a dying breed of hero—the man who relies on courage and physical ability to succeed. **(a)** Why is the necessity for Cal's brand of heroism fading in our society? **(b)** What sort of hero is replacing men like Cal?

WORD STUDY

Use your dictionary or the Glossary to answer the questions following each sentence.

1. With his broken leg, my father was in a *melancholy* humor.

How is *ch* pronounced in *melancholy*? What is the father's mood? What are the meanings of the two Greek words from which *melancholy* comes? Look up the word *humor*. How is the modern meaning of *melancholy* related to the old "humors" theory of medicine?

2. Dad lacked Cal Crawford's *arrogance*.

Could *arrogance* be used to describe a king or a beggar or both? What language gave us the word *arrogance*?

3. Moccasined men rode like *wary* kings.

Is *wary* related to *beware* or *war*? What two old English words contributed two meanings for *ware* to modern English? Do people still use both meanings of *ware*?

4. Cal stayed to defend the last *vestige* of his empire.

Which meaning of *vestige* is intended in this sentence? Why is the Latin word from which *vestige* comes a logical ancestor of the English word *vestige*?

THE AUTHOR

When Dorothy Johnson became an honorary member of Montana's Blackfeet tribe, an old medicine man bestowed his grandmother's name upon her: "Kills-both-places." The name is not entirely inappropriate to a writer who can so strongly affect both our emotions and intelligence.

Miss Johnson has spent most of her life in Montana and her interest in the West is evident in her fiction. Two of her western stories, "The Hanging Tree" and "The Man Who Shot Liberty Valance," have been made into movies.

Of "A Time of Greatness" she says: "Some of the details in this story are true. I was tremendously moved by one small statement in a biography of the famous mountain man, Jim Bridger: when he was old and blind, he used to kneel down and feel how tall the grain was growing. My stories always grow from an emotion. In this case it was deep pity.

"Jim Bridger, whose nickname was Old Gabe even when he was young, became Cal Crawford in the story because I did not want to stick to history. Jim Bridger did have a half-Indian daughter, whose life he saved with buffalo milk, as related here.

"I don't care to write about people I can't admire for at least one quality. I admire the people in this story because of their loyalty to one another. Such loyalty often results in sacrifice."

COURTESY OF THE AUTHOR

Sometimes caution is the better part of valor.

Advice to a Knight

T. H. JONES

Wear modest armor; and walk quietly
In woods, where any noise is treacherous.
Avoid dragons and deceptive maidens.

Be polite to other men in armor,
Especially the fierce ones, who are often strong.   5
Treat all old men as they might be magicians.

So you may come back from your wanderings,
Clink proud and stiff into the queen's court
To doff your helmet and expect her thanks.

The young queen is amused at your white hair,   10
Asks you to show your notched and rusty sword,
And orders extra straw for your bedding.

Tomorrow put on your oldest clothes,
Take a stout stick and set off again,
It's safer that way if no more rewarding.   15

From THE COLOUR OF COCKCROWING. Reprinted by permission of Granada Publishing Limited.

DISCUSSION

1. (a) Summarize the kinds of action which the speaker advises. **(b)** Are these the kinds of action one might expect from a heroic figure? Explain.

2. (a) What kind of person would you assume the giver of this advice is? Would you say he was young or old, cowardly or wise, gentle or fierce? **(b)** Briefly describe what you think he might look like.

3. Could you take any of the advice offered in the poem seriously? Which lines or phrases seem most meaningful to you? Why?

THE AUTHOR

T. H. Jones (1921–1965) was a Welsh poet. In a way he was very much like the modest knight he presents in his poem, a man who spurns the bold and daring in favor of the safer, if not more rewarding way.

*Two brothers built a plane in a bicycle shop
and with that machine made the world's first
practical airplane flight.
How does Dos Passos convey
the excitement of their achievement?*

The Campers at Kitty Hawk

JOHN DOS PASSOS

ON DECEMBER SEVENTEENTH, nineteen hundred and three, Bishop Wright, of the United Brethren, onetime editor of the *Religious Telescope*, received in his frame house on Hawthorn Street in Dayton, Ohio, a telegram from his boys Wilbur and Orville who'd gotten it into their heads to spend their vacations in a little camp out on the dunes of the North Carolina coast tinkering with a homemade glider they'd knocked together themselves. The telegram read:

> SUCCESS FOUR FLIGHTS THURSDAY MORNING ALL AGAINST TWENTY-ONE MILE WIND STARTED FROM LEVEL WITH ENGINE-POWER ALONE AVERAGE SPEED THROUGH AIR THIRTYONE MILES LONGEST FIFTYSEVEN SECONDS INFORM PRESS HOME CHRISTMAS

The figures were a little wrong because the telegraph operator misread Orville's hasty penciled scrawl.
But the fact remains
that a couple of young bicycle mechanics from Dayton, Ohio,
had designed, constructed, and flown
for the first time ever a practical airplane.

After running the motor a few minutes to heat it up, I released the wire that held the machine to the track and the machine started forward into the wind. Wilbur ran at the side of the machine holding the wing to balance it on the track. Unlike the start on the fourteenth, made in a calm, the machine facing a twentyseven-mile wind started very slowly.

From THE BIG MONEY—THE USA TRILOGY by John Dos Passos. Reprinted by permission of Elizabeth Dos Passos.

*. . . Wilbur was able to stay with it until it lifted from the track after
a forty-foot run. One of the lifesaving men snapped the camera for us,
taking a picture just as it reached the end of the track and the machine
had risen to a height of about two feet. . . . The course of the flight up
and down was extremely erratic, partly due to the irregularities of the
air, partly to lack of experience in handling this machine. A sudden dart
when a little over a hundred and twenty feet from the point at which
it rose in the air ended the flight. . . . This flight lasted only twelve seconds, but it was nevertheless the first in the history of the world in which
a machine carrying a man had raised itself by its own power into the
air in full flight, had sailed forward without reduction of speed, and had
finally landed at a point as high as that from which it started.*

A little later in the day the machine was caught in a gust of wind
and turned over and smashed, almost killing the coastguardsman who
tried to hold it down;
>it was too bad,
>but the Wright brothers were too happy to care;
>they'd proved that the thing flew.

*When these points had been definitely established, we at once packed
our goods and returned home, knowing that the age of the flyingmachine
had come at last.*

They were home for Christmas in Dayton, Ohio, where they'd been
born in the seventies of a family who had been settled west of the
Alleghenies since eighteen-fourteen; in Dayton, Ohio, where they'd been
to grammarschool and highschool and joined their father's church and
played baseball and hockey and worked out on the parallel bars and the
flying swing and sold newspapers and built themselves a printingpress out
of odds and ends from the junkheap and flown kites and tinkered with
mechanical contraptions and gone around town as boys doing odd jobs
to turn an honest penny.
>The folks claimed it was the Bishop's bringing home a helicopter,
a fiftycent mechanical toy made of two fans worked by elastic bands that
was supposed to hover in the air, that had got his two youngest boys
hipped on the subject of flight
>so that they stayed home instead of marrying the way the other
boys did, and puttered all day about the house picking up a living with
jobprinting,
>>bicyclerepair work,
>>sitting up late nights reading books on aerodynamics.
>Still they were sincere churchmembers, their bicycle business was
prosperous, a man could rely on their word. They were popular in Dayton.
>In those days flyingmachines were the big laugh of all the cracker-
barrel philosophers. Langley's and Chanute's[1] unsuccessful experiments
had been jeered down with an I-told-you-so that rang from coast to coast.

---

1. **Langley and Chanute,** Samuel P. Langley (1834–1906), pioneer in aeronautics, and Octave Chanute (1832–1910),
pioneer in glider experimentation.

The Wrights' big problem was to find a place secluded enough to carry on their experiments without being the horselaugh of the countryside. Then they had no money to spend;
    they were practical mechanics; when they needed anything they built it themselves.

    They hit on Kitty Hawk,
    on the great dunes and sandy banks that stretch south toward Hatteras seaward of Albemarle Sound,[2]
    a vast stretch of seabeach,
    empty except for a coastguard station, a few fishermen's shacks, and the swarms of mosquitoes and the ticks and chiggers in the crabgrass behind the dunes,
    and overhead the gulls and swooping terns, in the evening fishhawks and cranes flapping across the saltmarshes, occasionally eagles
    that the Wright brothers followed soaring with their eyes
    as Leonardo[3] watched them centuries before,
    straining his sharp eyes to apprehend
    the laws of flight.

    Four miles across the loose sand from the scattering of shacks, the Wright brothers built themselves a camp and a shed for their gliders. It was a long way to pack their groceries, their tools, anything they happened to need; in summer it was hot as blazes, the mosquitoes were bad;
    but they were alone there,
    and they'd figured out that the loose sand was as soft as anything they could find to fall in.
    There with a glider made of two planes and a tail in which they lay flat on their bellies and controlled the warp of the planes by shimmying their hips, taking off again and again all day from a big dune named Kill Devil Hill,
    They learned to fly.

    once they'd managed to hover for a few seconds
    and soar ever so slightly on a rising aircurrent,
    they decided the time had come
    to put a motor in their biplane.

    Back in the shop in Dayton, Ohio, they built an airtunnel, which is their first great contribution to the science of flying, and tried out model planes in it.
    They couldn't interest any builders of gasoline engines, so they had to build their own motor.
    It worked; after that Christmas of nineteen-three the Wright brothers weren't doing it for fun any more; they gave up their bicycle business,

---

2. **Hatteras . . . Albemarle Sound.** Cape Hatteras is east of Albemarle Sound, an inlet in the northeast coast of North Carolina.
3. **Leonardo,** Leonardo da Vinci (1452–1519), Italian artist and scientist who studied the principles of flight.

got the use of a big old cowpasture belonging to the local banker for practice flights, spent all the time when they weren't working on their machine in promotion, worrying about patents, infringements, spies, trying to interest government officials, to make sense out of the smooth involved heartbreaking remarks of lawyers.

In two years they had a plane that would cover twentyfour miles at a stretch round and round the cowpasture.

People on the interurban car used to crane their necks out of the windows when they passed along the edge of the field, startled by the clattering pop-pop of the old Wright motor and the sight of the white biplane like a pair of ironingboards one on top of the other chugging along a good fifty feet in the air. The cows soon got used to it.

As the flights got longer,
the Wright brothers got backers,
engaged in lawsuits,
lay in their beds at night sleepless with the whine of phantom millions, worse than mosquitoes at Kitty Hawk.

In nineteen-seven they went to Paris,
allowed themselves to be togged out in dress suits and silk hats,
learned to tip waiters,
talked with government experts, got used to gold braid and postponements and Vandyke beards[4] and the outspread palms of politicos.
For amusement
they played diabolo in the Tuileries Gardens.[5]

They gave publicized flights at Fort Myers, where they had their first fatal crackup, St. Petersburg, Paris, Berlin; at Pau[6] they were all the rage,
such an attraction that the hotelkeeper
wouldn't charge them for their room.
Alfonso of Spain shook hands with them and was photographed sitting in the machine.
King Edward watched a flight,
the Crown Prince insisted on being taken up,
the rain of medals began.

They were congratulated by the Czar
and the King of Italy and the amateurs of sport, and the society climbers and the papal titles,[7]
and decorated by a society for universal peace.

Aeronautics became the sport of the day.
The Wrights don't seem to have been very much impressed by the

---

4. *Vandyke beards*, small pointed beards worn by European men at the turn of the century.
5. *Tuileries* (twē′lər ēz) *Gardens,* the gardens which surround the Tuileries, a former royal palace in Paris. The palace was destroyed by fire in 1871, but the gardens remain.
6. *Pau* (pō), a winter resort in southwest France.
7. *papal titles,* men who bear titles of nobility conferred by the Pope in his capacity as sovereign of the Vatican.

upholstery and the braid and the gold medals and the parades of plush
horses;
    they remained practical mechanics
    and insisted on doing all their own work themselves,
    even to filling the gasolinetank.

    In nineteen-eleven they were back on the dunes
    at Kitty Hawk with a new glider.
    Orville stayed up in the air for nine and a half minutes, which re-
mained a long time the record for motorless flight.
    The same year Wilbur died of typhoidfever in Dayton.
    In the rush of new names; Farman, Blériot, Curtiss, Ferber, Esnault-
Peltrie, Delagrange⁸;
    in the snorting impact of bombs and the whine and rattle of shrapnel
and the sudden stutter of machineguns after the motor's been shut off
overhead,
    and we flatten into the mud
    and make ourselves small cowering in the corners of ruined walls,
    the Wright brothers passed out of the headlines;
    but not even headlines or the bitter smear of newsprint or the choke
of smokescreen and gas or chatter of brokers on the stockmarket or
barking of phantom millions or oratory of brasshats laying wreaths on
new monuments
    can blur the memory
    of the chilly December day
    two shivering bicycle mechanics from Dayton, Ohio,
    first felt their homemade contraption,
    whittled out of hickory sticks,
    gummed together with Arnstein's bicycle cement,
    stretched with muslin they'd sewn on their sister's sewingmachine
in their own backyard on Hawthorn Street in Dayton, Ohio,
    soar into the air
    above the dunes and the wide beach
    at Kitty Hawk.

✦ ✦ ✦ ✦ ✦ ✦

---

8. *Farman . . . Delagrange,* all were pioneers in flying.

DISCUSSION

1. **(a)** What overall impression of the Wright brothers does Dos Passos give you? **(b)** Find expressions the author uses to demonstrate the simplicity of their lives. **(c)** The author refers to the Wright brothers as "a couple of young bicycle mechanics from Dayton, Ohio." Would a description such as "two brilliant young men who devoted their lives to aeronautics" have been more suitable to the picture Dos Passos is creating of them? Why or why not?

2. **(a)** Does Dos Passos feel that the Wright brothers' personalities were changed by success? Find evidence to support your answer. **(b)** Does he admire the brothers as people, as scientists, or as both? How do you know?

3. **(a)** What picture of the brothers does Dos Passos create in the last eleven lines of the selection? **(b)** What contrast is there between these lines and the ten that precede them? **(c)** What is the point of this contrast?

4. Find a passage that contains words that have been run together and read it aloud. **(a)** What effect do the compound words have on your reading rate? **(b)** Why might Dos Passos have run these words together?

5. The various typographical devices Dos Passos uses make the selection attractive to the eye. He explained that he used these devices to "make the words stand up off the page." **(a)** Find a paragraph that has been set in the conventional manner. What similarities do you see between arrangement and content in this paragraph? **(b)** What kind of information is given in italics? **(c)** Do the italics lend a sense of importance or unimportance to the information? Explain. **(d)** Is the information that is given in the lines resembling poetry straight fact or Dos Passos' comments on the fact? **(e)** Do you think the unusual arrangement of the selection is suitable to what the author has to say? Why or why not?

6. **(a)** Does Dos Passos stick to facts in this account? **(b)** What facts does he use which are not important but add color and interest?

7. **(a)** Why are men like the Wright brothers considered heroes? **(b)** Do you think the necessity for their kind of heroism will ever die out? Why or why not?

WIDE WORLD PHOTOS

THE AUTHOR

While growing up, John Dos Passos (1896–1970) made trips all over the United States, for his father liked traveling and seeing new places. After graduating from Harvard, Dos Passos went to Spain to study architecture. But during World War I, he left his studies to serve as an ambulance driver for the French, and when America entered the conflict he joined the U.S. Medical Corps. His war experiences provided the material for *One Man's Initiation—1917*, his first book. Later he worked as a newspaper correspondent in Spain, Mexico, and the Near East.

Dos Passos was the author of plays, novels, and historical works. One of his novels is *U.S.A.*, a penetrating description of twentieth-century society. Placed throughout the novel are biographical sketches of famous Americans, similar in form to "The Campers at Kitty Hawk."

UNIT 2 Review

Part I

1. Literature and life both produce heroes, most of whom can be placed in one of several broad categories. Fit each of the following into the classification that best suits him. Then, explain why you think he fits there. In several cases, more than one hero will fit into a classification.

Harriet Tubman	*Hal*
the Wright brothers	*Buck*
Crooked-Thodoros	*Katya*
Cal Crawford	*Monkeyface*
Jimmy Bruce	

A. While not always totally admirable for his ideals and actions, he is sly and quick, and comes to the aid of his rival in an emergency. He conquers the forces of evil, not by great strength or fearlessness, but almost by mistake through some human action we recognize and sympathize with. Sometimes a clown, sometimes outwitted by others, he nevertheless comes out on top at the end.

B. He has a wild courage in his blood that often causes him to act without thinking of the consequences. He lives in an uncivilized society which recognizes him as a superior human being. He displays physical courage in a struggle with elements that endanger his community, and his heroic acts generally restore complete order. Although we admire him, we are seldom capable of displaying a courage equal to his.

C. He is either physically or mentally superior to most men, and he can usually influence society to some degree. His heroic acts can be motivated by personal desires or by a concern for the welfare of society. His abilities may exceed ours, but we feel free to criticize him.

D. He is our equal, and, like us, he conforms to the rules of society. Under ordinary circumstances, he behaves in a thoroughly ordinary manner. It takes a time of crisis or terror to bring out his heroic elements. His heroism can be prompted by either the wish for self-preservation or by love of mankind.

2. Name other heroes you know about who fit into one of the above classifications.

3. Many scientists who study human behavior claim that our heroes reflect the type of people we are. That is, if we admire persons who are power-hungry and ruthless, we ourselves aspire to be the same way. Name one figure who is a hero to a certain group and explain how that person reflects the desires and hopes of the people who admire him.

Part II

1. "The Rescue" and "The Pharmacist's Mate" are both suspenseful. What causes the suspense in each?

2. Do any of the selections in the unit have an unbelievable or inappropriate ending? Explain.

3. Trace the cause-and-effect relationships in the plot of "The Pharmacist's Mate." Can you find the same kind of relationship between incidents in "A Time of Greatness"? Explain.

4. Which selections in the unit are biographical? Which seems to stick closest to fact?

SUGGESTED READING

BAKER, RACHEL, *The First Woman Doctor.* (Messner) To enter the medical profession, Elizabeth Blackwell had to fight strong prejudice against women. Her struggle for equal rights opened the doors for the many women who followed her into medicine.

BENET, STEPHEN VINCENT and ROSEMARY *A Book of Americans.* (Holt) The accomplishments of many famous Americans are recounted in this sprightly collection of poetry.

DAUGHERTY, JAMES, *Marcus and Narcissa Whitman.* (Viking) When in 1836 Dr. Whitman and his wife Narcissa journeyed out to Oregon as missionaries, they knew their days would be difficult and dangerous, but they could not have dreamed that their heroic deeds would bring them undying fame.

GARST, SHANNON, *Jim Bridger, Greatest of the Mountain Men.* (Houghton) Jim Bridger could neither read nor write, but he knew the mountains and valleys of the West as other men know the streets of their town.

GOLLUMB, JOSEPH, *Albert Schweitzer: Genius in the Jungle.* (Vanguard) Turning away from the comforts and honors that were his as a musician, scholar, and physician, Schweitzer devoted his life to aiding the sick of West Africa.

GRAHAM, SHIRLEY, and GEORGE DEWEY LIPSCOMB, *Dr. George Washington Carver: Scientist.* (Messner) The life of this great scientist is a remarkable example of achievement and of service to mankind.

KUGELMASS, JOSEPH A., *Ralph J. Bunche, Fighter for Peace.* (Messner) The achievements of Ralph Bunche, who has been called the "United Nations' Peacemaker," will make you wonder how one man could accomplish so much in a lifetime.

MANN, ARTHUR WILLIAMS, *The Jackie Robinson Story.* (Grosset) The road that led Jackie Robinson from a sharecropper's farm to success was a rough, hard one to travel. Here is the story of the first Negro to become a major league baseball player.

MARRIOTT, ALICE, *Sequoyah, Leader of the Cherokees.* (Random) In this interesting biography of the famous Indian Sequoyah, emphasis is on his craftsmanship and his invention of an Indian alphabet.

OURSLER, FULTON and WILL, *Father Flanagan of Boys Town.* (Doubleday) Almost everyone has heard of Father Flanagan, but few realize how he struggled and fought for homeless and misplaced boys.

PETRY, ANN, *Harriet Tubman: Conductor on the Underground Railroad.* (Crowell) If you enjoyed the excerpt printed in the text, you'll want to read the rest of this well-written biography of a resolute woman.

WIBBERLEY, LEONARD, *The Life of Winston Churchill.* (Farrar) Churchill's colorful childhood, his hectic school years, and adventure-packed period of war service make absorbing reading.

WILLIAMS, BERYL, and SAMUEL EPSTEIN, *Francis Marion, Swamp Fox of the Revolution.* (Messner) The greatest guerrilla fighter of the American Revolution terrorized the entire British army in South Carolina by striking swiftly and then vanishing into the swamps. He won the first important victory of the Revolution.

WOOD, LAURA N., *Louis Pasteur.* (Messner) With all his success, Pasteur was a humble man. His patient experiments and painstaking research have contributed enormously to modern medicine. Also by Miss Wood is *Walter Reed, Doctor in Uniform* (Messner), the exciting story of the man who struggled to control yellow fever.

WYATT, EDGAR, *Cochise, Apache Warrior and Statesman.* (McGraw) The daring Cochise, chieftain of the Chiricahua Apaches, wanted peace. But peace was impossible, for there was too much provocation by both Indians and settlers.

A poem can create a mood, show a viewpoint, tell a story, reflect the poet's personality, or do all of these things at once. Discover the pleasure of sharing a poet's mood in this first group of poems.

POETRY I

Simultaneously

DAVID IGNATOW

Simultaneously, five thousand miles apart,
two telephone poles, shaking and roaring
and hissing gas, rose from their emplacements
straight up, leveled off and headed
for each other's land, alerted radar   5
and ground defense, passed each other
in midair, escorted by worried planes,
and plunged into each other's place,
steaming and silent and standing straight,
sprouting leaves.   10

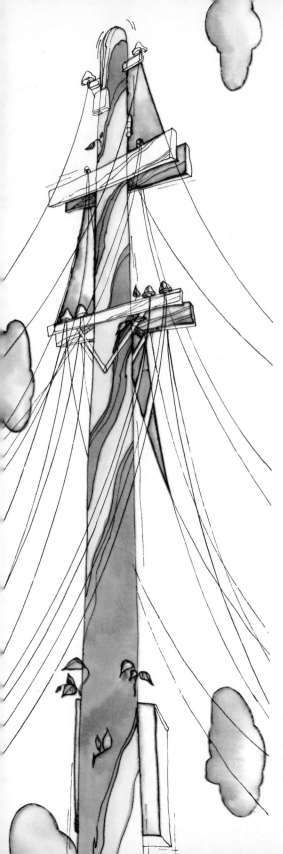

1. (a) What do the events described in the first seven lines suggest to you about the purpose of the "telephone poles"? **(b)** What kind of things do these "telephone poles" resemble? **(c)** What might be the significance of the distance between their "emplacements"? **(d)** Why might they be escorted by "worried planes"?

2. (a) What feeling or mood did the first seven lines of the poem give as you first read through them? **(b)** What details, words, or phrases influenced your mood?

3. (a) What change in mood occurs in the last two lines? **(b)** What words or word sounds help create this change? **(c)** What does the image of the "telephone poles" sprouting leaves suggest about the change that has overcome them?

THE AUTHOR

David Ignatow is a product of Brooklyn, New York, where his formal education came to an end upon his graduation from high school. He still lives in New York today, writing poetry and doing free-lance editing.

Among the literary figures he cites as influential in his development as a poet are Walt Whitman, Ernest Hemingway, and the poets of the Bible.

See
INFERENCES
*Handbook
of Literary
Terms
page 526*

The
Demon
of the
Gibbet

*FITZ-JAMES
O'BRIEN*

There was no west, there was no east,
    No star abroad for eyes to see;
And Norman spurred his jaded beast
    Hard by the terrible gallows tree.

"O, Norman, haste across this waste—   5
    For something seems to follow me!"
"Cheer up, dear Maud, for, thanked be God,
    We nigh have passed the gallows tree!"

He kissed her lip: then—spur and whip
    And fast they fled across the lea.   10
But vain the heel, and rowel steel—
    For something leaped from the gallows tree!

"Give me your cloak, your knightly cloak,
    That wrapped you oft beyond the sea!
The wind is bold, my bones are old,   15
    And I am cold on the gallows tree."

"O holy God! O dearest Maud,
    Quick, quick, some prayers—the best that be!
A bony hand my neck has spanned,
    And tears my knightly cloak from me!"   20

"Give me your wine, the red, red wine,
    That in the flask hangs by your knee!
Ten summers burst on me accurst,
    And I'm athirst on the gallows tree!"

"O Maud, my life, my loving wife!   25
    Have you no prayer to set us free?
My belt unclasps—a demon grasps,
    And drags my wine flask from my knee!"

"Give me your bride, your bonnie bride,
    That left her nest with you to flee!   30
O she hath flown to be my own,
    For I'm alone on the gallows tree!"

"Cling closer, Maud, and trust in God!
    Cling close—Ah, heaven, she slips from me!"
A prayer, a groan, and he alone   35
    Rode on that night from the gallows tree.

DISCUSSION

1. (a) What is a gibbet? (b) Which words and phrases help you infer the setting of the poem? (c) Why, when he nears the gallows tree, does Norman spur his horse?

2. (a) Who speaks in lines 5-6? (b) Who answers in lines 7-8?

3. Which words and phrases in lines 9-12 imply Norman's efforts to make the horse hurry?

4. (a) Who speaks in the lines set in italics? (b) What do you learn about this character? (c) What three things does he demand? (d) What reasons does he give for wanting each thing? (e) How does he get each?

THE AUTHOR

Fitz-James O'Brien's life began about 1828 in County Limerick, Ireland, and ended in 1862 in Cumberland, Virginia, where he died of tetanus six weeks after being wounded in the Civil War. As a young man, he wasted his entire inheritance during four years in London and Paris. Broke when he arrived in New York in 1852, he soon established himself as a writer of essays, poems, stories, including science fiction, and articles. When the Civil War began, O'Brien enlisted in the New York National Guard. He received special mention for gallantry at the Battle of Bloomery Gap shortly before he was wounded.

See
IMAGERY
*Handbook
of Literary
Terms
page 524*

Two views of stormy weather. How do they compare?

Rain

ROSS PARMENTER

The parts of trees,
leaves, twigs and moving boughs,
reveal the wind.

But rain can be most surely gauged
on the surface of still water.   5
The punctured holes
make clear the congregation of the drops,
and each circumference the size,
and force is manifest
in brief beads popping   10
above the spreading circles
linking the water
in a coat of living mail.

DISCUSSION

1.(a) What aspect of rain do the images in this poem focus on? **(b)** Which sense do they mainly appeal to?
2. (a) Restate lines 6–11 in your own words. **(b)** What does the poet mean when he describes the surface of the water as "a coat of living mail"?

THE AUTHOR

Ross Parmenter might best be described as a man who is versed in all the fine arts. He started his career in 1934 as a general reporter for the *New York Times.* Since then he has been a music editor, columnist, free-lance writer, and illustrator for his own books, among them works on language, anthropology, and Japanese Buddhist temples.

One A.M.

X. J. KENNEDY

The storm came home too blind to stand,
He thwacked down oaks like chairs,
Shattered a lake and in the dark
Head over heels downstairs
Rolled, and up grumbling, on his knees,   5
Made nine white tries to scratch
Against walls that kept billowing
The strict head of his match.

From THE NEW YORK TIMES BOOK OF VERSE. Reprinted by permission of the author.

DISCUSSION

1. (**a**) What inference about the behavior of the storm can you make from the first line of the poem? (**b**) What in the rest of the poem supports this inference?
2. What actual sights and sounds do the lines that follow refer to? (**a**) "thwacked down oaks like chairs" (**b**) "Head over heels downstairs Rolled" (**c**) "Made nine white tries to scratch Against walls that kept billowing The strict head of his match."
3. What storm sounds do the words or phrases in this poem imitate? Make a list of words or phrases that suggest such sounds and note the aspect of the storm each refers to.

THE AUTHOR

The *X* in X. J. Kennedy's name does not really stand for anything at all; it was simply chosen to distinguish the author from the Kennedy clan of political fame.

Although widely recognized as a poet, Kennedy does not spend all of his time writing poetry. Since 1956 he has been teaching English and creative writing courses at a number of universities and colleges.

It says a lot in a little

A poem is a record of experience to be shared. The poet sees or does or thinks or feels, and he passes along his observations and actions and ideas and emotions to the reader. This is what the prose writer does too, but the poet's job is a harder one. The prose writer can leisurely develop his theme, making abundant use of details. But the poet is held down by the conventions, or rules, of his form. He must evoke emotional and intellectual response in the fewest possible words, usually through careful use of language. He chooses his material with special care and screens his language for useless words. Careful selection and sifting result in *compression:* he says a lot in a little. For example:

There stood one—aside the seawashed shore and dared breakers to touch toes.

These two lines call a definite picture to mind. Try describing the scene in prose. About how many words does it take to create the same image?

Like anyone else, a poet uses words for their meaning. He often tries to pack more meaning into them than does the prose writer.

The poet is also concerned with the **connotations** of words, the emotions and associations they stir up in us. For example, what two very different pictures of, and responses to, a brook do you have in:

I chatter, chatter as I flow I babble on the pebbles . . .

and

I murmur under moon and stars . . .

Because the poet cuts away all needless words and packs the useful ones with all possible meaning and emotion, poetry should be read slowly and carefully. Every word has a purpose; to understand a poem fully, you have to be aware of the meaning and connotation that each word carries.

How well do you understand the following poem?

Apparently With No Surprise

EMILY DICKINSON

Apparently with no surprise
To any happy Flower
The Frost beheads it at its play—
In accidental power—
The blonde Assassin passes on—   5
The Sun proceeds unmoved
To measure off another Day
For an approving God.

What happens in the first three lines of the poem? Which word in line 2 implies a comparison between the flower and humans? What is unusual about the flower's response to being beheaded? What meanings does the word **accidental** carry with it? In what two ways does this reaction differ from the human response to death?

What is the literal meaning of "blonde Assassin" (line 5)? What other meanings might it have? What connotations does **blonde** carry with it? Would humans be more apt to describe death as **blonde** or **dark**? Why? What is the meaning of "proceeds unmoved" (line 6)? Why might the Sun and God accept death so readily? What criticism of human thinking is implied?

Two poems by Robert Frost . . .
What do they tell you about the speaker?

The Pasture / *ROBERT FROST*

I'm going out to clean the pasture spring;
I'll only stop to rake the leaves away
(And wait to watch the water clear, I may):
I sha'n't be gone long.—You come too.

I'm going out to fetch the little calf   5
That's standing by the mother. It's so young
It totters when she licks it with her tongue.
I sha'n't be gone long. —You come too.

DISCUSSION

1. (a) What kind of person does the speaker seem to be? (b) What are his feelings toward the person he is addressing? How can you tell?
2. (a) Which words in the poem give it its conversational tone? (b) Does punctuation add anything to the informality? Explain.
3. Frost began several collections of his work with "The Pasture." What additional invitation does this placement suggest?

Good-by and Keep Cold

ROBERT FROST

This saying good-by on the edge of the dark
And the cold to an orchard so young in the bark
Reminds me of all that can happen to harm
An orchard away at the end of the farm
All winter, cut off by a hill from the house.   5
I don't want it girdled by rabbit and mouse,
I don't want it dreamily nibbled for browse
By deer, and I don't want it budded by grouse.
(If certain it wouldn't be idle to call
I'd summon grouse, rabbit, and deer to the wall   10
And warn them away with a stick for a gun.)
I don't want it stirred by the heat of the sun.
(We made it secure against being, I hope,
By setting it out on a northerly slope.)
No orchard's the worse for the wintriest storm;   15
But one thing about it, it mustn't get warm.
How often already you've had to be told,
"Keep cold, young orchard. Good-by and keep cold.
Dread fifty above more than fifty below."
I have to be gone for a season or so.   20
My business awhile is with different trees,
Less carefully nurtured, less fruitful than these,
And such as is done to their wood with an ax —
Maples and birches and tamaracks.
I wish I could promise to lie in the night   25
And think of an orchard's arboreal plight
When slowly (and nobody comes with a light)
Its heart sinks lower under the sod.
But something has to be left to God.

1. Reread lines 1–11. **(a)** What is the "edge of the dark/And the cold"? **(b)** What things can happen to damage the orchard? **(c)** Explain the meaning of: "girdled by rabbit and mouse"; "nibbled for browse"; "budded by grouse." **(d)** What character traits does the speaker reveal in saying he would warn some dangers away "with a stick for a gun"?

2. Why does the speaker want the orchard to keep cold?

3. (a) Where is the speaker going? **(b)** What does he wish he could promise to do while he is gone?

4. (a) Summarize what the speaker is saying about the relationship between man and nature and God. **(b)** *Philosophy* means "love of wisdom." What is the evidence that the speaker in this poem is a philosopher?

5. In what ways is the speaker in "Good-by and Keep Cold" like the speaker in "The Pasture"? Find lines and phrases in each that indicate similarities.

Robert Frost (1874–1963) was a New England farmer who loved the earth and the things close to it. Rocky farms, lush woodlands, old houses, stone fences, and the rugged people who work the soil are the stuff his poems are made of. Frost was born in San Francisco, but his forebears for nine generations had been New Englanders. When the boy was ten, his father died, and the family returned to the Northeast, where Frost spent most of his life.

In 1892, Frost—the valedictorian of his high-school class—enrolled in college, found he didn't like it, and quit. During the next few years, he worked in a mill, took a tramping trip through the South, did some teaching and some newspaper work, and married Elinor White, his one-time rival for class valedictorian. In 1897, he tried college again and this time stayed two years. For the next eleven years, he farmed; then he spent four years teaching. Throughout this time he wrote poetry. According to his own calculations, he earned about two hundred dollars, in all, from his verse.

Attracted by the low cost of living in England, he went there with his family in 1912. One year later, he found a publisher for his first book, *A Boy's Will*. This as well as his second book, *North of Boston,* became popular, and he returned to America to find himself famous. Nevertheless, he resumed his old vocations—farming and teaching—and still found time to write poetry. Between 1912 and the year of his death, Frost won the Pulitzer Prize, an award given annually to the work judged to be the best in its field, four times.

Much has been written about Robert Frost—about his personality, his work, his philosophy, his magnificent appearance, his ability to captivate an audience completely. But a very short comment by Gwendolyn Brooks is perhaps one of the best word pictures of the man who called himself a farmer:

There is a little lightning in his eyes.
Iron at the mouth.
His brows ride neither too far up or down.

He is splendid. With a place to stand.

Some glowing in the common blood.
Some specialness within.[1]

---

1. "Of Robert Frost." Copyright © 1963 by Gwendolyn Brooks Blakely. From SELECTED POEMS by Gwendolyn Brooks. Reprinted by permission of Harper & Row, Publishers.

One poet shows you how to look at a circus
and another explains how to live
through a roller-coaster ride.

Toulouse-Lautrec, In the Circus Fernando, 1888. The Joseph Winterbotham Collection, Art Institute, Chicago.

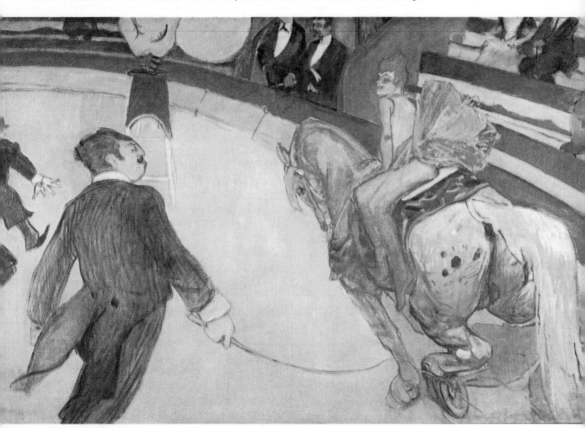

The Circus; Or One View of It

THEODORE SPENCER

Said the circus man, Oh what do you like
Best of all about my show —
The circular rings, three rings in a row,
With animals going around, around,
Tamed to go running round, around,   5
And around, round, around they go;
Or perhaps you like the merry-go-round,
Horses plunging sedately up,
Horses sedately plunging down,
Going around the merry-go-round;   10
Or perhaps you like the clown with a hoop,
Shouting, rolling the hoop around;
Or the elephants walking around in a ring
Each trunk looped to a tail's loop,
Loosely ambling around the ring;   15
How do you like this part of the show?
Everything's busy and on the go;
The peanut men cry out and sing,
The round fat clown rolls on the ground,
The trapeze ladies sway and swing,   20
The circus horses plunge around
The circular rings, three rings in a row;
Here they come, and here they go.
And here you sit, said the circus man,
Around in a circle to watch my show;   25
Which is show and which is you,
Now that we're here in this circus show,
Do I know? Do you know?
But hooray for the clowns and the merry-go-round,
The painted horses plunging round,   30
The live, proud horses stamping the ground,
And the clowns and the elephants swinging around;
Come to my show; hooray for the show,
Hooray for the circus all the way round!
Said the round exuberant circus man.   35
Hooray for the show! said the circus man.

Continued

DISCUSSION

1. The idea of roundness is constantly re-peated in the poem. Give examples that emphasize this concept.

2. What images of sound does the poet use?

3. (a) What does the second part of the title, "Or One View of It," suggest? **(b)** Where, in the poem, is the second view given? **(c)** What is the poet saying in these lines?

4. Why does some kind of rhyme scheme seem appropriate to a poem about a circus?

THE AUTHOR

Could you guess from "The Circus; Or One View of It" that Theodore Spencer (1902-1949) was a well-known critic of Shake-spearean tragedy, an authority on contem-porary literature, and a Harvard professor? Spencer included "The Circus; Or One View of It" in *The Paradox in the Circle*, a volume of poems he wrote to be read aloud. (A *paradox* is something that seems to be full of contradictions.) "The Circus; Or One View of It" may be regarded as a clue to Theodore Spencer's concern with the puzzles and contradictions of life.

WORD STUDY

Circus is a Latin word meaning "ring." In ancient Rome, a circus was a ring-shaped amphitheater used for chariot racing, ath-letic contests, gladiator matches, and pub-lic spectacles. The concept of a ring shape influences the meaning of other words from the Latin *circus,* including those listed below. Use each word in the sentence where it best fits. Then explain the connection between the meanings of these words and a ring shape. Use your dictionary if you aren't sure.

circle, circular, circulate, circulation, encircle.

1. That magazine has had a three-per-cent in-crease in _____ since July.

2. Using a stick, Jack drew a _____ in the dust.

3. Instead of the letter Sally expected, there was only a _____ in the mailbox.

4. This plastic model shows how the blood can _____.

5. The raiding party planned to _____ the camp.

The Contraption

MAY SWENSON

Going up is pleasant. It tips your chin,
and you feel tall and free
as if in control of, and standing in
a chariot, hands feeling the frisky

reins. But, doubled in your seat,   5
knuckled to the fun-car's handrails,
you mount baby-buggied, cleat by cleat,
to that humped apogee your entrails

aren't ready for. Wind in your
ears, clouds in your eyes, it's easy   10
to define the prophetic jelly at your core
as joy. The landscape of amusement goes queasy

only when the gilded buckboard juts straight out
over undippered air. A jaw of horror will split
you? Not yet. The route   15
becomes a roaring trough for the next hill

hairpinning higher. You wish you had
the chance to count how many ups,
downs and switchbacks the mad
rattler, rearing its steel hoops, has. The divan hiccups   20

over a straightaway now, at mild speed.
Then you look: Jolly carousel and ferris wheel, far
years beneath, are cruel gears you can be emptied
into over the side of the hellish sled. Star-

beaded sky! (It feels better to look higher.) How   25
did the morning, the whole blue-and-white day
go by in what seems one swoop? You vow
to examine the contraption and its fairway,

Continued

---

measure the system of gruesome twists,
the queer dimensions, if ever you get down. Going   30
down is a dull road. Your fists
loosen, pretend no longer, knowing

they grip no stick of purpose. The final chutes are
unspectacular, slower repetitious of past
excitements. A used and vulgar car   35
shovels you home in a puzzling gloom. The vast

agitation faded in your bowels, you think
that from the ground you'll trace the rim
your coaster sped and crawled, the sink
and rise, the reason for its shape. Grim   40

darkness now. The ride
is complete. You are positioned for discovery, but,
your senses gone, you can't see the upper arching works. Wide
silence. Midnight. The carnival is shut.

DISCUSSION

1. Who is the *you* in the poem?
2. (**a**) How does it feel to start upward in the contraption? (**b**) What does *baby-buggied* mean (line 7)? (**c**) What words in lines 9-12 indicate a thrilling ride is expected?
3. (**a**) How does it feel just before the first plunge downward (lines 12-14)? (**b**) What images in lines 15-17 show that the ride is fast and steep? (**c**) What is the "mad rattler" in lines 19-20? (**d**) Explain the use of *hiccups* in lines 20-21 to describe the motion of the contraption. (**e**) Why do the carousel and ferris wheel (lines 22-24) bring to mind thoughts of gears?
4. (**a**) What are the rider's feelings now that the ride is complete? (**b**) Compare and contrast the feeling you get from "The Circus; Or One View of It" with the feeling you get from "The Contraption."

THE AUTHOR

May Swenson was born and educated in Utah, but she has spent most of her career as a poet in New York. Her poems, recognized for their imagery and unusual observations, have been recorded, translated for publication in German and Italian anthologies, and set to music.

What incident does the poet remember as a . . .

Crystal Moment

ROBERT P. TRISTRAM COFFIN

Once or twice this side of death
Things can make one hold his
    breath.

From my boyhood I remember
A crystal moment of September.

A wooded island rang with sounds   5
Of church bells in the throats of
    hounds.

A buck leaped out and took the tide
With jewels flowing past each side.

With his high head like a tree
He swam within a yard of me.   10

I saw the golden drop of light
In his eyes turned dark with fright.

I saw the forest's holiness
On him like a fierce caress.

Fear made him lovely past belief,   15
My heart was trembling like a leaf.

He leaned towards the land and life
With need upon him like a knife.

In his wake the hot hounds churned,
They stretched their muzzles out and
    yearned.   20

They bayed no more, but swam and
    throbbed,
Hunger drove them till they sobbed.

Pursued, pursuers reached the shore
And vanished. I saw nothing more.

So they passed, a pageant such   25
As only gods could witness much,

Life and death upon one tether
And running beautiful together.

DISCUSSION

1. What incident does the poet describe in lines 5-24?
2. (a) Why is the comparison between the dogs' voices and the sound of church bells an especially effective image? (b) Find other good images in the poem.
3. According to lines 25-28, what does the speaker consider so dramatic about the brief scene?
4. The rhymes in this poem form a pattern called a *couplet*. (a) Which lines rhyme? (b) Where do most of the sentences end?
5. (a) Describe a crystal. (b) What do you think the poet means by a *crystal* moment?

What is it that makes some people unpopular,

misfits, or the last to be chosen? Why do some choose

not to be part of the crowd?

And why are some tormented for their beliefs, their

background, or their way of dress? What stuff are

their tormenters made of?

Or what of those who choose to question, shun

recognition, want no attention? What do they gain

by being different and what price must they pay

to be so?

These are but a few of the questions confronting . . .

THE OUTSIDER

See
THEME
*Handbook
of Literary
Terms
page 536*

*When Ellenwood came to Moon Dance,
he brought his own ideals and standards with him.
Why was he forced to fight for them?*

First Principal

A. B. GUTHRIE

THE FIRST MAN Lonnie Ellenwood saw to remember after the stage arrived at Moon Dance was Mr. Ross, the chairman of the school board.

The second was the man with the yellow eyes.

The first one stepped out and stood by the wheel as the driver checked the horses. His voice boomed up at Lonnie's father before they could get down. "Howdy there, Professor. I'm Ross. Glad to see you."

The man stood as high as a high-headed horse. He had a red face and bright blue eyes. "Howdy, Mrs. Ellenwood. How's Ohio?" He offered a hand to match the voice. "Hope you're going to like it here."

He stooped to shake hands with Lonnie. "Howdy there. Guess you're too young for your dad's new high school. Like to fish, Bub?" Lonnie smelled the evil smell of whisky on his breath. The man straightened and turned to Mr. Ellenwood. "We can go, soon's we get your plunder."

They stood in front of a frame hotel — Lonnie and his parents and Mr. Ross in a little group — and the grown people talked while they waited for the driver to hand down the baggage. A sign across the hotel said HERREN HOUSE. Another, below it, said BAR. The other buildings along the street were wooden, too, and mostly one-story. The dust that the stage had raised was settling back.

A line of men leaned against the front of the hotel, watching from under wide hats. Lonnie saw curiosity in their faces, and doubt and maybe dislike for the new principal and his wife and boy. At first he thought the men all looked alike — weathered cheeks, blue or black shirts, faded pants — and then he saw the man with the yellow eyes. They weren't exactly yellow, though, but pale brown, pale enough to look yellow, yellow and cold like a cat's. Under his nose was a cat's draggle of mustache.

The eyes caught Lonnie's and held them, and Lonnie felt a quick alarm, seeing bold and rude in them the veiled suspicions of the rest.

"Kind of raw country to you, I guess, Prof," Mr. Ross was saying, "but you'll get along." He took a cigar from the pocket of his unbuttoned vest and bit the end off it and spit it out. "Great country, Montana is, and bound to be better. We got a church already, like I told you in my letter, and now we'll have a high school. Yep, you'll get along."

Two of the men who lounged against the hotel were chewing tobacco, staining the plank sidewalk with thoughtful spurts of spit. A swinging door divided them, and a sweet-sour smell came from inside.

"Preacher's a fine man, or so they tell me," Mr. Ross went on. "He figured to be here, only a funeral came up."

Beside Mr. Ross, beside the shirt sleeves and the open vest, Mr. Ellenwood looked small and pale, and too proper in the new suit he'd bought in Cincinnati.

Lonnie's mother wasn't paying any attention to the watching men. She looked up and down the dusty street, at the board buildings that fronted up to it, and at the sky that arched over. She smiled down at Lonnie and touched him on the shoulder. "This is our new home, son."

He didn't answer. He wished he were back in Ohio, screened in the friendly woods and hills, away from this bare, flat land where even the sun seemed to stare at him.

Mr. Ross was still talking. "I got a team hitched around the corner. I'll ride you over. Hope you like the house we got for you."

The stage driver had set the baggage down. Mr. Ross grabbed hold of a bag and suitcase and an old telescope[1] and began walking along with Mrs. Ellenwood.

As Lonnie's father started to follow, carrying a box in one hand and a straw suitcase in the other, a man lurched from the door of the hotel and fell against him and caught his balance and went swaying up the street talking to himself.

When Lonnie brought his gaze back from the man, he saw his father leaning over. The suitcase had broken open and spilled towels and cold cream and powder and one of his mother's petticoats on the walk. Father was stuffing them back in, stuffing them in slowly one by one while blood colored his neck.

The men were laughing, not very loud but inside themselves while they tried to keep their mouths straight. Only the man with the yellow eyes really let his laughs come out. He was angled against the wall of the hotel, one booted foot laid across the other. His voice sounded in little jeering explosions.

Mr. Ellenwood didn't say anything. He went ahead stuffing things back into the suitcase and trying to make the lock catch afterwards.

Mr. Ross looked back and saw what had happened and turned around and returned. His face got redder than ever. To the one man he said, "Funny, ain't it, Chilter!"

"To me it is," the man answered and laughed again.

Mrs. Ellenwood was standing where Mr. Ross had left her. Lonnie saw an anxious look on her face.

Mr. Ellenwood finally got the lock to catch. He picked up the suitcase, and they started off again, the eyes following them and then being lost around a corner. Mr. Ross didn't speak until they had put the baggage in the buggy, and then all he said was, "Sorry, Prof."

Lonnie's father sat quietly while Mr. Ross cramped the wheel around

---

1. *telescope,* a traveling bag made up of two parts, the larger of which fits over the smaller.

and got straightened out. "It's all right." His voice was even. "It doesn't matter."

Mrs. Ellenwood smiled at Lonnie. "I guess it was funny, to everybody but us."

Mr. Ross grunted as if he didn't think so.

He came around the next day, the day before school was to open. "Like I told you," he promised Mr. Ellenwood, "next year we'll have a building, but the old hall'll have to do until then. You seen it? Everything shipshape?" He stood half a foot higher than Mr. Ellenwood. He was bigger, thicker, stronger, more assured. When he laughed he rattled the china that Lonnie's mother hadn't found a place for yet. He turned to Lonnie. "Your school don't start till next week, eh, Bub?"

He bit off the end of a cigar and lighted up and settled back in the rocking chair. "You're going to like it here, Prof. It ain't much, in a way, but in a way it is, too. Best damn people—excuse me—that ever lived, most of 'em. You'll see."

Mr. Ellenwood was nodding politely.

"Kind of rough, but you'll get on."

"Yes," Mr. Ellenwood said and waited for Mr. Ross to say more.

Mr. Ross took his cigar out and rolled it between his fingers. He studied it for a long time. "People'll take to you," he said slowly as if reading the words from the cigar, "soon as they learn you ain't being buffaloed."

"I don't know that I know what you mean."

"It's just a word, is all. Comes, I guess, because buffalo scare kind of easy."

"I see."

Mr. Ross squirmed in the rocker. He rolled the cigar some more, and then chewed on it and pulled and let

out a plume of smoke. "Some maybe ain't used to a man teaching school," he said, not looking at Mr. Ellenwood.

"I see."

"You'll get on. Mostly it's women who teach in this country."

"I see."

Mrs. Ellenwood came from the kitchen. She said good morning.

Mr. Ross lifted himself from the rocker. "Howdy, ma'am. Preacher been around yet, and Mrs. Rozzell?"

Mrs. Ellenwood nodded. "Yesterday."

"We liked them," Mr. Ellenwood said.

Lonnie's mother put her hand on his father's shoulder. "They insist Tom has to be superintendent of the Sunday school."

Mr. Ross nodded and smoked some more on his cigar. When he got up to go, Mr. Ellenwood stepped to the door with him. "We'll get on, as you say."

For what seemed a long time, Mr. Ross looked him up and down. Lonnie wondered if he saw a kind of chunky man, not very tall, with a pale complexion and sandy hair and the look of books and church about him, a man firm in the right but not forward, not hearty and sure like Mr. Ross himself.

"O' course," Mr. Ross said, "you'll get on." He put his cigar back in his mouth and closed the door.

It rained the next day, a cold misty rain that sifted out of the north. The air was still wet with drizzle that afternoon as Lonnie started out to meet his father on his return from school. The dirt trails that passed for streets were sticky with mud. At the crossings Lonnie hopped and skipped until he reached the plank sidewalk again, but even so he got mud on his shoes.

A little bunch of cattle was being herded down the street. Lonnie could

see the horseman behind them, reining to and fro to bring up the poky ones and flicking at them with his quirt.[2] The cattle had their heads stuck out, their eyes big with the strangeness of town, their mouths opening to a lost mooing. The voice of the driver as he herded them along came to Lonnie like a snarl.

For a minute he was frightened, seeing the cattle coming his way and the long horns gleaming white, and then he saw his father and felt safe and hurried along to meet him. Mr. Ellenwood was walking with half a dozen boys and girls. They were students, Lonnie guessed. He saw his father lift his head and turn his face toward the horseman. The boys and girls stopped. The rider pulled up, held his horse for a moment, and then reined over.

Lonnie had got close enough to hear. The rider said, "How was that, schoolteacher?"

Even before he saw for sure, Lonnie felt his insides tighten. The man was Chilter of the almost yellow eyes and the cat's mustache beneath.

"I asked you to stop that cursing."

Chilter spit, then asked, "Why so?"

Mr. Ellenwood made a little motion toward the boys and girls. "You can see why."

For a while the man didn't say anything. He sat on his horse, curbing it as it tried to step around, and let his gaze go over Mr. Ellenwood. He looked big, sitting there over everybody. "Why," he said, "I heard this was a free country."

Mr. Ellenwood stepped out into the mud. He didn't speak; he just stepped out into the mud, his face lifted and his gaze steady.

The cat eyes looked him over. They traveled down the street to the cattle. Lonnie saw that the bunch was loosening. Some had poked through the open gate of a front yard. Some had started up an alley. A man came out of a door and called from the front yard. "Hey, you, haze these steers away, will you?"

Mr. Ellenwood said, "These are just children."

The eyes came back to him. They looked him over again, slowly, yellow and cold and scornful. The man spit and dug his spurs into his horse. It threw some mud on Mr. Ellenwood as it lunged. When it had run a little way, Chilter jerked it up and turned in his saddle and lifted his hat and bobbed his head at Mr. Ellenwood as if speaking to a lady.

Mr. Ellenwood pulled back from the mud. He kept silent, walking home, even after the high-schoolers had dropped away one by one. Lonnie wanted to question him but felt closed off. And when finally the words came to his mouth, he would see the man turning and lifting his hat, like saying, "Excuse me, ma'am," and anger or shame or the fear in his stomach kept them unsaid. All he managed was, "Mother said to tell you she was meeting with the ladies of the church."

At home Mr. Ellenwood changed clothes and went out into the back yard and began to split wood for the kitchen range. Lonnie sat on the steps and watched.

It had quit drizzling. In the west the sun showed red through black clouds. The sharp smell of fall was in the air, the smell of summer done and things dying, of cold to come, of leaves that someone was trying to make into a bonfire.

Lonnie's father was still chopping wood when Mr. Ross came clattering

---

2. **quirt,** a riding whip with a braided leather lash and a short handle.

down the back steps. "Couldn't rouse anyone," Mr. Ross explained, "so I come on through, figuring you might be out here in back."

Mr. Ellenwood anchored the ax in the chopping block and turned to talk.

Mr. Ross bobbed his head toward Lonnie, and Mr. Ellenwood said, "You run in the house, son."

Lonnie backed up and lagged up the steps, but he didn't go in. He sat down on the porch, behind the low wall of it, and listened and now and then dared a look.

"Might as well tell you, Prof," Mr. Ross said, "that man Chilter's up to the saloon, making big medicine against you."

Mr. Ellenwood nodded, as if he expected it all the time.

"I don't know what to tell you."

"Nothing. It's all right."

"He's got a kind of a reputation as a bad actor."

"Oh."

"You got a gun or something?"

"I wouldn't want a gun."

"No?"

"No."

"You can't just hold quiet, and let him do whatever he figures on!"

"I'll just have to wait and see."

"I could stay with you, I guess." It was as if the words were being pulled out of Mr. Ross.

Mr. Ellenwood looked him in the eye. "Mr. Ross," he said, "a man has to hoe his own row, here or in Ohio."

"Good for you. I wasn't so sure about Ohio. I kind of wish you'd let me give you a six-shooter. I brought one along for you, just in case."

"No. Thanks."

"He ain't likely to use one. More likely to be fist fighting or wrastling, no holds barred."

"Anyhow, you go on."

"I might hang around, kind of out of sight."

"You go on."

Mr. Ross rolled his lower lip with his thumb and forefinger. "Damn if I ain't acting like a mother hen." He laughed without humor. "Good luck, Prof." He turned and walked away. Lonnie could see, before he rounded the corner of the house, that his face was troubled.

Later, out of the beginning dusk, the man came riding. Far off, before he could see him, Lonnie heard the quick suck of horse's hoofs in the mud. They might have been meaningless at first, just sounds that went along with other sounds like the creak of an axle and the cry of children and the whisper of wind, except that already Lonnie knew, and his stomach sickened and the blood raced in him.

He wanted to cry out, wanted to shout the man was coming, wanted to scream that here he was, forever identifiable now by the mere turn of a shoulder and the set of his head.

The man didn't speak. He just kept coming, his horse's feet dancing fancy in the mud.

Mr. Ellenwood raised his ax and saw him and tapped the ax head into the block and stood straight.

The man rode from the alley into the unfenced back yard, and for a minute Lonnie thought he meant to ride his father down. Then he saw the hand leap up and the butt of the quirt arching from it. The quirt came down to the sound of torn air.

A weal sprang out on Mr. Ellenwood's face. One second it wasn't there, and the next it was, like something magical, a red and purple weal swollen high as half a rope. It ran from the temple across the cheek and down the line of the jaw.

For one breath it was like looking at a picture, the horse pulled up, the quirt downswept from the hand, the weal hot and angry, and nothing

moving, everything caught up and held by the violence that had gone before.

The picture broke into sound and fury, father's hand shooting out and catching the man's arm and tearing him from his horse and the horse snorting and shying away and the man landing sprawled and gathering himself like a cat and raising the quirt high again while swear words streamed from his mouth.

Mr. Ellenwood was stepping, stepping forward, not back, stepping into the wicked whistle and cut of the quirt, his head up and his eyes fixed. There was a terrible rightness about him, a rightness so terrible and so fated that for a minute Lonnie couldn't bear to look, thinking of Stephen stoned[3] and Christ dying on the cross—of all the pale, good, thoughtful men foredoomed before the hearty.

He heard the whine of the quirt and the two men grunting and the whine of the quirt and feet slipping in the wet grass and breaths hoarse in the throat and the sound of the quirt again.

He heard the grunting and the slipping and the hoarse breathing, and all at once he remembered he didn't hear the quirt now, and he looked and saw it looping away, thrown by his father's hand. He saw his father's fists begin to work and heard the flat smacks of bone against flesh and saw the man try to shield himself and go down and get up and go down again. His eyes ran from side to side like a cornered animal's. He began crawling away. Rather than meet those fists again, he crawled away, beaten and silent, and climbed his horse and rode off.

Mr. Ellenwood watched him, then turned and saw Lonnie, who had come off the porch and down the steps. "Son," he said sternly, still panting, "I thought I told you to go inside."

From a distance Mr. Ross's voice, raised in a great whoop, came to Lonnie's ears.

"I did—I mean I couldn't. I just couldn't."

Lonnie watched his father's face, wanting, now that he had won, to see it loosen and light up and the weal bend to a smile.

"You're pale as paper, son."

"I didn't know if you could fight. I didn't know if you would think it was right to fight."

Mr. Ross's voice drowned out the answer. From across the street it boomed at them, the words sounding almost like hurrahs. "By God, Prof, you're all right!"

Mr. Ellenwood straightened and turned in the direction of the voice, and then turned back and looked at Lonnie and abruptly sat down on the step by him. "If a man has to fight, he has to fight, Lonnie."

Mr. Ross came marching through the mud, his big mouth open in a smile. "I saw it, Prof. I hung around. Damn me, if that ain't a bridge crossed!" He stuck out his hand.

Mr. Ellenwood took the hand and answered, "Thanks," but he didn't smile back. He looked at Mr. Ross and then looked off into space.

Mr. Ross said, "There's one man ain't going to be thinking education's so sissified."

Father nodded at the space he was looking into. "One," he said.

✦   ✦   ✦   ✦

---

3. *Stephen stoned.* Stephen, the first Christian martyr, was stoned to death because he would not renounce his religious beliefs.

1. (a) What is the first indication that the inhabitants of Moon Dance mistrust Ellenwood? (b) Why do they mistrust him? (c) How does the town's attitude influence Chilter's behavior toward Ellenwood?

2. Read the biography of A. B. Guthrie that appears below. (a) According to Guthrie, what is Lonnie's function in the story? (b) What insights into Mr. Ellenwood's character do Lonnie's feelings about him give you? Support your answer with specific lines from the story.

3. (a) Why does Ellenwood finally accept Chilter's challenge to fight? (b) What else might he have done? (c) Do you think he made the right choice in fighting Chilter? Why or why not?

4. (a) In what way does the setting influence the action in this story? (b) In what modern settings might this same kind of incident take place?

5. (a) Is there any indication that Ellenwood will be accepted in Moon Dance because of his victory over Chilter? (b) Is the ending of this story appropriate in terms of what comes before? Explain. (c) Is the ending happy, unhappy, or indeterminate? Why do you think so?

6. Which of the following best states the theme of this story? (a) If you're able to fight, you should do so or you will be thought of as a coward. (b) Many small communities in the old West demanded physical strength of their male members. (c) A man may be forced to prove himself by the rules of the society in which he lives—even when these rules are contrary to his own beliefs. How is the theme demonstrated in the story?

7. (a) What does the word *principal* in the title of this story mean? (b) Could the story have been called "First Principle"? Explain.

WORD STUDY

"He went ahead stuffing things back into the suitcase and trying to make the *lock* catch afterwards." In the preceding sentence, the word *lock* means "a fastening," but *lock* can mean "a tress of hair." Words that have the same spelling but are derived from different roots and differ widely in meaning are called *homographs*. Study each pair of sentences below, then explain how the homographs differ in meaning.

1. (a) How many times must I tell you not to leave your *skates* on the stairs! (b) I spent all day fishing, but caught only two *skates*.
2. (a) The *rent* is due on the first of the month. (b) Would you please patch the *rent* in my shirt?
3. (a) Don't bother saving that *junk*. (b) During our stay in Asia, we took a trip on a *junk*.
4. (a) My *gum* hasn't stopped bleeding since I left the dentist's office. (b) If you lean on that tree, you'll get *gum* on your clothes.
5. (a) After the trumpet solo, the drummer began a *tattoo*. (b) What kind of *tattoo* is that you have on your arm?
6. (a) I have an ache in my *temple*. (b) When in Greece, be sure to visit at least one *temple*.

THE AUTHOR

When A. B. Guthrie, Jr. and his parents moved to the Montana territory, it was a land of strong men and raw violence. The boy from Indiana saw the stuff that legends are made of happening around him; and, as an adult, he has filled books with stories of that wild country and the men who ruled it.

Most of Guthrie's fiction is based on actual occurrences. Of "First Principal" he says: "Though I know very well that a grounding in fact does not by itself enhance values in fiction, my story has a basis in fact. My father *did* come to Montana to teach in a day when male teachers were few in the cattle country and often were belittled because of their occupation. He *did* yank a bully off his horse, after a quirt slash across the face, and put the run on him. Only in pretending that I was a witness am I false to the facts. To make the story work, it seemed to me, I had to put myself in the position of a witness. Not only that, but I had to illuminate the story, through a child's feelings and observations, with the reflections of maturity. One man (one teacher, that is), in that time and place and atmosphere, had proved himself not a sissy. One!"

*Marty was an outsider with a single ambition—
to be accepted by the boys. What comment on life
does Murray Heyert make in this story of an ambition fulfilled?*

The New Kid

MURRAY HEYERT

BY THE TIME Marty ran up the stairs, past the dentist's office, where it smelled like the time his father was in the hospital, past the fresh paint smell, where the new kid lived, past the garlic smell from the Italians in 2D; and waited for Mommer to open the door; and threw his schoolbooks on top of the old newspapers that were piled on the sewing machine in the hall; and drank his glass of milk ("How many times must I tell you not to gulp! Are you going to stop gulping like that or must I smack your face!"); and set the empty glass in the sink under the faucet; and changed into his brown keds; and put trees into his school shoes ("How many times must I talk to you! God in Heaven—when will you learn to take care of your clothes and not make me follow you around like this!"); and ran downstairs again, past the garlic and the paint and the hospital smells; by the time he got into the street and looked breathlessly around him, it was too late. The fellows were all out there, all ready for a game, and just waiting for Eddie Deakes to finish chalking a base against the curb.[1]

From *Harper's Magazine* (June 1944). Reprinted by permission of Barthold Fles.
1. **chalking a base against the curb.** The boys are preparing for a game of punchball, a game similar to baseball but played with a tennis ball that is struck with a clenched fist rather than a bat.

Running up the street with all his might, Marty could see that the game would start any minute now. Out in the gutter Paulie Dahler was tossing high ones to Ray-Ray Stickerling, whose father was a bus driver and sometimes gave the fellows transfers so they could ride free. The rest were sitting on the curb, waiting for Eddie to finish making the base and listening to Gelberg, who was a Jew, explain what it meant to be bar-mitzvah'd,[2] like he was going to be next month.

They did not look up as Marty galloped up to them all out of breath. Eddie finished making his base and after looking at it critically a moment, with his head on one side, moved down toward the sewer that was home plate and began drawing a scoreboard alongside it. With his nose running from excitement Marty trotted over to him.

"Just going to play with two bases?" he said, wiping his nose on the sleeve of his lumber jacket, and hoping with all his might that Eddie would think he had been there all the while and was waiting for a game like all the other fellows.

Eddie raised his head and saw that it was Marty. He gave Marty a

---

2. *bar-mitzvah* (bär′mits′və) On his thirteenth birthday, a Jewish boy is considered to have reached the age of religious duty and responsibility. In a synagogue ceremony, he is recognized as a man with a man's responsibilities.

shove. "Why don't you watch where you're walking?" he said. "Can't you see I'm making a scoreboard!"

He bent over again and with his chalk repaired the lines that Marty had smudged with his sneakers. Marty hopped around alongside him, taking care to keep his feet off the chalked box. "Gimme a game, Eddie?" he said.

"What are you asking me for?" Eddie said, without looking up. "It ain't my game."

"Aw, come on, Eddie. I'll get even on you!" Marty said.

"Ask Gelberg. It's his game," Eddie said, straightening himself and shoving his chalk into his pants pocket. He trotted suddenly into the middle of the street and ran sideways a few feet. "Here go!" he hollered. "All the way!"

From his place up near the corner Paulie Dahler heaved the ball high into the air, higher than the telephone wires. Eddie took a step back, then a step forward, then back again, and got under it.

Marty bent his knees like a catcher, pounded his fist into his palm as though he were wearing a mitt, and held out his hands. "Here go, Eddie!" he hollered. "Here go!"

Holding the ball in his hand, and without answering him, Eddie walked toward the curb, where the rest of the fellows were gathered around Gelberg. Marty straightened his knees, put down his hands, and sniffling his nose, trotted after Eddie.

"All right, I'll choose Gelberg for sides," Eddie said.

Gelberg heaved himself off the curb and put on his punchball glove, which was one of his mother's old kid gloves, with the fingers and thumb cut off short. "Odds, once takes it," he said.

After a couple of preparatory swings of their arms they matched fingers. Gelberg won. He chose Albie Newbauer. Eddie looked around him and took Wally Reinhard. Gelberg took Ray-Ray Stickerling. Eddie took Wally Reinhard's brother, Howey.

Marty hopped around on the edge of the group. "Hey, Gelberg," he hollered, in a high voice. "Gimme a game, will you?"

"I got Arnie," Gelberg said.

Eddie looked around him again. "All right, I got Paulie Dahler."

They counted their men. "Choose you for up first," Gelberg said. Feeling as though he were going to cry, Marty watched them as they swung their arms, stuck out their fingers. This time Eddie won. Gelberg gathered his men around him and they trotted into the street to take up positions on the field. They hollered "Here go!" threw the ball from first to second, then out into the field, and back again to Gelberg in the pitcher's box.

Marty ran over to him. "Gimme a game, will you, Gelberg?"

"We're all choosed up," Gelberg said, heaving a high one to Arnie out in center field.

Marty wiped his nose on his sleeve. "Come on, gimme a game. Didn't I let you lose my Spaulding Hi-Bouncer down the sewer once?"

"Want to give the kid a game?" Gelberg called to Eddie, who was seated on the curb, figuring out his batting order with his men.

"Aw, we got the sides all choosed up!" Eddie said.

Marty stuck out his lower lip and wished that he would not have to cry. "You give Howey Reinhard a game!" he said, pointing at Howey sitting on the curb next to Eddie. "He can't play any better than me!"

"Yeah," Howey yelled, swinging back his arm as though he were going

to punch Marty in the jaw. "You couldn't hit the side of the house!"

"Yeah, I can play better than you any day!" Marty hollered.

"You can play left outside!" Howey said, looking around to see how the joke went over.

"Yeah, I'll get even on you!" Marty hollered, hoping that maybe they would get worried and give him a game after all.

With a fierce expression on his face, as if to indicate that he was through joking and now meant serious business, Howey sprang up from the curb and sent him staggering with a shove. Marty tried to duck, but Howey smacked him across the side of the head. Flinging his arms up about his ears Marty scrambled down the street; for no reason at all Paulie Dahler booted him in the pants as he went by.

"I'll get even on you!" Marty yelled, when he was out of reach. With a sudden movement of his legs Howey pretended to rush at him. Almost falling over himself in panic Marty dashed toward the house, but stopped, feeling ashamed, when he saw that Howey had only wanted to make him run.

For a while he stood there on the curb, wary and ready to dive into the house the instant any of the fellows made a move toward him. But presently he saw that the game was beginning, and that none of them was paying any more attention to him. He crept toward them again, and seating himself on the curb a little distance away, watched the game start. For a moment he thought of breaking it up, rushing up to the scoreboard and smudging it with his sneakers before anyone could stop him, and then dashing into the house before they caught him. Or grabbing the ball when it came near him and flinging it

down the sewer. But he decided not to; the fellows would catch him in the end, smack him and make another scoreboard or get another ball, and then he would never get a game.

Every minute feeling more and more like crying, he sat there on the curb, his elbow on his knee, his chin in his palm, and tried to think where he could get another fellow, so that they could give him a game and still have even sides. Then he lifted his chin from his palm and saw that the new kid was sitting out on the stoop in front of the house, chewing something and gazing toward the game; and all at once the feeling that he was going to cry disappeared. He sprang up from the curb.

"Hey, Gelberg!" he hollered. "If I get the new kid for even sides can I get a game?"

Without waiting for an answer he dashed down the street toward the stoop where the new kid was sitting.

"Hey, fellow!" he shouted. "Want a game? Want a game of punchball?"

He could see now that what the new kid was eating was a slice of rye bread covered with apple sauce. He could see, too, that the new kid was smaller than he was, and had a narrow face and a large nose with a few little freckles across the bridge. He was wearing Boy Scout pants and a brown woolen pullover, and on the back of his head was a skullcap made from the crown of a man's felt hat, the edge turned up and cut into sharp points that were ornamented with brass paper clips.

All out of breath he stopped in front of the new kid. "What do you say?" he hollered. "Want a game?"

The new kid looked at him and took another bite of rye bread. "I don't know," he said, with his mouth full of bread, turning to take another

look at the fellows in the street. "I guess I got to go to the store soon."

"You don't have to go to the store right away, do you?" Marty said, in a high voice.

The new kid swallowed his bread and continued looking up toward the game. "I got to stay in front of the house in case my mother calls me."

"Maybe she won't call you for a while," Marty said. He could see that the inning was ending, that they would be starting a new inning in a minute, and his legs twitched with impatience.

"I don't know," the new kid said, still looking up at the game. "Anyway, I got my good shoes on."

"Aw, I bet you can't even play punchball!" cried Marty.

The new kid looked at him with his lower lip stuck out. "Yeah, I can so play! Only I got to go to the store!"

Once more he looked undecidedly up toward the game. Marty could see that the inning was over now. He turned pleadingly to the new kid.

"You can hear her if she calls you, can't you? Can't you play just till she calls you? Come on, can't you?"

Putting the last of his rye bread into his mouth, the new kid got up from the stoop. "Well, when she calls me—" he said, brushing off the seat of his pants with his hand, "when she calls me I got to quit and go to the store."

As fast as he could run Marty dashed up the street with the new kid trailing after him. "Hey, I got another man for even sides!" he yelled. "Gimme a game now? I got another man!"

The fellows looked at the new kid coming up the street behind Marty.

"You new on the block?" Howey Reinhard asked, eyeing the Boy Scout pants, as Marty and the new kid came up to them.

"You any good?" Gelberg demanded, bouncing the ball at his feet and looking at the skullcap ornamented with brass paper clips. "Can you hit?"

"Come on!" Marty said. He wished that they would just give him a game and not start asking a lot of questions. "I got another man for even sides, didn't I?"

"Aw, we got the game started already!" Ray-Ray Stickerling hollered.

Marty sniffled his nose, which was beginning to run again, and looked at him as fiercely as he was able. "It ain't your game!" he yelled. "It's Gelberg's game! Ain't it your game, Gelberg?"

Gelberg gave him a shove. "No one said you weren't going to get a game!" With a last bounce of his ball he turned to Eddie, who was looking the new kid over carefully.

"All right, Eddie. I'll take the new kid and you can have Marty."

Eddie drew his arm back as though he were going to hit him. "Like fun! Why don't you take Marty, if you're so wise?"

"I won the choose-up!" Gelberg hollered.

"Yeah, that was before! I'm not taking Marty!"

"I won the choose-up, didn't I?"

"Well, you got to choose up again for the new kid!"

Marty watched them as they stood up to each other, each eyeing the other suspiciously, and swung their arms to choose. Eddie won.

"Cheating shows!" he yelled, seizing the new kid by the arm, and pulling him into the group on his side.

Trying to look like the ball players he had seen the time his father had taken him to the Polo Grounds,[3]

---

3. *Polo Grounds*, once a baseball stadium in the Bronx, New York.

Marty ran into the outfield and took the position near the curb that Gelberg had selected for him. He tried not to feel bad because Eddie had taken the new kid, that no one knew anything about, how he could hit, or anything; and that he had had to go to the loser of the choose-up. As soon as he was out in the field he leaned forward, with his hands propped on his knees, and hollered: "All right, all right, these guys can't hit!" Then he straightened up and pounded his fist into his palm as though he were wearing a fielder's glove and shouted: "Serve it to them on a silver platter, Gelberg! These guys are just a bunch of fan artists!" he propped his hands on his knees again, like a big-leaguer, but all the while he felt unhappy, not nearly the way he should have felt, now that they had finally given him a game. He hoped that they would hit to him, and he would make one-handed catches over his head, run way out with his back to the ball and spear them blind, or run in with all his might and pick them right off the tops of his shoes.

A little nervous chill ran through his back as he saw Paulie Dahler get up to hit. On Gelberg's second toss Paulie stepped in and sent the ball sailing into the air. A panic seized Marty as he saw it coming at him. He took a step nervously forward, then backward, then forward again, trying as hard as he could to judge the ball. It smacked into his cupped palms, bounced out and dribbled toward the curb. He scrambled after it, hearing them shouting at him, and feeling himself getting more scared every instant. He kicked the ball with his sneaker, got his hand on it, and straightening himself in a fever of fright, heaved it with all his strength at Ray-Ray on first. The moment the ball left his hand he knew he had done the wrong thing. Paulie was already on his way to second; and besides, the throw was wild. Ray-Ray leaped into the air, his arms flung up, but it was way over his head, bouncing beyond him on the sidewalk and almost hitting a woman who was jouncing a baby carriage at the door of the apartment house opposite.

With his heart beating the same way it did whenever anyone chased him, Marty watched Paulie gallop across the plate. He sniffled his nose, which was beginning to run again, and felt like crying.

"Holy Moses!" he heard Gelberg yell. "What do you want, a basket? Can't you hold on to them once in a while?"

"Aw, the sun was in my eyes!" Marty said.

"You wait until you want another game!" Gelberg shouted.

Breathing hard, Ray-Ray got back on first and tossed the ball to Gelberg. "Whose side are you on anyway?" he hollered.

Eddie Deakes put his hands to his mouth like a megaphone. "Atta-boy, Marty!" he yelled. "Having you out there is like having another man on our side!"

The other fellows on the curb laughed, and Howey Reinhard made them laugh harder by pretending to catch a fly ball with the sun in his eyes, staggering around the street with his eyes screwed up and his hands cupped like a sissy, so that the wrists touched and the palms were widely separated.

No longer shouting or punching his fist into his palm, Marty took his place out in the field again. He stood there, feeling like crying, and wished that he hadn't dropped that ball, or thrown it over Ray-Ray's head. Then, without knowing why, he looked up to see whether the new kid

was laughing at him like all the rest. But the new kid was sitting a little off by himself at one end of the row of fellows on the curb, and with a serious expression on his face gnawed at the skin at the side of his thumbnail. Marty began to wonder if the new kid was any good or not. He saw him sitting there, with the serious look on his face, his ears sticking out, not joking like the other fellows, and from nowhere the thought leaped into Marty's head that maybe the new kid was no good. He looked at the skinny legs, the Boy Scout pants, and the mama's boy shoes and all at once he began to hope that Eddie would send the new kid in to hit, so that he could know right away whether he was any good or not.

But Wally Reinhard was up next. He fouled out on one of Gelberg's twirls, and after him Howey popped up to Albie Newbauer and Eddie was out on first. The fellows ran in to watch Eddie chalk up Paulie's run on the scoreboard alongside the sewer. They were still beefing and hollering at Marty for dropping that ball, but he pretended he did not hear them and sat down on the curb to watch the new kid out in the field.

He was over near the curb, playing in closer than Paulie Dahler. Marty could see that he was not hollering "Here go!" or "All the way!" like the others, but merely stood there with that serious expression on his face and watched them throw the ball around. He held one leg bent at the ankle, so that the side of his shoe rested on the pavement, his belly was stuck out, and he chewed the skin at the side of his thumbnail.

Gelberg got up to bat. Standing in the pitcher's box, Eddie turned around and motioned his men to lay out. The new kid looked around him to see what the other fellows did, took a few steps backward, and then, with his belly stuck out again, went on chewing his thumb.

Marty felt his heart begin to beat hard. He watched Gelberg stand up to the plate and contemptuously fling back the first few pitches.

"Come on, gimme one like I like!" Gelberg hollered.

"What's the matter! You afraid to reach for them?" Eddie yelled.

"Just pitch them to me, that's all!" Gelberg said.

Eddie lobbed one in that bounced shoulder high. With a little sideways skip Gelberg lammed into it.

The ball sailed down toward the new kid. Feeling his heart begin to beat harder, Marty saw him take a hurried step backward, and at the same moment fling his hands before his face and duck his head. The ball landed beyond him and bounded up on the sidewalk. For an instant the new kid hesitated, then he was galloping after it, clattering across the pavement in his polished shoes.

Swinging his arms in mock haste, Gelberg breezed across the plate. "Get a basket!" he hollered over his shoulder. "Get a basket!"

Marty let his nose run without bothering to sniffle. He jumped up from the curb and curved his hands around his mouth like a megaphone. "He's scared of the ball!" he yelled at the top of his lungs. "He's scared of the ball! That's what he is, scared of the ball!"

The new kid tossed the ball back to Eddie. "I wasn't scared!" he said, moistening his lips with his tongue. "I wasn't scared! I just couldn't see it coming!"

With an expression of despair on his face Eddie shook his head. "Holy Moses! If you can't see the ball why do you try to play punchball?" He bounced the ball hard at his feet and

motioned Gelberg to send in his next batter. Arnie got up from the curb and wiping his hands on his pants walked toward the plate.

Marty felt his heart pounding in his chest. He hopped up and down with excitement and seizing Gelberg by the arm pointed at the new kid.

"You see him duck?" he yelled. "He's scared of the ball, that's what he is!" He hardly knew where to turn first. He rushed up to Ray-Ray, who was sitting on the curb making marks on the asphalt with the heel of his sneaker. "The new kid's scared to stop a ball! You see him duck!"

The new kid looked toward Marty and wet his lips with his tongue. "Yeah," he yelled, "didn't you muff one that was right in your hands?"

He was looking at Marty with a sore expression on his face, and his lower lip stuck out; and a sinking feeling went through Marty, a sudden sick feeling that maybe he had started something he would be sorry for. Behind him on the curb he could hear the fellows sniggering in that way they did when they picked on him. In the pitcher's box Eddie let out a loud cackling laugh.

"Yeah, the new kid's got your number!"

"The sun was in my eyes!" Marty said. He could feel his face getting red, and in the field the fellows were laughing. A wave of self-pity flowed through him.

"What are you picking on me for!" he yelled, in a high voice. "The sun was so in my eyes. Anyway, I ain't no yellowbelly! I wasn't scared of the ball!"

The instant he said it he was sorry. He sniffled his nose uneasily as he saw Gelberg look at Ray-Ray. For an instant he thought of running into the house before anything happened. But instead he just stood there, snif-fling his nose and feeling his heart beating, fast and heavy.

"You hear what he called you?" Paulie Dahler yelled at the new kid.

"You're not going to let him get away with calling you a yellowbelly, are you?" Eddie said, looking at the new kid.

The new kid wet his lips with his tongue and looked at Marty. "I wasn't scared!" he said. He shifted the soles of his new-looking shoes on the pavement. "I wasn't scared! I just couldn't see it coming, that's all!"

Eddie was walking toward the new kid now, bouncing the ball slowly in front of him as he walked. In a sudden panic Marty looked back toward the house where old lady Kipnis lived. She always broke up fights; maybe she would break up this one; maybe she wouldn't even let it get started. But she wasn't out on her porch. He sniffled his nose, and with all his might hoped that the kid's mother would call him to go to the store.

"Any kid that lets himself be called a yellowbelly must be a yellowbelly!" Albie Newbauer said, looking around him for approval.

"Yeah," Gelberg said. "I wouldn't let anyone call me a yellowbelly."

With a sudden shove Eddie sent the new kid scrambling forward toward Marty. He tried to check himself by stiffening his body and twisting to one side, but it was no use. Before he could recover his balance another shove made him stagger forward.

Marty sniffled his nose and looked at the kid's face close in front of him. It seemed as big as the faces he saw in the movies; and he could see that the kid's nose was beginning to run just like his own; and he could see in the corner of his mouth a crumb of the rye bread he had eaten on the stoop. For a moment the kid's eyes looked squarely

into Marty's, so he could see the little dark specks in the colored part around the pupil. Then the glance slipped away to one side; and all at once Marty had a feeling that the new kid was afraid of him.

"You gonna let him get away with calling you a yellowbelly?" he heard Eddie say. From the way it sounded he knew that the fellows were on his side now. He stuck out his jaw and waited for the new kid to answer.

"I got to go to the store!" the new kid said. There was a scared look on his face and he took a step back from Marty.

Paulie Dahler got behind him and shoved him against Marty. Although he tried not to, Marty couldn't help flinging his arms up before his face. But the new kid only backed away and kept his arms at his sides. A fierce excitement went through Marty as he saw how scared the look on the kid's face was. He thrust his chest up against the new kid.

"Yellowbelly!" he hollered, making his voice sound tough. "Scared of the ball!"

The new kid backed nervously away, and there was a look on his face as though he wanted to cry.

"Yeah, he's scared!" Eddie yelled.

"Slam him, Marty!" Wally Reinhard hollered. "The kid's scared of you!"

"Aw, sock the yellowbelly!" Marty heard Gelberg say, and he smacked the kid as hard as he could on the shoulder. The kid screwed up his face to keep from crying, and tried to back through the fellows ringed around him.

"Lemme alone!" he yelled.

Marty looked at him fiercely, with his jaw thrust forward, and felt his heart beating. He smacked the kid again, making him stagger against Arnie in back of him.

"Yeah, yellowbelly!" Marty hollered, feeling how the fellows were on his side, and how scared the new kid was. He began smacking him again and again on the shoulder.

"Three, six, nine, a bottle of wine, I can fight you any old time!" he yelled. With each word he smacked the kid on the shoulder or arm. At the last word he swung with all his strength. He meant to hit the kid on

the shoulder, but at the last instant, even while his arm was swinging, something compelled him to change his aim; his fist caught the kid on the mouth with a hard, wet, socking sound. The shock of his knuckles against the kid's mouth, and that sound of it, made Marty want to hit him again and again. He put his head down and began swinging wildly, hitting the new kid without any aim on the head and shoulders and arms.

The new kid buried his head in his arms and began to cry. "Lemme alone!" he yelled. He tried to rush through the fellows crowded around him. With all his might Marty smacked him on the side of the head. Rushing up behind him Arnie smacked him too. Paulie Dahler shoved the skullcap, with its paper clip ornaments, over the kid's eyes; and as he went by Gelberg booted him in the pants.

Crying and clutching his cap, the new kid scampered over to the curb out of reach.

"I'll get even on you!" he cried.

With a fierce expression on his face Marty made a sudden movement of his legs and pretended to rush at him. The kid threw his arms about his head and darted down the street toward the house. When he saw that Marty was not coming after him he sat down on the stoop; and Marty could see him rubbing his knuckles against his mouth.

Howey Reinhard was making fun of the new kid, scampering up and down the pavement with his arms wrapped around his head and hollering, "Lemme alone! Lemme alone!" The fellows laughed, and although he was breathing hard, and his hand hurt from hitting the kid, Marty had to laugh too.

"You see him duck when that ball came at him?" he panted at Paulie Dahler.

Paulie shook his head. "Boy, just wait until we get the yellowbelly in the schoolyard!"

"And on Halloween," Gelberg said. "Wait until we get him on Halloween with our flour stockings!" He gave Marty a little shove and made as though he were whirling an imaginary flour stocking around his head.

Standing there in the middle of the street, Marty suddenly thought of Halloween, of the winter and snowballs, of the schoolyard. He saw himself whirling a flour stocking around his head and rushing at the new kid, who scampered in terror before him hollering, "Lemme alone! Lemme alone!" As clearly as if it were in the movies, he saw himself flinging snowballs and the new kid backed into a corner of the schoolyard, with his hands over his face. Before he knew what he was doing, Marty turned fiercely toward the stoop where the new kid was still sitting, rubbing his mouth and crying.

"Hey, yellowbelly!" Marty hollered; and he pretended he was going to rush at the kid.

Almost falling over himself in fright the new kid scrambled inside the house. Marty stood in the middle of the street and sniffled his nose. He shook his fist at the empty doorway.

"You see him run?" he yelled, so loud that it made his throat hurt. "Boy, you see him run?" He stood there shaking his fist, although the new kid was no longer there to see him. He could hardly wait for the winter, for Halloween, or the very next day in the schoolyard.

DISCUSSION

1. (a) What does the manner in which the opening sentence is written reveal about Marty's feelings toward the game? **(b)** What do Eddie's and Gelberg's reluctance to have him on their teams reveal about his ability as a player?

2. (a) Which one of Marty's physical characteristics does the author emphasize? **(b)** What does this characteristic tell you about him?

3. (a) Describe Marty's actions when he learns that the new kid is a poor player, too. **(b)** What motivates Marty to act as he does? **(c)** What clue to his behavior toward the new kid is supplied by Howey Reinhard's actions and attitudes toward Marty? **(d)** What does Marty gain by bullying the new kid? **(e)** How much, if at all, are the other boys to blame for Marty's actions?

4. What reasons might the author have had for not giving the new kid a name?

5. Which of the following best states the theme of this story? **(a)** To gain a feeling of security and respect, weak people often persecute those weaker than themselves. **(b)** A new kid in a neighborhood usually has to undergo rough treatment before he is accepted. **(c)** Practically everyone is a bully at heart. Support your answer with logical arguments.

6. (a) Would Marty have been more believable if he had defended the new kid rather than picked on him? Why or why not? **(b)** Do you think the new kid may someday treat another boy the way Marty treated him? In answering this question, consider what you know of the new kid's character and the way in which the other boys behave.

FROM THE AUTHOR

"The New Kid" is an instance of a story getting away from its author. It was written just before the outbreak of World War II, and in its original concept it was to be the new kid's story. He was to be a boy whose family were refugees from Nazi Germany and who ultimately found himself again abused and tormented because his foreign-ness made him strange and different from the other boys on the block. But Marty—one of the tormentors—kept pushing more and more into the story and grew more and more interesting to me as a subject. In the end I found I had written an entirely different story from the one I started out to do.

The story took six weeks to write. Almost five were spent trying to force it into the original concept. Then, very suddenly, the present version went down on paper almost as fast as I could type it.

See
CONTRAST
*Handbook
of Literary
Terms
page 519*

*Fiona Farmer makes a break for freedom
and is bounced into a world she never knew existed.
What are the contrasts between that new world and her daily one?*

NANCY

ELIZABETH ENRIGHT

FIONA FARMER was seven years old. Her mother was forty-six, her father was fifty-five, her nurse was sixty-one, and her grandmother and grandfather with whom they were all spending the summer had reached such altitudes of age that no one remembered what they were. From these great heights Fiona was loved and directed.

She wore her hair as her mother had worn it in 1914, braided tight and tied back in pretzel loops with big stiff ribbons. In winter she was the only girl at school to wear a flannel petticoat and underwear with sleeves. Her mother read her all the books she had loved in her childhood: *Rebecca of Sunnybrook Farm*, and *The Five Little Peppers*, and *Under the Lilacs*. Her grandmother read her the books *she* had loved as a child: Macé's *Fairy Tales*, and Grimm's *Fairy Tales*, and *The Princess and Curdie*. On this mixed diet of decorum and brutality Fiona was rapidly turning into a "quaint little creature." She was a pensive child with large attentive eyes and rather elderly manners; all her

play was quiet, accompanied at times by nothing noisier than a low continuous murmuring, so it was strange that the ranks of dolls on her nursery shelves were scalped, and eyeless, like the victims of a Sioux massacre.

"What on earth does she do to them?" her mother said to Nana, the nurse. "Why, when I was little my dollies were really like babies to me. I took such *care* of them, I *loved* them so. . . ."

"I honestly don't know, Mrs. Farmer," Nana said. "She'll be as quiet as a mouse in here for hours at a time, and then I'll come in and find all this—this destruction! It seems so unlike her!"

Fiona's grandmother reproached her quietly. "How would you like it if your dear mother pulled all your hair out of your head and broke your arms and legs? Your dolls are your little responsibilities, your *children* in a way. . . ."

Her admonishments though fre-

quent were always mild. When Fiona scratched her head, or picked her nose, she would say: "That's not very pretty, dear, is it? We don't do those things, do we?" . . . She was a lofty, dignified, conventional lady, and she smelled like an old dictionary among whose pages many flowers have been dried and pressed. She taught Fiona how to make a sachet and a pomander ball and play parcheesi.

Fiona liked her grandfather the best. He was a man of wonderful patience and politeness, deaf as a post. Every morning she followed him out to the vegetable garden where, in his old loose button-down-the-front sweater and his white canvas golf hat that sagged in a ruffle around his head, he worked along the rows of beets and cabbages with his hoe and rake. Fiona followed at his heels, speaking ceaselessly; it did not matter to her that he never heard a word she said, she told him everything. Now and then he would stop, resting on his hoe handle, and look down at her appreciatively. "Well," he would say. "You're a pleasant little companion, aren't you?" Then he would reach out his old parched hand (he was so old that he never sweated any more) and give her a brittle tap or two on the shoulder or head, and he and Fiona would smile at each other out of a mutual feeling of benevolence.

Sooner or later, though, Nana's voice would begin to caw: "Fee-ona! Fee-ona!" and she would have to go back to the house to pick up her toys or change her dress or eat a meal, or some other dull thing.

Her grandparents' house was big and cool inside. All the rooms were full of greenish light reflected from the maple trees outdoors; the floors were dark and gleaming, the carpets had been taken up for the summer and the furniture had linen dresses

on. There was no dust anywhere, not even in the corners of the empty fireplaces, for Cora and Mary, the maids who had been there for thirty years, spent their lives seeing that there was not.

Cora had arthritis, and on Sundays when Fiona had noon dinner with the whole family she marveled at the extreme slowness with which the maid moved about the table, like a running-down toy. Her face looked very still and concentrated then, relaxing only when she served Fiona, whispering: "Eat it all up now, dear, every bit, so I can tell Mary."

Oh food! People were always speaking of food to Fiona; the Sunday dinners were a trial to toil through. "Eat it all up, dear," and "Clean your plate" were phrases that were ugly in her ears.

After Sunday dinner everyone went to sleep for a while and the house droned with different pitches of snoring. Wearing nothing but a pink wrapper Fiona would lie on the big white bed while Nana sat in an armchair by the window rattling the Sunday paper. Out of doors the cicadas sounded hot as drills; the lazy air coming in the window brought a smell of grass, and Fiona wished that Nana would fall asleep so that she could get up and find something to play with, but Nana would not fall asleep.

But once she did.

Once on Sunday after the usual slow massive dinner, as Fiona lay in the extremity of boredom counting mosquito bites and listening to herself yawn, she heard another sound; a new one that might promise much. Quietly she raised herself to her elbows, hardly daring to believe, and saw that the impossible had happened at last. Nana lay in the armchair, abandoned, with her head thrown back and her hair coming down and

her mouth wide open like that of a fish; a faint guttural sound came out of it each time she breathed.

A great light seemed to flood the room, and a voice from on high addressed Fiona: "Get up and dress, but do not put on your shoes. Carry them in your hand till you get outside, and close the front door quietly behind you."

Fiona got up at once, dressed with the silence and speed of light, and departed. The upstairs hall hummed and trumpeted with the noises of sleeping; no one heard her running down the stairs.

Out of doors it was bright and hot; she sat on the front step and put on her sandals with her heart galloping in her chest. Though old, the members of her family were tall, their legs were long as ladders, and if they came after her they would surely catch her. Leaving the sandal straps unbuckled, Fiona ran out of the gate and down the street, terrified and exhilarated. She ran till she was giddy and breathless, but when at last she stopped and looked behind her the street on which she found herself was still and empty; steeped in Sunday.

She walked for a long time. Her heart stopped racing and her breathing became comfortable again. Her fear, too, gave way to pleasure and pride. It was a beautiful afternoon. The street was very high with elms. The light that came through their roof of leaves was green and trembling like light through water. Fiona became a little crab crawling among the roots of seaweed. The parked cars were fishes which would eat her up, danger was everywhere. . . . She walked sideways, made claws out of her thumbs, hid behind trees, and felt that her eyes grew out on stems. But not for long. Suddenly, as sometimes happened, the fancy collapsed, betrayed her completely. There was no danger; the cars were cars only. Nothing was any better than real; in the end somebody would catch her and take her home or she would return of her own accord, driven by hunger or conscience, and everything would be as it had always been.

The houses sat back from their green laps of lawn, silent and substantial, regarding her like people wearing glasses. There was a smell of privet and hot asphalt in the still air; a boring smell. . . . Intolerable boredom amounting to anguish drove Fiona to turn abruptly and kick the iron palings of a fence that she was passing; a kick that hurt right through her shoe.

The big street came to an end finally at a small Civil War monument and branched out beyond it in three roads. She chose the right-hand one because there was a dog asleep on the sidewalk there, but when she got to him she saw the flies strolling up and down his face and he looked up at her balefully with a low ripple of sound in his throat and she hurried on.

This street had few trees; it was broader, and the houses, while farther apart, were shabbier. The afternoon sun was in her eyes, drawing her along the gilded road. The wind had sprung up, too, warm and lively, blowing from the west.

On the outskirts of the town she came upon her destination, though at first she did not realize it. For some time the wind had been bringing her great blasts of radio music; and she saw now that these had their source in a gray frame house that fairly trembled with melody. Though not small, this was the seediest of all the houses. It stood in the middle of a yard as full of tall grass as a field. There were paths through the field and bald patches where people had

stamped and trampled, and many souvenirs abandoned and half grown over: a rusted little wagon with no wheels, somebody's shoe, an old tire . . .

The house had a queer shape, fancy, but with everything coming off or breaking. Some of the shutters hung by one hinge only; the cupola on top was crooked and so was the porch from which half the palings were gone. The fence, too, had lost many of its pickets and stood propped against the tangle like a large comb with teeth missing; but it had kept its gate and hanging onto this and swinging slowly back and forth were three little girls. Fiona walked more slowly.

One of the girls had a bandanna tied tightly around her head but the other two regarded her from under untrimmed dusty bangs, like animals peering out from under ferns. The gate gave a long snarl of sound as they pushed it forward. "Where are you going?" said the tallest one.

Fiona could not be sure of the tone of this question: was it a friendly or a hostile challenge? She moved still more slowly touching each picket with her forefinger.

"No place," she said guardedly.

"What's your name?" demanded the girl with the bandanna. She smelled of kerosene.

"Fiona Farmer," said Fiona.

"That's a funny name. My name's Darlene, and hers is Pearl, and *hers* is Merle. Nancy is a nice name."

Fiona saw that all of them were wearing red nail polish and asked a question of her own.

"Are you all three sisters?"

"Yes, and there's more of us. *Them*," said Pearl, the tallest girl, jerking her head. "In the swing."

Beyond the house Fiona now saw for the first time an old double-rocker swing full of boys.

"There's Norman and Stanley and Earl," Darlene said. "And in the house we got a baby sister named Marilyn, and down to the picture theater we got a big sister named Deanna. Come on in."

"Will they let me swing in the swing?" said Fiona.

"Sure they will. *What* did you say your name was?"

"Fiona," she admitted. "Fiona Farmer."

"Gee," said Pearl.

"We'll call her Nancy," said Darlene, who, though younger, seemed to be a leader in her way. "Come on, Nancy, you wanna swing on the gate? Get off, Merle."

Merle got off obediently, sucking her thumb.

"I would like to swing in the *swing*," Fiona said.

She came into the yard gazing up at the tipsy cupola. "Can you get up there into that kind of little tower?"

"Sure," said Darlene. "Come on up and we'll show you."

Fiona followed them through the interesting grass in which she now saw a broken doll, somebody's garter, somebody's hat, and many weathered corncobs and beer cans.

On the porch which swayed when they walked on it there were a tough-looking baby buggy, two sleds, a bent tricycle, a lot of chairs and boxes and bushel baskets and peck baskets and a baby pen and a wagon wheel and some kindling wood. The screen door was full of holes and instead of a doorknob there was a wooden thread spool to turn.

The noise of music was stunning as they went indoors; it kept the Mason jars[1] ringing on the shelves. They walked right into it, into the thrilling heart of noise which was the kitchen,

---

1. *Mason jars,* jars used for canning fruits and vegetables. Mason is a brand name.

where a woman was sitting nursing a baby and shouting random conversation at an old, old woman with a beak nose.

The music ceased with a flourish and the radio announcer's tremendous tones replaced it, but this did not stop the shouted discourse of the woman with the baby. As the girls crossed the kitchen she turned for a moment to look at them, saw Fiona and said, "Who's she?"

"She's Nancy," called Darlene, against the radio.

"Who?"

"Nancy! She dropped in."

"That's Mom," Pearl said.

Fiona went over to the lady to shake her hand. She made her usual curtsy and said, "How do you do?"

Mom's hand felt limp and rather damp and startled. She was a big woman with a wide face and tired blue eyes.

"The old one's Gramma," Darlene said, so Fiona curtsied to the old lady too, and shook her hand which felt like a few twigs in a glove.

"And that's my father," Darlene added, a few seconds later when they had gone up the loud bare stairs to the next floor; Fiona peeked in the doorway of the dim strong-smelling room but all she saw of *him* was the soles of his socks and she heard him snoring.

"Just like at home," she said. "Sunday afternoon they all sleep."

"Heck, he sleeps all *day* on Sundays," Darlene said, and Fiona felt a little humiliated for her own father.

"This is Gramma's room." Pearl threw open the door. "She likes flowers."

The room was a jungle steeped in musky twilight. A vine of some kind had crawled all over the window and parts of the wall, and on the sill, the sash, the floor below, were pots and jars and coffee tins in which stout lusty plants were growing and flowering.

"How does she open the window at night?" Fiona wondered.

"*She* don't open no windows day or night," Darlene said. "Heck, she's *old*, she's gotta stay *warm*."

They went up another flight of stairs, narrow steep ones, crowded with magazines and articles of clothing and decayed toys. "Up here's where we sleep," Darlene said. "Us girls, all of us except Marilyn. Pearl and me and Merle sleep in the big bed and Deanna she sleeps in the cot. This is the attic like."

The big bed was made of iron with the post knobs missing. It dipped in the middle like a hammock and there, Fiona knew, the little girls would lie at night, dumped together in a tangle, quarreling or giggling in whispers.

"Look at all the comic books!" she cried, and indeed they lay everywhere in tattered profusion, a drift of stained, disordered leaves.

"We got about a hundred or a thousand of 'em, I guess," Pearl said. "You want some?"

"Could I really, Pearl? Could you spare them?"

"*Atom Annie's* a good one," Pearl said. "We got a lot about her, and here's one called *Hellray* that's real good, real scary. Take these."

Fiona looked at them longingly.

"I don't know if my mother—she doesn't like for me to have comics."

"Heck, why not?"

"Well, maybe this time she won't mind," Fiona said, taking the books, determined that everything would be all right for once. "Thank you very, very much, Darlene and Pearl."

"Here's the stairs to the lookout," Darlene said. "Get out of the way, Merle, you wait till last."

They climbed the ladder steps in

the middle of the room. Pearl pushed open the trap door and one by one they ascended into the tiny chamber.

It was a tipped little cubicle like a ship's cabin in stiff weather, and stiflingly hot. It seemed remote, high, cozy, and its four soiled windows showed four different views of the town faded and reduced as pictures in an old book. Flies buzzed and butted at the hot glass. Fiona felt disappointed when she saw the steeple of the church that stood across the street from her grandfather's house. She had not thought it was so near.

"Jump!" cried Darlene. They all began to jump, and the cupola jarred and trembled under the pounding.

"Won't it break?" cried Fiona, pounding with the rest. "Won't it fall off?"

"Naw, it won't break," Darlene called back. "It never did yet."

"But it might some day, though," shouted Pearl encouragingly.

It was fun to jump riotously and yell, as the tiny tower rocked and resounded.

There was an interruption from below.

"Get out of there!" bawled Mom up the stairs. "How many times I told you kids to stay down out of there! You want to get your backs broke? You want to get killed? You scram down!"

"Get out of the way, Merle, let Nancy go first," Pearl said.

Mom stood at the foot of the steps wearing the baby around her neck. Anxiety had made her furious. "That place ain't safe, you know that!" she cried. "How many times have I told you?" She gave Pearl a slap on the cheek and would have given one to Darlene, too, if Darlene had not bent her neck adroitly.

"You let me catch you up there one more time and I'll get your father to lick you good!"

"Aw, climb a tree," said Darlene.

Fiona was aghast. What would happen now?

But nothing happened. Merle still quietly sucked her thumb, Darlene and Pearl seemed cool and jaunty, and as they descended through the house Mom's anger dried up like dew.

"You kids want a snack?" she said. "You didn't eat since breakfast."

"Can Nancy stay?"

"Why sure, I guess. Why not?"

"Oh, thank you very, very much. . . . "

The kitchen, like the rest of the house, had a rich bold musty smell. It smelled of constant usage and memories of usage. It was crowded and crusted with objects: pots, pans, kettles, boxes, jars, cans, buckets, dippers. There were two alarm clocks, one lying on its side, and each asserting a different hour, and four big Coca-Cola calendars on the wall, none for the current year. The radio was still thundering music, and close beside it warming herself at the noise sat Gramma, dark as a crow, chewing and chewing on her empty gums.

The stove was named Ebony Gem, and behind it in a cardboard box there was something alive; something moved. . . .

"It's kittens," said Merle, removing her thumb from her mouth and speaking for the first time. "Our cat had kittens."

"Oh, let me see!" Fiona knelt by the box. There inside it lay a bland and happy group: mother cat with her yellow eyes half closed and her paws splayed out in pleasure; kittens lined up all along her, sucking.

Merle put out her little forefinger with its chipped red nail polish, stroking first one infant, then the next. "The black one's name is Blackie and

the white one's name is Whitey and we call *this* one Butch because he's so . . ."

"My father usually drowns them, all but one," Darlene interrupted. She bent her kerchiefed head close to Fiona's, so that there was a blinding smell of kerosene. "Tomorrow probly," she whispered. "We don't tell Merle, it makes her feel so bad." Then she raised her voice. "She knows it's going to happen but she don't know when, huh, Merle?"

"You could take one, Nancy," Merle said, still gazing at the kittens. "You could keep it and be good to it."

"Do you mean honestly and truly?"

Fiona's joy was suffocating.

"Any one? Any one at all?"

"Except Butch," Darlene said. "We're going to keep him to help with the rats."

"Could I have Blackie? Really for keeps?"

Merle plucked the dark little thing from the mother as if she were plucking off a burr and gave it to Fiona.

"I can feel its little tiny heart," Fiona said. "I'll give it milk all the time and brush its fur and it can sleep in the doll cradle. Oh look at its ears, oh Merle, oh thank you!"

Shamed by gratitude Merle put her thumb back in her mouth and looked away.

"You kids get out from under my feet," Mom said. "Sit up to the table now, it's all ready. Come on Mama, come on *boys!*" She opened the screen door and put her head out, shouting so hard that great cords stood out on her neck.

They sat around the big table with its oilcloth cover, everything in easy reach: cereal in paper boxes, sugar, catsup. . . . They had cornflakes and milk, Swiss cheese sand-wiches with catsup, cream soda in bottles, and little cakes out of a box with pink and green beads on them. Fiona ate everything.

"Nancy eats good, don't she, Mom?" Darlene said.

"I never had catsup before," said Fiona. "My, it certainly is delicious, isn't it?"

The table was a family battlefield. Fiona had never seen anything like it in her life. Stanley and Norman threw pieces of sandwich at each other, Earl took one of Merle's cakes and Merle cried and Mom slapped Earl; Darlene stole big swigs from Pearl's soda bottle, was loudly accused and loudly defended herself.

"You kids shut up," Mom said, eating over Marilyn's head and giving her occasional bits of cake dipped in tea. Gramma was the only quiet one; she sat bent over, all wrapped and absorbed in her old age, gazing into her cup as she drank from it with a long purring sound. Blackie was quiet, too, asleep in Fiona's lap. She kept one hand on his little velvet back. Mom pointed at Fiona with her spoon. "Looks like Margaret O'Brien[2] used to, don't she? The ribbons and all."

"Margaret who?" said Fiona.

"O'Brien, *you* know, the kid in the movies," Darlene said.

"Oh, I never go to movies," said Fiona. "I'm not allowed."

"Not allowed!" cried Darlene incredulously. "Heck, we go all the time, don't we, Mom? Even Deanna goes. We could take Nancy with us sometimes, couldn't we, Mom?"

"Maybe, if her folks say yes."

"Oh if I went with *you* it would be all right, I'm sure," cried Fiona joyously. Drunk with noise, strange flavors, gifts, and new friendship, she really believed this.

---

2. *Margaret O'Brien,* a child movie star, popular in the late 1940's and early 1950's.

Afterward, still with catsup on their upper lips, they went outdoors to play hide-and-seek.

"You be her partner, Stanley," ordered Darlene, who was "it." "You kind of look after her, she don't know our places to hide."

Then she hid her eyes with her arm, cast herself against a tree like a girl in grief, and began to count out loud.

"The cellar," hissed Stanley, grabbing Fiona's hand. He was a big eight-year-old boy, and still clutching the kitten Fiona ran with him willingly, hesitating only for a second at sight of the dark abyss. On the steps were many cans and beer crates, but Stanley led her safely down among these and into the black deep tunnel beyond. Fiona could feel that there were solid things all around them; probably more boxes, more beer crates, but she could see nothing. Stanley's hand was warm and firm, it just fitted hers, and she liked having him lead her.

"We can stop now," he said, "but keep quiet."

Darlene could still be heard, faintly. Her counting voice sounded deserted and defiant: "*Ninety*-five, *ninety*-six, *ninety*-seven" . . . The blackness throbbed and shimmered and the air had a dense aged smell.

"Coming, ready or not!" called the faraway defiant voice.

"We're safe here anyways," Stanley said. "She won't come down *here*, she's scared to." He laughed silently and gave Fiona's hand a squeeze. "There's rats down here."

"Oh no, oh no! Oh, Stanley, let's go up again," cried Fiona, tears of panic in her voice.

But Stanley held onto her hand. "You going to be a sissy too?" he demanded. "We got the *cat*, ain't we?"

Fiona strained the tiny kitten to her chest. Her heart was banging terribly and she wanted to cry but she would not. All around the rats were closing in, large as dogs and smiling strangely; smiling like people. She almost sobbed when Stanley said, "Now we can go, hurry up, and keep still!"

They were the first ones back.

For a long time they played and Stanley always was her partner. He knew the best places to hide: up in the boughs of a pear tree, under the porch steps, in the fearful little dark privy with its different-sized "family accommodations," and flat on their stomachs under the folded-back cellar door. Darlene was "it" till she caught Merle and Merle was "it" for hours. Fiona got spider webs in her mouth and gnats up her nose, tore her dress, scraped her knee, lost one hair ribbon, and gave the other to Merle, who had admired it.

When they were through with hide-and-seek they all got into the rocker swing and played gangsters. The swing leapt to and fro, to and fro, screaming wildly at the joints; surely it would break, and soon! That was the thrilling thing about this place: so many features of it—the tower, the swing, the porch—trembled at the edge of ruin, hung by a thread above the fatal plunge. Earl and Stanley and Norman leaned over the back of one of the seats firing at the enemy. "Step on it, you guys," yelled Stanley, "they got a gat!"

"They got a rod!" yelled Norman. "They got a lotta rods!"

"What's a rod?" cried Fiona. "What's a gat?"

"Guns he means," Darlene told her. "Rods and gats is guns."

"Shoot 'em, Stanley," yelled Fiona. "With your gat, shoot the eyes out of 'em!"

Clutching the clawing kitten to her collarbone, her hair in her open

mouth, she bawled encouragement to them. The swing accelerated ever more wildly: soon it would take off entirely, depart from its hinges, fly through the air, burn a hole through the sky! . . .

"Fee-ona Farmer!"

The cry was loud enough to be heard above all sounds of war and wind and radio music.

Beside the swing stood Nana, so tall, so highly charged with hurry and emotion, that the children stopped their play at once.

"Who's she?" Stanley asked.

"She's my nurse," Fiona murmured.

"Your nurse! What's the matter, are you sick?"

"No . . . she just—takes care of me."

"Takes *care* of you!"

"You get out of that swing and come this in-stant!"

Having struck the bottom of disgrace, Fiona stepped down and slowly went to Nana. From the swing the others watched as still as children posing for a photograph.

"Put down that cat and come at once."

"Oh no!" Fiona said. "It's mine, they gave it to me."

"Put. Down. That. Cat."

Darlene came to stand beside Fiona. "But we did give it to her, we want for her to have it."

Nana struck the kitten from Fiona's arms. "You will not take that creature home! It's filthy, it has fleas!"

"Oh my kitty!" shrieked Fiona, diving after Blackie, but Nana caught her wrist.

"You come!"

Fiona pulled, struggled, cast a glare of anguish at all the rapt photograph-faces in the swing.

"You should be punished. You should be whipped. Whipped!" Nana whistled the cruel words; Nana, who was never cruel! Her fingers on Fiona's wrist were hard.

"Let me say good-by to them, Nana, let me say good-by to their *mother!* You said I should *always* say good-by to the mother!"

"Not this time, this time it doesn't matter," Nana said. "You're going straight home and into the tub. Heaven knows what you will have caught!" Upon Fiona's friends she turned a single brilliant glance like one cold flash from a lighthouse.

There was nothing to commend Fiona's departure; dragged by the hand, whimpering, she looked back at her friends in desperation. "Oh, Darlene!"

But it was easy to see that Darlene had detached herself. "Good-by, Nancy," she said, not without a certain pride. She did not smile or say anything else, but her attitude showed Fiona and Nana that she had no need for either of them, could not be hurt by them, and would not think of them again. As they went out the gate she turned her back and skipped away, and Fiona heard the rocker swing resume its screaming tempo.

Halfway home Nana's recriminations began to modify, gradually becoming reproaches: "How could you have, Fiona, run away like that, why it's only by the grace of God I ever found you at all! And all the time I was half sick with worry I never said a word to your father and mother! I didn't want *them* to worry!"

Somewhere deep inside her Fiona understood exactly why Nana had said nothing to her parents, but she just kept on saying: "I want my kitty, I want my kitty."

Finally Nana said: "If you're a good girl maybe we'll get you another kitten."

"I don't want another, I want that one."

"Oh for pity's sakes, it had fleas, or worse. Anything belonging to the Fadgins would be bound to have—"

"Do you know them?"

"I know about them, everybody does. They're the dirtiest, the shift-lessest, the most down-at-the-heel tribe in this whole town!"

"They are not, they're nice, I love them!"

Nana relented a little. "Maybe it's hard not to be shiftless when you're that poor."

"They aren't poor. You should see all the things they've got! More than Grandmother's got in her whole house!"

"All right now, dearie, all right. We'll forget about it, shall we? It will be our secret and we'll never tell anyone because we don't want them to worry, do we? But you must promise me never, never to do such a thing again, hear?"

"I want my kitty," droned Fiona.

Her grandparents' house smelled cool and sweetish. There was a bowl of white and pink stock on the hall table and her grandmother's green linen parasol leaned in a corner among the pearly company of her grandfather's canes.

In the shaded living room Fiona saw her mother knitting and her grandmother at the piano playing the same kind of music she always played, with the loose rings clicking on her fingers.

"Is that my baby?" called her mother—but Nana answered hastily, "I'm getting her right into her bath, Mrs. Farmer. She's sim-ply fil-thy."

Upstairs Nana went in to run the water in the tub. Fiona kicked off one sandal, then the other. A terrible pain took hold of her; it began in her mind

and spread down to her stomach. She had never been homesick before and did not know what ailed her: she knew only that she wanted to sleep at night in a big twanging bed full of children and to eat meals at a crowded table where people threw bread at each other and drank pop. She wanted Stanley's hand to guide her and Darlene's voice to teach her and Blackie's purr to throb against her chest. . . .

Beyond the window she saw her grandfather's wilted golf hat bobbing among the cornstalks and escaped again, running on bare feet down the back stairs and out of doors across the billowing lawn which seemed to be colliding with the trees and sky and shadows, all flooded and dazzled with tears. Blindly she flung open the garden gate and pushed her way through the green-paper corn forest to her grandfather who dropped his hoe and held out his arms when he saw her face.

"Come here now," he said in his gentle deaf voice. "Well, well, this won't do, no it won't, not at all. Come sit here with Grandpa, sit here in the arbor. Did you hurt yourself?"

He led her to the seat under the green grape trellis where he sometimes rested from the hot sun. He put his arm around her shoulders, offering himself as a support for grief, and Fiona howled against his waistcoat till the wet tweed chapped her cheek and there was not a tear left in her. He did not interrupt or ask questions but kept patting her shoulder in a sort of sympathetic accompaniment to her sobs, which he could not hear but which he felt. What's the cause of it all, he wondered. A broken toy? A scolding? Children's tragedies, he thought, children's little tragedies: there are bigger ones in store for you, Fiona, a world of them. The thought

did not move him deeply; everyone must suffer, but for an instant he was not sorry to be old.

Fiona leaned against him and after a while between the hiccups left from sobbing she could hear the ancient heart inside his chest ticktocking steadily, as tranquil and unhurried as he was himself. All the wild performance of her sorrow had not quickened its tempo by a single beat, and this for some reason was a comfort.

The sound of her grandmother's music, sugary and elegant, came sparkling from the house, and upstairs in the bedroom or the hall Nana began to call. "Fee-ona?" she cried. "Oh, Fee-*ona*?"

There was a hint of panic in her voice, now, but no response came from under the green trellis: Fiona's grandfather could not hear the calling, and Fiona, for the time being, did not choose to answer.

(c) What might have been the author's purpose in pointing out these very different feelings?

5. (a) What contrasting attitudes do Fiona and the Fadgins display upon Fiona's departure? (b) What does the Fadgins' detachment tell you about them?

6. (a) How does Fiona feel while waiting for Nana to bathe her? (b) Why couldn't she possibly have felt this way before?

7. (a) What way of life did Fiona discover at the Fadgins'? (b) What important conflict in Fiona does this discovery cause? (c) What question about happiness does the author raise by demonstrating this conflict?

8. Which of the following is the theme of the story? (a) Children have to be allowed the companionship of others their own age. (b) Happiness is not dependent upon material things. (c) The things that bring happiness to one person are not always a source of happiness for the next.

9. Fiona loved the Fadgins. How would a child with a more normal upbringing probably react to them?

10. The author of this story makes much use of imagery. Point out uses of this device in the description of Fiona's walk (page 231). Are the images effective? Why or why not?

DISCUSSION

1. (a) Before Fiona meets the Fadgins, what kind of life does she lead? (b) Who is her one friend? (c) Why does she enjoy his company so much?

2. (a) How is the Fadgin house different from the Farmer house? (b) In what ways are the occupants different? (c) How do the attitudes toward adults differ in the two homes?

3. (a) Compare a meal at the Fadgins' to a Sunday dinner at the Farmers'. (b) Why does Fiona prefer the Fadgins' meal?

4. (a) Why is the kitten so important to Fiona? (b) Compare her feelings for the kitten with her attitude toward her dolls.

THE AUTHOR

Because Elizabeth Enright's father was a cartoonist and her mother an artist, it seemed natural that she should be interested in art. After studying at the School of Applied Art in Paris, Miss Enright began illustrating children's books. Only after she'd done the art work for several books written by other people, did she attempt to write one of her own. Her first book, *Kintu,* which she wrote and illustrated, was honored for its literary content as well as its art work. Her second, *Thimble Summer*, won the Newbery Medal.

Miss Enright wrote novels and short stories both for young people and adults. She illustrated her own books, and also a number written by other people.

How important is it to be important?

I'M NOBODY

EMILY DICKINSON

I'm nobody! Who are you?
Are you nobody, too?
Then there's a pair of us — don't tell!
They'd banish us, you know.

How dreary to be somebody!   5
How public, like a frog
To tell your name the livelong day
To an admiring bog.

DISCUSSION

1. (a) Whom does the speaker mean by "they" in line 4? (b) Why do "they" feel it's wrong to be a nobody? (c) Why might a person who chooses to be a nobody be forced to be an outsider?
2. (a) How does the speaker feel about being important? (b) Explain the comparison the speaker makes in the second stanza.
3. (a) What comment on human nature is made in this poem? (b) Do you agree or disagree with the speaker's view? Why?
4. Contrast the speaker's attitude in "I'm Nobody" with Marty's attitude in "The New Kid."

THE AUTHOR

Like the speaker in "I'm Nobody," Emily Dickinson had no wish to be important. She wrote her poems secretly on scraps of paper — used envelopes, backs of recipes. Some of these she copied on separate sheets out of which she made small packets, little books of her poems. The rest of her ragged manuscripts, she rolled up, tied with thread, and stuffed in drawers.

The first of Miss Dickinson's poems to appear in print was published without her permission. The publisher changed the poem in five places — a practice that disturbed the poet. At least two other works, published in a New England newspaper, were also altered without her consent.

Miss Dickinson's correspondence with a well-known writer indicates that she was interested in having her poems published only if they would be printed exactly as she had written them. She preferred that they be burned rather than tampered with. Because of her attitude, only four of her other poems were published during her lifetime. After she died, her sister, and later a niece, gathered her manuscripts for publication. Since 1890 her poetry has been widely read and greatly appreciated. Many consider her one of America's greatest poets.

*". . .You have no excuse for failure, son,"
said Graham's dad. What in Graham's account explains
why he would then try to fail?*

See
NARRATOR
*Handbook
of Literary
Terms*
page 529

win
or
lose

BRIAN GLANVILLE

IN LEIPZIG.[1] *A very hot day, one of those
days that burn the strength out of you
as you run. Sieloff, the big German, in
front of me, because I'd let him go in
front of me. And knowing that if I
wanted to catch him, I could still catch
him, but if I left it any longer, even two
seconds, then I couldn't. The most important race I'd ever run in my life, the
one that it meant most to win; and the
one it would mean most to lose. Because I could win it or lose it. It was up
to me. That was what I thought, as the
crowd started shouting him on. All
those thousands of East Germans. It's
not up to him; it's up to me. I could
win it, or I could lose it.*

Reprinted by permission of the author and BOYS' LIFE,
published by the Boy Scouts of America.

1. *Leipzig,* city in the southern half of East Germany.

I think the first time Dad took me out running I must have been about three. Running round a track, that is. The other, just running in the room or running round the garden, that began earlier, when I was two. Of course I can't remember it, but he's told me about it often enough, how he'd give me a candy if I could get right round the dining room in less than a minute. Two candies for under half-a-minute. "You should have seen yourself!" he says. "Especially if it was chocolate. You'd do anything for chocolate."

And of course, it's all in the books, the notebooks he's kept on me from the beginning, the great pile of them that he's got in his study. Records of everything, right back to the first day, even of how many times I ran round the garden and how long it took me. Incredible, really. Then, later on, my height; every month, we had that. My weight; every week. My pulse rate, when we started interval training—that was when I was 12. And later still, when we'd been out to the Sports Institute at Dusseldorf,[2] and he'd got taken with this German coach's theories, Emmerich, then there was a record of my heartbeats too.

The thing about Dad was, he was a runner himself in his time, but never as good as he'd wanted to be. He's told me about it so often, I know it almost by heart, now. "The thing is, Graham, I had ability, but I didn't have opportunity. You have ability, *and* you have opportunity, because I've seen to it that you *do* have opportunity. I always swore to myself, long before I met your mother, long before I got married, if ever I have a son, he's not going to be frustrated the way I was." And then I'd get all the old stuff about what a great runner he was as a boy, how he ran a mile in 4:45 when he was 16, which wasn't bad going in those days,

and then how the war came along and put an end to everything. He was called up almost straightaway and put into the Royal Engineers.[3]

"But it wasn't just the war," he'd say. "People like me, Graham, they never had a chance. I left school at 14 to be apprenticed, and after that it was work, work, work. I trained when I could. I'd go slogging round the streets before I'd had my breakfast, or else as soon as I got home; didn't matter how tired I was. I remember how people used to turn and laugh at me, running past them.

"Britain wasn't sports-minded then, Graham. At the Berlin Olympics,[4] this country was a laughing-stock. I remember every morning I looked at the times recorded by our athletes in the middle-distance races, and they were shameful times, son, most of them, times I knew I could have beaten with ease, if only I had had the chance to train—the way the Germans and the Finns and the Americans had. Paavo Nurmi; that was the runner I admired more than any other. The Flying Finn. This little man; there was nothing of him. But year after year he came in ahead of the world.

"Paavo Nurmi; and in England, Sidney Wooderson."

In fact he had pictures of both of them up, Nurmi in the dining room, Wooderson in his study. Wooderson had been a miler, a tiny little skinny fellow, you'd have thought he'd be pushed to run across the road, but he'd won the European Championship in 1946, or whenever it was. Anyway, before I was born.

"Sheer willpower," Dad used to

---

2. *Dusseldorf,* city on the Rhine River in West Germany.
3. *Royal Engineers,* the corps of engineers of the British Army.
4. *Berlin Olympics,* Olympic Games held in Berlin, Germany, in 1936.

say. "That man prevailed on sheer guts and determination. Now you, Graham, you have no excuse for failure, son. You are physically exceptional, and between us, we're going to see you have the right mental attitude, as well."

Dad was very hot on mental attitudes. And diet. And sleep. In fact, on practically everything that had to do with running, even in the most indirect way, even when it came to what I read, what films he thought I ought to see. As for television, he wouldn't have one in the house. Well, not for years, anyway. His idea was it was a distraction; instead of going out to train, you sat at home goggling at the box and filling up your mind with rubbish.

What changed him was when they started showing athletics on the box. First of all, he hired one. Just for the weekend, he said when he got it, just to watch the European Games, from Bucharest.[5] And then, just for the week. And after that, well, just for the month. He said, "After all, we've paid for a month," and so it stayed.

I was talking about that first time, though, that first time Dad took me out running at the track, over at Parliament Hill Fields, which was about the nearest, then, to where we were living. That I *do* remember, or rather, I remember things about it. Number one, I remember it being cold, I remember I was shivering; I didn't want to take my warm-up suit off, this little one he'd had specially made for me, but the old man insisted. I can imagine what he must have said, more or less, because I've had the same kind of thing dozens of times, over the years. "Look, son, look, Graham, let's do the thing properly, or let's not do it at all." So I took the warm-up suit off and I froze and I ran crying all the time and when we got home I was still shaking,

and Mum gave him the devil for making me do it.

Mum. It wasn't very often she got like that. Less and less over the years, in fact. Mostly Dad got his own way. She's small, always very quiet, she gives in too much. He's tall and thin, white hair and glasses. They married very young, started poor, then gradually got richer and richer till now, well, he's rich, Dad, that's the only word for it, and as for me, I'm the only child, born pretty late.

And I never went to school. It's hard to believe, isn't it? To be dead accurate, I did go just for a couple of years or so. I suppose it must have been during the time Dad was still wondering had I got it or hadn't I? Then when he'd decided that I had, it was out of school and private tutors, and if you think that was a pretty lonely kind of life, you're right. I hardly knew any other kids, really; the only time I'd meet them was when I was running against them.

I had quite a few different tutors. First it was women, later on it was men. The old man had it all worked out. He said, "This won't only benefit your running; in this way you'll get a better education, Graham. You'll learn more from them than you ever would at school."

Some I learned from and some I didn't. A lot of it may have been me. Whatever the old man said, he knew and I knew what the real point of it all was, it was to give me more time for running, and knowing it came first, what incentive was there to work hard at things like Math and Latin? History I quite enjoyed, particularly the way one strange bloke taught it to me, though he only stayed a couple of months.

His name was Buglass, and he was

---

5. *Bucharest,* capital city of Romania.

the first chap I ever met who actually made fun of running, which I'm sure was what made the old man get rid of him as quickly as he did. There were times when I'd egg him on, if Dad happened to be in the room, just because I liked hearing the two of them going at it. It was easy for Dad to make fun of Buglass, who looked as if he'd never done a day's exercise.

Buglass would say, "A sound mind in a healthy body, that was the Roman ideal, my dear Graham. You've achieved half of it, at the expense of the other. You have a superbly healthy body, and no mind at all."

"What about the Greeks?" Dad asked him. "Who invented the Olympic Games, then?"

Buglass said, "I have personally always regarded the Olympic Games as a most unfortunate aberration on the part of the Greeks. Of course I admire them. The Greeks were the exponents of the Golden Mean.[6] They engaged in sport purely to exercise their bodies. It was only in their period of decadence that they stooped to producing specialized athletes, like circus animals."

You should have seen the old man's face, then. Puce. "How can you achieve anything without specialization?" he said. If there was one thing he believed in, it was that.

"On the contrary," Buglass told him, "you achieve nothing through specialization except the specialty."

When I was 16, I took half-a-dozen of the O-level exams that you have to pass if you want to go on studying to try for a university. I passed in History, Geography, and English, and I failed the rest. Quite honestly, it didn't worry either of us, either the old man or me. I think our main reaction, his and mine, was that we were glad to get it out of the way. Now we could just concentrate on training.

That winter, we all three of us went out to Santa Barbara, to California, which was great, the sunshine and the beaches, instead of all the London cold and rain, even if the old man wouldn't let me swim much; he said it was bad for the running muscles. I trained with the Santa Barbara Striders, Dad had arranged that through his contacts. They had a very good coach there called Joe Watson who taught me a lot, he worked on my starts and my stride and my arm action. At that time, I was still doing the 100 yards, gradually moving up to competitive 220's, but Joe convinced me I'd never have the basic speed for the hundred. He said, "Shoot for the 220 the next couple of years, then when you're a little stronger, I reckon you'll be running the quarter."

Dad was always trying out different coaches. I suppose at the bottom of it was that he wanted to be my only coach, himself, just as he always was till I was about 14. But then I think he realized that he couldn't do it all alone; he needed professional coaches for me. At the same time, he couldn't reconcile himself to this, so what would happen, time and time again, was that he'd pick on a coach he'd think was fabulous, maybe in the States, maybe in England, maybe in Germany or Scandinavia, take me to this fellow, then, after a time, fall out with him.

As I grew up, Dad's attitude towards me changed quite a lot, I suppose. When I was just a kid, it was, "Do this, do that," but I shot up very quickly and got big, all the more so with the weight training that I hated when he first made me do it, so it got to be more, "Please, Graham," or, "I want you to do it for *me*, Graham." He was very fond of saying, when there

---

6. *Golden Mean,* safe, sensible way of doing things; the avoidance of extremes.

...e people there, "We're pals, we two, aren't we, Graham?"

In a way this made it harder for me, knowing he was expecting so much, not wanting to let him down. Every time I ran a race, I was running for the both of us, and the more I won, the more difficult it got, because people knew about me, they were keener to beat me; and because of all the publicity, too.

It started from the summer I turned 16 and set a new junior record for the hundred. I was running for the Ajax Club, then. I think if Dad had had his way I wouldn't have run for any club, but since I didn't go to school and couldn't compete in school championships, there was nothing else for it. With the clubs, it was more or less the same as with the coaches; I've never stayed with one for long, because Dad finished up quarreling with the officials—who, I must say, it's very easy to quarrel with. They wanted their way, he wanted his.

So after Ajax it was East London, and after that, Nemean. It got to the point where other athletes would say, "Well, how long will you be staying with us, then?" They were never very friendly to me, other athletes, and I suppose this was another thing that started me resenting Dad. They seemed to have the idea that I'd been spoon-fed. Dad would say, "They're jealous of you, son, that's all," and I suppose they were.

If *I'd* known that while I'd been slogging through school, somebody else had gone all over the world just to run and train, I'd probably have felt the same. All this stuff in the papers about "Britain's Test-Tube Runner," and "British Whiz Kid" didn't help much, either. But there was more to it, as well.

Dad's point was that this was simply something that had to be faced. He said, "Dilettantism, that's always been the curse of British sport, son. I fought against it while I was a runner, but it beat me. I'll fight against it now, and between us, we'll win."

We usually won—or rather, I usually won. It's hard to get out of the habit of saying "we," I'm so used to hearing Dad. First it was the Southern Junior, then the National Junior, then, when I was 17—last year, that was—the Nationals, the AAA's, all in the 220 yards. I remember afterwards all the newspapermen clustering round, it was at the White City; there's a little sort of bend there in the railings where runners come and talk to the press, I was terrified, to tell the truth, but Dad called me over there, and, as usual, he did all the talking.

"After this," he said, "Graham is turning to the 440. Our aim is the 400 meters in next year's European Games, isn't it, Graham?" All I could do was nod. As far as I was concerned, I was going to try the 440, I was going to run both distances for a time, then make up my mind which suited me best.

Dad told them, "Graham has the basic strength for the 440. He has speed and strength; the two great requisites. We have three years until the next Olympics, then he'll be 20, and I think he'll be capable of standing up to anybody in the world."

One of them asked him, "Don't you think he'll be a little young, Mr. Rogerson?"

"No," said Dad. "Don't forget Graham has been in training virtually since the age of three."

They made great play of that, I can tell you. It made me feel like a freak. Dad told me, "I did that for one reason, Graham, to set you a standard. It's often a wonderful idea to have a goal, even if in the end you don't achieve it. The mere fact you know it's

there means that you're striving toward it."

By this time, I was right in the middle of the whole athletics thing, where people didn't get at me for being single-minded, because everybody else was too. Some of them were so fanatical, I even thought at times perhaps I wasn't taking it seriously enough.

And now I know you're waiting for me to come to the race and tell you why I did what I did; which I shall. But everything I've said so far was necessary; it was all part of it. You can't understand what I did without knowing what had gone before.

It was in Leipzig, of course: the finals of the European 400 meters. I hated everything about that city, except for the stadium, which was a nice one, out among the trees, full of wooden benches. I hated the atmosphere, I hated the grayness of everything. I hated the loudspeakers in the streets that suddenly began spouting at you, even if you couldn't understand a word of it, and when they took us round their Sports Institute that they were so proud of, I didn't even like *that*. I'd seen things like it before, of course, but here, going round it, I suddenly remembered what my tutor, Buglass, had said that time. These athletes, they were what he said: circus animals. They did their tricks and you threw them a bun or a peanut.

The old man was with me, too, raving about everything. "Look at it, Graham. No wonder they produce so many champions. I've done this for you, but I've done it with my own money."

I think it must have been then that the idea came to me: I was going to lose. Yes, lose. You find that hard to believe, don't you? After all the preparation, all the victories. Lose—because if I lost, it would let me off the

hook. If I lost, it would free me from *him,* I could make up my own mind and maybe I'd decide to go on running, maybe I wouldn't; at least I'd have done something for myself. Because if this was the big one to win, then it had to be the big one to lose. And in this place that I hated: this Leipzig.

Then, when the moment came, I couldn't lose. As you know, I won, but what you don't know is how near I came to throwing it away; deliberately. I cruised through the heats, I coasted through the semifinals, and when it came to the final, I was running so well I knew there were only two of them who could live with me—Davidescu of Rumania, who got away quicker than me, and the East German, Sieloff, who had a better finish.

I admit I had a plan, and it was a strange plan. I was going to get off to a flying start, stay with Davidescu, lose him on the first bend, go into the straight neck and neck with Sieloff, pull ahead of him to show I could beat him if I wanted—even if I only showed myself—then let him go, and finish maybe third, even fourth.

Which was exactly how it went; until that last bit.

I stayed with Davidescu, just as I planned I would. I left him behind in the back straight, I was way out in front, and then I could hear Sieloff coming, on the outside. I held him all the way to the bend, then he caught me as we came into the home straight; then I clenched my teeth and gave it everything and got ahead of him again.

We were about 90 yards out when I eased up and let him pass me, but the moment he did, the moment I saw him ahead, something happened, like a reflex action: *snap!* I couldn't let him get away with it, it was just bred into me, all the years of slogging my guts out, and I went after him again,

even though what it meant was winning it twice. At 50 yards I was still a yard behind him. My chest felt as if it was bursting, my legs were turning to paper. Then I was right on his heels, then swerving round him, then level; then I was slinging myself at the tape, going through it, falling, knowing I'd won.

Afterwards I went on down into the interview room. It was packed with people. Dad was there; I couldn't look at him. So pleased. Beaming all over his face. One of the British reporters called out, "What next, Graham?" and I said, "Nothing's next, I've retired."

You could have heard a pin drop; or rather, you could once the Germans had explained to one another, once everyone had grasped it. This reporter asked, "Do you mean it, Graham? Are you serious?"

From the corner of my eye I could see Dad's face; the most astonished look I think I've ever come across. "Yes," I said, "I've never been more serious." Then I got up and walked out. I still didn't look at Dad. All I could think of was the talk we were going to have, hours and hours, like two records playing in turn. "I don't understand, Graham," he'd say. "I just don't understand you."

Outside in the sunshine, I suddenly realized something. I was happy. I was really happy. I could start running for myself, now.

DISCUSSION

1. (a) From whose point of view is this story told? (b) What impression does the speaker give of his father? of his mother? (c) What kind of person do you think the narrator is on the basis of what he says and does? Give examples.
2. (b) What does Buglass have to say about athletes? (b) Is there any indication that he might be prejudiced? What? (c) What kind of impression do Buglass's words make on the narrator's father? (d) At what point do Buglass's words take on meaning to the narrator? Do they influence him?
3. Would you call Graham's decision at the end of the story courageous or selfish? Explain.
4. (a) What changes in attitude toward his father does Graham experience as he grows up? (b) Does his father's attitude toward him change also? How? (c) Is there any possibility that the father will ever be able to understand Graham's decision to retire from competitive running? (d) Do you think Graham might ever return to competitive running?

THE AUTHOR

Sundays will find Brian Glanville kicking, dribbling, and if need be, elbowing his way up the field at the Wormwood Scrubs soccer club in London, England. A man of unlimited energy (he is one of the busiest and most prolific sports journalists in England), Glanville says of soccer, "Without it, I don't know what I'd do. Soccer is an essential part of my life."

His story, "Win or Lose," is about an athlete who must come to grips with his own needs and desires, and this emphasis on the human situation is characteristic of all Glanville's writing. "My column is for people who don't want to read about sport just as sport, but want to read about people and human experience."

*Joey knew his sister would be hurt
when he gave her the sled.
Why then didn't he act to prevent
her injury?*

THOMAS E. ADAMS

ALL THE ADVENTURE of the night and
snow lay before him: if only he could
get out of the house.

"You can't go out," his mother
said, "until you learn how to act like a
gentleman. Now apologize to your sister."

He stared across the table at his
sister.

"Go on," his mother said.

His sister was watching her plate.
He could detect the trace of a smile at
the corners of her mouth.

First published in *The Sewanee Review* LXIX, 1 (Winter,
1961). © 1961 by The University of the South. Reprinted
with the permission of the author and the publisher.

"I won't! She's laughing at me!" He saw the smile grow more pronounced. "Besides, she *is* a liar!"

His sister did not even bother to look up, and he felt from looking at her that he had said exactly what she had wanted him to say. He grew irritated at his stupidity.

"That settles it," his mother said calmly, without turning from the stove. "No outs for you."

He stared at his hands, his mind in a panic. He could feel the smile on his sister's face. His hand fumbled with the fork on his plate. "No," he said meekly, prodding a piece of meat with the fork. "I'll apologize."

His sister looked up at him innocently.

"Well?" said his mother. "Go on."

He took a deep breath. "I'm . . ." He met his sister's gaze. "I'm sorry!" But it came out too loudly, he knew.

"He is not," his sister said.

He clenched his teeth and pinched his legs with his fingers. "I am too," he said. It sounded good, he knew; and it was half over. He had control now, and he relaxed a bit and even said further: "I'm sorry I called you a liar."

"That's better," his mother said. "You two should love each other. Not always be fighting."

He paused strategically for a long moment.

"Can I go out now?"

"Yes," his mother said.

He rose from the table, glaring at his sister with a broad grin, calling her a liar with his eyes.

His hand plucked his jacket from the couch and swirled it around his back. The buttons refused to fit through the holes, so he let them go in despair. He sat down just long enough to pull on his shiny black rubbers. Finally he put on his gloves. Then with four proud strides he arrived at the door and reached for the knob.

"Put your hat on," his mother said without looking at him.

His face, toward the door, screwed and tightened with disgust. "Aw Ma."

"Put it on."

"Aw Ma, it's not that cold out."

"Put it on."

"Honest Ma, it's not that cold out."

"Are you going to put your hat on, or are you going to stay and help with the dishes?"

He sighed. "All right," he said. "I'll put it on."

The door to the kitchen closed on his back and he was alone in the cold gloom of the shed. Pale light streamed through the frosted window and fell against the wall where the sled stood. The dark cold room was silent, and he was free. He moved into the shaft of light and stopped when from the kitchen he heard the muffled murmur of his mother's voice, as if she were far away. He listened. The murmuring hushed and he was alone again.

The sled. It was leaning against the wall, its varnished wood glistening in the moonlight. He moved closer to it and he saw his shadow block the light, and he heard the cold cracking of the loose linoleum beneath his feet.

He picked it up. He felt the smooth wood slippery in his gloved hands. The thin steel runners shone blue in the light, as he moved one finger along the polished surface to erase any dust. He shifted the sled in his hands and stood getting the feel of its weight the way he had seen his brother hold a rifle. He gripped the sled tightly, aware of the strength in his arms; and he felt proud to be strong and alone and far away with the sled in the dark cold silent room.

The sled was small and light. But strong. And when he ran with it, he ran very quickly, quicker than anyone, because it was very light and

small and not bulky like other sleds. And when he ran with it, he carried it as if it were a part of him, as if he carried nothing in his arms. He set the rear end on the floor and let the sled lean against him, his hands on the steering bar. He pushed down on the bar and the thin runners curved gracefully because they were made of shiny blue flexible steel; and with them he could turn sharply in the snow, sharper than anyone. It was the best sled. It was his.

He felt a slight chill in the cold room, and in the moonlight he saw his breath in vapor rising like cigarette smoke before his eyes. His body shivered with excitement as he moved hurriedly but noiselessly to the door. He flung it open; and the snow blue and sparkling, and the shadows deep and mysterious, and the air silent and cold: all awaited him.

"Joey!" From the kitchen came his mother's voice. He turned toward the kitchen door and refused to answer.

"Joseph!"

"What!" His tone was arrogant, and a chill of fear rushed through his mind.

There was a long awful silence.

"Don't you forget to be home by seven o'clock." She hadn't noticed, and his fear was gone.

"All right!" he answered, ashamed of his fear. He stepped across the threshold and closed the door. Then he removed the hat and dropped it in the snow beside the porch.

He plodded down the alley, thrilling in the cold white silence—the snow was thick. The gate creaked as he pushed it open, holding and guiding the sled through the portal. The street was white, and shiny were the icy tracks of automobiles in the lamplight above, while between him and the light the black branches of trees ticked softly in the slight wind. In the gutters stood enormous heaps of snow, pale and dark in the shadows, stretching away from him like a string of mountains. He moved out of the shadows, between two piles of snow, and into the center of the street, where he stood for a moment gazing down the white road that gradually grew darker until it melted into the gloom at the far end.

Then he started to trot slowly down the street. Slowly, slowly gaining speed without losing balance. Faster he went now, watching the snow glide beneath his shiny black rubbers. Faster and faster, but stiffly, don't slip. Don't fall, don't fall: now! And his body plunged downward, and the sled whacked in the quiet and the white close to his eyes was flying beneath him as he felt the thrill of gliding alone along a shadowy street, with only the ski-sound of the sled in the packed snow. Then before his eyes the moving snow gradually slowed. And stopped. And he heard only the low sound of the wind and his breath.

Up again and start the trot. He moved to the beating sound of his feet along the ground. His breath came heavily and quickly, and matched the rhythm of his pumping legs, straining to carry the weight of his body without the balance of his arms. He reached a wild dangerous breakneck speed, and his leg muscles swelled and ached from the tension, and the fear of falling too early filled his mind; and down he let his body go. The white road rushed to meet him; he was off again, guiding the sled obliquely across the street toward a huge pile of snow near a driveway.

Squinting his eyes into the biting wind, he calculated when he would turn to avoid crashing. The pile, framed against the darkness of the sky, glistened white and shiny. It

loomed larger and larger before him. He steered the sled sharply, bending the bar; and the snow flew as the sled churned sideways, and he heard suddenly a cold metallic snap. He and the sled went tumbling over in the hard wet snow. He rolled with it and the steering bar jarred his forehead. Then the dark sky and snow stopped turning, and all he felt was the cold air stinging the bump on his forehead.

The runner had snapped; the sled was broken. He stared at the shiny smooth runner and touched the jagged edge with his fingers. He sat in the middle of the driveway, the sled cradled in his lap, running his fingers up and down the thin runner until he came to the jagged edge where it had broken.

With his fingers he took the two broken edges and fitted them back into place. They stuck together with only a thin crooked line to indicate the split. But it was like putting a broken cup together. He stared at it, and wished it would be all right and felt like crying.

He got up and walked slowly back down the street to his house. He sat down between the back bumper of a parked car and a pile of snow. Cradling the sled across his legs, he put the two edges together again and stared at them. He felt a thickness in his throat, and he swallowed hard to remove it, but it did not go away.

He leaned back, resting his head against the snowpile. Through his wet eyelids he saw the lamplight shimmering brightly against the sky. He closed his eyes and saw again the shiny graceful curve of the runner. But it was broken now. He had bent it too far; too far. With his hand he rubbed his neck, then his eyes, then his neck again. And he felt the snow coming wet through his pants. As he shifted to a new position, he heard the creaking of a gate. He turned toward the sound.

His sister was walking away from his house. He watched her move slowly across the street and into the grocery store. Through the plate-glass window he saw her talking with the storekeeper. He stared down at the runner. With his gloves off, he ran his fingers along the cold smooth surface and felt the thin breakline. He got up, brushed the snow off the seat of his pants, and walked to the gate to wait for his sister.

He saw her take a package from the man and come out of the store. She walked carefully on the smooth white, her figure dark in its own shadow as she passed beneath the streetlight, the package in her arm. When she reached the curb on his side, he rested his arms on the nose of the sled and exhaled a deep breath nervously. He pretended to be staring in the opposite direction.

When he heard her feet crunching softly in the snow, he turned. "Hi," he said.

"Hi," she said, and she paused for a moment. "Good sledding?"

"Uhuh," he said. "Just right. Snow's packed nice and hard. Hardly any slush at all." He paused. "I'm just resting a bit now."

She nodded. "I just went for some milk."

His fingers moved slowly down the runner and touched the joined edges.

"Well . . ." she said, about to leave.

His fingers trembled slightly, and he felt his heart begin to beat rapidly. "Do you want to take a flop?" In the still night air he heard with surprise the calm sound of his voice.

Her face came suddenly alive. "Can I? I mean, will you let me? Really?"

"Sure," he said. "Go ahead," and

he handed her the sled very carefully. She gave him the package.

He put the bag under his arm and watched her move out of the shadows of the trees and into the light. She started to trot slowly, awkwardly, bearing the sled. She passed directly beneath the light and then she slipped and slowed to regain her balance. The sled looked large and heavy in her arms and, seeing her awkwardness, he realized she would be hurt badly in the fall. She was moving away again, out of the reach of the streetlight, and into the gray haze farther down the road.

He moved to the curb, holding the bag tightly under his arm, hearing his heart pounding in his ears. He wanted to stop her, and he opened his mouth as if to call to her; but no sound came. It was too late: her dark figure was already starting the fall, putting the sled beneath her. Whack! And her head dipped with the front end jutting the ground, and the back of the sled and her legs rose like a seesaw and down they came with another muffled sound. The street was quiet, except for a low whimper that filled his ears.

He saw her figure rise slowly and move toward him. He walked out to meet her beneath the light. She held the sled loosely in one hand, the broken runner dangling, reflecting light as she moved.

She sobbed and looking up he saw bright tears falling down her cheeks, and a thin line of blood trickling down her chin. In the corner of her mouth near the red swelling on her lip, a little bubble of spit shone with the blood in the light.

He felt that he should say something but he did not speak.

"I'm . . . I'm sorry," she said and the bubble broke. "I'm sorry I . . . your sled." She looked down at the sled. "It'll never be the same."

"It'll be all right," he said. He felt that he ought to do something but he did not move. "I can get it soldered. Don't worry about it." But he saw from her expression that she thought he was only trying to make her feel better.

"No," she said, shaking her head emphatically. "No it won't! It'll always have that weak spot now." She began to cry very hard. "I'm sorry."

He made an awkward gesture of forgiveness with his hand. "Don't cry," he said.

She kept crying.

"It wasn't your fault," he said.

"Yes it was," she said. "Oh, yes it was."

"No!" he said. "No, it wasn't!" But she didn't seem to hear him, and he felt his words were useless. He sighed wearily with defeat, not knowing what to say next. He saw her glance up at him as if to see whether he were still watching her, then she quickly lowered her gaze and said with despair and anguish: "Oh . . . girls are so stupid!"

There was no sound. She was no longer crying. She was looking at the ground: waiting. His ears heard nothing; they felt only the cold silent air.

"No they aren't," he said half-heartedly. And he heard her breathing again. He felt he had been forced to say that. In her shining eyes he saw an expression he did not understand. He wished she would go in the house. But seeing the tears on her cheeks and the blood on her chin, he immediately regretted the thought.

She wiped her chin with her sleeve, and he winced, feeling rough cloth on an open cut. "Don't do that," his hand moved to his back pocket, "use my handkerchief."

She waited.

The pocket was empty. "I haven't got one," he said.

Staring directly at him, she patted gingerly the swollen part of her lip with the tips of her fingers.

He moved closer to her. "Let me see," he said. With his hands he grasped her head and tilted it so that the light fell directly on the cut.

"It's not too bad," she said calmly. And as she said it she looked straight into his eyes, and he felt she was perfectly at ease; while standing that close to her, he felt clumsy and out of place.

In his hands her head was small and fragile, and her hair was soft and warm; he felt the rapid pulsing of the vein in her temple; his ears grew hot with shame.

"Maybe I better go inside and wash it off?" she asked.

With his finger he wiped the blood from her chin. "Yes," he said, feeling relieved. "You go inside and wash it off." He took the sled and gave her the package.

He stared at the ground as they walked to the gate in silence. When they reached the curb he became aware that she was watching him.

"You've got a nasty bump on your forehead," she said.

"Yes," he said. "I fell."

"Let me put some snow on it," she said, reaching to the ground.

He caught her wrist and held it gently. "No," he said.

He saw her about to object. "It's all right. You go inside and take care of your lip." He said it softly but with his grip and his eyes he told her more firmly.

"All right," she said after a moment, and he released his hold. "But don't forget to put your hat on."

He stared at her.

"I mean, *before* you go back in the house."

They both smiled.

"Thanks for reminding me," he said, and he dropped the sled in the snow and hurried to hold the gate open for her.

She hesitated, then smiled proudly as he beckoned her into the alley.

He watched her walk away from him down the dark alley in the gray snow. Her small figure swayed awkwardly as she stepped carefully in the deep snow, so as not to get her feet too wet. Her head was bowed and her shoulders hunched and he humbly felt her weakness. And he felt her cold. And he felt the snow running cold down her boots around her ankles. And though she wasn't crying now, he could still hear her low sobbing, and he saw her shining eyes and the tears falling, saw her trying to stop them and them falling even faster. And he wished he had never gone sledding. He wished that he had never even come out of the house tonight.

The back door closed. He turned and moved about nervously kicking at the ground. At the edge of the curb he dug his hands deep into the cold wet snow. He came up with a handful and absently began shaping and smoothing it. He stopped abruptly and dropped it at his feet.

He did not hear it fall. He was looking up at the dark sky but he did not see it. He put his cold hands in his back pockets but he did not feel them. He was wishing that he were some time a long time away from now and somewhere a long way away from here.

In the corner of his eye something suddenly dimmed. Across the street in the grocery store the light was out: it was seven o'clock.

DISCUSSION

1. (a) What kind of tensions are evident between the characters as the story opens? **(b)** What might have caused these tensions? **(c)** Is Joe sincere in his first apology to his sister? **(d)** How do you think brother and sister feel toward each other at this point?

2. (a) What does the sled represent to Joe? What actions of his indicate this? **(b)** How does he feel about sledding at night?

3. (a) How does the sled get broken? **(b)** Describe the damage to the sled. **(c)** How does Joe feel about the break?

4. (a) How does Joe act toward his sister after she leaves the store? **(b)** Does his attitude toward her seem to have changed? **(c)** How does she react to his offer of the sled?

5. (a) What reasons might Joe have for offering his sister a "flop" on the sled? **(b)** How does he begin to feel as he sees her start to run with the sled? **(c)** Does he think of warning her?

6. (a) After she falls, what does Joe's sister think? **(b)** Does Joe let her keep thinking this? Do his words to her make any difference? Explain.

7. (a) How does Joe's attitude toward his sister change after seeing that she is hurt? Explain, using details from the story. **(b)** Why does Joe try to keep his sister's attention from the bump on his forehead?

8. (a) Who seems more mature and more in control near the end of the story, Joe or his sister? Explain. **(b)** Comment briefly on how Joe feels about himself and his actions.

LEIGH PHOTOGRAPHERS

THE AUTHOR

"Sled" was the first published piece of fiction by Thomas E. Adams, a young writer from New Jersey. It has proved to be a very popular work, reprinted in a number of magazines, and was once turned into a play that was broadcast in Europe by The Voice of America.

See
SYMBOL
*Handbook
of Literary
Terms
page 534*

*Sister Opal carried as a memory for the rest of her life
R. Sonnier's knowing look that dismissed her as a person
of no importance at all.*

THE BAROQUE MARBLE

E. A. PROULX

LATE AUTUMN RAIN again. Sister Opal woke up in a Polaroid yellow light with her head hanging off the bed all sideways. Down in the street children's voices slid under the window muffled and changed by the damp morning. Sister Opal thought the children sounded as if they were speaking Russian or Basque[1]—some queer, garbled language. She pretended she was in another country where she didn't know a word of the language and where she would have to make signs to get breakfast in a few minutes when she went downstairs. False panic began to rise in her, then subsided. From her position of suspension over the edge of the bed, the furniture looked darker, and the unfamiliar angle gave it a sinister look. The bureau loomed, a

skyscraper in dull, dark varnish. Perhaps there were tiny people and offices inside. The chair arms seemed to have clenched hands at their ends, like brown old men sitting anxiously in the doctor's office waiting to hear the bad news.

Sister Opal twisted her head around toward the yellow window. On the sill was a square glass jar of marbles, reddish brown, yellow and white glassies and a very large blue one. Most of them were mob marbles, as much alike as the faces of the crowd to

1. **Basque,** language of a people who live in and around the Pyrenees, a mountain range of northern Spain and southern France.

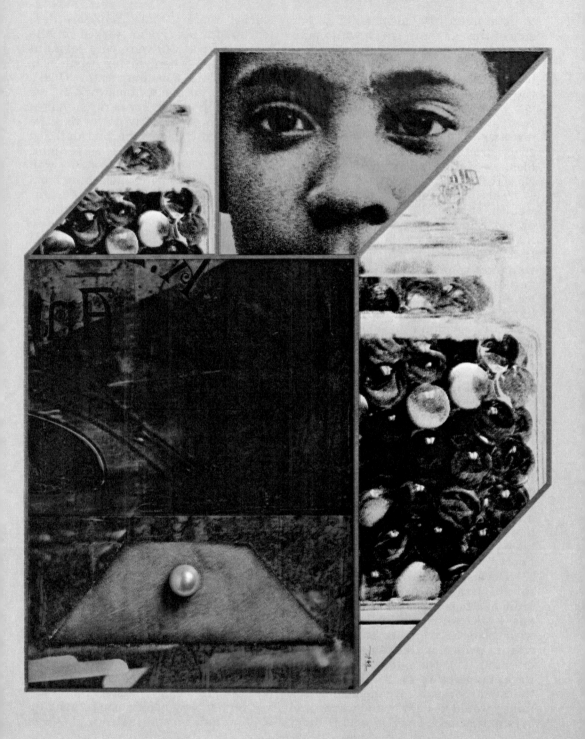

a dictator on his balcony. Off to one side of the jar there was a white marble, deformed and not a true round — a lopsided freak of a marble — her favorite one. When this marble sat alone on the splendor of Sister Opal's blue velvet best dress, it took on a silver, translucent glow. In the jar, it was dirty-white, opaque and with more space around it than the other marbles, as if they avoided getting too close to it.

The jar of marbles was a kind of wealth. It was the most Sister Opal owned. Eight hundred and forty-three marbles. She took a miser's satisfaction in pouring them out onto the bed, watching them roll into the valleys, gathering up their heavy, glassy weight, cold but soon warming in her hand. Each marble was individually beautiful. A kind of classic Greek perfection shone in their roundness. Under Sister Opal's father's magnifying glass the perfect marbles disclosed blemishes, pits and scratches. Sister Opal liked them unmagnified; in their smallness she found their greatest value.

She touched the shade and it leaped up, startled, to the top of the wooden roller where it chattered a few seconds in fright, and then clung, tightly wound. Her warm breath made a milky fog on the window glass and her warm finger wrote, "All the sailors have died of scurvy, yours truly, Opal Foote."

Downstairs, Sister Opal's family sat at the table. Dark and sullen, they crunched toast, stabbed at their eggs and made whirlpools in their coffee with spoons. Except for Sister Opal, it was a bad-tempered family in the mornings and the only conversations were mumbles to each other to pass the sugar or salt. By noontime the family would be chatty and warm, and by suppertime everyone was in high spirits. Sister Opal's four brothers (except for Roy, who worked on the night shift at GE) were very jovial at suppertime when Sister Opal was weary. This morning Sister Opal's father asked about homework. Sister Opal thought of homework as yellow leaves dropping softly down, like the yellow blank pages she had dropped into the wastepaper basket last night. Guilty, Sister Opal went outside with jammy toast, hearing something from her father about being home right after school to make up Roy's dinner pail and to start supper because Mama had to work late. Sister Opal sang a private song as she walked along the wet sidewalk hopping the shallow puddles which were out to ruin her good shoes.

Sailors died of scurvy, oh,
They threw them in the sea.
Pack Roy's dinner pail tonight
With a thermos bottle of tea.

The rain outside had transmuted to yellow light and threatened afternoon lightning. Somewhere Sister Opal had read that yellow was the favorite color of insane people. The woman down the street had had a nervous breakdown last summer only a week after her husband had painted their house yellow. Across the street some white boys from Sister Opal's class at school were walking in the same direction. They pushed and shoved each other. One of them yelled, "Hey, turkey!" at Sister Opal. Sister Opal laughed because their faces looked yellow. Immediately they became hostile, thinking she was laughing at their existence, their being. Sister Opal's dignity did not allow her to hear their jeers.

At three-thirty Sister Opal was not on her way back home to pack up Roy's dinner pail. Instead, she was

walking thoughtfully down Essex Street, peering into all the windows of the silver and antique shops. Art class that afternoon had completely enthralled Sister Opal. Mrs. Grigson had shown a film about ordinary people who started art collections with inexpensive things that became rare and valuable as time went by. Sister Opal envisioned herself someday in her own apartment with rare items of art in glass cases and white walls hung with glowing works of great artists which she, Sister Opal, had picked up years before for just a song. Even though she had only a few dollars in her savings account (a birthday present from her grandmother), and little hope of getting more, she was looking for something really good and fine on Essex Street. The film had indicated that all the people who built up enviable art collections had started off with the things they really liked. This was Sister Opal's primary mission: to find something she really liked. Then she would face the money problem. She had quite forgotten about Roy's empty dinner pail, the cold stove, and Mama working late.

As she splashed through the puddles of Essex Street, she dismissed old silver, all lumpy with twisted roses and crests, and dark with tarnish. She rejected the idea of collecting glass — too space-consuming and bothersome. She didn't really like sculpture, and she didn't know where she could buy real paintings or prints. The rain began again and Sister Opal's shoes were sodden and squishy. Past shops with small, dirty windows she went, discarding ceramics, carved wooden figures, vases, chandeliers, toy soldiers, andirons, dog-grates, lacquerware and crystal.

Then, in the window of R. Sonnier's, she saw *it*. On a piece of blue velvet, quite like Sister Opal's best dress, there lay a large, glowing, misshapen marble. Sister Opal drew in her breath and exhaled slowly. This was it. She would collect marbles, rare ones from China, ancient ones from Peru, Roman marbles, marbles Genghis Khan[2] had played with, marbles from Napoleon's[3] cabinets, from Istanbul and Alexandria, marbles of solid gold, of azure, of lapis lazuli, of wood and stone and jewel. And she would begin with the marble in this very window! In she marched, a thin black girl with wet shoes, whose older brother was going to go supperless on the night shift.

The shop inside was crowded with objects stacked on shelves, in corners or looming down from the ceiling, crumpled, dusty dark things. A fat, middle-aged white man was reading a book in a leather chair behind the counter. He looked up when the door opened and then back to his book. Sister Opal did not waste time looking around the shop. She marched briskly up to R. Sonnier, or as briskly as one can march with wet shoes.

"Excuse me, how much is that marble in the window, and do you have any other kinds?"

"*What* marble in the window? I haven't got any marble that I know of in there. This is an antique shop, not a toy store." Sister Opal went to the curtain that hung behind the window to give a background for the objects displayed and pulled it aside.

"There," she said simply, pointing to the fat, lucent sphere.

"Young lady," said R. Sonnier, highly amused, "that is *not* a marble. That is a baroque pearl, an antique baroque pearl, and even though I am letting it go at an unbelievably low

---

2. **Genghis Khan,** early 13th century Mongol leader who conquered much of Asia.
3. **Napoleon's,** Napoleon Bonaparte, French Emperor who in the early 19th century conquered a large part of Europe.

price, I doubt you could afford it." He looked her up and down, seeing the wet shoes, the cotton dress in late October, the brown skin and thinness that was Sister Opal. "It is for sale for four hundred and fifty dollars. A bargain for those who can afford such things. Marbles I believe you'll find at Woolworth's."

Sister Opal felt a horrible combination of shame, embarrassment, anger, pride and sadness rise in her. She carried as a memory for the rest of her life R. Sonnier's knowing look that dismissed her as a person of no importance at all. Sister Opal, in a burst of pride and fantasy, said in a haughty voice, "*I* prefer to think of baroque pearls as marbles. And I would definitely like *that* marble. Please save it for me because it might be quite a while before I can pick it up. My name is Opal Foote."

R. Sonnier digested this information and repeated, "Then you want me to save this baroque pearl for you? You intend to buy it?"

"Yes," said Sister Opal. "Opal Foote is the name." She gave him her address and then left with her shoes squelching softly. She was committed to the baroque marble which R. Sonnier was saving for her. Suddenly she remembered Roy's dinner pail and the gloomy apartment without one picture or really nice thing in it. There were only the family photographs kept in an old candy box and a plastic vase filled with plastic flowers. She ran home hoping that Roy hadn't left for work yet.

At the table that night Sister Opal's father looked on her with disfavor. His cheerful supper face was cloudy, and Sister Opal knew the storm would break before she poured out his coffee. Roy had had to go to work without any dinner, supper had been late

and Opal had broken three eggs by slamming the old refrigerator door so hard that the eggs had shot out of their aluminum nest and run all over everything inside. Sister Opal's father finished the last bit of mashed potato on his plate and leaned back, glaring at Sister Opal.

"Well, girl, how come you didn't get home to fix your brother's dinner pail or start the supper? Everybody in this family's got to do his part. Now I'm waiting to hear."

There was no escape. Sister Opal took a deep breath and began telling about the art class and Essex Street and the baroque pearl in R. Sonnier's shop. Her father's face was first incredulous, then angry, then sad. He said nothing for a long time. Opal sat miserably waiting for the lecture. Her brother Andrew got up and poured the coffee and patted Opal's shoulder as he passed behind her chair. Her father began to speak, slowly at first.

"Well, Sister, I think for a family in the kind of situation we got, where we all work to keep some kind of decency in our lives, and where we are trying to work toward an education for all you kids, an education of *some* kind, that any ideas about collecting art are just plain *crazy*. We are poor people and it's no use you pretending otherwise. Maybe someday your children, or more likely, grandchildren can collect art, but right now, girl, we can't gather enough money together to collect milk bottles! Wait!" (Sister Opal had uttered a furious "But!")

"Now just wait! I don't want to crush you down like a pancake. I *know* how you felt when that antique man looked you up and down and made his remarks. Every person in this family knows how you felt. And I understand how you answered him back pridefully about how you'd *get* that pearl or marble or whatever it is. But now, Opal,

you got to swallow your pride and forget that marble, or else you got to do something about it. You got any ideas? Because I personally do not."

"I am old enough and able enough to get a job after school in the evenings and earn enough money to *buy* that baroque pearl myself, and I am going to do it!" Opal spoke slowly.

Her father looked at Opal, sadder than ever, and said, "If you are old enough to get a job, Sister Opal, you are old enough to save that job money for college or for helping this big family to get along. How would it be if I decided to save the money I make at Quadrant for buying myself a Picasso[4] or something? Or suppose Roy decided not to kick in money for groceries and things but to buy himself a—a—harpsichord[5] or a statue?" The idea of big, quiet Roy, clumsy and inarticulate, buying himself a harpsichord or a statue sent half the table snorting with laughter. "Besides," continued her father, "who's going to pack up Roy's dinner pail and start the supper while you are at some job?"

Sister Opal's brother Andrew stood up. "I am sick and tired of hearing about Roy's dinner pail. I expect the sun isn't going to come up and set anymore—no, it's going to be Roy's dinner pail! I say that if Sister Opal sees more in life than groceries and trying to get along, she should at least have the chance to try. I can get home a little earlier and start supper myself, and Roy can pack up his *own* dinner pail. You've told us yourself, Papa, that if a person wants something bad enough, and works hard enough *for* it, he'll get it. I'm willing to see Opal get that baroque pearl. I wouldn't mind seeing a few nice things around here myself."

The great argument broke out and raged around the supper table and took on fresh vigor when Sister Opal's mother came in, tired and with a sharp edge to her tongue. The final resolution, near midnight, was that if Sister Opal got a job, she could save half the money for the baroque pearl and half for college. Sister Opal felt triumphant and like a real art collector.

It took her three days to find a job. She was to work at Edsall's drugstore after school until ten-thirty from Monday to Friday and all day Saturday. She dipped out ice cream, made sodas and cherry Cokes, mixed Alka-Seltzer for gray-faced men, sold cigars and newspapers, squeezed her homework in between customers and wiped off the sticky counter with a yellow sponge (Mr. Edsall had bought five hundred yellow sponges at a bargain sale the year before and Sister Opal got to despise those yellow sponges). She made change for people to use in the phone booth, she cleaned out the Pyrex coffeepots and made fresh coffee a thousand times a day, sold cough drops and throat lozenges all through the winter and dispensed little plastic hats to ladies when the spring rains came. She got home at eleven o'clock each night with aching legs and red eyes, and Sunday mornings she slept late, catching up. In little ways, her mother showed an extra tenderness for her only daughter's great desire for a beautiful object. Her father surprised Sister Opal by Scotch-taping a reproduction of a Picasso painting over the kitchen calendar. He had cut *The Three Musicians* out of an old magazine. When Roy said, "What's that!?" Sister Opal's father remarked loftily, "I always did like Picasso."

"Yeah," said Andrew to Roy, "at least he doesn't go in for harpsichords

4. **Picasso,** work by Pablo Picasso (1881–1973), important Spanish painter and sculptor.
5. **harpsichord,** musical instrument much like a piano except that the strings are plucked instead of hammered, causing a more delicate and tinkling sound.

and statues." This joke about harpsichords and statues was one that Roy had never quite fathomed, and he eventually grew so confused on the matter that he was convinced that he really did take an extraordinary interest in keyboard music and sculpture. It was even suspected by the family that on his night off he had once gone, not to a night baseball game, but to a concert.

Sister Opal's weeks turned into months, and the long drugstore nights dragged through winter into spring. She had two bank accounts, one for college money and one for the baroque pearl. In March on a Friday night, she had four hundred dollars in the school account, and four hundred fifty in the pearl account. It was enough. She got permission from Mr. Edsall to take the next day off to go to R. Sonnier's to buy the pearl.

Early in the morning Sister Opal woke to pale yellow spring sun. She leaped up with her heart beating hard and dressed the part of a baroque pearl buyer. Something special was needed. Her blue velvet best dress had been outgrown and remade during the winter into a blue velvet best skirt. She put it on and borrowed her mother's white silk blouse. She shined her shoes until the cracks didn't show and rushed downstairs to breakfast. Everybody knew she was going to buy the pearl that day but nobody said anything. The whole family was shy and quiet with anticipation. Andrew sat breathing quietly on his coffee.

At nine o'clock Sister Opal was walking along Essex Street. She went past the dusty windows displaying lumpy silverware, ceramic mugs with gold decorations, wooden candelabra from Spain, and then she came to R. Sonnier's shop. In his window there was a display of silver and gold watches and clocks under glass bells. Sister Opal smiled, thinking of the baroque pearl hidden secretly in a box, waiting for Sister Opal all those long months. She went inside. R. Sonnier sat in his chair behind the counter, reading a book. Nothing had changed. Stuff was still stacked to the ceiling, stuff still hung down to the floor. R. Sonnier looked up. His eyes were flat, incurious.

"Can I help you?"

"It's me, Mr. Sonnier. Opal Foote. I've come to get my baroque marble that you've been saving for me."

"What marble? I don't have any marbles."

Patiently Sister Opal explained about the baroque pearl she had asked him to save for her last fall, and then she expectantly waited for the shock of recognition, the rummaging in a desk drawer and the uncovering of the baroque pearl. She hadn't even yet seen it up close or held it. R. Sonnier looked annoyed.

"Listen, young lady, I had a baroque pearl last fall, and I sold it to a very nice lady who comes in here often to buy things. I never save anything except for my good customers. This lady paid me by check right away. I don't run any lay-away plan here, and that baroque pearl was priced at almost five hundred dollars."

"You sold it? But it was supposed to be *mine!* I worked after school all fall and winter long, and I earned the money for it!" Sister Opal pulled out her wad of money. R. Sonnier looked astounded.

"Little lady, how was I to know you were serious? We get people in here every day saying they like something and they'll be back the next day or next week. They never show up, never! So when somebody comes in and says I'll take that ring or that vase, here, here's the money, why I *sell* it to them. I'd go out of business if

I believed everything people tell me. But since you've worked all that time, maybe you'd like to see some nice earrings I've got, jade and . . ."

"No. I was starting a famous marble collection. I don't want anything else." Sister Opal tucked her worthless money away in her old purse and went out with her back straight and stiff.

She walked around downtown all day long, looking into bookstores, department stores, stationery shops, jewelry stores, boutiques, but nothing seemed attractive to her. She thought it was strange that all the times she hadn't had any money hundreds and hundreds of things in the store windows had looked so great and she had really wanted them. Now that she had a lot of money nothing interested her. She stared at the most exotic clothes without even a twinge of desire. Her beautiful baroque pearl belonged to somebody else; she didn't want any other thing. She put off going home as long as possible, but when the lights began to come on she knew it was time to go back.

The family was at supper. Every head turned to Sister Opal as she came in and slumped into her chair.

"Well!" boomed Roy, who didn't work Saturday nights. "Let's see that solid gold marble you got!" Sister Opal's mother, who saw something was wrong, said, "Well, what's the trouble, Sister? Was the store closed?" Sister Opal, who had not cried, or even felt much of anything except emptiness and loss, burst into a howl she didn't even know was inside her.

"He sold it to somebody else a long time ago-o-oo-o!" Between sobs, hiccups and tears dripping into her plate, Sister Opal told the family about R. Sonnier and how he had sold the pearl. Andrew was indignant and declared that if he was ever in the market for a baroque pearl, he would rather die in the gutter than buy it from R. Sonnier. But Sister Opal's father said judiciously, "Well, Sister, he didn't do it out of spite and meanness. He was just being businesslike. If you were a store man and somebody breezed in and said, 'Here, you hold on to that stuffed elephant for me, I'll be back someday and pay for it,' and a week later somebody else came in and said, 'Here, here's a thousand dollars for that stuffed elephant,' you *know* you are going to sell that elephant right there and then. Sister Opal, you should have checked back with that R. Sonnier every week or so, so that he'd know you were really serious about buying it. I know you're disappointed. I'm disappointed myself. I was looking forward to seeing that baroque pearl and knowing somebody in our family owned it." This brought a fresh howl from Sister Opal which her father silenced by continuing.

"As I see it, Sister, you can either curl up and die because you didn't get your fancy marble, or you can hurry up and quit crying and think about the future. Probably you should take that pearl money and put it with the college money so that you can study up on baroque pearls when you get to college. So you got to adopt a long range plan now and think about education and a career . . ."

Sister Opal heard her father talking on in a kindly way about his favorite subject, education and getting knowledge and getting ahead and having a career. She knew that most of what he was saying was sensible, but she had heard it all so many times she didn't want to hear it again. Her father didn't *know* how it felt to be a girl and to want a beautiful thing very badly. Sister Opal excused herself from the table and went up to her room. She flung herself on the bed

sideways and dangled her head off the edge, looking at the pale rectangle of the window. The marble jar was dark in the twilight and it glittered along one side from the reflected light of the street lamp. Sister Opal reached out for the marble jar, tipped the contents onto the bed with a rich, sensuous, rolling sound. Her thin hand slid through the marble pile in the darkening room until she touched the familiar lopsided marble. Warming it in the hollow of her hand, she could just make out its ephemeral glow, its waxy luster against the darkness of her hand and the darkness of the oncoming night. She rolled it slightly in her palm and said softly to the warmed, heavy marble, "Oh, what a beautiful baroque pearl."

✦ ✦ ✦ ✦

DISCUSSION

1. (a) Briefly give your impression of Sister Opal's character as presented through her thoughts and actions at the beginning of the story. (b) Does Sister Opal seem changed at the end of the story? Why or why not?
2. What reasons can you give for Sister Opal's actions in the last few paragraphs of the story?
3. (a) In what ways does Sister Opal's discovery of the baroque pearl change her life? the lives of those in her family? (b) Why does she want the pearl so badly? What reasons can you think of? (c) Does she learn anything from losing the pearl? Explain.
4. What does the baroque pearl symbolize to Sister Opal and her family? In your own interpretation of the story did it come to mean anything additional or different than what it means to these characters?
5. (a) What kind of man is R. Sonnier? In your response take into account both his attitude and Sister Opal's toward the baroque pearl. (b) In your opinion, is Sonnier's treatment of Sister Opal acceptable or unacceptable? (c)

Do you agree with Sister Opal's father's explanation of why Sonnier sold the pearl to someone else? Why or why not?
6. One reader of this story said, "Sister Opal is lucky to have a nearly perfect family who support and try to understand her; next to this her loss of the pearl is secondary." Do you agree? Explain.

WORD STUDY

Note the italicized word in each sentence below. In the list above the sentences, find the synonym of each italicized word. On a sheet of paper, after the appropriate numbers, write the correct synonym. If necessary, use the Glossary for help.

amble	slapdash
captivated	skein
distracted	jolly
sheen	sardonic
understand	furtive
reconcile	sensible

1. Sister Opal was usually weary by suppertime, but her brothers were always *jovial*.
2. She was so *enthralled* by the idea of becoming an art collector, Sister Opal spent the entire afternoon window shopping at art and antique stores.
3. Roy could not quite *fathom* the joke about statues and harpsichords which seemed somehow to revolve around him.
4. Although she knew that the explanation her father had given was a *judicious* one, Sister Opal was not consoled.
5. The lopsided marble had a *luster* not unlike that of the baroque pearl.

THE AUTHOR

This story by E. A. Proulx might well have taken place in any large city where young men work all night at industrial plants, where drugstores stay open until 10:30, and where whole sections of town are devoted to antique stores and silver shops. Yet, today, the author of this story (whose real name is Ann Lang) lives in the small town of St. Albans, Vermont, away from the busy pace and pressures of the city.

See
TONE
*Handbook
of Literary
Terms
page 537*

*The bird-watchers were a dull, but ladylike
group—until a pair of outsiders named McKenney
joined them. Ruth McKenney
tells of a real episode in her life.
What attitude does she
express toward it?*

a Loud Sneer for Our Feathered Friends

Ruth McKenney

FROM CHILDHOOD, my sister and I have had a well-grounded dislike for our friends the birds. We came to hate them when she was ten and I was eleven. We had been exiled by what we considered an unfeeling family to one of those loathsome girls' camps where Indian lore is rife and the management puts up neatly lettered signs reminding the clients to be Good Sports. From the moment Eileen and I arrived at dismal old Camp Hi-Wah, we were Bad Sports, and we liked it.

We refused to get out of bed when the bugle blew in the morning, we fought against scrubbing our teeth in public to music, we sneered when the flag was ceremoniously lowered at sunset, we avoided doing a good deed a day, we complained loudly about the food, which was terrible, and we bought some chalk once and wrote all over the Recreation Cabin, "We hate Camp Hi-Wah." It made a wonderful scandal, although unfortunately we were immediately accused of the crime. All the other little campers *loved* dear old Camp Hi-Wah, which shows you what kind of people they were.

The first two weeks Eileen and I were at Camp Hi-Wah, we sat in our cabin grinding our teeth at our counselor and writing letters to distant relatives. These letters were, if I say so myself, real masterpieces of double dealing and heartless chicanery. In our childish and, we hoped, appealing scrawl, we explained to Great-Aunt Mary Farrel and Second Cousin Joe Murphy that we were having such fun at dear Camp Hi-Wah making Indian pocketbooks.

"We would simply L-O-V-E to make you a pocketbook, dear Aunt Mary," we wrote, "only the leather costs $1 for a small pocketbook or $1.67 for a large size pocketbook, which is much nicer because you can carry more things in it, and the rawhide you sew it up with, just exactly the way the Indians did, costs 40 cents more. We burn pictures on the leather but that doesn't cost anything. If we O-N-L-Y had $1 or $1.67 and 40 cents for the rawhide, we could make you the S-W-E-L-L-E-S-T pocketbook."

As soon as we had enough orders for Indian pocketbooks with pictures

burnt on them, we planned to abscond with the funds sent by our trusting relatives and run away to New York City, where, as we used to explain dramatically to our cabin-mates, we intended to live a life of sin. After a few days, our exciting plans for our immediate future were bruited all over the camp, and admirers came from as far away as Cabin Minnehaha, which was way down at the end of Hiawatha Alley, just to hear us tell about New York and sin.

Fame had its price, however. One of the sweet little girls who lived in our cabin turned out to be such a Good Citizen ("Camp Hi-Wah Girls Learn to Be Good Citizens") that she told our dreadful secret to our counselor. Our mail was impounded for weeks, and worst of all, we actually had to make several Indian pocketbooks with pictures burnt on them. My pictures were all supposed to be snakes, although they were pretty blurred. Eileen specialized in what she believed to be the likeness of a werewolf, but Cousin Joe, who had generously ordered three pocketbooks, wrote a nice letter thanking Eileen for his pretty pocketbooks with the pretty pictures of Abraham Lincoln on them. We were terribly disgusted by the whole thing.

It was in this mood that we turned to birds. The handicraft hour at Camp Hi-Wah, heralded by the ten-thirty A.M. bugle, competed for popularity with the bird walks at the same hour. You could, as Eileen had already somewhat precociously learned how to say, name your own poison. After three weeks of burning pictures on leather, we were ready for anything, even our feathered friends.

So one hot morning in July, the two McKenney sisters, big and bad and fierce for their age, answered the bird-walk bugle call, leaving the Indian-pocketbook teacher to mourn her two most backward pupils. We were dressed, somewhat reluctantly, to be sure, in the required heavy stockings for posion ivy and brambles, and carried, each of us, in our dirty hands a copy of a guide to bird lore called *Bird Life for Children*.

Bird Life for Children was a volume that all the Good Citizens in Camp Hi-Wah pretended to find engrossing. Eileen and I thought it was stupefyingly dull. Our favorite literary character at the time was Dumas' Marguerite de Valois,[1] who took her decapitated lover's head home in a big handkerchief for old times' sake. Eileen, in those days, was always going to name her first girl child Marguerite de Valois.

Bird Life for Children was full of horrid pictures in full color of robins and pigeons and redbirds. Under each picture was a loathsomely whimsical paragraph describing how the bird in question spent his spare time, what he ate, and why children should love him. Eileen and I hated the book so, we were quite prepared to despise birds when we started off that morning on our first bird walk, but we had no idea of what we were going to suffer, that whole awful summer, because of our feathered friends. In the first place, since we had started off making leather pocketbooks, we were three weeks behind the rest of the Hi-Wah bird-lovers. They had been tramping through blackberry bushes for days and days and had already got the hang of the more ordinary bird life around camp, whereas the only bird I could identify at the time was the vulture. Cousin Joe took me to a zoo once, and there was a fine vulture

---

1. **Dumas' Marguerite de Valois.** Alexander Dumas, a French writer, wrote *Marguerite de Valois* in 1845. The real Marguerite de Valois was the wife of Henry IV, a sixteenth-century French king. However, she did not really perform the acts Dumas attributed to her in his book.

Blechman

there, a big, fat one. They fed him six live rats every day in lieu of human flesh. I kept a sharp eye out for a vulture all summer, but one never turned up at Camp Hi-Wah. Nothing interesting ever happened around that place.

On that first bird walk, Eileen and I trotted anxiously along behind the little band of serious-minded bird-lovers, trying desperately to see, or at least hear, even one bird, even one robin. But alas, while other bird-walkers saw, or pretended to see — for Eileen and I never believed them for a moment — all kinds of hummingbirds and hawks and owls and whatnot, we never saw or heard a single, solitary feathered friend, not one.

By the time we staggered into camp for lunch, with stubbed toes, scratched faces, and tangled hair, Eileen and I were soured for life on birds. Our bird logs, which we carried strapped to our belts along with the *Guide*, were still chaste and bare, while all the other little bird-lovers had fulsome entries, such as "Saw and heard redbird at 10:37 A.M. Molting."

Still, for the next three days we stayed honest and suffered. For three terrible mornings we endured being dolts among bird-walkers, the laughingstock of Camp Hi-Wah. After six incredibly tiresome hours, our bird logs were still blank. Then we cracked under the strain. The fourth morning we got up feeling grim but determined. We sharpened our pencils before we started off on the now-familiar trail through the second-growth forest.

When we got well into the woods and Mary Mahoney, the premier bird-walker of Camp Hi-Wah, had already spotted and logged her first redbird of the morning, Eileen suddenly stopped dead in her tracks.

"Hark!" she cried. She had read that somewhere in a book. "Quiet!" I echoed instantly.

The bird-walkers drew to a halt respectfully and stood in silence. They stood and stood. It was not good form even to whisper while fellow bird-walkers were logging a victim, but after quite a long time the Leader, whose feet were flat and often hurt her, whispered impatiently, "Haven't you got him logged yet?"

"You drove him away," Eileen replied sternly. "It was a yellow-billed cuckoo."

"A yellow-billed cuckoo?" cried the Leader incredulously.

"Well," Eileen said modestly, "at least *I* think it was." Then, with many a pretty hesitation and thoughtful pause, she recited the leading features of the yellow-billed cuckoo, as recorded in *Bird Life for Children*.

The Leader was terribly impressed. Later on that morning I logged a kingfisher, a red-headed woodpecker, and a yellow-bellied sapsucker, which was all I could remember at the moment. Each time, I kept the bird-walkers standing around for an interminable period, gaping into blank space and listening desperately to the rustle of the wind in the trees and the creak of their shoes as they went from one foot to another.

In a few days Eileen and I were the apple of our Leader's eye, the modest heroes of the Camp Hi-Wah bird walks. Naturally, there were base children around camp, former leading bird-walkers, who spread foul rumors up and down Hiawatha Alley that Eileen and I were frauds. We soon stopped this ugly talk, however. Eileen was the pitcher, and a very good one, too, of the Red Bird ball team and I was the first base. When Elouise Pritchard, the worst

gossip in Cabin Sitting Bull, came up to bat, she got a pitched ball right in the stomach. Of course it was only a soft ball, but Eileen could throw it pretty hard. To vary this routine, I tagged Mary Mahoney, former head bird-walker, out at first base, and Mary had a bruise on her thigh for weeks. The rumors stopped abruptly.

We had begun to get pretty bored with logging rare birds when the game took on a new angle. Mary Mahoney and several other bird-walkers began to see the same birds we did on our morning jaunts into the forest. This made us pretty mad, but there wasn't much we could do about it. Next, Mary Mahoney began to see birds we weren't logging. The third week after we joined the Camp Hi-Wah Bird Study Circle, everybody except the poor, dumb Leader and a few backward but honest bird-lovers was logging the rarest birds seen around Camp Hi-Wah in twenty years. Bird walks developed into a race to see who could shout "Hark!" first and keep the rest of the little party in fidgety silence for the next five minutes.

The poor bird-walk Leader was in agony. Her reputation as a bird-lover was in shreds. Her talented pupils were seeing rare birds right and left, while the best she could log for herself would be a few crummy old redbirds and a robin or so. At last our Leader's morale collapsed. It was the day when nearly everybody in the study circle swore that she saw and heard a bona-fide nightingale.

"Where?" cried our Leader desperately, after the fourth nightingale had been triumphantly logged in the short space of five minutes. Heartless fingers pointed to a vague bush. The Leader strained her honest eyes. No notion of our duplicity crossed her innocent, unworldly mind.

"I can't see any nightingale," our Leader cried, and burst into tears. Then, full of shame, she sped back to camp, leaving the Camp Hi-Wah bird-lovers to their nightingales and guilty thoughts.

Eileen and I ate a hearty lunch that noon because we thought we would need it. Then we strolled down Hiawatha Alley and hunted up Mary Mahoney.

"We will put the Iron Cross on you if you tell," Eileen started off, as soon as we found Mary.

"What's the Iron Cross?" Mary squeaked, startled out of her usual haughty poise.

"Never mind," I growled. "You'll find out if you tell."

We walked past Cabin Sitting Bull, past the flagpole, into the tall grass beyond the ball field.

"She'll tell," Eileen said finally.

"What'll we do?" I replied mournfully. "They'll try us at campfire tonight."

They did, too. It was terrible. We denied everything, but the Head of Camp, a mean old lady who wore middy blouses and pleated serge bloomers, sentenced us to no desserts and eight-o'clock bedtime for two weeks. We thought over what to do to Mary Mahoney for four whole days. Nothing seemed sufficiently frightful, but in the end we put the wart curse on her. The wart curse was simple but horrible. We dropped around to Cabin Sitting Bull one evening and in the presence of Mary and her allies we drew ourselves up to our full height and said solemnly in unison, "We put the wart curse on you, Mary Mahoney." Then we stalked away.

We didn't believe for a moment in the wart curse, but we hoped Mary would. At first she was openly con-

temptuous, but to our delight, on the fourth evening she developed a horrible sty on her eye. We told everybody a sty was a kind of a wart and that we had Mary in our power. The next day Mary broke down and came around to our cabin and apologized in choked accents. She gave Eileen her best hair ribbon and me a little barrel that had a picture of Niagara Falls inside it, if you looked hard enough. We were satisfied.

✦　✦　✦　✦

DISCUSSION

1. (a) Which sentence in the opening paragraph gives you the best clue to how the McKenney sisters behaved during their stay at camp? (b) Do you think the author wants to be taken seriously? Find words and phrases in the first three paragraphs to support your answer.
2. (a) How do the girls plan to escape from Camp Hi-Wah? (b) Where do they plan to go? (c) What happens to spoil their scheme?
3. (a) Why do the girls finally turn to bird-watching? (b) Why were they prepared to despise the birds?
4. (a) How do Ruth and Eileen behave during their first three days as bird-watchers? (b) What happens on the fourth day? (c) Describe the results of their plot.
5. What one victory did the sisters actually achieve during their stay at camp?
6. (a) What impression does Ruth McKenney give you of Camp Hi-Wah? (b) What is the overall tone of this selection? (c) By what various devices does she convey the tone?
7. What do you suppose Camp Hi-Wah thought of the McKenney girls?

WORD STUDY

For their own reasons, the McKenney girls pretended to be interested in *ornithology*, or the study of birds. A person who really knows a great deal about birds and their habits is called an *ornithologist*.

Words used to identify scientists often end with *-logist*. This suffix was created by combining *-logy* which means "a science" and *-ist,* or "one who is skilled in, or occupied with."

Combine each word part in the list below with the ending *-logist*. Then give the meaning of the word formed by joining the two parts.

1. *bio-* (from the Greek *bios,* or "life").
2. *archaeo-* (from the Greek *archaios,* or "ancient").
3. *geo-* (from the Greek *geo-,* or "earth").
4. *hydro-* (from the Greek *hydro-,* or "water").
5. *psycho-* (from the Greek *psyche,* or "soul, mind").

THE AUTHOR

Ruth McKenney claimed that it took her twenty years to learn how to spell the name of her home town—Mishawaka, Indiana. She and her sister Eileen grew up in Cleveland, Ohio, where they were once barred from Sunday school. Miss McKenney began her career in literature as a printer (she considered herself a pretty good one); later, she moved on to become a feature writer for a New York paper. In 1936 she began writing books.

According to Miss McKenney, she had very little sense of humor. But *My Sister Eileen*, from which "A Loud Sneer" is taken, is considered one of the funniest books written in this century. The book has been made into a Broadway play, a motion picture, and a musical comedy called *Wonderful Town*. In each form, it has delighted thousands.

The Boy Who Laughed at Santa Claus

OGDEN NASH

In Baltimore there lived a boy.
He wasn't anybody's joy.
Although his name was Jabez Dawes,
His character was full of flaws.
In school he never led his classes;   5
He hid old ladies' reading glasses;
His mouth was open when he chewed,
And elbows to the table glued.

He stole the milk of hungry kittens,
And walked through doors marked NO ADMITTANCE.   10
He said he acted thus because
There wasn't any Santa Claus.
Another trick that tickled Jabez
Was crying "Boo!" at little babies.
He brushed his teeth, they said in town,   15
Sideways instead of up and down.

Yet people pardoned every sin,
And viewed his antics with a grin,
Till they were told by Jabez Dawes,
"There isn't any Santa Claus!"   20
Deploring how he did behave,
His parents swiftly sought their grave.
They hurried through the portals pearly,
And Jabez left the funeral early.

Like whooping cough, from child to child,   25
He sped to spread the rumor wild:
"Sure as my name is Jabez Dawes
There isn't any Santa Claus!"
Slunk like a weasel or a marten
Through nursery and kindergarten,   30
Whispering low to every tot,
"There isn't any, no there's not!"

The children wept all Christmas Eve
And Jabez chortled up his sleeve.
No infant dared hang up his stocking   35
For fear of Jabez' ribald mocking.
He sprawled on his untidy bed,
Fresh malice dancing in his head,
When presently with scalp a-tingling,
Jabez heard a distant jingling.   40
He heard the crunch of sleigh and hoof
Crisply alighting on the roof.

What good to rise and bar the door?
A shower of soot was on the floor.
What was beheld by Jabez Dawes?   45
The fireplace full of Santa Claus!
Then Jabez fell upon his knees
With cries of "Don't!" and "Pretty please!"
He howled, "I don't know where you read it,
But anyhow, I never said it!"   50

"Jabez," replied the angry saint,
"It isn't I, it's you that ain't.
Although there is a Santa Claus,
There isn't any Jabez Dawes!"
Said Jabez then with impudent vim,   55
"Oh, yes there is; and I am him!
Your magic don't scare *me*, it doesn't" —
And suddenly he found he wasn't!

From grimy feet to grimy locks,
Jabez became a Jack-in-the-box,   60
An ugly toy with springs unsprung,
Forever sticking out his tongue.
The neighbors heard his mournful squeal;
They searched for him, but not with zeal.
No trace was found of Jabez Dawes,   65
Which led to thunderous applause,
And people drank a loving cup
And went and hung their stockings up.

All you who sneer at Santa Claus,
Beware the fate of Jabez Dawes,   70
That saucy boy who mocked the saint.
Donder and Blitzen licked off his paint.

1. (a) What are some of the offenses Jabez Dawes commits? (b) What reason does he give for his behavior? (c) How do people react to his pranks? (d) What is the one thing he does that people cannot accept?

2. (a) How does Jabez upset the community on Christmas Eve? (b) In what way does Santa get his revenge? (c) Do you consider the revenge appropriate? Why or why not?

3. (a) What is the "moral" of this poem? (b) What is the poet's attitude toward Jabez? (c) Do you think the poet wants to be taken seriously? Why or why not? (d) What is the overall tone of the poem? (e) What specific words and images help you understand the tone?

THE AUTHOR

Ogden Nash (1902–1971) poked fun at our way of life, our social customs, and at his own pet peeves. (Most of Nash's pet peeves begin with the letter p and include professors, politicans, parsley, and parties next door.) He used rhymes that were never meant to be and may never be again. He misspelled and mispronounced words to make them rhyme with others. He gleefully distorted meanings and invented new ones.

Nash was born in Rye, New York, but his family was originally from the South. By his own count he had ten thousand cousins in North Carolina alone. His great-great-grandfather was once governor of that state, and his great-great uncle had Nashville, Tennessee, named in his honor.

Nash attended Harvard for one year, spent one year as an instructor in a boys' school, and worked for two years as a bond salesman. After several jobs in publishing houses, Mr. Nash quit working for others and spent his time writing.

The Skunk

ROBERT P. TRISTRAM COFFIN

When the sun has slipped away
And the dew is on the day,
Then the creature comes to call
Men malign the most of all.

The little skunk is very neat   5
With his sensitive plush feet
And a dainty, slim head set
With diamonds on bands of jet.

He walks upon his evening's duty
Of declaring how that beauty   10
With her patterns is not done
At the setting of the sun.

He undulates across the lawn,
He asks nobody to fawn
On his graces. All that he   15
Asks is that men let him be.

He knows that he is very fine
In every clean and rippling line,
He is a conscious black and white
Little symphony of night.

DISCUSSION

1. (a) What does "diamonds on bands of jet" refer to? **(b)** What does the use of the word *undulates* in the fourth stanza suggest about the skunk's movements? **(c)** Would the word *walks* have been as effective? Why or why not? **(d)** Which other words and images in the poem help you understand the poet's feelings toward the skunk? **(e)** Describe the tone of this poem.

2. (a) According to the speaker, what opinion does the skunk have of himself? **(b)** What is the speaker's attitude toward the skunk's vanity?

THE AUTHOR

Robert P. Tristram Coffin was born in 1892 to a New England whaling family, and grew up on a farm near the ocean. Until his death in 1955, he spent his summers near the Maine coast, which he also used as the setting for some of his novels.

Coffin studied at Oxford, then taught at Wells College and later at Bowdoin College where he had once been a student himself. Often he used his talents as an artist to draw illustrations for his own books.

The street of a city can be a battlefield.
In this true selection,
Richard Wright tells how his mother taught him
one of the necessities demanded for survival
on such a street. In what tone does he
describe that incident?

HUNGER

Richard Wright

HUNGER stole upon me so slowly that at first I was not aware of what hunger really meant. Hunger had always been more or less at my elbow when I played, but now I began to wake up at night to find hunger standing at my bedside, staring at me gauntly. The hunger I had known before this had been no grim, hostile stranger; it had been a normal hunger that had made me beg constantly for bread, and when I ate a crust or two I was satisfied. But this new hunger baffled me, scared me, made me angry and insistent. Whenever I begged for food now my mother would pour me a cup of tea which would still the clamor in my stomach for a moment or two; but a little later I would feel hunger nudging my ribs, twisting my empty guts until they ached. I would grow dizzy and my vision would dim. I became less active in my play, and for the first time in my life I had to pause and think of what was happening to me.

"Mama, I'm hungry," I complained one afternoon.

"Jump up and catch a kungry," she said, trying to make me laugh and forget.

"What's a *kungry*?"

"It's what little boys eat when they get hungry," she said.

"What does it taste like?"

"I don't know."

"Then why do you tell me to catch one?"

"Because you said that you were hungry," she said, smiling.

I sensed that she was teasing me and it made me angry.

"But I'm hungry. I want to eat."

"You'll have to wait."

"But I want to eat now."

"But there's nothing to eat," she told me.

"Why?"

"Just because there's none," she explained.

"But I want to eat," I said, beginning to cry.

"You'll just have to wait," she said again.

"But why?"

"For God to send some food."

"When is He going to send it?"

"I don't know."

"But I'm hungry!"

She was ironing and she paused and looked at me with tears in her eyes.

"Where's your father?" she asked me.

I stared in bewilderment. Yes, it

"Hunger," an excerpt from pp. 13–16 of BLACK BOY by Richard Wright. Copyright 1945 by Richard Wright. Reprinted by permission of Harper & Row, Publishers.

was true that my father had not come home to sleep for many days now and I could make as much noise as I wanted. Though I had not known why he was absent, I had been glad that he was not there to shout his restrictions at me. But it had never occurred to me that his absence would mean that there would be no food.

"I don't know," I said.

"Who brings food into the house?" my mother asked me.

"Papa," I said. "He always brought food."

"Well, your father isn't here now," she said.

"Where is he?"

"I don't know," she said.

"But I'm hungry," I whimpered, stomping my feet.

"You'll have to wait until I get a job and buy food," she said.

As the days slid past the image of my father became associated with my pangs of hunger, and whenever I felt hunger I thought of him with a deep biological bitterness.

My mother finally went to work as a cook and left me and my brother alone in the flat each day with a loaf of bread and a pot of tea. When she returned at evening she would be tired and dispirited and would cry a lot. Sometimes, when she was in despair, she would call us to her and talk to us for hours, telling us that we now had no father, that our lives would be different from those of other children, that we must learn as soon as possible to take care of ourselves, to dress ourselves, to prepare our own food; that we must take upon ourselves the responsibility of the flat while she worked. Half frightened, we would promise solemnly. We did not understand what had happened between our father and our mother and the most that these long talks did to us was to make us feel a vague dread.

Whenever we asked why father had left, she would tell us that we were too young to know.

One evening my mother told me that thereafter I would have to do the shopping for food. She took me to the corner store to show me the way. I was proud; I felt like a grownup. The next afternoon I looped the basket over my arm and went down the pavement toward the store. When I reached the corner, a gang of boys grabbed me, knocked me down, snatched the basket, took the money, and sent me running home in panic. That evening I told my mother what had happened, but she made no comment; she sat down at once, wrote another note, gave me more money, and sent me out to the grocery again. I crept down the steps and saw the same gang of boys playing down the street. I ran back into the house.

"What's the matter?" my mother asked.

"It's those same boys," I said. "They'll beat me."

"You've got to get over that," she said. "Now, go on."

"I'm scared," I said.

"Go on and don't pay any attention to them," she said.

I went out of the door and walked briskly down the sidewalk, praying that the gang would not molest me. But when I came abreast of them someone shouted, "There he is!"

They came toward me and I broke into a wild run toward home. They overtook me and flung me to the pavement. I yelled, pleaded, kicked, but they wrenched the money out of my hand. They yanked me to my feet, gave me a few slaps, and sent me home sobbing. My mother met me at the door.

"They b-beat m-me," I gasped. "They t-t-took the m-money."

I started up the steps, seeking the shelter of the house.

"Don't you come in here," my mother warned me.

I froze in my tracks and stared at her.

"But they're coming after me," I said.

"You just stay right where you are," she said in a deadly tone. "I'm going to teach you this night to stand up and fight for yourself."

She went into the house and I waited, terrified, wondering what she was about. Presently she returned with more money and another note; she also had a long heavy stick.

"Take this money, this note, and this stick," she said. "Go to the store and buy those groceries. If those boys bother you, then fight."

I was baffled. My mother was telling me to fight, a thing that she had never done before.

"But I'm scared," I said.

"Don't you come into this house until you've gotten those groceries," she said.

"They'll beat me; they'll beat me," I said.

"Then stay in the streets; don't come back here!"

I ran up the steps and tried to force my way past her into the house. A stinging slap came on my jaw. I stood on the sidewalk, crying.

"Please, let me wait until tomorrow," I begged.

"No," she said. "Go now! If you come back into this house without those groceries, I'll whip you!"

She slammed the door and I heard the key turn in the lock. I shook with fright. I was alone upon the dark, hostile streets and gangs were after me. I had the choice of being beaten at home or away from home. I clutched the stick, crying, trying to reason. If I were beaten at home,

there was absolutely nothing that I could do about it; but if I were beaten in the streets, I had a chance to fight and defend myself. I walked slowly down the sidewalk, coming closer to the gang of boys, holding the stick tightly. I was so full of fear that I could scarcely breathe. I was almost upon them now.

"There he is again!" the cry went up.

They surrounded me quickly and began to grab for my hand.

"I'll kill you!" I threatened.

They closed in. In blind fear I let the stick fly, feeling it crack against a boy's skull. I swung again, lamming another skull, then another. Realizing that they would retaliate if I let up for but a second, I fought to lay them low, to knock them cold, to kill them so that they could not strike back at me. I flayed with tears in my eyes, teeth clenched, stark fear making me throw every ounce of my strength behind each blow. I hit again and again, dropping the money and the grocery list. The boys scattered, yelling, nursing their heads, staring at me in utter disbelief. They had never seen such frenzy. I stood panting, egging them on, taunting them to come on and fight. When they refused, I ran after them and they tore out for their homes, screaming. The parents of the boys rushed into the streets and threatened me, and for the first time in my life I shouted at grownups, telling them that I would give them the same if they bothered me. I finally found my grocery list and the money and went to the store. On my way back I kept my stick poised for instant use, but there was not a single boy in sight. That night I won the right to the streets of Memphis.

WIDE WORLD PHOTOS

THE AUTHOR

1. Describe the conditions under which the Wright family lived.

2. (**a**) In the first paragraph, to what does Wright compare his hunger? (**b**) What words and phrases help make that hunger seem real?

3. (**a**) Why didn't the Wrights have any food? (**b**) What feeling did hunger create in Wright toward his father?

4. (**a**) What sort of person was Richard's mother? (**b**) What were her motives for sending Richard out on the street with a stick? (**c**) How did she force him to be courageous? (**d**) What lesson did she teach him? (**e**) What do you think of her methods?

5. (**a**) As a child how did Wright feel about his mother's methods? (**b**) As an adult, did he change his attitude? How can you tell?

6. (**a**) Do you think Wright wrote this selection to arouse your pity? (**b**) If not, what might have been his reason for writing it? (**c**) What emotions does he reveal? (**d**) Describe the tone of "Hunger."

To Richard Wright, childhood meant hunger and unhappiness and endless moving. When Wright was five, his father deserted the family; and for the next five years, Mrs. Wright tried desperately to keep Richard and his brother with her. But the only work she could get was as a domestic, and domestics worked for starvation wages. For a time, she had to put her sons in an orphan asylum; when they refused to stay there, she borrowed from relatives to feed and shelter them. Finally, Mrs. Wright, who had been ill for years, grew completely paralyzed, and the two boys became wholly dependent on their relatives.

But Richard was rude and hard to manage. He could not get along with the aunts and uncles and cousins who wanted to make him over into a good boy. So, unlike his brother who lived with one family, Richard was shuffled from relative to relative, from town to town.

At fifteen, Richard discovered the joys of reading and he knew he wanted to be a writer. He wrote short stories which he showed to no one for fear of being ridiculed. He worked at whatever jobs were available until he had enough money to move to Chicago. It was there that he published his first book and wrote his most important works. In 1946, he went to Paris, where he continued to write. There he died in 1960. Today, Richard Wright is remembered for the realism and sensitivity of all his works.

On his first day at the new school in this strange country, Juan wore short pants and a jacket with an embroidered collar. When he saw the other boys in blue jeans and plaid shirts, he was afraid. He was different.

But at first, the other boys were kind to him. During the class period, they smiled at him from behind their books and at recess they invited him to join their game. But he did not know how to play it. They bombarded him with questions; he could not understand their rapid-fire English, their flat accents. In his frustration, he cried. Giggling nervously, the other boys stepped away.

During the lunch break, he stood at the edge of the playground and watched a group of boys play a game. Not understanding the rules, he tried to ask for explanations from a boy standing near him who was not playing either. But the boy shouted, "Foreigner! Dirty mama's boy foreigner!" Then another took up the name and soon it became a chant, but Juan did not retaliate. Instead, he moved on to another group on the other side of the playground. He knew that group was made up of foreigners like himself and he wished to seek shelter in it. They were happy to have him. He knew the game they played and some-one even spoke to him in his native tongue. Then a shout came across the playground: "Dirty foreigners playing with dirty mama's boy foreigner!" His new-found friends looked at him with hate; one pushed him away, saying, "Get away from us, mama's boy."

By the afternoon recess, everyone was laughing at him. He would not even have gone out on the playground if the teacher had not insisted that the fresh air was good for him.

1. (a) How does Juan feel upon entering the school and seeing the other boys? (b) Why does he feel this way?

2. (a) At first, how do the other boys treat Juan? (b) Why does their attitude toward him change?

3. (a) What sort of person is the boy who first calls Juan a name? Explain. (b) Why does he call Juan "mama's boy"?

4. (a) For what reason do the members of the second group of boys grow angry with Juan? (b) Note that the boy who pushes Juan calls him "mama's boy." Why doesn't he add *foreigner?*

5. (a) Is Juan at all responsible for the way in which he is treated? (b) Could he gain anything by fighting back? Why or why not?

6. Part of the feeling against Juan is caused by prejudice. (a) What does the word *prejudice* mean? (b) What are some of the common causes of prejudice? Base your answer on what you've learned in studying "The Outsider." (c) Why are Juan's class-mates prejudiced against him?

7. Juan becomes a *scapegoat*—a person who is made to bear the blame for the short-comings of others. (a) From what you've learned in this unit, give reasons why groups often need a common scapegoat. (b) How does a group usually behave toward a com-mon scapegoat? (c) Is there any means by which the scapegoat can win the approval of the group?

8. Compare each of the following:
   (a) Juan and the new kid
   (b) Juan's tormenters and Marty
   (c) Juan and Sister Opal
   (d) Juan and Joey's sister
   (e) Juan and Richard Wright

SUGGESTED READING

BALL, ZACHERY, *Swamp Chief.* (Holiday) A young Seminole Indian must choose between the primitive culture of his people and the cosmopolitan life of Miami.

BEIM, LORRAINE, *Carol's Side of the Street.* (Harcourt) A twelve-year-old girl encounters prejudice in a new neighborhood.

BENARY-ISBERT, MARGOT, *The Ark.* (Harcourt) In this story of post-war Germany, you'll share the despair of the five Lechows during nine months in refugee camps, and rejoice with them when they finally secure two rooms in which to live.

BRO, MARGUERITE H., *Su-Mei's Golden Year.* (Doubleday) A Chinese girl and her family lead in the modernization of their community.

GATES, DORIS, *Blue Willow.* (Viking) Janey Larkin travels with her father and stepmother who work as itinerant laborers. To Janey, who longs for stability and beauty in her life, the blue willow plate left to her by her mother is a symbol of her hopes.

HUGGINS, ALICE M., and HUGH L. ROBINSON, *Wan Fu: The Thousand Happinesses.* (McKay) One-Leg, a crippled Chinese beggar girl, yearns to be like the school children she sees. How she learns to read, finds a new way of life, and earns a new name make an interesting story.

KRUMGOLD, JOSEPH, *Onion John.* (Crowell) Andy befriends Onion John, a squatter on two acres allowed him in a New Jersey town. As Andy matures, he unwillingly finds himself on the side of adults who are organizing against Onion John.

LEE, MILDRED, *The Rock and the Willow.* (Lothrop) Enie, just going into high school, is a member of a large, poor family. The young girl yearns for a better life and secretly knows she will find it.

McILVAINE, JANE S., *The Sea Sprite.* (Macrae) Callie Pritchard comes home to Sea Haven to find that she no longer "fits in." Only after many blunders on her part does she come to an understanding with her friends.

MEANS, FLORENCE, *Knock On Any Door, Emmy.* (Houghton) Emmy and her itinerant family live in a pick-up truck that carries them from one work area to another. Emmy's wish to lead a normal life is achieved in this sympathetic and exciting story. *Shuttered Windows,* (Harcourt) also by Miss Means, tells the story of a young Northern Negro girl who moves to the South.

NEVILLE, EMILY, *Berries Goodman.* (Harper) A young boy discovers the meaning and power of prejudice when he becomes friendly with a Jewish classmate.

RICE, ALICE HEGAN, *Mrs. Wiggs of the Cabbage Patch.* (Appleton) This simple and amusing novel shows the good in human nature in the midst of poverty.

RICHTER, CONRAD, *Light in the Forest.* (Knopf) A white boy, reared among the Indians, is returned to his white parents. His love for the people who reared him causes many problems.

SHOTWELL, LOUISA R., *Roosevelt Grady.* (**Grosset) Action, love, hope, and humor fill the pages of this fascinating book about a migrant family who fight to "belong."

WIER, ESTER, *The Loner.* (McKay) A nameless boy finds companionship in a lonely old woman. While living with her, he earns the name David, slays his Goliath—a grizzly bear—and comes to understand himself.

**paperback and hardcover

UNIT 4

Fantasy changes ordinary people into

monsters,

pits humans against dragons,

awakens the dead, and foresees the future.

It gives human traits to animals,

causes wars between worlds,

creates thinking machines and invisible men.

Fantasy is a lure, an escape, an enticement

into the world of . . .

YESTERDAY AND TOMORROW

There is a fifth dimension beyond that which is known to man.
It is a dimension as vast as space, and as timeless as infinity.
It is the middle ground between light and shadow—
between science and superstition. And it lies between the pit of man's fears
and the summit of his knowledge.
This is the dimension of imagination.
It is an area which we call the Twilight Zone.

See
FANTASY
*Handbook
of Literary
Terms
page 521*

The Monsters Are Due on Maple Street

ROD SERLING

CHARACTERS

> NARRATOR   *John D*
> FIGURE ONE   *Steve C.*
> FIGURE TWO
> *Residents of Maple Street:*
> DON MARTIN   *Greg*
> STEVE BRAND   *John W*
> MYRA BRAND, *Steve's wife* — *Angela*
> PETE VAN HORN   *Phil D*
> CHARLIE   *Andy B*
> CHARLIE'S WIFE   *Alisa*
> TOMMY   *John*
> SALLY, *Tommy's mother*   *Becky*
> LES GOODMAN   *Andy*
> ETHEL GOODMAN, *Les' wife*   *Phaedra*
> MAN ONE
> WOMAN ONE
> WOMAN TWO

Act One

SCENE 1

[*Fade in on shot of the sky. The various nebulae and planet bodies stand out in sharp, sparkling relief. The camera begins a slow pan across the Heavens until it passes the horizon and is flush on the opening shot: residential street, day, medium close shot of sign which reads, "Maple Street." Pan down until we are shooting down at an angle toward the street below. It's a tree-lined, quiet, residential American street, very typical of the small town. The houses have front porches on which people sit and swing on gliders, conversing across from house to house. STEVE BRAND polishes his car parked in front of his house. His neighbor, DON MARTIN, leans against the fender watching him. A Good Humor man[1] rides a bicycle and is just in the process of stopping to sell some ice cream to a couple of kids. Two women gossip on the front lawn. Another man waters his lawn.*

Camera takes a slow dolly[2] down the street to pick up these various activities and we hear the NARRATOR'S voice.]

NARRATOR. Maple Street, U.S.A., late summer. A tree-lined little world of front porch gliders, hop scotch, the laughter of children, and the bell of an ice cream vendor.

[*There is a pause and the camera moves over to a shot of the Good Humor man and two small boys who are standing alongside just buying ice cream.*]

NARRATOR. At the sound of the roar and the flash of the light, it will be precisely six-forty-three P. M. on Maple Street.

[*At this moment one of the boys, TOMMY, looks up to listen to a sound of a tremendous screeching roar from overhead. A flash of light plays on both their faces and then it moves down the street past lawns and porches and rooftops and then disappears.*

A long angle shot[3] looking down the street as various people leave their porches and stop what they're doing to stare up at the sky.

A medium close shot of STEVE BRAND, the man who's been polishing his car; he stands there transfixed, staring upwards. He looks at DON MARTIN, his neighbor from across the street.]

STEVE. What was that? A meteor?

DON (*nods*). That's what it looked like. I didn't hear any crash though, did you?

STEVE (*shakes his head*). Nope. I didn't hear anything except a roar.

MRS. BRAND (*from her porch*). Steve? What was that?

STEVE (*raising his voice and looking toward the porch*). Guess it was a meteor, honey. Came awful close, didn't it?

MRS. BRAND. Too close for my money! Much too close.

[*The camera pans across the various porches to people who stand there watching and talking in low conversing tones.*]

NARRATOR. Maple Street. Six-forty-four P. M., on a late September evening. (*A pause.*) Maple Street in the last calm and reflective moment . . . before the monsters came!

[*A slow pan across the porches again interspersed with a medium close shot of a man screwing a light bulb on a front porch, then getting down off the stool to flick the switch and find that nothing happens.*

---

1. **Good Humor man,** traveling ice cream salesman employed by the Good Humor Corporation.
2. **slow dolly.** The camera takes pictures as it moves down the street mounted on a wheeled platform, or *dolly*.
3. **long angle shot,** picture covering a large area.

A medium shot of a man working on an electric power mower. He plugs in the plug, flicks on the switch of the power mower, off and on, with nothing happening.

A medium close shot through the window of a front porch of a woman pushing her finger back and forth on the dial hook. Her voice is indistinct and distant, but intelligible and repetitive.]

WOMAN ONE. Operator, operator, something's wrong on the phone, operator!

[A medium shot of MRS. BRAND *as she comes out on the porch and calls to* STEVE.]

MRS. BRAND *(calling).* Steve, the power's off. I had the soup on the stove and the stove just stopped working.

WOMAN ONE. Same thing over here. I can't get anybody on the phone either. The phone seems to be dead.

[A long angle shot, looking down on the street, as we hear the voices creep up from down below, small, mildly disturbed voices, highlighting these kinds of phrases.]

VOICE ONE. Electricity's off.

VOICE TWO. Phone won't work.

VOICE THREE. Can't get a thing on the radio.

VOICE FOUR. My power mower won't move, won't work at all.

VOICE FIVE. Radio's gone dead!

[A medium close shot of PETE VAN HORN, *a tall, thin man who is seen standing in front of his house.]*

VAN HORN. I'll cut through the back yard. . . . See if the power's still on on Floral Street. I'll be right back!

[A long shot of VAN HORN *as he walks past the side of his house and disappears into the back yard.*

The camera pans down slowly until we're looking at ten or eleven people standing around the street and overflowing up to the curb and side-

walk. *In the background is Steve Brand's car.]*

STEVE. Doesn't make sense. Why should the power go off all of a sudden *and* the phone line?

DON. Maybe some kind of an electrical storm or something.

CHARLIE. That don't seem likely. Sky's just as blue as anything. Not a cloud. No lightning. No thunder. No nothing. How could it be a storm?

WOMAN ONE. I can't get a thing on the radio. Not even the portable.[4]

[A medium close shot of the group as the people again murmur softly in wonderment and question.]

CHARLIE. Well, why don't you go downtown and check with the police, though they'll probably think we're crazy or something. A little power failure and right away we get all flustered and everything—

STEVE. It isn't just the power failure, Charlie. If it was, we'd still be able to get a broadcast on the portable.

[There's a murmur of reaction to this. STEVE *looks from face to face and then over to his car.]*

STEVE. I'll run downtown. We'll get this all straightened out.

[A track shot[5] follows STEVE *as he walks over to the car, gets in it, turns the key.*

A different angle, looking through the open car door. Beyond it we see the crowd watching him from the other side. STEVE *starts the engine. It turns over sluggishly and then just stops dead. He tries it again, and this time he can't get it to turn over. Then very slowly and reflectively he turns the key back to "off" and then slowly gets out of the car.*

A group shot as they stare at STEVE. *He stands for a moment by the car and then walks toward the group.]*

---

4. **portable,** battery-powered.
5. **track shot,** the camera moves along with the character.

STEVE. I don't understand it. It was working fine before——

DON. Out of gas?

STEVE (shakes his head). I just had it filled up.

WOMAN ONE. What's it mean?

CHARLIE. It's just as if . . . as if everything had stopped. (Then he turns toward STEVE.) We'd better walk downtown.

[Another murmur of assent to this.]

STEVE. The two of us can go, Charlie. (He turns to look back at the car.) It couldn't be the meteor. A meteor couldn't do this.

[He and CHARLIE exchange a look. Then they start to walk away from the group.

A medium close shot of TOMMY, a serious-faced young boy in spectacles who stands a few feet away from the group, halfway between them and the two men who start to walk down the sidewalk.]

TOMMY. Mr. Brand . . . you'd better not! (A medium close shot of the two men. The boy can be seen beyond them.)

STEVE. Why not?

TOMMY. They don't want you to.

[STEVE and CHARLIE exchange a grin and STEVE looks back toward the boy.]

STEVE. Who doesn't want us to?

TOMMY (jerks his head in the general direction of the distant horizon). Them!

STEVE. Them?

CHARLIE. Who are them?

TOMMY (very intently). Whoever was in that thing that came by overhead.

[A close shot of STEVE as he knits his brows for a moment, cocking his head questioningly. His voice is intense.]

STEVE. What?

TOMMY. Whoever was in that thing that came over. I don't think they want us to leave here.

[A moving shot of STEVE as he leaves CHARLIE and walks over to the boy. He kneels down in front of him. He forces his voice to remain gentle. He reaches out and holds the boy.]

STEVE. What do you mean? What are you talking about?

TOMMY. They don't want us to leave. That's why they shut everything off.

STEVE. What makes you say that? Whatever gave you that idea?

WOMAN ONE (from the crowd). Now isn't that the craziest thing you ever heard?

TOMMY (persistently but a little intimidated by the crowd). It's always that way, in every story I ever read about a ship landing from outer space.

WOMAN ONE (to the boy's mother, SALLY, who stands on the fringe of the crowd). From outer space yet! Sally, you better get that boy of yours up to bed. He's been reading too many comic books or seeing too many movies or something!

SALLY. Tommy, come over here and stop that kind of talk.

STEVE. Go ahead, Tommy. We'll be right back. And you'll see. That wasn't any ship or anything like it. That was just a . . . a meteor or something. Likely as not——(He turns to the group now trying to weight his words with an optimism he obviously doesn't feel but is desperately trying to instill in himself as well as the others.) No doubt it did have something to do with all this power failure and the rest of it. Meteors can do some crazy things. Like sun spots.

DON (picking up the cue). Sure. That's the kind of thing—like sun spots. They raise Cain with radio reception all over the world. And this thing being so close—why, there's no telling the sort of stuff it can do. (He wets his lips, smiles nervously.)

Go ahead, Charlie. You and Steve go into town and see if that isn't what's causing it all.

[*A track shot of* STEVE *and* CHARLIE *as they again continue to walk away from the group down the sidewalk.*

A medium close shot of the people as they watch silently.

A close shot of TOMMY *as he stares at them, biting his lips and finally calling out again.*]

TOMMY. Mr. Brand!

[*A long shot of the two men as they stop again. Tommy takes a step toward them.*]

TOMMY. Mr. Brand . . . please don't leave here.

[*A different angle, looking toward the people.* STEVE *and* CHARLIE *can be seen beyond them. They stop once again and turn toward the boy. There's a murmur in the crowd, a murmur of irritation and concern as if the boy were bringing up fears that shouldn't be brought up, words which carry with them a strange kind of validity that comes without logic but nonetheless registers and has meaning and effect. Again the murmur of reaction from the crowd.*

A medium close shot of TOMMY, *who is partly frightened and partly defiant as well.*]

TOMMY. You might not even be able to get to town. It was that way in the story. *Nobody* could leave. Nobody except——

STEVE. Except who?

TOMMY. Except the people they'd sent down ahead of them. They looked just like humans. And it wasn't until the ship landed that——(*The boy suddenly stops again conscious of his parents staring at him and of the sudden hush of the crowd.*)

SALLY (*in a whisper, sensing the antagonism of the crowd*). Tommy, please, son . . . honey, don't talk that way——

MAN ONE. That kid shouldn't talk that way . . . and we shouldn't stand here listening to him. Why, this is the craziest thing I ever heard of. The kid tells us a comic book plot and here we stand listening——

[*A long shot of* STEVE *as he walks toward the camera, and stops by the boy.*]

STEVE. Go ahead, Tommy. What kind of story was this? What about the people that they sent out ahead?

TOMMY. That was the way they prepared things for the landing. They sent four people. A mother and a father and two kids who looked just like humans . . . but they weren't.

[*There's another silence as* STEVE *looks toward the crowd and then toward* TOMMY. *He wears a tight grin.*]

STEVE. Well, I guess what we'd better do then is to run a check on the neighborhood and see which ones of us are really human.

[*There's laughter at this, but it's a laughter that comes from a desperate attempt to lighten the atmosphere. It's a release kind of laugh.*

A group shot of the people as they look at one another in the middle of their laughter.]

CHARLIE (*rubs his jaw nervously*). I wonder if Floral Street's got the same deal we got. (*He looks past the houses.*) Where is Pete Van Horn anyway? Didn't he get back yet?

[*Suddenly there's the sound of a car's engine starting to turn over.*

A long shot, looking across the street toward the driveway of LES GOODMAN'S *house. He's at the wheel trying to start the car.*

A reverse angle, looking toward the people.]

SALLY. Can you get started, Les?

[*A long shot looking toward* LES GOODMAN *as he gets out of the car, shaking his head.*]

GOODMAN. No dice.

[*A track shot follows him as he walks toward the group. He stops suddenly as behind him, inexplicably and with a noise that inserts itself into the silence, the car engine starts up all by itself.* GOODMAN *whirls around to stare toward it.*

A different angle of the car as it idles roughly, smoke coming from the exhaust, the frame shaking gently.

A close shot of GOODMAN *as his eyes go wide, and he runs over to his car.*

A different angle of the people as they stare toward the car.]

MAN ONE. He got the car started somehow. He got *his* car started!

[*A pan shot along the faces of the people as they stare, somehow caught up by this revelation and somehow, illogically, wildly, frightened.*]

WOMAN ONE. How come his car just up and started like that?

SALLY. All by itself. He wasn't anywhere near it. It started all by itself.

[DON *approaches the group, stops a few feet away to look toward Goodman's car and then back toward the group.*]

DON. And he never did come out to look at that thing that flew overhead. He wasn't even interested. (*He turns to the faces in the group, his face taut and serious.*) Why? Why didn't he come out with the rest of us to look?

CHARLIE. He always was an odd ball. Him and his whole family. Real odd ball.

DON. What do you say we ask him?

[*A different angle of the group as they suddenly start toward the house. In this brief fraction of a moment they take the first step toward performing a metamorphosis that changes people from a group into a mob. They begin to head purposefully across the street toward the house.* STEVE *stands in front of them. For a moment their fear almost turns their walk into a wild stam-*

pede, but STEVE'S *voice, loud, incisive and commanding makes them stop.*]

STEVE. Wait a minute . . . *wait a minute!* Let's not be a mob!

[*The people stop as a group, seem to pause for a moment and then much more quietly and slowly start to walk across the street.*

A full shot of GOODMAN'S *house and driveway. He stands there alone facing the people.*]

GOODMAN. I just don't understand it. I tried to start it and it wouldn't start. You saw me. All of you saw me.

[*And now just as suddenly as the engine started it stops, and there's a long silence that is gradually intruded upon by the frightened murmuring of the people.*]

GOODMAN. I don't understand. I swear . . . I don't understand. What's happening?

DON. Maybe you better tell us. Nothing's working on this street. Nothing. No lights, no power, no radio. (*And then meaningfully.*) Nothing except one car—*yours!*

[*A close shot of the people as they pick this up, and their murmuring becomes a loud chant filling the air with accusations and demands for action. Two of the men pass* DON *and head toward* GOODMAN *who backs away, backing into his car and now at bay.*]

GOODMAN. Wait a minute now. You keep your distance—all of you. So I've got a car that starts by itself —well, that's a freak thing—I admit it. But does that make me some kind of a criminal or something? I don't know why the car works—it just does!

[*This stops the crowd momentarily and* GOODMAN, *still backing away, goes toward his front porch. He goes up the steps and then stops to stand facing the mob.*]

GOODMAN. What's it all about, Steve?

STEVE (quietly). We're all on a monster kick, Les. Seems that the general impression holds that maybe one family isn't what we think they are. Monsters from outer space or something. Different than us. Fifth columnists[6] from the vast beyond. (He chuckles.) You know anybody that might fit that description around here on Maple Street?

GOODMAN. What is this, a gag or something? This a practical joke or something?

[A medium close shot of the car as suddenly the engine starts all by itself again, runs for a moment and stops. The people once again react.]

GOODMAN. Now that's supposed to incriminate me, huh? The car engine goes on and off and that really does it, doesn't it? (He looks around the faces of the people.) I just don't understand it . . . any more than any of you do! (He wets his lips, looking from face to face.) Look, you all know me. We've lived here five years. Right in this house. We're no different than any of the rest of you! We're no different at all . . . Really . . . this whole thing is just . . . just weird——

WOMAN ONE. Well, if that's the case, Les Goodman, explain why——(She stops suddenly, clamping her mouth shut.)

GOODMAN (softly). Explain what?

STEVE (interjecting). Look, let's forget this——

CHARLIE (over-lapping him). Go ahead, let her talk. What about it? Explain what?

WOMAN ONE (a little reluctantly). Well . . . sometimes I go to bed late at night. A couple of times . . . a couple of times I'd come out here on the porch and I'd see Mr. Goodman here in the wee hours of the morning standing out in front of his house . . . looking up at the sky.

(She looks around the circle of faces.) That's right, looking up at the sky as if . . . as if he were waiting for something. (A pause.) As if he were looking for something.

[There's a murmur of reaction from the crowd again.

An abrupt cut to a close shot of GOODMAN as he backs away.]

GOODMAN. She's crazy. Look I can explain that. Please . . . I can really explain that . . . she's making it up anyway. (Then he shouts.) I tell you she's making it up!

[He takes a step toward the crowd and they back away. He walks down the steps after them and they continue to back away. He's suddenly and completely left alone, and he looks like a man caught in the middle of a menacing circle as we fade to black.]

Act Two

SCENE 1

[Fade in on the street at night. The camera takes a slow pan down the sidewalk taking in little knots of people who stand around talking in low voices. At the end of each conversation they look toward Les Goodman's house. From the various houses we can see candlelight but no electricity, and there's an all-pervading quiet that blankets the whole area, disturbed only by the almost whispered voices of the people as they stand around. The camera pans over to one group where CHARLIE stands. He stares across at Goodman's house. Two men stand across the street from it in almost sentry-like poses.]

6. Fifth columnists, people who engage in spying, sabotage, and other revolutionary activities within the borders of a nation.

SALLY (*a little timorously*). It doesn't seem right, though, keeping watch on them. Why, he was right when he said he was one of our neighbors. Why I've known Ethel Goodman ever since they moved in. We've been good friends——

CHARLIE. That don't prove a thing. Any guy who'd spend his time lookin' up at the sky early in the morning—well there's something wrong with that kind of person. There's something that ain't legitimate. Maybe under normal circumstances we could let it go by, but these aren't normal circumstances. Why look at this street! Nothin' but candles. Why it's like goin' back into the dark ages or somethin'!

[*A track shot of* STEVE *from several yards down as he walks down the steps of his porch, walks down the street over to Les Goodman's house and then stops at the foot of the steps.* GOODMAN *stands there,* MRS. GOODMAN *behind him very frightened.*]

GOODMAN. Just stay right where you are, Steve. We don't want any trouble but this time if anybody sets foot on my porch—that's what they're going to get—trouble!

STEVE. Look, Les——

GOODMAN. I've already explained to you people. I don't sleep very well at night sometimes. I get up and I take a walk and I look up at the sky. I look at the stars!

MRS. GOODMAN. That's exactly what he does. Why this whole thing it's . . . it's some kind of madness or something.

STEVE (*nods grimly*). That's exactly what it is—some kind of madness.

CHARLIE'S VOICE (*shrill, from across the street*). You best watch who you're seen with, Steve! Until we get this all straightened out, you ain't exactly above suspicion yourself.

STEVE (*whirling around toward him*). Or you, Charlie. Or any of us, it seems. From age eight on up!

WOMAN ONE. What I'd like to know is—what are we gonna do? Just stand around here all night?

CHARLIE. There's nothin' else we *can* do! (*He turns back looking toward* STEVE *and* GOODMAN *again.*) One of 'em'll tip their hand. They *got* to.

STEVE (*raising his voice*). There's something you can do, Charlie. You could go home and keep your mouth shut. You could quit strutting around like a self-appointed hanging judge[7] and just climb into bed and forget it.

CHARLIE. You sound real anxious to have that happen, Steve. I think we better keep our eye on you too!

DON (*as if he were taking the bit in his teeth, takes a hesitant step to the front*). I think everything might as well come out now. (*He turns toward* STEVE.) Your wife's done plenty of talking, Steve, about how odd *you* are!

CHARLIE (*picking this up, his eyes widening*). Go ahead, tell us what she's said.

[*A long shot of* STEVE *as he walks toward them from across the street.*]

STEVE. Go ahead, what's my wife said? Let's get it *all* out. Let's pick out every idiosyncrasy of every single man, woman and child on the street. And then we might as well set up some kind of kangaroo court.[8] How about a firing squad at dawn, Charlie, so we can get rid of all the suspects. Narrow them down. Make it easier for you.

DON. There's no need gettin' so upset Steve. It's just that . . . well . . . Myra's talked about how there's

---

7. hanging judge, judge who consistently calls for the death penalty.
8. kangaroo court, term given to an unauthorized, on-the-spot mock trial in which heated emotion replaces reason and justice.

been plenty of nights you spent hours down in your basement workin' on some kind of radio or something. Well, none of us have ever *seen* that radio——

[*By this time* STEVE *has reached the group. He stands there defiantly close to them.*]

CHARLIE. Go ahead Steve. What kind of "radio set" you workin' on? I never seen it. Neither has anyone else. Who do you talk to on that radio set? And who talks to you?

STEVE. I'm surprised at you, Charlie. How come you're so dense all of a sudden? (*A pause.*) Who do I talk to? I talk to monsters from outer space. I talk to three-headed green men who fly over here in what look like meteors.

[*A medium long shot of Steve's house.* MRS. BRAND *steps down from the porch, bites her lip, calls out.*]

MRS. BRAND. Steve! Steve, please. (*Then looking around frightened, she walks toward the group.*) It's just a ham radio set, that's all. I bought him a book on it myself. It's just a ham radio set. A lot of people have them. I can show it to you. It's right down in the basement.

STEVE (*whirls around toward her*). Show them nothing! If they want to look inside our house—let them get a search warrant.

CHARLIE. Look, buddy, you can't afford to——

STEVE (*interrupting*). Charlie, don't start telling me who's dangerous and who isn't and who's safe and who's a menace. (*He turns to the group and shouts.*) And you're with him too—all of you! You're standing here all set to crucify—all set to find a scapegoat—all desperate to point some kind of a finger at a neighbor! Well now look friends, the only thing that's gonna happen is that we'll eat each other up alive——

[*He stops abruptly as* CHARLIE *suddenly grabs his arm.*]

CHARLIE (*in a hushed voice*). That's not the *only* thing that can happen to us.

[*Cut to a long shot, looking down the street. A figure has suddenly materialized in the gloom, and in the silence we can hear the clickety-clack of slow, measured footsteps on concrete as the figure walks slowly toward them. One of the women lets out a stifled cry. The young mother grabs her boy as do a couple of others.*]

TOMMY (*shouting, frightened*). It's the monster! It's the monster!

[*Another woman lets out a wail and the people fall back in a group staring toward the darkness and the approaching figure.*

A medium close shot of the people as they stand in the shadows watching. DON MARTIN *joins them carrying a shotgun. He holds it up.*]

DON. We may need this.

STEVE. A shotgun? (*He pulls it out of* DON'S *hand.*) Good Lord—will anybody think a thought around here? Will you people wise up? What good would a shotgun do against——

[CHARLIE *pulls the gun from* STEVE'S *hand.*]

CHARLIE. No more talk, Steve. You're going to talk us into a grave! You'd let whatever's out there walk right over us, wouldn't yuh? Well some of us won't!

[*He swings the gun around to point it toward the sidewalk. A long shot from behind the crowd looking toward the sidewalk as the dark figure continues to walk toward them.*

A reverse angle shot looking toward the group as they stand there, fearful, apprehensive, mothers clutching children, men standing in front of wives. CHARLIE *slowly raises the gun. As the figure gets closer he pulls the trigger. The sound explodes in the stillness.*

A long angle shot looking down at the figure who suddenly lets out a small cry, stumbles forward onto his knees and then falls forward on his face. DON, CHARLIE *and* STEVE *race forward over to him.* STEVE *is there first and turns the man over. The crowd gathers around them.*]

STEVE *(slowly looks up).* It's Pete Van Horn.

DON *(in a hushed voice).* Pete Van Horn! He was just gonna go over to the next block to see if the power was on——

WOMAN ONE. You killed him, Charlie. You shot him dead!

CHARLIE *(looks around at the circle of faces, his eyes frightened, his face contorted).* But . . . but I didn't know who he was. I certainly didn't know who he was. He comes walkin' out of the darkness—how am I supposed to know who he was? *(He grabs* STEVE.*)* Steve—you know why I shot! How was I supposed to know he wasn't a monster or something? *(He grabs* DON.*)* We're all scared of the same thing. I was just tryin' to . . . tryin' to protect my home, that's all! Look, all of you, that's all I was tryin' to do. *(He looks down wildly at the body.)* I didn't know it was somebody we knew! I didn't know——

[*There's a sudden hush and then an intake of breath in the group. Cut to a long shot across the street as all of the lights go on in one of the houses.*]

WOMAN ONE *(in a very hushed voice).* Charlie . . . Charlie . . . the lights just went on in your house. Why did the lights just go on?

DON. What about it Charlie? How come you're the only one with lights now?

GOODMAN. That's what I'd like to know.

[*A pause as they all stare toward* CHARLIE.]

GOODMAN. You were so quick to kill, Charlie, and you were so quick to tell us who we had to be careful of. Well, maybe you *had* to kill. Maybe Pete there was trying to tell us something. Maybe he'd found out something and came back to tell us who there was amongst us we should watch out for——

[CHARLIE *backs away from the group, his eyes wide with fright.*]

CHARLIE. No . . . no . . . it's nothing of the sort! I don't know why the lights are on. I swear I don't. Somebody's pulling a gag or something.

[*He bumps against* STEVE *who grabs him and whirls him around.*]

STEVE. A gag? A gag? Charlie there's a dead man on the sidewalk and you killed him! Does this thing look like a gag to you?

[CHARLIE *breaks away and screams as he runs toward his house.*]

CHARLIE. No! No! Please!

[*A man breaks away from the crowd to chase* CHARLIE.

A long angle shot looking down at them as the man tackles him and lands on top of him. The other people start to run toward them. CHARLIE *gets up on his feet, breaks away from the other man's grasp, lands a couple of desperate punches that push the man aside. Then he forces his way, fighting, through the crowd. He once again breaks free and jumps up on his front porch.*

A medium close shot of CHARLIE *on the front porch as a rock thrown from the group smashes a window alongside of him, the broken glass flying past him. A couple of pieces cut him. He stands there perspiring, rumpled, blood running down from a cut on the cheek. His wife breaks away from the group to throw herself into his arms. He buries his face against her. We can see the crowd converging on the porch.*]

VOICE ONE. It must have been him.

VOICE TWO. He's the one.

VOICE THREE. We got to get Charlie.

[*Another rock lands on the porch.* CHARLIE *pushes his wife behind him, facing the group.*]

CHARLIE. Look, look I swear to you . . . it isn't me . . . but I do know who it is . . . I swear to you, I do know who it is. I know who the monster is here. I know who it is that doesn't belong. I swear to you I know.

DON (*pushing his way to the front of the crowd*). All right, Charlie, let's hear it!

MAN TWO (*screaming*). Go ahead, Charlie, tell us.

CHARLIE. It's . . . it's the kid. It's Tommy. He's the one!

[*There's a gasp from the crowd as we cut to a shot of the mother holding the boy. The boy at first doesn't understand and then, realizing the eyes are all on him, buries his face against his mother,* SALLY.]

SALLY (*backs away*). That's crazy. That's crazy. He's only a boy.

WOMAN ONE. But he knew! He was the only one who knew! He told us all about it. Well how did he know? How *could* he have known?

[*The various people take this up and repeat the question aloud.*]

VOICE ONE. How could he know?

VOICE TWO. Who told him?

VOICE THREE. Make the kid answer.

[*The crowd starts to converge around the mother who grabs* TOMMY *and starts to run with him. The crowd starts to follow, at first walking fast, and then running after* SALLY *and* TOMMY.

A full shot of the street as suddenly CHARLIE'S *lights go off and the lights in another house go on. They stay on for a moment, and then from across the street other lights go on and then off again.*

Cut to a series of close shots of the people.]

MAN ONE (*shouting*). It isn't the kid . . . it's Bob Weaver's house.

WOMAN ONE. It isn't Bob Weaver's house, it's Don Martin's place.

CHARLIE. I tell you it's the kid.

DON. It's Charlie. He's the one.

[*Move into a series of tilt close ups[9] of various people as they shout, accuse, scream, interspersed with cuts of tilt shots of houses as the lights go on and off. Then, slowly, in the middle of this nightmarish morass of sight and sound the camera starts to pull away until once again we've reached the opening shot looking at the Maple Street sign from high above.*]

SCENE 2.

[*The camera continues to move away until we dissolve to a field. An angle shot looks toward the metal side of a space craft which sits shrouded in darkness. An open door throws out a beam of light from the illuminated interior. Two figures silhouetted against the bright lights appear. We get only a vague feeling of form but nothing more explicit than that.*]

FIGURE ONE. Understand the procedure now? Just stop a few of their machines and radios and telephones and lawn mowers . . . throw them into darkness for a few hours, and then just sit back and watch the pattern.

FIGURE TWO. And this pattern is always the same?

FIGURE ONE. With few variations. They pick the most dangerous enemy they can find . . . and it's themselves. And all we need do is sit back . . . and watch.

FIGURE TWO. Then I take it this place . . . this Maple Street . . . is not unique.

---

9. *tilt close ups,* shots from a tilted camera.

FIGURE ONE (*shaking his head*). By no means. Their world is full of Maple Streets. And we'll go from one to the other and let them destroy themselves. One to the other . . . one to the other . . . one to the other—

SCENE 3.
[*The camera pans up for a shot of the starry sky, and over this we hear the* NARRATOR'S *voice.*]

NARRATOR. The tools of conquest do not necessarily come with bombs and explosions and fall-out. There are weapons that are simply thoughts, attitudes, prejudices—to be found only in the minds of men. For the record, prejudices can kill and suspicion can destroy and a thoughtless, frightened search for a scapegoat has a fall-out all of its own for the children . . . and the children yet unborn. (*A pause.*) And the pity of it is . . . that these things cannot be confined to . . . The Twilight Zone!
[*Fade to black.*]

✦   ✦   ✦   ✦

DISCUSSION

1. (a) What is the setting of the play? (b) Name the details that make this setting seem ordinary or commonplace. (c) Why is it important for the setting to be quite ordinary?
2. (a) What incident begins the action of the play? (b) How does Tommy affect the action? (c) Why does the group listen to Tommy?
3. (a) List in order the characters on whom the group's suspicion falls. (b) For what reasons do the people accuse each of these characters?
4. What types of people do Steve and Charlie represent?
5. Reread the stage directions on page 290 concerning the "metamorphosis that changes people from a group into a mob." (a) What is the difference between a group and a mob? (b) Do the people on Maple Street continue the metamorphosis into a mob? Explain.
6. (a) Review the Handbook article on endings (page 520). Is the ending of the play happy, unhappy, or indeterminate? (b) What do you think will eventually happen to the people on Maple Street? Support your answer with evidence from the play.
7. (a) What is the "pattern" to which the space man refers (page 296, column 2, paragraph 8)? (b) State the theme of the play. (c) Do you agree with this view of human nature? Why or why not?
8. (a) What elements of fantasy does the play include? (b) Is fantasy essential to the development of this particular theme? Why or why not?
9. Read the interview with Serling (page 298). (a) Does the play illustrate his "awareness of human conflict"? Explain. (b) What examples from current television can you cite to prove or disprove Serling's belief that television writers wield power and influence over their audiences?

Questions put to a playwright

Mr. Serling, where do you get ideas for your television plays, and how do you prepare scripts?
I generally start with a rough theme or at least a semblance of a storyline. On occasion, I'll start with things as tenuous as a collection of interesting characters, or perhaps one or two characters. Or, I might even start a script based on nothing more than an exciting title. This, of course, varies tremendously with the nature of the material I'm using. If I'm doing a long and serious drama, I generally have a theme in mind. But if I'm dealing with something light, an interesting plot twist might trigger a story.

Generally, I write the whole script right from the top. But I write with an eye toward many, many rewrites. No writer ever writes the best he knows how the first time around. I think it was George Bernard Shaw[1] who said that a good play is never written, it's rewritten. And I subscribe to that.

Do you use personal background as a source for material?
Yes. I draw upon human and personal experiences, and I do so often because I write better when I'm dealing with a subject I know about. But in response to that age-old question as to whether a writer should limit himself to writing only of personal experiences—I don't subscribe to that. I think a good writer is an imaginative writer.

I do think, though, that when dealing with very special areas—contemporary areas like labor unions, or capitalists, or industrialists, or army men—the writer better be sure that he knows the language, the particular specialties, the highly individualized concepts that exist within given professions and areas and times.

While writing, do you try to aim for a particular segment of the population?
No, I never do. I don't aim for any segment—any intellectual group or any particular type of people. I write the best I know how, for what I assume to be a generally bright and astute audience—one that is eye level to me in every respect. I think the writer who begins to tailor for a particular audience segment runs the desperate risk of misreading who is listening to or reading him. It's my guess that a competent writer is a man who writes precisely that which he believes, that which he feels the necessity of writing, and does so in the best way he knows how.

Do you think of yourself as simply a storyteller, or as a modern moralist, a social critic?
I'm all these things; all writers are. All writers are storytellers. All, in a sense, take a position of morality—at least a position which they assume to be a moral one. And all writers are indeed social critics. Some champion certain areas—not to the exclusion of others, but pronouncedly in excess of others.

Is there any common theme in your own writing?
I think you'll find that I have an awareness of human conflict—people fighting other people on many levels other than physical. I'm constantly aware—having lived to a certain extent in this kind of environment—of the combat that human beings enter into with themselves and others. Of the various themes, I've tried to attack prejudice more than any other social evil. I've always felt that prejudice is probably the most damaging, the most jeopardizing, most fruitless of the human frailties. I think prejudice is a waste, and its normal end is violence.

Do you feel that by your writing you wield power and influence attitudes?
Indeed I do. I know I wield power, and I know I influence attitudes just as any writer does. But no more than any other writer, and probably a lot less than many. A writer always influences his audience, motivates them, evokes some kind of reaction from them.

Is your work meant to be entertaining—or is entertainment secondary to intent?
Needless to say, I want to entertain. But I think there is a semantics problem here. You know, a very solid melodrama—one that is heavy and brutal and very commentative on the tragedy of the times—might still be entertaining. I think it harks back to your question about aiming at a particular audience segment. I have no preoccupation, no awareness, of whether or not I'm entertaining—again, I'm writing a story as honestly and as effectively as I know how. And, if in the process I do entertain, or simply titillate, or appeal to, or make laugh, or make weep, or make think, I've done my job.

1. *George Bernard Shaw,* British playwright (1856–1950).

Enemies lurk in the garden,
terrorizing the neighborhood
—until Rikki-tikki-tavi arrives.
Note how the suspense builds as
Rikki fights his great war.

Rikki-tikki-tavi

RUDYARD KIPLING

THIS IS THE STORY of the great war that Rikki-tikki-tavi fought single-handed, through the bathrooms of the big bungalow in Segowlee cantonment.[1] Darzee the Tailorbird helped him, and Chuchundra the Muskrat, who never comes out into the middle of the floor, but always creeps round by the wall, gave him advice, but Rikki-tikki did the real fighting.

He was a mongoose, rather like a little cat in his fur and his tail, but quite like a weasel in his head and his habits. His eyes and the end of his restless nose were pink. He could scratch himself anywhere he pleased with any leg, front or back, that he chose to use. He could fluff up his tail till it looked like a bottle brush, and his war cry as he scuttled through the long grass was: *Rikk-tikk-tikki-tikki-tchk!*

One day, a high summer flood washed him out of the burrow where he lived with his father and mother, and carried him, kicking and clucking, down a roadside ditch. He found a little wisp of grass floating there, and clung to it till he lost his senses. When he revived, he was lying in the hot sun on the middle of a garden path, very draggled indeed, and a small boy was saying, "Here's a dead mongoose. Let's have a funeral."

"No," said his mother, "let's take him in and dry him. Perhaps he isn't really dead."

They took him into the house, and a big man picked him up between his

"Rikki-tikki-tavi" from THE JUNGLE BOOK by Rudyard Kipling. Reprinted by permission of Mrs. George Bambridge, Doubleday & Company, Inc., The Macmillan Company of Canada Ltd., and Macmillan & Co., Ltd.

1. **Segowlee** (sə gou'li) **cantonment,** the British military station at Segowlee, India.

finger and thumb and said he was not dead but half choked. So they wrapped him in cotton wool, and warmed him over a little fire, and he opened his eyes and sneezed.

"Now," said the big man (he was an Englishman who had just moved into the bungalow), "don't frighten him, and we'll see what he'll do."

It is the hardest thing in the world to frighten a mongoose, because he is eaten up from nose to tail with curiosity. The motto of all the mongoose family is "Run and find out," and Rikki-tikki was a true mongoose. He looked at the cotton wool, decided that it was not good to eat, ran all around the table, sat up and put his fur in order, scratched himself, and jumped on the small boy's shoulder.

"Don't be frightened, Teddy," said his father. "That's his way of making friends."

"Ouch! He's tickling under my chin," said Teddy.

Rikki-tikki looked down between the boy's collar and neck, snuffed at his ear, and climbed down to the floor, where he sat rubbing his nose.

"Good gracious," said Teddy's mother, "and that's a wild creature! I suppose he's so tame because we've been kind to him."

"All mongooses are like that," said her husband. "If Teddy doesn't pick him up by the tail, or try to put him in a cage, he'll run in and out of the house all day long. Let's give him something to eat."

They gave him a little piece of raw meat. Rikki-tikki liked it immensely, and when it was finished he went out into the veranda and sat in the sunshine and fluffed up his fur to make it dry to the roots. Then he felt better.

"There are more things to find out about in this house," he said to himself, "than all my family could find out in all their lives. I shall certainly stay and find out."

He spent all that day roaming over the house. He nearly drowned himself in the bathtubs, put his nose into the ink on a writing table, and burned it on the end of the big man's cigar, for he climbed up in the big man's lap to see how writing was done. At nightfall he ran into Teddy's nursery to watch how kerosene lamps were lighted, and when Teddy went to bed Rikki-tikki climbed up too. But he was a restless companion, because he had to get up and attend to every noise all through the night, and find out what made it. Teddy's mother and father came in, the last thing, to look at their boy, and Rikki-tikki was awake on the pillow.

"I don't like that," said Teddy's mother. "He may bite the child."

"He'll do no such thing," said the father. "Teddy is safer with that little beast than if he had a bloodhound to watch him. If a snake came into the nursery now——"

But Teddy's mother wouldn't think of anything so awful.

Early in the morning Rikki-tikki came to early breakfast in the veranda riding on Teddy's shoulder, and they gave him banana and some boiled egg. He sat on all their laps one after the other, because every well-brought up mongoose always hopes to be a house mongoose some day and have rooms to run about in; and Rikki-tikki's mother (she used to live in the general's house at Segowlee) had carefully told Rikki what to do if ever he came across white men.

Then Rikki-tikki went out into the garden to see what was to be seen. It was a large garden, only half cultivated, with bushes, as big as summer houses, of Marshal Niel roses, lime and orange trees, clumps of bamboos,

and thickets of high grass. Rikki-tikki licked his lips. "This is a splendid hunting ground," he said, and his tail grew bottle-brushy at the thought of it, and he scuttled up and down the garden, snuffing here and there till he heard very sorrowful voices in a thornbush. It was Darzee the Tailorbird and his wife. They had made a beautiful nest by pulling two big leaves together and stitching them up the edges with fibers, and had filled the hollow with cotton and downy fluff. The nest swayed to and fro, as they sat on the rim and cried.

"What is the matter?" asked Rikki-tikki.

"We are very miserable," said Darzee. "One of our babies fell out of the nest yesterday and Nag ate him."

"H'm," said Rikki-tikki, "that is very sad—but I am a stranger here. Who is Nag?"

Darzee and his wife only cowered down in the nest without answering, for from the thick grass at the foot of the bush there came a low hiss—a horrid cold sound that made Rikki-tikki jump back two clear feet. Then inch by inch out of the grass rose up the head and spread hood of Nag, the big black cobra, and he was five feet long from tongue to tail. When he had lifted one-third of himself clear of the ground, he stayed balancing to and fro exactly as a dandelion tuft balances in the wind, and he looked at Rikki-tikki with the wicked snake's eyes that never change their expression, whatever the snake may be thinking of.

"Who is Nag?" said he. "*I* am Nag. The great God Brahm[2] put his mark upon all our people, when the first cobra spread his hood to keep the sun off Brahm as he slept. Look, and be afraid!"

He spread out his hood more than ever, and Rikki-tikki saw the specta-cle mark on the back of it that looks exactly like the eye part of a hook-and-eye fastening. He was afraid for the minute, but it is impossible for a mongoose to stay frightened for any length of time, and though Rikki-tikki had never met a live cobra before, his mother had fed him on dead ones, and he knew that all a grown mongoose's business in life was to fight and eat snakes. Nag knew that too and, at the bottom of his cold heart, he was afraid.

"Well," said Rikki-tikki, and his tail began to fluff up again, "marks or no marks, do you think it is right for you to eat fledglings out of a nest?"

Nag was thinking to himself, and watching the least little movement in the grass behind Rikki-tikki. He knew that mongooses in the garden meant death sooner or later for him and his family, but he wanted to get Rikki-tikki off his guard. So he dropped his head a little, and put it on one side.

"Let us talk," he said. "You eat eggs. Why should not I eat birds?"

"Behind you! Look behind you!" sang Darzee.

Rikki-tikki knew better than to waste time in staring. He jumped up in the air as high as he could go, and just under him whizzed by the head of Nagaina, Nag's wicked wife. She had crept up behind him as he was talking, to make an end of him. He heard her savage hiss as the stroke missed. He came down almost across her back, and if he had been an old mongoose he would have known that then was the time to break her back with one bite; but he was afraid of the terrible lashing return stroke of the cobra. He bit, indeed, but did not bite long enough, and he jumped clear of the whisking tail, leaving Nagaina torn and angry.

2. **The great God Brahm** (bräm), the supreme god of the Hindu religion, usually known as *Brahma* (brä'mə).

"Wicked, wicked Darzee!" said Nag, lashing up as high as he could reach toward the nest in the thornbush. But Darzee had built it out of reach of snakes, and it only swayed to and fro.

Rikki-tikki felt his eyes growing red and hot (when a mongoose's eyes grow red, he is angry), and he sat back on his tail and hind legs like a little kangaroo, and looked all round him, and chattered with rage. But Nag and Nagaina had disappeared into the grass. When a snake misses its stroke, it never says anything or gives any sign of what it means to do next. Rikki-tikki did not care to follow them, for he did not feel sure that he could manage two snakes at once. So he trotted off to the gravel path near the house, and sat down to think. It was a serious matter for him.

If you read the old books of natural history, you will find they say that when the mongoose fights the snake and happens to get bitten, he runs off and eats some herb that cures him. That is not true. The victory is only a matter of quickness of eye and quickness of foot—snake's blow against mongoose's jump—and as no eye can follow the motion of a snake's head when it strikes, this makes things much more wonderful than any magic herb. Rikki-tikki knew he was a young mongoose, and it made him all the more pleased to think that he had managed to escape a blow from behind.

It gave him confidence in himself, and when Teddy came running down the path, Rikki-tikki was ready to be petted. But just as Teddy was stooping, something wriggled a little in the dust, and a tiny voice said: "Be careful. I am Death!" It was Karait, the dusty brown snakeling that lies for choice on the dusty earth; and his bite is as dangerous as the cobra's. But he is so small that nobody thinks of him, and so he does the more harm to people.

Rikki-tikki's eyes grew red again, and he danced up to Karait with the peculiar rocking, swaying motion that he had inherited from his family. It looks very funny, but it is so perfectly balanced a gait that you can fly off from it at any angle you please, and in dealing with snakes this is an advantage.

If Rikki-tikki had only known, he was doing a much more dangerous thing than fighting Nag, for Karait is so small, and can turn so quickly, that unless Rikki bit him close to the back of the head, he would get the return stroke in his eye or his lip. But Rikki did not know. His eyes were all red, and he rocked back and forth, looking for a good place to hold. Karait struck out. Rikki jumped sideways and tried to run in, but the wicked little dusty gray head lashed within a fraction of his shoulder, and he had to jump over the body, and the head followed his heels close.

Teddy shouted to the house: "Oh, look here! Our mongoose is killing a snake." And Rikki-tikki heard a scream from Teddy's mother. His father ran out with a stick, but by the time he came up, Karait had lunged out once too far, and Rikki-tikki had sprung, jumped on the snake's back, dropped his head far between his forelegs, bitten as high up the back as he could get hold, and rolled away. That bite paralyzed Karait, and Rikki-tikki was just going to eat him up from the tail, after the custom of his family at dinner, when he remembered that a full meal makes a slow mongoose, and if he wanted all his strength and quickness ready, he must keep himself thin. He went away for a dust bath under the castor-oil

bushes, while Teddy's father beat the dead Karait.

"What is the use of that?" thought Rikki-tikki. "I have settled it all."

And then Teddy's mother picked him up from the dust and hugged him, crying that he had saved Teddy from death, and Teddy's father said that he was a providence, and Teddy looked on with big scared eyes. Rikki-tikki was rather amused at all the fuss, which, of course, he did not understand. Teddy's mother might just as well have petted Teddy for playing in the dust. Rikki was thoroughly enjoying himself.

That night at dinner, walking to and fro among the wineglasses on the table, he might have stuffed himself three times over with nice things. But he remembered Nag and Nagaina, and though it was very pleasant to be patted and petted by Teddy's mother, and to sit on Teddy's shoulder, his eyes would get red from time to time, and he would go off into his long war cry of *"Rikk-tikk-tikki-tikki-tchk!"*

Teddy carried him off to bed and insisted on Rikki-tikki sleeping under his chin. Rikki-tikki was too well bred to bite or scratch, but as soon as Teddy was asleep he went off for his nightly walk round the house, and in the dark he ran up against Chuchundra the Muskrat creeping around by the wall. Chuchundra is a broken-hearted little beast. He whimpers and cheeps all the night, trying to make up his mind to run into the middle of the room. But he never gets there.

"Don't kill me," said Chuchundra, almost weeping. "Rikki-tikki, don't kill me!"

"Do you think a snake-killer kills muskrats?" said Rikki-tikki scornfully.

"Those who kill snakes get killed by snakes," said Chuchundra, more sorrowfully than ever. "And how am I

to be sure that Nag won't mistake me for you some dark night?"

"There's not the least danger," said Rikki-tikki. "But Nag is in the garden, and I know you don't go there."

"My cousin Chua the Rat told me—" said Chuchundra, and then he stopped.

"Told you what?"

"H'sh! Nag is everywhere, Rikki-tikki. You should have talked to Chua in the garden."

"I didn't—so you must tell me. Quick, Chuchundra, or I'll bite you!"

Chuchundra sat down and cried till the tears rolled off his whiskers. "I am a very poor man," he sobbed. "I never had spirit enough to run out into the middle of the room. H'sh! I mustn't tell you anything. Can't you *hear*, Rikki-tikki?"

Rikki-tikki listened. The house was as still as still, but he thought he could just catch the faintest *scratch-scratch* in the world—a noise as faint as that of a wasp walking on a windowpane—the dry scratch of a snake's scales on brick work.

"That's Nag or Nagaina," he said to himself, "and he is crawling into the bathroom sluice. You're right, Chuchundra; I should have talked to Chua."

He stole off to Teddy's bathroom, but there was nothing there, and then to Teddy's mother's bathroom. At the bottom of the smooth plaster wall there was a brick pulled out to make a sluice for the bath water, and as Rikki-tikki stole in by the masonry curb where the bath is put, he heard Nag and Nagaina whispering together outside in the moonlight.

"When the house is emptied of people," said Nagaina to her husband, "*he* will have to go away, and then the garden will be our own again. Go in quietly, and remember that the big

man who killed Karait is the first one to bite. Then come out and tell me, and we will hunt for Rikki-tikki together."

"But are you sure that there is anything to be gained by killing the people?" said Nag.

"Everything. When there were no people in the bungalow, did we have any mongoose in the garden? So long as the bungalow is empty, we are king and queen of the garden; and remember that as soon as our eggs in the melon bed hatch (as they may tomorrow), our children will need room and quiet."

"I had not thought of that," said Nag. "I will go, but there is no need that we should hunt for Rikki-tikki afterwards. I will kill the big man and his wife, and the child if I can, and come away quietly. Then the bungalow will be empty, and Rikki-tikki will go."

Rikki-tikki tingled all over with rage and hatred at this, and then Nag's head came through the sluice, and his five feet of cold body followed it. Angry as he was, Rikki-tikki was very frightened as he saw the size of the big cobra. Nag coiled himself up, raised his head, and looked into the bathroom in the dark, and Rikki could see his eyes glitter.

"Now, if I kill him here, Nagaina will know; and if I fight him on the open floor, the odds are in his favor. What am I to do?" said Rikki-tikki-tavi.

Nag waved to and fro, and then Rikki-tikki heard him drinking from the biggest water jar that was used to fill the bath. "That is good," said the snake. "Now, when Karait was killed, the big man had a stick. He may have that stick still, but when he comes in to bathe in the morning he will not have a stick. I shall wait here till he comes. Nagaina — do you hear me? — I shall wait here in the cool till daytime."

There was no answer from outside, so Rikki-tikki knew Nagaina had gone away. Nag coiled himself down, coil by coil, round the bulge at the bottom of the water jar, and Rikki-tikki stayed still as death. After an hour he began to move, muscle by muscle, toward the jar. Nag was asleep, and Rikki-tikki looked at his big back, wondering which would be the best place for a good hold. "If I don't break his back at the first jump," said Rikki, "he can still fight. And if he fights — O Rikki!" He looked at the thickness of the neck below the hood, but that was too much for him; and a bite near the tail would only make Nag savage.

"It must be the head," he said at last; "the head above the hood. And, when I am once there, I must not let go."

Then he jumped. The head was lying a little clear of the water jar, under the curve of it; and, as his teeth met, Rikki braced his back against the bulge of the red earthenware to hold down the head. This gave him just one second's purchase, and he made the most of it. Then he was battered to and fro as a rat is shaken by a dog — to and fro on the floor, up and down, and around in great circles, but his eyes were red and he held on as the body cart-whipped over the floor, upsetting the tin dipper and the soap dish and the flesh brush, and banged against the tin side of the bath.

As he held he closed his jaws tighter and tighter, for he made sure he would be banged to death, and, for the honor of his family, he preferred to be found with his teeth locked. He was dizzy, aching, and felt shaken to pieces when something went off like a thunderclap just behind him. A hot

wind knocked him senseless and red fire singed his fur. The big man had been wakened by the noise, and had fired both barrels of a shotgun into Nag just behind the hood.

Rikki-tikki held on with his eyes shut, for now he was quite sure he was dead. But the head did not move, and the big man picked him up and said, "It's the mongoose again, Alice. The little chap has saved *our* lives now."

Then Teddy's mother came in with a very white face, and saw what was left of Nag, and Rikki-tikki dragged himself to Teddy's bedroom and spent half the rest of the night shaking himself tenderly to find out whether he really was broken into forty pieces, as he fancied.

When morning came he was very stiff, but well pleased with his doings. "Now I have Nagaina to settle with, and she will be worse than five Nags, and there's no knowing when the eggs she spoke of will hatch. Goodness! I must go and see Darzee," he said.

Without waiting for breakfast, Rikki-tikki ran to the thornbush where Darzee was singing a song of triumph at the top of his voice. The news of Nag's death was all over the garden, for the sweeper had thrown the body on the rubbish heap.

"Oh, you stupid tuft of feathers!" said Rikki-tikki angrily. "Is this the time to sing?"

"Nag is dead—is dead—is dead!" sang Darzee. "The valiant Rikki-tikki caught him by the head and held fast. The big man brought the bang stick, and Nag fell in two pieces! He will never eat my babies again."

"All that's true enough. But where's Nagaina?" said Rikki-tikki, looking carefully round him.

"Nagaina came to the bathroom sluice and called for Nag," Darzee went on, "and Nag came out on the end of a stick—the sweeper picked him up on the end of a stick and threw him upon the rubbish heap. Let us sing about the great, the red-eyed Rikki-tikki!" And Darzee filled his throat and sang.

"If I could get up to your nest, I'd roll your babies out!" said Rikki-tikki. "You don't know when to do the right thing at the right time. You're safe enough in your nest there, but it's war for me, down here. Stop singing a minute, Darzee."

"For the great, the beautiful Rikki-tikki's sake I will stop," said Darzee. "What is it, O Killer of the terrible Nag?"

"Where is Nagaina, for the third time?"

"On the rubbish heap by the stables, mourning for Nag. Great is Rikki-tikki with the white teeth."

"Bother my white teeth! Have you ever heard where she keeps her eggs?"

"In the melon bed, on the end nearest the wall, where the sun strikes nearly all day. She hid them there weeks ago."

"And you never thought it worthwhile to tell me? The end nearest the wall, you said?"

"Rikki-tikki, you are not going to eat her eggs?"

"Not eat exactly, no. Darzee, if you have a grain of sense you will fly off to the stables and pretend that your wing is broken, and let Nagaina chase you away to this bush. I must get to the melon bed, and if I went there now she'd see me."

Darzee was a feather-brained little fellow who could never hold more than one idea at a time in his head. And just because he knew that Nagaina's children were born in eggs like his own, he didn't think at first that it was fair to kill them. But his wife was a sensible bird, and she knew that co-

bra's eggs meant young cobras later on. So she flew off from the nest, and left Darzee to keep the babies warm, and continue his song about the death of Nag. Darzee was very like a man in some ways.

She fluttered in front of Nagaina by the rubbish heap and cried out, "Oh, my wing is broken! The boy in the house threw a stone at me and broke it." Then she fluttered more desperately than ever.

Nagaina lifted up her head and hissed. "You warned Rikki-tikki when I would have killed him. Indeed and truly, you've chosen a bad place to be lame in." And she moved toward Darzee's wife, slipping along over the dust.

"The boy broke it with a stone!" shrieked Darzee's wife.

"Well! It may be some consolation to you when you're dead to know that I shall settle accounts with the boy. My husband lies on the rubbish heap this morning, but before night the boy in the house will lie very still. What is the use of running away? I am sure to catch you. Little fool, look at me!"

Darzee's wife knew better than to do *that*, for a bird who looks at a snake's eyes gets so frightened that she cannot move. Darzee's wife fluttered on, piping sorrowfully, and never leaving the ground, and Nagaina quickened her pace.

Rikki-tikki heard them going up the path from the stables, and he raced for the end of the melon patch near the wall. There, in the warm litter above the melons, very cunningly hidden, he found twenty-five eggs, about the size of a bantam's eggs, but with whitish skins instead of shells.

"I was not a day too soon," he said, for he could see the baby cobras curled up inside the skin, and he knew that the minute they were hatched

they could each kill a man or a mongoose. He bit off the tops of the eggs as fast as he could, taking care to crush the young cobras, and turned over the litter from time to time to see whether he had missed any. At last there were only three eggs left, and Rikki-tikki began to chuckle to himself, when he heard Darzee's wife screaming:

"Rikki-tikki, I led Nagaina toward the house, and she has gone into the veranda, and — oh, come quickly — she means killing!"

Rikki-tikki smashed two eggs, and tumbled backward down the melon bed with the third egg in his mouth, and scuttled to the veranda as hard as he could put foot to the ground. Teddy and his mother and father were there at early breakfast, but Rikki-tikki saw that they were not eating anything. They sat stone-still, and their faces were white. Nagaina was coiled up on the matting by Teddy's chair, within easy striking distance of Teddy's bare leg, and she was swaying to and fro, singing a song of triumph.

"Son of the big man that killed Nag," she hissed, "stay still. I am not ready yet. Wait a little. Keep very still, all you three! If you move I strike, and if you do not move I strike. Oh, foolish people, who killed my Nag!"

Teddy's eyes were fixed on his father, and all his father could do was to whisper, "Sit still, Teddy. You mustn't move. Teddy, keep still."

Then Rikki-tikki came up and cried, "Turn round, Nagaina. Turn and fight!"

"All in good time," said she, without moving her eyes. "I will settle my account with *you* presently. Look at your friends, Rikki-tikki. They are still and white. They are afraid. They dare not move, and if you come a step nearer I strike."

"Look at your eggs," said Rikki-tikki, "in the melon bed near the wall. Go and look, Nagaina!"

The big snake turned half around, and saw the egg on the veranda. "Ah-h! Give it to me," she said.

Rikki-tikki put his paws one on each side of the egg, and his eyes were blood-red. "What price for a snake's egg? For a young cobra? For a young king cobra? For the last—the very last of the brood? The ants are eating all the others down by the melon bed."

Nagaina spun clear round, forgetting everything for the sake of the one egg. Rikki-tikki saw Teddy's father shoot out a big hand, catch Teddy by the shoulder, and drag him across the little table with the teacups, safe and out of reach of Nagaina.

"Tricked! Tricked! Tricked! *Rikk-tck-tck!*" chuckled Rikki-tikki. "The boy is safe, and it was I—I—I that caught Nag by the hood last night in the bathroom." Then he began to jump up and down, all four feet together, his head close to the floor. "He threw me to and fro, but he could not shake me off. He was dead before the big man blew him in two. I did it! *Rikki-tikki-tck-tck!* Come then, Nagaina. Come and fight with me. You shall not be a widow long."

Nagaina saw that she had lost her chance of killing Teddy, and the egg lay between Rikki-tikki's paws. "Give me the egg, Rikki-tikki. Give me the last of my eggs, and I will go away and never come back," she said, lowering her hood.

"Yes, you will go away, and you will never come back. For you will go to the rubbish heap with Nag. Fight, widow! The big man has gone for his gun. Fight!"

Rikki-tikki was bounding all round Nagaina, keeping just out of reach of her stroke, his little eyes like hot coals. Nagaina gathered herself together and flung out at him. Rikki-tikki jumped up and backward. Again and again and again she struck, and each time her head came with a whack on the matting of the veranda and she gathered herself together like a watch spring. Then Rikki-tikki danced in a circle to get behind her, and Nagaina spun round to keep her head to his head, so that the rustle of her tail on the matting sounded like dry leaves blown along by the wind.

He had forgotten the egg. It still lay on the veranda, and Nagaina came nearer and nearer to it, till at last, while Rikki-tikki was drawing breath, she caught it in her mouth, turned to the veranda steps, and flew like an arrow down the path, with Rikki-tikki behind her. When the cobra runs for her life, she goes like a whiplash flicked across a horse's neck. Rikki-tikki knew that he must catch her, or all the trouble would begin again.

She headed straight for the long grass by the thornbush, and as he was running Rikki-tikki heard Darzee still singing his foolish little song of triumph. But Darzee's wife was wiser. She flew off her nest as Nagaina came along, and flapped her wings about Nagaina's head. If Darzee had helped her they might have turned her, but Nagaina only lowered her hood and went on. Still, the instant's delay brought Rikki-tikki up to her, and as she plunged into the rat-hole where she and Nag used to live, his little white teeth were clenched on her tail, and he went down with her—and very few mongooses, however wise and old they may be, care to follow a cobra into its hole.

It was dark in the hole; and Rikki-tikki never knew when it might

open out and give Nagaina room to turn and strike at him. He held on savagely, and stuck out his feet to act as brakes on the dark slope of the hot, moist earth.

Then the grass by the mouth of the hole stopped waving, and Darzee said, "It is all over with Rikki-tikki! We must sing his death song. Valiant Rikki-tikki is dead! For Nagaina will surely kill him underground."

So he sang a very mournful song that he made up on the spur of the minute, and just as he got to the most touching part, the grass quivered again, and Rikki-tikki, covered with dirt, dragged himself out of the hole leg by leg, licking his whiskers. Darzee stopped with a little shout. Rikki-tikki shook some of the dust out of his fur and sneezed. "It is all over," he said. "The widow will never come out again." And the red ants that live between the grass stems heard him, and began to troop down one after another to see if he had spoken the truth.

Rikki-tikki curled himself up in the grass and slept where he was—slept and slept till it was late in the afternoon, for he had done a hard day's work.

"Now," he said, when he awoke, "I will go back to the house. Tell the Coppersmith, Darzee, and he will tell the garden that Nagaina is dead."

The Coppersmith is a bird who makes a noise exactly like the beating of a little hammer on a copper pot. The reason he is always making it is because he is the town crier to every Indian garden, and tells all the news to everybody who cares to listen. As Rikki-tikki went up the path, he heard his "attention" notes like a tiny dinner gong, and then the steady *"Ding-dong-tock!* Nag is dead—*dong!* Nagaina is dead! *Ding-dong-tock!"* That set all the birds in the garden

singing, and the frogs croaking, for Nag and Nagaina used to eat frogs as well as little birds.

When Rikki got to the house, Teddy and Teddy's mother (she looked very white still, for she had been fainting) and Teddy's father came out and almost cried over him; and that night he ate all that was given him till he could eat no more, and went to bed on Teddy's shoulder, where Teddy's mother saw him when she came to look late at night.

"He saved our lives and Teddy's life," she said to her husband. "Just think, he saved all our lives."

Rikki-tikki woke up with a jump, for the mongooses are light sleepers.

"Oh, it's you," said he. "What are you bothering for? All the cobras are dead. And if they weren't, I'm here."

Rikki-tikki had a right to be proud of himself. But he did not grow too proud, and he kept that garden as a mongoose should keep it, with tooth and jump and spring and bite, till never a cobra dared show its head inside the walls.

DISCUSSION

1. How does Rikki prove the family motto "Run and find out" fits him?
2. (a) Why do the snakes want to get rid of Teddy and his parents? (b) How does Rikki put an end to each of their plans?
3. Review the Handbook article on suspense (page 534). (a) At what point in the story is suspense first aroused? (b) Which of Rikki's battles thrilled you most? Why? (c) What methods of suspense does Kipling use? Find examples in the story to support your answer.
4. The biographical sketch of Kipling notes that his animal stories are similar to those he heard from his Indian nurses. Is there anything about the way "Rikki-tikki-tavi" is

written that suggests the author is talking to an audience? Explain.

5. Choose from the following words those that best describe the narrator's tone and give reasons for your choices: *amused, cold, affectionate, critical, pitying, admiring, gloomy, ridiculing.*

6. (a) What details in the story about the habits of animals are factual? **(b)** What human characteristics does Kipling give the animals? **(c)** Review the Handbook article on methods of characterization (page 516). Which methods does Kipling use? Find examples of each.

7. (a) In the second and third paragraphs on page 299, which give a physical description of Rikki, to which of your senses do the images appeal? **(b)** Find images appealing to your sense of sound in the passages dealing with Nag and Nagaina (page 301, column 1, paragraph 4, and column 2, paragraph 5). **(c)** In the scene describing the fight with Nag (page 305, column 2, paragraphs 3 and 4), which images appeal to physical feeling?

WORD STUDY

Because India was for many years a British colony, a number of Indian words have become common expressions in the English language. For example, our word *punch,* referring to a beverage made of several liquids mixed together, comes from *panc,* the Hindu word for "five," probably because of the number of ingredients in the drink. The words listed in the left-hand column below have all come to us from India. Match them with their original Indian meanings given at the right. Use your dictionary if necessary.

1. *veranda*
2. *bungalow*
3. *cot*
4. *shampoo*
5. *bangle*
6. *cashmere*
7. *pajamas*
8. *loot*

a. he robs
b. leg + garment
c. house
d. bracelet
e. to press, knead, clean
f. bed frame
g. thatched roof, porch
h. a goat-raising country

FPG

THE AUTHOR

Rudyard Kipling (1865–1936), who was born to English parents in Bombay, India, spent his first six years in Lahore, India. During those years, his native nurses entertained him with tales of jungle animals —tales much like those he himself wrote later.

Like most British children in foreign countries, Kipling was sent to England for his schooling. When he returned to India at the age of seventeen, he found an outlet for his writing talent by working on a newspaper. As a reporter, he traveled throughout the country and grew to know it as few outsiders do.

In 1889, Kipling left India and set out to see the rest of the world. While in America, he met and married an American woman. For five years, the Kiplings lived in Vermont; later, they settled permanently in England, where Kipling continued his writing.

Today, Kipling is remembered throughout the world for his poems and tales of India. Of special interest are his *Just-So Stories, The Jungle Book,* and *The Second Jungle Book,* all of which deal with animals. *Kim,* an adventure story about an English orphan in India, and *Captains Courageous,* the story of a spoiled American boy on a fishing schooner, are also favorite reading.

Macavity: The Mystery Cat

T. S. ELIOT

MACAVITY's a Mystery Cat: he's called the Hidden Paw—
For he's the master criminal who can defy the Law.
He's the bafflement of Scotland Yard, the Flying Squad's despair[1]:
For when they reach the scene of crime—*Macavity's not there!*

Macavity, Macavity, there's no one like Macavity,   5
He's broken every human law, he breaks the law of gravity.
His powers of levitation would make a fakir stare,[2]
And when you reach the scene of crime—*Macavity's not there!*
You may seek him in the basement, you may look up in the air—
But I tell you once and once again, *Macavity's not there!*   10

Macavity's a ginger cat, he's very tall and thin;
You would know him if you saw him, for his eyes are sunken in.
His brow is deeply lined with thought, his head is highly domed;
His coat is dusty from neglect, his whiskers are uncombed.
He sways his head from side to side, with movements like a snake;   15
And when you think he's half asleep, he's always wide awake.

Macavity, Macavity, there's no one like Macavity,
For he's a fiend in feline shape, a monster of depravity.
You may meet him in a by-street, you may see him in the square—
But when a crime's discovered, then *Macavity's not there!*   20

He's outwardly respectable. (They say he cheats at cards.)
And his footprints are not found in any file of Scotland Yard's.
And when the larder's looted, or the jewel-case is rifled,
Or when the milk is missing, or another Peke's[3] been stifled,
Or the greenhouse glass is broken, and the trellis past repair—   25
Ay, there's the wonder of the thing! *Macavity's not there!*

From OLD POSSUM'S BOOK OF PRACTICAL CATS, copyright, 1939, by T. S. Eliot; renewed, 1967, by Esme Valerie Eliot. Reprinted by permission of Harcourt Brace Jovanovich, Inc. and Faber and Faber Ltd.

1. *Scotland Yard . . . Flying Squad's despair.* The Flying Squad, a group prepared to travel anywhere on short notice, is a section of the criminal investigation department of Scotland Yard, the headquarters of the London police.
2. *His powers . . . would make a fakir stare.* His ability to rise and float in the air (*levitate*) would surprise even a *fakir*, a Hindu who renounces all worldly pleasures for religious reasons.
3. *Peke.* A Pekingese is a tiny, Oriental breed of dog.

And when the Foreign Office⁴ finds a Treaty's gone astray,
Or the Admiralty⁵ loses some plans and drawings by the way,
There may be a scrap of paper in the hall or on the stair—
But it's useless to investigate—*Macavity's not there!*
And when the loss has been disclosed, the Secret Service say: 30
"It *must* have been Macavity!"—but he's a mile away.
You'll be sure to find him resting, or a-licking of his thumbs,
Or engaged in doing complicated long division sums.

Macavity, Macavity, there's no one like Macavity,   35
There never was a cat of such deceitfulness and suavity.
He always has an alibi, and one or two to spare:
At whatever time the deed took place—MACAVITY WASN'T THERE!
And they say that all the Cats whose wicked deeds are widely known
(I might mention Mungojerrie, I might mention Griddlebone⁶)   40
Are nothing more than agents for the Cat who all the time
Just controls their operations: the Napoleon of Crime!

---

4. *Foreign Office,* the department of the government that deals with foreign affairs. It is comparable to the U.S. State Department.
5. *Admiralty,* the government department that handles commerce and shipping affairs.
6. *Mungojerrie, Griddlebone,* characters in *Old Possum's Book of Practical Cats,* in which "Macavity" is included.

DISCUSSION

1. (a) Why is Macavity called "the mystery cat"? (b) What does the name *Macavity* suggest to you?
2. (a) How do Macavity's crimes vary in degree of importance? Cite examples. (b) Why is it impossible to prosecute him for his deeds?
3. (a) What lines in the poem are repeated? (b) Why do you think T. S. Eliot repeats them?

THE AUTHOR

Both England and America claim a part in T. S. Eliot (1888–1965), perhaps the most influential twentieth-century poet in the English language. A quiet, reserved man, Eliot was born in St. Louis, Missouri. After making a brilliant record at Harvard, he moved to England in 1914 and remained there for the rest of his life. He became a British subject in 1927.

In 1948 Eliot won the Nobel Prize in Literature, the highest award any author can receive. He is the only American-born poet to be so honored.

Much of Eliot's poetry is complex and intellectual, but "Macavity" comes from an amusing volume of poems, *Old Possum's Book of Practical Cats.*

See
SATIRE
Handbook
of Literary
Terms
page 532

"She was horribly good," said the bachelor
and his audience sat up in surprise.
What does Saki satirize in this tale of . . .

The Storyteller

H. H. MUNRO

IT WAS a hot afternoon, and the railway carriage was correspondingly sultry, and the next stop was at Templecombe, nearly an hour ahead. The occupants of the carriage were a small girl, and a smaller girl, and a small boy. An aunt belonging to the children occupied one corner seat, and the further corner seat on the opposite side was occupied by a bachelor who was a stranger to their party, but the small girls and the small boy emphatically occupied the compartment.

Both the aunt and the children were conversational in a limited, persistent way, reminding one of the attentions of a housefly that refused to be discouraged. Most of the aunt's remarks seemed to begin with "Don't," and nearly all of the children's remarks began with "Why?" The bachelor said nothing out loud.

"Don't, Cyril, don't," exclaimed the aunt, as the small boy began smacking the cushions of the seat, producing a cloud of dust at each blow.

"Come and look out of the window," she added.

The child moved reluctantly to the window. "Why are those sheep being driven out of that field?" he asked.

"I expect they are being driven to another field where there is more grass," said the aunt weakly.

"But there is lots of grass in that field," protested the boy. "There's nothing else but grass there. Aunt, there's lots of grass in that field."

"Perhaps the grass in the other field is better," suggested the aunt fatuously.

"Why is it better?" came the swift, inevitable question.

"Oh, look at those cows!" exclaimed the aunt. Nearly every field along the line had contained cows or bullocks, but she spoke as though she were drawing attention to a rarity.

"Why is the grass in the other field better?" persisted Cyril.

The frown on the bachelor's face was deepening to a scowl. He was a hard, unsympathetic man, the aunt decided in her mind. She was utterly unable to come to any satisfactory decision about the grass in the other field.

The smaller girl created a diversion by beginning to recite "On the Road to Mandalay." She only knew the first line, but she put her limited knowledge to the fullest possible use. She repeated the line over and over again in a dreamy but resolute and very audible voice; it seemed to the bachelor as though someone had had a bet with her that she could not repeat the line aloud two thousand times without stopping. Whoever it was who had made the wager was likely to lose his bet.

"Come over here and listen to a story," said the aunt, when the bachelor had looked twice at her and once at the communication cord.[1]

The children moved listlessly toward the aunt's end of the carriage. Evidently her reputation as a story-teller did not rank high in their estimation.

In a low, confidential voice, interrupted at frequent intervals by loud, petulant questions from her listeners, she began an unenterprising and deplorably uninteresting story about a little girl who was good, and made friends with everyone on account of her goodness, and was finally saved from a mad bull by a number of rescuers who admired her moral character.

"Wouldn't they have saved her if she hadn't been good?" demanded the bigger of the small girls. It was exactly the question that the bachelor had wanted to ask.

"Well, yes," admitted the aunt lamely, "but I don't think they would have run quite so fast to her help if they had not liked her so much."

"It's the stupidest story I've ever heard," said the bigger of the small girls, with immense conviction.

"I didn't listen after the first bit, it was so stupid," said Cyril.

The smaller girl made no actual

---

1. **communication cord,** cord pulled to signal the engineer to stop the train in case of an emergency.

comment on the story, but she had long ago recommenced a murmured repetition of her favorite line.

"You don't seem to be a success as a storyteller," said the bachelor suddenly from his corner.

The aunt bristled in instant defense at this unexpected attack.

"It's a very difficult thing to tell stories that children can both understand and appreciate," she said stiffly.

"I don't agree with you," said the bachelor.

"Perhaps *you* would like to tell them a story," was the aunt's retort.

"Tell us a story," demanded the bigger of the small girls.

"Once upon a time," began the bachelor, "there was a little girl called Bertha, who was extraordinarily good."

The children's momentarily aroused interest began at once to flicker; all stories seemed dreadfully alike, no matter who told them.

"She did all that she was told, she was always truthful, she kept her clothes clean, ate milk puddings as though they were jam tarts, learned her lessons perfectly, and was polite in her manners."

"Was she pretty?" asked the bigger of the small girls.

"Not as pretty as any of you," said the bachelor. "But she was horribly good."

There was a wave of reaction in favor of the story; the word *horrible* in connection with goodness was a novelty that commended itself. It seemed to introduce a ring of truth that was absent from the aunt's tales of infant life.

"She was so good," continued the bachelor, "that she won several medals for goodness, which she always wore pinned onto her dress. There was a medal for obedience, another medal for punctuality, and a third for good behavior. They were large metal medals, and they clinked against one another as she walked. No other child in the town where she lived had as many as three medals, so everybody knew that she must be an extra good child."

"Horribly good," quoted Cyril.

"Everybody talked about her goodness, and the Prince of the country got to hear about it, and he said that as she was so very good she might be allowed once a week to walk in his park, which was just outside the town. It was a beautiful park, and no children were ever allowed in it, so it was a great honor for Bertha to be allowed to go there."

"Were there any sheep in the park?" demanded Cyril.

"No," said the bachelor, "there were no sheep."

"Why weren't there any sheep?" came the inevitable question arising out of that answer.

The aunt permitted herself a smile, which might almost have been described as a grin.

"There were no sheep in the park," said the bachelor, "because the Prince's mother had once had a dream that her son would either be killed by a sheep or else by a clock falling on him. For that reason the Prince never kept a sheep in his park or a clock in his palace."

The aunt suppressed a gasp of admiration.

"Was the Prince killed by a sheep or by a clock?" asked Cyril.

"He is still alive, so we can't tell whether the dream will come true," said the bachelor unconcernedly. "Anyway, there were no sheep in the park, but there were lots of little pigs running all over the place."

"What color were they?"

"Black with white faces, white with black spots, black all over, gray

with white patches, and some were white all over."

The storyteller paused to let the full idea of the park's treasures sink into the children's imaginations; then he resumed:

"Bertha was rather sorry to find that there were no flowers in the park. She had promised her aunts, with tears in her eyes, that she would not pick any of the kind Prince's flowers, and she had meant to keep her promise, so of course it made her feel silly to find that there were no flowers to pick."

"Why weren't there any flowers?"

"Because the pigs had eaten them all," said the bachelor promptly. "The gardeners had told the Prince that you couldn't have pigs and flowers, so he decided to have pigs and no flowers."

There was a murmur of approval at the excellence of the Prince's decision; so many people would have decided the other way.

"There were lots of other delightful things in the park. There were ponds with gold and blue and green fish in them, and trees with beautiful parrots that said clever things at a moment's notice, and humming birds that hummed all the popular tunes of the day. Bertha walked up and down and enjoyed herself immensely, and thought to herself, 'If I were not so extraordinarily good I should not have been allowed to come into this beautiful park and enjoy all there is to be seen in it,' and her three medals clinked against one another as she walked and helped to remind her how very good she really was. Just then an enormous wolf came prowling into the park to see if it could catch a fat little pig for its supper."

"What color was it?" asked the children, amid an immediate quickening of interest.

"Mud-color all over, with a black tongue and pale gray eyes that gleamed with unspeakable ferocity. The first thing that it saw in the park was Bertha; her pinafore was so spotlessly white and clean that it could be seen from a great distance. Bertha saw the wolf and saw that it was stealing toward her, and she began to wish that she had never been allowed to come into the park. She ran as hard as she could, and the wolf came after her with huge leaps and bounds. She managed to reach a shrubbery of myrtle bushes, and she hid herself in one of the thickest of the bushes. The wolf came sniffing among the branches, its black tongue lolling out of its mouth and its pale gray eyes glaring with rage. Bertha was terribly frightened, and thought to herself: 'If I had not been so extraordinarily good, I should have been safe in town at this moment.'

"However, the scent of the myrtle was so strong that the wolf could not sniff out where Bertha was hiding, and the bushes were so thick that he might have hunted about in them for a long time without catching sight of her; so he thought he might as well go off and catch a little pig instead. Bertha was trembling very much at having the wolf prowling and sniffing so near her, and as she trembled the medal for obedience clinked against the medals for good conduct and punctuality. The wolf was just moving away when he heard the sound of the medals clinking and stopped to listen; they clinked again in a bush quite near him. He dashed into the bush, his pale gray eyes gleaming with ferocity and triumph, and dragged Bertha out and devoured her to the last morsel. All that was left of her were her shoes, bits of clothing, and the three medals for goodness."

"Were any of the little pigs killed?"

"No, they all escaped."

"The story began badly," said the smaller of the two girls, "but it had a beautiful ending."

"It is the most beautiful story that I ever heard," said the bigger of the small girls, with immense decision.

"It is the *only* beautiful story I have ever heard," said Cyril.

A dissentient opinion came from the aunt.

"A most improper story to tell to young children! You have undermined the effect of years of careful teaching."

"At any rate," said the bachelor, collecting his belongings preparatory to leaving the carriage, "I kept them quiet for ten minutes, which was more than you were able to do."

"Unhappy woman!" he observed to himself as he walked down the platform of Templecombe station. "For the next six months or so those children will assail her in public with demands for an improper story!"

✦　✦　✦　✦

DISCUSSION

1. (a) What elements does the bachelor's story have in common with the usual fairy tale? (b) What is the first indication that his story will be different? (c) Why does his story have a "ring of truth" that is "absent from the aunt's tales"? (d) What features of his story are very different from the ordinary children's story?

2. (a) What kind of person is the aunt? (b) Judging from her disapproval of the man's story, what does she believe the purpose of children's stories should be? Do you agree or disagree? Explain.

3. Read lines that you find amusing in Saki's description of the children's behavior and the aunt's attempts to handle her charges.

4. (a) What or who are the objects of Saki's satire? (b) Would you describe his satire as *bitter, amused,* or *scornful*?

5. (a) Why do the children find the man's story so much more satisfying than their aunt's? (b) How does Mark Twain's saying, "The hardest thing to endure is a good example," apply to the story?

THE AUTHOR

The bachelor in the train compartment who delights the children but confounds their aunt could almost be H(ector) H(ugh) Munro himself, one of the world's master storytellers. His tales, which often blend humor with an element of gruesomeness, and frequently contain characters who play tricks on each other, usually end in a surprising way.

"Saki," the name of a character who, in a twelfth-century Persian poem, carries wine to guests seated on the lawn, is Munro's pen name. Born in Burma, he left that country when his mother died. After his education in England, he and his father traveled throughout Europe. Later Saki became a writer and published his first collection of short stories in 1904. He enlisted as a private during World War I and was killed in action in 1916.

Sometimes nonsense seems to make sense.

Jabberwocky

LEWIS CARROLL

'TWAS brillig, and the slithy toves
   Did gyre and gimble in the wabe;
All mimsy were the borogoves,
   And the mome raths outgrabe.

"Beware the Jabberwock, my son!   5
   The jaws that bite, the claws that catch!
Beware the Jubjub bird, and shun
   The frumious Bandersnatch!"

He took his vorpal sword in hand;
   Long time the manxome foe he sought—   10
So rested he by the Tumtum tree,
   And stood awhile in thought.

And, as in uffish thought he stood,
   The Jabberwock, with eyes of flame,
Came whiffling through the tulgey wood,   15
   And burbled as it came!

One, two! One, two! And through and through
   The vorpal blade went snicker-snack!
He left it dead, and with its head
   He went galumphing back.   20

"And hast thou slain the Jabberwock?
   Come to my arms, my beamish boy!
O frabjous day! Callooh! Callay!"
   He chortled in his joy.

'Twas brillig and the slithy toves   25
   Did gyre and gimble in the wabe;
All mimsy were the borogoves,
   And the mome raths outgrabe.

Glossary of Jabberwocky Terms

The following glossary of the invented words in *Jabberwocky* is compiled from ingenious definitions given by Humpty Dumpty in Carroll's *Through the Looking Glass*. The last definition is found in the *Preface* to *The Hunting of the Snark*.

Brillig, four o'clock in the afternoon—the time when you begin broiling things for dinner.

Slithy, lithe and slimy. *Lithe* is the same as *active*. It is like a portmanteau—there are two meanings packed up into one word.

Toves, animals something like badgers—they're something like lizards—and they're something like corkscrews. They make their nests under sundials; also they live on cheese.

Gyre, to go round and round like a gyroscope.

Gimble, to make holes like a gimlet.

Wabe, a grass-plot round a sun-dial; so called because it goes a long way before it, a long way behind it, and a long way beyond it on each side.

Mimsy, flimsy and miserable; another portmanteau word.

Borogove, a thin, shabby-looking bird with its feathers sticking out all round—something like a live mop.

Mome. Humpty says that he is uncertain of the meaning of this word; but he thinks it's "short for *from home*—meaning that they'd lost their way."

Rath, a sort of green pig.

Outgrabe, past tense of *outgribe,* meaning to make a noise like something between bellowing and whistling, with a kind of sneeze in the middle.

Frumious, another portmanteau word meaning fuming and furious.

DISCUSSION

1. Summarize the action described in the poem.
2. *Chortle,* coined by Lewis Carroll in "Jabberwocky," is now a perfectly acceptable word. It is a blend of *chuckle* and *snort*. (**a**) *Galumph,* too, is listed in Webster's unabridged dictionary. Of what two words is it a blend? (**b**) How would you explain the nonsense words not defined on the glossary list?
3. What do you think the Jabberwock might look like?
4. Why do you suppose this nonsense poem has remained so popular throughout the years?

THE AUTHOR

Charles Lutwidge Dodgson (1832–1898), better known by his pen name of Lewis Carroll, was a mathematician. Yet there was another side to his nature for which he is remembered today. Shy with adults, Dodgson felt more at home with children. And this understanding of young people combined with a lively imagination won him a place among the most famous English authors.

To amuse a little girl named Alice Liddell, Dodgson wrote a dream story called *Alice in Wonderland* and published it under the name Lewis Carroll. Suddenly famous, he wrote Alice into another story, *Through the Looking Glass,* in which she has a series of adventures on a giant chessboard. These two books are Carroll's best-known works.

Carroll knew and loved poetry almost as much as he loved children. During his time, English children were often required to memorize poems that taught lessons; this memory work was supposed to teach them how to be good. Carroll enjoyed rewriting the moral poems, changing them into nonsense. "Jabberwocky" is not based on a particular poem, but it is characteristic of its author's humor and imagination.

"Surely, I have not slept here all night,"
thought Rip as he woke up in a mountain forest.

Rip Van Winkle

WASHINGTON IRVING

WHOEVER has made a voyage up the Hudson must remember the Kaatskill mountains. They are a dismembered branch of the great Appalachian family, and are seen away to the west of the river, swelling up to a noble height, and lording it over the surrounding country. Every change of season, every change of weather, indeed, every hour of the day, produces some change in the magical hues and shapes of these mountains, and they are regarded by all the good wives, far and near, as perfect barometers. When the weather is fair and settled, they are clothed in blue and purple, and print their bold outlines on the clear evening sky; but, sometimes, when the rest of the landscape is cloudless, they will gather a hood of gray vapors about their summits, which, in the last rays of the setting sun, will glow and light up like a crown of glory.

At the foot of these fairy mountains, the voyager may have descried the light smoke curling up from a village, whose shingle roofs gleam among the trees, just where the blue tints of the upland melt away into the fresh green of the nearer landscape. It is a little village, of great antiquity, having been founded by some of the Dutch colonists, in the early times of the province, just about the beginning of the government of the good Peter Stuyvesant[1] (may he rest in peace!) and there were some of the houses of the original settlers standing within a few years,[2] built of small yellow bricks brought from Holland, having latticed windows and gabled fronts, surmounted with weathercocks.

In that same village, and in one of these very houses (which, to tell the precise truth, was sadly time-worn and weather-beaten), there lived many years since, while the country was yet a province of Great Britain, a simple good-natured fellow, of the name of Rip Van Winkle. He was a descendant of the Van Winkles who figured so gallantly in the chivalrous days of Peter Stuyvesant, and accompanied him to the siege of Fort Christina.[3] He inherited, however, but little of the martial character of his ancestors. I have observed that he was a

---

1. **Peter Stuyvesant** (stī'və sənt), a Dutchman who, from 1646 to 1664, was governor of the Colony of New Amsterdam, later New York.
2. **within a few years,** only a few years ago.
3. **the siege of Fort Christina** (kris tē' nə), a long-continued attack on a Swedish fort on the Delaware River. The fort was taken by the Dutch in 1654.

simple good-natured man; he was, moreover, a kind neighbor, and an obedient henpecked husband. Indeed, to the latter circumstance might be owing that meekness of spirit which gained him such universal popularity; for those men are most apt to be obsequious and conciliating abroad, who are under the discipline of shrews at home. Their tempers, doubtless, are rendered pliant and malleable in the fiery furnace of domestic tribulation; and a curtain lecture[4] is worth all the sermons in the world for teaching the virtues of patience and long-suffering. A termagant wife may, therefore, in some respects, be considered a tolerable blessing; and if so, Rip Van Winkle was thrice blessed.[5]

Certain it is, that he was a great favorite among all the good wives of the village, who, as usual, with the amiable sex, took his part in all family squabbles; and never failed, whenever they talked those matters over in their evening gossipings, to lay all the blame on Dame Van Winkle. The children of the village, too, would shout with joy whenever he approached. He assisted at their sports, made their playthings, taught them to fly kites and shoot marbles, and told them long stories of ghosts, witches, and Indians. Whenever he went dodging about the village, he was surrounded by a troop of them, hanging on his skirts, clambering on his back, and playing a thousand tricks on him with impunity; and not a dog would bark at him throughout the neighborhood.

The great error in Rip's composition was an insuperable aversion to all kinds of profitable labor. It could not be from the want of assiduity or perseverance; for he would sit on a wet rock, with a rod as long and heavy as a Tartar's lance,[6] and fish all day without a murmur, even though he should not be encouraged by a single nibble. He would carry a fowling-piece on his shoulder for hours together, trudging through woods and swamps, and up hill and down dale, to shoot a few squirrels or wild pigeons. He would never refuse to assist a neighbor even in the roughest toil, and was a foremost man at all country frolics for husking Indian corn, or building stone fences; the women of the village, too, used to employ him to run their errands, and to do such little odd jobs as their less obliging husbands would not do for them. In a word Rip was ready to attend to anybody's business but his own; but as to doing family duty, and keeping his farm in order, he found it impossible.

In fact, he declared it was of no use to work on his farm; it was the most pestilent little piece of ground in the whole country; everything about it went wrong, and would go wrong, in spite of him. His fences were continually falling to pieces; his cow would either go astray, or get among the cabbages; weeds were sure to grow quicker in his fields than anywhere else; the rain always made a point of setting in just as he had some outdoor work to do; so that though his patrimonial estate had dwindled away under his management, acre by acre, until there was little more left than a mere patch of Indian corn and potatoes, yet it was the worst-conditioned farm in the neighborhood.

His children, too, were as ragged and wild as if they belonged to nobody. His son Rip, an urchin begotten in his own likeness, promised to inherit the habits, with the old clothes

4. *curtain lecture,* a wife's scolding of her husband within the bed curtains; that is, in bed.
5. *Rip Van Winkle was thrice blessed.* Dame Van Winkle scolded three times as much as most wives who henpeck their husbands.
6. *Tartar's lance.* The Tartars (tar′tərz), a group of fierce Mongols and Turks who overran Asia and eastern Europe in the Middle Ages, fought with heavy lances or spears.

of his father. He was generally seen trooping like a colt at his mother's heels, equipped in a pair of his father's cast-off galligaskins,[7] which he had much ado to hold up with one hand, as a fine lady does her train in bad weather.

Rip Van Winkle, however, was one of those happy mortals, of foolish, well-oiled dispositions, who take the world easy, eat white bread or brown, whichever can be got with least thought and trouble, and would rather starve on a penny than work for a pound. If left to himself, he would have whistled life away in perfect contentment; but his wife kept continually dinning in his ears about his idleness, his carelessness, and the ruin he was bringing on his family. Morning, noon, and night, her tongue was incessantly going, and everything he said or did was sure to produce a torrent of household eloquence. Rip had but one way of replying to all lectures of the kind, and that, by frequent use, had grown into a habit. He shrugged his shoulders, shook his head, cast up his eyes, but said nothing. This, however, always provoked a fresh volley from his wife; so that he was fain to draw off his forces, and take to the outside of the house—the only side which belongs to a henpecked husband.

Rip's sole domestic adherent was his dog Wolf, who was as much henpecked as his master; for Dame Van Winkle regarded them as companions in idleness, and even looked upon Wolf with an evil eye, as the cause of his master's going so often astray. True it is, in all points of spirit befitting an honorable dog, he was as courageous an animal as ever scoured the woods—but what courage can withstand the ever-enduring and all-besetting terrors of a woman's tongue? The moment Wolf entered the house his crest fell, his tail drooped to the ground, or curled between his legs, he sneaked about with a gallows air, casting many a sidelong glance at Dame Van Winkle, and at the least flourish of a broomstick or ladle, he would fly to the door.

Times grew worse and worse with Rip Van Winkle as years of matrimony rolled on; a tart temper never mellows with age, and a sharp tongue is the only edged tool that grows keener with constant use. For a long time he used to console himself, when driven from home, by frequenting a kind of perpetual club of the sages, philosophers, and other idle personages of the village; which held its sessions on a bench before a small inn, designated by a rubicund portrait of His Majesty George the Third.[8] Here they used to sit in the shade through a long lazy summer's day, talking listlessly over village gossip, or telling endless sleepy stories about nothing. But it would have been worth any statesman's money to have heard the profound discussions that sometimes took place, when by chance an old newspaper fell into their hands from some passing traveller. How solemnly they would listen to the contents, as drawled out by Derrick Van Bummel, the schoolmaster, a dapper learned little man, who was not to be daunted by the most gigantic word in the dictionary; and how sagely they would deliberate upon public events some months after they had taken place.

The opinions of this junto were completely controlled by Nicholas Vedder, a patriarch of the village, and landlord of the inn, at the door of which he took his seat from morning till night, just moving sufficiently to avoid the sun and keep in the shade

---

7. **galligaskins** (gal ə gas'kənz), loose, wide trousers.
8. **His Majesty George the Third,** ruler of England and the colonies at the time of the Revolutionary War.

of a large tree; so that the neighbors could tell the hour by his movements as accurately as by a sundial. It is true he was rarely heard to speak, but smoked his pipe incessantly. His adherents, however (for every great man has his adherents), perfectly understood him, and knew how to gather his opinions. When anything that was read or related displeased him, he was observed to smoke his pipe vehemently, and to send forth short, frequent and angry puffs; but when pleased, he would inhale the smoke slowly and tranquilly, and emit it in light and placid clouds; and sometimes, taking the pipe from his mouth, and letting the fragrant vapor curl about his nose, would gravely nod his head in token of perfect approbation.

From even this stronghold the unlucky Rip was at length routed by his termagant wife, who would suddenly break in upon the tranquillity of the assemblage and call the members all to naught; nor was that august personage, Nicholas Vedder himself, sacred from the daring tongue of this terrible virago, who charged him outright with encouraging her husband in habits of idleness.

Poor Rip was at last reduced almost to despair; and his only alternative, to escape from the labor of the farm and clamor of his wife, was to take gun in hand and stroll away into the woods. Here he would sometimes seat himself at the foot of a tree, and share the contents of his wallet[9] with Wolf, with whom he sympathized as a fellow-sufferer in persecution. "Poor Wolf," he would say, "thy mistress leads thee a dog's life of it; but never mind, my lad, whilst I live thou shalt never want a friend to stand by thee!" Wolf would wag his tail, look wistfully in his master's face, and if dogs can feel pity I verily believe he reciprocated the sentiment with all his heart.

In a long ramble of the kind on a fine autumnal day, Rip had unconsciously scrambled to one of the highest parts of the Kaatskill mountains. He was after his favorite sport of squirrel shooting, and the still solitudes had echoed and re-echoed with the reports of his gun. Panting and fatigued, he threw himself, late in the afternoon, on a green knoll, covered with mountain herbage, that crowned the brow of a precipice. From an opening between the trees he could overlook all the lower country for many a mile of rich woodland. He saw at a distance the lordly Hudson, far, far below him, moving on its silent but majestic course, with the reflection of a purple cloud, or the sail of a lagging bark, here and there sleeping on its glassy bosom, and at last losing itself in the blue highlands.

On the other side he looked down into a deep mountain glen, wild, lonely, and shagged, the bottom filled with fragments from the impending cliffs, and scarcely lighted by the reflected rays of the setting sun. For some time Rip lay musing on this scene; evening was gradually advancing; the mountains began to throw their long blue shadows over the valleys; he saw that it would be dark long before he could reach the village, and he heaved a heavy sigh when he thought of encountering the terrors of Dame Van Winkle.

As he was about to descend, he heard a voice from a distance, hallooing, "Rip Van Winkle! Rip Van Winkle!" He looked round, but could see nothing but a crow winging its solitary flight across the mountain. He thought his fancy must have deceived him, and turned again to descend, when he heard the same cry ring

9. **wallet**, a bag or knapsack for carrying provisions.

through the still evening air; "Rip Van Winkle! Rip Van Winkle!"—at the same time Wolf bristled up his back, and giving a low growl, skulked to his master's side, looking fearfully down into the glen. Rip now felt a vague apprehension stealing over him; he looked anxiously in the same direction, and perceived a strange figure slowly toiling up the rocks, and bending under the weight of something he carried on his back. He was surprised to see any human being in this lonely and unfrequented place, but supposing it to be someone of the neighborhood in need of his assistance, he hastened down to yield it.

On nearer approach he was still more surprised at the singularity of the stranger's appearance. He was a short square-built old fellow, with thick bushy hair, and a grizzled beard. His dress was of the antique Dutch fashion—a cloth jerkin strapped round the waist—several pairs of breeches, the outer one of ample volume, decorated with rows of buttons down the sides, and bunches at the knees. He bore on his shoulder a stout keg, that seemed full of liquor, and made signs for Rip to approach and assist him with the load. Though rather shy and distrustful of this new acquaintance, Rip complied with his usual alacrity; and mutually relieving one another, they clambered up a narrow gully, apparently the dry bed of a mountain torrent. As they ascended, Rip every now and then heard long rolling peals, like distant thunder, that seemed to issue out of a deep ravine, or rather cleft, between lofty rocks toward which their rugged path conducted. He paused for an instant, but supposing it to be the muttering of one of those transient thundershowers which often take place in mountain heights, he proceeded. Passing through the ravine, they came to a hollow, like a small amphitheatre, surrounded by perpendicular precipices, over the brinks of which impending trees shot their branches, so that you only caught glimpses of the azure sky and the bright evening cloud. During the whole time Rip and his companion had labored on in silence; for though the former marvelled greatly what could be the object of carrying a keg of liquor up this wild mountain, yet there was something strange and incomprehensible about the unknown, that inspired awe and checked familiarity.

On entering the amphitheatre, new objects of wonder presented themselves. On a level spot in the centre was a company of odd-looking personages playing at nine-pins. They were dressed in a quaint outlandish fashion; some wore short doublets, others jerkins, with long knives in their belts, and most of them had enormous breeches, of similar style with that of the guide's. Their visages too, were peculiar: one had a large beard, broad face, and small piggish eyes: the face of another seemed to consist entirely of nose, and was surmounted by a white sugarloaf hat,[10] set off with a little red cock's tail. They all had beards, of various shapes and colors. There was one who seemed to be the commander. He was a stout old gentleman, with a weather-beaten countenance; he wore a laced doublet, broad belt and hanger, high crowned hat and feather, red stockings, and high-heeled shoes, with roses[11] in them. The whole group reminded Rip of the figures in an old Flemish painting, in the parlor of Dominie Van Schaick, the village parson, and which had been brought over from Holland at the time of the settlement.

10. *sugarloaf hat,* cone-shaped hat.
11. *roses,* rosettes, or ribbon in the shape of roses.

What seemed particularly odd to Rip was, that though these folks were evidently amusing themselves, yet they maintained the gravest faces, the most mysterious silence, and were, withal, the most melancholy party of pleasure he had ever witnessed. Nothing interrupted the stillness of the scene but the noise of the balls, which, whenever they were rolled, echoed along the mountains like rumbling peals of thunder.

As Rip and his companion approached them, they suddenly desisted from their play, and stared at him with such fixed statue-like gaze, and such strange, uncouth, lacklustre countenances, that his heart turned within him, and his knees smote together. His companion now emptied the contents of the keg into large flagons, and made signs to him to wait upon the company. He obeyed with fear and trembling, they quaffed the liquor in profound silence, and then returned to their game.

By degrees Rip's awe and apprehension subsided. He even ventured, when no eye was fixed upon him, to taste the beverage, which he found had much of the flavor of excellent Hollands.[12] He was naturally a thirsty soul, and was soon tempted to repeat the draught. One taste provoked another; and he reiterated his visits to the flagon so often that at length his senses were overpowered, his eyes swam in his head, his head gradually declined, and he fell into a deep sleep.

On waking, he found himself on the green knoll whence he had first seen the old man of the glen. He rubbed his eyes—it was a bright sunny morning. The birds were hopping and twittering among the bushes, and the eagle was wheeling aloft, and breasting the pure mountain breeze. "Surely," thought Rip, "I have not slept here all night." He recalled the occurrences before he fell asleep. The strange man with a keg of liquor—the mountain ravine—the wild retreat among the rocks—the woebegone party at nine-pins—the flagon—"Oh! that flagon! that wicked flagon!" thought Rip—"What excuse shall I make to Dame Van Winkle!"

He looked round for his gun, but in place of the clean well-oiled fowling-piece, he found an old firelock lying by him, the barrel incrusted with rust, the lock falling off, and the stock worm-eaten. He now suspected that the grave roysters[13] of the mountain had put a trick upon him, and, having dosed him with liquor had robbed him of his gun. Wolf, too, had disappeared, but he might have strayed away after a squirrel or partridge. He whistled after him and shouted his name, but all in vain; the echoes repeated his whistle and shout, but no dog was to be seen.

He determined to revisit the scene of the last evening's gambol, and if he met with any of the party, to demand his dog and gun. As he rose to walk, he found himself stiff in the joints, and wanting in his usual activity. "These mountain beds do not agree with me," thought Rip, "and if this frolic should lay me up with a fit of the rheumatism, I shall have a blessed time with Dame Van Winkle." With some difficulty he got down into the glen: he found the gully up which he and his companion had ascended the preceding evening; but to his astonishment a mountain stream was now foaming down it, leaping from rock to rock, and filling the glen with babbling murmurs. He, however, made shift to scramble up its sides, working his toilsome way through thickets of birch, sassafras, and witch hazel, and sometimes tripped up or

12. *Hollands,* Dutch gin.
13. *roysters,* merry-makers.

entangled by the wild grapevines that twisted their coils or tendrils from tree to tree, and spread a kind of network in his path.

At length he reached to where the ravine had opened through the cliffs to the amphitheatre; but no traces of such opening remained. The rocks presented a high impenetrable wall over which the torrent came tumbling in a sheet of feathery foam, and fell into a broad deep basin, black from the shadows of the surrounding forest. Here, then, poor Rip was brought to a stand. He again called and whistled after his dog; he was only answered by the cawing of a flock of idle crows, sporting high in air about a dry tree that overhung a sunny precipice; and who, secure in their elevation, seemed to look down and scoff at the poor man's perplexities. What was to be done? The morning was passing away, and Rip felt famished for want of his breakfast. He grieved to give up his dog and gun; he dreaded to meet his wife; but it would not do to starve among the mountains. He shook his head, shouldered the rusty firelock, and, with a heart full of trouble and anxiety, turned his steps homeward.

As he approached the village he met a number of people, but none whom he knew, which somewhat surprised him, for he had thought himself acquainted with everyone in the country round. Their dress, too, was of a different fashion from that to which he was accustomed. They all stared at him with equal marks of surprise, and whenever they cast their eyes upon him, invariably stroked their chins. The constant recurrence of this gesture induced Rip, involuntarily, to do the same, when, to his astonishment, he found his beard had grown a foot long!

He had now entered the skirts of the village. A troop of strange children ran at his heels, hooting after him, and pointing at his gray beard. The dogs, too, not one of which he recognized for an old acquaintance, barked at him as he passed. The very village was altered; it was larger and more populous. There were rows of houses which he had never seen before, and those which had been his familiar haunts had disappeared. Strange names were over the doors—strange faces at the windows—everything was strange. His mind now misgave him; he began to doubt whether both he and the world around him were not bewitched. Surely this was his native village, which he had left but the day before. There stood the Kaatskill mountains—there ran the silvery Hudson at a distance—there was every hill and dale precisely as it had always been—Rip was sorely perplexed—"That flagon last night," thought he, "has addled my poor head sadly."

It was with some difficulty that he found the way to his own house, which he approached with silent awe, expecting every moment to hear the shrill voice of Dame Van Winkle. He found the house gone to decay—the roof fallen in, the windows shattered, and the doors off the hinges. A half-starved dog that looked like Wolf was skulking about it. Rip called him by name, but the cur snarled, showed his teeth, and passed on. This was an unkind cut indeed—"My very dog," sighed poor Rip, "has forgotten me!"

He entered the house, which, to tell the truth, Dame Van Winkle had always kept in neat order. It was empty, forlorn, and apparently abandoned. This desolateness overcame all his connubial fears—he called loudly for his wife and children—the lonely chambers rang for a moment with his voice, and then all again was silence.

He now hurried forth, and has-

tened to his old resort, the village inn — but it too was gone. A large rickety wooden building stood in its place, with great gaping windows, some of them broken and mended with old hats and petticoats, and over the door was painted, "the Union Hotel, by Jonathan Doolittle." Instead of the great tree that used to shelter the quiet little Dutch inn of yore, there was now reared a tall naked pole, with something on the top that looked like a red night-cap,[14] and from it was fluttering a flag, on which was a singular assemblage of stars and stripes — all this was strange and incomprehensible. He recognized on the sign, however, the ruby face of King George, under which he had smoked so many a peaceful pipe; but even this was singularly metamorphosed. The red coat was changed for one of blue and buff, a sword was held in the hand instead of a sceptre, the head was decorated with a cocked hat, and underneath was painted in large characters, GENERAL WASHINGTON.

There was, as usual, a crowd of folk about the door, but none that Rip recollected. The very character of the people seemed changed. There was a busy, bustling, disputatious tone about it, instead of the accustomed phlegm and drowsy tranquillity. He looked in vain for the sage Nicholas Vedder, with his broad face, double chin, and fair long pipe, uttering clouds of tobacco smoke instead of idle speeches; or Van Bummel, the schoolmaster, doling forth the contents of an ancient newspaper. In place of these, a lean, bilious-looking fellow, with his pockets full of handbills, was haranguing vehemently about rights of citizens — elections — members of congress — liberty — Bunker's Hill — heroes of seventy-six — and other words, which were a perfect

Babylonish jargon[15] to the bewildered Van Winkle.

The appearance of Rip, with his long grizzled beard, his rusty fowling-piece, his uncouth dress, and an army of women and children at his heels, soon attracted the attention of the tavern politicians. They crowded round him, eyeing him from head to foot with great curiosity. The orator bustled up to him, and, drawing him partly aside, inquired "on which side he voted?" Rip stared in vacant stupidity. Another short but busy little fellow pulled him by the arm, and, rising on tip-toe, inquired in his ear, "whether he was Federal or Democrat?"[16] Rip was equally at a loss to comprehend the question; when a knowing, self-important old gentleman, in a sharp cocked hat, made his way through the crowd, putting them to the right and left with his elbows as he passed, and planting himself before Van Winkle, with one arm akimbo, the other resting on his cane, his keen eyes and sharp hat penetrating, as it were, into his very soul, demanded in an austere tone, "what brought him to the election with a gun on his shoulder, and a mob at his heels, and whether he meant to breed a riot in the village?" — "Alas! gentlemen," cried Rip, somewhat dismayed, "I am a poor quiet man, a native of the place, and a loyal subject of the king, God bless him!"

Here a general shout burst from the bystanders — "A tory![17] a tory! a spy! a refugee! hustle him! away with

---

14. **red night-cap**, the liberty cap, first worn by the freed slaves in ancient Rome and later adopted by the American revolutionists. Its display here shows Doolittle's sympathy with the revolutionists' goals.
15. **Babylonish jargon**, incomprehensible speech, a reference to the Tower of Babel in Babylon. God punished the builders' ambition to reach Heaven by changing their language into new and different languages so that they could not understand each other. [Genesis 11:1–9]
16. **Federal or Democrat**, two political parties formed shortly after the Revolutionary War.
17. **tory**, person favoring English rule during the Revolution.

him!" It was with great difficulty that the self-important man in the cocked hat restored order; and, having assumed a tenfold austerity of brow, demanded again of the unknown culprit, what he came there for, and whom he was seeking? The poor man humbly assured him that he meant no harm, but merely came there in search of some of his neighbors, who used to keep about the tavern.

"Well—who are they?—name them."

Rip bethought himself a moment, and inquired, "Where's Nicholas Vedder?"

There was a silence for a little while, when an old man replied, in a thin piping voice, "Nicholas Vedder! why, he is dead and gone these eighteen years! There was a wooden tombstone in the churchyard that used to tell all about him, but that's rotten and gone too."

"Where's Brom Dutcher?"

"Oh, he went off to the army in the beginning of the war; some say he was killed at the storming of Stony Point[18]—others say he was drowned in a squall at the foot of Anthony's Nose.[19] I don't know—he never came back again."

"Where's Van Bummel, the schoolmaster?"

"He went off to the wars too, was a great militia general, and is now in congress."

Rip's heart died away at hearing of these sad changes in his home and friends, and finding himself thus alone in the world. Every answer puzzled him, too, by treating of such enormous lapses of time, and of matters which he could not understand: war—congress—Stony Point;—he had no courage to ask after any more friends, but cried out in despair, "Does nobody here know Rip Van Winkle?"

"Oh, Rip Van Winkle!" exclaimed two or three, "Oh, to be sure! that's Rip Van Winkle yonder, leaning against the tree."

Rip looked, and beheld a precise counterpart of himself, as he went up the mountain: apparently as lazy, and certainly as ragged. The poor fellow was now completely confounded. He doubted his own identity, and whether he was himself or another man. In the midst of his bewilderment, the man in the cocked hat demanded who he was, and what was his name?

"God knows," exclaimed he, at his wit's end; "I'm not myself—I'm somebody else—that's me yonder—no—that's somebody else got into my shoes—I was myself last night, but I fell asleep on the mountain, and they've changed my gun, and everything's changed, and I'm changed, and I can't tell what's my name, or who I am."

The bystanders began now to look at each other, nod, wink significantly, and tap their fingers against their foreheads. There was a whisper, also, about securing the gun, and keeping the old fellow from doing mischief, at the very suggestion of which the self-important man in the cocked hat retired with some precipitation. At this critical moment a fresh comely woman pressed through the throng to get a peep at the gray-bearded man. She had a chubby child in her arms, which, frightened at his looks, began to cry. "Hush, Rip," cried she, "hush, you little fool; the old man won't hurt you." The name of the child, the air of the mother, the tone of her voice, all awakened a train of recollection in his

---

18. *Stony Point,* a fort in New York, taken in 1779 by the American general, "Mad Anthony" Wayne.
19. *Anthony's Nose,* a mountain across the Hudson River from West Point Academy. According to Irving, it was named for Anthony Van Corlear, the legendary trumpeter for Stuyvesant.

mind. "What is your name, my good woman?" asked he.

"Judith Gardenier."

"And your father's name?"

"Ah, poor man, Rip Van Winkle was his name, but it's twenty years since he went away from home with his gun, and never has been heard of since—his dog came home without him; but whether he shot himself, or was carried away by the Indians, nobody can tell. I was then but a little girl."

Rip had but one more question to ask; but he put it with a faltering voice:

"Where's your mother?"

"Oh, she too had died but a short time since; she broke a blood vessel in a fit of passion at a New England peddler."

There was a drop of comfort, at least, in this intelligence. The honest man could contain himself no longer. He caught his daughter and her child in his arms. "I am your father!" cried he—"Young Rip Van Winkle once—old Rip Van Winkle now!—Does nobody know poor Rip Van Winkle?"

All stood amazed, until an old woman, tottering out from among the crowd, put her hand to her brow, and peering under it in his face for a moment, exclaimed, "Sure enough! it is Rip Van Winkle—it is himself!—Welcome home again, old neighbor—Why, where have you been these twenty long years?"

Rip's story was soon told, for the whole twenty years had been to him but as one night. The neighbors stared when they heard it; some were seen to wink at each other, and put their tongues in their cheeks: and the self-important man in the cocked hat, who, when the alarm was over, had returned to the field, screwed down the corners of his mouth, and shook his head—upon which there was a

general shaking of the head throughout the assemblage.

It was determined, however, to take the opinion of old Peter Vanderdonk, who was seen slowly advancing up the road. He was a descendant of the historian of that name, who wrote one of the earliest accounts of the province. Peter was the most ancient inhabitant of the village, and well versed in all the wonderful events and traditions of the neighborhood. He recollected Rip at once, and corroborated his story in the most satisfactory manner. He assured the company that it was a fact, handed down from his ancestor the historian, that the Kaatskill mountains had always been haunted by strange beings. That it was affirmed that the great Hendrick Hudson, the first discoverer of the river and country, kept a kind of vigil there every twenty years, with his crew of the Half-moon; being permitted in this way to revisit the scenes of his enterprise, and keep a guardian eye upon the river, and the great city called by his name.[20] That his father had once seen them in their old Dutch dresses playing at nine-pins in a hollow of the mountain; and that he himself had heard, one summer afternoon, the sound of their balls, like distant peals of thunder.

To make a long story short, the company broke up, and returned to the more important concerns of the election. Rip's daughter took him home to live with her; she had a snug, well-furnished house, and a stout cheery farmer for a husband, whom Rip recollected for one of the urchins that used to climb upon his back. As to Rip's son and heir, who was the ditto of himself, seen leaning against the tree, he was employed to work on the farm; but evinced an hereditary

20. *great city . . . name.* Hudson was a shipping center in Irving's day.

disposition to attend to anything else but his business.

Rip now resumed his old walks and habits; he soon found many of his former cronies, though all rather the worse for the wear and tear of time; and preferred making friends among the rising generation, with whom he soon grew into great favor.

Having nothing to do at home, and being arrived at that happy age when a man can be idle with impunity, he took his place once more on the bench at the inn door, and was reverenced as one of the patriarchs of the village, and a chronicle of the old times "before the war." It was some time before he could get into the regular track of gossip, or could be made to comprehend the strange events that had taken place during his torpor. How that there had been a revolutionary war—that the country had thrown off the yoke of old England—and that, instead of being a subject of His Majesty George the Third, he was now a free citizen of the United States. Rip, in fact, was no politician; the changes of states and empires made but little impression on him; but there was one species of despotism under which he had long groaned, and that was—petticoat government. Happily that was at an end; he had got his neck out of the yoke of matrimony, and could go in and out whenever he pleased without dreading the tyranny of Dame Van Winkle. Whenever her name was mentioned, however, he shook his head, shrugged his shoulders, and cast up his eyes; which might pass either for an expression of resignation to his fate, or joy at his deliverance.

He used to tell his story to every stranger that arrived at Mr. Doolittle's hotel. He was observed, at first, to vary on some points every time he told it, which was, doubtless, owing to his having so recently awaked. It at last settled down precisely to the tale I have related, and not a man, woman, or child in the neighborhood, but knew it by heart. Some always pretended to doubt the reality of it, and insisted that Rip had been out of his head, and that this was one point on which he always remained flighty. The old Dutch inhabitants, however, almost universally gave it full credit. Even to this day they never hear a thunderstorm of a summer afternoon about the Kaatskill, but they say Hendrick Hudson and his crew are at their game of nine-pins; and it is a common wish of all henpecked husbands in the neighborhood, when life hangs heavy on their hands, that they might have a quieting draught out of Rip Van Winkle's flagon.

DISCUSSION

1. (a) What are some of Rip Van Winkle's character traits? (b) What reason does he give for not tending his farm? (c) Why is the inn his favorite place of refuge? (d) Describe the various friends he joins there.

2. (a) What kind of person is Dame Van Winkle? (b) How do her husband and Wolf respond to her?

3. (a) Describe the merry-makers. (b) How does Rip get involved with them?

4. (a) What is Rip's first concern on waking up? (b) What are the earliest clues that he's been gone longer than overnight? (c) How does he explain these mysteries to himself?

5. (a) When does Rip finally realize what has happened to him? (b) How is he received by the villagers at first? (c) Why does their opinion of him change? (d) How do they later regard him?

6. (a) What great change has occurred in the country during Rip's absence? (b) Has village life changed in a manner proportionate to the upheaval in the nation? Explain.

7. (a) Who is the narrator of the story? (b) How might the story have differed had it been told by Rip? by an unsympathetic neighbor?

8. (a) At what characteristics of the villagers is Irving poking fun in the following sentences:

1. Certain it is, that he was a great favorite among all the good wives of the village, who, as usual, with the amiable sex, took his part in all family squabbles; and never failed, whenever they talked these matters over in their evening gossipings, to lay all the blame on Dame Van Winkle (page 324).

2. But it would have been worth any statesman's money to have heard the profound discussions that sometimes took place, when by chance an old newspaper fell into their hands from some passing traveller (page 325).

(b) Find passages in the description of Rip and his wife that are satirical in tone. (c) Would you describe the tone of Irving's satire as *sneering, broadly comic, protesting,* or *teasing*? Explain.

9. Irving was interested in painting as well as in writing. (a) What images in the opening description of the setting are especially picturesque? (b) Point out word pictures in the description of Nicholas Vedder's pipe (page 326) and the mountain stream (page 328). (c) What other passages contain vivid imagery?

10. (a) Where and when does the story occur? (b) What details in the introduction help prepare you for a mysterious fantasy? (c) Does the setting influence the action of the story? Explain.

WORD STUDY

Language is constantly changing. The italicized expressions in the following sentences from "Rip Van Winkle" were commonly used in America a hundred or more years ago; today they are not so familiar. Try to determine from context the meaning of each of the italicized words. Use your dictionary if there are insufficient clues in the sentence.

1. He was *fain* to draw off his forces, and take to the outside of the house—the only side which, in truth, belongs to a henpecked husband.
2. He saw at a distance the sail of a lagging *bark.*
3. Some wore short *doublets*, others *jerkins*, with long knives in their belts, and most of them had enormous *breeches.*
4. He repeated his visits to the *flagon* so often that at length his senses were overpowered.
5. But in place of the clean, well-oiled *fowling-piece*, he found an old *firelock* lying by him.
7. On waking, he found himself on the green knoll *whence* he had first seen the old man of the glen.
8. He *made shift* to scramble up its sides.

THE AUTHOR

As a boy, Washington Irving (1783–1859) spent a good deal of his time in the Dutch sector of New York City listening to the Hollanders tell the tales and legends of their homeland. Later, these stories provided him with ideas for "Rip Van Winkle" and many of his other works.

Irving began his literary career in 1802 with a series of humorous letters written for a New York newspaper. In 1808, his *Knickerbocker's History of New York,* an only partially fictitious account of the Dutch establishment in the city, won him a reputation as a fine author. Yet it was only after his brothers' importing business went bankrupt, some years later, that Irving decided to earn his living by writing.

In 1815 Irving went to England, where he traveled about writing stories and essays that he at length published in a volume entitled *The Sketch Book.* The book, which included "Rip Van Winkle," was an instant success in Europe as well as in America, Englishmen finally conceding that America had at last produced a first-rate author. *The Sketch Book* was soon followed by *Tales of a Traveller.*

Seventeen years after leaving America, Irving returned to New York State and bought a large estate on the Hudson River. With the exception of four years spent as the United States minister to Spain, he remained there until his death.

*At Milne's mixed-up court there's a Prince who isn't dashing
and a Princess with not one, but two, fairy godmothers.
In this most unlikely kingdom
things aren't quite what you'd expect. . . .*

The Ugly Duckling

A. A. MILNE

CHARACTERS

THE KING
THE QUEEN
THE PRINCESS CAMILLA
THE CHANCELLOR
DULCIBELLA
THE PRINCE SIMON
CARLO

SCENE: *The Throne Room of the Palace; a room of many doors, or, if preferred, curtain-openings: simply furnished with three thrones for Their Majesties and Her Royal Highness the PRINCESS CAMILLA—in other words, with three handsome chairs. At each side is a long seat: reserved, as it might be, for His Majesty's Council (if any), but useful, as today, for other purposes. The KING is asleep on his throne with a handkerchief over his face. He is a king of any country from any story-book, in whatever costume you please. But he should be wearing his crown.*

A VOICE *(announcing)*. His Excellency, the Chancellor! *(The* CHANCELLOR, *an elderly man in horn-rimmed spectacles, enters, bowing. The* KING *wakes up with a start and removes the handkerchief from his face.)*

KING *(with simple dignity)*. I was thinking.

CHANCELLOR *(bowing)*. Never, Your Majesty, was greater need for thought than now.

KING. That's what I was thinking. *(He struggles into a more dignified position.)* Well, what is it? More trouble?

CHANCELLOR. What we might call the old trouble, Your Majesty.

KING. It's what I was saying last night to the Queen. "Uneasy lies the head that wears a crown,"[1] was how I put it.

CHANCELLOR. A profound and original thought, which may well go down to posterity.

KING. You mean it may go down well with posterity. I hope so. Remind me to tell you some time of another

---

1. **Uneasy . . . crown,** a line from Shakespeare's play, *Henry IV, Part II.*

little thing I said to Her Majesty: something about a fierce light beating on a throne.[2] Posterity would like that, too. Well, what is it?

CHANCELLOR. It is in the matter of Her Royal Highness' wedding.

KING. Oh . . . yes.

CHANCELLOR. As Your Majesty is aware, the young Prince Simon arrives today to seek Her Royal Highness' hand in marriage. He has been travelling in distant lands and, as I understand, has not—er—has not—

KING. You mean he hasn't heard anything.

CHANCELLOR. It is a little difficult to put this tactfully, Your Majesty.

KING. Do your best, and I will tell you afterwards how you got on.

CHANCELLOR. Let me put it this way. The Prince Simon will naturally assume that Her Royal Highness has the customary—so customary as to be in my own poor opinion, slightly monotonous—has what one might call the inevitable—so inevitable as to be, in my opinion again, almost mechanical—will assume, that she has the, as *I* think of it, faultily faultless, icily regular, splendidly—

KING. What you are trying to say in the fewest words possible is that my daughter is not beautiful.

CHANCELLOR. Her beauty is certainly elusive, Your Majesty.

KING. It is. It has eluded you, it has eluded me, it has eluded everybody who has seen her. It even eluded the Court Painter. His last words were, "Well, I did my best." His successor is now painting the view across the water-meadows from the West Turret. He says his doctor has advised him to keep to landscape.

CHANCELLOR. It is unfortunate, Your Majesty, but there it is. One just cannot understand how it can have occurred.

KING. You don't think she takes after *me*, at all? You don't detect a likeness?

CHANCELLOR. Most certainly not, Your Majesty.

KING. Good. Your predecessor did.

CHANCELLOR. I have often wondered what happened to my predecessor.

KING. Well, now you know. (*There is a short silence.*)

CHANCELLOR. Looking at the bright side, although Her Royal Highness is not, strictly speaking, beautiful—

KING. Not, truthfully speaking, beautiful—

CHANCELLOR. Yet she has great beauty of character.

KING. My dear Chancellor, we are not considering Her Royal Highness' character, but her chances of getting married. You observe that there is a distinction.

CHANCELLOR. Yes, Your Majesty.

KING. Look at it from the suitor's point of view. If a girl is beautiful, it is easy to assume that she has, tucked away inside her, an equally beautiful character. But it is impossible to assume that an unattractive girl, however elevated in character, has, tucked away inside her, an equally beautiful face. That is, so to speak, not where you want it—tucked away.

CHANCELLOR. Quite so, Your Majesty.

KING. This doesn't, of course, alter the fact that the Princess Camilla is quite the nicest person in the Kingdom.

CHANCELLOR (*enthusiastically*). She is indeed, Your Majesty. (*Hurriedly.*) With the exception, I need hardly say, of Your Majesty—and Her Majesty.

KING. Your exceptions are tolerated for their loyalty and condemned for their extreme fatuity.

2. **fierce . . . throne,** a reference to a line from a poem about King Arthur by Alfred, Lord Tennyson (1809–1892).

CHANCELLOR. Thank you, Your Majesty.

KING. As an adjective for your King, the word "nice" is ill-chosen. As an adjective for Her Majesty, it is—ill-chosen. *(At which moment* HER MAJESTY *comes in. The* KING *rises. The* CHANCELLOR *puts himself at right angles.)*

QUEEN *(briskly).* Ah. Talking about Camilla? *(She sits down.)*

KING *(returning to his throne).* As always, my dear, you are right.

QUEEN *(to the* CHANCELLOR*).* This fellow, Simon—What's he like?

CHANCELLOR. Nobody has seen him, Your Majesty.

QUEEN. How old is he?

CHANCELLOR. Five-and-twenty, I understand.

QUEEN. In twenty-five years he must have been seen by somebody.

KING *(to the* CHANCELLOR*).* Just a fleeting glimpse.

CHANCELLOR. I meant, Your Majesty, that no detailed report of him has reached this country, save that he has the usual personal advantages and qualities expected of a Prince, and has been travelling in distant and dangerous lands.

QUEEN. Ah! Nothing gone wrong with his eyes? Sunstroke or anything?

CHANCELLOR. Not that I am aware of, Your Majesty. At the same time, as I was venturing to say to His Majesty, Her Royal Highness' character and disposition are so outstandingly—

QUEEN. Stuff and nonsense. You remember what happened when we had the Tournament of Love last year.

CHANCELLOR. I was not myself present, Your Majesty. I had not then the honour of—I was abroad, and never heard the full story.

QUEEN. No; it was the other fool. They all rode up to Camilla to pay their homage—it was the first time they had seen her. The heralds blew their trumpets, and announced that she would marry whichever Prince was left master of the field when all but one had been unhorsed. The trumpets were blown again, they charged enthusiastically into the fight, and—*(The* KING *looks nonchalantly at the ceiling and whistles a few bars.)*—don't do that.

KING. I'm sorry, my dear.

QUEEN *(to the* CHANCELLOR*).* And what happened? They all simultaneously fell off their horses and assumed a posture of defeat.

KING. One of them was not quite so quick as the others. I was very quick. I proclaimed him the victor.

QUEEN. At the Feast of Betrothal held that night—

KING. We were all very quick.

QUEEN. The Chancellor announced that by the laws of the country the successful suitor had to pass a further test. He had to give the correct answer to a riddle.

CHANCELLOR. Such undoubtedly is the fact, Your Majesty.

KING. There are times for announcing facts, and times for looking at things in a broad-minded way. Please remember that, Chancellor.

CHANCELLOR. Yes, Your Majesty.

QUEEN. I invented the riddle myself. Quite an easy one. What is it which has four legs and barks like a dog? The answer is, "A dog."

KING *(to the* CHANCELLOR*).* See that?

CHANCELLOR. Yes, Your Majesty.

KING. It isn't difficult.

QUEEN. He, however, seemed to find it so. He said an eagle. Then he said a serpent; a very high mountain with slippery sides; two peacocks; a moonlight night; the day after tomorrow—

KING. Nobody could accuse him of not trying.

QUEEN. *I* did.

KING. I *should* have said that nobody could fail to recognize in his attitude an appearance of doggedness.

QUEEN. Finally he said "Death." I nudged the King—

KING. Accepting the word "nudge" for the moment, I rubbed my ankle with one hand, clapped him on the shoulder with the other, and congratulated him on the correct answer. He disappeared under the table, and, personally, I never saw him again.

QUEEN. His body was found in the moat next morning.

CHANCELLOR. But what was he doing in the moat, Your Majesty?

KING. Bobbing about. Try not to ask needless questions.

CHANCELLOR. It all seems so strange.

QUEEN. What does?

CHANCELLOR. That Her Royal Highness, alone of all the Princesses one has ever heard of, should lack that invariable attribute of Royalty, supreme beauty.

QUEEN *(to the* KING*).* That was your Great-Aunt Malkin. She came to the christening. You know what she said.

KING. It was cryptic. Great-Aunt Malkin's besetting weakness. She came to *my* christening—she was one hundred and one then, and that was fifty-one years ago. *(To the* CHANCELLOR.*)* How old would that make her?

CHANCELLOR. One hundred and fifty-two, Your Majesty.

KING *(after thought).* About that, yes. She promised me that when I grew up I should have all the happiness which my wife deserved. It struck me at the time—well, when I say "at the time," I was only a week old—but it did strike me as soon as anything could strike me—I mean of that nature—well, work it out for yourself, Chancellor. It opens up a most interesting field of speculation. Though naturally I have not liked to go into it at all deeply with Her Majesty.

QUEEN. I never heard anything less cryptic. She was wishing you extreme happiness.

KING. I don't think she was *wishing* me anything. However.

CHANCELLOR *(to the* QUEEN*).* But what, Your Majesty, did she wish Her Royal Highness?

QUEEN. Her other godmother—on my side—had promised her the dazzling beauty for which all the women in my family are famous— *(She pauses, and the* KING *snaps his fingers surreptitiously in the direction of the* CHANCELLOR.*)*

CHANCELLOR *(hurriedly).* Indeed, yes, Your Majesty. *(The* KING *relaxes.)*

QUEEN. And Great-Aunt Malkin said—*(To the* KING.*)*—what were the words?

KING.

> *I give you with this kiss*
> *A wedding day surprise.*
> *Where ignorance is bliss*
> *'Tis folly to be wise.*[3]

I thought the last two lines rather neat. But what it *meant*—

QUEEN. We can all see what it meant. She was given beauty—and where is it? Great-Aunt Malkin took it away from her. The wedding day surprise is that there will never be a wedding day.

KING. Young men being what they are, my dear, it would be much more surprising if there *were* a wedding day. So how—*(The* PRINCESS *comes in. She is young, happy, healthy, but not beautiful. Or let us say that by some trick of make-up or arrangement of hair she seems plain*

---

3. *Where ignorance . . . be wise,* from "On a Distant Prospect of Eton College," by Thomas Gray (1716–1771).

to us: unlike the princess of the story-books.)

PRINCESS *(to the* KING*)*. Hello, darling! *(Seeing the others.)* Oh, I say! Affairs of state? Sorry.

KING *(holding out his hand)*. Don't go, Camilla. *(She takes his hand.)*

CHANCELLOR. Shall I withdraw, Your Majesty?

QUEEN. You are aware, Camilla, that Prince Simon arrives today?

PRINCESS. He has arrived. They're just letting down the drawbridge.

KING *(jumping up)*. Arrived! I must—

PRINCESS. Darling, you know what the drawbridge is like. It takes at *least* half an hour to let it down.

KING *(sitting down)*. It wants oil. *(To the* CHANCELLOR*.)* Have *you* been grudging it oil?

PRINCESS. It wants a new drawbridge, darling.

CHANCELLOR. Have I Your Majesty's permission—

KING. Yes, yes. *(The* CHANCELLOR *bows and goes out.)*

QUEEN. You've told him, of course? It's the only chance.

KING. Er—no. I was just going to, when—

QUEEN. Then I'd better. *(She goes to the door.)* You can explain to the girl; I'll have her sent to you. You've told Camilla?

KING. Er—no. I was just going to, when—

QUEEN. Then you'd better tell her now.

KING. My dear, are you sure—

QUEEN. It's the only chance left. *(Dramatically to heaven.)* My daughter! *(She goes out. There is a little silence when she is gone.)*

KING. Camilla, I want to talk seriously to you about marriage.

PRINCESS. Yes, father.

KING. It is time that you learnt some of the facts of life.

PRINCESS. Yes, father.

KING. Now the great fact about marriage is that once you're married you live happy ever after. All our history books affirm this.

PRINCESS. And your own experience too, darling.

KING *(with dignity)*. Let us confine ourselves to history for the moment.

PRINCESS. Yes, father.

KING. Of course, there *may* be an exception here and there, which, as it were, proves the rule; just as—oh, well, never mind.

PRINCESS *(smiling)*. Go on, darling. You were going to say that an exception here and there proves the rule that all princesses are beautiful.

KING. Well—leave that for the moment. The point is that it doesn't matter *how* you marry, or *who* you marry, as long as you *get* married. Because you'll be happy ever after in any case. Do you follow me so far?

PRINCESS. Yes, father.

KING. Well, your mother and I have a little plan—

PRINCESS. Was that it, going out of the door just now?

KING. Er—yes. It concerns your waiting-maid.

PRINCESS. Darling, I have several.

KING. Only one that leaps to the eye, so to speak. The one with the—well, with everything.

PRINCESS. Dulcibella?

KING. That's the one. It is our little plan that at the first meeting she should pass herself off as the Princess—a harmless ruse, of which you will find frequent record in the history books—and allure Prince Simon to his—that is to say, bring him up to the—in other words, the wedding will take place immediately afterwards, and as quietly as

possible—well, naturally in view of the fact that your Aunt Malkin is one hundred and fifty-two; and since you will be wearing the family bridal veil—which is no doubt how the custom arose—the surprise after the ceremony will be his. Are you following me at all? Your attention seems to be wandering.

PRINCESS. I was wondering why you needed to tell me.

KING. Just a precautionary measure, in case you happened to meet the Prince or his attendant before the ceremony; in which case, of course, you would pass yourself off as the maid—

PRINCESS. A harmless ruse, of which, also, you will find frequent record in the history books.

KING. Exactly. But the occasion need not arise.

A VOICE (announcing). The woman Dulcibella!

KING. Ah! (To the PRINCESS.) Now, Camilla, if you just retire to your own apartments, I will come to you there when we are ready for the actual ceremony. (He leads her out as he is talking, and as he returns calls out:) Come in, my dear! (DULCIBELLA comes in. She is beautiful, but dumb.) Now don't be frightened, there is nothing to be frightened about. Has Her Majesty told you what you have to do?

DULCIBELLA. Y-yes, Your Majesty.

KING. Well now, let's see how well you can do it. You are sitting here, we will say. (He leads her to a seat.) Now imagine that I am Prince Simon. (He curls his moustache and puts his stomach in. She giggles.) You are the beautiful Princess Camilla whom he has never seen. (She giggles again.) This is a serious moment in your life, and you will find that a giggle will not be helpful. (He goes to the door.) I am announced: "His Royal Highness Prince Simon!" That's me being announced. Remember what I said about giggling. You should have a faraway look upon the face. (She does her best.) Farther away than that. (She tries again.) No, that's too far. You are sitting there, thinking beautiful thoughts—in maiden meditation, fancy-free,[4] as I remember saying to Her Majesty once . . . speaking of somebody else . . . fancy-free, but with the mouth definitely shut—that's better. I advance and fall upon one knee. (He does so.) You extend your hand graciously—graciously; you're not trying to push him in the face—that's better, and I raise it to my lips—so—and I kiss it—(He kisses it warmly.)—no, perhaps not so ardently as that, more like this (He kisses it again.) and I say, "Your Royal Highness, this is the most—er—Your Royal Highness, I shall ever be—no—Your Royal Highness, it is the proudest—" Well, the point is that he will say it, and it will be something complimentary, and then he will take your hand in both of his, and press it to his heart. (He does so.) And then—what do you say?

DULCIBELLA. Coo![5]

KING. No, not Coo.

DULCIBELLA. Never had anyone do that to me before.

KING. That also strikes the wrong note. What you want to say is, "Oh, Prince Simon!" . . . Say it.

DULCIBELLA (loudly). Oh, Prince Simon!

KING. No, no. You don't need to shout until he has said "What?" two or three times. Always consider the possibility that he isn't deaf. Softly, and giving the words a dying fall, letting them play around his head like a flight of doves.

4. in . . . fancy-free, a line from Shakespeare's play, A Midsummer Night's Dream.
5. Coo, a British expression of delight.

DULCIBELLA (still a little over-loud). O-o-o-o-h, Prinsimon!

KING. Keep the idea in your mind of a flight of *doves* rather than a flight of panic-stricken elephants, and you will be all right. Now I'm going to get up, and you must, as it were, *waft* me into a seat by your side. *(She starts wafting.) Not* rescuing a drowning man, that's another idea altogether, useful at times, but at the moment inappropriate. Wafting. Prince Simon will put the necessary muscles into play—all you require to do is to indicate by a gracious movement of the hand the seat you require him to take. Now! *(He gets up, a little stiffly, and sits next to her.)* That was better. Well, here we are. Now, I think you give me a look: something, let us say, halfway between the breathless adoration of a nun[6] and the voluptuous abandonment of a woman of the world; with an undertone of regal dignity, touched, as it were, with good comradeship. Now try that. *(She gives him a vacant look of bewilderment.)* Frankly, that didn't quite get it. There was just a little something missing. An absence, as it were, of all the qualities I asked for, and in their place an odd resemblance to an unsatisfied fish. Let us try to get it another way. Dulcibella, have you a young man of your own?

DULCIBELLA *(eagerly, seizing his hand).* Oo, yes, he's ever so smart, he's an archer, well not as you might say a real archer, he works in the armoury, but old Bottlenose, *you* know who I mean, the Captain of the Guard, says the very next man they ever has to shoot, my Eg shall take his place, knowing Father and how it is with Eg and me, and me being maid to Her Royal Highness and can't marry me till he's a real soldier, but ever so loving, and funny like, the things he says. I said to him once, "Eg," I said—

KING *(getting up).* I rather fancy, Dulcibella, that if you think of Eg all the time, *say* as little as possible, and, when thinking of Eg, see that the mouth is not more than partially open, you will do very well. I will show you where you are to sit and wait for His Royal Highness. *(He leads her out. On the way he is saying:)* Now remember—waft—waft—not hoick.[7] (PRINCE SIMON wanders in from the back unannounced. He is a very ordinary-looking young man in rather dusty clothes. He gives a deep sigh of relief as he sinks into the king's throne. CAMILLA, a new and strangely beautiful CAMILLA, comes in.)

PRINCESS *(surprised).* Well!

PRINCE. Oh, hello!

PRINCESS. Ought you?

PRINCE *(getting up).* Do sit down, won't you?

PRINCESS. Who are you, and how did you get here?

PRINCE. Well, that's rather a long story. Couldn't we sit down? You could sit here if you liked, but it isn't very comfortable.

PRINCESS. That is the King's Throne.

PRINCE. Oh, is that what it is?

PRINCESS. Thrones are not meant to be comfortable.

PRINCE. Well, I don't know if they're meant to be, but they certainly aren't.

PRINCESS. Why were you sitting on the King's Throne, and who are you?

PRINCE. My name is Carlo.

PRINCESS. Mine is Dulcibella.

PRINCE. Good. And now couldn't we sit down?

---

6. **breathless . . . nun,** a paraphrase of a line from "It Is a Beauteous Evening," a poem by William Wordsworth (1770–1850).

7. **hoick,** jerk or yank.

PRINCESS (*sitting down on the long seat to the left of the throne, and, as it were, wafting him to a place next to her*). You may sit here, if you like. Why are you so tired? (*He sits down.*)

PRINCE. I've been taking very strenuous exercise.

PRINCESS. Is that part of the long story?

PRINCE. It is.

PRINCESS (*settling herself*). I love stories.

PRINCE. This isn't a story really. You see, I'm attendant on Prince Simon, who is visiting here.

PRINCESS. Oh? I'm attendant on Her Royal Highness.

PRINCE. Then you know what he's here for.

PRINCESS. Yes.

PRINCE. She's very beautiful, I hear.

PRINCESS. Did you hear that? Where have you been lately?

PRINCE. Travelling in distant lands —with Prince Simon.

PRINCESS. Ah! All the same, I don't understand. Is Prince Simon in the Palace now? The drawbridge *can't* be down yet!

PRINCE. I don't suppose it is. *And* what noise it makes coming down!

PRINCESS. Isn't it terrible?

PRINCE. I couldn't stand it any more. I just had to get away. That's why I'm here.

PRINCESS. But how?

PRINCE. Well, there's only one way, isn't there? That beech tree, and then a swing and a grab for the battlements, and don't ask me to remember it all— (*He shudders.*)

PRINCESS. You mean you came across the moat by that beech tree?

PRINCE. Yes. I got so tired of hanging about.

PRINCESS. But it's terribly dangerous!

PRINCE. That's why I'm so exhausted. Nervous shock. (*He lies back.*)

PRINCESS. Of course, it's different for me.

PRINCE (*sitting up*). Say that again. I must have got it wrong.

PRINCESS. It's different for me, because I'm used to it. Besides, I'm so much lighter.

PRINCE. You don't mean that *you*—

PRINCESS. Oh yes, often.

PRINCE. And I thought I was a brave man! At least, I didn't until five minutes ago, and now I don't again.

PRINCESS. Oh, but you are! And I think it's wonderful to do it straight off the first time.

PRINCE. Well, *you* did.

PRINCESS. Oh no, not the first time. When I was a child.

PRINCE. You mean that you crashed?

PRINCESS. Well, you only fall into the moat.

PRINCE. Only! Can you *swim?*

PRINCESS. Of course.

PRINCE. So you swam to the castle walls, and yelled for help, and they fished you out and walloped you. And next day you tried again. Well, if *that* isn't pluck—

PRINCESS. Of course I didn't. I swam back, and did it at once; I mean I tried again at once. It wasn't until the third time that I actually did it. You see, I was afraid I might lose my nerve.

PRINCE. Afraid she might lose her nerve!

PRINCESS. There's a way of getting over from this side, too; a tree grows out from the wall and you jump into another tree—I don't think it's quite so easy.

PRINCE. Not quite so easy. Good. You must show me.

PRINCESS. Oh, I will.

PRINCE. Perhaps it might be as well if you taught me how to swim first. I've often heard about swimming, but never—

PRINCESS. You can't swim?

PRINCE. No. Don't look so surprised. There are a lot of other things which I can't do. I'll tell you about them as soon as you have a couple of years to spare.

PRINCESS. You can't swim and yet you crossed by the beech tree! And you're *ever* so much heavier than I am! Now who's brave?

PRINCE *(getting up)*. You keep talking about how light you are. I must see if there's anything in it. Stand up! *(She stands obediently and he picks her up.)* You're right, Dulcibella. I could hold you here forever. *(Looking at her.)* You're very lovely. Do you know how lovely you are?

PRINCESS. Yes. *(She laughs suddenly and happily.)*

PRINCE. Why do you laugh?

PRINCESS. Aren't you tired of holding me?

PRINCE. Frankly, yes. I exaggerated when I said I could hold you for ever. When you've been hanging by the arms for ten minutes over a very deep moat, wondering if it's too late to learn how to swim—*(He puts her down.)*—what I meant was that I should *like* to hold you forever. Why did you laugh?

PRINCESS. Oh, well, it was a little private joke of mine.

PRINCE. If it comes to that, I've got a private joke too. Let's exchange them.

PRINCESS. Mine's very private. One other woman in the whole world knows, and that's all.

PRINCE. Mine's just as private. One other man knows, and that's all.

PRINCESS. What fun. I love secrets. . . . Well, here's mine. When I was born, one of my godmothers promised that I should be very beautiful.

PRINCE. How right she was.

PRINCESS. But the other one said this:

I give you with this kiss
A wedding day surprise.
Where ignorance is bliss
'Tis folly to be wise.

And nobody knew what it meant. And I grew up very plain. And then, when I was about ten, I met my godmother in the forest one day. It was my tenth birthday. Nobody knows this—except you.

PRINCE. Except us.

PRINCESS. Except us. And she told me what her gift meant. It meant that I *was* beautiful—but everybody else was to go on being ignorant, and thinking me plain, until my wedding day. Because, she said, she didn't want me to grow up spoilt and wilful and vain, as I should have done if everybody had always been saying how beautiful I was; and the best thing in the world, she said, was to be quite sure of yourself, but not to expect admiration from other people. So ever since then my mirror has told me I'm beautiful, and everybody else thinks me ugly, and I get a lot of fun out of it.

PRINCE. Well, seeing that Dulcibella is the result, I can only say that your godmother was very, very wise.

PRINCESS. And now tell me *your* secret.

PRINCE. It isn't such a pretty one. You see, Prince Simon was going to woo Princess Camilla, and he'd heard that she was beautiful and haughty and imperious—all *you* would have been if your godmother hadn't been so wise. And being a very ordinary-looking fellow himself, he was afraid she wouldn't think much of him, so he suggested to one of his attendants, a man called Carlo, of extremely attractive appearance, that *he* should pretend to be the Prince, and win the Princess' hand; and then at the last moment they would change places—

PRINCESS. How would they do that?

PRINCE. The Prince was going to have been married in full armour—with his visor down.

PRINCESS (laughing happily). Oh, what fun!

PRINCE. Neat, isn't it?

PRINCESS (laughing). Oh, very . . . very . . . very.

PRINCE. Neat, but not so terribly funny. Why do you keep laughing?

PRINCESS. Well, that's another secret.

PRINCE. If it comes to that, I've got another one up my sleeve. Shall we exchange again?

PRINCESS. All right. You go first this time.

PRINCE. Very well. I am not Carlo. (Standing up and speaking dramatically.) I am Simon!—ow! (He sits down and rubs his leg violently.)

PRINCESS (alarmed). What is it?

PRINCE. Cramp. (In a mild voice, still rubbing.) I was saying that I was Prince Simon.

PRINCESS. Shall I rub it for you? (She rubs.)

PRINCE (still hopefully). I am Simon.

PRINCESS. Is that better?

PRINCE (despairingly). I am Simon.

PRINCESS. I know.

PRINCE. How did you know?

PRINCESS. Well, you told me.

PRINCE. But oughtn't you to swoon or something?

PRINCESS. Why? History records many similar ruses.

PRINCE (amazed). Is that so? I've never read history. I thought I was being profoundly original.

PRINCESS. Oh, no! Now I'll tell you my secret. For reasons very much like your own the Princess Camilla, who is held to be extremely plain, feared to meet Prince Simon. Is the draw-bridge down yet?

PRINCE. Do your people give a faint, surprised cheer every time it gets down?

PRINCESS. Naturally.

PRINCE. Then it came down about three minutes ago.

PRINCESS. Ah! Then at this very moment your man Carlo is declaring his passionate love for my maid, Dulcibella. That, I think, is funny. (So does the PRINCE. He laughs heartily.) Dulcibella, by the way, is in love with a man she calls Eg, so I hope Carlo isn't getting carried away.

PRINCE. Carlo is married to a girl he calls "the little woman," so Eg has nothing to fear.

PRINCESS. By the way, I don't know if you heard, but I said, or as good as said, that I am the Princess Camilla.

PRINCE. I wasn't surprised. History, of which I read a great deal, records many similar ruses.

PRINCESS (laughing). Simon!

PRINCE (laughing). Camilla! (He stands up.) May I try holding you again? (She nods. He takes her in his arms and kisses her.) Sweetheart!

PRINCESS. You see, when you lifted me up before, you said, "You're very lovely," and my godmother said that the first person to whom I would seem lovely was the man I should marry; so I knew then that you were Simon and I should marry you.

PRINCE. I knew directly when I saw you that I should marry you, even if you were Dulcibella. By the way, which of you am I marrying?

PRINCESS. When she lifts her veil, it will be Camilla. (Voices are heard outside.) Until then it will be Dulcibella.

PRINCE (in a whisper). Then good-bye, Camilla, until you lift your veil.

PRINCESS. Good-bye, Simon, until you raise your visor. (The KING and QUEEN come in arm-in-arm, followed by CARLO and DULCIBELLA,

john evans

also arm-in-arm. The CHANCELLOR *precedes them, walking backwards, at a loyal angle.)*

PRINCE *(supporting the* CHANCELLOR *as an accident seems inevitable).* Careful! *(The* CHANCELLOR *turns indignantly round.)*

KING. Who and what is this? More accurately, who and what are all these?

CARLO. My attendant, Carlo, Your Majesty. He will, with Your Majesty's permission, prepare me for the ceremony. *(The* PRINCE *bows.)*

KING. Of course, of course!

QUEEN *(to* DULCIBELLA*).* Your maid, Dulcibella, is it not, my love? *(DUL-CIBELLA nods violently.)* I thought so. *(To* CARLO.*) She* will prepare Her Royal Highness. *(The* PRINCESS *curtsies.)*

KING. Ah, yes. Yes. *Most* important.

PRINCESS *(curtsying).* I beg pardon, Your Majesty, if I've done wrong, but I found the gentleman wandering—

KING *(crossing to her).* Quite right, my dear, quite right. *(He pinches her cheek, and takes advantage of this kingly gesture to say in a loud whisper)* We've pulled it off! *(They sit down; the* KING *and* QUEEN *on their thrones,* DULCIBELLA *on the princess' throne.* CARLO *stands behind* DULCIBELLA, *the* CHANCELLOR *on the right of the* QUEEN, *and the* PRINCE *and* PRINCESS *behind the long seat on the left.)*

CHANCELLOR *(consulting documents).* H'r'm! Have I Your Majesty's authority to put the final test to His Royal Highness?

QUEEN *(whispering to the* KING*).* Is this safe?

KING *(whispering).* Perfectly, my dear. I told him the answer a minute ago. *(Over his shoulder to* CARLO.*)* Don't forget. *Dog. (Aloud.)* Proceed, Your Excellency. It is my desire that the affairs of my country should ever be conducted in a strictly constitutional manner.

CHANCELLOR *(oratorically).* By the constitution of the country, a suitor to Her Royal Highness' hand cannot be deemed successful until he has given the correct answer to a riddle. *(Conversationally.)* The last suitor answered incorrectly, and thus failed to win his bride.

KING. By a coincidence he fell into the moat.

CHANCELLOR *(to* CARLO*).* I have now to ask Your Royal Highness if you are prepared for the ordeal?

CARLO *(cheerfully).* Absolutely.

CHANCELLOR. I may mention, as a matter, possibly, of some slight historical interest to our visitor, that by the constitution of the country the same riddle is not allowed to be asked on two successive occasions.

KING *(startled).* What's that?

CHANCELLOR. This one, it is interesting to recall, was propounded exactly a century ago, and we must take it as a fortunate omen that it was well and truly solved.

KING *(to the* QUEEN*).* I may want my sword directly.

CHANCELLOR. The riddle is this. What is it which has four legs and mews like a cat?

CARLO *(promptly).* A dog.

KING *(still more promptly).* Bravo, bravo! *(He claps loudly and nudges the* QUEEN, *who claps too.)*

CHANCELLOR *(peering at his documents).* According to the records of the occasion to which I referred, the correct answer would seem to be—

PRINCESS *(to the* PRINCE*).* Say something, quick!

CHANCELLOR.—not dog, but—

PRINCE. Your Majesty, have I permission to speak? Naturally His Royal Highness could not think of justifying himself on such an occasion, but

I think that with Your Majesty's gracious permission, I could—

KING. Certainly, certainly.

PRINCE. In our country, we have an animal to which we have given the name "dog," or, in the local dialect of the more mountainous districts, "doggie." It sits by the fireside and purrs.

CARLO. That's right. It purrs like anything.

PRINCE. When it needs milk, which is its staple food, it mews.

CARLO *(enthusiastically)*. Mews like nobody's business.

PRINCE. It also has four legs.

CARLO. One at each corner.

PRINCE. In some countries, I understand, this animal is called a "cat." In one distant country to which His Royal Highness and I penetrated it was called by the very curious name of "hippopotamus."

CARLO. That's right. *(To the PRINCE.)* Do you remember that ginger-coloured hippopotamus which used to climb onto my shoulder and lick my ear?

PRINCE. I shall never forget it, sir. *(To the KING.)* So you see, Your Majesty—

KING. Thank you. I think that makes it perfectly clear. *(Firmly to the CHANCELLOR.)* You are about to agree?

CHANCELLOR. Undoubtedly, Your Majesty. May I be the first to congratulate His Royal Highness on solving the riddle so accurately?

KING. You may be the first to see that all is in order for an immediate wedding.

CHANCELLOR. Thank you, Your Majesty. *(He bows and withdraws. The KING rises, as do the QUEEN and DULCIBELLA.)*

KING *(to CARLO)*. Doubtless, Prince Simon, you will wish to retire and prepare yourself for the ceremony.

CARLO. Thank you, sir.

PRINCE. Have I Your Majesty's permission to attend His Royal Highness? It is the custom of his country for Princes of the royal blood to be married in full armour, a matter which requires a certain adjustment—

KING. Of course, of course. *(CARLO bows to the KING and QUEEN and goes out. As the PRINCE is about to follow, the KING stops him.)* Young man, you have a quality of quickness which I admire. It is my pleasure to reward it in any way which commends itself to you.

PRINCE. Your Majesty is ever gracious. May I ask for my reward *after* the ceremony? *(He catches the eye of the PRINCESS, and they give each other a secret smile.)*

KING. Certainly. *(The PRINCE bows and goes out. To DULCIBELLA.)* Now, young woman, make yourself scarce. You've done your work excellently, and we will see that you and your—what was his name?

DULCIBELLA. Eg, Your Majesty.

KING.—that you and your Eg are not forgotten.

DULCIBELLA. Coo! *(She curtsies and goes out.)*

PRINCESS *(calling)*. Wait for me, Dulcibella!

KING *(to the QUEEN)*. Well, my dear, we may congratulate ourselves. As I remember saying to somebody once, "You have not lost a daughter, you have gained a son." How does he strike you?

QUEEN. Stupid.

KING. They made a very handsome pair, I thought, he and Dulcibella.

QUEEN. Both stupid.

KING. I said nothing about stupidity. What I *said* was that they were both extremely handsome. That is the important thing. *(Struck by a sudden idea.)* Or isn't it?

QUEEN. What do *you* think of Prince Simon, Camilla?

PRINCESS. I adore him. We shall be so happy together.

KING. Well, of course you will. I told you so. Happy ever after.

QUEEN. Run along now and get ready.

PRINCESS. Yes, mother. *(She throws a kiss to them and goes out.)*

KING *(anxiously).* My dear, have we been wrong about Camilla all this time? It seemed to me that she wasn't looking *quite* so plain as usual just now. Did *you* notice anything?

QUEEN *(carelessly).* Just the excitement of the marriage.

KING *(relieved).* Ah, yes, that would account for it.

✦   ✦   ✦   ✦

DISCUSSION

1. (a) Why did Great-Aunt Malkin hide Camilla's beauty from the world? (b) Do you agree with her idea? Why or why not? (c) How does Camilla show that she is "quite the nicest person in the kingdom"?

2. How princely is Simon?

3. (a) How does the Chancellor conduct himself with the King and Queen? Cite examples to illustrate your answer. (b) Is the Chancellor a fool, as the Queen suggests?

4. (a) What are the King's beliefs about beauty and about marriage? (b) What new idea suddenly strikes him at the end of the play?

5. The opening dialogue between the King and the Chancellor sets the tone of the play. (a) What evidence is there to suggest that the King believes the famous lines he quotes are original with him? (b) How does the Chancellor react to these quotations? (c) What other lines in the opening dialogue are humorous to you?

6. Which lines of the King's instructions to Dulcibella seem especially funny?

7. One source of humor is *incongruity,* or inappropriateness. In "The Ugly Duckling," for example, the King's sleeping with a handkerchief over his face is funny because it is incongruous with our usual concept of a king as stately and dignified. Much of the comedy of "The Ugly Duckling" is dependent on the incongruity between real life and storybook life. What is incongruous about each of the following?

   a. The Queen's saying "Don't do that" to the King, who is whistling while she talks (page 339).

   b. The slowness of the drawbridge (page 341).

   c. Dulcibella's efforts to act like a princess (pages 342–343).

   d. Prince Simon's leg cramp (page 346).

8. What elements of fantasy does the play have?

9. **(a)** What storybook characteristics is Milne satirizing in the play? **(b)** Does Milne criticize any aspects of real life? If so, what is he criticizing? **(c)** Which of the following words best describes the tone of the author's satire: *sneering, serious, light-hearted, critical?* Explain.

10. **(a)** Which of the following characteristics do you think an actor portraying the King should adopt? Give reasons for your choices.

dignity	*pride*
seriousness	*humility*
gaiety	*understanding*
sense of humor	*efficiency*
peevishness	*kindness*
vanity	*self-importance*
wickedness	

(b) Which qualities would apply to the Queen?

WORD STUDY

A dialogue similar to the following might have occurred between the King and Queen after the King's discouraging attempt to teach Dulcibella princesslike behavior. Read the speeches and, with the aid of context clues, find in the list below a synonym for each italicized word. Consult your dictionary if necessary.

warm	*secretly*
discourtesy	*hopeless*
foolish	*baffling*
sameness of sound	*heavy*
unavoidably	*suspiciously*
trick	

KING. My dear! That Dulcibella is such a bubble-brain! The stupidity of her *fatuous* talk will surely drive the prince away and ruin our crafty *ruse*. All she can say is "Coo!" and that in a constant *monotone* as varied as the whine of a mosquito. All my efforts just now were frustrated. I told her

to practice gazing at me with a burning, *ardent* expression, for example—and she turns on me the cold, glassy stare of a fish. I told her she must not call attention to herself after the wedding, but sneak *surreptitiously* away—but she moves with all the delicacy of a troupe of elephants. She'll give us all away; and Prince Simon will find the solution to the riddle just as *elusive* as all the others did.

QUEEN. Oh, dear. It sounds hopeless. Our poor, dear Camilla will *inevitably* die an old maid.

WIDE WORLD PHOTOS

THE AUTHOR

A. A. Milne (1882–1956) wanted to be remembered for such serious writing as *Peace With Honor,* his book condemning war. Yet he is known all over the world for something far different—warm, light-hearted stories featuring Winnie the Pooh, a character whose adventures have signaled bedtime for thousands of children. One of Winnie the Pooh's friends, Christopher Robin, was named for Milne's own son.

Milne was born in London, and after graduating from college in 1903 he became a journalist. Three years of thrifty living in cheap, uncomfortable rooms were followed by a successful career as assistant editor of one of England's leading magazines. After serving in World War I he became a free-lance writer and produced a number of plays and novels. *The Perfect Alibi,* a mystery play, and *The Red House Mystery,* a satirical detective novel, are two of his best-known adult works.

THE UGLY DUCKLING **351**

*What can a robot
teach a man about life?*

VIRTUOSO

HERBERT GOLDSTONE

"SIR?"

The Maestro[1] continued to play, not looking up from the keys.

"Yes, Rollo?"

"Sir, I was wondering if you would explain this apparatus to me."

The Maestro stopped playing, his thin body stiffly relaxed on the bench. His long supple fingers floated off the keyboard.

"Apparatus?" He turned and smiled at the robot. "Do you mean the piano, Rollo?"

"Virtuoso" by Herbert Goldstone. Reprinted by permission of the author.
1. Maestro (mīs′ trō), a master composer or teacher of music. [Italian]

"This machine that produces varying sounds. I would like some information about it, its operation and purpose. It is not included in my reference data."

The Maestro lit a cigarette. He preferred to do it himself. One of his first orders to Rollo when the robot was delivered two days before had been to disregard his built-in instructions on the subject.

"I'd hardly call a piano a machine, Rollo," he smiled, "although technically you are correct. It is actually, I suppose, a machine designed to produce sounds of graduated pitch and tone, singly or in groups."

"I assimilated that much by observation," Rollo replied in a brassy baritone which no longer sent tiny tremors up the Maestro's spine. "Wires of different thickness and tautness struck by felt-covered hammers activated by manually operated levers arranged in a horizontal panel."

"A very cold-blooded description of one of man's nobler works," the Maestro remarked dryly. "You make Mozart and Chopin mere laboratory technicians."

"Mozart? Chopin?" The duralloy sphere that was Rollo's head shone stark and featureless, its immediate surface unbroken but for twin vision lenses. "The terms are not included in my memory banks."

"No, not yours, Rollo," the Maestro said softly. "Mozart and Chopin are not for vacuum tubes and fuses and copper wire. They are for flesh and blood and human tears."

"I do not understand," Rollo droned.

"Well," the Maestro said, smoke curling lazily from his nostrils, "they are two of the humans who compose, or design successions of notes—varying sounds, that is, produced by the piano or by other instruments, machines that produce other types of sounds of fixed pitch and tone.

"Sometimes these instruments, as we call them, are played, or operated, individually: sometimes in groups—orchestras, as we refer to them—and the sounds blend together, they harmonize. That is, they have an orderly, mathematical relationship to each other which results in. . . ."

The Maestro threw up his hands.

"I never imagined," he chuckled, "that I would some day struggle so mightily, and so futilely, to explain music to a robot!"

"Music?"

"Yes, Rollo. The sounds produced by this machine and others of the same category are called music."

"What is the purpose of music, sir?"

"Purpose?"

The Maestro crushed the cigarette in an ash tray. He turned to the keyboard of the concert grand and flexed his fingers briefly.

"Listen, Rollo."

The wraithlike fingers glided and wove the opening bars of "Clair de Lune," slender and delicate as spider silk. Rollo stood rigid, the fluorescent light over the music rack casting a bluish jeweled sheen over his towering bulk, shimmering in the amber vision lenses.

The Maestro drew his hands back from the keys and the subtle thread of melody melted reluctantly into silence.

"Claude Debussy," the Maestro said. "One of our mechanics of an era long past. He designed that succession of tones many years ago. What do you think of it?"

Rollo did not answer at once.

"The sounds were well formed," he replied finally. "They did not jar my auditory senses as some do."

The Maestro laughed. "Rollo, you

may not realize it, but you're a wonderful critic."

"This music, then," Rollo droned. "Its purpose is to give pleasure to humans?"

"Exactly," the Maestro said. "Sounds well formed, that do not jar the auditory senses as some do. Marvelous! It should be carved in marble over the entrance of New Carnegie Hall."

"I do not understand. Why should my definition—?"

The Maestro waved a hand. "No matter, Rollo. No matter."

"Sir?"

"Yes, Rollo?"

"Those sheets of paper you sometimes place before you on the piano. They are the plans of the composer indicating which sounds are to be produced by the piano and in what order?"

"Just so. We call each sound a note; combinations of notes we call chords."

"Each dot, then, indicates a sound to be made?"

"Perfectly correct, my man of metal."

Rollo stared straight ahead. The Maestro felt a peculiar sense of wheels turning within that impregnable sphere.

"Sir, I have scanned my memory banks and find no specific or implied instructions against it. I should like to be taught how to produce these notes on the piano. I request that you feed the correlation between those dots and the levers of the panel into my memory banks."

The Maestro peered at him, amazed. A slow grin traveled across his face.

"Done!" he exclaimed. "It's been many years since pupils helped gray these ancient locks, but I have the feeling that you, Rollo, will prove

a most fascinating student. To instill the Muse[2] into metal and machinery . . . I accept the challenge gladly!" He rose, touched the cool latent power of Rollo's arm.

"Sit down here, my Rolleindex Personal Robot, Model M-e. We shall start Beethoven spinning in his grave—or make musical history."

More than an hour later the Maestro yawned and looked at his watch.

"It's late," he spoke into the end of the yawn. "These old eyes are not tireless like yours, my friend." He touched Rollo's shoulder. "You have the complete fundamentals of musical notation in your memory banks, Rollo. That's a good night's lesson, particularly when I recall how long it took me to acquire the same amount of information. Tomorrow we'll attempt to put those awesome fingers of yours to work."

He stretched. "I'm going to bed," he said. "Will you lock up and put out the lights?"

Rollo rose from the bench. "Yes, sir," he droned. "I have a request."

"What can I do for my star pupil?"

"May I attempt to create some sounds with the keyboard tonight? I will do so very softly so as not to disturb you."

"Tonight? Aren't you—?" Then the Maestro smiled. "You must pardon me, Rollo. It's still a bit difficult for me to realize that sleep has no meaning for you."

He hesitated, rubbing his chin. "Well, I suppose a good teacher should not discourage impatience to learn. All right, Rollo, but please be careful." He patted the polished mahogany. "This piano and I have been together

---

2. **Muse,** one of the nine Greek goddesses of the fine arts and sciences. Here, the expression is extended to mean musical inspiration in general.

for many years. I'd hate to see its teeth knocked out by those sledge-hammer digits of yours. Lightly, my friend, very lightly."

"Yes, sir."

The Maestro fell asleep with a faint smile on his lips, dimly aware of the shy, tentative notes that Rollo was coaxing forth.

Then gray fog closed in and he was in that half-world where reality is dreamlike and dreams are real. It was soft and feathery and lavender clouds and sounds were rolling and washing across his mind in flowing waves.

Where? The mist drew back a bit and he was in red velvet and deep and the music swelled and broke over him.

He smiled.

My recording. Thank you, thank you, thank—

The Maestro snapped erect, threw the covers aside.

He sat on the edge of the bed, listening.

He groped for his robe in the darkness, shoved bony feet into his slippers.

He crept, trembling uncontrollably, to the door of his studio and stood there, thin and brittle in the robe.

The light over the music rack was an eerie island in the brown shadows of the studio. Rollo sat at the keyboard, prim, inhuman, rigid, twin lenses focused somewhere off into the shadows.

The massive feet working the pedals, arms and hands flashing and glinting—they were living entities, separate, somehow, from the machined perfection of his body.

The music rack was empty.

A copy of Beethoven's "Appassionata" lay closed on the bench. It had been, the Maestro remembered, in a pile of sheet music on the piano.

Rollo was playing it.

He was creating it, breathing it, drawing it through silver flame.

Time became meaningless, suspended in midair.

The Maestro didn't realize he was weeping until Rollo finished the sonata.

The robot turned to look at the Maestro. "The sounds," he droned. "They pleased you?"

The Maestro's lips quivered. "Yes, Rollo," he replied at last. "They pleased me." He fought the lump in his throat.

He picked up the music in fingers that shook.

"This," he murmured. "Already?"

"It has been added to my store of data," Rollo replied. "I applied the principles you explained to me to these plans. It was not very difficult."

The Maestro swallowed as he tried to speak. "It was not very difficult. . . ." he repeated softly.

The old man sank down slowly onto the bench next to Rollo, stared silently at the robot as though seeing him for the first time.

Rollo got to his feet.

The Maestro let his fingers rest on the keys, strangely foreign now.

"Music!" he breathed. "I may have heard it that way in my soul. I know Beethoven did!"

He looked up at the robot, a growing excitement in his face.

"Rollo," he said, his voice straining to remain calm. "You and I have some work to do tomorrow on your memory banks."

Sleep did not come again that night.

He strode briskly into the studio the next morning. Rollo was vacuuming the carpet. The Maestro preferred carpets to the new dust-free plastics, which felt somehow profane to his feet.

The Maestro's house was, in fact, an oasis of anachronisms in a desert of contemporary antiseptic efficiency.

"Well, are you ready for work, Rollo?" he asked. "We have a lot to do, you and I. I have such plans for you, Rollo — great plans!"

Rollo, for once, did not reply.

"I have asked them all to come here this afternoon," the Maestro went on. "Conductors, concert pianists, composers, my manager. All the giants of music, Rollo. Wait until they hear you play."

Rollo switched off the vacuum and stood quietly.

"You'll play for them right here this afternoon." The Maestro's voice was high-pitched, breathless. "The 'Appassionata' again, I think. Yes, that's it. I must see their faces!

"Then we'll arrange a recital to introduce you to the public and the critics and then a major concert with one of the big orchestras. We'll have it telecast around the world, Rollo. It can be arranged.

"Think of it, Rollo, just think of it! The greatest piano virtuoso of all time . . . a robot! It's completely fantastic and completely wonderful. I feel like an explorer at the edge of a new world."

He walked feverishly back and forth.

"Then recordings, of course. My entire repertoire, Rollo, and more. So much more!"

"Sir?"

The Maestro's face shone as he looked up at him. "Yes, Rollo?"

"In my built-in instructions, I have the option of rejecting any action which I consider harmful to my owner," the robot's words were precise, carefully selected. "Last night you wept. That is one of the indications I am instructed to consider in making my decisions."

The Maestro gripped Rollo's thick, superbly molded arm.

"Rollo, you don't understand. That was for the moment. It was petty of me, childish!"

"I beg your pardon, sir, but I must refuse to approach the piano again."

The Maestro stared at him, unbelieving, pleading.

"Rollo, you can't! The world must hear you!"

"No, sir." The amber lenses almost seemed to soften.

"The piano is not a machine," that powerful inhuman voice droned. "To me, yes. I can translate the notes into sounds at a glance. From only a few I am able to grasp at once the composer's conception. It is easy for me."

Rollo towered magnificently over the Maestro's bent form.

"I can also grasp," the brassy monotone rolled through the studio, "that this . . . music is not for robots. It is for man. To me it is easy, yes . . . . It was not meant to be easy."

✦   ✦   ✦   ✦

DISCUSSION

DISCUSSION

1. Why does the Maestro object when Rollo refers to the piano as a *machine* and an *apparatus?*

2. (**a**) What is the Maestro's first reaction to Rollo's musical ability? (**b**) Why does he weep on hearing Rollo play? (**c**) Why do you think he wants Rollo to perform in public? (**d**) Is the Maestro vain, as Goldstone suggests in the article in the next column?

3. (**a**) Why does Rollo reject the Maestro's plan for him? (**b**) Is Rollo's reaction to the Maestro's request emotional or mechanical? Explain.

4. Which of the following sentences best states the theme of the story? Give reasons for your choice. (**a**) Robots will be common items in the future. (**b**) True art is the result of human pain and struggle. (**c**) Machines can produce greater art than men can.

5. Do you think fantasy is a good way of presenting the theme? Why or why not?

WORD STUDY

In 1920, the Czechoslovakian playwright Karel Capek wrote *R.U.R.*, a play about a rebellion at Rossum's Universal Robots, a factory that manufactures mechanical men for cheap labor. The theme of Capek's play is the loss of human individuality in the mechanized twentieth century. For his play, Capek drew on the Czech word for "work," *robota,* to invent the now familiar word *robot.*

Like *robot*, the six words listed below are familiar terms in the Machine Age. Use your dictionary to answer the following questions about their origins.

automation	*jet*
technology	*nuclear*
atom	*astronaut*

1. Which word is a recent blending of a Greek word meaning *self-acting* and the Latin word for *work?*

2. Which word comes from *nut* in Latin?

3. Which word combines the Greek words for *star* and *ship?*

4. Which word is derived from the French verb *to throw?*

5. Which word comes from a Greek word used to describe an object so small it can't be divided?

6. Which word combines the Greek words meaning *study* or *treatment* and *art* or *craft?*

FROM THE AUTHOR

"Virtuoso," which was written one quiet night in 1952, is one of a small handful of short stories I have had published and my own overwhelming favorite. It was actually the result of a vague idea that had been perking for a year or two. Originally, I toyed with the notion of a story about a famous concert pianist who had hurt his hands and tried to fake a performance by having records play off stage while he pretended to play at the keyboard. For one reason or another, it just didn't jell and, without warning, my old love for science fiction stepped in and took over. I used to gorge myself on rocket ships and space travel when they were still fiction. The idea of a robot learning to play a piano and becoming an instant master just hit me and the story wrote itself. The original title was "Finale," by the way, but the magazine that accepted it already had a story by that name scheduled and suggested "Virtuoso."

Music is big in the Goldstone family and I wrote with some amateurish familiarity with the subject. I'm not familiar with robots, but neither is anyone else, so I felt on safe grounds. That's one advantage to imaginative fiction. Nobody can argue with you.

In a way, I was sorry the story ended the way it did. Rollo was understandably out to protect the Maestro's vanity, but it would have been great to see Rollo perform with the New York Philharmonic. Oh well.

Metropolitan Nightmare

STEPHEN VINCENT BENÉT

IT RAINED quite a lot that spring. You woke in the morning
And saw the sky still clouded, the streets still wet,
But nobody noticed so much, except the taxis
And the people who parade. You don't, in a city.
The parks got very green. All the trees were green   5
Far into July and August, heavy with leaf,
Heavy with leaf and the long roots boring and spreading,
But nobody noticed that but the city gardeners
And they don't talk.
             Oh, on Sundays, perhaps you'd notice:
Walking through certain blocks, by the shut, proud houses   10
With the windows boarded, the people gone away,
You'd suddenly see the queerest small shoots of green
Poking through cracks and crevices in the stone
And a bird-sown flower, red on a balcony,
And then you made jokes about grass growing in the streets   15
And politics and grass-roots[1] — and there were songs
And gags and a musical show called "Hot and Wet."
It all made a good box[2] for the papers. When the flamingo
Flew into a meeting of the Board of Estimate,
The new mayor acted at once and called the photographers.   20
When the first green creeper crawled upon Brooklyn Bridge,
They thought it was ornamental. They let it stay.

That was the year the termites came to New York
And they don't do well in cold climates — but listen, Joe,
They're only ants, and ants are nothing but insects.   25
It was funny and yet rather wistful, in a way
(As Heywood Broun pointed out in the *World-Telegram*)[3]
To think of them looking for wood in a steel city.
It made you feel about life. It was too divine.
There were funny pictures by all the smart, funny artists   30
And Macy's[4] ran a terribly clever ad:
"The Widow's Termite"[5] or something.

"Metropolitan Nightmare" from THE SELECTED WORKS OF STEPHEN VINCENT BENÉT. Holt, Rinehart and Winston, Inc. Copyright, 1933, by Stephen Vincent Benét. Copyright renewed © 1961, by Rosemary Carr Benét. Reprinted by permission of Brandt & Brandt.
1. **grass-roots,** a term used in politics to refer to all the ordinary citizens of a political district, here used as a pun.
2. **box,** feature story set off by lines in a newspaper.
3. **Heywood Broun . . . World Telegram,** a popular columnist who wrote for the New York *World-Telegram*.
4. **Macy's,** large New York department store.
5. **"Widow's Termite,"** a word play on "widow's mite," a term from the Bible referring to any small contribution willingly given by a poor person. [Mark 12:42]

There was no
Disturbance. Even the Communists didn't protest
And say they were Morgan hirelings.[6] It was too hot,
Too hot to protest, too hot to get excited,   35
An even African heat, lush, fertile and steamy,
That soaked into bone and mind and never once broke.
The warm rain fell in fierce showers and ceased and fell.
Pretty soon you got used to it always being that way.

You got used to the changed rhythm, the altered beat,   40
To people walking slower, to the whole bright
Fierce pulse of the city slowing, to men in shorts,
To the new sun-helmets from Best's[7] and the cops' white uniforms,
And the long noon-rest in the offices, everywhere.
It wasn't a plan or anything. It just happened.   45
The fingers tapped slower, the office-boys
Dozed on their benches, the bookkeeper yawned at his desk.
The A.T.&T.[8] was the first to change the shifts
And establish an official siesta-room;
But they were always efficient. Mostly it just   50
Happened like sleep itself, like a tropic sleep,
Till even the Thirties[9] were deserted at noon
Except for a few tourists and one damp cop.
They ran boats to see the big lilies on the North River
But it was only the tourists who really noticed   55
The flocks of rose-and-green parrots and parakeets
Nesting in the stone crannies of the Cathedral.
The rest of us had forgotten when they first came.

There wasn't any real change, it was just a heat spell,
A rain spell, a funny summer, a weather-man's joke,   60
In spite of the geraniums three feet high
In the tin-can gardens of Hester and Desbrosses.[10]
New York was New York. It couldn't turn inside out.
When they got the news from Woods Hole about the Gulf Stream,[11]
The *Times* ran an adequate story.   65
But nobody reads those stories but science-cranks.

---

6. *Even the Communists . . . Morgan hirelings.* Even the Communists didn't accuse the termites of working for J. Pierpont Morgan, the wealthy New York capitalist.
7. *Best's,* New York department store.
8. *A.T.&T.,* the huge American Telephone and Telegraph Corporation.
9. *Thirties,* the garment district in New York from 30th to 39th streets. Its principal thoroughfare is 34th Street, where both the Empire State Building and Macy's stand.
10. *Hester and Desbrosses,* slum districts.
11. *Woods Hole . . . Gulf Stream.* The Marine Biological Laboratory is at Woods Hole, a town on the eastern tip of Cape Cod in Massachusetts; the Gulf Stream, the Atlantic Ocean current originating in the Gulf of Mexico, affects weather in the United States and western Europe. The laboratory has noted a definite alteration in the Gulf current, indicating a permanent change in climate.

Until, one day, a somnolent city-editor
Gave a new cub the termite yarn to break his teeth on.
The cub was just down from Vermont, so he took his time.
He was serious about it. He went around. 70
He read all about termites in the Public Library
And it made him sore when they fired him.
                                    So, one evening,
Talking with an old watchman, beside the first
Raw girders of the new Planetopolis Building
(Ten thousand brine-cooled offices, each with shower) 75
He saw a dark line creeping across the rubble
And turned a flashlight on it.
                                "Say, buddy," he said,
"You better look out for those ants. They eat wood, you know,
They'll have your shack down in no time."
                              The watchman spat.
"Oh, they've quit eating wood," he said in a casual voice, 80
"I thought everybody knew that."
                          —And, reaching down,
He pried from the insect jaws the bright crumb of steel.

DISCUSSION

1. (a) What changes described in lines 1–39 indicate that New York is turning into a tropical area? (b) How do various residents react to these changes?
2. How do living and working habits change, according to lines 40–58?
3. What is the feeling among the population when the climate change is officially noted?
4. Why is the reporter fired?
5. (a) What is the watchman's attitude toward the termites? (b) What does the last line of the poem imply about the future?
6. (a) Why does the author repeat the words "Nobody noticed," "It just happened," and "You got used to it"? (b) Whose attitude, the watchman's or the reporter's, represents that of people in general? Explain. (c) State the theme of the poem in a sentence or two.
7. (a) What makes "Metropolitan Nightmare" a fantasy? (b) Is fantasy an effective way for Benét to make his point? Explain.

THE AUTHOR

Stephen Vincent Benét (1898–1943) was the son of a dedicated army man from whom he inherited a great love for the United States. His strong feelings for his native land influenced his writing: many of his short stories and poems deal with the glory and the heroism of America's past. Nevertheless, he was also aware of the shortcomings of humanity, as evident in works such as "Metropolitan Nightmare."

At thirteen Benét won his first literary prize —three dollars in a poetry-writing contest. At thirty-one, with *John Brown's Body,* a poem about the Civil War, he won the Pulitzer Prize.

As a young man, Benet traveled in Paris, where he met Rosemary Carr. After their marriage, they collaborated in many writings, their best-known joint effort being *A Book of Americans,* a collection of poems about America's heroes.

UNIT 4 *Review*

Part 1

1. (a) In your opinion, which selections in the unit would the aunt in "The Storyteller" have judged most suitable for young people? least suitable? Give reasons for your answers. **(b)** Which would her nieces and nephew have most enjoyed? Why?

2. (a) In which selections does the fantasy fall into the realm of future possibility? **(b)** Which selections contain incredible events of magic and the supernatural? **(c)** Which selections introduce fantasy into the animal kingdom?

3. (a) What criticisms of people are made in "The Monsters Are Due on Maple Street" and "Metropolitan Nightmare"? **(b)** Do you think these criticisms are justified? Explain.

Part 2

The Government of Mars
Department of Studies in
Solar System Societies
Bureau of Earth Studies
American Section

Report # 17
To: All Department Heads
From: Agent Hwholl
Subject: Ingestion ("eating"), further customs of.

For this report I chose to observe two of the human species, one male and one female, engaged in ingestion at a "restaurant." The first curious matter occurred when the "waiter" appeared at the table. The male inquired of the female what she desired. She replied in a normal tone of voice that she would have "roast beef medium rare." The male then turned to the waiter and said, "She will have roast beef medium rare"—the exact words used by the female. Because I had no diffi-culty in understanding her, the only explanation I can propose for the male's repetition is that perhaps waiters are a class of individuals not attuned to tones of female speech.

Next in peculiarity was the manner of consuming meat. Each took a pronged utensil ("fork") in one hand, and a flat blade ("knife") in the other, cut off a small square of meat, laid down knife, changed fork to other hand, inserted piece in mouth, and chewed. Immediately afterward, each again changed fork to other hand, picked up knife, cut off another small square, laid down knife, changed fork to other hand, and inserted in the mouth another piece. The strange things about this operation are the apparently pointless efforts involved in cutting one piece at a time and shuffling fork from hand to hand. I can offer no theories for these actions.

Also unaccountable is the way in which both creatures maintained one of their appendages under the table at all times (except, of course, during cutting)—almost as though they were reluctant to offend the other with the sight of it. . . .

1. What makes the preceding article a fantasy?

2. (a) What is the author satirizing in the selection? **(b)** How do the efforts of the Martian to find reasons for the humans' behavior help emphasize the point of the satire?

3. Point out examples of exaggeration used to create humor.

4. How would you describe the tone of the article?

SUGGESTED READING

BRADBURY, RAY, *The Martian Chronicles.* (Doubleday) A master of science fiction tells a series of frightening stories about an expedition to Mars in the twenty-first century.

CLEMENS, SAMUEL, *A Connecticut Yankee in King Arthur's Court.* (**Harper) A practical Yankee finds himself an associate of King Arthur and his Knights of the Round Table in this amusing novel by one of America's best storytellers.

CROSS, JOHN KIER, *The Angry Planet.* (Coward) A Scottish scientist and an English novelist take off for Mars in their privately constructed spaceship only to discover that they have three stowaways aboard. All five of the space travelers collaborate to produce this account of their other-worldly adventures.

GRAHAME, KENNETH, *The Wind in the Willows.* (**Scribner) This is an imaginative story about Water Rat, who enjoys messing around in boats, Toad, who is enthusiastic about caravans and cars, and Badger, who is ruled by boyish impulses.

HEINLEIN, ROBERT A., *Rolling Stones.* (Scribner) One of the most popular of the science-fiction writers tells an amusing story of a family who starts out for an asteroid in a second-hand spaceship.

IRVING, WASHINGTON, *The Bold Dragoon and Other Ghostly Tales,* selected and edited by A. C. Moore. (Knopf) Washington Irving was a master at creating an atmosphere of the fantastic in his out-of-this-world tales. These five of his best are guaranteed to make shivers tingle your spine.

JONES, LOUIS, *Spooks of the Valley.* (Houghton) Hudson River Valley ghost stories are not only absorbing in themselves; they also give picturesque information about bygone days in the region. Among the famous "spooks" who appear are Captain Kidd, Aaron Burr, and others who helped make tradition and history.

LAWSON, MARIE, *Strange is the Sea.* (Viking) Gathered here are a number of strange legends and superstitions of the sea. Watery ghosts will chill your blood as rapidly as do the kind who haunt the earth.

L'ENGLE, MADELEINE, *Wrinkle in Time.* (Farrar) Meg, her brother, and a friend go in search of Meg's father, a scientist who disappeared while engaged in secret work for the government. Their search takes them to a planet ruled by hostile beings.

MERRILL, JEAN, *The Pushcart War.* (**Grosset) The author reports on a war that takes place in 1976 between the truck drivers and pushcart peddlers of New York City. Tacks and pea shooters are the peddlers' weapons in this funny satire on modern life.

SAINT-EXUPÉRY, ANTOINE DE, *The Little Prince.* (Houghton) The author meets the Little Prince when he is forced to land his plane in the Sahara. The prince is from another planet, and while talking of his own world and the others he visited on the way to earth, he and the author contemplate the important things in life.

SERLING, ROD, *Rod Serling's Twilight Zone,* adapted by Walter B. Gibson. (Grosset) Reality is suspended in these thirteen stories based on the popular television series.

VERNE, JULES, *20,000 Leagues Under the Sea.* (Scribner *Associated Booksellers) This amazing book, written during the nineteenth century, tells the tale of Captain Nemo and his submarine Nautilus.

WIBBERLEY, LEONARD, *The Mouse that Roared.* (Doubleday *Dell) A tiny nation in need of money declares war on the United States because that country is known to be good to its defeated enemies. By a series of freak accidents, the small nation wins the war. If you like satire, you'll enjoy this humorous, yet thoughtful, book.

*paperback
**paperback and hardcover

*A word can be made to suggest many things
beyond its usual meanings.
A few lines arranged in a careful structure
can reveal an idea.
A poem, no matter how short, can probe deeply
into emotion and thought and
human experience.*

POETRY II

Poets provide new insights into old tales . . .

The Builders

SARA HENDERSON HAY

I told them a thousand times if I told them once:
Stop fooling around, I said, with straw and sticks;
They won't hold up; you're taking an awful chance.
Brick is the stuff to build with, solid bricks.
You want to be impractical, go ahead.   5
But just remember, I told them; wait and see.
You're making a big mistake. Awright, I said,
But when the wolf comes, don't come running to me.

The funny thing is, they didn't. There they sat,
One in his crummy yellow shack, and one   10
Under his roof of twigs, and the wolf ate
Them, hair and hide. Well, what is done is done.
But I'd been willing to help them, all along,
If only they'd once admitted they were wrong.

DISCUSSION

1. (a) Who is the speaker in this poem? **(b)** What is the first clue to his identity? **(c)** What story is he telling?
2. (a) What do the words, "What is done is done" indicate about the speaker's attitude toward his brothers? **(b)** Why is he telling this story? **(c)** Does he succeed in his purpose? Explain.
3. Which of the following characteristics does the speaker reveal: **(a)** self-righteousness; **(b)** concern for others; **(c)** selfishness; **(d)** practicality; **(e)** guilt. Defend your answers with logical arguments.
4. (a) Which lines summarize the point the speaker is making? **(b)** How does this version of the old story differ from the original? **(c)** What application does Miss Hay's version have to people?

The Fox and the Grapes / *MARIANNE MOORE*

A fox of Gascon, though some say of Norman descent,[1]
When starved till faint gazed up at a trellis to which grapes were tied —
    Matured till they glowed with a purplish tint
    As though there were gems inside.
Now grapes were what our adventurer on strained haunches chanced to crave,
    But because he could not reach the vine   6
He said, "These grapes are sour; I'll leave them for some knave."
Better, I think, than an embittered whine.

THE AUTHOR

The language of poetry, said Marianne Moore (1887–1972) substitutes "compactness for confusion." Miss Moore, whose poetry says a great deal with a few words, won many awards for her work, including the Pulitzer Prize. Fascinated by everything that happened around her, she revealed in her writing keen insights into men and nature. As both poet and woman she "watched life with affection."

DISCUSSION

1. (a) Summarize the incident described in this poem. (b) What doubt does the speaker express in the first line? (c) Does his doubt give the incident an air of reality or unreality? Explain.
2. (a) What image does the poet give you of the grapes? (b) Does the image help you understand the fox's predicament?
3. The speaker does not merely report the facts; he comments on them. (a) What tone does he adopt as commentator? (b) Find words and phrases that indicate his attitude. For example, what does he suggest by the expression, "our adventurer"?
4. The fable on which this poem is based usually ends with a line such as, "It is easy to despise what you cannot have." Does the last line of the poem suggest the same meaning? Explain.

"The Fox and the Grapes" translated by Marianne Moore. From THE MARIANNE MOORE READER. ALL Rights Reserved. Reprinted by permission of The Viking Press, Inc.
1. **Gascon . . . Norman descent.** The speaker is unsure of what part of France the fox comes from. Gascony and Normandy are names of provinces in southwestern and northern France, respectively.

See
FIGURATIVE LANGUAGE
Handbook
of Literary
Terms
page 522

Three views of death
by three different poets . . .

Requiem for a Modern Croesus

LEW SARETT

To him the moon was a silver dollar, spun
Into the sky by some mysterious hand; the sun
Was a gleaming golden coin——
    His to purloin;
The freshly minted stars were dimes of delight   5
Flung out upon the counter of the night.

In yonder room he lies,
With pennies on his eyes.

DISCUSSION

1. Look up *requiem* and *Croesus* in the Glossary. What does the title of the poem tell you about its subject?
2. (a) What sort of person was the dead man? **(b)** Point out figurative expressions that help define his character. **(c)** Why are they appropriate to a "modern Croesus"?
3. (a) Which of the following words describes the speaker's attitude toward the dead man: *cold; sympathetic; pitying*? **(b)** What does the speaker's choice of details contribute to your understanding of his attitude?
4. (a) What contrast does the poet point out with the literal statement made in the closing couplet? **(b)** What theme is implied by this contrast?

THE AUTHOR

Lew Sarett (1888–1954), who was for many years a teacher, spent much of his youth working as a guide and forest ranger. These experiences helped him to develop a great love for the earth and the things that grow and live upon it. He preferred simple, honest people to the type described in the above poem. Much of Sarett's poetry is about nature; the American Indians were another of his favorite subjects.

From COVENANT WITH EARTH by Lew Sarett. Edited and copyrighted, 1956, by Alma Johnson Sarett. Gainesville: University of Florida Press, 1956. Reprinted by permission of Mrs. Sarett.

To a Dead Goldfish

O. B. HARDISON, JR.

Stirring with oars of filmy gold
The glassy tide that round him rolled,
He ruled two quarts of universe
And gave no subject ground to curse.

The snail in peace devoured the slime,   5
The seed toward heaven did greenly climb,
The fry disported in the deep,
Knowing their lord the watch did keep.

Splendid to see, upon his flanks
Grew golden scales in glittering ranks;   10
His gills were red, his belly white,
And from his regal eyes, a light

Appeared to stream. Serene, benign,
His sovereign touch would calm the brine,
And even unhallowed Tabby's claw   15
Recoiled from him in holy awe.

Still would he rule and swim, but Fate
(which must to all men soon or late)
Gave him the last and bitter cup:
Now see him floating, bottoms up.

DISCUSSION

1. What are the "two quarts of universe" that the goldfish ruled?
2. (a) Trace the various ways in which the goldfish is compared to a ruler. (b) What kind of ruler was he?
3. (a) What impression do you get of the goldfish in the first four stanzas of the poem? (b) How is this impression altered in lines 17–20? (c) What tone does the poet give the poem through this complete reversal? (d) Does the poem have a theme, or a moral, or is it simply meant to amuse? Explain.

Artifact

SHEILA PRITCHARD

Our dog died last winter
on Abraham Lincoln's birthday to be exact.
Disease: this culture;
specific: traffic.

And a path beneath the apple tree 5
tamped by her running feet
winds dank under the comparatively permanent sun
now northward moving reminding the apple tree and the codling moth
that time of sleep and frost is done.

I wonder and I remember 10
other springs, other romances,
for she was a restless hunter
able to leap fences:
she made chances, baited with love for curious life.

The prancing squirrel who burrows the cherry tree kernels, 15
advances freed from her furious threat and rebuff.
A bone she buried may turn up among the lilies,
and I shall walk under the apple tree over her furrow.

DISCUSSION

1. (a) Explain when and how the dog died. (b) Why is culture referred to as a *disease*? (c) In view of the situation is the word used appropriately? Why or why not?

2. (a) What inferences can you make from stanza 2 as to the time of year in which the poem is set? (b) Is "comparatively permanent" a good description of the sun in this particular season? (c) What is described as "northward moving" (line 8)?

3. (a) What does the speaker recall in stanza 3? (b) What does "made chances" reveal about the dog's spirit? (c) Would "took chances" reveal the same characteristics?

4. (a) What may happen to remind the speaker of the dog? (b) What other reminders of her remain?

5. In archaeology, remnants of past civilizations are called *artifacts*. What is the "artifact" in this poem?

6. Read "From the Author," in which the poet comments on "Artifact." (a) According to the poet, what ideas does she wish to bring to mind by mentioning the bone? (b) In what way is the title an indication that the poem is more than a remembrance of a pet?

FROM THE AUTHOR

A real experience predated "Artifact," for our German short-hair pointer, Wrinkles, four years old, dug out during a thaw in February, and was run over on a nearby street. That spring I could see, as green spread over the yard, the path she'd made from countless journeys about, and in pulling a weed near the Madonna lilies, a rotty old bone did turn up. *Then,* I thought of, or felt, the impact of the past on our land—the archaeological panorama everywhere just under the surface, and under the surface of our minds too, and the poem began. I know I mean more than just our Wrink and her personality—and it was interesting to see what I did have to say, in that poem. For you never know till the end, or till you find out what the end is, and what it's saying.

It doesn't have to rhyme

A poem is what the poet chooses to make it, and it doesn't have to rhyme unless he wants it to. Because the earliest poems we learn are nursery rhymes and jingles, most of us first associate poetry with rhyme. But people identify poetry by many qualities, and much poetry has no rhyme at all.

Just as different kinds of games have their own rules, so different kinds of poems have theirs. You can't play any kind of game well unless you know the rules; poetry becomes more enjoyable when you understand what guideline or pattern the poet is following.

Much poetry written before the twentieth century conformed to very strict rules, or *forms.* But a modern poet sometimes decides that the meaning and emotion he wants to express don't fit into a traditional form. In such a case, the poet is free to develop a new form to fit what he wants to say.

Let's examine just a few of the many ways of putting a poem together. A poet can use rhyme to help create mood and melody:

*On either side the river lie
Long fields of barley and of
    rye,
That clothe the world and
    meet the sky;
And through the field the
    road runs by
To many towered
    Camelot.*

Or, if he wishes, he may use words whose meaning and sound combine to establish a mood and create a melody:

*Summer seething with silly-
    simple days
Suns seemingly under bur-
    nished branches . . .*

He may use a very regular rhythm:

*By the shores of Gitche
    Gumee
By the shining Big-Sea-
    Water
Stood the wigwam of No-
    komis,
Daughter of the moon,
    Nokomis.*

Or an irregular rhythm:

*I saw in Louisiana a live-
    oak growing,
All alone stood it and the
    moss hung down from
    the branches,*

*Without any companion it
    grew there uttering
    joyous leaves of dark
    green,
And its look, rude, unbend-
    ing, lusty, made me
    think of myself. . .*

He can use sounds to make a poem move slowly:

*Thou watchest the last
    oozings hours by
    hours . . .*

Or rapidly:

*And wretches hang that jury-
    men may dine . . .*

The poet should use the sound patterns and rhythm and movement that are best suited to his subject matter. For example, a grief-stricken poet would not write:

*Grief is here, grief is there.
Grief is round us every-
    where.*

Can you point out what is inappropriate about these two lines?

Read the following poem to see if you can determine not only what kind of visits the poet is describing, but how he creates a mood and a melody:

Visits

VERN RUTSALA

Strangers invade
the dim façades.
The cracked leather
flanks of suitcases
mutter like saddles.   5
Cousins test each other
on chinning bars
before their heights
are measured back to back.
And soon the houses change: 10
Daybeds convert
themselves obsequiously
to night duties.
Rooms are disarrayed:
Like weak triangles   15
metal coat hangers
on door knobs
ring the dim tunes
of all reunions.

Who are the visitors? How can you tell? Do they come often? What one word answers this question? What seems to be the poet's feeling toward the kind of visits he describes? Explain.

There are no rhyming lines in "Visits," but Rutsala sets up definite sound patterns by repeating certain letters and letter combinations. Where is the **d** sound in **invade** (line 1) repeated? What words echo the vowel sound in **tunes** (line 18)? What other sound patterns are noticeable? Are the letter sounds in the poem light-sounding? If not, what are they? Are they in keeping with the poet's attitude?

Does the poem have a regular or an irregular rhythm? Does the rhythm seem suitable to the poem? Why or why not? Try reading the poem aloud. Do the short lines make you read in a flowing manner or an abrupt one? Is the length of the lines in keeping with the visits? Explain.

Does the poem move rapidly or slowly? Which sounds do the most to influence the movement? Is the movement in keeping with the idea expressed in the poem?

In your opinion, has the poet used the rules appropriate to what he has to say? Be sure you can defend your answer with logical arguments.

In summary, the poet should use the form that best fits his subject matter. He can use an existing set of rules or invent his own. Whichever he does, the poem should be based on careful repetition of rhythms and sounds; but the rhythm doesn't necessarily have to be regular, and the sound patterns don't necessarily have to be rhymes.

Stubborness is sometimes so satisfying.

Time Out

JOHN MONTAGUE

The donkey sat down on the roadside
Suddenly, as though tired of carrying
His cross. There was a varnish
Of sweat on his coat, and a fly
On his left ear. The tinker   5
Beating him finally gave in,
Sat on the grass himself, prying
His coat for his pipe. The donkey
(not beautiful but more fragile
than any swan, with his small   10
front hooves folded under him)
Gathered enough courage to raise
That fearsome head, lip in a daisy,
As if to say—slowly, contentedly—
Yes, there is a virtue in movement,   15
But only in going so far, so fast,
Sucking the sweet grass of stubbornness.

From TIDES by John Montague. Published by the Swallow Press. Reprinted by permission of
the author.

1. (a) What kind of condition is the donkey in? **(b)** What does the poet mean when he says that the donkey sat down "as though tired of carrying His cross"? **(c)** What other indications of the donkey's condition are there in the poem? **(d)** Is there any indication that the donkey may have been abused?

2. (a) What is the donkey figuratively compared to in lines 8–11? **(b)** Have you ever thought of a donkey as "fragile" before? What image makes him seem so? **(c)** Are there any indications that the donkey might sometimes be strong, as well?

3. (a) Restate the last three lines of the poem in your own words. **(b)** What in your opinion could be so satisfying about being stubborn?

Though born in New York City, John Montague has spent much of his life living and writing in Ireland.

His poetry, the chief interest of his literary career, is widely respected and has frequently been praised. In addition to his literary interests, Montague has been a film critic for a Dublin newspaper, a Paris correspondent for the *Irish Times,* and a visiting lecturer at the University of California at Berkeley.

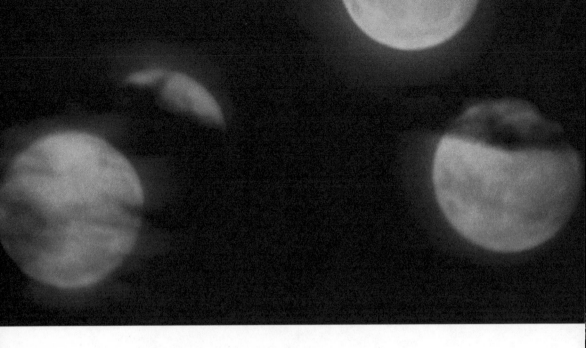

who knows if the moon's
a balloon,coming out of a keen city
in the sky—filled with pretty people?
(and if you and i should

get into it,if they   5
should take me and take you into their balloon,
why then
we'd go up higher with all the pretty people

than houses and steeples and clouds:
go sailing   10
away and away sailing into a keen
city which nobody's ever visited,where

always
      it's
           Spring)and everyone's   15
in love and flowers pick themselves

who knows if the moon's / *E. E. CUMMINGS*

1. (a) What might the speaker think the "pretty people" are like? **(b)** Which images in the poem describe the world of the "pretty people"?

2. Parentheses are used to set off a qualifying or explaining expression in a sentence. Cummings' parentheses enclose almost two-thirds of his entire poem. Read the poem, eliminating the lines enclosed in the parentheses. Then, read only the part which is enclosed. **(a)** What does the poem say when you eliminate the part in parentheses? **(b)** What does the part in the parenthe-ses talk about? **(c)** Read the enclosed lines with expression suitable for these emotions: (1) a wish (almost childlike) to adventure to a new place; (2) an it-doesn't-matter-much feeling; (3) a depressed feeling. Which of the three seems the best considering the total poem? Why?

3. The speaker describes a "keen city which nobody's ever visited." **(a)** Do you think he considers this city "keen" because no-body has ever visited it? Why or why not? **(b)** Why does the speaker seem to suggest a visit to the city?

Fish in tanks
and animals in cages . . .
do they reflect the limitations of man?

At the Aquarium

MAX EASTMAN

Serene the silver fishes glide,
Stern-lipped, and pale, and wonder-eyed!
As through the aged deeps of ocean,
They glide with wan and wavy motion!
They have no pathway where they go.   5
They flow like water to and fro.
They watch with never-winking eyes,
They watch with staring, cold surprise,
The level people in the air,
The people peering, peering there: 10
Who also wander to and fro,
And know not why or where they go,
Yet have a wonder in their eyes,
Sometimes a pale and cold surprise.

DISCUSSION

1. (a) In your own words, tell what picture you get of the fish in the first ten lines. **(b)** How, in the fishes' eyes, might the observers be "level people in the air"?

2. (a) What comparison does the poet make in lines 11–14? **(b)** What comment on human life does it suggest? **(c)** Is the comparison a valid one? Why or why not?

FROM THE AUTHOR

This poem was conceived in 1911 in the Aquarium at Naples, Italy, one of the first public aquariums in which the walls themselves were made of glass, so that people coming in could look straight through at the fish as though dwelling with them under the sea. The first two lines of the poem came to me then and remained in my mind—perhaps also in a notebook—for some four years. Then one day in New York when I had rented a hall-bedroom in which to do my writing apart from family and friends, and had made one of my great (though frail) resolutions to devote my life to poetry, recalling this poem which had been waiting so long for its birth, I sat down and, tranquilly recollecting the emotion, composed it.

Thoughts in a Zoo

COUNTEE CULLEN

They in their cruel traps, and we in ours,
Survey each other's rage, and pass the hours
Commiserating each the other's woe,
To mitigate his own pain's fiery glow.
Man could but little proffer in exchange   5
Save that his cages have a larger range.
That lion with his lordly, untamed heart
Has in some man his human counterpart,
Some lofty soul in dreams and vision wrapped,
But in the stifling flesh securely trapped.   10
Gaunt eagle whose raw pinions stain the bars
That prison you, so men cry for the stars!
Some delve down like the mole far underground,
(Their nature is to burrow, not to bound),
Some, like the snake, with changeless slothful eye,   15
Stir not, but sleep and smoulder where they lie.
Who is most wretched, these caged ones, or we,
Caught in a vastness beyond our sight to see?

DISCUSSION

1. (a) Who are "they" (line 1)? **(b)** Who are "we"? **(c)** What do "they" and "we" have in common?

2. Reword the general statement the speaker makes in lines 5–6.

3. (a) List the four specific comparisons the speaker makes in lines 7–16. **(b)** What kind of person is compared to the lion? **(c)** According to the speaker, how are some people like the eagle? **(d)** Explain the comparison between certain types of men and the mole. **(e)** What sort of people are like the snake?

4. (a) Which lines contain the poem's theme? **(b)** State the theme in a sentence or two. **(c)** What are the similarities in theme between "Thoughts in a Zoo" and "At the Aquarium"?

THE AUTHOR

During his short life, Countee Cullen (1903–1946) became a prominent poet. Though he wrote drama and prose as well as poetry, he is best remembered for his powerful lyrics, which explore the attitudes of men toward one another and the world about them, and reveal both the joyous and sorrowful aspects of the black American heritage

Cullen grew up in New York City, the adopted son of a Methodist minister. In addition to writing poetry, he taught French, and edited a anthology of poetry by black Americans, titled *Caroling Dusk*. Once, when talking about why he wrote poetry, he remarked, "Most things I write I do for the sheer joy of music in them."

*Three poets give
some uncommon insights
into common subjects.*

Street Window / *CARL SANDBURG*

The pawn-shop man knows hunger,
And how far hunger has eaten the heart
Of one who comes with an old keepsake.
Here are wedding rings and baby bracelets,
Scarf pins and shoe buckles, jeweled garters,   5
Old-fashioned knives with inlaid handles,
Watches of old gold and silver,
Old coins worn with finger-marks.
They tell stories.

DISCUSSION

1. Explain the meaning of the first three lines.
2. Pick one of the items in the window. What story does it suggest to you?

From CORNHUSKERS by Carl Sandburg. Copyright 1918 by Holt, Rinehart and Winston, Inc. Copyright 1946 by Carl Sandburg. Reprinted by permission of Holt, Rinehart and Winston, Inc. and Jonathan Cape Ltd.

Primer Lesson / *CARL SANDBURG*

Look out how you use proud words.
When you let proud words go, it is
　　not easy to call them back.
They wear long boots, hard boots; they
　　walk off proud; they can't hear you　　5
　　calling——
Look out how you use proud words.

DISCUSSION

1. What does the speaker mean by "proud words"?
2. What warning does the speaker give users of "proud words"?
3. (a) In what sense do "proud words" wear "long boots, hard boots"? (b) Is this figurative expression appropriate? Why or why not?
4. What effect does the poet achieve by placing the word *calling* in a line by itself?
5. (a) What is the meaning of *primer?* (b) Why might Sandburg consider his warning a "primer lesson"?

THE AUTHOR

In the late nineteenth century, a number of Swedish immigrants with the surname Johnson were living in Galesburg, Illinois. To avoid confusion, August Johnson, a blacksmith with a railroad-construction gang, changed his name to Sandburg. It is likely, however, that August's son, Carl, would have been pleased with the more ordinary name, for he views his poetry as an expression of the experiences, thoughts, and dreams of ordinary people.

Because his family was poor, Carl Sandburg (1878–1967) left school at thirteen to drive a milk truck. While still in his teens he traveled around the country in box cars, making friends with hoboes and working when he needed money. Later, he worked his way through college, did some more traveling —this time as a salesman—and finally took a job in Chicago. That city and its people are the subject of some of his best poems.

Sandburg's talents were not limited to poetry: he wrote children's books, was a noted collector of folklore who did much to popularize folk music, and won recognition as an historian with his six-volume biography of Lincoln. He wrote one of his Lincoln books, *Abe Lincoln Grows Up,* especially for young people.

The Forecast / *DAN JAFFE*

Perhaps our age has driven us indoors
We sprawl in the semi-darkness, dreaming sometimes
Of a vague world spinning in the wind.
But we have snapped our locks, pulled down our shades,
Taken all precautions. We shall not be disturbed.   5
If the earth shakes, it will be on a screen;
And if the prairie wind spills down our streets
And covers us with leaves, the weatherman will tell us.

DISCUSSION

1. (a) What is the meaning of "our age" (line 1)? (b) In what ways might "our age" influence our activities?

2. (a) What kind of forecast is the speaker describing? (b) By what means will we receive it? (c) What has it replaced in our lives?

3. (a) What is the speaker's attitude toward the kind of life he is describing? How can you tell?
(b) Is he at all optimistic about the people who have snapped their locks and pulled down their shades? Explain.

"The Forecast" by Dan Jaffe. Reprinted by permission.

Held Back / *LAURIE ABRAMS*

We oh so badly wish to go
Beyond our fence, beyond to grow,
Yet stopped because of age and such
We're asked to "slow" and use a crutch
Of beaten path and "parents' know,"   5
And so we limp
       And grow too slow.

DISCUSSION

1. Several words and phrases in the poem suggest more than one meaning or thought. Discuss the implications of the following: **(a)** "beyond our fence"; **(b)** "such"; **(c)** "use a crutch/Of beaten path"; **(d)** "so we limp." **2.** Describe the speaker's attitudes and age.

3. (a) What is the tone of the poem? **(b)** Can you find a dominant sound in the poem? **(c)** If so, what is it, and does it weaken or enforce the tone? Explain.

UNIT 5

IN THE BEGINNING . . .
(*a unit of folk literature*)

INTRODUCTION BY SUSAN TAUBES

*To the ancients, the sun, which lit the world when
it arose in the east and blackened it when it sank
into the west, was a majestic and powerful god.
Lightning, and earthquakes, and erupting volcanoes
were the revenge of supernatural beings against
mortals who had aroused their wrath. A small, but
cunning animal was to be more greatly feared than
a huge beast for the cunning one could influence
the spirits. Primitive peoples believed that each
of nature's creatures, forces, and objects had its
own distinct personality. And they told stories*

about the adventures of these things, and of their roles in men's lives.

For untold ages the art of storytelling flourished among people of all races. Throughout the ancient world a rich oral tradition existed prior to the adoption of writing. And, up until comparatively recent times, oral tales continued to be an important form of entertainment and vehicle of culture wherever writing was unknown or literacy the privilege of a few. These stories were not the invention of any one person, but of the collective imagination of a tribe or nation. They did not spring into being, but developed over hundreds of years. They did not remain the same, but changed with time and circumstance and the whims of storytellers. The sum total of these stories which a particular group created for itself is called that people's *folk literature*.

Myths, or stories about gods, spirits, and the origin of things, form an important part of every people's folk literature. This world with its earth, sky, sun, moon, and stars, its variety of living things, its human institutions and customs, has been a source of wonder and perplexity to men always and everywhere. Myths provided answers to such questions as: How did the world come into being? Why must men work, grow old, and die? How did the sun and moon get into the sky? The myths, or answers to these and many more questions prompted by nature and social customs, varied from culture to culture, for each society made its own decisions about the roles man and supernatural beings played in setting up the world and its laws. Every group made its own balance sheet of good and evil. And each decided for itself which factors in men's lives were governed by choice and which were controlled by unrelenting fate.

Another type of story found in the folk literature of most peoples is the *animal tale*. Whether told in Europe, Africa, or America, the animal tale's fa-

vorite theme is how one beast outwits another in situations that listeners could easily apply to themselves. Practical advice or warning is either stated or implied in these tales. Their lessons are geared to survival, and the rewards usually go to the crafty rather than the strong. Like myths, animal tales often explain how various animals acquired certain habits and physical traits. These explanations tend to be moral. Woodpeckers, for example, have long beaks because their ancestor, a snoopy old woman, was punished with a beak with which to pick up insects she had let out of a bag after being warned not to do so.

The *dilemma tale*, which raises a question without providing an answer, is a third form of folk story. For example, in one African story, bat is called to account by the animal community for claiming to be a bird when it profited him to do so, and a beast when *that* was to his advantage. The double-dealing bat gets a clever lawyer to argue his case; the lawyer claims his client's behavior is correct because he really is part bird, part beast. Does bat win? We don't know, for the story merely presents both sides of the case and allows the audience to decide the verdict among themselves.

All peoples tell stories about their *heroes*. The typical hero of myth is a supernatural being, or at least a being of divine descent. He is often reared by foster parents, and upon reaching manhood he embarks on a series of perilous adventures. Along the path of his quest he meets with many obstacles he must overcome and monsters he must slay or subdue or escape by trickery. He attempts and endures things that seem impossible by ordinary standards. A hero may be either a man or an animal. He may be a benefactor of mankind or a mischievous trickster concerned only with his own wants, or a combination of both. The mythic hero seldom receives aid from anyone; the quality that

helps him to triumph—whether it is physical strength, cunning, or magic—is his own.

The European *fairy tale*, which came into existence after the spread of Christianity, has very probably grown out of older folk literature. Many of its incidents are like those found in ancient myths, and its characters sometimes betray traces of gods. The fairy tale, however, differs from myth in meaning. This difference in meaning can be most easily seen by comparing the fairy-tale hero with the mythic hero. Unlike the highborn hero of myth, the fairy-tale hero starts at the bottom of the social scale. He is a mere mortal, often an unloved orphan or stepchild, with all the odds against him. His success depends entirely upon the help of others. Modesty, kindness, innocence, childlike trust, and obedience are the virtues required of him; he can have no faults. He rises from obscurity to fortune and lives "happily ever after." In his world, the good are always rewarded and the evil are always punished. The adventures of the mythic hero, on the other hand, symbolize the real life struggles everyone must go through and the conflicts each must resolve to attain happiness and maturity. Whether the mythic hero's goals are good or evil, he is admired for achieving them.

The relation of a people to their traditional stories varied from culture to culture. Some people considered their stories holy, and their preservation a sacred duty. This is illustrated in a story the Seneca Indians told: "You must keep these stories as long as the world lasts," the Storytelling stone tells the people. "Tell them to your children and grandchildren generation after generation." Other peoples recognized their stories as fiction. The Ashanti tribe of Africa, for example, began every tale with: "We do not really mean, we do not really mean, that what we are going to say is true." In Sudanese storytelling sessions, the narrator and

his listeners agreed before starting a tale that it was not to be taken literally:

"I'm going to tell a story," the storyteller said.

"Right!" the audience answered.

"It's a lie!"

"Right!"

"But not everything in it is false!"

"Right!"

The story lived through the storyteller's art. Each teller of tales adapted his stories to the needs and interests of his audience, making additions and omissions at will. Sometimes he acted the stories out; sometimes he introduced snatches of song into the narration and invited the audience to join him in singing. He did not develop his characters as a modern writer does; instead, he simply defined them by their station in life and by how they behaved and what they accomplished. Thus, the maiden was "beautiful," the prince "charming," the fox "cunning," and the woodcutter "strong and humble." Similarly, the storyteller merely indicated the setting of a story: a road, a forest, the king's palace.

The stories in this unit are only a sampling from the vast number of tales told in different parts of the world. Of unknown age and authorship, they have been handed down, by word of mouth, through countless generations. Some may have traveled across oceans and continents, carried by traders, adventurers, armies, nomads, and wandering minstrels. Only in the course of the last century have they been written down by the folklorists and anthropologists who collected them.

Apart from the light these ancient stories throw on the past, they have a unique fascination of their own. For they were first created when the world was younger and man was a simpler creature. And they have come down through untold ages to offer their original freshness to today's complex world.

"What does it mean to tell stories?"
the orphan asked the stone. And the
stone answered, "It is telling what
happened a long time ago." What does
the orphan learn from the stone that
speaks?

The Storytelling Stone

[*NORTH AMERICA*]

IN A SENECA[1] VILLAGE lived a boy whose father and mother died when he was only a few weeks old. The little boy was cared for by a woman who had known his parents. She gave him the name of *Poyeshao*[2]

The boy grew to be a healthy, active little fellow. When he was old enough, his foster mother gave him a bow and arrows, and said, "It is time for you to learn to hunt. Tomorrow morning, go to the woods and kill all the birds you can find."

Taking cobs of dry corn, the woman shelled off the kernels and parched them in hot ashes; and the next morning she gave the boy some of the corn for his breakfast and rolled up some in a piece of buckskin and told him to take it with him, for he would be gone all day and would get hungry.

Poyeshao started off and was very successful. At noon he sat down and rested and ate some of the parched corn; then he hunted till the middle of the afternoon. When he began to work toward home he had a good string of birds.

The next morning *Poyeshao*'s foster mother gave him parched corn for breakfast and while he was eating she told him that he must do his best when hunting, for if he became a good hunter, he would always be prosperous.

The boy took his bow and arrows and little bundle of parched corn and went to the woods; again he found plenty of birds. At midday he ate his

From the book SENECA INDIAN MYTHS by Jeremiah Curtin. Copyright, 1923, by E. P. Dutton & Co., Inc. Renewal, 1951, by Jeremiah Curtin Cardell. Reprinted by permission of the publishers.
1. *Seneca* (sen'ə kə), one of a tribe of Iroquoian Indians, formerly of western New York.
2. *Poyeshao*[n] (poi'ə shôN), orphan.

corn and thought over what his foster mother had told him. In his mind he said, "I'll do just as my mother tells me; then sometime I'll be able to hunt big game."

Poyeshao^n hunted till toward evening, then went home with a larger string of birds than he had the previous day. His foster mother thanked him, and said, "Now you have begun to help me get food."

Early the next morning the boy's breakfast was ready and as soon as he had eaten it, he took his little bundle of parched corn and started off. He went farther into the woods and at night came home with a larger string of birds than he had the second day. His foster mother praised and thanked him.

Each day the boy brought home more birds than the previous day. On the ninth day he killed so many that he brought them home on his back. His foster mother tied the birds in little bundles of three or four and distributed them among her neighbors.

The tenth day the boy started off, as usual, and, as each day he had gone farther for game than on the preceding day, so now he went deeper into the woods than ever. About midday the sinew that held the feathers to his arrow loosened. Looking around for a place where he could sit down while he took the sinew off and wound it on again, he saw a small opening and near the center of the opening a high, smooth, flat-topped, round stone. He went to the stone, sprang up onto it, and sat down. He unwound the sinew and put it in his mouth to soften; then he arranged the arrow feathers and was about to fasten them to the arrow when a voice, right there near him, asked, "Shall I tell you stories?"

Poyeshao^n looked up expecting to see a man. Not seeing anyone he looked behind the stone and around it; then he again began to tie the feathers to his arrow.

"Shall I tell you stories?" asked a voice right there by him.

The boy looked in every direction, but saw no one. Then he made up his mind to watch and find out who was trying to fool him. He stopped work and listened and when the voice again asked, "Shall I tell you stories?" he found that it came from the stone; then he asked, "What is that? What does it mean to tell stories?"

"It is telling what happened a long time ago. If you will give me your birds, I'll tell you stories."

"You may have the birds."

As soon as the boy promised to give the birds, the stone began telling what happened long ago. When one story was told, another was begun. The boy sat, with his head down, and listened. Toward night the stone said, "We will rest now. Come again tomorrow. If anyone asks about your birds, say that you have killed so many that they are getting scarce and you have to go a long way to find one."

While going home the boy killed five or six birds. When his foster mother asked why he had so few birds, he said that they were scarce; that he had to go far for them.

The next morning *Poyeshao*^{n} started off with his bow and arrows and little bundle of parched corn, but he forgot to hunt for birds; he was thinking of the stories the stone had told him. When a bird lighted near him he shot it, but he kept straight on toward the opening in the woods. When he got there he put his birds on the stone, and called out, "I've come! Here are birds. Now tell me stories."

The stone told story after story. Toward night it said, "Now we must rest till tomorrow." On the way home the boy looked for birds, but it was late and he found only a few.

That night the foster mother told her neighbors that when *Poyeshao^n* first began to hunt he had brought home a great many birds, but now he brought only four or five after being in the woods from morning till night. She said there was something strange about it; either he threw the birds away or gave them to some animal, or maybe he idled time away, didn't hunt. She hired a boy to follow *Poyeshao^n* and find out what he was doing.

The next morning the boy took his bow and arrows and followed *Poyeshao^n*, keeping out of his sight and sometimes shooting a bird. *Poyeshao^n* killed a good many birds; then, about the middle of the forenoon, he suddenly started off toward the East, running as fast as he could. The boy followed till he came to an opening in the woods and saw *Poyeshao^n* climb up and sit down on a large round stone; he crept nearer and heard talking. When he couldn't see the person to whom *Poyeshao^n* was talking, he went up to the boy and asked, "What are you doing here?"

"Hearing stories."

"What are stories?"

"Telling about things that happened long ago. Put your birds on this stone and say, 'I've come to hear stories.'"

The boy did as told and straightway the stone began. The boys listened till the sun went down; then the stone said, "We will rest now. Come again tomorrow."

On the way home *Poyeshao^n* killed three or four birds.

When the woman asked the boy she had sent why *Poyeshao^n* killed so few birds, he said, "I followed him for a while, then I spoke to him, and after that we hunted together till it was time to come home. We couldn't find many birds."

The next morning the elder boy said, "I'm going with *Poyeshao^n* to hunt, it's sport." The two started off together. By the middle of the forenoon each boy had a long string of birds. They hurried to the opening, put the birds on the stone, and said, "We have come. Here are the birds! Tell us stories."

They sat on the stone and listened to stories till late in the afternoon; then the stone said, "We'll rest now till tomorrow."

On the way home the boys shot every bird they could find, but it was late and they didn't find many.

Several days went by in this way; then the foster mother said, "Those boys kill more birds than they bring home," and she hired two men to follow them.

The next morning, when *Poyeshao^n* and his friend started for the woods, the two men followed. When the boys had a large number of birds, they stopped hunting and hurried to the opening. The men followed and, hiding behind trees, saw them put the birds on a large round stone, then jump up and sit there, with their heads down, listening to a man's voice; every little while they said, "Um!"

"Let's go there and find out who is talking to those boys," said one man to the other. They walked quickly to the stone and asked, "What are you doing, boys?"

The boys were startled, but *Poyeshao^n* said, "You must promise not to tell anyone."

They promised; then *Poyeshao^n* said, "Jump up and sit on the stone."

The men seated themselves on the stone; then the boy said, "Go on with the story; we are listening."

The four sat with their heads down and the stone began to tell stories. When it was almost night, the stone said, "Tomorrow all the people

in your village must come and listen to my stories. Tell the chief to send every man, and have each man bring something to eat. You must clean the brush away so the people can sit on the ground near me."

That night *Poyeshao* told the chief about the storytelling stone, and gave him the stone's message. The chief sent a runner to give the message to each family in the village.

Early the next morning everyone in the village was ready to start. *Poyeshao* went ahead and the crowd followed. When they came to the opening, each man put what he had brought, meat or bread, on the stone; the brush was cleared away, and everyone sat down. When all was quiet, the stone said, "Now I will tell you stories of what happened long ago. There was a world before this. The things that I am going to tell about happened in that world. Some of you will remember every word that I say, some will remember a part of the words, and some will forget them all—I think this will be the way, but each man must do the best he can. Hereafter you must tell these stories to one another—now listen."

Each man bent his head and listened to every word the stone said. Once in a while the boys said, "Um!" When the sun was almost down, the stone said, "We'll rest now. Come tomorrow and bring meat and bread."

The next morning, when the people gathered around the stone, they found that the meat and bread they had left there the day before was gone. They put the food they had brought on the stone, then sat in a circle and waited. When all was quiet the stone began. Again it told stories till the sun was almost down; then it said, "Come tomorrow. Tomorrow I will finish the stories of what happened long ago."

Early in the morning the people of the village gathered around the stone, and, when all was quiet, the stone began to tell stories, and it told till late in the afternoon; then it said, "I have finished! You must keep these stories as long as the world lasts; tell them to your children and grandchildren generation after generation. One person will remember them better than another. When you go to a man or a woman to ask for one of these stories, carry something to pay for it, bread or meat, or whatever you have. I know all that happened in the world before this; I have told it to you. When you visit one another, you must tell these things, and keep them up always. I have finished."

And so it has been. From the stone came all the knowledge the Senecas have of the world before this.

✦　✦　✦　✦

DISCUSSION

1. **(a)** What are the "stories" the stone tells the people? **(b)** Why do you think the Senecas believed that they learned their history from a stone? Explain.

2. **(a)** What character traits does the orphan reveal? **(b)** How do these help him to learn his people's stories? **(c)** Would any of his actions be considered wrong in present-day society? **(d)** Why didn't the Senecas frown upon the boy's behavior? (Refer back to pages 385–386 of the unit introduction if you need help in answering this question.)

3. **(a)** Why do you think the stone demands birds in exchange for its stories? **(b)** According to the stone, how were future storytellers to be treated by the rest of the tribe? **(c)** Why might the Senecas have felt the storyteller should be honored?

4. There is a great deal of repetition in "The Storytelling Stone." Why is repetition necessary in a story that is told orally?

WORD STUDY

In the morning, *Poyeshao*ⁿ awoke to a *breakfast* of corn kernels parched in hot ashes. What two words make up the word *breakfast*? What is the literal meaning of *breakfast*? Is *breakfast* a good word for the early morning meal?

Breakfast is a *compound*, a word made up of two or more other words. After a compound word has been used for some time, we come to think of it as having its own meaning as though the parts had never existed separately. The word *breakfast*, for example, calls to mind a particular event without suggesting the ideas conveyed by the elements making up the word.

Like *breakfast*, many English compounds tell their own stories. Define each of the following by using your knowledge of the words that make up the compound. Check the accuracy of your definitions in a dictionary.

boathouse	greengrocer	outcast
daredevil	houseboat	pushball
dog-eared	kill-joy	spendthrift

Primitive peoples told stories about the genesis, or creation, of the world and the gods who made it. What kind of god created the world of the Blackfoot?

The Blackfoot Genesis

[*NORTH AMERICA*]

ALL ANIMALS of the Plains[1] at one time heard and knew him, and all birds of the air heard and knew him. All things that he had made understood him when he spoke to them—the birds, the animals, and the people.

Old Man was traveling about, south of here, making the people. He came from the south, traveling north, making animals and birds as he passed along. He made the mountains, prairies, timber, and brush first. So he went along, traveling northward, making things as he went, putting rivers here and there, and falls on them, putting red paints here and there in the ground—fixing up the world as we see it today. He made the Milk River and crossed it, and, being tired, went up on a little hill and lay down to rest. As he lay on his back, stretched out on the ground, with arms extended, he marked himself out with stones—the shape of his body, head, legs, arms, and everything. There you can see those rocks today. After he had rested, he went on northward, and stumbled over a knoll and fell down on his knees. Then he said, "You are a bad thing to be stumbling against"; so he raised up two large buttes there, and named them the Knees, and they are called so to this day. He went on farther north, and with some of the rocks he carried with him he built the Sweet Grass Hills.

Old Man covered the Plains with grass for the animals to feed on. He marked off a piece of ground, and in it he made to grow all kinds of roots and berries—camass, wild carrots,

"The Blackfoot Genesis" is reprinted with the permission of Charles Scribner's Sons from BLACKFOOT LODGE TALES by George Bird Grinnell (1892).
1. *Plains,* the Great Plains. Although situated in Montana near the northwestern limit of the Great Plains, the Blackfoot shared the culture of the Plains tribes.

wild turnips, sweetroot, bitterroot, service berries, bull berries, cherries, plums, and rosebuds. He put trees in the ground. He put all kinds of animals on the ground. When he made the bighorn with its big head and horns, he made it out on the prairie. It did not seem to travel easily on the prairie; it was awkward and could not go fast. So he took it by one of its horns, and led it up into the mountains, and turned it loose; and it skipped about among the rocks and went up fearful places with ease. So he said, "This is the place that suits you; this is what you are fitted for, the rocks, and the mountains." While he was in the mountains, he made the antelope out of dirt, and turned it loose, to see how it would go. It ran so fast that it fell over some rocks and hurt itself. He saw that this would not do, and took the antelope down on the prairie, and turned it loose; and it ran away fast and gracefully, and he said, "This is what you are suited to."

One day Old Man determined that he would make a woman and a child; so he formed them both—the woman and the child, her son—of clay. After he had molded the clay in human shape, he said to the clay, "You must be people," and then he covered it up and left it, and went away. The next morning he went to the place and took the covering off, and saw that the clay shapes had changed a little. The second morning there was still more change, and the third still more. The fourth morning he went to the place, took the covering off, looked at the images, and told them to rise and walk; and they did so. They walked down to the river with their Maker, and then he told them that his name was Na'pi.[2]

As they were standing by the river, the woman said to him, "How is it? Will we always live, will there be no end to it?" He said: "I have never thought of that. We will have to decide it. I will take this buffalo chip and throw it in the river. If it floats, when people die, in four days they will become alive again; they will die for only four days. But if it sinks, there will be an end to them." He threw the chip into the river, and it floated. The woman turned and picked up a stone, and said: "No, I will throw this stone in the river; if it floats we will always live, if it sinks people must die, that they may always be sorry for each other." The woman threw the stone into the water, and it sank. "There," said Old Man, "you have chosen. There will be an end to them."

It was not many nights after that the woman's child died, and she cried a great deal for it. She said to Old Man: "Let us change this. The law that you first made, let that be the law."

He said: "Not so. What is made law must be law. We will undo nothing that we have done. The child is dead, but it cannot be changed. People will have to die."

That is how we came to be people. It is he who made us.

The first people were poor and naked, and did not know how to get a living. Old Man showed them the roots and berries, and told them that they could peel the bark off some trees and eat it, that it was good. He told the people that the animals should be their food, and gave them to the people, saying, "These are your herds." He said: "All these little animals that live in the ground —rats, squirrels, skunks, beavers—are good to eat. You need not fear to eat of their flesh." He made all the birds that fly, and told the people that there was no harm in their flesh, that it

2. *Na'pi* (Nä'pe), Old Man. In this tale, the Old Man takes the form of the Great Spirit, or creator.

could be eaten. The first people that he created he used to take about through the timber and swamps and over the prairies, and show them the different plants. Of a certain plant he would say, "The root of this plant, if gathered in a certain month of the year, is good for a certain sickness." So they learned the power of all herbs.

In those days there were buffalo. Now the people had no arms, but those black animals with long beards were armed; and once, as the people were moving about, the buffalo saw them, and ran after them, and hooked them, and killed and ate them. One day, as the Maker of the people was traveling over the country, he saw some of his children, that he had made, lying dead, torn to pieces and partly eaten by the buffalo. When he saw this he was very sad. He said: "This will not do. I will change this. The people shall eat the buffalo."

He went to some of the people who were left, and said to them, "How is it that you people do nothing to these animals that are killing you?" The people said: "What can we do? We have no way to kill these animals, while they are armed and can kill us." Then said the Maker: "That is not hard. I will make you a weapon that will kill those animals." So he went out, and cut some service berry shoots, and brought them in, and peeled the bark off them. He took a larger piece of wood, and flattened it, and tied a string to it, and made a bow. Now, as he was the master of all birds and could do with them as he wished, he went out and caught one, and took feathers from its wing, and split them, and tied them to the shaft of wood. He tied four feathers along the shaft, and tried the arrow at a mark, and found that it did not fly well. He took these feathers off and put on three; and

when he tried it again, he found that it was good. He went out and began to break sharp pieces off the stones. He tried them, and found that the black flint stones made the best arrow points, and some white flints. Then he taught the people how to use these things.

Then he said: "The next time you go out, take these things with you, and use them as I tell you, and do not run from these animals. When they run at you, as soon as they get pretty close, shoot the arrows at them, as I have taught you; and you will see that they will run from you or will run in a circle around you."

Now, as people became plenty, one day three men went out onto the plain to see the buffalo, but they had no arms. They saw the animals, but when the buffalo saw the men, they ran after them and killed two of them, but one got away. One day after this, the people went on a little hill to look about, and the buffalo saw them, and said, "There is some more of our food," and they rushed on them. This time the people did not run. They began to shoot at the buffalo with the bows and arrows Na'pi had given them, and the buffalo began to fall; but in the fight a person was killed.

At this time these people had flint knives given them, and they cut up the bodies of the dead buffalo. It is not healthful to eat the meat raw, so Old Man gathered soft, dry, rotten driftwood and made punk of it, and then got a piece of hard wood, and drilled a hole in it with an arrow point, and gave them a pointed piece of hard wood, and taught them how to make fire with fire sticks, and to cook the flesh of these animals and eat it.

They got a kind of stone that was in the land, and then took another harder stone and worked one upon the other, and hollowed out the softer one,

and made a kettle of it. This was the fashion of their dishes.

Also Old Man said to the people: "Now, if you are overcome, you may go and sleep, and get power. Something will come to you in your dream that will help you. Whatever these animals tell you to do, you must obey them, as they appear to you in your sleep. Be guided by them. If anybody wants help, if you are alone and traveling, and cry aloud for help, your prayer will be answered. It may be by the eagles, perhaps by the buffalo, or by the bears. Whatever animal answers your prayer, you must listen to him."

That was how the first people got through the world, by the power of their dreams.

After this, Old Man kept on, traveling north. Many of the animals that he had made followed him as he went. The animals understood him when he spoke to them, and he used them as his servants. When he got to the north point of the Porcupine Mountains, there he made some more mud images of people, and blew breath upon them, and they became people. He made men and women. They asked him, "What are we to eat?" He made many images of clay in the form of buffalo. Then he blew breath on these, and they stood up; and when he made signs to them, they started to run. Then he said to the people, "Those are your food." They said to him, "Well, now, we have those animals; how are we to kill them?" "I will show you," he said. He took them to the cliff, and made them build rock piles; and he taught them how to drive buffalo over a cliff.

After he had taught those people these things, he started off again, traveling north, until he came to where Bow and Elbow rivers meet. There he made some more people, and taught them the same things. From here he again went on northward. When he had come nearly to the Red Deer's River, he reached the hill where Old Man sleeps. There he lay down and rested himself. The form of his body is to be seen there yet.

When he awoke from his sleep, he traveled farther northward and came to a fine high hill. He climbed to the top of it, and there sat down to rest. He looked over the country below him, and it pleased him. Before him the hill was steep, and he said to himself, "Well, this is a fine place for sliding; I will have some fun," and he began to slide down the hill. The marks where he slid down are to be seen yet, and the place is known to all people as the "Old Man's Sliding Ground."

This is as far as the Blackfeet followed Old Man. The Crees know what he did farther north.

In later times once, Na'pi said, "Here I will mark you off a piece of ground," and he did so. Then he said: "There is your land, and it is full of all kinds of animals, and many things grow in this land. Let no other people come into it. This is for you five tribes.[3] When people come to cross the line, take your bows and arrows, your lances and your battle axes, and give them battle and keep them out. If they gain a footing, trouble will come to you."

Our forefathers gave battle to all people who came to cross these lines, and kept them out. Of late years we have let our friends, the white people, come in, and you know the result. We, his children, have failed to obey his laws.

+ + + +

3. **five tribes.** The five tribes are the Blackfoot, their relatives the Bloods and the Piegans, and the Gros Ventres (grō väN'trəs) and Sarsis, members of the Plains tribes.

DISCUSSION

1. (a) According to the Blackfoot, what did Old Man create first? **(b)** How did he make the first people? **(c)** Try to explain why the belief that man was formed from clay is a nearly universal one.

2. (a) What is Old Man's first test to determine whether people should die? **(b)** What do you think keeps the woman from accepting the results of Old Man's test? **(c)** Why does she later ask Old Man to reverse the law she helped make? **(d)** Why does he refuse to do so?

3. What did the Blackfoot seem to consider the most important things in life? Base your answer on the things Old Man teaches his people.

4. (a) What, according to Old Man, is the purpose of sleep? **(b)** Which of the Blackfoot beliefs was probably responsible for their faith in the guidance provided by animals who appeared in dreams?

5. (a) Show how Old Man displays such human characteristics as: *lack of foresight, concern for others, kindness, sense of humor,* and *need for relaxation.* **(b)** Is Old Man an all-knowing being, incapable of error? Support your answer with lines from the story. **(c)** What godlike traits does Old Man possess?

6. In your own words, describe the Blackfoot concept of their god and his role in men's lives.

WORD STUDY

Idioms are phrases or expressions whose meaning cannot be understood from the ordinary definitions of the words. For example, "I've been fired" is an idiom meaning "I've lost my job." But a person unfamiliar with idiomatic English would not know what was meant by this expression.

Perhaps because of the major role fire has played in man's history, the word *fire* is the basis of many idiomatic expressions. Find the idiom in each of the following sentences and express the thought in literal terms. Then, explain how each idiom is related to the idea of "flame, heat, and light caused by burning."

1. Since neither manager agreed with his decision, the umpire was caught between two fires.
2. If you have any questions, just fire away.
3. Why bother getting fired up over such a trivial incident?
4. My team will go through fire and water to win that championship.
5. You are playing with fire by taking that attitude.
6. There's a man who will set the world on fire someday.
7. The politician is under fire from the newspapers again.

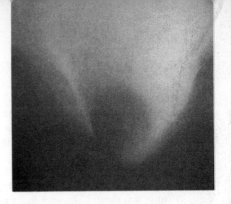

*Answers to some universal questions
are given in the six myths that follow.
Why did these questions plague
primitive man the world over?*

How the Lame Boy Brought Fire from Heaven

[AFRICA]

IN THE BEGINNING of the world, Obassi Osaw[1] made everything but he did not give fire to the people who were on earth.

Etim'Ne[2] said to the Lame Boy: "What is the use of Obassi Osaw sending us here without any fire? Go therefore and ask him to give us some." So the Lame Boy set out.

Obassi Osaw was very angry when he got the message, and sent the boy back quickly to earth to reprove Etim for what he had asked. In those days the Lame Boy had not become lame, but could walk like other people.

When Etim'Ne heard that he had angered Obassi Osaw, he set out himself for the latter's town and said: "Please forgive me for what I did yesterday. It was by accident." Obassi would not pardon him, though he stayed for three days begging forgiveness. Then he went home.

When Etim reached his town the boy laughed at him. "Are you a chief," said he, "yet could get no fire? I myself will go and bring it to you. If they will give me none, I will steal it."

That very day the lad set out. He reached the house of Obassi Osaw at evening time and found the people preparing food. He helped with the work, and when Obassi began to eat, knelt down till the meal was ended.

The master saw that the boy was useful and did not drive him out of the house. After he had served for several days, Obassi called to him and said: "Go to the house of my wives and ask them to send me a lamp."

The boy gladly did as he was bidden, for it was in the house of the wives that fire was kept. He touched nothing, but waited until the lamp was given him, then brought it back with all speed. Once, after he had stayed for many days among the servants,

1. **Obassi Osaw** (o bäs′sĕ ō′sô), the creator.
2. **Etim′Ne** (e′tim′ne), a tribal chief.

Obassi sent him again, and this time one of the wives said: "You can light the lamp at the fire." She went into her house and left him alone.

The boy took a brand and lighted the lamp; then he wrapped the brand in plantain leaves and tied it up in his cloth, carried the lamp to his master, and said: "I wish to go out for a certain purpose." Obassi answered: "You can go."

The boy went to the bush outside the town where some dry wood was lying. He laid the brand amongst the dry wood, and blew till it caught alight. Then he covered it with plantain stems and leaves to hide the smoke, and went back to the house. Obassi asked: "Why have you been so long?" And the lad answered: "I did not feel well."

That night when all the people were sleeping, the thief tied his clothes together and crept to the end of town where the fire was hidden. He found it burning, and took a glowing brand and some firewood and set out homeward.

When earth was reached once more the lad went to Etim and said: "Here is the fire which I promised to bring you. Send for some wood, and I will show you what we must do."

So the first fire was made on earth. Obassi Osaw looked down from his house in the sky and saw the smoke rising. He said to his eldest son Akpan Obassi: "Go, ask the boy if it is he who has stolen the fire."

Akpan came down to earth and asked as his father had bidden him. The lad confessed: "I was the one who stole the fire. The reason why I hid it was because I feared."

Akpan replied: "I bring you a message. Up till now you have been able to walk. From today you will not be able to do so any more."

That is the reason why the Lame Boy cannot walk. He it was who first brought fire to earth from Obassi's home in the sky.

How Raven Helped the Ancient People

[NORTH AMERICA]

LONG AGO, near the beginning of the world, Gray Eagle was the guardian of the sun and moon and stars, of fresh water, and of fire. Gray Eagle hated people so much that he kept these things hidden. People lived in darkness, without fire and without fresh water.

Gray Eagle had a beautiful daughter, and Raven fell in love with her. At that time Raven was a handsome young man. He changed himself into a snow-white bird, and as a snow-white bird he pleased Gray Eagle's daughter. She invited him to her father's lodge.

When Raven saw the sun and the moon and the stars and fresh water hanging on the sides of Eagle's lodge, he knew what he should do. He watched for his chance to seize them when no one was looking. He stole all of them, and a brand of fire also, and flew out of the lodge through the smoke hole.

As soon as Raven got outside, he hung the sun up in the sky. It made so much light that he was able to fly far out to an island in the middle of the ocean. When the sun set, he fastened the moon up in the sky and hung the stars around in different places. By this new light he kept on flying, carrying with him the fresh water and the brand of fire he had stolen.

He flew back over the land. When he had reached the right place, he dropped all the water he had stolen. It fell to the ground and there became the source of all the fresh-water streams and lakes in the world. Then Raven flew on, holding the brand of fire in his bill. The smoke from the fire blew back over his white feathers and made them black. When his bill began to burn, he had to drop the firebrand. It struck rocks and went into the rocks. That is why, if you strike two stones together, fire will drop out.

Raven's feathers never became white again after they were blackened by the smoke from the firebrand. That is why Raven is now a black bird.

From INDIAN LEGENDS OF THE PACIFIC NORTHWEST by R. E. Clark. Originally published by the University of California Press; reprinted by permission of The Regents of the University of California.

Man Chooses Death   [*AFRICA*]

ONE DAY God asked the first human couple who then lived in heaven what kind of death they wanted, that of the moon or that of the banana. Because the couple wondered in dismay about the implications of the two modes of death, God explained to them: the banana puts forth shoots which take its place and the moon itself comes back to life. The couple considered for a long time before they made their choice. If they elected to be childless they would avoid death, but they would also be very lonely, would themselves be forced to carry out all the work, and would not have anybody to work and strive for. Therefore they prayed to God for children, well aware of the consequences of their choice. And their prayer was granted. Since that time man's sojourn is short on this earth.

"Man Chooses Death" from THE ORIGIN OF DEATH by H. Abrahamsson. Copyright 1951. Reprinted by permission of Studia Ethnographica Upsaliensia.

The Origin of Death   [*AFRICA*]

THE MOON, it is said, once sent an insect to men, saying, "Go to men and tell them, 'As I die, and dying live; so you shall also die, and dying live.'"

The insect started with the message, but, while on his way, was overtaken by the hare, who asked, "On what errand are you bound?"

The insect answered, "I am sent by the Moon to men, to tell them that as she dies and dying lives, so shall they also die and dying live."

The hare said, "As you are an awkward runner, let me go." With these words he ran off, and when he reached men, he said, "I am sent by the Moon to tell you, 'As I die and dying perish, in the same manner you also shall die and come wholly to an end.'"

The hare then returned to the Moon and told her what he had said to men. The Moon reproached him angrily, saying, "Do you dare tell the people a thing which I have not said?"

With these words the Moon took up a piece of wood and struck the hare on the nose. Since that day the hare's nose has been slit, but men believe what Hare had told them.

From AN AFRICAN TREASURY edited by Langston Hughes. © 1960 by Langston Hughes. Used by permission of Crown Publishers, Inc.

Why the Sun and the Moon Live in the Sky

[AFRICA]

MANY YEARS AGO the sun and the water were great friends, and both lived on the earth together. The sun very often used to visit the water, but the water never returned his visits. At last the sun asked the water why it was that he never came to see him in his house. The water replied that the sun's house was not big enough, and that if he came with his people he would drive the sun out.

The water then said, "If you wish me to visit you, you must build a very large compound; but I warn you that it will have to be a tremendous place, as my people are very numerous and take up a lot of room."

The sun promised to build a very big compound, and soon afterward he returned home to his wife, the moon, who greeted him with a broad smile when he opened the door. The sun told the moon what he had promised the water, and the next day he commenced building a huge compound in which to entertain his friend.

When it was completed, he asked the water to come and visit him.

When the water arrived, he called out to the sun and asked him whether it would be safe for him to enter, and the sun answered, "Yes, come in, my friend."

The water then began to flow in, accompanied by the fish and all the water animals.

Very soon the water was knee-deep, so he asked the sun if it was still safe, and the sun again said, "Yes," so more water came in.

When the water was level with the top of a man's head, the water said to the sun, "Do you want more of my people to come?"

The sun and the moon both answered, "Yes," not knowing any better, so the water flowed in, until the sun and moon had to perch themselves on the top of the roof.

Again the water addressed the sun, but, receiving the same answer, and more of his people rushing in, the water very soon overflowed the top of the roof, and the sun and the moon were forced to go up into the sky, where they have remained ever since.

The Man Who Acted As the Sun

[NORTH AMERICA]

ONCE UPON A TIME there lived a woman some distance up Bellacoola River.[1] She refused the offers of marriage from the young men of the tribe, because she desired to marry the Sun. She left her village and went to seek the Sun. Finally she reached his house and married the Sun. After she had been there one day, she had a child. He grew very quickly, and on the second day of his life he was able to walk and to talk. After a short time he said to his mother, "I should like to see your mother and your father"; and he began to cry, making his mother feel homesick. When the Sun saw that his wife felt downcast and that his son was longing to see his grandparents, he said, "You may return to the earth

Reprinted from TALES OF THE NORTH AMERICAN INDIANS by Stith Thompson. Reprinted by permission of Indiana University Press.

1. *Bellacoola* (bel′ə ku′lə) *River*, a small river in northwestern North America which gets its name from the Bellacoola Indians, who formerly occupied a large territory on the coast of British Columbia.

to see your parents. Descend along my eyelashes." His eyelashes were the rays of the Sun, which he extended down to his wife's home, where they lived with the woman's parents.

The boy was playing with the children of the village, who were teasing him, saying that he had no father. He began to cry and went to his mother, whom he asked for bow and arrows. His mother gave him what he requested. He went outside and began to shoot his arrows toward the sky.

The first arrow struck the sky and stuck in it; the second arrow hit the notch of the first one; and thus he continued until a chain was formed, extending from the sky down to the place where he was standing. Then he ascended the chain. He found the house of the Sun, which he entered. He told his father that the boys had been teasing him, and he asked him to let him carry the sun. But his father said, "You cannot do it. I carry many torches. Early in the morning and late in the evening I burn small torches, but at noon I burn the large ones." The boy insisted on his request. Then his father gave him the torches, warning him at the same time to observe carefully the instructions that he was giving him in regard to their use.

Early the next morning, the young man started on the course of the sun, carrying the torches. Soon he grew impatient and lighted all the torches at once. Then it grew very hot. The trees began to burn, and many animals jumped into the water to save themselves, but the water began to boil. Then his mother covered the people with her blanket and thus saved them. The animals hid under stones. The ermine crept into a hole, which, however, was not quite large enough, so that the tip of its tail protruded from the entrance. It was scorched, and since that time the tip of the ermine's tail has been black. The mountain goat hid in a cave, hence its skin is perfectly white. All the animals that did not hide were scorched and therefore have black skins, but the skin on their lower side remained lighter. When the Sun saw what was happening, he said to his son, "Why do you do so? Do you think it is good that there are no people on the earth?"

The Sun took him and cast him down from the heavens, saying, "You shall be the mink, and future generations of man shall hunt you."

Why the Sun and the Moon Live in the Sky
The Man Who Acted As the Sun

1. (a) What is the relationship between the sun and the moon in "Why the Sun and the Moon Live in the Sky"? **(b)** What typical characteristics of married couples are responsible for their move to the sky?
2. (a) Is the tone of "Why the Sun and the Moon Live in the Sky" humorous or serious? Explain. **(b)** Find examples of repetition in the story and explain their purposes. **(c)** How do you think an oral storyteller might tell this tale? (Refer back to page 387 of the unit introduction for help in answering this question.)
3. (a) In "The Man Who Acted As the Sun," what are the sun's eyelashes? **(b)** What are its torches?
4. (a) What instructions did the sun probably give the young man in "The Man Who Acted As the Sun"? **(b)** What was the result of the boy's failure to follow the instructions? **(c)** What various questions does this myth answer?
5. What very different pictures of the sun's personality do you get in these two myths?

How the Lame Boy Brought Fire from Heaven
How Raven Helped the Ancient People

1. (a) What origins are explained in these two myths? **(b)** Why were the questions answered in these myths especially important to primitive peoples? **(c)** In the mythologies of many peoples, the essentials of life are stolen from a being who does not want to share them with mankind. Why do you think many primitive peoples imagined these essentials had to be stolen?
2. (a) What was the Lame Boy's motive in stealing the fire? **(b)** Why did Raven steal? **(c)** What part did trickery play in each thief's success?
3. (a) Do you suppose the people who heard these stories considered Lame Boy and Raven villains or heroes? Why? **(b)** If they were heroes, why were they punished?
4. Like Old Man, Obassi Osaw and Gray Eagle had power over people. How did the ways in which Obassi and Gray Eagle used their power differ from the ways in which Old Man used his?

Man Chooses Death
The Origin of Death

1. (a) Restate the choice given people in "Man Chooses Death." **(b)** Why do the people choose as they do?
2. (a) In "The Origin of Death," what does the Moon mean by, "As I die, and dying live, so you shall also die, and dying live"? **(b)** Why then, according to this myth, do people die forever?
3. (a) Compare these two stories with the Blackfoot explanation of how death came into the world. **(b)** In your opinion, which explanation expresses the best attitude toward death? Why?

The Art

of the

Primitives

Primitive man, who listened to the stories you have been reading, worshiped many gods and revered the spirits of his tribal ancestors. These gods and spirits gave him crops to eat and animals to hunt and children to love and care for him. They protected him against accident, disease, and death. They gave him strength and cunning in battle, and wisdom in family and tribal matters. But a man was not endowed with these gifts until he proved himself worthy of them. The favors of the supernatural beings had to be petitioned, and the gods demanded that ceremonies be directed to them out of honor and gratitude.

The immortals could not be seen by men's eyes, and often they lived in a distant world of their own. To bring them closer to men, primitive peoples often used carvings and sculptures as symbols of various gods and spirits. Through the worship of these art objects, the primitives conveyed their love, respect, fears, and needs, to the immortals.

Never in primitive cultures was art simply a source of pleasure. To the primitive man, art objects were necessary forms made for the religious, social, and economic needs of the community. Every figure, mask, and ceremonial object had its own particular function. Every design that was painted on the body had a purpose. Even the materials the primitive artist used were chosen for the blessings they were thought to contain.

Some African tribes, for example, believed in the dualism of life: at death the spirit leaves its used-up body and thereafter dwells in objects prepared for it by the community. Very often, these dwelling places were wooden statues, which had enormous heads. When the tribe needed the advice of the spirit who dwelt in the statue, a priest would take it in his hands and call the dead man's name until he was seized with convulsions and strange sounds came from his mouth. Then the tribe knew the spirit had taken possession of the priest and was sending the wanted message to the people. But the people treated the statue with respect only so long as it aided them. If the statue's advice proved faulty, they concluded that the spirit had abandoned it. In their eyes, the statue then became a worthless piece of wood which they angrily broke into pieces and cast aside.

The North American Indians also believed that the spirit lived on after the body had perished. In most Indian traditions, the spirit went to the land of the dead—but only if the man had lived a

moral life. To prove that a man had been good, the Indians buried certain prescribed objects with a body, among them pottery vessels, stone pipes, and small figures. These paraphernalia not only assured the dead man a place in the land of the dead; they also showed the tribe's respect for him and were protection against his spirit's returning to harm the living.

The peoples of the Pacific Islands used secret ceremonial objects in rituals performed over the body of an enemy killed in battle. The objects helped them to absorb the qualities and strengths of a courageous man whose life forces had not been completely used at the moment of death.

All over the world, masks were used to draw the spirits of ancestors into communication with a tribe and to repel the threats of demons. Animal masks were used in dances designed to comfort the souls of game killed in hunting and to protect the tribe from thieves. There were masks for every purpose—to collect debts, end wars, settle quarrels, bring rain, help women bear children, and cure illness. Huge and terrifying masks were worn by men's secret societies in the rituals they performed by moonlight to initiate boys into manhood. In dramas performed for secret purposes, masked dancers played the part of souls returned from the dead. Masks were respected and feared, and those with the most solemn functions were offered sacrifices.

Many primitive peoples, in both the Old and the New Worlds, believed the individual had an important relationship to some plant, animal, or inanimate object—his *totem*. (When, in

"The Blackfoot Genesis," Old Man tells the people to seek help from the animals who come to them in dreams, he is actually assigning them totems.) In areas where totemism was highly developed, primitive men commissioned artists to make elaborately carved and painted totem poles. These poles were a mark of identification and were very similar in function to a European coat of arms.

Some art objects served much more practical purposes. Pottery, for example, was important as a cooking utensil. In most primitive tribes pottery making was confined to women, and in many areas men were prohibited from practicing the art. One African group did not even allow men to speak to a woman who was making pottery for fear such an action would harm the tribe.

In a few cultures, every man was required to make certain art objects during his lifetime. But generally the artist was a professional who worked on a commission. His client was a tribal leader or a spokesman for a group that needed his services. Before he began work on an object, the artist took part in no activities that might give him pleasure. He retired to the wilderness for a period of solitude so that he could achieve a frame of mind in which he could produce work that would benefit the whole tribe.

The primitive artist worked mostly in wood, which he often treated as a living thing. Because he believed that cutting caused pain to the wood, he begged the forgiveness of the spirits that lived in it as he worked.

The artist's tools, his observations of people and nature, and his tribe's physical and spiritual needs were basically the same the world over. Artists in widely separated countries used the same materials—wood, clay, stone, vegetable and mineral pigments. Geometric forms based on the circle and square are found in the art of all primitive peoples. The whirls made by the wind, the zig-zag course of lightning, the waves on water are basic to nature all over the world. And these designs, adapted from natural surroundings, are common to the art of all primitive peoples. Thus there is, in the art of the primitives, a universal pattern.

The work of the primitive artist is neither polished nor refined. But it is vigorous and strong and has about it a simplicity that has greatly influenced the art of the world.

Six animal tales —
what moral does each have for humans?

How the Animals Got Their Color [AFRICA]

THE COLOR of all the animals is said to have been painted on by the meercat.[1] The meercat said to the animals, "If anyone will kill a buck and bring me the meat, I will paint color on him."

The hyena heard him, so he went and killed a buck; he ate all the meat himself and took the bones to the meercat.

The meercat said, "Lie down." The hyena knelt down and the meercat painted ugly marks on him, saying, "If anyone cheats me, I do the same to him."

The leopard went out hunting and killed a buck and brought it to the meercat unskinned. The meercat told him to kneel down and painted him a beautiful color, saying, "If anyone keeps his word with me, I will do the same to him."

The story is finished.

How the Animals Got Their Tails [AFRICA]

IT IS SAID that animals were created without tails by their maker. The Maker one day called them to come and select what tails would suit them. The first group of animals appeared and selected the long and best tails. The second group came and received good tails. The last group were the hares, who are very lazy, and they told the other animals to pick out tails for them. The other animals, having taken the best tails for themselves, brought the short and ugly tails for the hares. If you want a thing well done, do it yourself.

The story is finished.

From THE BAVENDA by H. A. Stayt. Published by the Oxford University Press, Inc., under the auspices of the International African Institute.
1. *meercat,* a burrowing, flesh-eating mammal similar in size and shape to the mongoose.

Why There Are Cracks in Tortoise's Shell

MR. TORTOISE, who was married to Mrs. Tortoise, had in Vulture a friend who was constant in visiting him. But, having no wings, Tortoise was unable to return the visits, and this upset him. One day he bethought himself of his cunning and said to his wife, "Wife!"

Mrs. Tortoise answered, "Hello, husband! What is it?"

Said he, "Don't you see, wife, that we are becoming despicable in Vulture's eyes?"

"How despicable?"

"Despicable, because it is despicable for me not to visit Vulture. He is always coming here and I have never yet been to his house—and he is my friend."

Mrs. Tortoise replied, "I don't see how Vulture should think us despicable unless we could fly as he does and then did not pay him a visit."

But Mr. Tortoise persisted. "Nevertheless, wife, it is despicable."

Said his wife, "Very well, then, sprout some wings and fly and visit your friend Vulture."

Mr. Tortoise answered, "No, I shan't sprout any wings because I was not born that way."

"Well," said Mrs. Tortoise, "what will you do?"

"I shall find a way," he replied.

"Find it then," said Mrs. Tortoise, "and let us see what you will do."

Later Tortoise said to his wife, "Come and tie me up in a parcel with a lump of tobacco and, when Vulture arrives, give it to him and say it is tobacco to buy grain for us." So Mrs. Tortoise took some palm leaf and made him into a parcel and put him down in the corner.

At his usual time, Vulture came to pay his visit and said, "Where's your husband gone, Mrs. Tortoise?"

"My husband has gone some distance to visit some people, and he left hunger here. We have not a bit of grain in the house."

Vulture said, "You are in trouble indeed, not having any grain."

Mrs. Tortoise replied, "We are in such trouble as human beings never knew." And she went on: "Vulture, at your place is there no grain to be bought?"

"Yes," said he, "any amount, Mrs. Tortoise."

She brought the bundle and said, "My husband left this lump of tobacco thinking you would buy some grain with it for us and bring it here."

Vulture willingly took it and returned to his home in the heights. As he was nearing his native town he was surprised to hear a voice saying, "Untie me, I am your friend Tortoise. I said I would pay a visit to you."

But Vulture, in his surprise, let go his hold of the bundle and down crashed Tortoise to the earth, *pididipididi*, his shell smashed to bits, and he died. And so the friendship between Tortoise and Vulture was broken: and you can still see the cracks in Tortoise's shell.

From THE ILA-SPEAKING PEOPLES OF NORTHERN RHODESIA (Volume 2) by Edwin W. Smith and A. Murray Dale. Reprinted by permission of Macmillan, London and Basingstoke.

Why the Woodpecker Has a Long Beak

[*ROMANIA*]

KNOW THAT the woodpecker was originally not a bird but an old woman with a very long nose, which she put into everybody's pots and pans, sniffing about, eavesdropping, inquisitive, and curious about everything whether it belonged to her or not, adding a little in her tale-bearing and taking off a bit from another tale, and so making mischief among her neighbours. When God saw her doings, he took a huge sack and filled it with midges, beetles, ants, and all kinds of insects, and, tying it tightly, gave it to the old woman, and said to her: "Now, take this sack and carry it home, but beware of opening it, for if your curiosity makes you put your nose into it you will find more than you care for, and you will have trouble without end."

"Heaven forbid," replied the old hag, "that I should do such a thing; I am not going against the will of God. I shall be careful."

So she took the sack on her back and started trotting home, but whilst she was carrying it her fingers were already twitching, and she could scarcely restrain herself, so no sooner did she find herself a short distance away than she sat down in a meadow and opened the sack. That was just what the insects wanted, for no sooner did she open it than they started scrambling out and scampered about the field, each one running his own way as fast as its little legs would carry it. Some hid themselves in the earth, others scrambled under the grass, others, again, went up the trees, and all ran away as fast as they could.

When the old woman saw what had happened, she got mightily frightened, and tried to gather the insects to pack them up again, and put them back into the sack. But the insects did not wait for her. They knew what to do, and a good number escaped into the field. Some she was able to catch, and these she packed into the sack, and tied it up. Then came the Voice of God, who asked her what she had done, and if that was the way she kept her promise.

"Where are the insects, beetles, and midges, which I gave you to carry? From this moment you shall change into a bird and go about picking up all these insects until you get my sack full again, and only then can you become a human being again." And so she changed into a woodpecker; the long beak is the long nose of the old woman, and she goes about hunting for these midges, beetles, and ants, in the hope of filling up the sack, when she would again resume her human shape. But to this very day she has not completed her task, and has remained the woodpecker.

From ROUMANIAN BIRD AND BEAST STORIES by Dr. Moses Gaster. Reprinted by permission of The Folklore Society.

The Dog, the Snake, and the Cure of Headache

[*ROMANIA*]

ONCE UPON A TIME, I do not know how it came about, the dog had a frightful headache, such a headache as he had never had before. It nearly drove him mad, and he ran furiously hither and thither, not knowing what to do to get rid of it. As he was running wildly over a field, he met a snake that was lying there coiled up in the sun.

"What is the matter that you are running about like a madman, brother?" asked the snake.

"Sister, I cannot stop to speak to you. I am clean mad with a splitting headache, and I do not know how to be rid of it."

"I know a remedy," said the snake. "It is excellent for the headache of a dog, but it is of no good to me who am also suffering greatly from a headache."

"Never mind you, what am I to do?"

"You go yonder and eat some of the grass, and you will be cured of the headache."

The dog did as the snake had advised him. He went and ate the grass, and soon felt relieved of his pain.

Now, do you think the dog was grateful? No such luck for the snake. On the contrary, a dog is a dog, and a dog he remains. And why should he be better than many people are? He did as they do, and returned evil for good. Going to the snake, he said, "Now that my headache is gone, I feel much easier; I remember an excellent remedy for the headaches of snakes."

"And what might it be?" asked the snake eagerly.

"It is quite simple. When you feel your head aching, go and stretch full length across the highroad and lie still for a while, and the pain is sure to leave you."

"Thank you," said the simpleton of a snake, and she did as the dog had advised her. She stretched herself full length across the highroad and lay still, waiting for the headache to go.

The snake had been lying there for some time, when it so happened that a man came along with a stout cudgel in his hands. To see the snake and to bruise her head was the work of an instant. And the snake had no longer any headache. The cure proved complete. And ever since that time, when a snake has a headache it goes and stretches across the highroad. If its head is crushed, then no other remedy is wanted, but if the snake escapes unhurt, it loses its headache.

From ROUMANIAN BIRD AND BEAST STORIES by Dr. Moses Gaster. Reprinted by permission of The Folklore Society.

Why the Stork Has No Tail

[ROMANIA]

NOW FLORIA[1] had once shown kindness to a stork, who afterward turned out to be the king of the storks. In return the stork gave Floria a feather, which, when taken up at any time of danger, would bring the stork to him and help him. Thus it came to pass that the hero, finding himself in danger, remembered the gift of the stork. He took out the feather from the place where he had hidden it, and waved it. At once the stork appeared and asked Floria what he could do for him. He told him the king had ordered him to bring the water of life and the water of death.[2]

The stork replied that if it could possibly be got he would certainly do it for him. Returning to his palace, the stork, who was the king of the storks, called all the storks together, and asked them whether they had seen or heard or been near the mountains that knock against one another, at the bottom of which are the fountains of the water of life and death.

All the young and strong looked at one another, and not even the oldest one ventured to reply. He asked them again, and then they said they had never heard or seen anything of the waters of life and death. At last there came from the rear a stork, lame on one foot, blind in one eye, and with a shrivelled-up body, and with half of his feathers plucked out. And he said, "May it please Your Majesty, I have been there where the mountains knock one against the other, and the proofs of it are my blinded eye, and

my crooked leg." When the king saw him in the state in which he was, he did not even take any notice of him.

Turning to the other storks, he said: "Is there anyone among you who, for my sake, will run the risk, and go to these mountains and bring the water?" Not one of the young and strong, and not even any of the older ones who were still strong replied. They all kept silence. But the lame stork said to the king, "For your sake, O Master King, I will again put my life in danger and go." The king again did not look at him, and turning to the others repeated his question; but when he saw that they all kept silence, he at last turned to the stork and said to him: "Dost thou really believe, crippled and broken as thou art, that thou wilt be able to carry out my command?"

"I will certainly try," he said.

"Wilt thou put me to shame?" the king again said.

"I hope not; but thou must bind on my wings some meat for my food, and tie the two bottles for the water to my legs."

The other storks, on hearing his words, laughed at what they thought his conceit, but he took no notice of it. The king was very pleased, and did as the stork had asked. He tied on his wings a quantity of fresh meat, which

---

From ROUMANIAN BIRD AND BEAST STORIES by Dr. Moses Gaster. Reprinted by permission of The Folklore Society.
1. *Floria*, a folk hero.
2. *water of life . . . death.* The early Romanians believed that when the water of death was poured over a dead body, it would heal all wounds. The water of life restored breath to the healed body.

would last him for his journey, and the two bottles were fastened to his legs. He said to him, "A pleasant journey."

The stork, thus prepared for his journey, rose up into the heavens, and away he went straight to the place where the mountains were knocking against one another and prevented anyone approaching the fountains of life and death. It was when the sun had risen as high as a lance that he espied in the distance those huge mountains which, when they knocked against one another, shook the earth and made a noise that struck fear and terror into the hearts of those who were a long distance away.

When the mountains had moved back a little before knocking against one another, the stork wanted to plunge into the depths and get the water. But there came suddenly to him a swallow from the heart of the mountains, and said to him, "Do not go a step further, for thou art surely lost."

"Who art thou who stops me in my way?" asked the stork angrily.

"I am the guardian spirit of these mountains, appointed to save every living creature that has the misfortune to come near them."

"What am I to do then to be safe?"

"Hast thou come to fetch the water of life and death?"

"Yes."

"If that be so, then thou must wait till noon, when the mountains rest for half an hour. As soon as thou seest that a short time has passed and they do not move, then rise up as high as possible into the air, and drop down straight to the bottom of the mountains. There standing on the ledge of the stone between the two waters, dip thy bottles into the fountains and wait until they are filled. Then rise as thou hast got down, but beware lest thou touchest the walls of the mountains or even a pebble, or thou art lost."

The stork did as the swallow had told him; he waited till the noontide, and when he saw that the mountains had gone to sleep, he rose up into the air, and, plunging down into the depth, he settled on the ledge of the stone and filled his bottles. Feeling that they had been filled, he rose with them as he had got down, but when he had reached almost the top of the mountains, he touched a pebble. No sooner had he done so, when the two mountains closed furiously upon him; but they did not catch any part of him, except the tail, which remained locked up fast between the two peaks of the mountains.

With a strong movement he tore himself away, happy that he had saved his life and the two bottles with the waters of life and death, not caring for the loss of his tail.

And he returned the way he had come, and reached the palace of the king of the storks in time for the delivery of the bottles. When he reached the palace, all the storks were assembled before the king, waiting to see what would happen to the lame and blind one who had tried to put them to shame. When they saw him coming back, they noticed that he had lost his tail, and they began jeering at him and laughing, for he looked all the more ungainly, from having already been so ugly before.

But the king was overjoyed with the exploit of his faithful messenger; and he turned angrily on the storks and said, "Why are you jeering and mocking? Just look round and see where are your tails. And you have not lost them in so honourable a manner as this, my faithful messenger." On hearing this they turned round, and lo! one and all of them had lost their tails.

And this is the reason why they have remained without a tail to this very day.

DISCUSSION

1. **(a)** What power does the meercat have in "How the Animals Got Their Color"? **(b)** What happens to the leopard and the hyena? **(c)** What moral, applicable to humans, is contained in the one's reward, the other's punishment?

2. **(a)** What picture of the hare do you get from "How the Animals Got Their Tails"? **(b)** In what other African story in this unit does the hare have the same characteristics? **(c)** Compare the African impression of the hare with the picture created of him in other stories you've read and in cartoons you've seen.

3. **(a)** How are Tortoise and his wife ("Why There Are Cracks in Tortoise's Shell") like the sun and the moon in "Why the Sun and the Moon Live in the Sky"? **(b)** What social customs do the Africans seem to be commenting on in these two stories?

4. What human traits are criticized in "Why the Woodpecker Has a Long Beak"?

5. **(a)** Describe the characteristics of the dog and the snake as illustrated in "The Dog, the Snake, and the Cure of Headache." **(b)** Are these traits usually associated with these animals? Explain. **(c)** Does this tale contain a moral? If so, what is it?

6. In "Why the Stork Has No Tail," what are the "mountains that knock against one another"?

7. **(a)** What traits does the old stork share with the typical mythic hero? **(b)** What does he have in common with the fairy-tale hero? **(c)** What kind of people are represented by the storks who refuse to perform the deed but jeer the old stork?

8. Basing your answer on what you have learned from this group of animal tales, defend or criticize this statement: Primitive peoples were very much aware of man's faults, and they believed the tale was a good vehicle for correcting them.

WORD STUDY

Just as the Romanians associated the woodpecker with an inquisitive old woman, we often give a person the name of some animal whose qualities he is thought to share. Thus, a crafty fellow may be called a *fox,* and a glutton might be labeled a *pig.* What qualities would the persons given each of the following names possess?

sheep	*horse*	*pigeon*	*magpie*
monkey	*goose*	*lion*	*snake*
bookworm	*beaver*	*cat*	*bear*
bull	*bee*	*parrot*	*dog*

Three dilemma tales present problems for you to consider. . .

The Leftover Eye

[AFRICA]

PAY HEED TO THIS TALE. This is a tale of things that have never happened. But we will suppose these things did happen for certainly there are such things possible.

This is a tale of a man who was blind. His mother, too, was blind. His wife and his wife's mother were also blind. They dwelt together in a wretched condition; their farm was poor and their house was badly built. They consulted together and decided to go away. They would journey until they came to some place where their lot would be better.

They set out and traveled along the road. As they walked, the man stumbled over something. He picked it up and felt it, and then he knew he had come upon seven eyes. He immediately gave two eyes to his wife, and then took two for himself. Of the three eyes remaining to him, he gave one to his mother and another to his wife's mother. He was left with one eye in his hand. This was a startling thing. Here was his mother with her one eye looking at him hopefully. There was his wife's mother with her one eye looking at him hopefully. To whom should he give the leftover eye?

If he gives the eye to his mother he will forever be ashamed before his wife and her mother. If he gives it to his wife's mother, he will fear the angry and disappointed heart of his own mother. A mother, know you, is not something to be played with.

This is difficult indeed. Here is the sweetness of his wife. She is good and loving. How can he hurt her? Yet his mother, too, is a good mother and loving. Can he thus injure her? Which would be easier, and which would be the right way to do this thing?

If this thing would come to you, which would you choose?

Reprinted by permission of the publisher, Horizon Press, from YES AND NO: THE INTIMATE FOLKLORE OF AFRICA by Alta Jablow. Copyright 1961.

The Two Strangers

[AFRICA]

TWO STRANGERS entered a village just as night was falling. They sought out the chief to greet him, according to custom, and to ask him for a place to spend the night. The chief replied, "Welcome, O strangers. We welcome you. There is a guesthouse in which you may sleep and there is food for you to eat. But know that in this village there is a custom of long standing. Strangers may sleep here, but on pain of death they may not snore. Remember this well, for if you snore you will be killed as you sleep." The chief then took the strangers to the guesthouse and they composed themselves for the night's rest.

The visitors had not been asleep for long when one of them began to snore: "Vo, vo, vo." His companion awoke. He heard also, "Ts, ts, ts." This was the sound the villagers made sharpening their knives. The stranger then knew that they were getting ready to kill the snorer. He thought quickly of a way that he might save his companion. As one stranger snored, "Vo, vo, vo," the other stranger composed a song:

Vo, vo, lio, vo. Vo, vo, lio, vo.
We walked on the road.
We came to this town.
We were welcomed.
Vo, vo, lio, vo.
Vo, vo, lio, vo.

He sang this song with a strong voice and the people could not hear the snoring above the song. They let their knives fall and began to dance. The drums were brought out and played. The people took up the song and sang. All the people, women, children, the chief, and all the men, came to join the dance.

All that night one stranger snored, one stranger sang, and the towns-people danced and played.

In the morning the strangers went to bid farewell to the chief before they took to the road again. The chief wished them a good journey and pressed a good-sized purse into their hands. "I give you this present of money for your fine song. Because of you, strangers, we spent the night in dance and play. We are grateful."

The strangers went out of the village. Once again on the road, they began to argue. How should the money be shared? The snorer said, "It is to me that the larger portion should fall. If I had not snored, you would not have been moved to compose the song, and we should have received no present at all."

The singer said, "True. If you had not snored, I would not have composed the song, but if I had not, you would have been killed. The people were already sharpening their knives. So I should certainly get the larger portion of the money." Thus they argued and could not decide. Can you?

Reprinted by permission of the publisher, Horizon Press, from YES AND NO: THE INTIMATE FOLKLORE OF AFRICA by Alta Jablow. Copyright 1961.

A Tug-of-War

[AFRICA]

TORTOISE considered himself a great personage. He went about calling attention to his greatness. He said to people, "We three, Elephant, Hippopotamus, and I, are the greatest, and we are equal in power and authority."

Thus he boasted, and his boasts came to the ears of Elephant and Hippopotamus. They listened and then they laughed. "Pooh, that's nothing. He is a small person of no account, and his boasting can only be ignored."

The talebearer returned to Tortoise telling him what the two great ones had said. Tortoise grew very vexed indeed. "So, they despise me, do they? Well, I will just show them my power. I am equal to them, and they will know it before long! They will yet address me as Friend." And he set off.

He found Elephant in the forest, lying down; and his trunk was eight miles long, his ears as big as a house, and his four feet large beyond measure. Tortoise approached him and boldly called out, "Friend, I have come! Rise and greet me. Your Friend is here."

Elephant looked about astonished. Then spying Tortoise, he rose up and asked indignantly, "Tortoise, small person, whom do you address as Friend?"

"You. I call you Friend. And are you not, Elephant?"

"Most certainly I am not," replied the Elephant in anger. "Besides, you have been going about and saying certain things about your great power —that it is equal to mine. How do you come to talk in such a way?"

Tortoise then said, "Elephant, don't get angry. Listen to me. True, I addressed you as Friend and said we were equal. You think that because you are of such a great size, you can surpass me, just because I am small? Let us have a test. Tomorrow morning we will have a tug-of-war."

Said Elephant, "What is the use of that? I can mash you with one foot."

"Be patient. At least try the test." And when Elephant unwillingly consented, Tortoise added, "When we tug, if one pulls the other, he shall be considered greater, and if neither overpulls, then we are equal, and will call each other Friend."

Then Tortoise cut a very long vine and brought one end to Elephant. "This end is yours. I will go off with my end to a certain spot; and we will begin to tug, and neither of us will stop to eat or sleep, until one pulls the other over, or the vine breaks." And he went off with the other end of the vine and hid it on the outskirts of the town where Hippopotamus lived.

Hippopotamus was bathing in the river and Tortoise shouted to him, "Friend, I have come! You! Come ashore! I am visiting you!"

There was a great splashing as Hippopotamus came to shore, bellow-

ing angrily, "You are going to get it now! Whom do you call Friend?"

"Why, you, of course. There is no one else here, is there?" answered Tortoise. "But do not be so quick to fight. I do not fear your size. I say we are equals, and if you doubt me, let us have a trial. Tomorrow morning we will have a tug-of-war. He who shall overcome the other, shall be the superior. But if neither is found superior, then we are equals and will call each other Friend." Hippopotamus thought the plan was absurd, but finally he consented.

Tortoise then brought his end of the vine to Hippopotamus and said, "This end is yours. And now I go. Tomorrow when you feel a pull on the vine, know that I am ready at the other end. Then you begin to tug, and we will not eat or sleep until the test is ended."

In the morning, Tortoise went to the middle of the vine and shook it. Elephant immediately grabbed his end, Hippopotamus caught up his end, and the tugging began. Each pulled at the vine mightily and it remained taut. At times it was pulled in one direction, and then in the other, but neither was overpulling the other.

Tortoise watched the quivering vine, laughing in his heart. Then he went away to seek for food, leaving the two at their tug, and hungry. He ate his bellyful of mushrooms and then went comfortably to sleep.

Late in the afternoon he rose and said, "I will go and see whether those fools are still pulling." When he went there the vine was still stretched taut, with neither of them winning. At last, Tortoise nicked the vine with his knife. The vine parted, and at their ends Elephant and Hippopotamus, so suddenly released, fell with a great crash onto the ground.

Tortoise started off with one end

of the broken vine. He came on Elephant looking doleful and rubbing a sore leg. Elephant said, "Tortoise, I did not know you were so strong. When the vine broke I fell over and hurt my leg. Yes, we are really equals. Strength is not because the body is large. We will call each other Friend."

Most pleased with this victory over Elephant, Tortoise then went off to visit Hippopotamus, who looked sick and was rubbing his head. Hippopotamus said, "So, Tortoise, we are equal. We pulled and pulled and despite my great size I could not surpass you. When the vine broke I fell and hurt my head. Indeed, strength has no greatness of body. We will call each other Friend."

After that, whenever they three and the others met in council, the three sat together on the highest seats. And always they addressed each other as Friend.

Do you think they were really equal?

DISCUSSION

1. (a) Explain the problem raised in each of the dilemma tales you have just read. (b) Which, in your opinion, raises the most meaningful question? (c) In each case, how would you answer the question? (d) Do you think the Africans who first heard these stories would agree with your solutions? Why or why not?

2. What are the values of this type of story to a society that has no written laws to serve as guides for the people?

3. (a) Do the characters in these stories seem concerned with moral behavior? (b) What attitude toward physical strength and brute force do the stories reveal? (c) According to these tales, what seems to be the prime virtue of the African hero?

The Origin of Speech

How did language begin? What were the first words of human speech like?

The origin of language is an unsolved problem that has puzzled men for centuries. It was once supposed that man was created a talking animal, and some scholars maintained that God taught people how to speak. But these views are no longer in favor, for experts are sure that language, as we know it, is a human invention.

The Greek historian, Herodotus, writing a little more than twenty centuries ago, tells a story of an Egyptian king who attempted to find the original language. The king placed two very young children in the care of a shepherd, who was ordered to prevent them from hearing a single spoken word and to report the words they invented when they became old enough to talk.

One day, or so the story goes, the children came to the shepherd and said a word he did not know. He reported it to the king's learned men who decided it was *becos*, the Phrygian word for "bread." The king concluded the children had used the word to let the shepherd know they were hungry, and that the Phrygian language to which it belonged was the original form of human speech.

This story may be fiction rather than fact, but, true or not, it illustrates a theory of the beginning of language which has been popular down to recent times. The "ding-dong theory," as it is called, held that language was originally an instinctive reaction to such internal needs as hunger and thirst and such outward forces as heat and wind and rain.

A second theory was that words originally came from efforts to imitate sounds which primitive man heard. For example, one might imitate the howling of a wolf or the barking of a dog, and the sounds might be made to serve as names for these creatures. If a man imitated a wolf's howl and at the same time pointed to a hill, he might be understood to mean he saw a wolf on the hill. If someone were bitten by a dog, he might point to the wound and imitate a dog's bark to indicate the source of his injury. This theory has been called, in ridicule, the "bow-wow theory." Although some words do appear to have been formed by imitation, a complete language couldn't have been built this way.

Another theory is that exclamations or interjections were the original source of language. A feeling of pain, of anger, of disgust, of fear, or of some other emotion frequently causes a vocal sound. According to the interjectional, or "pooh-pooh theory," such sounds were the instinctive beginnings of speech. Believers in this theory claimed that the sounds were gradually expanded to express ideas as well as emotions.

Since movements of the hands and head are often used to convey ideas, the theory developed that the earliest efforts to talk were merely vocal sounds which accompanied various gestures. Those who believed this explanation maintained that ideas were conveyed through gestures; only later did the accompanying vocal sounds come to stand for the ideas originally expressed by the gestures. Some American Indian tribes do make extensive use of gestures as a means of communication. But it would be quite difficult to prove that primitive man developed the power to express any considerable number of ideas in this manner.

Still another once-popular theory is that the primitives made a great many vocal sounds for the mere pleasure of doing so, just as infants do, and that certain sounds finally took on the nature of words. For example, a vocal sound or group of sounds often made by one person might come to serve as a name for him. Other sounds or groups of sounds might come to be associated with particular objects or actions, and in this way the basis of a language might develop.

None of these theories is generally accepted as correct. No satisfactory answer to the question, "How did language begin?" has ever been given. But language experts and word lovers keep looking for one.

*Can the crafty spider of this tale
really be called a hero?*

The Separation of God from Man

[AFRICA]

IN THE BEGINNING of days Wulbari[1] and man lived close together and Wulbari lay on top of Mother Earth. Thus it happened that, as there was so little space to move about in, man annoyed the divinity, who in disgust went away and rose up to the present place where one can admire him but not reach him.

He was annoyed for a number of reasons. An old woman, while making her *fufu*[2] outside her hut, kept on knocking Wulbari with her pestle. This hurt him and, as she persisted, he was forced to go higher out of her reach. Besides, the smoke of the cooking fires got into his eyes so that he had to go farther away.

Established in his new setting, Wulbari formed a court in which the animals were his chief attendants. Everything seemed to run smoothly for a time until one day Ananse, the spider,[3] who was Captain of the Guard, asked Wulbari if he would give him one corncob. "Certainly," Wulbari said, but he wanted to know what Ananse wished to do with only one corncob.

And Ananse said, "Master, I will bring you a hundred slaves in exchange for one corncob."

At this, Wulbari laughed.

But Ananse meant what he said, and he straightway took the road from the sky down to the earth, and there he asked the way from Krachi to Yendi.[4] Some men showed him the road and Ananse set out. That evening he had gone as far as Tariasu.[5] There he asked the chief for a lodging, and a house was shown him. And when it was time to go to bed, he took the corncob and asked the chief where he could put it for safekeeping. "It is the corn of Wulbari; he has sent me on a message to Yendi, and this corncob I must not lose."

So the people showed him a good place in the roof, and everyone went to sleep. But Ananse arose in the night and gave the corn to the fowls and, when day broke, he asked for the cob and lo! it was all eaten and destroyed. So Ananse made a great fuss and was not content till the people of Tariasu had given him a great basket

---

1. *Wulbari* (wôl bär'ə), the creator.
2. *fufu*, an African food made of grain.
3. *Ananse* (ä nans'), *the spider.* In African folklore, the spider is often pictured as being cunning and ruthless. His role is very similar to that of the fox in European literature.
4. *Krachi* (krä'chi) *to Yendi* (yen'di), towns on the Gold Coast of West Africa.
5. *Tariasu* (tä ri ä'sü), a tribal village in West Africa.

of corn. Then he continued on his way and shortly sat down by the roadside, as he was weary from carrying so great a load.

Presently there came along a man with a live fowl in his hand which he was bringing back from his field. Ananse greeted him and they soon became friends. Ananse said that he liked the fowl—in fact, he liked it so much that he would give the whole load of corn in exchange if the man would agree. Such a proposal was not to be met with every day; the fellow agreed, and Ananse went on his way carrying the fowl with him.

That night he reached Kpandae,[6] and he went and saluted the chief from whom he begged a night's lodging. This was readily granted and Ananse, being tired, soon went to bed. First, however, he showed his fowl to the people and explained that it was the fowl of Wulbari and that he had to deliver it to Yendi. They were properly impressed with this information and showed Ananse a nice, quiet fowl house where it would be perfectly safe. Then all went to bed.

But Ananse did not sleep. As soon as he heard everyone snoring, he arose and took his fowl and went outside the village and there sacrificed the poor bird. Leaving the corpse in the bush and placing some of the blood and feathers on the chief's own doorpost, he went back to bed.

At cockcrow Ananse arose and began shouting and crying out that the fowl of Wulbari was gone, that he had lost his place as Captain of the Guard, and that the unfortunate village of Kpandae would most certainly be visited by misfortune. The hullabaloo brought everyone outside, and by this time it was daylight. Great indeed was the clamor when the people learned what the fuss was about, and then suddenly Ananse pointed to the feathers and blood on the chief's doorpost.

There was no use denying the fact —the feathers were undoubtedly those of the unfortunate fowl, and just then a small boy found its body. It was evident to all that their own chief had been guilty of a sacrilege too dreadful to think about. They, therefore, one and all, came and begged Ananse to forgive them and to do something or other to divert the approaching calamity, which everyone thought must be inevitable.

Ananse at last said that possibly Wulbari would forgive them, if they gave him a sheep to take to Yendi.

"Sheep!" cried the people. "We will give you any number of sheep so long as you stop this trouble."

Ananse was satisfied with ten sheep and he went his way.

He had no further adventures until he reached the outskirts of Yendi with his sheep. He was a little tired, however, and sat down outside the village and allowed his sheep to graze. He was still resting when there came toward him a company of people, wailing and weeping. They bore with them a corpse, and when Ananse saluted them and asked what they were doing, they said that a young man had died and that they were now carrying him back to his village for burial.

Ananse asked if the village was far, and they said it was far. Then he said that it was more than likely that the body would rot on the road, and they agreed. He then suggested that they should give him the corpse and in exchange he would give them the ten sheep. This was a novel kind of business deal, but it sounded all right and, after a little while, the company of young men agreed and they went off with the sheep, leaving their dead brother with Ananse.

---

6. *Kpandae* (kə pan'dì), a tribal village.

The latter waited until nightfall and then walked into the town, carrying with him the corpse. He came to the house of the chief of Yendi and saluted that mighty monarch, and begged for a small place where he could rest. He added: "I have with me as companion the son of Wulbari. He is his favorite son, and, although you know me as the Captain of Wulbari's Host, yet I am only as a slave to this boy. He is asleep now, and as he is so tired I want to find a hut for him."

This was excellent news for the people of Yendi and a hut was soon ready for the favorite son of Wulbari.

Ananse placed the corpse inside and covered it with a cloth so that it seemed verily like a sleeping man. Ananse then came outside and was given food. He feasted himself well and asked for some food for Wulbari's son. This he took into the hut where, being greedy, he finished the meal and came out bearing with him the empty pots.

Now the people of Yendi asked if they might play and dance, for it was not often that a son of Wulbari came to visit them. Ananse said that they might, for he pointed out to them that the boy was an extraordinarily hard sleeper and practically nothing could wake him—that he himself, each morning, had had to flog the boy until he woke, and that shaking was no use, nor was shouting. So they played and they danced.

As the dawn came, Ananse got up and said it was time for him and Wulbari's son to be up about their business. So he asked some of the chief's own children who had been dancing to go in and wake the son of Wulbari. He said that, if the young man did not get up, they were to flog him, and then he would surely be aroused. The children did this, but Wulbari's son did not wake. "Hit harder, hit harder!" cried Ananse, and the children did so. But still Wulbari's son did not wake.

Then Ananse said that he would go inside and wake him himself. So he arose and went into the hut and called to Wulbari's son. He shook him, and then he made the startling discovery that the boy was dead. Ananse's cries drew everyone to the door of the compound, and there they learned the dreadful news that the sons of their chief had beaten Wulbari's favorite child to death.

Great was the consternation of the people. The chief himself came and saw and was convinced. He offered to have his children killed; he offered to kill himself; he offered everything imaginable. But Ananse refused and said that he could think of nothing that day, as his grief was too great. Let the people bury the unfortunate boy and perhaps he, Ananse, would devise some plan by which Wulbari might be appeased.

So the people took the dead body and buried it.

That day all Yendi was silent, as all men were stricken with fear.

But in the evening Ananse called the chief to him and said, "I will return to my father, Wulbari, and I will tell him how the young boy has died. But I will take all the blame on myself and I will hide you from his wrath. You must, however, give me a hundred young men to go back with me, so that they can bear witness as to the boy's death."

Then the people were glad, and they chose a hundred of the best young men and made them ready for the long journey to the abode of Wulbari.

Next morning Ananse arose and, finding the young men ready for the road, he went with them back to Krachi and from there he took them up to Wulbari.

The latter saw him coming with the crowd of youths and came out to greet him. And Ananse told him all that he had done and showed how from one single corncob Wulbari had now got a hundred excellent young slaves.

Now Ananse got very conceited over this deed and used to boast greatly about his cleverness. One day he even went so far as to say that he possessed more sense than Wulbari himself. It happened that Wulbari overheard this, and he was naturally annoyed at such presumption. So, next day, he sent for his captain and told him that he must go and fetch him *something*. No further information was forthcoming, and Ananse was left to find out for himself what Wulbari wanted.

All day Ananse thought and thought, and in the evening Wulbari laughed at him and said, "You must bring me *something*. You boast everywhere that you are my equal, now prove it."

So next day Ananse arose and left the sky on his way to find *something*. Presently he had an idea and, sitting down by the wayside, he called all the birds together. From each one he borrowed a fine feather and then dismissed them. Rapidly he wove the feathers into a magnificent garment and then returned to Wulbari's town. There he put on this wonderful feather robe and climbed up the tree over against Wulbari's house. Soon Wulbari came out and saw the garishly colored bird. It was a new bird to him, so he called all the people together and asked them the name of the wonderful bird. But none of them could tell, not even the elephant, who knows all that is in the far, far bush. Someone suggested that Ananse might know, but Wulbari said that, unfortunately, he had sent him away on an errand. Everyone wanted to know the errand and Wulbari laughed and said, "Ananse has been boasting too much and I heard him say that he has as much sense as I have. So I told him to go and get me *something*." Everyone wanted to know what this *something* was, and Wulbari explained that Ananse would never guess what he meant, for the *something* he wanted was nothing less than the sun, the moon, and darkness.

The meeting then broke up amid roars of laughter at Ananse's predicament and Wulbari's exceeding cleverness. But Ananse, in his fine plumes, had heard what was required of him and, as soon as the road was clear, descended from his tree and made off to the bush.

There he discarded his feathers and went far, far away. No man knows quite where he went, but, wherever he went, he managed to find the sun and the moon and the darkness. Some say that the python gave them to him, others are not sure. In any case, find them he did and, putting them into his bag, he hastened back to Wulbari.

He arrived at his master's house late one afternoon and was greeted by Wulbari who asked Ananse if he had brought back *something*.

"Yes," said Ananse, and went to his bag and drew out darkness. Then all was black and no one could see. Thereupon he drew out the moon and all could see a little again. Then last he drew out the sun, and some who were looking at Ananse saw the sun and they became blind, and some who saw only a little of it were blinded in one eye. Others, who had their eyes shut at the moment, were luckier, so they lost nothing of their eyesight.

Thus it came about that blindness was brought into the world, because Wulbari wanted *something*.

DISCUSSION

1. (a) Who is Wulbari? **(b)** Why does he move into the sky? **(c)** Does Wulbari try to punish the people for forcing him off the earth? **(d)** Does he seem hurt by their behavior toward him? **(e)** What, in general, seems to be his attitude toward people?

2. (a) After Wulbari moves to the sky, what position does Ananse, the spider, hold in his court? **(b)** Early in the story, what task does Ananse set for himself? **(c)** Why does he want to accomplish this feat? **(d)** Explain how he goes about doing so.

3. (a) What task does Wulbari set for Ananse? **(b)** Why does Ananse want to carry out the assignment? **(c)** What is the result of Ananse's completion of the second task?

4. (a) List Ananse's chief character traits. **(b)** How do they help him to perform his tasks?

5. (a) Consider the tone of this tale; then, describe what you think to be the storyteller's attitude toward Ananse. **(b)** Do you think his audience shared his feelings? Why or why not? **(c)** How do you feel about Ananse?

WORD STUDY

For what reason might the Africans have associated the spider with cunning? Traits associated with animals have added many verbs to our language. For instance, because dogs can be very persistent when they want attention, *to dog* has come to mean *to follow*. Explain each of the following, using your dictionary if necessary.

to henpeck   *to rat*   *to outfox*
to ape   *to worm*   *to hound*

Dourak finds a flying ship
and adventures into a fairy-tale world.
How do Dourak's adventures differ
from Ananse's exploits?

The Flying Ship

[RUSSIA]

IN A WILD and lonely region of the great empire of Russia, there lived an old couple who had three sons. They loved the first and the second dearly, for these were quick-witted and prudent beyond their years; but they had no love to spare for the youngest, whom they nicknamed "Dourak," the fool, and whom they regarded as a dreamer and a good-for-nothing.

Now it chanced that the Tsar then ruling over Russia had an only daughter of great beauty, whom many Princes came to woo. So he sent forth a proclamation to every corner of his dominions that whoever could make a Flying Ship should marry the Tsarevna—the daughter of the Tsar.

The eldest son of the old couple, and the second son, about this time decided to leave home and go and seek their fortunes. Their mother wept and kissed them, and gave each of them a flask of wine to cheer him on the way, and a bundle full of the best food she could afford. When they had gone Dourak had an even harder life than before, for his father and mother were always lamenting that their two wise and witty sons should be far away, while only this stupid fellow remained at home.

So at last Dourak decided that he, too, would go and seek his fortune.

"Whatever happens to me," he thought to himself, "I cannot be more unlucky than I am here. And perhaps I may find how Flying Ships are made. And then I should marry the Tsarevna. Tomorrow I will go forth."

When he told his mother that he, too, was bent upon seeking his fortune she laughed at him, and told him that the wolves that lived in the great dark forest would gobble him up. She wished Dourak to remain at home, not because she had any love for him, but because she could make him work for her, chopping wood and gathering sticks, and digging and weeding their little plot of garden.

Dourak, however, was determined to go. So the old woman gave him neither a kiss nor a blessing, but thrust a bundle with a piece of bread and a flask of water into his hands, and turned him roughly out of the house.

Poor Dourak trudged and trudged through the great dark forest, and at last he met a very old man, who asked him whither he was bound.

"I am going to seek my fortune, father," returned the young man.

"But what if you should not find it?"

"Whatever happens to me, I cannot be more unlucky than I was at home."

The old man looked keenly at Dourak. "Last week," said he, "I met two young men in this forest, neither of whom would give me a bite or a sup from the bundle of food which each carried. You also have some food. Are you as hardhearted as they?"

"Truly, sir," said Dourak, "I would gladly give you all that I have — I fear there is not enough for two — but dry bread and plain water may not seem to you worth the having."

"Let us sit down under this tree," suggested the old man, "and do you untie your bundle. What God gives, man must take, and be thankful."

Poor Dourak blushed as he untied the knot, for he was ashamed to offer such miserable fare to a stranger; but when the knot *was* untied, he was astonished to find that instead of bread and water his bundle contained white rolls, and sausages, and a flask of red wine.

He and his new friend crossed themselves, and said grace, and shared the good things fairly between them. When they had finished, the old man asked, "Have you any plan by which you hope to make your fortune?"

"Well," said Dourak, simply, "the Tsar has promised his daughter to the man who can make a Flying Ship."

"Can *you* make such a ship?"

"Not I. But maybe I might find the place where they are made."

"Where is that place?"

"God alone knows! I can but look for it, father."

The old man smiled. "Listen, Dourak," said he, "go into the forest, follow the first path you see, stop at the first tree at the path's end, cross yourself three times, strike the tree once with your axe, then lie down with your face to the ground and wait. Only remember this. Fly where you will, but take on board whomever you meet by the way."

Dourak thanked his friend warmly, and hurried into the forest. At the end of the path he found a tall and beautiful fir tree. There he stopped, and carefully obeyed the advice which the old man had given him. As he lay with his face against the ground he fell fast asleep. After a time he woke up, and there, instead of the fir tree, he saw a beautiful ship, of polished and painted wood, with sails shaped like the wings of a bird.

Dourak jumped into the ship, and it immediately rose into the air and flew toward Moscow, where the Tsar held his Court. Dourak peeped over the side and saw a man far below, lying with his ear pressed to the ground. He took the helm and steered the ship downward, and called out, "Good day, uncle! What are you doing?"

"Good day, my lad! I am listening to what is going on in the wide world."

"Will you come with me in my ship?"

"Gladly!"

So Dourak helped him to climb on board.

When they had flown a little farther they saw a man hopping on one

foot, while the other was tied up against his ear.

"Good day, uncle," cried Dourak, "why do you tie one of your legs against your ear?"

"Because if I were to untie it I should go halfway round the world in one stride."

"Come with us." And he came.

The ship flew, and flew, and presently they saw a man taking aim with a gun, though there was neither bird nor beast to be seen.

"God save you, uncle," quoth Dourak, "are you shooting at nothing?"

"Not I. I am aiming at a bird a hundred leagues away. That's what *I* call good sport."

"Come with us, uncle." And he came.

They flew, and flew, and presently they saw a man with a sackful of bread on his back.

"Whither bound, uncle?" asked Dourak.

"To get some bread for my dinner."

"Have you not got enough in that sack?"

"Indeed I have not. I could eat all *that* at one gulp."

"Come with us, Mr. Gobbler." And he came.

They flew, and flew, and they saw a man standing by a lake.

"Fair befall you, uncle," cried Dourak, "what do you seek?"

"Some water to drink."

"Why, there is a whole lake in front of you!"

"*That*? Oh, I should empty *that* at one draught."

"Come with us, Mr. Thirstyman." And he came.

They flew, and flew, and next they spied a man carrying a heap of straw.

"Whither bound with that straw, uncle?" inquired Dourak.

"To the village."

"Is there no straw in your village?"

"There is none like this. If you scatter it on the hottest midsummer day, the weather will become freezingly cold, and snow will begin to fall."

"Come with us, Mr. Strawmonger." And he came.

They flew, and flew, and soon they saw a man with a bundle of wood.

"Good morrow, uncle," said Dourak, "why are you taking wood into the forest where there is plenty already?"

"This is the most unusual wood, my young friend. Wherever it is scattered, an army will spring up."

"Come with us, Mr. Woodman." And he came.

They flew, and flew, and at last they reached the beautiful city of Moscow, with its clanging belfries and its many-coloured domes. The Tsar was looking out of his palace window, and saw the Flying Ship, and as he looked, it circled thrice and came down in a field not far away. Greatly excited, he sent one of his most fleet-footed servants to find out who was the captain of the vessel, "For," thought His Imperial Majesty, "whoever he may be, he can claim the hand of my daughter, the Tsarevna."

The servant soon returned, and the news he brought alarmed the Tsar. He declared that the ship carried a crew of seven very odd-looking men, and that their leader was a simple peasant lad, in patched and threadbare clothes.

"This is exceedingly awkward," exclaimed the Tsar. "The only thing to be done is to give the fellow some impossible tasks to perform. Go," he exclaimed to his Lord High Chamberlain, "go and tell him that before I have finished my dinner he must bring me some water that lives and sings."

Now the first of Dourak's fellow travellers, he with the keen ear, heard what the Tsar was saying, and told the others.

"Alas," cried Dourak, "I see that I am to be as unlucky here as I was at home! Where could I find such water? And if I knew where, might it not take me a whole lifetime to fetch it?"

"Have no fear," said the hopping man, "I know where it is. And if I untie my leg I can bring it to you in a twinkling."

So when the Lord High Chamberlain arrived with the imperial message, Dourak replied, "His Majesty shall be obeyed."

And the hopping man untied his leg, and in one stride he reached the distant country where the living river flows, and sings as it flows. When he had filled a jar with the singing water the hopping man felt tired. "I have plenty of time for a nap," he thought. So he lay down by the river bank beside a mill wheel, and fell asleep.

Time passed, and his companions in the Flying Ship began to feel anxious. Then he with the keen ear laid himself flat on the ground and listened. "I hear a mill wheel turning, and I hear a man snoring," said he. The marksman shaded his eyes with his hand. "I can see the mill," he said. So he raised his gun to his shoulder, took careful aim, and sent a bullet through the roof of the mill, which awoke the hopping man with its noise. Up jumped the hopping man, seized his jar, made one long stride, and was back in Moscow before the Tsar had finished his dinner.

Instead of being pleased at this prompt fulfilment of his commands, the Tsar was furious. He sent word to Dourak that before he could claim the hand of the Tsarevna he and his comrades must eat at one sitting twenty roast oxen and twenty loaves of bread.

"Alas," cried Dourak, "why, for my part, I could not eat *one!*"

"Be of good cheer," said his fellow traveller, Mr. Gobbler, "that will be a mere snack for *me.*"

So they brought the twenty roast oxen and the twenty large loaves, and the Gobbler ate them all up in a trice. "All very well," he remarked, when he had finished, "but the Tsar might have sent me a little more while he was about it."

Then the Tsar commanded Dourak to drink forty barrels of red wine, each barrel holding forty buckets.

"Woe is me," cried Dourak, "I am as unlucky as ever!"

"Not so," said his fellow traveller, Mr. Thirstyman. "It will seem a mere thimbleful to me."

So when the Tsar's servants brought the forty barrels of wine, the thirsty man drained all the wine at a draught. "Very good," he remarked, wiping his lips, "but not enough of it!"

Then the Tsar became desperate, and cast about in his mind for some way of ridding himself of this tiresome Dourak. He sent word that before the Tsarevna's future husband could be presented to her he would no doubt wish to have a bath, and to array himself in new garments. And then he gave orders to his servants that they should heat the bath so hot that no man could come out of it alive.

He with the keen ear overheard these orders, and told the fellow traveller with the bundle of straw. So when Dourak, obeying the royal command, wended his way to the imperial bathroom, the Strawmonger said, "I am coming with you." And he went with him.

It was fearfully hot in the bathroom, after the Tsar's servants had locked the door on the outside, and great clouds of steam rose from the bath.

Then Dourak's fellow traveller scattered some of his straw on the floor, and immediately the water in the bath froze, and Dourak was fain to clamber up onto the top of the stove lest he too should be frozen.

The next morning, when the Tsar's servants came and unlocked the door, they found Dourak perched on the stove, singing and whistling, not a whit the worse for his ordeal of fire and ice.

When tidings of these things reached the Tsar he was greatly alarmed and perplexed. How *could* he rid himself of this stubborn fellow? Then he had an idea. "Go," he said to his Lord High Chamberlain, "go and tell Dourak that he may now come and claim the hand of my daughter, but that *when* he comes he must come at the head of a great army."

This message reduced Dourak to despair. "When I was at home," he exclaimed, "I was unlucky, and I had no friends. Now, though I have seven friends I am still unlucky. What the Tsar asks is impossible."

"Nothing of the sort," cried his seventh fellow traveller with the bundle of wood. "You have forgotten *me!* Fear nothing. Tell the Lord High Chamberlain to inform the Tsar that you will come at the head of an army, as he desires, but that if he refuses you the hand of the Tsarevna, you will command your troops to lay siege to Moscow."

That night the seventh fellow traveller went out into the open plain,

beyond the walls of the city, and scattered his faggots far and wide. And the next morning, when the Tsar looked out of his palace window he heard the braying of trumpets and the thunder of drums, and saw the glint of swords and breastplates and helmets, and the gay columns of banners and military attire.

"I can do no more," cried the Tsar. "He must marry the Tsarevna!"

So he sent his servants to Dourak, and they gave him a bath of perfumed water, and combed his locks with a comb of gold, and clothed him in the gorgeous robes of a Tsar's son. And nobody would have recognized poor Dourak, the despised and neglected Dourak, in the handsome youth who rode on horseback at the head of an army to claim the hand of the Tsarevna. All the seven fellow travellers were invited to the wedding feast, and for once in their lives the Gobbler had enough to eat, and the thirsty man had so much to drink that even *he* wished for no more.

As for the Tsarevna, she was very happy as the wife of Dourak, and grew to love him as truly as he did her; and he, whose own father and mother had cared nothing for him, became a great favourite with his father-in-law and mother-in-law, the parents of the Tsarevna, his bride.

DISCUSSION

1. (a) What is the modern equivalent of Dourak's flying ship? (b) Why does Dourak want a flying ship?

2. Reread the description of the fairy-tale hero given in the introduction (page 386). (a) In what ways is Dourak's home life like the typical fairy-tale hero's background? (b) What are the odds against Dourak?

3. (a) Explain how Dourak demonstrates the following traits: *kindness, modesty, obedience, innocence,* and *childlike trust.* (b) What other characteristics does he display?

4. (a) Describe the various people who aid Dourak and tell how they do so. (b) Does Dourak ever do anything for himself? (c) What role does fate play in his success?

5. (a) From your own knowledge of fairy tales, tell why the Tsar is a typical villain. (b) Is his final acceptance of Dourak also typical? Why or why not? (c) Is the princess the type usually found in fairy tales? Explain.

6. Who is more of a hero, Dourak or Ananse, the spider? Why?

7. (a) Defend or criticize this statement: Though the fairy tale is generally less fantastic than the mythic tale, myths have more meaning in the real world. (b) Point out differences in attitudes toward life between the people who created Ananse and those who created Dourak.

*A man confounds his wife and
saves his treasure.
What traits
help him to accomplish
these feats?*

Fish
in
the
Forest

[RUSSIA]

IN TILLING THE GROUND a labourer found a treasure, and carrying it home, said to his wife, "See! Heaven has sent us a fortune. But where can we conceal it?" She suggested he should bury it under the floor, which he did accordingly.

Soon after this the wife went out to fetch water, and the labourer reflected that his wife was a dreadful gossip, and by tomorrow night all the village would know their secret. So he removed the treasure from its hiding place and buried it in his barn, beneath a heap of corn. When the wife came back from the well, he said to her quite gravely, "Tomorrow we shall go to the forest to seek fish; they say there's plenty there at present."

"What! Fish in the forest?" she exclaimed.

"Of course," he rejoined; "and you'll see them there." Very early next morning he got up, and took some fish, which he had concealed in a basket. He went to the grocer's and bought a quantity of sweet cakes. He also caught a hare and killed it. The fish and cakes he disposed of in different parts of the wood, and the hare he hooked on a fishing line, and then threw it in the river. After breakfast he took his wife with him into the wood, which they had scarcely entered when she found a pike, then a perch, and then a roach, on the ground. With exclamations of surprise, she gathered up the fish and put them in her basket. Presently they came to a pear tree, from the branches of which hung sweet cakes. "See!" she cried. "Cakes on a pear tree!"

"Quite natural," replied he; "it

has rained cakes, and some have remained on this tree; travellers have picked up the rest." Continuing their way to the village, they passed near a stream.

"Wait a little," said the husband; "I set my line early this morning, and I'll look if anything is caught on it." He then pulled in the line, and behold, there was a hare hooked on to it!

"How extraordinary!" cries the good wife; "a hare in the water!"

"Why," says he, "don't you know there are hares in the water as well as rats?"

"No, indeed, I knew it not." They now returned home, and the wife set about preparing all the nice eatables for supper. In a day or two the labourer found from the talk of his acquaintances that his finding the treasure was no secret in the village, and in less than a week he was summoned to the castle. "Is it true," says the lord, "that you have found a treasure?"

"It is not true," was the reply.

"But your wife has told me all."

"My wife does not know what she says—she is mad, My Lord."

Hereupon, the woman cries, "It is the truth, My Lord! He has found a treasure and buried it beneath the floor of our cottage."

"When?"

"On the eve before the day when we went into the forest to look for fish."

"What do you say?"

"Yes; it was on the day that it rained cakes; we gathered a basketful of them, and coming home, my husband fished a fine hare out of the river." My lord declared the woman to be an idiot; nevertheless he caused his servants to search under the labourer's cottage floor, but nothing was found there, and so the shrewd fellow secured his treasure.

✦   ✦   ✦   ✦

DISCUSSION

1. Is the laborer in this story more like Dourak, or more like Ananse? Explain.
2. (a) Why might the laborer have been considered heroic by the Russian peasants who created him? (b) Is he heroic in today's sense of the word? Why or why not?
3. (a) Does this tale teach a lesson? If so, what is it? (b) Do you consider the story true to life? Why or why not?

1. Discuss the ways in which the following tale is typical of primitive literature in terms of (**a**) its subject matter; (**b**) the attitudes it reveals; (**c**) the lesson it teaches.

THE DOG'S WISDOM/Africa

One day nine dogs went out to hunt. On the path they met a Lion who said that he too was on a hunt, and suggested that they join forces and hunt together. The dogs agreed, and they hunted together all day. By nightfall they had caught ten antelopes. The Lion said, "We must now go and find some person wise enough to divide this meat among us in a proper fashion."

One of the dogs said, "Why is that necessary? This does not require any special person of great wisdom. Are we not ten? We have caught ten antelopes, hence a fair division is that we each take one."

In an instant the Lion rose, and with his great hand he struck the bold dog and blinded him.

The other dogs were cowed and impressed. Then one of them ventured, "No, no, our brother was wrong. That was not a proper division of the meat. The Lion is King of the World, and if we leave nine of the antelopes to him, they will be ten. For us, we are nine and if we take an antelope, so shall we be ten. That is the best division!"

The Lion was pleased and strutted about saying, "You are not a fool like your brother. Such a very wise dog. How did you come by this great wisdom?"

And the dog replied, "When you struck my brother and blinded him, King Lion."

2. In the introduction, Susan Taubes talks about five different types of primitive stories: *myth, animal tale, dilemma tale, hero tale,* and *fairy tale.* Fit each of the titles in the next column into its proper category and tell why it belongs there:

(**a**) "How the Lame Boy Brought Fire from Heaven"
(**b**) "The Dog, the Snake, and the Cure of Headache"
(**c**) "The Blackfoot Genesis"
(**d**) "The Separation of God from Man"
(**e**) "Fish in the Forest"
(**f**) "The Two Strangers"

3. On the basis of what you have read in this unit, defend or criticize these statements:
(**a**) The people of the primitive tribes of Africa were realists who believed that an intelligent being could almost always best those who were stronger but duller.
(**b**) In their account of how things came to be, the Blackfoot Indians showed they were more dependent upon supernatural aids than upon their own abilities.
(**c**) The subject matter of European fairy tales is proof that the people who created them approached life very unrealistically.
(**d**) The American Indians seemed much closer to their gods than the Africans did to theirs.
(**e**) The sole purpose of dilemma tales was to set up standards of behavior.
(**f**) Animal tales taught practical survival rather than moral codes.
(**g**) The tone of the selections in this unit is proof that primitive peoples saw no entertainment values in their stories; instead, they always looked upon them as serious forms of instruction.

4. Of all the stories in the unit, which do you think has the most application to modern man? Be sure you can defend your answer with logical arguments.

Reprinted by permission from NOTES ON THE FOLK-LORE OF THE FJORT by R. E. Dennet. Published by The Folklore Society, London.

SUGGESTED READING

BIRCH, CYRIL, *Chinese Myths and Fantasies.* (Walck) Ghosts, magicians, demons, and a fox woman are a few of the characters in this collection of tales from one of the world's oldest civilizations.

COLUM, PADRAIC, *Children of Odin.* (Houghton) Suspenseful adventures of the gods of ancient Norway are told in rhythmic prose. Colum has also edited *A Treasury of Irish Folklore* (Crown) and the classic *The Arabian Nights* (Macmillan).

COOLIDGE, OLIVIA, *Legends of the North.* (Houghton) The god Odin, chief of Asgard, and his sons, red-bearded Thor and Baldur the Beautiful, storm through the pages of this collection of exciting episodes from ancient Scandinavian literature.

COURLANDER, HAROLD, and ALBERT PREMPEH, *The Hat-Shaking Dance and Other Tales from the Gold Coast.* (Harcourt) More stories about Ananse, the clever spider, including one that explains the humorous reason for his baldness, are found in this collection of tales from West Africa. Also by Courlander are *The Tiger's Whisker and Other Tales and Legends of the South Pacific* (Harcourt) and *The Cow-Tail Switch and Other West African Stories* (Holt).

DOWNING, CHARLES, *Russian Tales and Legends.* (Walck) Snowy steppes and dark forests form the settings of these Slavic stories.

FELDMAN, SUSAN (editor), *The Storytelling Stone.* (*Dell) More "how" and "why" stories such as you read in this unit are found in this collection of folklore of the North American Indians. Miss Feldman has also edited *African Tales and Legends* (*Dell).

FINGER, CHARLES J., *Tales from Silver Lands.* (Doubleday) During his travels among the Indians of South America, the author heard these legends of how Na-Ha defeated the wild, hairy undersea folk and how the rat lost its beautiful horse's tail.

GAER, JOSEPH, *Fables of India.* (Little) A harebrained monkey, a talkative tortoise, and a fox in saint's clothing are some of the actors in these stories from classical Indian literature.

GUILLOT, RENÉ, *Guillot's African Folk Tales,* translated by Gwen Marsh. (Watts) Among these West African tales is the story of how the animals lost the gift of fire because they believed it to be an animal like themselves, needing to be fed.

HAYES, WILLIAM D., *Indian Tales of the Desert People.* (McKay) The desert people whose folk tales are retold in this book are the Pima Indians of Arizona.

LEACH, MARIA (editor), *The Rainbow Book of American Folk Tales and Legends.* (World) In this broad sampling of American folklore are tall tales, ghost stories, legends, and Indian tales. Also by Miss Leach is *The Beginning: Creation Myths Around the World* (Funk), a collection including the Hindu myth of the golden egg and the Japanese chronicle of the first god, the One Who Stands Forever over the World.

McALPINE, HELEN and WILLIAM, *Japanese Tales and Legends.* (Walck) You will find similarities between these Oriental legends and the more familiar ones of the West.

MACMILLAN, CYRUS, *Glooskap's Country and Other Indian Tales.* (Walck) The Micmac Indians of Canada entertained each other with these stories about how Bear and Deer fought on the rainbow and dyed the autumn leaves with their blood, and why Glooskap, the creator, punished the bullfrog with a croaking voice.

MÜLLER-GUGGENBÜHL, FRITZ, *Swiss-Alpine Folk-tales,* translated by Katharine Potts. (Walck) Included with the familiar legend of William Tell are other Swiss favorites about Ida, the hermit-countess, and the wandering ghost, the Key Maiden.

SEREDY, KATE, *The White Stag.* (Viking) This is a collection of simple but charming Hungarian folk tales, including hero tales about the founding of Hungary.

*paperback

UNIT 6

All over the earth

  people live and work and dream and laugh and suffer.

  They journey back and forth or wait for those who

  travel to return.

  They build and destroy.

  They struggle against nature or each other or themselves.

  They ask questions. They seek answers.

  They experience the joy and despair of being human.

Between your experiences and theirs

There are . . .

PARALLELS

The cold war between the hippos and Laurie's father turns suddenly hot.
What makes the conflict humorous?

My Father
and the
Hippopotamus

LEON HUGO

MY FATHER'S FARM was in the bush-veld of the eastern Transvaal,[1] about thirty miles from the Kruger National Park. Wild animals therefore were common in our daily lives. They were nearly all, in their peculiar ways, destructive. Jackals stole my mother's chickens, koodoo[2] broke the fencing round the farm, giraffes entangled their necks in the telephone wires and lions occasionally carried off a cow. Sometimes they were dangerous. A lion once ate a herdboy instead of a heifer, and I still remember with a shudder the time I picked up a green stick which hissed, twisted, and bit my thumb.

Against most wild beasts my father had to wage unceasing war. On the whole he won—except against the hippos. The Letaba River ran through one end of our farm, and during the winter, when in its lower reaches the water level dropped, hippos would move upstream from the game reserve and settle on our farm. They always had. They sneaked in during the night,

sank softly into one of the deep pools in the river, and having done so announced their arrival with an amiable deep bellow. That would start my father's annual dance of rage on the veranda. It used to frighten me nearly out of my wits, but never the hippos, which was not surprising as they were a mile away. I still remember thinking (when I was eight): "If you could see my dad now, you hippos, you'd clear out before tomorrow. Gee, he's mad!"

My father may well have seemed so to me (my sister was too young to notice and my mother used merely to sigh), but as I grew older I began to realize that his roarings and stampings and vows to blow all hippopotamuses to kingdom come were simply excessive face-saving devices. He knew, I grew to know, and the hippos must

From *Blackwood's Magazine* (February 1960). Reprinted by permission of William Blackwood & Sons Limited.
1. *bushveld . . . Transvaal* (trans väl'). A bushveld is an area of grassy plains and scrubby bushes; the Transvaal is a northeastern province of the Union of South Africa.
2. *koodoo,* a large African antelope, usually spelled *kudu.*

have guessed, that he could do nothing.

For one thing there were strict laws about the shooting of hippos; and for another, when on the mornings following their arrival my father stamped down to the river, there was never a sign of one. The reeds were crushed, of course, and the riverbank looked as though it had been put through a mincing-machine, but none of us ever saw a single shining rump or head above the silent green surface. My father always swore that the animals were near. He could feel, he said, the calculating gaze of sleepy hippos lurking among the reeds on the opposite bank. Occasionally he would hear a sniff or a coarse gurgle, and that made him angrier than ever. He would walk up and down the bank cursing, and daring any hippo to show its face, until my mother sent a message to say that breakfast was ready.

After these formalities there was nothing my father could do except see that fires round the lands were kept going during the night. These usually protected the crops from the hippos' darkling gambols, but during their two-month stay my father was an anxious and overworked man.

"Give me a herd of stampeding buffalo, rather," he once remarked bitterly. "At least you can see them. But these damn hippos! I wish," he added wistfully, "I could catch one—just one—with its pants down. I'd teach it who's boss. By golly, I would!"

His chance came, I remember, on a Sunday.

The hippos had been making a dreadful noise the night before: an army of swine would have been nightingales in comparison. The crashing splashes, the snorts, grunts and squeals coming up to us through the dark in blasts of shattering sound, pointed to a hippopotamus frolic of unprecedented scope. To add to the pandemonium our two dogs, which were kept chained in the back yard, started howling. My father, with visions before him of a concerted hippo attack on his crops, if not on our very house, made four journeys on foot round his lands to see that the farm hands were keeping the fires going; and although he took a powerful flashlight with him—and a servant carrying a rifle—caught only one gray fleeting form in the beam of the torch.

When he came in for the fourth time he looked as though he had had enough. "They can eat everything," he muttered. "Everything—I don't care any more. There's enough for them anyway. About a ton of tomatoes per belly. I hope. . . ."

"Oh, John, I'm sure it will be all right," said my mother.

"I hope they burst, I do. I really do." My father spoke very calmly. "Laurie," he said to me, "shut the dogs up."

My sister, as I walked out, said, "Daddy, has a hippo got a curly tail like a piggy's?" When I came in again she was crying and my father had gone to bed.

A tremendous yell woke me the next morning. I shot up in bed to hear flat native feet pounding through the garden toward the house, the yell repeated, and then a burst of insane giggling. I was out in the passage in a moment and saw Matiba, my mother's kitchen boy, still giggling as he banged on my parents' bedroom door.

"What's the matter, Matiba?" I cried.

He only rolled his eyes and continued his giggle until my father opened the door.

"What is it?" my father growled.

Matiba managed to point to the garden. We hurried to the veranda. It was still early, but the sun had risen

enough to make the garden fairly easy to see: particularly the cause of old Matiba's fright; for Nature, as though to heighten the effect, had directed through the trees a shaft of golden light onto the fishpond. Cosily basking in this, half-submerged in the water, was a hippopotamus, fast asleep.

My mother called, "What is it, John?"

"A hippo," said my father, extraordinarily calm.

"A what?"

"I said a hippo," said my father.

"Good heavens!" said my mother. After a pause she called out, "Where?"

"In your fishpond."

There was another pause from my mother, a long one. Then, "The poor goldfish!" we heard her gasp.

My father laughed shortly. "Laurie," he said, "fetch my rifle."

My mother was on the veranda when I got back. She looked pale. I handed my father the rifle. "You aren't going to shoot it, are you, John?" she said.

My father opened the breech. "I jolly well am," he answered grimly.

Sunlight had swept in a flood into the garden by then, and we could see our visitor down to the last wrinkle on its hide. It was a calf, a small one, weighing about eight hundred pounds, and it fitted snugly into the pond, like a round balloon wedged in a tin can. As my father raised the rifle to his shoulder the hippo moved. Water splashed out of the pond as it snuggled in more deeply; and then it yawned, opening its jaws to cavernous proportions and displaying a set of young but immense canines.

I waited, holding my breath for the report of the rifle.

"How will you get it out?" my mother asked.

A spasm ran through my father's body, and for a moment it looked as though he would still pull the trigger. But he did not. Slowly he lowered the rifle. "What did you say?" he said softly.

"How are you going to get it out?"

"Quite simple, dear," said my father patiently. "We'll pull it out."

"You couldn't."

"Couldn't?"

"You couldn't possibly drag a huge beast that weighs thousands of pounds out without ruining the fishpond."

I could see by the look on my father's face that my mother had presented a poser. "We'll hack it up first," he suggested.

"You will not," said my mother firmly. "I'm not having any hippos cut up in my front garden, and anyway I think it's horrid and cruel. He's only a calf."

My father said, "If you want the goldfish to have a playmate, dear, just say so and we'll leave little Jumbo[3] to have his wallow."

"That's not a Jumbo," remarked my sister, who had joined us.

"You're quite right, darling," my mother told her. "Daddy's just being altogether ridiculous."

In the fishpond the hippo belched, not softly.

"No," my mother went on. "What you've got to do is get rid of it without ruining the pond or flowers. I've slaved for years in this garden and I'm not going to stand by and let you destroy it just because you can't get rid of a baby hippo."

"You make me sound so ineffectual," my father grumbled, but he was, I think, secretly glad that he could not conscientiously go on with the killing. "Matiba," he said, "call the boys."

The natives came running from

---

3. **Jumbo,** an elephant. The name comes from a famous elephant named Jumbo, exhibited in P. T. Barnum's circus during the late nineteenth century.

their huts, all of them agog. Stealthily we crept up to one side of the sleeping hippo. As we drew closer we could hear it breathing, slow and deep, with the faintest rumbling snore.

"Now!" yelled my father, and the din started. In addition to ten or so full-blooded yells, empty paraffin tins clashed under smiting sticks and my father's rifle cracked five times as he fired into the air. Altogether it was a most discordant and satisfying noise, and it seemed to electrify our hippo.

It stood up in the pond. Drops shook from it in a silver shower and a goldfish slid from its rump into the water. And it bellowed. Awed by the majesty of that blast we fell silent. We looked at the hippo, it at us. There was something regal about a hippo, even a baby one. We squirmed under its angry gaze. Then, as we silently watched, it sniffed, blinked, and settled slowly back into the pond.

We started our noise again, of course, but shamefacedly and with much less gusto; in any case the more we shouted and banged, the deeper into the pond did the hippo try to get. Only a circlet of rump, its ears, eyes and snout remained above the water eventually. We gave up after half an hour when jabs (with a very long pole) had produced no effect beyond indignant snorts and showers of spray.

"No good," my father whispered, as he and I returned to the house, and the natives, strangely quiet, to their huts for their day off. "We'll have to think of something else."

Breakfast was a silent meal. Even my sister, after mentioning sadly that hippos' tails were straight, said nothing. Shortly afterwards my mother left for church, but before driving off she asked my father to promise not to kill the hippo. Which he did, rather irritably.

My father spent the greater part of the morning staring pensively at the hippo in the pond. Finally he said, "We'll have to drag it out, all the same," and went to fetch the truck. He brought it round, reversed it between the trees surrounding the garden to as near the pond as he could go.

"This is what we do, Laurie," he said. "Tie this rope to the bumper and loop the other end round the blighter's neck. If I can't manage a dead one, a live hippo's going to find itself doing a damn quick sprint out of that pond."

I was only ten then, but I saw a difficulty at once. "Who's going to put the rope round its neck?" I asked.

"Matiba, of course; who else?" said my father, surprised. "Call him."

I did. Matiba came running from the kitchen. We told him what we wanted him to do and he started running again.

"Oh, well," said my father, when the wails of the objecting domestic had faded in the bush. "I'll do it myself."

First we tied the rope to the rear bumper; then my father made a wide noose of the other end and advanced slowly toward the pond. The hippo watched him suspiciously, snorting softly. It was wide-awake and clearly still annoyed.

I heard my father talking to it. "Steady now, boy. Don't worry, we don't want to hurt you. Just pull your head off at the worst. . . ." Carefully he inched forward to within about three yards of the pond. "Steady. . . !" He threw the rope. It was a good shot and the noose dropped over the hippo's ears. For a second my father looked quite pleased. Then the hippo bellowed straight into his face and wrenched its head upwards. My father catapulted back into a bed of flowers where he lay cursing; but in jerking its head the hippo had helped the noose to fall

farther over its ears and round its neck.

It was some moments before I could bring my father to realize this happy accident. When he did, though, he cheered up considerably, and after a few furtive flicks on the slack of the rope, the noose was reasonably tight round the hippo's neck.

"Well," my father remarked as we climbed into the truck, "that's nearly that. But one thing's got me slightly bothered."

"What?" I asked.

"Once we've got him out he'll still be attached to us—to the truck. Can't let the fellow go with twenty yards of good rope still round his neck."

The vision of a baby hippo permanently tied to the back of our truck made me long for its realization; but I saw with regret that it could hardly be practical.

"Anyway," my father continued happily, switching on, "we'll deal with that when it comes up." He revved the engine and slowly let in the clutch. The truck moved forward.

I could not see, sitting beside my father, but could feel when the rope tautened. We could hear too. Behind us, from the fishpond, came tremendous splashings and snorts of rage. The engine hummed, raced, roared; the wheels screamed in the earth. Then we shot away, bounded away rather, like an impala, and thundered along the car track toward the river.

"Golly!" my father yelled jubilantly. "He can run! Thirty—and not the slightest strain. . . ." A few seconds passed and then a worried look came into his face. He slowly braked.

We climbed out to look. There was no baby hippo behind us and no rope. There was no rear bumper.

Up to that moment my father had been exceptionally calm. But the strain began to tell on him then and I grew a little afraid. He got very red in the face and started muttering through clenched teeth. As we drove back to the farmhouse I felt glad I was not that poor hippopotamus.

"You going to shoot him now, Dad?" I ventured.

"No, damn it!" my father roared. "I'll get him out alive if it takes me a week!"

The hippo was in the pond, the rope was still round its neck—the torn-off rear bumper skulked in a flower bed—and my sister was sitting on her haunches beside the pond gazing earnestly into the hippo's eyes. They seemed to be getting on well together; so well, in fact, that she strongly objected when my father, swooping on her like a bird of prey, carried her into the house and locked her up.

"Untie that rope!" he yelled at me as he disappeared through the doorway. Shaking, I ran to obey, but his rage had so unnerved me that by the time he came back I had not managed a single knot. Up to then I had been enjoying myself immensely; now I began rather to dislike my father for spoiling the fun.

"You're an idiot," he informed me stridently. He pushed me aside, tried to untie the rope himself, tore his thumbnail, cursed, and cut the rope. I felt a little better.

He passed me the severed end. "Hold this," he said. "I'm getting under the truck to tie it to the axle." He glared at the hippo. "Just let him try to pull the axle off!" he snarled. "Hand me the rope when I'm ready."

He slid under the rear end of the truck. I was standing facing the pond. A sudden inexplicable gust of warm air struck the back of my neck and I swung round.

I question whether there is anything more conducive to a lightning upsurge of adrenalin than the sudden

sight, from twelve inches, of an adult hippopotamus. The ancient wicked eyes, the primeval face, the enormous expanse of a two-and-a-half-ton amphibian, all make for extremely rapid action. A tree was close at hand. I was up it in about a millionth of a second, staring down, goggle-eyed and dumb, at the hippopotamus cow that had appeared from nowhere at my shoulder. She gave me a perfunctory glance before turning. The part of my father that protruded from the back of the truck caught her eye. She bent her head to examine it.

It was horrible. There I was up the tree, quite speechless with fright, expecting her to open her mouth and bite my father's backside off. But she merely gave a long, interested sniff and my father said, "What the devil are you doing, Laurie?" and wriggled pettishly. Then he said, "All right, give me the rope," and his hand strayed out. The hippopotamus sniffed at that.

My father, sensing that something was near and thinking it was the rope, said, "Damn it, give it to me," and grabbed. His fingers closed unerringly on the hippo's snout.

I found my voice at last. "Daddy," I squeaked, "get underneath! Get underneath!"

He did not. His hand seemed riveted to that snout; and some strange power, instead of sending him slithering for safety under the truck, brought him ineluctably out into the open. They stared at one another for what seemed ages, my father and that female hippopotamus, deep into one another's eyes; then my father let go and giggled, while the hippo breathed long, slow exploratory breaths and twitched her ears. My father rose slowly to his feet, murmuring noncommittally, "Good chap, good old girl," only just restraining himself from patting her on the head. Then the hippo opened her mouth.

What happened next was too quick for me to see. It was a blur of action and there was my father just beneath me in the tree gasping, "Get higher you fool, higher!" and I crying, "I can't, I'm stuck!" and my father appearing magically in the fork above my head and the hippo looking disappointedly up at him, as though she regretted not having tried a piece of human while the going was good. But if that was her thought it was only a passing one, for she turned almost immediately to the fishpond and grunted.

The calf squeaked in reply and squirmed. The mother—the new arrival must have been that—grunted again, more peremptorily, the young hippo slowly emerged, leaving a trail of destruction through my mother's dahlias. As it reached her she bit it, not viciously but with enough vigor to make the calf squeal sharply, spring aside, and start off at a smart gallop for the river. Without a glance up at us, she followed.

As they reached the trees the calf tossed its head and the noose flew free of its neck. In another moment the two animals had disappeared.

We climbed down and without a word to one another slunk into the house. . . .

The first rain of the season fell that night and the hippos left the river pool. They never came back. But five years had to pass before my father (avoiding my eye) dared boast that he had taught them a lesson.

✦   ✦   ✦   ✦

DISCUSSION

1. What annual problem do the hippos create?

2. (a) What are the various plans for driving the young hippo away? **(b)** Why does each fail?

3. (a) What does Laurie mean in saying that his father's "roarings and stampings" were only "face-saving devices"? **(b)** Why does his father eventually claim to have taught the hippos "a lesson"? **(c)** Is this a natural reaction? Explain.

4. How might the tone of the story have differed if the father had been the narrator?

5. (a) Which events in the story are funniest to you? **(b)** What do the reactions of Laurie's mother and sister add to the humor?

6. How might Laurie's father be compared to a suburban home owner?

7. According to the author's letter, how "true" is his story?

WORD STUDY

Vigorous verbs enliven description. The vividness of "My Father and the Hippopotamus" comes in part from the author's choice of appropriate verbs.

In the following sentences from the story, explain how the verb which the author uses (the first in each italicized pair) enables you to visualize the action more clearly than does the second.

1. They [the hippos] (*sneaked, came*) in during the night.

2. . . . my father (*stamped, walked*) down to the river. . . .

3. Cosily (*basking, lying*) in this [the fishpond], half-submerged in the water, was a hippopotamus, fast asleep.

4. Then, "The poor goldfish!" we heard her (*gasp, say*).

5. Water splashed out of the pond as it [the hippo] (*snuggled, settled*) in more deeply.

6. He (*glared, looked*) at the hippo.

7. "Just let him try to pull the axle off!" he (*snarled, said*).

8. My father said, "What the devil are you doing, Laurie?" and (*wriggled, moved*) pettishly.

FROM THE AUTHOR

I grew up in the eastern Transvaal (a Province or "State" of South Africa), not far from the "bushveld" and the famous wildlife sanctuary, the Kruger National Park.

For the benefit of pupils whose knowledge of Africa begins and ends with the epithet "darkest"—lions do *not* prowl through the streets of our towns and hippos do *not* settle into fishponds—except in fiction, which this story is, of course. But the story is "true" in the sense that hippos are remarkably nomadic creatures. They sometimes leave their normal home in rivers for long stretches of time and appear in most unexpected places. One hippo, popularly called Huberta, became a legend in her lifetime. She covered many hundreds of miles in the course of her wanderings, showed herself in several country towns, and was (I should imagine) well on her way to become a National Institution when a trigger-happy ignoramus shot her. Less spectacular is an incident of my boyhood: a baby hippo suddenly appeared in a nearby dam. No one knew where it had come from or how it had got there. Perhaps this was the source of my story, although I wrote the piece in London—come to think of it, I was riding on top of a London Transport 'bus when the idea first occurred to me!

CONSTANCE STUART PHOTOGRAPHY

Mama Is a Sunrise

EVELYN TOOLEY HUNT

When she comes slip-footing through the door,
    she kindles us
    like lump coal lighted,
    and we wake up glowing.
She puts a spark even in Papa's eyes   5
and turns out all our darkness.

When she comes sweet-talking in the room,
    she warms us
    like grits and gravy,
    and we rise up shining.   10
Even at night-time Mama is a sunrise
that promises tomorrow and tomorrow.

From THE LYRIC (1972). Reprinted by permission of the author.

DISCUSSION

1. (a) List some of the phrases which describe Mama's effect on her family. **(b)** What kind of impression of her do you get from these phrases?
2. What does the speaker mean by the statement, "She . . . turns out all our darkness"?
3. Who do you assume the speaker of the poem is?

THE AUTHOR

"It's fun!" says Evelyn Tooley Hunt about writing poetry. She has been composing verse since she was a little girl, but she began offering her poems to editors just a few years ago. Since 1955 she has had more than 350 poems published. Though she writes some free verse, she prefers the challenge of fitting her ideas to the pattern of a definite rhyme and rhythm.

See
IRONY OF SITUATION
*Handbook
of Literary
Terms
page 528*

*Don Lollo was excessively fond of his fine new jar.
Look for irony in this story of the calamities that befall him
as he tries to preserve his treasure.*

THE JAR

LUIGI PIRANDELLO

THE OLIVE CROP was a bumper one that year: the trees had flowered luxuriantly the year before, and, though there had been a long spell of misty weather at the time, the fruit had set well. Lollo Zirafa[1] had a fine plantation on his farm at Primosole.[2] Reckoning that the five old jars of glazed earthenware which he had in his wine cellar would not suffice to hold all the oil of that harvest, he had placed an order well beforehand at Santo Stefano di Camastra,[3] where they are made. His new jar was to be of greater capacity—breast-high and pot-bellied; it would be the mother superior to the little community of five other jars.

I need scarcely say that Don Lollo Zirafa had had a dispute with the potter concerning this jar. It would indeed be hard to name anyone with whom he had not picked a quarrel; for every trifle—be it merely a stone that had fallen from his boundary wall, or a handful of straw—he would shout out to the servants to saddle his mule, so that he could hurry to the town and file a suit. He had half ruined himself, because of the large sums he had had to spend on court fees and lawyers' bills, bringing actions against one person after another, which always ended in his having to pay the costs of both sides. People said that his legal adviser grew so tired of seeing him appear two or three times a week that he tried to reduce the frequency of his visits by making him a present of a volume which looked like a prayer

1. *Lollo Zirafa* (lô′lō zē rä′fä).
2. *Primosole* (prē mō sō′lä).
3. *Santo Stefano di Camastra* (sän′tō stä′fä nō dē kä mä′strä).

book; it contained the judicial code —the idea being that he should take the trouble to see for himself what the rights and wrongs of the case were before hurrying to bring a suit.

Previously, when anyone had a difference with him, they would try to make him lose his temper by shouting out: "Saddle the mule!" but now they changed it to: "Go and look up your pocket code!" Don Lollo would reply: "That I will, and I'll break the lot of you, you swine!"

In the course of time, the new jar, for which he had paid the goodly sum of four florins,[4] duly arrived; until room could be found for it in the wine cellar, it was lodged in the crushing-shed for a few days. Never had there been a finer jar. It was quite distressing to see it lodged in that foul den, which reeked of stale grape juice and had that musty smell of places deprived of light and air.

It was now two days since the harvesting of the olives had begun, and Don Lollo was almost beside himself, having to supervise not only the men who were beating down the fruit from the trees, but also a number of others who had come with mule loads of manure to be deposited in heaps on the hillside, where he had a field in which he was going to sow beans for the next crop. He felt that it was really more than one man could manage. He was at his wits' ends whom to attend to. Cursing like a trooper, he vowed he would exterminate, first this man and then that, if an olive—one single olive —was missing. He almost talked as if he had counted them one by one, on his trees. Then he would turn to the muleteers and utter the direst threats as to what would happen, if any one heap of manure were not exactly the same size as the others. A little white cap on his head, his sleeves rolled up and his shirt open at the front, he

rushed here, there, and everywhere; his face was a bright red and poured with sweat, his eyes glared about him wolfishly, while his hands rubbed angrily at his shaven chin, where a fresh growth of beard always sprouted the moment the razor had left it.

At the close of the third day's work, three of the farm hands—rough fellows with dirty, brutish faces—went to the crushing-shed; they had been beating the olive trees and went to replace their ladders and poles in the shed. They stood aghast at the sight of the fine new jar in two pieces, looking for all the world as if someone had caught hold of the bulging front and cut it off with a sharp sweep of the knife.

"Oh, my God! look! look!"

"How on earth has that happened?"

"My holy aunt! When Don Lollo hears of it! The new jar! What a pity, though!"

The first of the three, more frightened than his companions, proposed to shut the door again at once and to sneak away very quietly, leaving their ladders and poles outside leaning up against the wall; but the second took him up sharply.

"That's a stupid idea! You can't try that on Don Lollo. As like as not he'd believe we broke it ourselves. No, we will stay here!"

He went out of the shed and, using his hands as a trumpet, called out: "Don Lollo! Oh! Don LOLLOOOOO!"

When the farmer came up and saw the damage, he fell into a towering passion. First he vented his fury on the three men. He seized one of them by the throat, pinned him against the wall, and shouted, "By the Virgin's blood, you'll pay for that!"

The other two sprang forward

---

4. **four florins** (flôr′ənz), about four dollars, at the time of the story.

in wild excitement, fell upon Don Lollo and pulled him away. Then his mad rage turned against himself; he stamped his feet, flung his cap on the ground, and slapped his cheeks, bewailing his loss with screams suited only for the death of a relation.

"The new jar! A four-florin jar! Brand new!"

Who could have broken it? Could it possibly have broken of itself? Certainly someone must have broken it, out of malice or from envy at his possession of such a beauty. But when? How? There was no sign of violence. Could it conceivably have come in a broken condition from the pottery? No, it rang like a bell on its arrival.

As soon as the farm hands saw that their master's first outburst of rage was spent, they began to console him, saying that he should not take it so to heart, as the jar could be mended. After all, the break was not a bad one, for the front had come away all in one piece, a clever riveter could repair it and make it as good as new. Zi' Dima Licasi[5] was just the man for the job; he had invented a marvelous cement made of some composition which he kept a strict secret—miraculous stuff! Once it had set, you couldn't loosen it, even with a hammer. So they suggested that, if Don Lollo agreed, Zi' Dima Licasi should turn up at daybreak and—as sure as eggs were eggs —the jar would be repaired and be even better than a new one.

For a long time Don Lollo turned a deaf ear to their advice—it was quite useless, there was no making good the damage—but in the end he allowed himself to be persuaded, and punctually at daybreak Zi' Dima Licasi arrived at Primosole, with his outfit in a basket slung on his back. He turned out to be a misshapen old man with swollen crooked joints, like the stem of an ancient Saracen olive tree. To ex-

tract a word from him, it looked as if you would have to use a pair of forceps on his mouth. His ungraceful figure seemed to radiate discontent or gloom, due perhaps to his disappointment that no one had so far been found willing to do justice to his merits as an inventor. For Zi' Dima Licasi had not yet patented his discovery; he wanted to make a name for it first by its successful application. Meanwhile he felt it necessary to keep a sharp lookout, lest someone steal the secret of his process.

"Let me see that cement of yours," began Don Lollo in a distrustful tone, after examining him from head to foot for several minutes.

Zi' Dima declined, with a dignified shake of the head.

"You'll see its results."

"But, will it hold?"

Zi' Dima put his basket on the ground and took out from it a red bundle composed of a large cotton handkerchief, much the worse for wear, wrapped round and round something. He began to unroll it very carefully, while they all stood round watching him with close attention. When at last, however, nothing came to light save a pair of spectacles with bridge and sides broken and tied up with string, there was a general laugh. Zi' Dima took no notice, but wiped his fingers before handling the spectacles, then put them on and, with much solemnity, began his examination of the jar, which had been brought outside onto the threshing floor. Finally he said, "It'll hold."

"But I can't trust cement alone," Don Lollo stipulated. "I must have rivets as well."

"I'm off," Zi' Dima promptly replied, standing up and replacing his basket on his back.

---

5. *Zi' Dima Licasi* (zē dē'mä lē kä'sē). *Zi'* or *zio* means "uncle."

Don Lollo caught hold of his arm. "Off? Where to? You've got no more manners than a pig! Just look at this pauper putting on an air of royalty! Why! you wretched fool, I've got to put oil in that jar, and don't you know that oil oozes? Yards and yards to join together, and you talk of using cement alone! I want rivets—cement and rivets. It's for me to decide."

Zi' Dima shut his eyes, closed his lips tightly and shook his head. People were all like that—they refused to give him the satisfaction of turning out a neat bit of work, performed with artistic thoroughness and proving the wonderful virtues of his cement.

"If," he said, "the jar doesn't ring as true as a bell once more. . . ."

"I won't listen to a word," Don Lollo broke in. "I want rivets! I'll pay you for cement and rivets. How much will it come to?"

"If I use cement only. . . ."

"My God! what an obstinate fellow! What did I say? I told you I wanted rivets. We'll settle the terms after the work is done. I've no more time to waste on you."

And he went off to look after his men.

In a state of great indignation Zi' Dima started on the job and his temper continued to rise as he bored hole after hole in the jar and in its broken section—holes for his iron rivets. Along with the squeaking of his tool went a running accompaniment of grunts which grew steadily louder and more frequent; his fury made his eyes more piercing and bloodshot and his face became green with bile. When he had finished that first operation, he flung his borer angrily into the basket and held the detached portion up against the jar to satisfy himself that the holes were at equal distances and fitted one another; next he took his pliers and cut a length of iron wire in-

to as many pieces as he needed rivets, and then called to one of the men who were beating the olive trees to come and help him.

"Cheer up, Zi' Dima!" said the laborer, seeing how upset the old man looked.

Zi' Dima raised his hand with a savage gesture. He opened the tin which contained the cement and held it up towards heaven, as if offering it to God, seeing that men refused to recognize its value. Then he began to spread it with his finger all round the detached portion and along the broken edge of the jar. Taking his pliers and the iron rivets he had prepared, he crept inside the open belly of the jar and instructed the farm hand to hold the piece up, fitting it closely to the jar as he had himself done a short time previously. Before starting to put in the rivets, he spoke from inside the jar, "Pull! Pull! Tug at it with all your might! . . . You see it doesn't come loose. Curses on people who won't believe me! Knock it! Yes, knock it! . . . Doesn't it ring like a bell, even with me inside it? Go and tell your master that!"

"It's for the top dog to give orders, Zi' Dima," said the man with a sigh, "and it's for the underdog to carry them out. Put the rivets in. Put 'em in."

Zi' Dima began to pass the bits of iron through the adjacent holes, one on each side of the crack, twisting up the ends with his pliers. It took him an hour to put them all in, and he poured with sweat inside the jar. As he worked, he complained of his misfortune, and the farm hand stayed near, trying to console him.

"Now help me to get out," said Zi' Dima, when all was finished. But large though its belly was, the jar had a distinctly narrow neck—a fact which Zi' Dima had overlooked, being so ab-

sorbed in his grievance. Now, try as he would, he could not manage to squeeze his way out. Instead of helping him, the farm hand stood idly by, convulsed with laughter. So there was poor Zi' Dima, imprisoned in the jar which he had mended and—there was no use in blinking at the fact—in a jar which would have to be broken to let him out, and this time broken for good.

Hearing the laughter and shouts, Don Lollo came rushing up. Inside the jar Zi' Dima was spitting like an angry cat.

"Let me out," he screamed, "for God's sake! I want to get out! Be quick! Help!"

Don Lollo was quite taken aback and unable to believe his own ears.

"What? Inside there? He's riveted himself up inside?"

Then he went up to the jar and shouted out to Zi' Dima, "Help you? What help do you think I can give you? You stupid old dodderer, what d'you mean by it? Why couldn't you measure it first? Come, have a try! Put an arm out . . . that's it! Now the head! Up you come! . . . No, no, gently! . . . Down again . . . Wait a bit! . . . Not that way . . . Down, get down . . . How on earth could you do such a thing? . . . What about my jar now? . . .

"Keep calm! Keep calm!" he recommended to all the onlookers, as if it was they who were becoming excited and not himself. . . .

"My head's going round! Keep calm! This is quite a new point! Get me my mule!"

He rapped the jar with his knuckles. Yes, it really rang like a bell once again.

"Fine! Repaired as good as new. You wait a bit!" he said to the prisoner; then instructed his man to be off and saddle the mule. He rubbed his forehead vigorously with his fingers

and continued, "I wonder what's the best course. That's not a jar, it's a contrivance of the devil himself. . . . Keep still! Keep still!" he exclaimed, rushing up to steady the jar, in which Zi' Dima, now in a towering passion, was struggling like a wild animal in a trap.

"It's a new point, my good man, which the lawyer must settle. I can't rely on my own judgment. Where's that mule? Hurry up with the mule! I'll go straight there and back. You must wait patiently; it's in your own interest. Meanwhile, keep quiet, be calm! I must look after my own rights. And, first of all, to put myself in the right, I fulfill my obligation. Here you are! I am paying you for your work, for a whole day's work. Here are your five lire.[6] Is that enough?"

"I don't want anything," shouted Zi' Dima. "I want to get out!"

"You shall get out, but meanwhile I, for my part, am paying you. There they are—five lire." He took the money out of his waistcoat pocket and tossed it into the jar, then enquired in a tone of great concern, "Have you had any lunch? . . . Bread and something to eat with it, at once! . . . What! You don't want it? Well, then throw it to the dogs! I shall have done my duty when I've given it to you."

Having ordered the food, he mounted and set out for the town. His wild gesticulations made those who saw him galloping past think that he might well be hastening to shut himself up in a lunatic asylum.

As luck would have it, he did not have to spend much time in the anteroom before being admitted to the lawyer's study; he had, however, to wait a long while before the lawyer could finish laughing after the matter had been related to him. Annoyed at the

---

6. *lire* (lē'rä). At the time of the story, a lira was worth about twenty cents.

amusement he caused, Don Lollo said irritably, "Excuse me, but I don't see anything to laugh at. It's all very well for your Honor, who is not the sufferer, but the jar is my property."

The lawyer continued to laugh and then made him tell the story all over again, just as it had happened, so that he could raise another laugh out of it. "Inside, eh? So he's riveted himself inside? And what did Don Lollo want to do? To ke—to ke—keep him there inside—ha! ha! ha!—keep him there inside, so as not to lose the jar?"

"Why should I lose it?" cried Don Lollo, clenching his fists. "Why should I put up with the loss of my money, and have people laughing at me?"

"But don't you know what that's called?" said the lawyer at last. "It's called 'wrongful confinement.'"

"Confinement? Well, who's confined him? He's confined himself! What fault is that of mine?"

The lawyer then explained to him that the matter gave rise to two cases: on the one hand he, Don Lollo, must straightway liberate the prisoner, if he wished to escape from being prosecuted for wrongful confinement; while, on the other hand, the riveter would be responsible for making good the loss resulting from his lack of skill or his stupidity.

"Ah!" said Don Lollo, with a sigh of relief. "So he'll have to pay me for my jar?"

"Wait a bit," remarked the lawyer. "Not as if it were a new jar, remember!"

"Why not?"

"Because it was a broken one, badly broken, too."

"Broken! No, Sir. Not broken. It's perfectly sound now and better than ever it was—he says so himself. And if I have to break it again, I shall not be able to have it mended. The jar will be ruined, Sir!"

The lawyer assured him that that point would be taken into account and that the riveter would have to pay the value which the jar had in its present condition. "Therefore," he counselled, "get the man himself to give you an estimate of its value first."

"I kiss your hands," Don Lollo murmured, and hurried away. On his return home towards evening, he found all his laborers engaged in a celebration around the inhabited jar. The watch dogs joined in the festivities with joyous barks and capers. Zi' Dima had not only calmed down, but had even come to enjoy his curious adventure and was able to laugh at it, with the melancholy humor of the unfortunate.

Don Lollo drove them all aside and bent down to look into the jar.

"Hallo! Getting along well?"

"Splendid! An open-air life for me!" replied the man. "It's better than in my own house."

"I'm glad to hear it. Meanwhile I'd like you to know that that jar cost me four florins when it was new. How much do you think it is worth now?"

"With me inside it?" asked Zi' Dima.

The rustics laughed.

"Silence!" shouted Don Lollo. "Either your cement is of some use or it is of no use. There is no third possibility. If it is of no use, you are a fraud. If it is of some use, the jar, in its present condition, must have a value. What is that value? I ask for your estimate."

After a space for reflection, Zi' Dima said, "Here is my answer: if you had let me mend it with cement only—as I wanted to do—first of all I should not have been shut up inside it and the jar would have had its original value, without any doubt. But spoilt by these rivets, which had to be done from inside, it has lost most of its value. It's

worth a third of its former price, more or less.

"One-third! That's one florin, thirty-three cents."

"Maybe less, but not more than that."

"Well," said Don Lollo. "Promise me that you'll pay me one florin, thirty-three cents."

"What?" asked Zi' Dima, as if he did not grasp the point.

"I will break the jar to let you out," replied Don Lollo. "And—the lawyer tells me—you are to pay me its value according to your own estimate —one florin thirty-three."

"I? Pay?" laughed Zi' Dima, "I'd sooner stay here till I rot!" With some difficulty he managed to extract from his pocket a short and peculiarly foul pipe and lighted it, puffing out the smoke through the neck of the jar.

Don Lollo stood there scowling. The possibility that Zi' Dima would no longer be willing to leave the jar had not been foreseen either by himself or by the lawyer. What step should he take now? He was on the point of ordering them to saddle the mule, but reflected that it was already evening.

"Oh ho!" he said. "So you want to take up your abode in my jar! I call upon all you men as witnesses to his statement. He refuses to come out, in order to escape from paying. I am quite prepared to break it. Well, as you insist on staying there, I shall take proceedings against you tomorrow for unlawful occupancy of the jar and for preventing me from my rightful use of it."

Zi' Dima blew out another puff of smoke and answered calmly, "No, your Honor. I don't want to prevent you at all. Do you think I am here because I like it? Let me out and I'll go away gladly enough. But as for paying, I wouldn't dream of it, your Honor."

In a sudden access of fury Don Lollo made to give a kick at the jar but stopped in time. Instead he seized it with both hands and shook it violently, uttering a hoarse growl.

"You see what fine cement it is," Zi' Dima remarked from inside.

"You rascal!" roared Don Lollo. "Whose fault is it, yours or mine? You expect me to pay for it, do you? You can starve to death inside first. We'll see who'll win."

He went away, forgetting all about the five lire which he had tossed into the jar that morning. But the first thing Zi' Dima thought of doing was to spend that money in having a festive evening, in company with the farm hands, who had been delayed in their work by that strange accident, and had decided to spend the night at the farm, in the open air, sleeping on the threshing floor. One of them went to a neighboring tavern to make the necessary purchases. The moon was so bright that it seemed almost day—a splendid night for their carousal.

Many hours later Don Lollo was awakened by an infernal din. Looking out from the farmhouse balcony, he could see in the moonlight what looked like a gang of devils on his threshing floor; his men, all roaring drunk, were holding hands and performing a dance round the jar, while Zi' Dima, inside it, was singing at the top of his voice.

This time Don Lollo could not restrain himself, but rushed down like a mad bull and, before they could stop him, gave the jar a push which started it rolling down the slope. It continued on its course, to the delight of the intoxicated company, until it hit an olive tree and cracked in pieces, leaving Zi' Dima the winner in the dispute.

✦   ✦   ✦   ✦

DISCUSSION

1. Why does Don Lollo say his jar is "a contrivance of the devil himself"?

2. An *obsession* is an idea or feeling on which a person constantly dwells. **(a)** What obsession of Don Lollo's do the phrases "Saddle the mule" and "Go and look up your pocket code" refer to? **(b)** What other exaggerated traits does Don Lollo possess?

3. (a) In what way is Zi' Dima as obsessed as Don Lollo? **(b)** How is Zi' Dima's obsession related to his imprisonment in the jar?

4. What do the physical appearances of Don Lollo and Zi' Dima add to the humor of the story?

5. (a) Explain the lawyer's advice to Don Lollo. **(b)** What is Zi' Dima's reaction to this advice? **(c)** How does Zi' Dima's attitude affect Don Lollo?

6. What is ironic about the final fate of the jar?

WORD STUDY

Read each sentence below. Then answer the questions that follow, using context clues, structure clues, and the Glossary to do so.

1. The olive crop was a *bumper* one that year: the trees had flowered luxuriantly the year before, and . . . the fruit had set well.

Why would an olive grower be pleased with a *bumper* crop? What context clues helped you determine the meaning of *bumper*?

2. In course of time, the new jar, for which he had paid the goodly sum of four florins, *duly* arrived.

Is *duly* related to *dull*? How is *duly* pronounced?

3. Zi' Dima turned out to be a *misshapen* old man with swollen crooked joints, like the stem of an ancient olive tree.

Is Zi' Dima a tall, upright old man? What context clues indicate the meaning of *misshapen*? How is it pronounced?

4. "Just look at this *pauper* putting on an air of royalty! . . . Why! you wretched beggar!"

Pauper means **(a)** a poor person; **(b)** a person of the upper classes; **(c)** a man of wealth and wisdom.

5. But the first thing Zi' Dima thought of doing was to spend the money in having a festive evening. . . . The moon was so bright it seemed almost day—a splendid night for their *carousal*.

What is a *carousal*? What context clues helped you to your decision? How is *carousal* pronounced? How does it differ in pronunciation and meaning from *carousel*? Are both words derived from the same root?

THE AUTHOR

Luigi Pirandello (1867–1936) was unknown as a writer until after World War I, when his play *Six Characters in Search of an Author* brought him sudden fame.

Pirandello came from a well-to-do family who lived in a backward, violent section of Italy where each man had to defend his own rights. Thus, he was early impressed by the injustice and cruelty in people. His life was not an easy one. Added to the hardships caused by his father's business failure was the insanity of his wife, whom Pirandello cared for at home.

Interested in the inner man, Pirandello explored the personalities of characters usually by placing them in fantastic rather than realistic situations. Today Pirandello is considered one of the most influential playwrights of the twentieth century.

They're called petits bébés[1] *in France. . .*
but they're still just kids.

On Hearing French Children Speak French

IRWIN EDMAN

Children—a well-known circumstance—
Speak French extremely well in France;
Their accent, to the wondering ear,
Is perfect, and their diction clear.

But when I watch them at their play,   5
They might be kids in Deal, N.J.
Like girls and boys one sees about
At home, they tumble, run, and shout;
Like others of their age and ilk,
They dote on sweets, they thrive on milk;   10
They are, their mothers sadly sigh,
With strangers always very shy.
Petits bébés, as here they're styled,
Cry very like my neighbor's child.

I, noting thus what's said and done,   15
Judge the world is, or should be, one;
It is the planet's blackest blot
That it should be—and that it's not.

Reprinted by permission; copyright 1949 The New Yorker Magazine, Inc.
1. *petits bébés* (pə tē′ bā bā′), little babies; children.

DISCUSSION

1. What does the speaker judge to be "the planet's blackest blot"?
2. Why does watching the children in France lead him to make this judgment?

THE AUTHOR

Students came in crowds to hear Professor Irwin Edman's lectures on philosophy at New York's Columbia University. Many considered him a "born teacher." He was also one of America's most popular essayists, and his clear and witty articles on men and ideas frequently appeared in leading magazines.

Edman occasionally lectured at Harvard, and abroad in Brazil, France, and England. But for most of his life he was exclusively a New Yorker. Born there in 1896, he studied at Columbia and remained after his graduation to teach philosophy until his death in 1954.

Why would a wife raise flocks of chickens in the yard,
yet refuse her husband even one egg?
Notice the ways in which the playwright portrays Fortunata and Mateo.

Fortunata writes a letter

THEODORE APSTEIN

[*The scene is the kitchen in a very small adobe house in a Central American town. The red stone floor is partially covered with straw mats, for this room also serves as a dining and living room for its owners,* FORTUNATA *and* MATEO GUTIERREZ.[1]

The long, tiled charcoal stove with four burners takes up the length of one of the walls. Above the stove, large nails and hooks hold earthenware pots and pans of varying colors and sizes. The table and chairs have never been painted, but two large baskets and a wicker rocking chair add color to the room. A rudimentary window, which has shutters but no glass panes, looks out on the street. There is a door to the street and another one to the patio.

Although there is an atmosphere of poverty here, the room is rather clean, considering that MATEO'S *wife,* FORTUNATA, *does all the work herself. But, then, there are no children in this humble household to make things untidy.*

MATEO *is an unassuming man in his fifties. The hot sun has wrinkled and toasted his copper-colored face, and his straight black hair has a gray streak here and there. He wears old black trousers and a white shirt without a collar, but with a patch which shows its age.*

MATEO *has just come in from the street. He takes off his straw hat and sniffs the odors carried by the steam from the stove. He proceeds to lift the lid from one of the earthenware pots on the fire, and puts it down with disgust. He repeats this action with another pot, as* FORTUNATA *comes in from the patio carrying a pail of water which is too heavy for her.*

FORTUNATA *is a small woman who has never been very healthy. Age has*

1. **Fortunata** (fôr tü nä′tä) . . . **Mateo** (mä te′ô) **Gutierrez** (gü tyer′es).

not been as kind to her as it has to her husband. Her fifty years show on her face and on her body. Instinctively FORTUNATA is neat, but it's a neatness which almost comes from within, for she persistently lets her slip show under her skirt and never manages to do a good job of combing her hair. A cheap cotton dress and old sandals are all she needs to wear around the house—and it's all she does wear.]

FORTUNATA. You are home, eh?

MATEO. Sí.[2]

FORTUNATA. And curious about my food?

MATEO (drops the lid with a sneer). Ah! Your food! I was curious if you have a heart. (FORTUNATA says nothing. She empties some of the water from the pail into a pot.) You made mole.[3]

FORTUNATA. You can smell.

MATEO. But what is mole without a chicken?

FORTUNATA. You ask me? Mole without a chicken is a very hot sauce.

MATEO. For dinner I get a very hot sauce! Hah!

FORTUNATA. You will get tortillas,[4] beans, rice and a very hot sauce. It is better than to have beans and rice without mole.

MATEO. Maybe so. But with a chicken. . . .

FORTUNATA. If you like a chicken so much, you will buy one maybe. (She goes on about her business at the stove. With a straw fan, she starts blowing in front of the burner to keep the coals glowing.)

MATEO. As I thought, you do not have a heart. (He goes to the patio door.) How many chickens you have out there?

FORTUNATA. You can count them.

MATEO. I do. One hundred and three. One hundred and three chickens; but I have to eat mole without meat.

FORTUNATA. It is no good to torture yourself like this, Mateo. For three months every night you tell me this, and every night I explain to you that you will not eat one of those chickens.

MATEO. They are sacred maybe?

FORTUNATA. No. I sold one to the Señora Ramirez[5] today, and she will probably eat it.

MATEO. Bueno[6]—then why I cannot?

FORTUNATA. If you pay me like Señora Ramirez, you can have any chicken you like. And I say you are welcome and I cook it for you.

MATEO. You know I have no money, Fortunata. On the first of the month I give you all I make. Today is the twelfth.

FORTUNATA. You give to me all you make—except for what you drink away. Sí, sí, on the first of the month! I know.

MATEO. A man has to have some fun.

FORTUNATA. Some day you will be sorry, Mateo. Dios[7], He watches you. (Outside a whistle is heard.) You hear? (She rushes to the door and opens it.) It is only Pepe,[8] the neighbor's idiot boy. I think maybe the postman. . . .

MATEO (laughs). The postman? Sí, you wait for him many days now. Who you think will write you a letter, hm?

FORTUNATA (closes the door). I will not tell you who. But somebody will write me soon or he will hear from me again.

MATEO (mocks her). Again, eh? You write once already?

FORTUNATA (goes back to the stove, none too eager to discuss this matter with MATEO). Sí, one letter.

2. Sí (sē), yes.
3. mole (mū′le), a rich sauce of chocolate and spices.
4. tortillas (tôr tē′yäs), round, flat corn cakes.
5. Señora Ramirez (se nyô′rä rä mēr′es), Mrs. Ramirez.
6. Bueno (bwe′nô), good.
7. Dios (dē′ôs), God.
8. Pepe (pe′pe).

MATEO. In your old age you are becoming a very strange woman, Fortunata. You write letters, you bring chickens home from I do not know where. . . .

FORTUNATA. Do not talk so much, and give this to the chickens. (She hands him a pan full of grain.)

MATEO. The chickens get food—oh, si—but your husband he does not matter. (He goes to the patio door, opens it, pushes the pan into the patio and comes back into the room.)

FORTUNATA. You matter—as much as you deserve to matter, Mateo. You are a lazy old man.

MATEO. Santo Dios![9] From eight o'clock in the morning until four in the afternoon, every day, I work in the museum and you say I am lazy!

FORTUNATA. You work! You sit near the door and you sell tickets. Only half the time people get in free because you are asleep.

MATEO. That is not true.

FORTUNATA (her thoughts on herself). Work is what I have to do. All my life.

MATEO (pleads with her). Por favor,[10] do not begin that. You have not talked about all your misery for a long time.

FORTUNATA (indignant). But still I am miserable! (She starts setting the table.) I must buy some herb tea and drink it again. My bones are sick in my back and in my arms. Still I must wake up before the sun is up. To make food for you before you go—to what you call your work. Ave Maria![11] And as soon as you go, I must think about your supper and to wash the floors and the clothes . . . .

MATEO. And to take care of your chickens who make the patio dirty. Do not forget that!

FORTUNATA (with a blissful smile). Ah, the chickens!

MATEO (irritated by her affection for the chickens). You are sick in your head, that is where you are sick, Fortunata. And one other thing; if the police find out—about the chickens—they will not understand. No, señora, they will think you are a thief. Fortunata, where do you get the chickens?

FORTUNATA. If I stole them, nobody noticed. It is three months ago. (She smiles to herself, knowing that this will irritate MATEO further.)

MATEO. All my life I am an honest man. People accuse me of being lazy maybe, but never of stealing anything. Now I must have an old wife who is a thief!

FORTUNATA (peacefully). Close your mouth, Mateo. Very well you know the police would be here a hundred times if I steal one chicken. And a hundred and three chickens? The whole government would come to arrest me. (She puts a steaming pot on the table.) Good beans. Eat.

MATEO (sits down at the table, slowly). Somebody give you the chickens?

FORTUNATA. I buy them! I tell you that every day. I buy them!

MATEO. You have no money, Fortunata. I know how much money I bring to you. It is enough for beans and rice and sometimes mole, but not for one hundred and three chickens—not for one half chicken!

FORTUNATA. Still, one morning I wake up and I want to buy chickens. I went to the market and I buy them.

MATEO (eats his beans). To steal money is worse than to steal chickens.

FORTUNATA. I do not steal money, Mateo. (A whistle is heard again. FORTUNATA runs to the door.)

---

9. Santo (sän'tô) Dios, Holy God.
10. Por favor (pôr fä vôr'), please.
11. Ave Maria (ä've mä rē'ä), Hail Mary, a phrase used here as an exclamation.

MATEO. First you complain about sickness in your bones and then you run like a young *muchacha*.[12] Three months ago you cannot do that.

FORTUNATA *(opens the door)*. Three months ago I was ready to die. Now I cannot afford to die. *(Looks outside.)* It is the postman.

MATEO *(goes on eating)*. Probably he is weighed down with letters for you.

FORTUNATA *(almost as if praying)*. I must hear. I must hear. There is no time to waste.

MATEO. What?

FORTUNATA *(slowly lowers her head and closes the door)*. He passed by.

MATEO. No letter?

FORTUNATA *(in defeat)*. No letter.

MATEO *(a little sorry for her, after all)*. Maybe you eat some beans, *si*?

FORTUNATA. No, I do not want food. *(She watches him eat, and suddenly turns her disappointment about the letter into anger against* MATEO.*)* You are a pig, Mateo. Eat, eat—that is all you do!

MATEO. Maybe I must stop eating to please you? It is my fault that the *señora* does not get her letter? Hah! I do not know even who it is that must write to you!

FORTUNATA *(violently fans the fire)*. I will write again. *Si, señor*,[13] I will write again!

MATEO. Fortunata, are you writing maybe to borrow money for the chickens?

FORTUNATA *(almost throws two pans on the table, as she faces her husband)*. Once and for all, Mateo, I tell you I buy the chickens with money. With money which I have! You do not understand that? *Bueno*, and I am a sick woman. Twenty-nine years ago I look at you and I say to myself, "Fortunata, this man he will never make you rich." This is what I say to myself twenty-nine years ago, one month after our matrimony took place. But eighteen years ago I look at you again and this time I say to myself, "Fortunata, this man will not even make enough money to bury you." I am a sick woman, Mateo, and I start to worry about my funeral. Do you know what happens to people who have no money to be buried?

MATEO. No. I do not like to know such things. They make me feel bad.

FORTUNATA. It is good for you to think about it when you spend your money on drink. If you die and have no money for the funeral, the government they send a truck and they throw you in with many other dead people. Then they take you to the cemetery and put you in the earth.

MATEO. That they do to the rich people also.

FORTUNATA. *Si*, but they put them in the earth alone. You they put together with all the dead people on the truck! *(She shudders.)*

MATEO *(not at all horrified)*. Maybe that is not so bad. Maybe that is for dead people not to be so lonely.

FORTUNATA. Do not be disrespectful, Mateo!

MATEO. Who tells you all this story about dead people?

FORTUNATA. Don Fabian, the night watchman of the cemetery. He knows.

MATEO. Hm. *(He pushes his plate aside.)* Anyway, I do not think it is nice for you to talk to me about dead people when I eat.

FORTUNATA. You ask me about the money.

MATEO *(regains interest in the conversation)*. Oh, *si*, the money.

FORTUNATA *(dishes some rice into* MATEO'S *plate)*. Eighteen years ago I start saving money for my fu-

---

12. *muchacha* (mü chä'chä), young girl.
13. *señor* (se nyôr'), mister or sir.

neral. Our children are dead and you never make enough money, so I know that when I die—no funeral. I save very carefully, Mateo, two hundred and seventy-eight pesos.[14]

MATEO (*shocked and astonished*). Two hundred and seventy . . . Fortunata!

FORTUNATA. I hide it from you. It is my secret, eh? You never know.

MATEO (*not without admiration*). You are a bad woman, Fortunata. You do not give me enough to eat so you can have a nice funeral.

FORTUNATA. What is more important, my soul or your stomach?

MATEO (*frankly*). I do not know. (*Curious.*) Where you hide this fortune?

FORTUNATA. That I will not tell you.

MATEO. But you have no money now.

FORTUNATA. I have some. A few chickens I sell—and many eggs.

MATEO. And to me, not even one egg.

FORTUNATA. When the letter comes, Mateo, I will give you one egg. One fresh egg. How do you wish that I fix it?

MATEO. I will think about that—when the letter comes.

FORTUNATA. You have no faith, Mateo. (*She goes back to the stove and gives him a plateful of* mole.) The *mole* is good today, thick, sweet and hot. (*She tastes it herself.*)

MATEO. Fortunata, there is one thing I do not understand. If you save money for eighteen years to give yourself a nice funeral, why do you spend it on chickens?

FORTUNATA. I explain this in the letter.

MATEO. But to me you cannot explain?

FORTUNATA. One night I have a bad dream, Mateo, and when I wake up in the morning I say to myself, "Fortunata, you have no right to hide that money in your kitchen floor. . . ." (*No sooner has she said* this than she realizes that she has given part of her secret away. MATEO *immediately gets up and starts scrutinizing the kitchen floor.*) You will not find it, Mateo. I have a good place. (MATEO *continues his search.*) So I say to myself, "Fortunata, you have no right to keep this money and not use it when children are starving—little children who are helpless, who are too young to work." That is what I say to myself.

MATEO. That is the trouble—always you are speaking to yourself, Fortunata. Where are these children?

FORTUNATA. In the countries that had the war, the terrible war. (*With a disgusted look at* MATEO.) You work in the museum. Do you not see the pictures on the wall? They are near where you sit—like big announcements in color.

MATEO. Huh?

FORTUNATA. You have your eyes closed all the time, Mateo. *Dios mío*,[15] they are pictures of hungry children, cold children. They say to me, "Help, Fortunata, help!" This is what gave me a bad dream, Mateo, a very bad dream. Because I remember our Genaro[16] who died when he was less than a year, because we have no food for him.

MATEO. That is when I fight in the Revolution.

FORTUNATA. *Sí*, and while you fight we lose all the children. (*She sighs heavily and puts that thought out of her mind.*) And I think—if I can help these children who lost their mothers and fathers in the war—if I can, then I must, no, Mateo? First, I wished to send my money, but it is

14. **pesos** (pe'sôs). The peso is a unit of currency used in Spain and Latin America. Its worth varies from country to country.
15. **Dios mío** (mē'ô), my God.
16. **Genaro** (he nä'rô).

not much, two hundred and seventy-eight pesos.

MATEO. Not much?

FORTUNATA. For so many children. But if I buy chickens with the money, I can raise more chickens. I sell the eggs and buy more—and I can send chickens, many chickens.

MATEO *(is moved. He says nothing at first, but he takes* FORTUNATA'S *head in his hands and kisses her hair).* I am glad I marry you, Fortunata.

FORTUNATA *(embarrassed).* You are an old fool. Please leave me alone. And sit down to finish your supper.

MATEO. I think maybe I am not so hungry.

FORTUNATA. Mateo, I make the *mole* for you. Now, you eat!

MATEO. First you take my appetite away from me, and then you tell me to eat! *(And another thought comes to his mind.)* Fortunata, what happens if I die?

FORTUNATA. If you are good enough, you go to Heaven. If not . . . .

MATEO. This I know. But my body, what happens to it? What kind of funeral?

FORTUNATA. You save money for your funeral?

MATEO. No.

FORTUNATA. Then you do not have a funeral.

MATEO. You are a very selfish woman.

FORTUNATA. I save only for mine.

MATEO. From my money!

FORTUNATA. Anyway, now I spend it.

MATEO *(laughs).* So, Fortunata, if you die . . . .

FORTUNATA. You laugh if I die?

MATEO. No, I think it is funny that eighteen years you hide your money. One day you die and you have no funeral because nobody knows you have this money.

FORTUNATA. I am not so stupid, Mateo. All the time I tell Father Anto-

nio where the money is hidden and what it is for.

MATEO *(incensed).* So! Father Antonio you tell, but I do not know in my own house where the money is.

FORTUNATA. If I tell you, you spend it. Even if you do not spend it before, you do it on the day of the funeral—*si, si,* you buy drinks instead of coffin, flowers . . . .

MATEO *(angry).* If you die now, Fortunata, you know what I do? I bury you with your chickens.

FORTUNATA. Hm! The chickens will go when the letter comes.

MATEO. But I do not think there is any letter.

FORTUNATA *(aggressively).* He will answer me!

MATEO. Who? Who you write to? Father Antonio?

FORTUNATA. I see Father Antonio every Sunday. Why write to him? No. I write to the *Presidente.*[17]

MATEO. The *Presidente?* The *Presidente* of what?

FORTUNATA. You fool! What other *Presidente* is there? The *Presidente* of our country!

MATEO. You write to the *Presidente* of our country! *Madre mía!*[18] You are crazy, Fortunata! You lose your head!

FORTUNATA. I have to ask somebody, no, to help me send the chickens to the hungry children?

MATEO. Somebody? *(With angry laughter.)* So she asks the *Presidente!* He is the only "somebody" she can think of! The *Presidente* she asks!

FORTUNATA *(simply).* It is his duty.

MATEO. Naturally! He has nothing else to do. He will come and pack the chickens in a crate and ship them for you.

---

17. Presidente (pre sē den'te).
18. Madre mía (mä'dre mē'ä), my mother, a phrase used as an exclamation.

FORTUNATA *(matter-of-factly)*. He does not have to do it himself.

MATEO. For this I am certain he will thank you. When I see these chickens the first time, I know they will bring to me trouble.

FORTUNATA. Always you think about yourself. What do you have to do with this? It is not your funeral money; it is mine. It is not your letter . . . .

MATEO. It is my wife that you are! I am — responsible — for you.

FORTUNATA. Never before you know this! Huh! I am responsible for myself, *señor*, and if the *Presidente* does not like my letter, I tell him I write it with no help from you. Now, you drink your coffee. *(Which she hands to him in a large cup.)*

MATEO *(sits down and tries to take a sip, but his indignation forces him to put his cup down again)*. To the *Presidente!* She writes to the *Presidente!* Not to the mayor, no. Not to the *gobernador!* No, not to the *ministro!*[19] No, *señor*, my old woman has to write to the *Presidente* himself!

FORTUNATA. One time in my life I have a right to disturb him, I think.

MATEO. You think, huh?

FORTUNATA. I help to make him *Presidente*, no? I vote and I force you to vote. I think . . .

MATEO. You think? You do not think! A letter to the *Presidente!* The postman takes it to him, you think, and says, "Here, *Señor Presidente*, here is a letter to you from Fortunata Gutierrez." *(Irately he drinks his coffee.)*

FORTUNATA. No. Probably some helper of the *Presidente* reads the letter first. Maybe many helpers. That is why it takes such a long time.

MATEO. Thousands of helpers, Fortunata, the whole government! Do you know how busy the *Presidente* is? He is the busiest man in all the country — and you know how many people are in this country?

FORTUNATA *(sincere in her ignorance)*. No.

MATEO *(He doesn't know either)*. *Bueno* — there are very many, more than you can count. If all write to the *Presidente* . . .

FORTUNATA. But they do not all write. Only I write. And only one time. But I think maybe I write again. I make a mistake in my first letter.

MATEO. In the grammar?

FORTUNATA. About that I do not know. But maybe it is a mistake that I tell the *Presidente* so much about me — and you.

MATEO. You tell him about me?

FORTUNATA. Naturally. I have to explain why I save funeral money all my life.

MATEO. What you explain, eh, Fortunata?

FORTUNATA. I tell him the truth. That you are a lazy man who likes to drink and would not give me a decent funeral.

MATEO *(distressed)*. To the *Presidente!* She ruins my good name!

FORTUNATA. I am afraid I complain so much in the letter he feels sorry for me and wants to leave the chickens here.

MATEO *(exasperated)*. I hope so!

FORTUNATA. I cannot touch one of those chickens for myself.

MATEO. I touch it for you.

FORTUNATA. You forget the hungry children?

MATEO *(somewhat ashamed)*. *Bueno*, I remember. *(Then, with a new idea.)* But, Fortunata, what are these chickens to so many children?

FORTUNATA. I cannot take care of

---

19. **gobernador** (gô ber nä dôr') . . . **ministro** (mē nes′ trō), governor and chief of a government department, respectively.

everybody, Mateo, but if fifty children have something to eat two, three days, it is good, no? It is more important than how an old woman is buried. *(But she doesn't like to dwell on this.)* Mateo, your supper will be cold. *(As* MATEO *sits down to eat, a great commotion is heard outside.* FORTUNATA *goes to the window and looks out.)* So many people! All the neighbors are in the street. What is this?

MATEO. A fire maybe?

[*He gets up and joins her at the window.*]

FORTUNATA. Look, Mateo, a beautiful automobile!

MATEO. A black automobile.

[*This with an ominous voice.*]

FORTUNATA *(with admiration)*. Oh! *Ave María*, never in my life I see such a nice automobile.

MATEO. Fortunata, look! A man he comes out of the black automobile.

FORTUNATA. On our street what can he do? He is dressed in so good a suit!

MATEO. Fortunata! He is coming here!

FORTUNATA *(alarmed)*. Mateo!

MATEO. He is the police!

FORTUNATA *(looks out again)*. He has no uniform.

MATEO. He is a detective. They do not have uniforms. He comes to take you to the prison. Maybe me also. That is what happens when you write letters to the *Presidente*.

FORTUNATA. I do nothing wrong. Nobody will take me to the prison. [*There's a knock on the door.*]

MATEO *(looks out the window again)*. All the neighbors look at this house. Oh, you will ruin me, Fortunata.

The shame, *Madre mía*, the shame! *(There's another knock on the door. FORTUNATA looks at MATEO, and knows she'll have to open it. She does. A very well-dressed GENTLE-MAN comes in.)* Señor, you probably made a mistake. . .

GENTLEMAN. I am looking for *Señora* Fortunata Gutierrez.

MATEO. Why?

FORTUNATA. Close your mouth, Mateo! *(To the GENTLEMAN.)* I am Fortunata Gutierrez, and this is my husband, Mateo Gutierrez, but he is not to blame for anything.

GENTLEMAN. It seems to me he would be proud to share the blame for this. *(From his brief case he produces a long document which bears a gold seal and a red ribbon.)*

MATEO. The order for your arrest!

GENTLEMAN *(smiles)*. No, a long letter from the *Presidente*.

FORTUNATA *(holds on to the doorknob, afraid of falling)*. Mateo, bring me a chair! *(MATEO looks dumbfounded; doesn't know what to do.)* A chair, you fool, before I faint! *(MATEO quickly complies. FORTUNATA sits down, but springs up at once.)* Señor, I am very rude. You please sit down.

GENTLEMAN. *Gracias,*[20] *Señora* Gutierrez, but you're the one who is excited. Anyway, I only have a few minutes. Then I must return to the train which will take me back to the *Presidente*. Won't you sit down? *(FORTUNATA does.)* The letter is quite long, so I will leave it with you to read by yourself.

FORTUNATA *(as she takes the letter from the GENTLEMAN'S hands)*. Gracias, señor. But please, you tell me the *Presidente* he says no or *sí?*

GENTLEMAN. He says *sí.*

FORTUNATA. Now I am happy.

GENTLEMAN. He also wishes to thank you for your kind thoughts. But the letter will tell you all that in better words than I have at my command.

FORTUNATA *(gets up)*. Maybe you drink one cup of coffee here?

GENTLEMAN. No, *gracias*, but I see you have some *mole*. If I could taste that . . . .

FORTUNATA *(runs to get a plate)*. Naturally, *señor*.

MATEO. You will pardon my Fortunata, *señor*, but there is no chicken in the *mole*.

GENTLEMAN. We are saving the chickens for a better purpose. *(MATEO supposes he should smile. He does.)* By the way, *señora*, tomorrow a truck will come here to pick up the chickens.

[*Meanwhile* FORTUNATA *has given him a plate full of* mole *and* tortillas.]

FORTUNATA. The house is yours, señor, if you wish to sit down.

GENTLEMAN. *(eats)*. Hm. Hm. *(Sits down.)* Muy bueno!*[21]

[*Obviously he is pleased with the food, which is rather a surprise to* MATEO.]

MATEO. Fortunata, you are a very good woman.

[*He tries to put his arm around her, but she pushes him away, embarrassed to have such intimacies occur in front of an illustrious stranger. She begins to unfold the letter and reads.* MATEO *looks over her shoulder. The* GENTLEMAN *eats and watches them.*]

FORTUNATA *(tears in her eyes)*. The *Presidente* writes a beautiful letter.

GENTLEMAN. Your letter was very beautiful too, *señora*. *(He rises.)* I wish I could stay for a full meal, but the *Presidente* has other duties for me. *(He shakes FORTUNATA'S hand.)* You are the sort of woman we are proud of, *Señora* Gutierrez. *(Now he shakes MATEO'S hand.)* And you are

---

20. *Gracias* (grä′sē äs), thank you.
21. *Muy* (mü′i) *bueno*, very good.

a very lucky man, *señor. (He goes to the door and turns back.)* The *Presidente* will be sorry he did not come himself—when I tell him how good your *mole* is.

[*He goes out.*]

FORTUNATA *(At first she is speechless. She sits down with the letter in her hand, but she can't read. She is crying).* Mateo. Mateo.

MATEO *(soothingly).* Sí, sí, it is too much for my Fortunata. Tomorrow they will take the chickens away, but the letter you can keep always.

FORTUNATA. Sí, but I think . . . *(She dries her tears and rises.)* Mateo, now you will see where I hide the money, because I must count it.

MATEO. Naturally.

FORTUNATA. Later I will find a new place to hide it.

[*She lifts a stone from the floor and takes out a handkerchief. She unties the knots as she places it on the table.* MATEO *watches the bills and coins come out of the little bundle.*]

MATEO. You are rich, Fortunata!

FORTUNATA *(counts).* Ninety, one hundred, one hundred—hm—one hundred and twenty—hm—hm.

MATEO *(scratches his head).* So much money in my own house and I do not know it!

FORTUNATA. Two hundred and eighty-three *pesos*, Mateo. That is five more than when I start. Mateo, I am happy! I can buy sixty new chickens. With the eggs I sell, I buy more chickens. In one month I write again to the *Presidente* . . . .

MATEO. You are a woman of business, Fortunata.

FORTUNATA. Tomorrow, after they take the chickens away, I must go to the market. *(She replaces the money in her handkerchief.)* Maybe I wait until you finish your work, and then you help me.

[*She is about to replace the money in the floor, but looks at* MATEO *and decides it's safer to hide it in her bosom.*]

MATEO. But, Fortunata, if you spend all this money on new chickens, you will have nothing for your funeral.

FORTUNATA. It is good business, the chickens. I will make the money back. And, anyway, Mateo, I do not feel like dying!

[*She goes to the stove.*]

MATEO *(amazed by this old woman of his).* No?

FORTUNATA. I will make for you something good, Mateo—three fried eggs!

[MATEO *settles down at the table in happy expectation, as* FORTUNATA *breaks the first egg into a skillet.*]

CURTAIN

1. (a) Why does Fortunata start saving for her funeral? **(b)** What brings about her change of plans?

2. (a) What kind of person is Fortunata? Cite passages from the play to illustrate your answer. **(b)** Describe Mateo's character traits, drawing on the play for evidence. **(c)** Review the Handbook article on methods of characterization (page 516). Which methods does the playwright use in portraying Mateo and Fortunata?

3. What does the gentleman mean in describing Fortunata's letter as "beautiful"?

4. (a) Do you agree with the gentleman that Mateo is lucky in his wife? Why or why not? **(b)** Do you think Fortunata is lucky or unlucky in Mateo? Explain.

5. (a) What is Fortunata's attitude toward funerals after the gentleman's visit? **(b)** Why has her project altered her outlook on life?

6. Is the Gutierrez' poverty important to the plot? Explain.

7. (a) What creates the main suspense of the play? **(b)** Is the happy ending appropriate? Why or why not?

8. Could the action of "Fortunata Writes a Letter" have occurred in a setting other than Latin America? Explain.

WORD STUDY

Throughout the play, Fortunata and Mateo go back and forth to the *patio* offstage. The Spanish word *patio* originally meant a courtyard open to the sky. But in recent years it has become increasingly common for Americans to call their backyard terraces *patios*. *Patio* is only one of many Spanish words that have become familiar English expressions since Spanish colonists settled in the southern and southwestern parts of the United States three hundred years ago.

Perhaps the *vaquero* (literally "cow man" in Spanish) of the southwestern plains brought the greatest number of Spanish terms into our language. Match the well-known Western-American terms at right with their Spanish ancestors in the left-hand column. Explain how each grew to have its present meaning, using your dictionary for help.

1.	*la reata* (the rope)	**a.**	palomino
2.	*bronco* (wild, rough)	**b.**	rodeo
3.	*corro* (ring)	**c.**	lariat
4.	*lazo* (noose)	**d.**	ranch
5.	*paloma* (dove)	**e.**	lasso
6.	*rancho* (group of persons who eat together)	**f.**	bronco
7.	*rodear* (go around)	**g.**	corral

THE AUTHOR

When he was eight years old, Russian-born Theodore Apstein settled in Mexico with his parents. His eleven years there as a youth, and brief visits since, have instilled in him a continuing interest in America's southern neighbors.

Apstein declares that two things led to the writing of "Fortunata." One is his love for the people of Mexico and Central America, the other an incident of several years ago. While he was working briefly for the United Nations Relief and Rehabilitation Administration, he noticed a touching letter from a woman who, like Fortunata, wanted to help the poverty-stricken children of the world. "Her scheme was different from Fortunata's," Apstein writes, "but the idea for the play was born there."

His dramas, one of which he translated into Spanish for production in Mexico City, have appeared both on and off Broadway. Apstein also writes frequently for dramatic television programs.

See
IRONIC TONE
*Handbook
of Literary
Terms
page 528*

*When news came in 1704
of the British victory over the French
at the German village of Blenheim,
the people of England cheered for joy.
How does the poet, writing a century later, regard the event?*

The Battle of Blenheim   /*ROBERT SOUTHEY*

IT WAS a summer evening;
  Old Kaspar's work was done,
And he before his cottage door
  Was sitting in the sun;
And by him sported on the green 5
His little grandchild Wilhelmine.

She saw her brother Peterkin
  Roll something large and round,
Which he beside the rivulet
  In playing there had found. 10
He came to ask what he had found,
That was so large, and smooth, and
    round.

Old Kaspar took it from the boy,
  Who stood expectant by; 14
And then the old man shook his head,
  And with a natural sigh,
" 'Tis some poor fellow's skull," said
    he,
"Who fell in the great victory.

"I find them in the garden,
  For there's many here about; 20
And often, when I go to plow,
The plowshare turns them out;
For many thousand men," said he,
"Were slain in that great victory."

"Now tell us what 'twas all about," 25
  Young Peterkin, he cries;
And little Wilhelmine looks up
  With wonder-waiting eyes;
"Now tell us all about the war,
And what they fought each other
    for." 30

"It was the English," Kaspar cried,
  "Who put the French to rout;
But what they fought each other for,
  I could not well make out;
But everybody said," quoth he, 35
"That 'twas a famous victory.

"My father lived at Blenheim then,
  Yon little stream hard by;
They burnt his dwelling to the
    ground.
  And he was forced to fly; 40
So with his wife and child he fled,
Nor had he where to rest his head.

"With fire and sword the country
    round
  Was wasted far and wide,
And many a childing mother then,   45
  And new-born baby, died;
But things like that, you know, must
    be
At every famous victory.

"They say it was a shocking sight
  After the field was won;   50
For many thousand bodies here
  Lay rotting in the sun;
But things like that, you know, must
    be
After a famous victory.

"Great praise the Duke of Marlboro'
    won,   55
  And our good Prince Eugene."[1]
"Why, 'twas a very wicked thing!"
  Said little Wilhelmine.
"Nay, nay, my little girl," quoth he;
"It was a famous victory.   60

"And everybody praised the Duke
  Who this great fight did win."
"But what good came of it at last?"
  Quoth little Peterkin.
"Why, that I cannot tell," said he;   65
"But 'twas a famous victory."

---

1. *Duke of Marlboro' . . . Prince Eugene.* The English forces, led by the Duke of Marlborough, were allied to the Austrians, commanded by Prince Eugene.

DISCUSSION

1. (a) How had the war affected old Kaspar's family and neighbors? (b) What is Kaspar's attitude toward the battle? (c) How does his attitude contrast with that of the children?
2. Why does Kaspar continue to repeat the phrase "a famous victory" in his explanation to the children?
3. (a) Whose attitude, Kaspar's or the children's, reflects the poet's own feeling? How do you know? (b) Why is the tone of this poem considered ironic?

THE AUTHOR

The English poet Robert Southey (1774–1843) claimed to have spent his years at Oxford University studying swimming and boating. Whether or not his claim is true, he did have some difficulty in settling down to serious work. After a few unsuccessful projects including the study of law, he went to Portugal for a time to study literature. Finally, he began writing for a popular English magazine, to which he contributed over one hundred articles, his subjects ranging widely from relief of the poor to Spanish literature.

Southey also wrote poetry. In 1813 he became poet laureate (the official national poet) of England, a post he held for thirty years. He wrote more than fifty volumes of prose and verse; "The Battle of Blenheim" is one of his most admired works.

After the graveyard was finished,
he yearned for only one more thing.
Can you infer what Papa's ambition led him to want?

THE GRAVEYARD

LYSANDER KEMP

MY FATHER was a good man, but once when I was a small boy, suddenly he was ambitious. I know it is excellent to be ambitious, if you have the right head for it, but my father had the wrong head. His ambition was not money, or a grand home with glass in the windows, it was a graveyard for our small village. I can smile now but it was trouble and grief at the time, till he was not ambitious.

We lived in a humble adobe house in Ixtlapan, three mountain ridges out from San Pedro Jalpa.[1] There is a dirt road to Ixtlapan now, and a bus every day, and many more houses, some of them of brick, but in those days the village was cut off by the ridges and you could reach San Pedro Jalpa, the large town with the market, only on horse or burro or your own feet. It was much work to bring crops and wares to the market over the three ridges, and to bring our dead to the graveyard to be buried.

My father was a farmer for most of the year, though he was also the *cohetero* of our village, that is, he made the *cohetes*,[2] the skyrockets, for the Day of the Cross and the Sixteenth of September[3] and the other special days. He was a good farmer, raising papayas for the market and corn and beans for ourselves, and we were poor but we were contented. Then suddenly he was ambitious.

He had brought papayas to the market in San Pedro Jalpa on a burro, riding another himself, and had sold them and come home weary. But the old father of Eufemio Bernal had died on that day, and he was related to our family, so on the next day my father had to climb the three ridges to San Pedro and back all over again, this time on foot with the little funeral pro-

From *The Virginia Quarterly Review*, Summer 1956. Reprinted by permission of the author and *The Virginia Quarterly Review*.
1. *Ixtlapan* (ēst lä pän') . . . *San Pedro Jalpa* (sän pä'drō häl'pä), villages in central Mexico.
2. *cohetero* (kō ā tā'rō) . . . *cohetes* (kō ā'tās).
3. *Day of the Cross . . . September,* a religious festival and Mexican Independence Day, respectively.

cession. He grumbled to my mother all the way there, though she tried to hush him. Finally, on the way back, he said to Mateo Rosa, the oldest and most respected man in Ixtlapan, and a cousin to the corpse, that it was a perfect shame to lug a body over the mountains like a load of fruit in a box, and to bury it away in a strange place.

Mateo was riding a burro, because he was so old. He was a man of dignity. He had a white beard and he sat on the burro as if it were a fine prancing horse, and his custom was to think a moment before he spoke. So now he thought a moment, squinting out at my father from under his wide sombrero, and said, "But why not? All the dead of Ixtlapan are buried in San Pedro Jalpa."

"True," my father said, talking upward because Mateo was on the burro, "but it is a disgrace, all this lugging them over the three ridges."

"It is not respectful to the dead," Mateo replied after a little pause, "if you begrudge them the trouble."

"Yes, it is true. But I am respectful to the dead, and that is why I say all this toting is a disgrace, we should bury them in Ixtlapan."

Mateo thought a moment. "No," he said, "we always bury our dead in San Pedro Jalpa." His tone was very final and that ought to have been the end of it, because the *costumbres*,[4] the customs, are very important in Mexico with the *indios*,[5] and we were all *indios* at least partly.

But now my father was ambitious for Ixtlapan, and he said, "Why? The dead are our own dead. We should bury them at home where they belong."

"No, no, it is impossible."

"Why?"

And for once, Mateo forgot to think a moment, for the answer was so perfectly simple. "Why? Because we have no graveyard in Ixtlapan."

My father was waiting for this, like a hawk in the air. He could not speak against the *costumbres* without danger, because they are so strong, but he could answer this. "True, we have none. So we should build one, it is very simple, and bring the priest from San Pedro to make it holy, and then we can bury our dead properly at home."

Mateo thought hard for a long time, and I remember wondering if he was going to answer at all. He stared straight ahead over the ears of his burro, and finally he said, "No, all the dead of Ixtlapan are buried in San Pedro." But he said it without hope, and of course my father promptly said, "Yes, because we have no graveyard. So we should build our own. That is what I say."

Mateo thought again, for a terribly long time, and said, "It is not the *costumbre*. But it is possible." Then he closed his mouth and spoke nothing more the whole way back, and I knew that my father had won a victory. I was tired but I swaggered a little as I walked, for old Mateo's mind was as hard to move as any of the three ridges.

In the days following, my father spoke his ambition to the men of the village, one at a time, in the same way he had spoken it to Mateo Rosa. All of them argued against it, because it was not the *costumbre*, but my father talked them all down. He was a quiet man, usually, and all this talking astonished the village. My mother made a joke of it, telling him he was becoming a *politico*,[6] but he paid no attention to her. Finally the men agreed to

---

4. *costumbres* (kōs tüm′bräs).
5. *indios* (in′dyos), Indians.
6. *politico* (po lēt′ē ko), politician.

meet at my father's house the next Sunday afternoon, to choose the proper place for a graveyard.

When Sunday came the men gathered outside our house, and even old Mateo was there. He still said it was a wrong idea, but he thought that if there was to be a graveyard anyhow, the wisest man in Ixtlapan should at least help to choose the right place for it. The men talked for a while, then they began walking around the village, pointing this way and that, while my brothers and I tagged along. Some of the men asked their questions of Mateo, but some of them turned to my father for his thought.

All of them knew, of course, that there was only one proper place for a graveyard, the low hill just outside the village to the north. But nobody mentioned it for a long time, because it was a pleasure to talk about the other places and show how they were not good.

At last my uncle Francisco Padilla, who had a weak leg and hated all this tramping about, said, "Look, why not the little hill over there?"

"Over where?" my father asked.

"Over there where I am pointing," my uncle said, pointing at it.

"Possibly, possibly," my father said. "Let us go over and look. It is very possible."

They all climbed up the little hill, and after peering around and discussing it they decided it was exactly right. There was some brush on it, and some *nopal*[7] cactus, so they agreed to meet the next Sunday afternoon to clear it off, and to begin building the wall the Sunday following.

And that was the way it happened. After the brush and the *nopales* were cleared off, they figured out how many bricks of adobe they needed for the wall, and how many roof tiles to run around the top of it for a protection against the season of rains. Then they figured out how many adobes and roof tiles each man was to bring. Then, Sunday by Sunday, they brought what they decided and built the wall.

On the last Sunday, when the wall was finished, my uncle said to the others as they all stood admiring it, "Now we can rest on Sundays in the afternoon."

"True," my father said, "if you can think of nothing better to do." He was not sympathetic with my uncle's weak leg. "But the graveyard is not finished yet. It is still only a piece of ground and a wall. We have to dedicate it."

"Yes," Mateo Rosa said. "With the priest from San Pedro Jalpa, to make it holy."

"Good," my uncle said. "When?"

There was an argument then about the proper time for a fiesta to dedicate it. The other men wanted to hold the fiesta on the next Sunday, but my father and Mateo agreed for once and they argued that to dedicate a graveyard properly, first you must have a corpse.

"Why a corpse?" asked young Ocampo, turning to Mateo. Young Ocampo was too fond of tequila, and was always drunk at fiestas, and on many nights between them.

Mateo thought a moment. "Because," he said, "you must always have a corpse to dedicate a graveyard."

"Yes," my father said. "Will the priest come all the way from San Pedro, over the three ridges, to bless a mere empty piece of earth, if we have no corpse to put into it?"

"I think he will," Ocampo said. "If we pay him, he will come."

---

7. **nopal** (nō päl′), cactus with scarlet flowers. The plural is *nopales*.

"Be careful of your tongue," Mateo said.

Ocampo looked surprised. "I am only speaking the truth," he said.

"No," Mateo said, very angry, "because you must have a suitable corpse to dedicate a graveyard. It is the *costumbre*."

Then Ocampo remembered that Mateo was the oldest, wisest, and most respected man in Ixtlapan, and held his tongue.

"Good," my father said, "we all agree. As soon as we have a corpse I will ride to San Pedro for the priest, and the fiesta will be the day he comes, whenever it may be."

"Good, good," Mateo said, looking hard at Ocampo. "And who wishes to say more?" Nobody spoke a word, and so it was decided.

My father was a busy man during the week that followed, because there was work in the fields and in his spare time he made *cohetes* for the fiesta of the graveyard. The *cohetes* he made were rockets that explode in the air, and he made almost fifty of them, bringing back more powder from San Pedro Jalpa on market day.

To make a *cohete* of that kind, first you need a tube of cane, as thick as your big toe and as long as your long finger. You put in the explosion first, then the powder to send it up, and you fasten a piece of paper over the end to keep the powder in. You wrap the tube with twine, and tie it to a straight stick or switch the length of your arm, and it is finished. When you shoot if off, you hold it in your hand by the tube, pointing up, and touch a smouldering corncob to the paper that holds in the powder. It begins to shoot orange flame and rushes up out of your hand into the sky, and explodes with a puff of white smoke and a loud noise.

My father finished the last of the *cohetes* on the next Sunday. "There," he said, bundling them all together and placing them in a corner, "now we are ready for the fiesta. All we need is the corpse."

"Hush," my mother said, "you should not speak of death like that."

"If it comes, it comes," he said. "And then we hold the fiesta. That was my meaning."

"It will come too soon, whenever it comes."

"It is true," he said.

But after that, my father began to think about the corpse. I was too young and silly to know it, but I saw later that my mother knew it. I was the next-to-oldest son, and my older brother and I worked in the fields with my father, and when we came home to supper on Monday, my father asked, "And is everybody well?"

"Yes," my mother said. "Chole broke the water jug." Soledad[8] was my one sister.

"I mean," he said, "is anybody sick?"

"No, we are well."

"Good. But I mean, is anybody sick in Ixtlapan?"

"How am I to know? Am I a doctor?"

"You cackle enough with the other hens, you ought to know what is happening."

"If you want," she said, "I will run around to every house in the morning, and bring you a report."

"Now you are speaking foolishly."

"It is true. So stop your foolish questions and eat your supper."

"Good," he said, "good."

He never asked these questions again, and while I was listening to them the thought of the graveyard and the corpse was not in my head.

---

8. **Chole** (chō'lä) . . . **Soledad** (sō lä däd'). *Chole* is a nickname for *Soledad.*

But I remember that he sometimes inspected the bundle of *cohetes* in the evening, to be sure he had made them properly, and a few times we walked out to the graveyard on a Sunday morning to inspect the wall and stare at the mountains that stood all around our small valley.

Then, after many weeks had passed, Mateo Rosa took sick. When we came home from the fields in the late afternoon, my mother said, "Mateo's wife told me he is sick with a bad cough. It began in the night."

"Who?" my father asked. "Old Mateo Rosa?"

"Yes."

"Is the cough bad?"

"I said it was."

"Poor old man. I am going to visit him."

"Good. But first, eat your supper."

"How can I eat, woman, when my old friend is dying?"

"He is not dying, he is simply coughing."

"Poor old man," he said, shaking his head. But he ate his supper. When it was finished he put on his good sombrero and slung his folded serape[9] across his shoulder.

"Papá," I said, "I want to come."

"Yes, why not?"

Of course my brothers and Chole wanted to come too, but my father said no, I asked first, and he could not take a mob to a deathbed. So my father and I walked over to old Mateo's house in the cool darkness. We stopped a moment outside the door, to listen, but there was no sound within. "Poor old man," my father whispered and rapped on the door. There was a cough, and then a rustling, and then Mateo's wife, who was bent over like the letter C, peeped out at us and silently let us in.

Old Mateo was lying stretched out on his *petate*,[10] his reed sleeping-mat, with his black serape over him for a blanket. This is how the *indio* sleeps, on his *petate* on the dirt floor, and this is how he dies. Mateo began to cough weakly, and in the yellow candlelight he looked as if he were a corpse already.

"Good evening," my father said. "My woman tells me you are a little sick, and I have come to visit you."

Mateo coughed and gasped. "Thank you," he said at last, in a voice we could hardly hear. "I am dying."

"Nonsense, man," my father said. "You are too stubborn to die, you old burro."

Mateo tried to chuckle at that, but it only set him to gasping again.

"What you need," my father said, "is a bottle of good medicine. I am going to ride to San Pedro for it in the morning."

"No," Mateo said, but he could not say more because of the cough, and his wife grasped my father's arm and said, "Thank you, you are very kind, he needs the medicine."

"It is nothing. I am happy to serve an old friend. May you pass a good night, Mateo."

The old man nodded from his *petate*, and his wife thanked my father again as we left. Then we walked home in the darkness.

"He is a sick man," my father said.

"Yes."

"That cough is very bad."

"Papá, I think he is dying."

"Who knows? Possibly he is dying. Surely he is a sick man. And an old man too."

The next morning my father bor-

---

9. **serape** (sā rä′pä), a shawl or blanket, often having bright colors, worn by Spanish-American Indians.
10. **petate** (pä tä′tä).

rowed my uncle's good horse, because it was not so slow as the burros, and rode to San Pedro Jalpa, and came home in the afternoon with the bottle of medicine. My brother and I stayed home from the fields that day, and my father told me to return the horse to my uncle. "I hope I am not too late," he said to my mother. "It was difficult to find the right medicine. How is old Mateo?"

"He is better," she said. "The coughing is better, and he sat in the sun a little this morning."

"Good. I am happy to hear it." Then he walked away, over to Mateo's house. I wanted to ask him if I could come along again, but I stood watching him.

"He is tired," my mother said.

"It is true," I said. I returned the horse to my uncle and came home, and my mother asked me to sweep the *zaguán*,[11] the entryway. I was sweeping it with the twig broom when my father came back from Mateo's house. He was walking very slowly, and I wondered if Mateo was bad again, or perhaps a dead man. I stopped sweeping and asked, "How is Don Mateo, Papá?" but he did not look at me, he walked past me into the patio without answering. I dropped the broom and followed him.

"Well," my mother said, turning from the charcoal fire where she was cooking the supper, "how is he?"

My father stood looking at the coals a moment, as if he had not heard her. "He is better." His voice sounded strange, and I thought how tired he must be, from riding to San Pedro Jalpa and back. "He is much better, he is up and about."

"Good," my mother said. "Did you give him the medicine?"

"Yes. Yes, I gave him the medicine. He laughed, and said it was not necessary now, but he would try a lit-

tle anyhow. For the taste, he said. To see how it tasted."

"Good," my mother said, fanning the charcoal with the reed fan. "We live in a healthy village."

"Yes. I am happy." He took off his good sombrero and hung it on the nail where he kept it. "I am very happy."

Suddenly the thought of the new graveyard and the bundle of *cohetes* and the need of a proper corpse for the fiesta came into my silly head.

"Papá," I blurted without thinking, "you *wanted* him to die."

My father turned and looked at me, without speaking a word. His eyes frightened me as he walked toward me, because they were burning like the coals of the fire, but I could not run and he swung his open hand and struck me on the side of the head. I fell backward and my head hit the stone *metate*,[12] the platform for grinding corn, and I cannot remember anything of what happened in the next minutes.

When I could know anything again, my mother was cleaning the gash in my head, and my father was not in the house. My head hurt me badly, and I was as weak as old Mateo had been the night before, but after the gash was clean and the bleeding stopped, I felt better and wanted to eat supper.

My father came back into the house in a few minutes, frowning and silent, and we ate supper. None of us said a word, not even Chole, for a long time, and my father would not look at any of us. Finally I said, "Papá."

He looked at me then.

"Papá," I mumbled, "I am sorry. It was a bad thing to say."

He stared at me for a moment, and then he stood up and walked out

---

11. *zaguán* (sä gwän').
12. *metate* (mä tä′tä).

of the house again. The tears came into my eyes, and my head was hurting worse than before. "Is he angry again?" I asked my mother.

"No," she said. "No, he is not angry."

I was huddled up on my *petate*, but not asleep because of the pain in my wound, when my father came back into the house. He walked straight to the far end of the patio, fetched a long dry corncob from the little heap of them, and came over to the cooking fire with it. He fanned up the dying coals, thrust one end of the corncob into them until it was smouldering, and gathered up the bundle of *cohetes* from the corner in one arm. He looked at my mother and myself, as if calling to us to come, and strode out of the house. I threw off my serape and stood up, though I was dizzy for a moment, and my mother woke up Chole and my brothers, and we followed my father out into the dark street.

"Is he drunk?" my older brother whispered to my mother.

"No," she said. "Be still."

My father had set down the bundle of *cohetes* in the middle of the street, and we watched him pick up a *cohete*, hold it out before him, and touch the red glow of the corncob to the paper. The *cohete* spouted flame at his feet and shot hissing and wobbling up, up into the black sky, streaming fire behind it, and exploded high over us with a brilliant flash and a roar. He picked up another and fired it, and another, another, till the night rocked with the noise of them. None of us spoke, though Chole clapped her hands after each explosion.

Of course the village dogs had all begun barking after the first *cohete*, and after the third or fourth the house doors opened all over Ixtlapan, the people gazing out in astonishment. Then they came to where we stood, some of them running, some walking as if still asleep. In a little while almost the whole village, the young and the old, was clustered around us.

My father paid them no attention at all. "Are you crazy, man?" my uncle shouted, and young Ocampo asked what the fiesta was, he would have brought tequila if he had known there was a fiesta, but my father was deaf and dumb to them, he shot off his *cohetes*, while the bundle shrank and the street smelled of powder-smoke.

Finally Mateo Rosa came forward. He was still coughing a little but he was not a corpse, and he took my father's arm, stopping him.

"Come," old Mateo said. "Tell us the occasion. We are your friends."

"They are my own *cohetes*," my father said. "I bought the powder and I made them. Now I want to shoot them off, so I am shooting them off." He shook himself free and shot off more of them.

Mateo retreated a little, and consulted hard with my uncle and my mother. "He is crazy," my uncle said, tapping his brow. "Anybody can see he is crazy, wasting all those *cohetes* like that. We ought to stop him." My mother said nothing.

There were only five *cohetes* left, no more, when Mateo stepped forward and clutched my father's arm again. "Look," he said, "the village thinks you are crazy. Even your wife's own brother thinks it. Tell us the occasion. You woke us up, now you must tell us why."

"Good," my father said. "I made them to celebrate death. Now I am celebrating life. It is better to celebrate life, true?"

Mateo coughed, to show that he was still a sick man, and therefore not quite so wise as it was his custom to

be. "You are speaking in riddles," he said.

"I am celebrating your recovery, then," my father said. "Is it clear now?"

"My recovery?"

"Yes."

Mateo thought for a moment. "Thank you," he said.

"It is nothing. We are happy you are well again. That is all."

"But the graveyard," my uncle said. "What about the fiesta for the graveyard?"

"I hope it stands empty forever," my father said. He looked at my mother and gave a little laugh. "This woman says we live in a healthy village, so perhaps it is possible. Stand back, Mateo."

Old Mateo stepped back and stood beside my mother smiling, while my father shot off the last five *cohetes*. We all watched in silence as they rushed upward and burst among the stars.

✦   ✦   ✦   ✦

DISCUSSION

1. Why does the father suddenly want to build a graveyard?
2. (a) Why is Mateo's approval of the project important? (b) What are Mateo's reasons for rejecting the idea? (c) How does the father answer his objections?
3. Review the Handbook article on inferences (page 526). (a) From which of the father's actions can you infer his yearning for a corpse even before Mateo's illness? (b) Find lines that indicate his desire for Mateo's death and his disappointment at his recovery.

(c) What can you infer from the mother's saying "he is tired"?
4. (a) How does the boy's accusation affect his father? (b) Do you think the father is conscious of his desire? Why or why not? (c) Why has the graveyard become so important to him?
5. Why does he set off all the *cohetes*?
6. (a) What is the narrator's attitude toward his father? toward his father's project? How can you tell? (b) What does he mean in saying that his father had the "wrong head" for ambition?
7. (a) State the theme of the story. (b) What ambitions with similarly unfortunate consequences might an American father have?
8. In the article below, Lysander Kemp says he tried "to give the prose a Spanish feeling." Find lines in the story that seem to you to contain such a Spanish flavor.

FROM THE AUTHOR

"The Graveyard" is based on an anecdote I heard in Buffalo some eight years before I wrote the story. The Brazilian wife of a friend of mine told me that in a little village in Brazil the villagers built a graveyard, waited for someone to die so that it could be inaugurated properly, and finally got so impatient that they held a fiesta in the graveyard anyway. There was a lot of drinking, which led to a free-for-all machete fight. When it was over, there were seven corpses to be planted! This true anecdote stuck in my mind, and when, after living for several years in a Mexican village, I decided to try my hand at a story with a Mexican scene and cast, I reshaped the anecdote to my own purposes. The characters are all imaginary; the setting is the village in which I was living. In writing it, I tried to give the prose a Spanish feeling, but without giving the characters a phony Hollywood accent. As for the personages, I tried to interpret certain aspects of the Mexican character as I then understood it; and after having lived another nine years in Mexico, I see no reason to change anything.

Stuffed with people, the train crawled across the hot Spanish plains.
Note how the author's use of figurative language
gives life to the journey, the land, and his fellow travelers.

⊕⊕⊕⊕⊕⊕⊕⊕⊕⊕⊕⊕⊕⊕⊕⊕⊕⊕⊕⊕⊕⊕⊕⊕⊕⊕⊕⊕⊕⊕⊕⊕⊕⊕⊕⊕⊕

A Ride through Spain

TRUMAN CAPOTE

CERTAINLY the train was old. The seats sagged like the jowls of a bulldog, windows were out and strips of adhesive held together those that were left; in the corridor a prowling cat appeared to be hunting mice, and it was not unreasonable to assume his search would be rewarded.

Slowly, as though the engine were harnessed to elderly coolies,[1] we crept out of Granada.[2] The southern sky was as white and burning as a desert; there was one cloud, and it drifted like a traveling oasis.

We were going to Algeciras, a Spanish seaport facing the coast of Africa. In our compartment there was a middle-aged Australian wearing a soiled linen suit; he had tobacco-colored teeth and his fingernails were unsanitary. Presently, he informed us that he was a ship's doctor. It seemed curious, there on the dry, dour plains of Spain, to meet someone connected with the sea. Seated next to him there were two women, a mother and daughter. The mother was an over-stuffed, dusty woman with sluggish, disapproving eyes and a faint mustache. The focus for her disapproval fluctuated; first, she eyed me rather strongly because, as the sunlight fanned brighter, waves of heat blew through the broken windows and I had removed my jacket—which she considered, perhaps rightly, discourteous. Later on, she took a dislike to the young soldier who also occupied our compartment. The soldier, and the woman's not very discreet daughter, a buxom girl with the scrappy features of a prizefighter, seemed to have agreed to flirt. Whenever the wandering cat appeared at our door, the daughter pretended to be frightened, and the soldier would gallantly shoo the cat into the corridor: this by-play gave them frequent opportunity to touch each other.

The young soldier was one of many on the train. With their tasseled caps set at snappy angles, they hung about in the corridors smoking sweet black cigarettes and laughing confidentially. They seemed to be en-

1. **coolies,** unskilled Oriental laborers.
2. **Granada** (grä nä′dä), the capital city of Granada, a district in southern Spain.

joying themselves, which apparently was wrong of them, for whenever an officer appeared the soldiers would stare fixedly out the windows, as though enraptured by the landslides of red rock, the olive fields and stern stone mountains. Their officers were dressed for a parade, many ribbons, much brass; and some wore gleaming, improbable swords strapped to their sides. They did not mix with the soldiers, but sat together in a first-class compartment, looking bored and rather like unemployed actors. It was a blessing, I suppose, that something finally happened to give them a chance at rattling their swords.

The compartment directly ahead was taken over by one family: a delicate, attenuated, exceptionally elegant man with a mourning ribbon sewn around his sleeve, and, traveling with him, six thin, summery girls, presumably his daughters. They were beautiful, the father and his children, all of them, and in the same way: hair that had a dark shine, lips the color of pimentos, eyes like sherry. The soldiers would glance into their compartment, then look away. It was as if they had seen straight into the sun.

Whenever the train stopped, the man's two youngest daughters would descend from the carriage and stroll under the shade of parasols. They enjoyed many lengthy promenades, for the train spent the greatest part of our journey standing still. No one appeared to be exasperated by this except myself. Several passengers seemed to have friends at every station with whom they could sit around a fountain and gossip long and lazily. One old woman was met by different little groups in a dozen-odd towns —between these encounters she wept with such abandon that the Australian doctor became alarmed: why

no, she said, there was nothing he could do, it was just that seeing all her relatives made her so happy.

At each stop cyclones of barefooted women and somewhat naked children ran beside the train sloshing earthen jars of water and furrily squalling *Agua!*[3] *Agua!* For two *pesetas*[4] you could buy a whole basket of dark runny figs, and there were trays of curious white-coated candy doughnuts that looked as though they should be eaten by young girls wearing Communion dresses. Toward noon, having collected a bottle of wine, a loaf of bread, a sausage and a cheese, we were prepared for lunch. Our companions in the compartment were hungry, too. Packages were produced, wine uncorked, and for a while there was a pleasant, almost graceful festiveness. The soldier shared a pomegranate with the girl, the Australian told an amusing story, the witch-eyed mother pulled a paper-wrapped fish from between her bosoms and ate it with a glum relish.

Afterwards, everyone was sleepy; the doctor went so solidly to sleep that a fly meandered undisturbed over his open-mouthed face. Stillness etherized the whole train; in the next compartment the lovely girls leaned loosely, like six exhausted geraniums; even the cat had ceased to prowl, and lay dreaming in the corridor. We had climbed higher, the train moseyed across a plateau of rough yellow wheat, then between the granite walls of deep ravines where wind, moving down from the mountains, quivered in strange, thorny trees. Once, at a parting in the trees, there was something I'd wanted to see, a castle on a hill, and it sat there like a crown.

---

3. *Agua!* (ä′gwä), water.
4. *pesetas* (pā sā′täs), units of Spanish money worth about two cents apiece.

It was a landscape for bandits. Earlier in the summer, a young Englishman I know (rather, know of) had been motoring through this part of Spain when, on the lonely side of a mountain, his car was surrounded by swarthy scoundrels. They robbed him, then tied him to a tree and tickled his throat with the blade of a knife. I was thinking of this when, without preface, a spatter of bullet fire strafed the dozy silence.

It was a machine gun. Bullets rained in the trees like the rattle of castanets, and the train, with a wounded creak, slowed to a halt. For a moment there was no sound except the machine gun's cough. Then, "Bandits!" I said, in a loud dreadful voice.

"*Bandidos!*"[5] screamed the daughter.

"*Bandidos!*" echoed her mother, and the terrible word swept through the train like something drummed on a tomtom. The result was slapstick in a grim key. We collapsed on the floor, one cringing heap of arms and legs. Only the mother seemed to keep her head; standing up, she began systematically to stash away her treasures. She stuck a ring into the buns of her hair and, without shame, hiked up her skirts and dropped a pearl-studded comb into her bloomers. Like the cryings of birds at twilight, airy twitterings of distress came from the charming girls in the next compartment. In the corridor the officers bumped about yapping orders and knocking into each other.

Suddenly, silence. Outside, there was the murmur of wind in leaves, of voices. Just as the weight of the doctor's body was becoming too much for me, the outer door of our compartment swung open, and a young man stood there. He did not look clever enough to be a bandit.

"*Hay un médico en el tren?*"[6] he said, smiling.

The Australian, removing the pressure of his elbow from my stomach, climbed to his feet. "I'm a doctor," he admitted, dusting himself. "Has someone been wounded?"

"*Sí*, Señor. An old man. He is hurt in the head," said the Spaniard, who was not a bandit: alas, merely another passenger. Settling back in our seats, we listened, expressionless with embarrassment, to what had happened. It seemed that for the last several hours an old man had been stealing a ride by clinging to the rear of the train. Just now he'd lost his hold, and a soldier, seeing him fall, had started firing a machine gun as a signal for the engineer to stop the train.

My only hope was that no one remembered who had first mentioned bandits. They did not seem to. After acquiring a clean shirt of mine which he intended to use as a bandage, the doctor went off to his patient, and the mother, turning her back with sour prudery, reclaimed her pearl comb. Her daughter and the soldier followed after us as we got out of the carriage and strolled under the trees where many passengers had gathered to discuss the incident.

Two soldiers appeared carrying the old man. My shirt was wrapped around his head. They propped him under a tree and all the women clustered about, vying with each other to lend him their rosary; someone brought a bottle of wine, which pleased him more. He seemed quite happy, and moaned a great deal. The children who had been on the train circled around him giggling.

We were in a small wood that

---
5. *Bandidos!* (bän dē′dōs).
6. *Hay un médico en el tren?* Is there a doctor on the train?

smelled of oranges. There was a path, and it led to a shaded promontory: from here, one looked across a valley where sweeping stretches of scorched golden grass shivered as though the earth were trembling. Admiring the valley, and the shadowy changes of light on the hills beyond, the six sisters, escorted by their elegant father, sat with their parasols raised above them like guests at a *fête champêtre*.[7] The soldiers moved around them in a vague, ambitious manner; they did not quite dare to approach, though one brash, sassy fellow went to the edge of the promontory and called: "*Yo te quiero mucho*."[8] The words returned with the hollow sub-music of a perfect echo, and the sisters, blushing, looked more deeply into the valley.

A cloud, somber as the rocky hills, had massed in the sky, and the grass below stirred like the sea before a storm. Someone said he thought it would rain. But no one wanted to go: not the injured man, who was well on his way through a second bottle of wine, nor the children who, having discovered the echo, stood happily caroling into the valley. It was like a party, and we all drifted back to the train as though each of us wished to be the last to leave. The old man, with my shirt like a grand turban on his head, was put into a first-class carriage and several eager ladies were left to attend him.

In our compartment, the dark, dusty mother sat just as we had left her. She had not seen fit to join the party. She gave me a long, glittering look. "*Bandidos*," she said, with a surly, unnecessary vigor.

The train moved away so slowly butterflies flew in and out the windows.

---

7. *fête champêtre* (fet shäm pe′trə), country festival.
8. *Yo te quiero mucho.* I like you very much.

DISCUSSION

1. (a) Describe the people with whom the narrator shares a compartment. (b) Which person makes the most vivid impression on you? Why?

2. (a) What leads the narrator to assume that the travelers are threatened by bandits? (b) Describe the effects of his shout. (c) How does the mood of the travelers, after they learn the truth, contrast with their earlier reaction? (d) Why are they reluctant to reboard the train?

3. Explain the image created by each of the following figurative expressions: (a) "The seats sagged like the jowls of a bulldog. . . ." (b) ". . . as though the engine were harnessed to elderly coolies. . . ." (c) ". . . one cloud . . . drifted like a traveling oasis." (d) "The soldiers would glance into their [the girls'] compartment, then look away . . . as if they had seen straight into the sun." (e) ". . . cyclones of barefooted women and . . . children ran beside the train. . . ." (f) ". . . the lovely girls leaned loosely, like six exhausted geraniums. . . ." (g) ". . . sweeping stretches of scorched golden grass shivered as though the earth were trembling."

4. (a) What general impressions of Spanish life do you gain from Capote's account? (b) What differences might there be between this ride and one on an American train?

THE AUTHOR

Truman Capote was born in New Orleans in 1924. After his schooling in New York, he worked in the art department of *The New Yorker* magazine. In 1948 his first novel brought the young man quick popularity. Later works, such as *In Cold Blood*, a chilling account of a murder case, have enlarged his reputation as a fine writer.

Capote, who is deeply concerned with style, finds satisfaction in his work only after much rewriting.

A young Chinese wife writes to her husband
who has traveled far away to sell his tea and salt, paper and silk.
The poem, written more than twelve hundred years ago,
traces the effect of time on her feelings for her husband.
How are people today akin to this girl of centuries past?

The River Merchant's Wife: A Letter

LI T'AI-PO
(Translated by Ezra Pound)

While my hair was still cut straight across my forehead
I played about the front gate, pulling flowers.
You came by on bamboo stilts, playing horse,
You walked about my seat, playing with blue plums.
And we went on living in the village of Chokan[1]:   5
Two small people, without dislike or suspicion.

At fourteen I married My Lord you.
I never laughed, being bashful.
Lowering my head, I looked at the wall.[2]
Called to, a thousand times, I never looked back.   10

At fifteen I stopped scowling,
I desired my dust to be mingled with yours
For ever and for ever and for ever.
Why should I climb the lookout?

At sixteen you departed,   15
You went into far Ku-to-yen,[3] by the river of swirling eddies,
And you have been gone five months.
The monkeys make sorrowful noise overhead.[4]
You dragged your feet when you went out.

From PERSONAE by Ezra Pound. Copyright 1926, 1954 by Ezra Pound. Reprinted with permission of the
publisher, New Directions, and Arthur V. Moore, literary agent.
1. *Chokan,* (chō kän'), a village outside Nanking, a large city in eastern China, on the Yangtze River, longest
in China.
2. *Lowering my head . . . wall.* Traditionally, Chinese girls modestly looked away at the very mention
of marriage.
3. *Ku-to-yen,* a deep, dangerous gorge, edged by high cliffs, at the upper part of the Yangtze River, near
Tibet.
4. *monkeys . . . overhead.* Gibbons, small tailless monkeys, are as common in this area of China as squirrels are in parts of North America. They spend most of their time in trees, and make an eerie, wailing sound.

By the gate now, the moss is grown, the different mosses, 20
Too deep to clear them away!
The leaves fall early this autumn, in wind.
The paired butterflies are already yellow with August
Over the grass in the West garden;
They hurt me. I grow older. 25
If you are coming down through the narrows of the river Kiang,
Please let me know beforehand,
And I will come out to meet you,
As far as Cho-fu-Sa.[5]

---

5. **Cho-fu-Sa,** Long Wind Sands, a beach several hundred miles up the Yangtze from Nanking.

DISCUSSION

1. What kind of relationship between the two people is described in the first stanza?
2. (**a**) What can you infer from the expression "My Lord" (line 7) about the role of the Chinese husband? (**b**) How are the girl's feelings in lines 7–10 different from those expressed in lines 1–6? (**c**) What explanation can you give for her attitude?
3. What is the young wife's attitude after one year of marriage?
4. The lookout mentioned in line 14 is a hill beside the Yangtze River where, according to legend, a wife who had kept a long daily watch for her husband and his boat was finally turned to stone. What inference about the young wife's view of the future can you make from line 14?
5. (**a**) What does line 19 imply about the husband's attitude toward his trip? (**b**) How do lines 20–21 show that time has passed? (**c**) Why does the wife say that the butterflies in pairs hurt her? (**d**) What does she mean in saying "I grow older"? (**e**) What does her offer to meet her husband imply about her feelings?
6. In what ways does this ancient poem apply to people today?

THE AUTHOR

Li T'ai-Po (701–762), whom many consider the greatest Chinese poet of all time, lived during the T'ang dynasty, when China was the most advanced and prosperous nation in the world. He spent three years at the worldly, conspiracy-filled court of the Emperor. But for most of his life, instead of working to support his family, he roamed around China with carefree, fun-loving friends. Nevertheless, his many poems about love, friendship, and the delights of wine brought him recognition in his own lifetime and a great reputation through later centuries.

*Dark, snow-covered streets in Russia
form the setting of the old sleigh-driver's lonely search.
Can you anticipate how it will end?*

Misery

ANTON CHEKHOV

THE TWILIGHT OF EVENING. Big flakes of wet snow are whirling lazily about the street lamps, which have just been lighted, and lying in a thin soft layer on roofs, horses' backs, shoulders, caps. Iona Potapov, the sledge-driver,[1] is all white like a ghost. He sits on the box without stirring, bent as double as the living body can be bent. If a regular snowdrift fell on him it seems as though even then he would not think it necessary to shake it off. . . . His little mare is white and motionless too. Her stillness, the angularity of her lines, and the stick-like straightness of her legs make her look like a halfpenny gingerbread horse. She is probably lost in thought. Anyone who has been torn away from the plough, from the familiar gray landscapes, and cast into this slough, full of monstrous lights, of unceasing uproar and hurrying people, is bound to think.

It is a long time since Iona and his nag have budged. They came out

of the yard[2] before dinnertime and not a single fare yet. But now the shades of evening are falling on the town. The pale light of the lamps changes to a vivid color, and the bustle of the street grows noisier.

"Sledge to Vyborgskaya!" Iona hears. "Sledge!"

Iona starts, and through his snow-plastered eyelashes sees an officer in a military overcoat with a hood over his head.

"To Vyborgskaya," repeats the officer. "Are you asleep? To Vyborgskaya!"

In token of assent Iona gives a tug at the reins which sends cakes of snow flying from the horse's back and shoulders. The officer gets into the

---

"Misery" from THE SCHOOLMISTRESS AND OTHER STORIES by Anton Tchehov, translated by Constance Garnett. Reprinted by permission of Harper & Row, Publishers, Inc., David Garnett and Chatto and Windus Ltd.

1. sledge-driver, cab driver who uses a sleigh, or *sledge,* as a vehicle.
2. yard, enclosure where the cabmen live and maintain their equipment.

sledge. The sledge-driver clicks to the horse, cranes his neck like a swan, rises in his seat, and more from habit than necessity brandishes his whip. The mare cranes her neck, too, crooks her stick-like legs, and hesitatingly sets off. . . .

"Where are you shoving, you devil?" Iona immediately hears shouts from the dark mass shifting to and fro before him. "Where the devil are you going? Keep to the r-right!"

"You don't know how to drive! Keep to the right," says the officer angrily.

A coachman driving a carriage swears at him; a pedestrian crossing the road and brushing the horse's nose with his shoulder looks at him angrily and shakes the snow off his sleeve. Iona fidgets on the box as though he were sitting on thorns, jerks his elbows, and turns his eyes about like one possessed, as though he did not know where he was or why he was there.

"What rascals they all are!" says the officer jocosely. "They are simply doing their best to run up against you or fall under the horse's feet. They must be doing it on purpose."

Iona looks at his fare and moves his lips. . . . Apparently he means to say something, but nothing comes but a sniff.

"What?" inquires the officer.

Iona gives a wry smile, and straining his throat, brings out huskily: "My son . . . er . . . my son died this week, sir."

"H'm! What did he die of?"

Iona turns his whole body around to his fare, and says:

"Who can tell! It must have been from fever. . . . He lay three days in the hospital and then he died. . . . God's will."

"Turn round, you devil!" comes out of the darkness. "Have you gone cracked, you old dog? Look where you are going!"

"Drive on! drive on! . . ." says the officer. "We shan't get there till tomorrow going on like this. Hurry up!"

The sledge-driver cranes his neck again, rises in his seat, and with heavy grace swings his whip. Several times he looks round at the officer, but the latter keeps his eyes shut and is apparently disinclined to listen. Putting his fare down at Vyborgskaya, Iona stops by a restaurant, and again sits huddled up on the box. . . . Again the wet snow paints him and his horse white. One hour passes, and then another. . . .

Three young men, two tall and thin, one short and hunchbacked, come up, railing at each other and loudly stamping on the pavement with their goloshes.

"Cabby, to the Police Bridge!" the hunchback cries in a cracked voice. "The three of us, . . . twenty kopecks!"[3]

Iona tugs at the reins and clicks to his horse. Twenty kopecks is not a fair price, but he has no thoughts for that. Whether it is a rouble[4] or whether it is five kopecks does not matter to him now so long as he has a fare. . . . The three young men, shoving each other and using bad language, go up to the sledge, and all three try to sit down at once. The question remains to be settled: Which are to sit down and which one is to stand? After a long altercation, ill-temper, and abuse, they come to the conclusion that the hunchback must stand because he is the shortest.

"Well, drive on," says the hunchback in his cracked voice, settling himself and breathing down Iona's neck.

3. **kopecks,** units of Russian currency, at the time of the story worth not quite one cent each.
4. **rouble,** usually spelled *ruble,* then worth approximately seventy-five cents.

"Cut along! What a cap you've got, my friend! You wouldn't find a worse one in all Petersburg. . . ."[5]

"He-he! . . . he-he! . . ." laughs Iona. "It's nothing to boast of!"

"Well, then, nothing to boast of, drive on! Are you going to drive like this all the way? Eh? Shall I give you one in the neck?"

"My head aches," says one of the tall ones. "At the Dukmasovs' yesterday Vaska and I drank four bottles of brandy between us."

"I can't make out why you talk such stuff," says the other tall one angrily. "You lie like a brute."

"Strike me dead, it's the truth! . . ."

"It's about as true as that a louse coughs."

"He-he!" grins Iona. "Me-er-ry gentlemen!"

"Tfoo! the devil take you!" cries the hunchback indignantly. "Will you get on, you old plague, or won't you? Is that the way to drive? Give her one with the whip. Hang it all, give it her well."

Iona feels behind his back the jolting person and quivering voice of the hunchback. He hears abuse addressed to him, he sees people, and the feeling of loneliness begins little by little to be less heavy on his heart. The hunchback swears at him, till he chokes over some elaborately whimsical string of epithets and is overpowered by his cough. His tall companions begin talking of a certain Nadyezhda Petrovna. Iona looks round at them. Waiting till there is a brief pause, he looks round once more and says:

"This week . . . er . . . my . . . er . . . son died!"

"We shall all die, . . ." says the hunchback with a sigh, wiping his lips after coughing. "Come, drive on! drive on! My friends, I simply cannot stand crawling like this! When will he get us there?"

"Well, you give him a little encouragement . . . one in the neck!"

"Do you hear, you old plague? I'll make you smart. If one stands on ceremony with fellows like you one may as well walk. Do you hear, you old dragon? Or don't you care a hang what we say?"

And Iona hears rather than feels a slap on the back of his neck.

"He-he! . . . ." he laughs. "Merry gentlemen. . . . God give you health!"

"Cabman, are you married?" asks one of the tall ones.

"I? He-he! Me-er-ry gentlemen. The only wife for me now is the damp earth. . . . He-ho-ho! . . . The grave that is! . . . Here my son's dead and I am alive. . . . It's a strange thing, death has come in at the wrong door. . . . Instead of coming for me it went for my son. . . ."

And Iona turns round to tell them how his son died, but at that point the hunchback gives a faint sigh and announces that, thank God! they have arrived at last. After taking his twenty kopecks, Iona gazes for a long while after the revelers, who disappear into a dark entry. Again he is alone and again there is silence for him. . . . The misery which has been for a brief space eased comes back again and tears his heart more cruelly than ever. With a look of anxiety and suffering Iona's eyes stray restlessly among the crowds moving to and fro on both sides of the street: can he not find among those thousands someone who will listen to him? But the crowds flit by heedless of him and his misery. . . . His misery is immense, beyond all bounds. If Iona's heart were to burst and his misery to flow out, it would flood the whole

5. **Petersburg,** St. Petersburg, now Leningrad, the capital of Russia until 1917.

world, it seems, but yet it is not seen. It has found a hiding-place in such an insignificant shell that one would not have found it with a candle by daylight. . . .

Iona sees a house-porter with a parcel and makes up his mind to address him.

"What time will it be, friend?" he asks.

"Going on for ten. . . . Why have you stopped here? Drive on!"

Iona drives a few paces away, bends himself double, and gives himself up to his misery. He feels it is no good to appeal to people. But before five minutes have passed he draws himself up, shakes his head as though he feels a sharp pain, and tugs at the reins. . . . He can bear it no longer.

"Back to the yard!" he thinks. "To the yard!"

And his little mare, as though she knew his thoughts, falls to trotting. An hour and a half later Iona is sitting by a big dirty stove. On the stove, on the floor, and on the benches are people snoring. The air is full of smells and stuffiness. Iona looks at the sleeping figures, scratches himself, and regrets that he has come home so early. . . .

"I have not earned enough to pay for the oats, even," he thinks. "That's why I am so miserable. A man who knows how to do his work, . . . who has had enough to eat, and whose horse has had enough to eat, is always at ease. . . ."

In one of the corners a young cabman gets up, clears his throat sleepily, and makes for the water bucket.

"Want a drink?" Iona asks him.

"Seems so."

"May it do you good. . . . But my son is dead, mate. . . . Do you hear? This week in the hospital. . . . It's a queer business. . . ."

Iona looks to see the effect produced by his words, but he sees nothing. The young man has covered his head over and is already asleep. The old man sighs and scratches himself. . . . Just as the young man had been thirsty for water, he thirsts for speech. His son will soon have been dead a week, and he has not really talked to anybody yet. . . . He wants to talk of it properly, with deliberation. . . . He wants to tell how his son was taken ill, how he suffered, what he said before he died, how he died. . . . He wants to describe the funeral, and how he went to the hospital to get his son's clothes. He still has his daughter Anisya in the country. . . . And he wants to talk about her too. . . . Yes, he has plenty to talk about now. His listener ought to sigh and exclaim and lament. . . . It would be even better to talk to women. Though they are silly creatures, they blubber at the first word.

"Let's go out and have a look at the mare," Iona thinks. "There is always time for sleep. . . . You'll have sleep enough, no fear. . . ."

He puts on his coat and goes into the stables where his mare is standing. He thinks about oats, about hay, about the weather. . . . He cannot think about his son when he is alone. . . . To talk about him with someone is possible, but to think of him and picture him is insufferable anguish. . . .

"Are you munching?" Iona asks his mare, seeing her shining eyes. "There, munch away, munch away. . . . Since we have not earned enough for oats, we will eat hay. . . . Yes, . . . I have grown too old to drive. . . . My son ought to be driving, not I. . . . He was a real cabman. . . . He ought to have lived. . . ."

Iona is silent for a while, and

then he goes on: "That's how it is, old girl. . . . Kuzma Ionitch is gone. . . . He said good-by to me. . . . He went and died for no reason. . . . Now, suppose you had a little colt, and you were own mother to that little colt. . . . And all at once that same little colt went and died. . . . You'd be sorry, wouldn't you? . . ."

The little mare munches, listens, and breathes on her master's hands. Iona is carried away and tells her all about it.

DISCUSSION

1. (a) What things does Iona long to tell someone? (b) How does he want a listener to respond? (c) Is his wish to talk a natural desire? Explain.
2. (a) How does each of Iona's passengers respond to his efforts to tell about his son? (b) Why do they react in this way? (c) What is Iona's attitude toward the abusive shouts of his passengers and the crowds in the street?
3. Review the Handbook article on endings (page 520). Why would a happy ending be inappropriate for "Misery"?
4. Which method of characterization is most important in the author's portrayal of Iona? Justify your answer.
5. State the theme of the story in a sentence or two.
6. (a) In what ways might Iona be compared to an American city dweller? (b) Would the story be as effective if Iona were a cab driver in today's world of machines? Explain.
7. (a) Point out several images in the opening paragraph of the story. (b) What does this description lead you to believe the tone of the story will be? Why?
8. Why do you think Chekhov tells his story entirely in the present tense?

WORD STUDY

A number of familiar English words are derived from the names of animals. Read the following word histories. Then explain how each of these words is related to its original root word. You will need to use your imagination.

1. *chivalry.* *Chivalry* is derived from the French word *cheval,* or "horse," an animal usually ridden in the Middle Ages only by knights.
2. *canopy.* *Canopy* comes from the Greek work *konopeion,* a couch with curtains. The Greeks formed *konopeion* from their word for "gnat," *konops.*
3. *chenille.* *Chenille* is a kind of velvety yarn, popularly used in bedspread fabric. The word comes from *chenille,* the French word for "caterpillar."
4. *muscle.* *Muscle* is derived from the Latin word *muscula,* meaning "muscle." The Romans, though, coined their word from *mus,* or "mouse." What does the appearance of rippling muscles remind you of?
5. *cab.* *Cab* comes from the French *cabriolet,* a type of light carriage. *Cabriolet* is in turn derived from *caper,* the Latin word for "goat."

THE AUTHOR

To finance his medical education at Moscow University as well as support his family, Anton Chekhov (1860–1904) dashed off hundreds of comic sketches and stories for various periodicals. He began practicing medicine in 1884, and soon won praise for putting down an epidemic of cholera. But poor health and lack of interest kept him from being very busy as a doctor.

Chekhov wrote more than six hundred stories altogether, but his plays brought him the greatest recognition. Two of his best-known dramas are *The Cherry Orchard* and *The Three Sisters.*

As in "Misery," Chekhov illustrates in his work the hardships of individuals, whom he treats with insight, humor, and compassion.

Who is the victor in the conflicts between old Mrs. Wang
and her two very different enemies?

The Old Demon

PEARL S. BUCK

OLD MRS. WANG knew of course that there was a war. Everybody had known for a long time that there was war going on and that Japanese were killing Chinese. But still it was not real and no more than hearsay since none of the Wangs had been killed. The Village of Three Mile Wangs on the flat banks of the Yellow River, which was old Mrs. Wang's clan village, had never even seen a Japanese. This was how they came to be talking about Japanese at all.

It was evening and early summer, and after her supper Mrs. Wang had climbed the dike steps, as she did every day, to see how high the river had risen. She was much more afraid of the river than of the Japanese. She knew what the river would do. And one by one the villagers had followed her up the dike, and now they stood staring down at the malicious yellow water, curling along like a lot of snakes, and biting at the high dike banks.

"I never saw it as high as this so early," Mrs. Wang said. She sat down on a bamboo stool that her grandson, Little Pig, had brought for her, and spat into the water.

"It's worse than the Japanese, this old devil of a river," Little Pig said recklessly.

"Fool!" Mrs. Wang said quickly. "The river god will hear you. Talk about something else."

So they had gone on talking about the Japanese. . . . How, for instance, asked Wang, the baker, who was old Mrs. Wang's nephew twice removed, would they know the Japanese when they saw them?

Mrs. Wang at this point said positively, "You'll know them. I once saw a foreigner. He was taller than the eaves of my house and he had mud-colored hair and eyes the color of a fish's eyes. Anyone who does not look like us — that is a Japanese."

Everybody listened to her since she was the oldest woman in the village and whatever she said settled something.

Then Little Pig spoke up in his disconcerting way. "You can't see them, Grandmother. They hide up in the sky in airplanes."

Reprinted by permission of Harold Ober Associates Incorporated and Methuen & Company, Ltd. from TODAY AND FOREVER. Copyright 1939 by Pearl S. Buck.

Mrs. Wang did not answer immediately. Once she would have said positively, "I shall not believe in an airplane until I see it." But so many things had been true which she had not believed—the Empress, for instance, whom she had not believed dead, was dead. The Republic, again, she had not believed in because she did not know what it was. She still did not know, but they had said for a long time there had been one. So now she merely stared quietly about the dike where they all sat around her. It was very pleasant and cool, and she felt nothing mattered if the river did not rise to flood.

"I don't believe in the Japanese," she said flatly.

They laughed at her a little, but no one spoke. Someone lit her pipe—it was Little Pig's wife, who was her favorite, and she smoked it.

"Sing, Little Pig!" someone called.

So Little Pig began to sing an old song in a high, quavering voice, and old Mrs. Wang listened and forgot the Japanese. The evening was beautiful, the sky so clear and still that the willows overhanging the dike were reflected even in the muddy water. Everything was at peace. The thirty-odd houses which made up the village straggled along beneath them. Nothing could break this peace. After all, the Japanese were only human beings.

"I doubt those airplanes," she said mildly to Little Pig when he stopped singing.

But without answering her, he went on to another song.

Year in and year out she had spent the summer evenings like this on the dike. The first time she was seventeen and a bride, and her husband had shouted to her to come out of the house and up the dike, and she had come, blushing and twisting her hands together, to hide among the women while the men roared at her and made jokes about her. All the same, they had liked her. "A pretty piece of meat in your bowl," they had said to her husband. "Feet a trifle big," he had answered deprecatingly. But she could see he was pleased, and so gradually her shyness went away.

He, poor man, had been drowned in a flood when he was still young. And it had taken her years to get him prayed out of Buddhist purgatory. Finally she had grown tired of it, what with the child and the land all on her back, and so when the priest said coaxingly, "Another ten pieces of silver and he'll be out entirely," she asked, "What's he got in there yet?"

"Only his right hand," the priest said, encouraging her.

Well, then, her patience broke. Ten dollars! It would feed them for the winter. Besides, she had had to hire labor for her share of repairing the dike, too, so there would be no more floods.

"If it's only one hand, he can pull himself out," she said firmly.

She often wondered if he had, poor silly fellow. As like as not, she had often thought gloomily in the night, he was still lying there, waiting for her to do something about it. That was the sort of man he was. Well, some day, perhaps, when Little Pig's wife had had the first baby safely and she had a little extra, she might go back to finish him out of purgatory. There was no real hurry, though. . . .

"Grandmother, you must go in," Little Pig's wife's soft voice said. "There is a mist rising from the river now that the sun is gone."

"Yes, I suppose I must," old Mrs. Wang agreed. She gazed at the river a moment. That river—it was full of good and evil together. It would water the fields when it was curbed and

checked, but then if an inch were allowed it, it crashed through like a roaring dragon. That was how her husband had been swept away—careless, he was, about his bit of the dike. He was always going to mend it, always going to pile more earth on top of it, and then in a night the river rose and broke through. He had run out of the house, and she had climbed on the roof with the child and had saved herself and it while he was drowned. Well, they had pushed the river back again behind its dikes, and it had stayed there this time. Every day she herself walked up and down the length of the dike for which the village was responsible and examined it. The men laughed and said, "If anything is wrong with the dikes, Granny will tell us."

It had never occurred to any of them to move the village away from the river. The Wangs had lived there for generations, and some had always escaped the floods and had fought the river more fiercely than ever afterward.

Little Pig suddenly stopped singing.

"The moon is coming up!" he cried. "That's not good. Airplanes come out on moonlight nights."

"Where do you learn all this about airplanes?" old Mrs. Wang exclaimed. "It is tiresome to me," she added, so severely that no one spoke. In this silence, leaning upon the arm of Little Pig's wife, she descended slowly the earthen steps which led down into the village, using her long pipe in the other hand as a walking stick. Behind her the villagers came down, one by one, to bed. No one moved before she did, but none stayed long after her.

And in her own bed at last, behind the blue cotton mosquito curtains which Little Pig's wife fastened securely, she fell peacefully asleep.

She had lain awake a little while thinking about the Japanese and wondering why they wanted to fight. Only very coarse persons wanted wars. In her mind she saw large coarse persons. If they came one must wheedle them, she thought, invite them to drink tea, and explain to them, reasonably—only why should they come to a peaceful farming village. . . ?

So she was not in the least prepared for Little Pig's wife screaming at her that the Japanese had come. She sat up in bed muttering, "The tea bowls—the tea—"

"Grandmother, there's no time!" Little Pig's wife screamed. "They're here—they're here!"

"Where?" old Mrs. Wang cried, now awake.

"In the sky!" Little Pig's wife wailed.

They had all run out at that, into the clear early dawn, and gazed up. There, like wild geese flying in autumn, were great birdlike shapes.

"But what are they?" old Mrs. Wang cried.

And then, like a silver egg dropping, something drifted straight down and fell at the far end of the village in a field. A fountain of earth flew up, and they all ran to see it. There was a hole thirty feet across, as big as a pond. They were so astonished they could not speak, and then, before anyone could say anything, another and another egg began to fall and everybody was running, running. . . .

Everybody, that is, but Mrs. Wang. When Little Pig's wife seized her hand to drag her along, old Mrs. Wang pulled away and sat down against the bank of the dike.

"I can't run," she remarked. "I haven't run in seventy years, since before my feet were bound. You go on. Where's Little Pig?" She looked

around. Little Pig was already gone. "Like his grandfather," she remarked, "always the first to run."

But Little Pig's wife would not leave her, not, that is, until old Mrs. Wang reminded her that it was her duty.

"If Little Pig is dead," she said, "then it is necessary that his son be born alive." And when the girl still hesitated, she struck at her gently with her pipe. "Go on—go on," she exclaimed.

So unwillingly, because now they could scarcely hear each other speak for the roar of the dipping planes, Little Pig's wife went on with the others.

By now, although only a few minutes had passed, the village was in ruins and the straw roofs and wooden beams were blazing. Everybody was gone. As they passed they had shrieked at old Mrs. Wang to come on, and she had called back pleasantly:

"I'm coming—I'm coming!"

But she did not go. She sat quite alone watching now what was an extraordinary spectacle. For soon other planes came, from where she did not know, but they attacked the first ones. The sun came up over the fields of ripening wheat, and in the clear summery air the planes wheeled and darted and spat at each other. When this was over, she thought, she would go back into the village and see if anything was left. Here and there a wall stood, supporting a roof. She could not see her own house from here. But she was not unused to war. Once bandits had looted their village, and houses had been burned then, too. Well, now it had happened again. Burning houses one could see often, but not this darting silvery shining battle in the air. She understood none of it—not what those things were, nor how they stayed up in the sky. She

simply sat, growing hungry, and watching.

"I'd like to see one close," she said aloud. And at that moment, as though in answer, one of them pointed suddenly downward, and, wheeling and twisting as though it were wounded, it fell head down in a field which Little Pig had ploughed only yesterday for soybeans. And in an instant the sky was empty again, and there was only this wounded thing on the ground and herself.

She hoisted herself carefully from the earth. At her age she need be afraid of nothing. She could, she decided, go and see what it was. So, leaning on her bamboo pipe, she made her way slowly across the fields. Behind her in the sudden stillness two or three village dogs appeared and followed, creeping close to her in their terror. When they drew near to the fallen plane, they barked furiously. Then she hit them with her pipe.

"Be quiet," she scolded, "there's already been noise enough to split my ears!"

She tapped the airplane.

"Metal," she told the dogs. "Silver, doubtless," she added. Melted up, it would make them all rich.

She walked around it, examining it closely. What made it fly? It seemed dead. Nothing moved or made a sound within it. Then, coming to the side to which it tipped, she saw a young man in it, slumped into a heap in a little seat. The dogs growled, but she struck at them again and they fell back.

"Are you dead?" she inquired politely.

The young man moved a little at her voice, but did not speak. She drew nearer and peered into the hole in which he sat. His side was bleeding.

"Wounded!" she exclaimed. She took his wrist. It was warm, but inert, and when she let it go, it dropped

against the side of the hole. She stared at him. He had black hair and a dark skin like a Chinese and still he did not look like a Chinese.

"He must be a Southerner," she thought. Well, the chief thing was, he was alive.

"You had better come out," she remarked. "I'll put some herb plaster on your side."

The young man muttered something dully.

"What did you say?" she asked. But he did not say it again.

"I am still quite strong," she decided after a moment. So she reached in and seized him about the waist and pulled him out slowly, panting a good deal. Fortunately he was rather a little fellow and very light. When she had him on the ground, he seemed to find his feet; and he stood shakily and clung to her, and she held him up.

"Now if you can walk to my house," she said, "I'll see if it is there."

Then he said something, quite clearly. She listened and could not understand a word of it. She pulled away from him and stared.

"What's that?" she asked.

He pointed at the dogs. They were standing growling, their ruffs up. Then he spoke again, and as he spoke he crumpled to the ground. The dogs fell on him, so that she had to beat them off with her hands.

"Get away!" she shouted. "Who told *you* to kill him?"

And then, when they had slunk back, she heaved him somehow onto her back; and, trembling, half carrying, half pulling him, she dragged him to the ruined village and laid him in the street while she went to find her house, taking the dogs with her.

Her house was quite gone. She found the place easily enough. This was where it should be, opposite the

water gate into the dike. She had always watched that gate herself. Miraculously it was not injured now, nor was the dike broken. It would be easy enough to rebuild the house. Only, for the present, it was gone.

So she went back to the young man. He was lying as she had left him, propped against the dike, panting and very pale. He had opened his coat and he had a little bag from which he was taking out strips of cloth and a bottle of something. And again he spoke, and again she understood nothing. Then he made signs and she saw it was water he wanted, so she took up a broken pot from one of many blown about the street, and, going up the dike, she filled it with river water and brought it down again and washed his wound, and she tore off the strips he made from the rolls of bandaging. He knew how to put the cloth over the gaping wound and he made signs to her, and she followed these signs. All the time he was trying to tell her something, but she could understand nothing.

"You must be from the South, sir," she said. It was easy to see he had education. He looked very clever. "I have heard your language is different from ours." She laughed a little to put him at his ease, but he only stared at her somberly with dull eyes. So she said brightly, "Now if I could find something for us to eat, it would be nice."

He did not answer. Indeed he lay back, panting still more heavily, and stared into space as though she had not spoken.

"You would be better with food," she went on. "And so would I," she added. She was beginning to feel unbearably hungry.

It occurred to her that in Wang, the baker's shop, there might be some bread. Even if it were dusty with

fallen mortar, it would still be bread. She would go and see. But before she went she moved the soldier a little so that he lay in the edge of shadow cast by a willow tree that grew in the bank of the dike. Then she went to the baker's shop. The dogs were gone.

The baker's shop was, like everything else, in ruins. No one was there. At first she saw nothing but the mass of crumpled earthen walls. But then she remembered that the oven was just inside the door, and the door frame still stood erect, supporting one end of the roof. She stood in this frame, and, running her hand in underneath the fallen roof inside, she felt the wooden cover of the iron caldron. Under this there might be steamed bread. She worked her arm delicately and carefully in. It took quite a long time, but, even so, clouds of lime and dust almost choked her. Nevertheless she was right. She squeezed her hand under the cover and felt the firm smooth skin of the big steamed bread rolls, and one by one she drew out four.

"It's hard to kill an old thing like me," she remarked cheerfully to no one, and she began to eat one of the rolls as she walked back. If she had a bit of garlic and a bowl of tea—but one couldn't have everything in these times.

It was at this moment that she heard voices. When she came in sight of the soldier, she saw surrounding him a crowd of other soldiers, who had apparently come from nowhere. They were staring down at the wounded soldier, whose eyes were now closed.

"Where did you get this Japanese, Old Mother?" they shouted at her.

"What Japanese?" she asked, coming to them.

"This one!" they shouted.

"Is he a Japanese?" she cried

in the greatest astonishment. "But he looks like us—his eyes are black, his skin——"

"Japanese!" one of them shouted at her.

"Well," she said quietly, "he dropped out of the sky."

"Give me that bread!" another shouted.

"Take it," she said, "all except this one for him."

"A Japanese monkey eat good bread?" the soldier shouted.

"I suppose he is hungry also," old Mrs. Wang replied. She began to dislike these men. But then, she had always disliked soldiers.

"I wish you would go away," she said. "What are you doing here? Our village has always been peaceful."

"It certainly looks very peaceful now," one of the men said, grinning, "as peaceful as a grave. Do you know who did that, Old Mother? The Japanese!"

"I suppose so," she agreed. Then she asked, "Why? That's what I don't understand."

"Why? Because they want our land, that's why!"

"Our land!" she repeated. "Why, they can't have our land!"

"Never!" they shouted.

But all this time while they were talking and chewing the bread they had divided among themselves, they were watching the eastern horizon.

"Why do you keep looking east?" old Mrs. Wang now asked.

"The Japanese are coming from there," the man replied who had taken the bread.

"Are you running away from them?" she asked, surprised.

"There are only a handful of us," he said apologetically.

"We were left to guard a village —Pao An, in the county of ——"

"I know that village," old Mrs.

Wang interrupted. "You needn't tell me. I was a girl there. How is the old Pao who keeps the teashop in the main street? He's my brother."

"Everybody is dead there," the man replied. "The Japanese have taken it—a great army of men came with their foreign guns and tanks, so what could we do?"

"Of course, only run," she agreed. Nevertheless she felt dazed and sick. So he was dead, that one brother she had left! She was now the last of her father's family.

But the soldiers were straggling away again leaving her alone.

"They'll be coming, those little black dwarfs," they were saying. "We'd best go on."

Nevertheless, one lingered a moment, the one who had taken the bread, to stare down at the young wounded man, who lay with his eyes shut, not having moved at all.

"Is he dead?" he inquired. Then, before Mrs. Wang could answer, he pulled a short knife out of his belt. "Dead or not, I'll give him a punch or two with this—"

But old Mrs. Wang pushed his arm away.

"No, you won't," she said with authority. "If he is dead, then there is no use in sending him into purgatory all in pieces. I am a good Buddhist myself."

The man laughed. "Oh well, he is dead," he answered; and then, seeing his comrades already at a distance, he ran after them.

A Japanese, was he? Old Mrs. Wang, left alone with this inert figure, looked at him tentatively. He was very young, she could see, now that his eyes were closed. His hand, limp in unconsciousness, looked like a boy's hand, unformed and still growing. She felt his wrist but could discern no pulse. She leaned over him and held

to his lips the half of her roll which she had not eaten.

"Eat," she said very loudly and distinctly. "Bread!"

But there was no answer. Evidently he was dead. He must have died while she was getting the bread out of the oven.

There was nothing to do then but to finish the bread herself. And when that was done, she wondered if she ought not to follow after Little Pig and his wife and all the villagers. The sun was mounting and it was growing hot. If she were going, she had better go. But first she would climb the dike and see what the direction was. They had gone straight west, and as far as eye could look westward was a great plain. She might even see a good-sized crowd miles away. Anyway, she could see the next village, and they might all be there.

So she climbed the dike slowly, getting very hot. There was a slight breeze on top of the dike and it felt good. She was shocked to see the river very near the top of the dike. Why, it had risen in the last hour!

"You old demon!" she said severely. Let the river god hear it if he liked. He was evil, that he was—so to threaten flood when there had been all this other trouble.

She stooped and bathed her cheeks and her wrists. The water was quite cold, as though with fresh rains somewhere. Then she stood up and gazed around her. To the west there was nothing except in the far distance the soldiers still half-running, and beyond them the blur of the next village, which stood on a long rise of ground. She had better set out for that village. Doubtless Little Pig and his wife were there waiting for her.

Just as she was about to climb down and start out, she saw something on the eastern horizon. It was

at first only an immense cloud of dust. But, as she stared at it, very quickly it became a lot of black dots and shining spots. Then she saw what it was. It was a lot of men—an army. Instantly she knew what army.

"That's the Japanese," she thought. Yes, above them were the buzzing silver planes. They circled about, seeming to search for someone.

"I don't know who you're looking for," she muttered, "unless it's me and Little Pig and his wife. We're the only ones left. You've already killed my brother Pao."

She had almost forgotten that Pao was dead. Now she remembered it acutely. He had such a nice shop— always clean, and the tea good and the best meat dumplings to be had and the price always the same. Pao was a good man. Besides, what about his wife and his seven children? Doubtless they were all killed, too. Now these Japanese were looking for her. It occurred to her that on the dike she could easily be seen. So she clambered hastily down.

It was when she was about halfway down that she thought of the water gate. This old river—it had been a curse to them since time began. Why should it not make up a little now for all the wickedness it had done? It was plotting wickedness again, trying to steal over its banks. Well, why not? She wavered a moment. It was a pity, of course, that the young dead Japanese would be swept into the flood. He was a nice-looking boy, and she had saved him from being stabbed. It was not quite the same as saving his life, of course, but still it was a little the same. If he had been alive, he would have been saved. She went over to him and tugged at him until he lay well near the top of the bank. Then she went down again.

She knew perfectly how to open the water gate. Any child knew how to open the sluice for crops. But she knew also how to swing open the whole gate. The question was, could she open it quickly enough to get out of the way?

"I'm only one old woman," she muttered. She hesitated a second more. Well, it would be a pity not to see what sort of a baby Little Pig's wife would have, but one could not see everything. She had seen a great deal in this life. There was an end to what one could see, anyway.

She glanced again to the east. There were the Japanese coming across the plain. They were a long clear line of black, dotted with thousands of glittering points. If she opened this gate, the impetuous water would roar toward them, rushing into the plains, rolling into a wide lake, drowning them, maybe. Certainly they could not keep marching nearer and nearer to her and to Little Pig and his wife who were waiting for her. Well, Little Pig and his wife—they would wonder about her—but they would never dream of this. It would make a good story—she would have enjoyed telling it.

She turned resolutely to the gate. Well, some people fought with airplanes and some with guns, but you could fight with a river, too, if it were a wicked one like this one. She wrenched out a huge wooden pin. It was slippery with silvery green moss. The rill of water burst into a strong jet. When she wrenched one more pin, the rest would give way themselves. She began pulling at it, and felt it slip a little from its hole.

"I might be able to get myself out of purgatory with this," she thought, "and maybe they'll let me have that old man of mine, too. What's a hand of his to all this? Then we'll—"

The pin slipped away suddenly, and the gate burst flat against her and

knocked her breath away. She had only time to gasp, to the river:

"Come on, you old demon!"

Then she felt it seize her and lift her up to the sky. It was beneath her and around her. It rolled her joyfully hither and thither, and then, holding her close and enfolded, it went rushing against the enemy.

DISCUSSION

1. How is old Mrs. Wang regarded by the villagers?
2. (a) Why does old Mrs. Wang say she doubts the existence of the Japanese and airplanes? (b) Describe her attitude toward each of the following: her husband and grandson; warfare in general; the bombing of the village; death. (c) Which method of characterization is most important in revealing these attitudes? Support your answer with evidence from the story.
3. (a) Why does old Mrs. Wang help the wounded soldier? (b) Does her behavior toward him change when she learns that he is Japanese? Explain.
4. (a) What are her motives in opening the water gate? (b) Is flooding the village logical, after her earlier kindness to the wounded Japanese? Why or why not?
5. (a) What is the role of the river in the lives of the Wangs? (b) How does the river's part in the conclusion of the story contrast with its earlier role?
6. Does old Mrs. Wang triumph or suffer defeat in the end? Explain your answer.
7. How is old Mrs. Wang similar to the river merchant's wife?

WORD STUDY

The Yellow River in "The Old Demon" is described as *malicious*. What does this mean? *Malicious* is a form of the word *malice*, which comes from the Latin word *malus*, meaning "poor" or "evil."

The Latin *mal-* is found in many English words. Read the sentences below and explain how the italicized word in each is related to "evil" or "poor" in meaning.
1. An unhappy patient accused Dr. Ache of *malpractice*.
2. The humane society was on hand to make certain that the animals were not *maltreated*.
3. My father told me to stop behaving like a *malcontent* and cut my hair, or he'd cut my allowance.
4. We own a contented cat and a *maladjusted* poodle.
5. Throughout the world, millions of people suffer from *malnutrition*.
6. The calf was *malformed* at birth.
7. An editorial charged the mayor with *maladministration*.

THE AUTHOR

At one time Pearl Buck (1892–1973) was as much at home in China as in America. Though born in West Virginia, she went to China with her missionary parents when she was only five months old. Her college years were spent back in the United States, but a few years later, Mrs. Buck returned to China to teach for five years.

Pearl Buck's first book appeared in 1930. A year later she published *The Good Earth,* a novel about China. A best-seller for nearly two years, *The Good Earth* was made into both a play and a movie, and has been translated into more than thirty languages. In 1938 she won the Nobel Prize in Literature for her "rich and genuine portrayals of Chinese peasant life." She was the first American woman to receive the Nobel award.

Part 1

1. Each sentence below tells of something that took place in one of the selections in this unit. **(a)** In what country or region does each action occur? **(b)** How might the details of each sentence be changed to describe a parallel situation in the United States?

1. A man is frustrated in his efforts to combat the hippopotamuses that annually threaten his crops.
2. Passengers on a train take up the cry of "Bandidos!" when mysterious gunfire is heard.
3. An old woman dreams of offering tea to her country's enemies, hoping to persuade them to stop the war.
4. In attempting to repair an olive oil jar, a man seals himself up inside the container.
5. A sledge driver finds only his horse to tell about his son's death.
6. A woman omits the meat from her husband's *mole* in order to earn money to help homeless children in other countries.

2. (a) In which selections is the author's purpose, at least in part, to portray the characteristics of a particular nationality? What are those characteristics? **(b)** What are some of the foreign customs you learned of through the selections in the unit? **(c)** Do you think the qualities portrayed in the Evelyn Tooley Hunt poem are "American" or "universal"? Discuss.

3. (a) What two selections are concerned with war? **(b)** Do both express the same attitude toward war? Explain.

4. Three of the important characters in the unit are wives. **(a)** Which—old Mrs. Wang or the river merchant's wife—can be more accurately compared with Fortunata? **(b)** How might Fortunata react to the situations faced by the Chinese women? Give reasons based on your knowledge of her character for your answer.

5. The selections in this unit develop many ideas about human nature. Match the titles below on the right with the appropriate subjects given at left. (Some titles may fit more than one subject.)

1. Man's cruelty
2. Man's ambition
3. Man's self-sacrifice
4. Man's faithfulness
5. Man's struggle with nature

a. "Fortunata Writes a Letter"
b. "The Graveyard"
c. "The River Merchant's Wife"
d. "The Old Demon"
e. "Misery"
f. "Mama Is a Sunrise"

6. Reread the paragraphs describing various types of heroes, page 187. **(a)** In which of these classifications do Fortunata and old Mrs. Wang fit? **(b)** Do any other characters in the unit, male or female, show elements of heroism? Cite evidence from the selections to support your answer.

Part 2

Several selections from preceding units of this book contain examples of irony of situation. **(a)** In "The Dubbing of General Garbage," how is Lennie's pride in his sword ironic? **(b)** What is the irony in John Thomas' careful grooming of Curly in "The Lesson"? **(c)** Why is finding the guitar in the boat ("Death by Drowning") ironic? **(d)** What irony is implied in the last lines of "Old Age Sticks"? **(e)** What is ironic about the little girl's fate in the story told by the bachelor in "The Storyteller"?

SUGGESTED READING

BAGNOLD, ENID, *National Velvet.* (Morrow *Grosset) An English girl wins a horse in the village lottery and enters it in the exciting Grand National Steeplechase.

BENARY-ISBERT, MARGOT, *Castle on the Border.* (Harcourt) Sixteen-year-old Leni, who dreams of becoming an actress, discovers more vital concerns when she becomes involved with the daring East German refugees sheltered by her aunt and uncle in their ancient family castle.

BENNETT, JACK, *Mister Fisherman.* (Little) Danger confronts old fisherman Pillay and a spoiled teenager when they are lost at sea off the coast of South Africa.

BOOTH, ESMA RIDEOUT, *Kalena.* (McKay) Kalena is an African girl whose life is changed when she learns about Western ways at the mission school.

CHRISMAN, ARTHUR, *Shen of the Sea.* (Dutton) These amusing stories about China include the legend of Ah Mee, who accidentally invented printing because he loved jam.

CLARK, ANN NOLAN, *Santiago.* (Viking) A twelve-year-old Guatemalan boy is torn between remaining among the comforts of modern civilization and returning to his native Indian village.

CROCKETT, LUCY HERNDON, *Pong Choolie, You Rascal.* (Holt) A messenger for the North Korean Communists, Pong Choolie learns about democracy from American GI's.

DALY, MAUREEN, *Twelve Around the World.* (Dodd) The author interviews teenagers from all over the world and relates their ideas on manners, customs, food, and fun.

EDELMAN, LILY, *Israel: New People in an Old Land.* (Nelson) The description of the resettlement and growth of Israel is illustrated with maps and photos.

FENTON, EDWARD, *The Golden Doors.* (Doubleday) Wayne and Alida, newly arrived in Florence, meet Bruno before the great bronze doors of the Baptistery and explore the old city with him.

LEWIS, ELIZABETH FOREMAN, *Young Fu of the Upper Yangtze.* (Holt) China in the 1920's, a land of old customs and "foreign" innovations, is the setting for the story of Young Fu, a country boy who comes to the city to learn the art of working with copper.

LEWIS, MILDRED, *The Honorable Sword.* (Houghton) Two Japanese brothers determine to avenge their family and regain the Honorable Sword of the House of Yori.

LORENZ, CLARISSA, *Junket to Japan.* (Little) Sixteen-year-old Peter Bell from Massachusetts goes to Tokyo as an American Field Service exchange student.

NAJAFI, NAJMEH, *Persia Is My Heart,* edited by Helen Hinckley. (Harper) A Moslem girl, who became the first woman dress designer in Persia, tells about life in her country, now Iran.

NORDHOFF, CHARLES, *The Pearl Lagoon.* (Little) Battles with pirates and sharks add excitement to this tale of a pearl-diving cruise in the South Seas.

RANKIN, LOUISE, *Daughter of the Mountains.* (Viking) In an adventurous journey to find her lost dog, a girl travels all the way from Tibet to Calcutta, India.

REYNOLDS, QUENTIN, *The Battle of Britain.* (Random) A famous war correspondent tells about his experiences with the men of the Royal Air Force who fought to defend Britain against German bombs in 1940.

RITCHIE, RITA, *The Golden Hawks of Genghis Khan.* (Dutton) To regain a fine strain of stolen falcons and avenge his father's death, Jalair makes a daring journey to the land of the Mongols. This story is set in the thirteenth century.

SHIPPEN, KATHARINE, *New Found World.* (Viking) In her portrayal of daily life in Latin America, the author gives special attention to the peoples of Argentina, Brazil, Haiti, Mexico, and Peru.

*paperback

HANDBOOK
of literary terms

BIOGRAPHY

Percy Bysshe Shelley, the great English poet, lived from 1792 to 1822. Throughout his short life he had "a passion for reforming the world." His poetry sang of his zeal for freedom and liberty. An early example of this enthusiasm occurred while he was at Eton, the aristocratic school for boys. He refused to participate in "fagging," the custom which required younger boys to perform chores for the older students. Shelley's rebelliousness often caused him to be persecuted while at Eton—indeed, during his entire life. He refused to be an unquestioning member of society, preferring instead to follow his own sense of justice.

1. Which of the following phrases best summarizes the purpose of the preceding paragraph? **(a)** to give information about the life and personality of the poet Shelley; **(b)** to entertain the reader with an amusing account of Shelley's peculiarities; **(c)** to describe an exciting and suspenseful episode in Shelley's life; **(d)** to convince the reader of Shelley's amazing genius

2. What aspect of Shelley's character is emphasized in the above paragraph?

Fagging was an organized affair at Eton, not, as at Sion House School,[1] a case of individual whim.

These facts were retailed to Shelley, the novice, by this one and that one. But, to his mind, fagging smacked of nothing but tyranny and oppression—two things he had vowed to take a stand against. He would have none of it. He listened in silent scorn until, one late summer morning, a violent storm broke upon his head.

He was told off as fag[2] to one Henry Matthews, a Fifth Form[3] boy, inclined to bully savagely. Matthews called him into his study in a genuine temper one morning. He wanted it put in order for the day and was prepared to take peremptory measures with the new boy. First, he gave him the broom. "You sweep this room out and get it clean!" said he.

Shelley flatly refused to do this work. Matthews stood, glaring angrily, first at him, then at the room. He had come back from breakfast to find it just as frowzy as when he left it, the carpet covered with lint, the mantel and chairs thick with dust, the candlesticks covered with grease. Slowly and wrathfully his eyes measured Shelley, who stood before him, having defiantly dropped with a thud the broom that the older lad had thrust into his hands. They were indeed a contrast—Matthews, heavily strong and hardy, every muscle toughened by cricket and football; Shelley, slender, willowy,

somewhat round-shouldered, his eyes just now flashing as if they were sparks blown from a forge.

As the broom fell to the floor, Matthews' self-control broke down. "Oh, that's your game, is it?" he roared, seizing Shelley's wrist, which was nearly dislocated by the cruel twist he gave it. "Here's where you get the flogging you've deserved for so long, you slinking hound, you shirker, with your fine pride and your nose in the air. You dare refuse to fag for me? Say it then, say it!"

The other's voice, clear and high, rose like a peacock's. "I despise fagging. It's only work for slaves. Why should we younger ones have to do it? You force us into it against our will. Rank injustice. You flogged Horter the other day for hard-boiling an egg. I'm no slave, and I'll not fag for you nor any one else. I'll not stir a step."

Shelley's resolution was beyond dispute. Matthews flew at him, attempting to pin his arms down to his sides, before throwing him for a beating. But Shelley had learned from his bullyings at Sion House to be exceedingly nimble. His lighter weight gave him an advantage. Before Matthews could get hold of him, he adroitly tripped up the older boy and threw him. Matthews fell heavily on his own hearthrug, overtaken and surprised by the swift attack. His prey slipped through the half-open door and fled, deerlike, down the long corridor. . . .*

1. What fact stated in the first article has been more fully developed in the second?

2. The incident described in the second selection occurred over one hundred and fifty years ago, long before the writer was born. Which of the following sentences are probably imagined details? Explain your reasons for believing these sentences to be imaginary. **(a)** "Fagging was an organized affair at Eton . . ." **(b)** "He listened in silent scorn . . ." **(c)** "He was told off as fag to one Henry Matthews . . ." **(d)** "Slowly and wrathfully his eyes measured Shelley . . ." **(e)** ". . . his eyes just now flashing as if they were sparks . . ."

3. Which of the two selections about Shelley is the more interesting? Why?

---

*Reprinted by permission of Dodd, Mead & Company, Inc. from THE BOY SHELLEY by Laura Benét. Copyright 1937 by Dodd, Mead & Company, Inc. Copyright renewed 1965 by Laura Benét.
1. Sion House School, the school that Shelley had previously attended.
2. told off as fag, assigned to perform chores.
3. Fifth Form, grade level for boys aged fifteen or sixteen.

An account of a person's life written by another person is a *biography*. Usually, a biographer's chief purpose is to inform the reader about his subject's activities and character.

To make his informative account more interesting, the biographer often uses some techniques of fiction. The author of the second selection about Shelley made her account more exciting by selecting a particularly significant event in the poet's life and developing it in such detail the reader feels he is taking part in the action. Although the situation and the characters themselves are factual, Laura Benét probably invented details about how Shelley and Matthews looked and spoke. These imaginary details help the reader become more involved with Shelley and Matthews as persons than does the factual statement that Shelley refused to fag for Matthews.

Since the most important element of biography is truthfulness, however, the biographer has to be careful that his imagined scenes are in keeping with known facts.

BIOGRAPHY: an account of a person's life written by another person. Sometimes a biographer tries to make his work more interesting by adding imaginary details to a particular incident.

CHARACTERIZATION

I. Methods of Characterization

Gray hair sticking up in damp wisps around her red face, Ma plodded heavily across the kitchen floor.

A little boy, no older than six, stood directly in her path licking from his fingers the remains of something sticky. Noticing him, she barked, "Git outa my way. I've told you a hundred times to stay outa here. Where in the devil's your sister?"

The child finished licking, then looked up and smilingly revealed a partially toothless mouth. "I dunno, Mama." He edged toward her and flung his arms as far around her as they would reach and pressed his face into her voluminous skirt.

She reached down to pat his head, thinking how much he looked like his shiftless father, and wondering if she could somehow keep this last one from turning out like the others.

1. What does the author tell you about the woman's appearance?
2. What do you learn about her from what she says and does?
3. What does the boy's behavior toward her indicate about her personality?
4. What does the author's description of the woman's thoughts tell you about her attitude toward life?

Characterization is the technique a writer uses to help you become acquainted with a person, or *character*, in his writing. Basically, there are four *methods of characterization*. Three of these methods are similar to the ways in which you learn about a person in real life. You learn something about a person from his physical appearance; you decide whether you like or dislike him by what he says and does; you listen to opinions others have of him. A writer describes a character's *physical appearance, his speech and actions,* and the *attitudes of other characters toward him.* In addition, an author may use another method which is not open to you. While you cannot read a person's mind, a writer can tell you about a character's *inner thoughts and feelings.*

II. Motivation

Sid flung open the door and rushed out into the cold rain, singing at the top of his voice and dancing around in circles.

Our first reaction to reading about someone capering in the rain would probably be one of puzzlement. Often, we need to know the reasons for a person's action before we can understand and accept that action. Which of the following might help explain Sid's behavior?

1. He has passed an important exam.
2. He has learned that his dog is ill.
3. He has lost his billfold.
4. He has been turned down for a date.
5. He has won the grand prize in a contest.

After the waitress had taken their order, Cynthia returned to the hangnail on her thumb. The boy across from her said, "Nice place, don't you think?" She swallowed and murmured, "Yes, I do," so softly he had to lean forward to hear. She didn't look up. Then the boy said, "Have you ever eaten at The Flame?" She shook her head, eyes still lowered, and he added lamely, "It's nice." Why can't she loosen up, Jack wondered. He searched his mind for something more to say, found nothing. Suddenly, he heard a sharp clunk and a startled cry from the girl. Water dripped onto her lap. She sat for a moment, her nail-bitten hands covering her reddening face. Then she leaped to her feet and stumbled through the restaurant and out the door.

1. What personality traits does Cynthia display?
2. What led to her flight from the restaurant?
3. Is it probable that a girl like Cynthia would run away from an embarrassing situation? Why or why not?

4. Would it have been more believable for her to have laughed and accepted her misfortune easily? Explain.

Joe grasped the bills handed him through the teller's window and said to Tim, "Boy, do I love payday. Best day of the week. Come on, I'll show you that heap I got my eye on." The two boys left the building, Joe keeping up a steady rain of chatter.

"It sure burns me up to give my old man ten dollars every week. It could get me some decent clothes." He pulled at the sleeve of his jacket. "I'm sick of this mangy coat."

"My gosh, Joe, you just bought it a month ago and you got plenty others hanging in your closet."

"Okay, okay, I know," said Joe, "but what's money for except to have a good time with?"

They passed a blind man selling pencils. When he heard their voices, the beggar quavered, "Help a poor old blind man." Joe, without hesitation, gave the old man three ten-dollar bills, and said jovially, "There you are, old fellow."

1. What character traits does Joe reveal in the first four paragraphs of the above anecdote?

2. Considering what you know about him, is his action in the last paragraph believable? Why or why not?

3. What action might Joe have been more likely to take?

A careful writer does not allow characters to act haphazardly, nor does he have them carry out certain actions merely to advance the plot. Instead, he gives characters sound reasons for acting as they do.

The way in which a character acts is generally determined by what he wants, by what happens to him, and, of course, by his personality and character traits. A writer's description of a character and of the situations which cause the character to act is called *motivation*. (For example, Cynthia's flight from the restaurant was motivated by embarrassment and self-consciousness.) Sometimes an author states a character's motives directly, but more often he only suggests them. When a character has been skillfully motivated, the reader tends to accept his actions without question for they seem natural and real. But when a character is poorly motivated, the reader rejects him as unbelievable.

METHODS OF CHARACTERIZATION: the techniques an author uses to reveal the personality and character of a fictional person. An author reveals a character's personality and traits by describing his (*1*) physical appearance; (*2*) speech and actions; (*3*) inner thoughts and feelings; and (*4*) his effect on other characters. These methods can be used in any combination.

MOTIVATION: the combination of character traits and circumstances that causes a character to act in a certain manner. In good writing, the reader can find valid reasons for the characters' behavior.

CONFLICT

Blinking against the glare of sunlight from the lake, I tried to decide if the little red bobber had moved. I wiped the perspiration out of my eyes and strained to see; yes, the bobber dipped! Hastily, I jerked on the pole and felt a sharp tug as the fish began to fight the hook imbedded in its mouth.

What is "I" struggling against in the paragraph above? Is his struggle physical or mental?

Tony, hidden in the shadows a block away, watched Nick hurl the brick at the darkened window. What if somebody should see them, he wondered. But Nick had said nobody would come if they hurried. Nick was a great guy, a great friend to have—or would be. Yet, even if he did go into that house with Nick and no one knew, how could he ever look into his father's eyes again? But then, actually, what was so awful about going into an empty house just to have a look around? Who would it hurt? Tony's mind whirled.

Between what two alternatives is Tony struggling? Is his struggle taking place outside of him or within him?

LEHMAN (*with a heavy sigh*). Well, but that's just the way it is. We haven't figured out any other way of dealing with kids like him. A boy who would beat up a teacher is simply—
OLNEY (*pleading*). Aw, come off it. He didn't "beat him up," he only hit him once or twice—didn't even faze him. Well, what'd you do if someone called you a name like that in front of everybody? This is a kid who don't know any different—he's been fighting all his life.
LEHMAN (*patiently*). I know all that. But you can't let him off the hook because of his background.

What is Olney struggling for? Who opposes him? Is this opposition physical or mental? Explain.

At first, Bev wasn't sure she'd heard the knocking, but then she heard it again. She frowned as she stood uncertainly in the middle of the room. Again there was a knock, only this time it was a pounding, and along with it a man's voice pleading, "Please let me in. I'm in trouble. HELP!" She frowned, remembering her mother's usual parting speech: "Do NOT, under any circumstances, let anyone in while I'm gone." Her mother always said that, and, until now, Bev had never felt any urge to disobey.

Is Bev's an inner or outer struggle? Between what opposite courses of action is she torn?

Most fiction contains some type of struggle, or *conflict*, between opposing forces. A conflict may be physical, intellectual, emotional, or moral. It can be as obvious and simple as the struggle between the man and the fish. Or, it can be as subtle and complex as the debate between Lehman and Olney. A character may be in conflict with an *external* force such as another character, nature, or society. Or, he may undergo an inner conflict during which he battles with some element of his own personality.

> **CONFLICT:** a struggle between opposing forces; a clash of actions, ideas, desires or values. A conflict may take place between a character and an outside force or within the character himself.

CONTRAST

An unusual sight startles visitors to bustling West Berlin. Next to a tall, angular modern church constructed of steel and stone stands old Kaiser Wilhelm Cathedral. Such a combination of old and new would not be unusual, but for one thing. While the new building gleams with freshness and careful maintenance, Kaiser Wilhelm is a hollow shell. From crumbling walls its bombed-out, vacant windows stare down at passers-by, in silent testimony to the horrors of war.

1. How do the two churches differ from each other?
2. Why do you suppose the Germans left Kaiser Wilhelm Cathedral standing?
3. What silent comment on war and peace do these buildings make?

His mother had fallen asleep. Her breathing hardly stirred the sheets covering her thin body. Don bent over, kissed her, and eased himself out the door. He went down the hall, trying to keep his shoes from clacking on the gray tiled floor. While he waited for the elevator, which whirred up as softly as everything else moved in the hospital, he became conscious of the stuffy silence of the place. A white-uniformed nurse walked by, her face expressionless, her tread muffled by her rubber-soled white oxfords.

When he pulled open the front door, the sunlight momentarily blinded him and the squeals and shrieks of a group of children playing "Red Rover" across the street shocked his ears. High heels clicking, a girl in a floppy red hat and bright blue dress swished past. Life whistled, honked, shouted,

and laughed in energetic confusion all around the somber building where his mother lay quietly dying.

1. What are the differences between the hospital and the scene outside it? Find specific details in each scene that develop these differences.
2. What idea suggested in the very last sentence is reinforced by these contrasting details?

The two churches in Berlin and the hospital and the scene outside it are examples of *contrast,* the striking difference between two things. When two very different objects are set side by side in contrast to each other, each tends to illuminate or emphasize the characteristics of the other. White seems whiter, for example, when it appears next to black. A sudden noise makes a person more conscious of the silence that preceded or followed the noise. To heighten the effect they wish to achieve, authors frequently use contrast to point out the differences between such things as ways of life, settings, and personalities.

> **CONTRAST:** a striking difference between two things. Its purpose in literature is to heighten effect.

ENDINGS

Directly below is a summary of the first part of a short story. Read through it carefully.

Carl Yonkers and his wife, Hilda, owned and operated a modest hardware store in a small Nebraska farming town. They were admired for their devotion to their small business, for they had been known to spend up to sixteen hours a day in the store. The merchandise was always in place, the counters always sparkled, and, as someone said, you could almost eat off the floor.

Carl and Hilda were both in their forties when Lewis, their only child, was born. For the first time, the store took a secondary position in the Yonkers' lives, and Lewis quickly became their reason for living. Helpful, cheerful, the head of his class, Lewis was a favorite of all who knew him.

At seventeen Lewis announced that he was going to be a writer, and he enrolled in a large New York university to learn his craft.

The elder Yonkers waited for his letters anxiously, and he did not disappoint them. Every day he wrote—serious explanations of his goals in life, amusing anecdotes on the eccentricities of New Yorkers, graphic descriptions of the city by night. And always, his letters contained information about a young man named Ben Hurley whom he had met during his first week at school and who had quickly become his best friend.

But one day there was no letter, and then it was a week since Lewis had written. On the eighth night, the Yonkers were awakened by a knock at the door. Carl Yonkers opened it to find a strange young man standing there. It was Ben Hurley and he had come with terrible news. Lewis was missing; the police presumed he had drowned and the river was being dragged in the hope of finding his body. Ben had wanted to tell the Yonkers personally because he had felt that it would be the most merciful way to break the news to them.

Following are three different endings for this story. Read through all three and then answer the questions below.

A. The Yonkers were heartbroken by the news. Ben, who shared their grief, dropped out of school to stay with them. During the course of his stay, the Yonkers grew to know and love Ben. When they learned that he had no parents of his own, they asked him to be their son. They knew that Lewis would have approved of such an action. Ben agreed, and although the Yonkers never forgot Lewis, Ben was a comfort and a joy to them.

B. After Ben had delivered his message and gone, the Yonkers discussed the tragedy that had befallen them. They decided that there was nothing left to live for. Before they went back to bed, they turned on the gas stove. They fell asleep, knowing they would never awaken again.

C. The Yonkers were struck mute by the news about their son. Their lack of an outward show of grief made Ben extremely uncomfortable and he left as soon as possible. Carl Yonkers slipped into his trousers and went over to the hardware store. His wife followed him there. Wordlessly, they busied themselves by straightening out merchandise, dusting, rearranging displays.

1. Which of the endings is best suited to the story? Defend your answer with logical arguments based on what you know about the Yonkers.

2. Which ending is second best? Why do you think so?

3. Do you find any of the endings unbelievable? Why or why not?

FANTASY

Young children's favorite stories are usually those that end, in effect, with the phrase: ". . . and they lived happily ever after." But not all literature presents a happy ending. The purpose of the serious writer is to render a believable view of life as he sees it. To do so, he manages his subjects and characters so as to make some comment on life. He depicts life's defeats as well as its triumphs and, therefore, much good literature ends unhappily.

In life, some problems are never completely solved. Consequently, a piece of literature can have an *indeterminate* ending—one in which the conflict is partially reduced but not actually solved. Which of the endings to the Yonkers' story is happy? Which is unhappy? Which is indeterminate? In each case, explain your answer.

The excellence of an ending should not be judged by whether it is happy, unhappy, or indeterminate, but by whether it is logical in terms of what comes before it. A person's character is partially revealed by the way the author introduces him and by the setting in which he initially appears. Character is further revealed by the way the person reacts in a problem situation. If there is too great a difference between the person as he has been introduced and as he later behaves, he becomes unbelievable. A character's traits, then, should determine how he goes about contending with a problem.

Sometimes, however, an author allows a weak character to overcome a huge problem simply because he feels his readers will prefer a happy ending. In doing so, he is cheating the reader because he is not showing him people as they really are and life as it really is.

> **ENDINGS:** An ending to a piece of fiction can be happy, unhappy, or indeterminate. An ending should be judged by whether it is logical in terms of what has come before it.

The other day I overheard two fat, prosperous fleas talking as they sunned themselves on my dog Risty's back. Among the normal complaints about having to work too hard, nagging wives, and smart-alecky children, they got to discussing their tastes in food. And one made an illuminating observation:

"You know," he said, "I just can't understand all this fuss about pedigrees, blue blood, and so on. When you get right down to it, champions don't taste much different from strays."

1. What is the point of the flea's remark? How does it apply to other situations?
2. Do you believe that fleas can talk? Does the fact that a flea is speaking make his idea less worth while?

Mysteriously, the storm arose. Since the Chicago weather bureau had repeatedly broadcast assurances of a fine day for sailing, Gene was astonished to see, just as he was preparing to start back, the black cloud that plunged the afternoon into night. Almost as abruptly the breeze became a gale, turning the boat's gentle bobbing into violent lurching. A mammoth wave arose like a whale and crashed over him. Choking and struggling, Gene was dragged down into the lake. A great tiredness overwhelmed him. Some time later, he opened his eyes to see a bright, golden sky glowing through the branches of a strange-looking tree. Next Gene stared at his watch. Its hands were racing around the watch face, measuring the hours like seconds. . . .

1. What improbable events have occurred in the preceding paragraph? What is the first indication that this is not a story of ordinary action?
2. Which of the following phrases probably best describes the author's purpose:
(a) to tell an exciting but improbable adventure
(b) to study a complicated character
(c) to illustrate a theme about the weakness of man
(d) to make fun of weather bureau predictions

In real life, fleas don't talk and sudden storms don't plunge people into strange worlds. But *fantasy* is fiction that deals with make-believe

worlds, imaginary creatures, or impossible situations.

Fantasy has various purposes. Sometimes the author aims only to amuse you, excite you, perhaps even scare you a bit. At other times, he uses fantasy to express an idea about real life—a theme.

An author has the freedom to write in any way he wishes about any subject he chooses. The author of fantasy may exercise his imagination more freely than most writers; but the good reader acknowledges his privilege to do so. He coöperates with the author by willingly accepting his basic situations and characters, no matter how impossible or fantastic they may seem. Only after the reader has accepted the author's initial ideas does he have the right to evaluate the work in terms of its literary merit. In other words, the good reader doesn't condemn a story simply because it is about a witch. Rather, he accepts the existence of the witch and judges the story by the same standards he would use to judge a story about a more probable character.

FANTASY: fiction that contains impossible situations, events, or characters. Fantasy includes fables, fairy tales, ghost stories, and science fiction. It often, though not always, develops a theme.

FIGURATIVE LANGUAGE

Police! A siren clawed at the night's surface. As if playing at blindman's buff, a search light, like an illuminated finger, swung around the corner, groped for the scene of disturbance, found it. A young patrolman, tautly stitched together by muscle, leaped from the car. Uncertain as to why he had been called, he swallowed up the crowd with a curious glance. A stringy woman, with skin like weather-beaten newspaper, stepped forward. "Thank God, you've come. There's been a shooting. . . ."

1. In your own words, relate the happenings in the above paragraph.
2. Explain the meaning of each of the following as it is used in the paragraph:
(a) siren clawed at the night's surface
(b) playing at blindman's buff
(c) like an illuminated finger
(d) groped for the scene
(e) tautly stitched together by muscle
(f) he swallowed up the crowd
(g) stringy
(h) skin like weather-beaten newspaper
3. Do you think the paragraph would be more, or less, interesting to read if the writer had said exactly what he meant? Why?

The author of the above paragraph has combined ideas, images, and facts in such a way as to make his comments doubly clear and forceful. To do this, he has used *figurative language* rather than literal language. Literal language is that which uses words in their usual meaning, without exaggeration or imagination. Figurative language departs from ordinary language to make meaning more vivid. In figurative language words are given unusual or exaggerated meanings. Two things that seem unlike each other are compared and the reader suddenly sees similarities between them:

Her hair drooped round her pallid cheeks
Like seaweed on a clam.

Do these lines call a pretty or a grotesque picture to mind? Would they be more suitable in describing a drowned girl, or one with a new hair style? Why?

Forces of nature are given human qualities:

I saw you toss the kites on high
And blow the birds about the sky;
And all around I heard you pass,
Like ladies' skirts across the grass —
O wind, a-blowing all day long,
O wind, that sings so loud a song!

What human characteristics does the poet give the wind? Is the wind a gentle or a violent one? How can you tell?

Appropriate figurative language expresses an idea or experience vividly, forcefully, and briefly. It has a quality of freshness about it. (For example, "sweet as sugar" is not a good figure of speech simply because it is overused.) Sometimes figurative language may seem even more direct than literal language because it helps the reader grasp important ideas immediately.

Poets, especially, use figurative language to suggest an idea in a few words. Below are excerpts from some well-known poems. Read each excerpt and then answer the questions that follow:

I will kill thee a hundred and fifty ways.

1. What emotion is the poet expressing?
2. Why is the statement considered figurative?

Disdain and scorn ride sparkling in her eyes.

1. Describe the girl's eyes in literal terms.
2. What kind of person might the girl be?

Like a lobster boiled, the morn
From black to red began to burn.

1. What kind of day is suggested?
2. Explain the meaning of the second line.

Day after day, day after day,
We stuck, nor breath nor motion;
As idle as a painted ship
Upon a painted ocean.

1. Is the ship moving slowly or standing still? How can you tell?
2. Explain the meaning of: "As idle as a painted ship/Upon a painted ocean."

. . . the Lady stretch'd a vulture throat
And shot from crooked lips a haggard smile.

1. Describe the Lady's smile in literal terms.

2. In the first line, the Lady's throat is compared to a vulture's. Is the comparison to a vulture carried out in the second line?
3. What does the word *shot* suggest about the way in which the Lady smiled?

Life's but a walking shadow; a poor player
That struts and frets his hour upon the stage,
And then is heard no more: it is a tale
Told by an idiot, full of sound and fury,
Signifying nothing.

1. To what three things does the speaker compare life?
2. What attitude does the speaker express toward life?

To be effective, figurative language has to fit the situation. For example, if the figurative expression includes a comparison, the things that are compared must be alike in some way, and the general effect of the comparison must be appropriate. In which of the following does the effect of the comparison fit the situation? Be sure you can defend your answers.

1. Streams of rain formed prison bars.
2. Remember those lovely, lazy days of Spring, when the sun snarled like a mad dog at a new-green world?
3. Grief is a wilted lily.
4. Only music relaxed him. Its soft sounds were a fist beating against his ear.
5. The sea strangled him with cold, wet hands.
6. The sergeant, death, is strict in his arrest.

FIGURATIVE LANGUAGE: any language which deviates from literal language so as to furnish novel effects or fresh insights into the subject being discussed.

IMAGERY

Describe what you can see, hear, feel, taste, or smell when you think of:

a bonfire
a dill pickle
a heavy wool blanket
thunder
a hot fudge sundae
a hat

When you consider what a word suggests, you form pictures and sense impressions in your imagination. Such pictures or sense impressions are called *images*.

Some words are too general to suggest similar images in the minds of different people. For example, while you and your classmates probably had somewhat similar images of thunder, your images of a hat may have been quite different. Some of you may have visualized a man's hat, others a woman's hat; some may have seen a policeman's or a fisherman's hat. One way of helping others form an image closer to yours is by using specific words, such as *cap,* or *sombrero;* another way is adding details, such as *a grass-green hat overflowing with artificial daisies.*

In the following paragraph, notice the specific words and details that the writer uses to create vivid pictures and thus give a clearer picture of mountain climbing than if he had merely reported facts.

Up. Pressure on the rope circling my waist was a reminder. Thin, chill air seared inside my nostrils and seemed to dull the brain, too. It was hard to separate tastes of dust and snow in the dry, stinging mixture that the wind whipped against my face. I could just barely remember the outline of the mountain, gleaming and jagged, against a piercing blue, cloudless sky. Now, only stretches of raw earth, broken rock, and grainy snow remained real. I struggled upward; my hands were numb, rope-burned claws. Sounds of breathing and scraping and of tumbling bits of rock and dirt were unnaturally loud in the icy stillness. A dim, even drone told me that far to the east, above and beyond the peak that was our goal, an airplane soared.

1. What visual images are mentioned in this paragraph?

2. What sounds are indicated?
3. Is there anything that you might taste?
4. What parts describe physical feelings?
5. Are there any smells in the scene?

The good writer chooses images with extreme care. Rather than use as many as possible, he selects only those that help the reader interpret the poem or story, and he arranges them in such order as to convey certain attitudes and feelings. He avoids trite, commonplace, and exaggerated expressions; his images are fresh, vivid, and sometimes even startling.

In the following poem, Donald Hall uses images to introduce a place many of us have never seen. Read all of "Caribbean" to get a general idea of the poem.

CARIBBEAN

DONALD HALL

Montego Bay
in its quick curve
listens
to the plane, waiting
for the cross of silver to   5
soften down.
In the air, above,
past the frail
wing and the gauze
glint of the propellers,   10
we see the thick
curve of the green:
the aqua-
marine!
This is the Caribbean   15
Sea, and the Bay
which gathers into
its shallows all
measures of green,
until, in the sun, the   20
patches declare
communities of depth, from
bright to sombre.
Touch them,

To see if your impression of the scene is in keeping with the images the poet uses, read the poem in sections, answering the questions as you go.

"Caribbean" by Donald Hall from *Poetry* (June 1958). Reprinted by permission of Curtis Brown, Ltd. Copyright © 1958 by Donald Hall.

Montego Bay
in its quick curve
listens
to the plane, waiting
for the cross of silver to   5
soften down.

1. Describe the shape of Montego Bay as seen from the plane.
2. How does this shape resemble a listening position?
3. What sound is heard?
4. Explain the phrase "cross of silver."
5. What words indicate that the plane might descend?

In the air, above,
past the frail
wing and the gauze
glint of the propellers,   10
we see the thick
curve of the green:
the aqua-
marine!

6. Are "we" on the ground or inside the plane?
7. Does the flying plane seem light and delicate or heavy and powerful?
8. Why would looking through moving propellers be like looking through gauze?
9. What do "we" see beyond parts of the plane?

This is the Caribbean   15
Sea, and the Bay
which gathers into
its shallows all
measures of green,
until, in the sun, the   20
patches declare
communities of depth, from
bright to sombre.
Touch them.

10. What color is the water that Montego Bay collects?
11. How does the sunlight help to show where the water is shallow and where it is deeper?
12. What could you reach out and touch, especially if the plane were descending?
13. What general impression of Montego Bay does the poet give you?
14. What details in the poem has the artist depicted in the illustration below? What details not found in the poem has he added?

IMAGERY: concrete words or details that appeal to the senses. Words that cause a scene to flash before the reader's eye or summon up a sudden sound or smell give a written work a sense of reality.

INFERENCES

Suppose an author writes a story in which he wants to reveal the personality of a girl named Peg. He has Peg write the following letter to a sick friend:

Hi Marge!

I'm awfully sorry to hear you've been sick and in the hospital for two weeks. I've been meaning to come see you—I really have—but I've been terribly, *terribly* busy. Did you know·I replaced you in the class play? Rehearsals are a ball!

I suppose you're living a life of luxury—nurses to wait on you hand and foot, good-looking interns to watch over you. Boy! some people have all the luck. I guess a healthy little nobody like me just doesn't rate.

I hope you don't mind, but Eddie asked me to the prom. I ran into him the other day, and asked who he was taking—I knew you couldn't go. You probably won't be able to do much more than light walking for months. Anyway, he said he'd asked Gloria. Now, I know you wouldn't want him to take *her*—you'd probably never see him again (ha ha). So, I convinced him to take me. I'm sure you'd prefer that he took a friend of yours.

Could I ask you one teensy little favor? Could I wear the dress you bought for the prom? After all, it won't do you any good just hanging in the closet. And pink is my best color.

Seriously, I hope you get better soon.

Do you think you'll be able to rejoin the cheerleading squad this year?

Love,

Peg

Listed below are some conclusions you might draw about Peg. Which conclusions are clearly supported by evidence in the letter? Which conclusions can be guessed from the evidence? From the evidence, which conclusions seem untrue? For which conclusions is there nothing in the letter to support the statement as true or false?

1. Peg is really concerned about Marge's illness.

2. Peg is jealous of Marge.

3. Peg has probably never been in a hospital.

4. Peg has no sympathy for others.

5. Peg would like to be in a hospital herself.

6. Peg is very shy with people.

7. Peg is forward with other people.

8. Peg thinks of herself as unimportant.

9. Peg would like to be important.

10. Peg is very practical and doesn't like to see anything go to waste.

11. Peg takes advantage of her friends.

12. Peg would like to replace Marge as a cheerleader.

What information can you find in the poem that follows?

HAWK
LAURIE ABRAMS

```
There sits beneath the tree
      Hawk
   whose brownwing gathers reddust
      as he hobbles.
He came to us old,                              5
            he is older now. And
Men
      with dustbig boots and broad shoulders
            ask
                  "his age." And          10
Children
      his "whereabouts."
We tell children
            tall tales.
We tell men                                     15
            "it is unknown" and
      what we do know.

Hawk came one day
   hobbled from off the road
      with a dragging wing.                      20
We splinted; it healed.
We had to keep the dogs away.
      They yapped.

Then Hawk could fly . . .
   We saw him.                                   25
But in our presence
      (even with the splint removed)
he dragged his wing.

Funny,
      we thought                                 30
      as we caught frogs to feed him
            and·patted his head.
We have grown fond of the old bird.
```

"Hawk" by Susan Laurie Abrams. Copyright, 1967 by Scott Foresman & Co.

1. What might be the setting of this poem? How can you tell?

2. Which of these feelings does the speaker express for the hawk: (a) sympathy; (b) dislike; (c) admiration; (d) affection? Explain.

3. What kind of person does the speaker seem to be? Why do you think so?

4. (a) What does the hawk pretend? (b) Which lines explain why he does so?

5. (a) What does the speaker mean by "Funny" (line 29)? Explain.

The authors of the letter and poem used indirect clues to suggest or *imply* certain information. To understand fully what they have written, you had to read between the lines to find the implications from which to draw logical conclusions, or *inferences*.

Many writers—especially writers of short stories, plays, and poems—often depend on implications to convey important information. A writer may expect you to infer matters of setting and action. On the basis of what characters do and say, he may expect you to recognize how the characters feel, what kind of people they are, and why they act as they do. To understand fully what you read, you must be alert to what the author implies; you have to be able to read between the lines and draw logical inferences from indirect clues.

> **INFERENCES:** reasonable and intelligent conclusions drawn from hints or implications provided by the author.

IRONY

I. Irony of Situation

Cyril Scott of 474 Rose St. was killed last evening when his car was struck at the intersection of Rose and Grant by a vehicle driven by Charles Keney, 23, of 543 Lane Ave.

Keney, cited for failure to stop at the intersection and for driving while intoxicated, was booked at city jail and released on bail.

The son of missionary parents, Scott spent his youth in Africa, where he hunted wild game. After schooling in England, he tested experimental automobiles on the continent for several years. A veteran of over a hundred bombing missions in World War II, Scott recently worked as a test pilot for Aircanes Aviation.

Killed a block from his home, Scott, 44, leaves a wife and three sons.

1. What is unexpected about the manner of Cyril Scott's death?

2. Considering the kind of life he had led, what would have been a more appropriate way for him to die?

Irony of situation is the term given to an occurrence contrary to what one would expect. Cyril's death is ironic because it is so ordinary; a sensational death in connection with any one of his dangerous occupations would have been more likely. Irony of situation, so frequent in real life, is often effectively employed in the plots of literary works.

II. Ironic Tone

"What a nice guy you are," Tom said, as his brother Bill seized the last slice of cake and stuffed it into his mouth.

Tom says his brother is nice. What does he really mean?

Tom's comment to his brother is an example of *verbal irony,* a device, like irony of situation, that involves contrast. In verbal irony, the speaker says the opposite of what he really means or what he thinks is true. All of us speak ironically at times; for example, if you say, "What a great day!" when caught in a downpour, you are using verbal irony. You indicate what you really mean by the expression on your face and your tone of voice.

The new American ideal is speed. To date, the best way for Americans to fulfill that ideal is to use the modern expressway. One problem remains, however: how best to deal with traitors to the swift way of life. Feeble attempts to handle such disloyalty are found in recent expressway laws forbidding anyone to go *below* a minimum speed limit. Ideally, though, anyone un-American enough to drive slowly and thus deny the merit of our fast-paced living deserves nothing less than death. Come to think of it, that's what he'll probably get if he stays on that highway long enough. Perhaps there's not such a problem after all.

NARRATOR

The writer of the preceding paragraph claims that driving slowly is un-American. Is this his real attitude toward speed and the modern expressway? Explain.

In literature, verbal irony may extend beyond a single statement to include the author's entire attitude; this is known as *ironic tone*. In other words, the writer's real attitude contrasts with the attitude he pretends to have. He may pretend to be admiring, unsuspecting, or perhaps even stupid. But he provides details about characters, events, and situations that, taken together, express his real feeling. For example, the author of the paragraph about speed makes a pretense of praising rapid driving, but the total effect is to condemn the speed that costs so many lives. No one would seriously accuse a slow driver of being un-American.

By writing ironically, the author can often convey his ideas more subtly, and thereby more effectively, than he could by making direct critical statements. Irony is therefore a regular device of satire.

IRONY: a contrast between what is said and what is meant. The author's tone is ironic when he veils his real attitude behind a mask of innocence or admiration. Irony is a frequent device of satire.

IRONY OF SITUATION: an event contrary to that which is expected or appropriate.

A Town Mouse went to visit his cousin in the country. The Country Mouse welcomed him heartily, and when it came time to dine, served his guest the best of his bread and cheese. But the Town Mouse, unaccustomed to such meager fare, was unhappy with the meal. He invited the Country Mouse to come to town and dine with him. The Country Mouse accepted his worldly cousin's offer and soon they were supping upon the finest jams and jellies, cakes and ales. Suddenly, their happy feast was interrupted by two dogs who came bounding into the room and frightened the cousins into the walls of the house. "Good-by," said the visitor from the country, and he began to take his leave. "But you've just arrived," said his host. "Didn't you enjoy the meal I served you? Didn't you prefer it to your molding bread and bits of cheese?" "Yes," admitted his cousin, "but I prefer, most of all, to eat in peace." The Town Mouse failed to understand his cousin's feelings; he was willing to give up peaceful surroundings for good food. And all this just goes to prove that everyone is convinced his ways are best.

In the above, an author tells the tale of the two cousins who saw things differently. Because he wished to show us both sides of the situation, he tells it from the point of view of an observer not directly involved in the incident.

But the author doesn't have to remain an impartial observer. He can, if he wishes, get inside one of his characters and tell the story through that character's eyes. When the author has a character tell a story, he allows the character's feelings and attitudes to affect the way it is told. Suppose the author of "The Town Mouse and the Country Mouse" had chosen to have one of the cousins tell his tale. It might read something like this:

I went to visit my cousin in the country, who seemed quite happy to see me. But when it came time to dine, he served me nothing but day-old bread and molding cheese crumbs. At first taken aback by this show of inhospitality, I soon learned that this was all the poor wretch had to offer. Out of sheer politeness, I ate a few meager scraps, but my stomach objected to them violently. Then, as nicely as possible, I said: "Cousin, you need a change in your diet. Come with me to town and I

shall feed you delicacies fit for gods." Of course, I made it very clear that I found nothing wrong with the humble fare he offered, and that I simply thought he might enjoy a change. At my descriptions of my daily meals, the dear fool began to water at the mouth—so much did he crave to share my supper. He insisted that we be off immediately and would not give me a chance to rest my weary legs from the long journey I had just made. When we arrived at my stately residence in town, he went straight into the dining room. His eyes did bulge at the sight of that room and the lovely things to eat therein! He set to gorging himself upon jams and jellies, cakes and ales. I was about to comment —jokingly of course—on his lack of table manners when, suddenly, the dogs of the house began to bark playfully, whereupon my cowardly cousin screamed, "What's that?" and dropped a piece of cake from his mouth. Ignoring that display of ill-breeding, and wishing to put him at ease, I answered soothingly, "Why, it's only the dogs supplying music for our dinner." But my country-bumpkin cousin did not find my little jest humorous, and when the dogs entered the room, the ill-mannered creature scurried ahead of me into my domicile in the wall where he dripped blueberry jam on my floor; you know what a stain that makes. "Good-by," my cousin said. "What, are you going so soon?" I asked. "There is really nothing to worry about for, after all, a mouse can outrun a clumsy hound. Stay and finish your supper, dear Cousin." But he would not listen to my reassurances or my pleadings and he was off without a thank-you. Ah and alas, some mice will never learn that one can't have the best unless one is willing to make little sacrifices.

1. From whose point of view is this version of the story told?
2. What kind of picture does the story-teller give you of his cousin? Point out words and phrases that create that picture.
3. Does the storyteller make any direct statements about his own character and personality? What impression does he make on you? What creates this impression?
4. How does the concluding statement in this version differ from the concluding statement in the first version?
5. Do you think the mouse telling the second version has told any deliberate lies? What has he failed to see?
6. How might this story differ if it were told by the other mouse? What conclusion might he come to?

The person who tells a story is called the *narrator*. If the narrator is the author, he usually remains an anonymous observer who seldom makes any references to himself. But if the author allows one of the characters to narrate the story, that character always refers to himself as "I."

It's important to recognize who the narrator is, for his personal feelings and attitudes affect the way the story is told.

> **NARRATOR:** the person who tells a story. The author may tell the story directly or he may tell it through one of his characters. When an author allows a character to tell a story, it is limited to what that character can see, hear, think, and express. He lets that character's personal feelings affect the way the story is told.

PLOT

Let's suppose that an author decides to write a story about revenge. Our imaginary author bases his story on a violent quarrel between two men—Jacob Newcomber and Claude Erskine. Listed below are the events the author wants to include in the story. Arrange them in the order in which they would most likely happen.

(a) Jacob Newcomber and Claude Erskine quarrel over the ownership of a piece of land.

(b) When Claude escapes the sheriff, Jacob's son, George, swears personal vengeance against the man who murdered his father.

(c) George is tried and sent to prison.

(d) Claude flees the scene of his crime.

(e) George tracks down Claude and shoots him.

(f) The quarrel degenerates into a fight in which Claude kills Jacob.

(g) George is sought and captured for the murder of Claude.

1. What is the main idea in the story outlined above?

2. Are any of the incidents unrelated to the main idea? Explain.

3. What is the purpose of incident **c**? of incident **d**?

4. Why is it necessary that incident **f** come before incident **b**?

5. Explain how the action in incident **e** causes the action in incident **g**.

Just as the navigator on an airplane charts the course of his aircraft, so an author charts the course of his story. He arranges incidents in a logical order that builds up to a peak of excitement. Such a plan, or pattern of action, is called a *plot*.

But a good plot is not just a series of exciting incidents. If the plot of a story is a good one, each incident in it will meet the following requirements:

1. It will have a purpose. That purpose may be to reveal character, complicate the problems or conflicts, advance the action, or

supply necessary background information. An incident may have more than one purpose.

2. It will grow naturally out of incidents that come before it and lead naturally into incidents that follow it.

3. It will be related to the main idea in the story.

PLOT: the pattern of incidents which make up a story. In a good plot, each incident has a purpose, grows out of the incidents that precede it and leads into those that follow, and is related to the main idea in the story.

SATIRE

While sorting through some old papers the other day, I unearthed a tattered brochure from my old college, Midwestern University. During my collegiate days, M.U. enthusiastically joined the national crusade to improve physical fitness. Rereading the brochure's description of the school's physical education program, I painfully recalled my athletic experiences there.

The school optimistically launched its attack on flabby muscles by introducing freshmen to the most strenuous sports imaginable: soccer, softball, and hockey. Besides risking heart attack and lung failure in actual play, merely getting out on the field was dangerous—players were constantly charging into each other, falling down, being walloped by wild balls, or slashed with wayward hockey sticks. Moreover, these outdoor sports were invariably offered in earliest spring, just when mud was at its gluiest and slipperiest, and wind howled its fiercest through gossamer gym suits.

Swimming, though, was the school's surefire way of doing us in. Though the pool was indoors, it wasn't unusual to find scattered sheets of ice floating on the surface. For swimming, like the field sports, was calculatedly scheduled during coldest weather. Thus we consistently trudged the campus nursing aching muscles, sniffles, and sore throats.

1. What aspects of the school's physical education program are described in the paragraphs above?
2. Which of the following phrases best summarizes the author's purpose?
(a) to praise his university in order to encourage other students to go there
(b) to poke fun at the school's athletic program by exaggerating its weaknesses
(c) to protest courses in physical education at the university level
(d) to persuade the reader of the need for physical exercise by describing the awkwardness and poor health of his college friends

TWO BLIND MICE

PAUL DEHN

Two blind mice
See how they run!
They each ran out of the lab with an oath,
For the scientist's wife had injected them both.
Did you ever see such a neat little growth   5
On two blind mice?

1. To what aspect of modern society does the author object in the preceding verse?
2. He speaks of a "neat little growth" as though he admired the scientist's experimentation. What is really his attitude?
3. From the following list of words, choose the one that best describes his tone: *amused; protesting; teasing; affectionate; sad; scornful.*

Satire is a kind of writing that criticizes something by making fun of it. Its purpose is to expose the weakness or wrongs of people, ideas, customs, or organizations, usually to reform them. A writer may ridicule his subject by exaggerating, or magnifying, its foolish characteristics. Often a satiric author makes his point by seeming to praise his subject, whereas his real attitude is the very opposite. Paul Dehn, for example, is dismayed by animal experimentation, although he calls a cancerous growth "neat" and "little."

Depending on the significance of the subject, the tone of a satiric piece of writing can be gentle, amused, bitter, or cutting. The author of the paragraphs about physical education, for instance, is amused at his school's failure to build athletes, while Dehn is acid in his comment on one feature of modern life.

Satire can be an effective means for a writer to call for improvements in society.

> **SATIRE:** literature that ridicules people, ideas, customs, or organizations, in order to expose their follies or evils and thereby to correct them. Exaggeration is a frequent device of satire. Often a satiric author's point is very different from the attitude he seems to be expressing. The tone of satire may range from gentle humor to sharp bitterness.

"Two Blind Mice" from RHYMES FOR A MODERN NURSERY by Paul Dehn. ©PUNCH, London.

SETTING

Scene: the sitting room of the Adams house in Indianapolis about 1900.

At center back is a dark red velvet sofa. Screen door at right opens onto porch. At right stands a big round table covered with a dark cloth. Windows, on either side of door at right and of sofa at back, are curtained in lace. Walls are papered in a somber dark red and brown design. The room is lighted by a center gas chandelier and a painted china oil lamp on the round table.

Curtain opens on Lavinia, seated on sofa, earnestly speaking to her brother, Edward, who stands looking out window to right of sofa.

1. The three paragraphs above are stage directions for a play. When and where is the play to take place?

2. If the first paragraph were omitted, what details in the second could give you a fairly clear picture of when and where the play is to take place?

Setting is the word used to indicate time, location, and general environment. The place setting might be, as in the stage directions above, merely one room. Or it might be a city, or a countryside. The time setting might be a particular day, a season of the year, or a period in history. Although a playwright customarily states the time and place of his drama, in other forms of literature, the author usually informs the reader about the background of his story through scattered details that hint at time and location.

Sometimes the setting aids our understanding of people in a story by revealing something about their personalities:

Ann pulled her diary out of the bookcase and carefully realigned the remaining books in a straight row. She sat down and reflectively put the tip of a freshly sharpened pencil in her mouth while rereading yesterday's entry. The spotless mirror above her reflected a neat, pink bedroom. The pink quilted nylon bedspread was folded down three times without a trace of a wrinkle or lump. An orderly group of bottles and jars stood in the exact center of the top of the dresser. None of the bottles was empty.

1. Is the above more likely to be happening in 1866 or 1966? How do you know?

2. What is the place described in the paragraph?

3. What impression of Ann do you get from the paragraph? What specific details helped form this impression?

Sometimes setting shapes the plot by causing events to occur:

Rain drumming on the roof of the cabin awoke Tom and Kathleen. Minutes later they were fully dressed and standing outside in the clearing, anxiously examining the black sky. There was no lightning, no thunder, nothing but the steady downpour in the darkness.

"We're in for it now, I guess, Kathy. The river'll be up to our door by morning." Without replying, Kathy bowed her head in resignation and turned back toward the cabin. Tom followed her and they entered together. Silently they began gathering up some of their more movable possessions—dishes, pictures, quilts—which Tom carried out to the wagon.

1. Where does the preceding action occur?

2. Approximately when does it take place?

3. What words or phrases hint at the time of the action?

4. How does the setting influence the action?

SETTING: the time, place, and general environment in which a piece of fiction occurs. Details of setting may be either stated or suggested. Although the first purpose of setting in modern fiction is to serve as a background for the action, it can also be used to reveal character and shape events.

SUSPENSE

The cluster of frightened children watched the spacecraft touch down on their playground. They waited speechless as it jolted to a stop and the loud buzzing of its rockets changed to a steady tick. A scaly green hand slid open a panel near the top of the craft. . . .

At this point, what do you most want to know: (a) exactly how the sliding panel operates; (b) the feelings of the person with the green hand; (c) what happens next?

The element in a story that makes us ask "What's going to happen next?" and "What's the reason for all this?" and "How will things turn out?" is called *suspense*. One common method of creating suspense is to introduce an element of mystery into the material. Because mystery arouses our curiosity, we read on for an explanation.

Another way to create suspense is to involve a character in an uncomfortable or dangerous situation. We read because we want to find out how the character contends with his problem. This kind of suspense can be created by tying anyone to a log and tossing that log into a wild river near a treacherous rapids. But the suspense will be much greater if the reader's excitement over what will happen next is combined with strong feelings for the person tied to the log. The author arouses this additional suspense by making the character seem lifelike. If the author is especially skilled, he need not place the character in a situation that is anywhere nearly so dangerous as the log episode above. He can keep us interested simply by getting us involved in the feelings and problems of the people he creates.

> **SUSPENSE:** the element in a literary work that keeps the reader wanting to know what happens next. Suspense can be created through the use of mystery, conflict, or characterization.

SYMBOL

What does each of the following suggest to you?

> the American flag
> a handshake
> a heart
> a million dollars
> a four-leaf clover
> a clenched fist
> a policeman's uniform

Each of the above has some special meaning to most people. This meaning may be the same for everyone: the four-leaf clover, for example, almost always suggests luck and good fortune. Or, the meaning may vary from person to person—as is the case with the policeman's uniform. To a law-abiding citizen, a police uniform suggests protection and security. To a thief, the same uniform stands for authority that is to be feared and outwitted. Few of us think of a policeman in uniform as just another man.

The four-leaf clover, the police uniform, and the rest of the items listed above are *symbols*. A symbol may be an object, a person, an action, a situation—anything that has a meaning of its own but suggests other emotional meanings as well.

In addition to the symbols we share with others, most of us have private symbols to which we attach values and meanings others don't see in them. Read the following ads taken from the lost and found column of a newspaper.

LOST: Small gold pin with two green stones in center. A gift from my husband. Pin has little monetary worth but high sentimental value. Reward.

LOST: Black alligator wallet containing papers, pictures and money. Finder may keep papers and pictures, but please return money. I need it to pay my bills.

1. Why does the woman who ran the ad for the gold pin want it back? What might it symbolize to her?
2. Is the money a symbol to the man who ran the second ad? Why or why not?

Characters in literature can also have their own private symbols. You can usually recognize literary symbols by paying careful attention to the objects, persons, or situations for which a character has special feelings. By analyzing the character's attitude toward these objects, persons, or situations, you can determine what they symbolize to him as well as understand him more fully.

Printed below are three excerpts from short stories. Try to find the symbol in each.

He hadn't anticipated any trouble when he'd taken the night watchman's job. But lately he'd been reading about the robberies in other warehouses in the area. Invariably, the watchmen were beaten up—it seemed to be an important part of the thief's method of operation. "Well," he thought, "tonight's a good night for a robbery. Fog, deserted streets, and probably not a patrol car in the area." He knew his job was a dangerous one, and, for a moment, he was terribly frightened. Then he felt the pressure of his gun against his hip, and was suddenly smug in his safeness.

1. What sort of person does the watchman seem to be?
2. What has been happening in other warehouses in the area?
3. What is the watchman carrying with him? What does that object symbolize to him?

It isn't that I hate my sister—nobody could hate Deb. But I certainly wish that once—just once—she'd behave like a normal human being and do something wrong. As far back as I can remember, I've been compared with her. And I don't have to tell you that I'm always the loser in those little comparisons. Parents, teachers—even *friends*—are constantly saying, "Why can't you be more like Deb?" They tell me she's so "helpful," or "pretty," or "popular" or "orderly" or "graceful" or "intelligent" or "courteous." It's not that I don't try—I really do—but, after all, I'm just a plain, ordinary human. What I'd like to know is this: what did I do that was so wrong that I had to be given so great a punishment as a faultless sister?

1. What kind of person does the speaker seem to be?
2. What are the speaker's feelings toward her sister?
3. What does Deb symbolize to her sister?

"How old are you?" the woman asked.
"Eleven, ma'am."
"Aren't you getting too big for this sort of thing? I've got two kids younger 'en you who wouldn't be caught dead out trick or treatin'. Some of you kids never grow up."
The boy said nothing, merely held his empty sack open in front of her.
Thinking she had failed in her attempt to shame the boy, the woman sullenly tossed a popcorn ball into the sack and slammed the door.
But the boy's pride had been hurt. She's not going to make me grow up any faster than I feel like doing, he thought. If I want to act like a kid, I will. He reached into the bag for the popcorn ball, unwrapped it, and put it up to his mouth. It had a delicious, sugary smell, but—for some reason—he couldn't bear to take a bite out of it. Holding it away from himself, he stared at it defiantly. It seemed to be echoing the woman's words, to be laughing at him. He tossed it into a nearby mud puddle and watched it grow ugly as it absorbed the brown water. Feeling he had won some sort of victory, he went on to the next house.

1. What is the woman's attitude toward the eleven-year-old trick or treater?
2. How does she make the boy feel?
3. Why can't he eat the popcorn ball?
4. What does the ball symbolize to him?
5. Why does he feel better after he throws the ball away?

> **SYMBOL:** a person, place, event, or object which has a meaning in itself but suggests other emotional meanings as well. A particular symbol may mean different things to different people.

THEME

FABLE

RALPH WALDO EMERSON

The mountain and the squirrel
Had a quarrel,
And the former called the latter "Little
Prig";
Bun[1] replied,   5
"You are doubtless very big;
But all sorts of things and weather
Must be taken in together,
To make a year
And a sphere.   10
And I think it no disgrace
To occupy my place.
If I'm not so large as you,
You are not so small as I,
And not half so spry.   15

I'll not deny you make
A very pretty squirrel track;
Talents differ; all is well and wisely put;
If I cannot carry forests on my back,
Neither can you crack a nut."

1. In which lines does the squirrel speak? What arguments does he give in defense of his size?
2. Do the squirrel's arguments apply only to the differences between squirrels and mountains? Explain.
3. What idea about life does the poet express in this poem? Find the line that best states his idea.

The idea, or point, or general truth about life that a piece of fiction reveals is called its *theme*. Sometimes, as in the poem above, an author states his theme directly. But, more often, he merely implies it. To find the theme in a piece of literature, ask yourself what it reveals to you about life or nature or people.

In some parts of Mexico, hot springs and cold springs are found side by side. The women often boil their clothes in the hot springs and rinse them in the cold. A tourist who had been watching the women at work remarked to his Mexican companion, "I suppose they think nature is pretty generous to them."

"No," replied the other. "They grumble because there isn't any soap."

1. What do the women's grumblings tell you about their outlook on life?
2. Is this outlook held only by Mexican laundresses, or do others share it?
3. Who, in general, might the grumbling women represent?
4. Which of the following best states the theme of the anecdote? (**a**) Don't ask for too much from life. (**b**) Be satisfied with what you have. (**c**) Many are never satisfied with what they have.

If you chose either statement (**a**) or (**b**), you found a moral, rather than a theme, in the anecdote. Actually, the author gives no indication that he feels people should be happy with what they have. In assuming he does, you've drawn principles from your own life and made them the author's.

A moral and a theme are not the same. A moral is a lesson, a rule to live by. A theme is a comment on life, a description of how people act — not how they should act — and the effect their actions have upon themselves and others.

> **THEME:** an idea about life expressed in a literary work. A theme may sometimes be stated directly, but, more often, it is implied. A theme, or a comment on life, should not be confused with a moral, or rule to live by.

---

1. Bun, a name often applied to a squirrel in Emerson's time.

TONE

Don't you *dare* move an inch before I tell you to!
Please stay right there until I come back.

1. How are the two statements above similar?
How are they different?

2. Read each statement aloud as you think it
might be spoken.

Read through the following verses, paying
careful attention to the way the authors use
words.

Climb upon my knee, Sonny boy;
Though you're only three, Sonny boy . . .
When there are gray skies,
I don't mind the gray skies
You make them blue, Sonny boy.[1]

Let's straighten this out, my little man,
And reach an agreement if we can.
I entered your house an honored guest.
My shoes are shined and my trousers
    are pressed,
And I won't stretch out and read you
    the funnies.   5
And I won't pretend that we're Easter
    bunnies . . .
You may take a sock at your daddy's
    tummy
Or climb all over your doting mummy,
But keep your attention to me in check
Or, sonny boy, I will wring your neck. . . .[2]

1. To whom is the speaker in each poem
talking?

2. What two very different attitudes toward
boys are expressed in these poems?

3. Point out words and phrases that helped
you understand the attitude in each.

Everything ever said is expressed in some
tone of voice. The tone in which we speak
helps listeners to understand our feelings on
the subject we're talking about.

An author also expresses a *tone* in his
writing. Sometimes he will write in anger,
and his choice of short, tense-sounding
words will indicate his tone. Or, to point up
the ridiculousness of a situation, he may say
the opposite of what he means. In short,
his tone may be despairing, triumphant,
admiring, affectionate, gay, defiant, resentful,
amused, or as many variations as there are
emotions.

Tone in literature has much the same
purpose as tone of voice: it helps readers
understand the author's attitude toward
his subject. To understand a work of literature completely, you must sense its tone.

To determine the tone of a literary selection
analyze the words and details the author
uses and the ways in which he portrays
characters and describes events. For example, a paragraph containing words such
as *grim, gray, bleak, dejected, beaten,* might
have an unhappy or despairing tone. A
description like "beautiful as night" or
"graceful as a swan" might convey the
author's admiration for his subject.

> **TONE:** an author's attitude toward his
> subject as expressed in a literary work.
> Tone is conveyed through the author's
> choice of words and details and his
> descriptions of characters and events.

---

1. "Sonny Boy" by Al Jolson, Bud DeSylva, Lew Brown
and R. Henderson. Copyright 1928 by DeSylva, Brown &
Henderson, Inc. Copyright renewed, assigned to Chappell
& Co., Inc. Used by permission of Chappell & Co., Inc. and
Campbell Connelly & Co. Limited.
2. Copyright 1931, by Ogden Nash. Excerpted from "To a
Small Boy Standing on My Shoes While I Am Wearing
Them" from FAMILY REUNION by Odgen Nash, by per-
mission of Little, Brown and Co., and J. M. Dent &
Sons Ltd.

COMPOSITION GUIDE

LEARNING TO WRITE is like learning to skate. It helps to have someone tell you how it is done, but you learn the skill only through your own efforts. The composition lessons that follow will give you a chance to develop your skills as a writer. All the lessons are related to the literature in the anthology, and most of them ask you to write about this literature. Some draw upon the selections in the text for practice in describing, explaining, and interpreting. Some ask for your opinion on ideas expressed by an author or character. Others give you the opportunity to tell of a personal experience that is similar to an incident in a selection.

There are thirty-two lessons in the composition guide. Some of the lessons contain a second optional assignment for students especially interested in writing. Since the optional assignment is usually more difficult than the regular one, it should be done only with your teacher's permission.

Printed below are the unit titles and the composition lessons designed to accompany each unit.

UNIT 1: STANDPOINT
 1: Persuasion
 2: Description
 3: Character Sketch
 4: Opinion

UNIT 2: A GALLERY OF HEROES
 5: Character Sketch
 6: Explanation
 7: Interview
 8: Opinion

POETRY I
 9: News Story
10: Description
11: Interpretation

UNIT 3: THE OUTSIDER
12: Persuasion
13: Comparison and Contrast
14: Narration
15: Narration
16: Opinion

UNIT 4: YESTERDAY AND TOMORROW
17: Character Sketch
18: Explanation
19: News Story
20: Character Sketch
21: Opinion

POETRY II
22: Interpretation
23: Narration
24: Opinion

UNIT 5: IN THE BEGINNING. . .
25: Explanation
26: Description
27: Opinion
28: Comparison and Contrast

UNIT 6: PARALLELS
29: Reviews
30: Explanation
31: Character Sketch
32: Evaluation

LESSON 1

Persuasion

Based on "The Dubbing of General Garbage," "Speed Adjustments," and "Thanksgiving Hunter," pages 4–23.

In "The Dubbing of General Garbage," Mrs. Gorkin and Mr. Gauss disagree on whether or not Lee should surrender his sword to Grant. By uncontrolled crying, Mrs. Gorkin finally persuades the principal that her viewpoint is the right one. Tears may not be the best argument, but they are one way of persuading others. How else might Mrs. Gorkin have had her way?

What if it had been Herbie instead of Mr. Gauss who pointed out the fault in the play? Considering Mrs. Gorkin's personality, how might she have "persuaded" Herbie?

The purpose in *persuasive writing* is the same as in persuasive speech: to convince someone to accept a particular opinion or idea. But in writing, methods such as those Mrs. Gorkin employs with Mr. Gauss will usually convince no one. If you are to persuade others that your opinion is to be taken seriously, you must organize your arguments logically, present your facts clearly, and give examples to enforce your position. Listed below are three statements presenting a particular viewpoint. Pick the statement with which you most strongly agree. Then write one paragraph defending the viewpoint it presents. Be sure to use concrete examples and logical arguments.

1. Lennie Krieger is a bully who deserved to be humiliated.
2. Children should be reasoned with rather than spanked.
3. Hunting should be outlawed.

Before you begin to write, review in your language text the qualities that a good paragraph must have. After you have written a first draft of your composition, read it over carefully. Is it well organized? Is it grammatically correct? Can you improve the structure of any of the sentences? Your language text will help answer questions about the mechanics of grammar and will give you useful hints on how to improve the structure of sentences. If you are doubtful about the spelling of a word, check it in a dictionary. Are your arguments logical? Can you defend each of your points? Revise accordingly. Remember revision is an important part of writing.

LESSON 2

Description

Based on "Strawberry Ice Cream Soda" and "Beauty Is Truth," pages 24–41.

Eddie preferred the city to the country because there was a lot more going on in the city.

Compare the above statement with the fifth paragraph of "Strawberry Ice Cream Soda" (page 25). Which gives you a better idea of why Eddie likes the city better than the country?

In writing description, you should use specific details that will help your readers grasp the feeling of whatever you are describing. But writing good description is not simply a matter of filling a paragraph with details. Only those details necessary to convey a clear picture of the subject being described should be used. Are there any unnecessary details in Shaw's description of the New York streets?

In both "Strawberry Ice Cream Soda" and "Beauty Is Truth" the authors describe outdoor scenes. Their descriptions are so good that even if

we have never seen the things they talk about we can visualize them.

Find a picture of an outdoor scene in a magazine or book. How does the picture make you feel? What are the most important things in the scene? During what season is the scene set? What time of day is it? Write a description of the scene for class members who haven't seen the actual picture. After you have revised your description, read it to your classmates. Then show them the picture. Do others feel your description is accurate?

LESSON 3

Character Sketch

Based on "The Lesson" and "The Pheasant Hunter," pages 42–67.

When you finished reading "The Lesson," you knew that John Thomas is so devoted to his pets that he thinks of them as being almost human. But there are many things about John Thomas you do not know —such as whether he does well in school, likes sports, or makes friends easily.

In a short story, there is seldom enough room to develop all of a character's traits fully. Thus, a short-story writer often emphasizes a particularly strong trait in each of his characters. Which of Jo's traits does Jessamyn West emphasize? What is Mayo Maloney's chief characteristic?

Write a paragraph focused on the outstanding trait of either Mr. Hobhouse or Mike Maloney. Begin with a topic sentence in which you highlight this trait; for example, "Mr. Hobhouse is a very practical man." Develop the paragraph from your topic sentence by giving exact details, vivid examples, or any sort of ex-

planation which will illustrate your subject's chief trait. (For further information on how to develop a topic sentence, refer to your language text.)

OPTIONAL ASSIGNMENT

Write one paragraph about the most important trait of a classmate you know well. Start with a topic sentence; then give details and examples which illustrate this particular trait. If you wish, you might avoid using your subject's name. After you have written and carefully revised your composition, read it to the rest of the class. Are others able to recognize your subject? If not, what did you do wrong?

LESSON 4

Opinion

Based on "The Pheasant Hunter," "Old Age Sticks," and "The Gift," pages 56–91.

In the opening paragraphs of "The Pheasant Hunter," William Saroyan describes Mayo Maloney as "a perfectly normal boy." In saying this, Saroyan is expressing an opinion; throughout the rest of the story he supplies evidence to back up his belief. After you had finished reading "The Pheasant Hunter," did you agree or disagree with the author's opinion? Why?

In reading, you often find yourself reacting to ideas and opinions expressed by a writer. Sometimes you agree with what he has to say; at other times you feel his ideas are completely wrong. Few of us ever have the chance to meet a writer and exchange opinions with him. But what if you were given that opportunity? What would you say to Saroyan, for

example, about how a perfectly normal eleven-year-old boy acts?

In "The Pheasant Hunter," "Old Age Sticks," and "The Gift," the writers express opinions about the relationship between adults and children. Their views are summarized in the three statements below. Read through the statements and choose the one with which you most strongly disagree. Then write a paragraph in which you give your opinion on the subject. Direct your statements at the author who holds the opposing view.

Begin by rewriting the statement to express your viewpoint. For example, if you disagree with Saroyan, you might start like this: "Conflicts between generations often arise not because parents have forgotten their own youth, but because they remember how hard they had to work to get the things they wanted." Use an example from your own reading or experience to support your attitude.

1. Conflicts between generations often arise because parents forget what they were like at their child's age. (William Saroyan holds this viewpoint in "The Pheasant Hunter." If you choose to disagree with this opinion, make Saroyan the audience for your paragraph.)
2. The relationship between parents and children is a kind of war which parents will inevitably win because children grow up to accept their elders' viewpoints. (If this is the statement you disagree with, Cummings will be your audience.)
3. It is very difficult for a father to be both a good friend and a strict disciplinarian to his children. (John Steinbeck expresses this opinion by showing us the relationship between Jody and his father. If you disagree with Steinbeck's viewpoint, explain your own feelings to him.)

LESSON 5
Character Sketch

Based on "Swinger," "Speaking: The Hero," "The Rescue," "The Companion," and "The Two Hoaxers," pages 96–128.

Before you read these selections you might have had some notions about what a typical hero was like. But as you can probably tell, there is nothing typical about the heroes of the stories and poems listed above. Some of the characters are forced into heroic acts, some reject the whole idea of heroism itself and ask only to be left alone, some are heroes without ever knowing it, and some are heroic in spite of their every effort to be otherwise.

But our culture also deals in stereotypes. TV, movies, and newspapers tend to portray heroes (whether they are athletes, detectives, entertainers, or politicians), as coming out of the same mold. Because we are so influenced by the media, it seems worthwhile to investigate these typical heroes so that we might better understand them.

Listed below are three types of people. Pick the type you know the most about and imagine a person you think is typical of it. What does your typical person look like? How does he dress? How does he walk and talk? Does he have any peculiar or interesting habits? Write a one-paragraph description of that person. (In each case, an audience is given to help you know what kind of details and language to use.)

1. The typical hero in television Westerns. (Your audience is an adult who seldom views this kind of show. You should avoid mentioning specific actors and programs that your reader may not know.)

2. The typical popular American singer. (Your audience is an English pen pal of your own age and sex. You can use informal language, but don't use any American slang which an English person might not understand.)

3. The typical major-league baseball pitcher. (Your audience is a friend who shares your interest in the sport. Because your friend is familiar with baseball, you can use baseball terms and specific names.)

LESSON 6

Explanation

Based on the selection from Harriet Tubman *and "The Pharmacist's Mate,"* pages 129–164.

In "The Pharmacist's Mate," the characters use a great many sea and medical terms. Because these terms belong to specialized professions, the editors explained their meanings in footnotes. If you were asked to explain these terms to a younger child, you would have to simplify them even further; you would need to use words and examples your listener could understand.

Write a paragraph based on one of the two suggestions below for an audience of fourth-graders. Use simple sentences and words that should be familiar to your readers.

1. Throughout the selection from *Harriet Tubman*, Ann Petry has included details that tell you how the Underground Railroad functioned. Read through the selection carefully, listing the details that add to your understanding of the Railroad. Write a one-paragraph explanation of how the Railroad worked, based on these details. Remember that your audience is probably unfamiliar with the people involved in the system. Therefore, if you mention particular people, be sure to tell who they were and what part they played in helping slaves to escape.

2. On the day Jimmy Bruce operates on Tommy, the sea is very rough; the men responsible for maneuvering the submarine have a hard time keeping it steady. Scattered throughout the play is information on how they do so. Skim the play and make a list of the details that help you understand how the sub is held level. Then write one paragraph explaining the process. Since your readers probably know little about submarines, you should avoid using technical terms. If you must use them, insert context clues that will help your readers understand the terms. (For information on context clues, see your language text and pages 32–33 of this book.)

LESSON 7

Interview

Based on "A Time of Greatness" and "Advice to a Knight," pages 165–179.

An interview with Richard Eberhart is printed on page 55 of *Projection in Literature*. Read through the questions that were asked of Mr. Eberhart. If you were interviewing the poet, would you ask him the same things? If not, what would you ask?

A good interviewer does not just ask questions; he asks the *right* questions. He might, for example, ask Eberhart about modern poetry, for that is a subject the poet would know a good deal about. He would not, however, question him about modern painting, for this form of art is not Eberhart's field.

Suppose you are a reporter for a Boston newspaper who has been sent

to interview Cal Crawford. Make up three questions that you feel will add to your Eastern readers' understanding of Cal and that the mountain man will enjoy answering. Then, put yourself in Crawford's place and answer the questions as you think he might have replied to them. Write up your interview in the form shown on page 55 of the text.

OPTIONAL ASSIGNMENT

In the five stanzas of T. H. Jones' poem you are given a glimpse of the character of a gentle, old knight. But the poem suggests more, and you can embellish the picture of this hero with some fanciful questions in an imaginary interview. Take both the part of interviewer and interviewee and write at least three questions and answers. Record them in the form shown on page 55.

LESSON 8

Opinion

Based on "A Gallery of Heroes," pages 94–187.

Because the word *hero* means different things to different people, a poll of class members would probably reveal that few considered every character in this unit truly heroic. In the next column are four opinions on what makes a real hero. Weigh each statement carefully; then pick the opinion with which you most strongly agree or disagree. You can use one of the statements as your topic sentence, or you can rewrite the statement to suit your own purposes. Then support your viewpoint with logical arguments and use one concrete example to reinforce it. Limit your discussion to one paragraph.

1. You call our scientists heroes, but I call them what they really are—villains.
2. To be a hero requires more courage than wisdom.
3. No man is truly heroic if his courageous actions benefit himself.
4. Anyone who can face the problems of the modern world without trying to run away from them is worthy of the title *hero*.

After you have written and revised your composition, compare your work with that of a classmate who took an opposing stand. Which of you has given sounder reasons for your opinion?

LESSON 9

News Story

Based on "Simultaneously" and "The Demon of the Gibbet," pages 190–193.

The first paragraph of almost every good newspaper story contains the answers to five questions: Who? What? Where? When? Why? Newspapers make such summaries of the news for the benefit of those people who want the most important information without reading the entire story. Thus, the first paragraph in a story about a robbery might summarize what happened in a statement that reads something like this:

John Edward Hobbins of 1244 Willow Road was attacked by two armed men while walking from his train stop to his home last night. The thieves fled with Hobbins' brief case, which contained what he termed "highly valuable papers." They seemed to have no interest in money, for they did not take Hobbins' wallet containing three hundred dollars.

Write the opening paragraph of one of the following stories for your local newspaper.

1. A front-page story of international news that describes the events suggested in David Ignatow's poem "Simultaneously" (you will have to depend on your own interpretation of the events). Be sure to tell why this incident took place, who was responsible for the decisions taken, when and where it took place, and what the final outcome was.

2. A news story about the bride who is stolen by the demon. Tell who the bride was, what happened to her, where and when and why it happened. Be sure that no opinions are stated as facts.

LESSON 10

Description

Based on "Rain," "One A.M.," "The Pasture," and "Good-by and Keep Cold," pages 194–199.

Poets are very observant people. They recognize that man feels insignificant when he comes up against nature's immense power. They see similarities between beauty and drabness. They sense the unusual in the things most of us consider very ordinary. When a poet writes his observations down, he helps his readers see what he has seen.

How observant are you? Pay a visit to your local hardware store, supermarket, or drug store. Pick one counter in the store that especially interests you. To which of your senses does this counter have the greatest appeal?

Write one paragraph in which you describe your favorite counter in terms of what you either see, hear, smell, or feel there. Try to include details that other people might not notice. Use plenty of vivid imagery to help classmates share your observations.

LESSON 11

Interpretation

Based on "Poetry I," pages 189–205.

The supplementary article entitled "It Says a Lot in a Little" (page 196) points out that a poem often contains ideas that most readers cannot grasp in one hurried reading. What, for example, is Coffin saying in "Crystal Moment"? Is the poem merely a recollection of a sight the poet found both beautiful and horrible? Does Coffin fill the poem with images only to help readers share his memory? Or does the author use these images to develop an idea?

The best way of finding out whether you really understand the meaning of a poem is to write your own interpretation of it. Forcing yourself to find words to pin down your ideas will clarify your thinking.

Select one of the poems in this section of poetry. Read and reread the poem until every line is clear to you and fits into the idea of the poem as a whole. Then write one paragraph explaining the meaning of the poem.

LESSON 12

Persuasion

Based on "First Principal" and "The New Kid," pages 208–227.

A. B. Guthrie and Murray Heyert both present, in their fiction, thought-provoking comments on the individual and society. Through their imaginary characters the authors make clear what they consider to be some of the flaws in real man's make-up. The following statements are summaries of some ideas implied in these two stories:

1. Children place so much emphasis on physical ability that they often overlook other good qualities in people.
2. A person's pride often leads him to search out those who seem weak in order to make them the object of his scorn.
3. Because many people are suspicious of individualists, they try to force those who are different into the patterns of the majority.

Choose one of these statements. Consider it carefully, weighing the evidence for and against the ideas it presents. Then write a paragraph in which you present arguments that either support or oppose the statement.

Direct your writing at a classmate who disagrees with you. After you have written and revised your composition, present it to the person you have chosen as your audience. Do your arguments convince him that your viewpoint is worth serious consideration?

OPTIONAL ASSIGNMENT

In "The New Kid," Murray Heyert uses a group of young boys who are playing a game of punchball to develop his theme. What comment on life does Heyert make through these boys and their game? Does Heyert's comment apply to adults, also?

Write one paragraph in which you try to prove or disprove that adults, like children, need to feel they are better than someone else. Use an incident that you have seen or have read about to support your argument.

If you wish, you might, in a separate paragraph, explain why you think people need to feel more important than someone else. Should you choose to write such a paragraph, base your explanation on fact as well as opinion.

LESSON 13

Based on "The New Kid," "Nancy," and "Win or Lose," pages 216–248.

If you happened to see Marty and the new kid on the block sitting together on an apartment house stoop, what similarities would you notice between them? What differences might you see? Who is Marty more like: the new kid or the other boys on the block?

Reread "The New Kid" and as you do, jot down notes about the differences and similarities between both Marty and the new kid and Marty and the other boys. Develop those notes into a composition of four separate paragraphs; two to describe the differences between the characters and two to describe the similarities. For help on how to write comparison and contrast see the Handbook entry on contrast (page 519).

As an alternative project you could contrast and compare the forces which work on Graham and alternately push him to run harder or seek to pull him away from competitive running. Start by describing the two characters who represent these opposing forces.

If you would like to try your skill at a more difficult assignment, write two paragraphs in which you compare and contrast Fiona Farmer with a seven-year-old girl you know. Be sure to use specific details and concrete examples in your writing. Include information about family background, and attitudes toward pets and playthings. Is your seven-year-old friend, for example, content with quietly playing house, or is she more apt to be found climbing trees? Are her parents careful to see that she is polite at all times, or do they occasionally permit her to forget her manners?

LESSON 14

Narration

Based on "Sled" and "The Baroque Marble," pages 249–264.

Narration is one of the commonest forms of writing. We use it whenever we write an account of some personal experience. Biographers use it in telling about someone's life. Short-story writers use it in relating events in the lives of fictional characters. The first purpose of narration is to interest or entertain the reader.

In "The Baroque Marble," E. A. Proulx uses narration to tell of a certain incident in Opal Foote's life. Although the story revolves around Opal's dreams of a pearl, we also learn quite a bit about the rest of the Footes. Knowing what you do about the Foote family, write a short narrative account of one of the following incidents that might have taken place.

1. Brother Roy is laid off work at GE.
2. Mama is ill and requires an operation that will cost $800, almost all of Opal's yearly earnings.
3. Opal, unable to buy her pearl, spends all of her money on a Picasso painting for her father.

If you prefer to write about "Sled," put yourself in the position of Joey's sister and write a short account of the evening when the sled broke. Be sure to consider exactly what his sister thinks about breaking the sled and if she has any suspicions about her brother.

OPTIONAL ASSIGNMENT
Jack and Jill went up the hill
To fetch a pail of water,
Jack fell down and broke his crown,
And Jill came tumbling after.

This rhyme is an impartial account of what happened to Jack and Jill. It simply states the facts; it places the blame for the accident on no one.

But what caused Jack to fall and break his crown? Did Jill trip him, perhaps? Why did Jill tumble after him? Did Jack grab onto Jill as he began to fall? Whose fault was the accident? Put yourself in either Jack's or Jill's place and write one paragraph giving your view of what happened.

LESSON 15

Narration

Based on "A Loud Sneer for Our Feathered Friends," "The Boy Who Laughed at Santa Claus," and "The Skunk," pages 265–274.

Ruth McKenney begins "A Loud Sneer for Our Feathered Friends" by stating: "From childhood, my sister and I have had a well-grounded dislike for our friends, the birds." In the remainder of the selection, Miss McKenney explains why and how she and Eileen came to dislike birds. She illustrates her explanation by relating humorous incidents that both entertain and inform.

How do you feel about birds? Is there any particular incident that led to your feelings? Do you dislike cats? If so, what caused you to dislike them?

Try writing one or two paragraphs on one of the following subjects, or on any other subject about which you have strong feelings. Begin with a topic sentence in which you state your opinions on the subject. Then relate the incident that led to this feeling.

green vegetables	*dentists' drills*
big dogs	*school cafeterias*
comic books	*gym classes*

LESSON 16

Opinion

Based on "The Outsider," pages 206–280.

The good reader responds to good literature. It causes him to think, to see the world from a new standpoint, to compare his own ideas with those held by the author. The selections in this unit are particularly apt to lead you into weighing the authors' ideas, since in each of them the writer comments upon some aspect of life.

Listed below are several quotations taken from selections in the unit. Choose the quotation about which you have an idea you would like to develop. You may comment on the quotation, telling why you agree or disagree with the idea it expresses. You may simply explain the idea in more detail. Or you may use an example from your own life to prove or disprove the validity of the author's idea. Confine your comment to a single paragraph.

1. Children's tragedies, he thought, children's little tragedies: there are bigger ones in store for you, Fiona, a world of them. The thought did not move him deeply; everyone must suffer, but for an instant he was not sorry to be old. (Enright, "Nancy," pages 239–240.)

2. How dreary to be somebody! (Dickinson, "I'm Nobody," page 241.)

3. He was wishing that he were some time a long time away from now and somewhere a long way away from here. (Adams, "Sled," page 254.)

4. "I say that if Sister Opal sees more in life than groceries and trying to get along, she should at least have the chance to try." (Proulx, "The Baroque Marble," page 261.)

LESSON 17

Character Sketch

Based on "The Monsters Are Due on Maple Street," pages 284–297.

If the dialogue in a play is good, a character's words can reveal much about his personality, his outlooks, and his attitudes. The words a character uses and the way in which he speaks to another character may indicate something about the speaker's education, his social position, and his aggressiveness—or lack of it. The statements others make about this character add to your knowledge of him. The actions the character performs, the opinions he expresses, and the things he fights for are also important sources of information about him.

With these ideas in mind, consider the following characters from Serling's "The Monsters Are Due on Maple Street":

Don Martin
Steve Brand
Charlie

Choose the character who interests you most or the one you believe you understand best. Go through the play again, studying carefully everything the character says and does and everything others say about him. Make brief notes of all the details and write out quotations that are especially significant in explaining the kind of person this character really is. Before you begin writing, use an outline to get your ideas in proper order. (Your language text will give you some ideas on how to make good outlines.)

In writing this character sketch, try to present as complete and well-rounded a portrait as possible. What do the character's speech and his

manner show you about his education? What are his good qualities? What are his faults? Use brief quotations from the play to help make your ideas clear. End your composition with a short paragraph giving your total impression of the character. Your entire composition should not be more than 300 words in length.

After you have revised your composition, compare your work with the interpretation made by a classmate who has written about the same individual. If you do not agree, produce evidence from the play to support your opinion.

LESSON 18

Explanation

Based on "Rikki-tikki-tavi" and "Macavity," pages 299–313.

In the course of the story "Rikki-tikki-tavi," Rudyard Kipling has sprinkled many details about how Rikki stalks Nag and Nagaina, how he fights them, and how he finally kills them.

Reread the story, writing down all the details that help you understand Rikki's methods. Then write an explanation, one paragraph in length, of how a mongoose hunts, fights, and kills a snake. You will probably explain the subject more clearly if you imagine you are addressing a reader who is not familiar with the facts you are presenting.

OPTIONAL ASSIGNMENT

One of the big puzzles in "Macavity" is how the mystery cat always manages to have fled the scene of his crime before the police arrive. How does he do it? In one paragraph, write an explanation of how you think Macavity makes his getaway. Let your imagination work.

LESSON 19

News Story

Based on "The Storyteller" and "Rip Van Winkle," pages 314–335.

If the editors of the newspaper that Rip and his cronies read at the inn had heard about Van Winkle's strange adventure, they surely would have sent someone to get a story. Imagine you are a reporter sent to interview Rip about his long sleep. Remember that Rip does not know as much about what happened to him as the readers of Irving's story do. Write a short news story based only on what Rip could tell you.

In writing a news story, keep your sentences and paragraphs short. Your statements should be very exact and clearly worded. This particular story may contain three paragraphs:

1. Perhaps only a sentence in length, this paragraph should summarize all the important facts in the story: *Who* did *what, when, where,* and *why?* (Be sure no opinion is stated as fact.)
2. This paragraph should present more details about the most important fact, usually either the *who* or the *what.* (You might, for example, give more details about the men Rip met in the mountains and what they did to him.)
3. The third paragraph may summarize other details related to less important facts. (Here you could tell how Rip's friends and family feel about his return.)

If you would like to base your composition on "The Storyteller," imagine that the prince had invited the press to view his park when he opened it. Pretend you were among the reporters in attendance and write a newspaper story in which you describe the park's most important features.

LESSON 20

Character Sketch

Based on "The Ugly Duckling," pages 336–351.

Before you had read very far in "The Ugly Duckling," you very likely had a strong mental picture of each major character. Some of these mental images probably resembled people you have seen in movies and on television. From the list below, select three characters you visualize clearly.

Decide what movie, stage, or television personality you would cast for each one. Then write a composition of three paragraphs naming your candidates to play these three parts. Explain why you think these actors fit the roles you have assigned them.

Chancellor *Dulcibella*
King *Princess Camilla*
Queen *Prince Simon*

LESSON 21

Opinion

Based on "Yesterday and Tomorrow," pages 282–361.

In studying the Handbook article on fantasy (pages 521–522), you learned that writers often use improbable situations and characters to make important comments on real life. In the next column are some quotations from various selections in Unit Four. Read through the quotations and pick the one on which you have the strongest feelings. You may comment on the quotation, telling why you agree or disagree with it. You may explain the comment in more detail. Or you may use an example from your own life to prove the truth of the author's idea.

1. For the record, prejudices can kill and suspicion can destroy and a thoughtless, frightened search for a scape-goat has a fall-out all of its own for the children . . . and the children yet unborn. (Serling, "The Monsters Are Due on Maple Street," page 247.)

2. Darzee was a feather-brained little fellow who could never hold more than one idea at a time in his head. . . . Darzee was very like a man in some ways. (Kipling, "Rikki-tikki-tavi," pages 306–307.)

3. If a girl is beautiful, it is easy to assume that she has, tucked away inside her, an equally beautiful character. But it is impossible to assume that an unattractive girl, however elevated in character, has, tucked away inside her, an equally beautiful face. (Milne, "The Ugly Duckling," page 333.)

4. . . . the best thing in the world, she [Great-Aunt Malkin] said, was to be quite sure of yourself, but not to expect admiration from other people. (Milne, "The Ugly Duckling," page 345.)

5. It [music] was not meant to be easy. (Goldstone, "Virtuoso," page 356.)

6. It rained quite a lot that spring. You woke in the morning/And saw the sky still clouded, the streets still wet,/ But nobody noticed so much, except the taxis/And the people who parade. You don't, in a city. (Benét, "Metropolitan Nightmare," page 358.)

LESSON 22

Interpretation

Based on "The Builders," "The Fox and the Grapes," "Requiem for a Modern Croesus," "To a Dead Goldfish," and "Artifact," pages 364–369.

From the group of poems listed above choose the one to which you react most strongly—the one in which idea and tone communicate themselves to you clearly and forcefully—and write a paragraph or more on it. Explain first the idea expressed in the poem. Then describe the emotion you feel upon reading the poem and explain which elements in the poem caused this feeling in you. A personal experience may have helped stimulate your reaction to the poem. If so, refer to your experience in the paragraph.

After you have written a first draft of the composition, read it over carefully. Are your ideas relevant to the poem and to the assignment? Have you used a variety of sentence lengths, or is your writing monotonous? Do the important ideas stand out? Did you use any sentence fragments by mistake? Do too many sentences begin with the same word? Revise accordingly.

OPTIONAL ASSIGNMENT

Marianne Moore in "The Fox and the Grapes" and Sara Henderson Hay in "The Builders" have both taken old nursery tales and altered them to make observations on modern life. Choose a popular fable or nursery rhyme and try rewriting it with a fresh, unusual twist. For example, you might write about the spider who was admired for his perserverance in the face of defeat, and show him dying as a result, thereby proving that, at times, it may be wise to give up on a task entirely.

LESSON 23

Narration

Based on "Time Out," "Who Knows If the Moon's," "At the Aquarium," and "Thoughts in a Zoo," pages 372–377.

The poet in "Time Out" views a simple scene but imagines the thoughts of a tired donkey in a confrontation with his master. In "Who Knows If the Moon's," someone looks at the moon and imagines a fantastic journey he might take in it. While visiting an aquarium, a man sees similarities between the aimless swimming of the fish and man's life. Another man visits a zoo and thinks that people, like animals, live in cages.

Take a walk in one of the places listed below, and write a short narrative account of what you see in your wanderings. Look for the unusual and emphasize one particularly interesting thing: a hot-dog vendor's wagon; an overheard conversation; an especially friendly dog; children at play; trees in the wind, or anything else that captures your attention. Make your account as vivid as possible by using imagery and comparison and contrast. If you can think of some figurative expressions which seem both fresh and appropriate, use them.

1. A walk between your home and the school.
2. A walk through a park.
3. A walk in a zoo.
4. A walk through a city street.
5. A walk in the country.
6. A walk in the school corridor between classes.
7. A walk through the halls of an office building.
8. A walk along a lake.
9. A walk among the book shelves in your library.

LESSON 24

Opinion

Based on "Poetry II," pages 363–381.

Even if everything you read is written in English, you "translate" it; that is, you change the words into a set of meanings that have personal significance for you. When you communicate ideas from your own reading to others, you again perform the translation process. Now you state the ideas as you understand them in words your listener will understand.

Listed below are quotations from some of the poems contained in the second poetry section. Read through the list carefully and choose the quotation which states an idea about which you feel deeply. How can you best explain this idea to a friend? One way is to draw on your own experience for concrete examples. Begin by stating the idea in your own words; then write a single paragraph on the subject you have chosen.

1. He said, "These grapes are sour; I'll leave them for some knave."/ Better, I think, than an embittered whine. (Moore, "The Fox and the Grapes," page 365.)
2. The people . . . also wander to and fro./And know not why or where they go,/Yet have a wonder in their eyes,/Sometimes a pale and cold surprise. (Eastman, "At the Aquarium," page 376.)
3. Who is more wretched, these caged ones, or we,/Caught in a vastness beyond our sight to see? (Cullen, "Thoughts in a Zoo," page 377.)
4. Look out how you use proud words. (Sandburg, "Primer Lesson," page 379.)
5. Perhaps our age has driven us indoors. (Jaffe, "The Forecast," page 380.)

LESSON 25

Explanation

Based on the selections from "In the Beginning . . ." on pages 388–407.

Suppose you were a primitive man who knew nothing about chemistry, physics, and the earth sciences. Your lack of knowledge would not prevent you from wondering about the things that happened around you, and your curiosity might lead you to make up explanations that answered your questions. One African tribe, for instance, in explaining the presence of the sun and moon in the sky, reasoned that they had overextended themselves while entertaining friends.

Using only the information available to primitive peoples, make up an answer to one of the following questions. Remember that your audience will hear rather than read your tale, so keep your sentences simple and use plenty of vigorous verbs.

1. Why is there thunder?
2. Why does the sun sink into the west at night?
3. Why do men walk on two legs instead of four?
4. Why does the moon change its shape?
5. Why does the tiger fear fire?
6. Why aren't men covered with fur like other creatures?
7. What causes rain?
8. What holds up the earth?
9. Why aren't babies born in eggs?
10. Why can't men fly like the birds?
11. What causes the tide?
12. What are the stars and how did they get into the sky?
13. What causes a volcano?
14. What is the purpose of clouds?
15. Where do men go after death?

LESSON 26
Description

Based on the selections from "In the Beginning . . ." on pages 411–418.

The people who made up the animal tales placed the blame for what happened to certain animals on the animals themselves. Hares, for example, have short, ugly tails simply because they are lazy creatures. Snakes get crushed because they are stupid. Tortoises have cracks in their shells because one of their ancestors spoke up at the wrong time, causing Vulture to drop him from the sky. Storks have no tails because they once laughed at the noblest among them.

But how do the animals in these stories feel toward the tales people tell about them? How might they describe what happened to them? Would a spokesman for the hares say that his family have short tails because they are shy, retiring types who were pushed aside by bigger animals when tails were distributed? Put yourself in the place of one of the following animals and give your own description of how you came to be as you are.

Hare	*Woodpecker*
Hyena	*Snake*
Tortoise	*Stork*

OPTIONAL ASSIGNMENT

In "The Dog, the Snake, and the Cure of Headache," the storyteller says: "Now, do you think the dog was grateful? No such luck for the snake. On the contrary, a dog is a dog, and a dog he remains. And why should he be better than many people are? He did as they do, and returned evil for good." Is this a fair comment? Do people really return evil for good? Write one paragraph either defending or opposing the storyteller's statement.

LESSON 27
Opinion

Based on "The Leftover Eye," "The Two Strangers," and "A Tug-of-War," pages 419–423.

African storytellers presented dilemmas for their audiences to puzzle over, argue about, and solve. Listed below are some dilemmas for you to consider. Read through all three and pick the one that interests you most. In a composition no more than two paragraphs in length present your solution to the dilemma you have chosen. Be sure to make clear why you think your solution is the best one.

1. If it were up to you to decide whether people should always have to tell the truth or whether they should be allowed to lie, what would your decision be?
2. If you could be either wealthy but hated or poor but admired, which would you choose?
3. If you could be either handsome (beautiful) or wise, which would you choose to be?

LESSON 28
Comparison and Contrast

Based on "The Separation of God from Man," "The Flying Ship," and "Fish in the Forest," pages 425–439.

While studying Unit Two ("A Gallery of Heroes") you probably developed some strong opinions on what makes a hero. In a composition three paragraphs in length, compare and contrast your concept of heroism with what you have learned about primitive peoples' admiration for the trickster hero. Organize your composition according to the following outline:

Paragraph One: Discuss the similarities between your idea of the hero and the primitive concept.

Paragraph Two: Point out the differences between your typical hero and the trickster hero.

Paragraph Three: Explain why and how your own beliefs have been altered by primitive concepts.

If you prefer, you might write a composition in which you compare and contrast the fairy-tale hero with heroes in more recent fiction. In writing this composition, use examples drawn from selections in the text.

LESSON 29
Reviews

Based on "My Father and the Hippopotamus," "Mama is a Sunrise," "The Jar," and "Fortunata Writes a Letter," pages 444–475.

Many newspapers and magazines employ people to review books, films, television programs, plays, and concerts. Basically, a reviewer's job is to give reasons why he feels others should or should not read a certain book, or view a certain show, or attend a certain performance or event. But a reviewer cannot merely say, for example, "This is a bad book; I wouldn't recommend it to anyone." He must point out *why* he thinks it is bad: Do the characters seem unreal? Is the plot faulty? Does the author write poorly? And a reviewer cannot just summarize the plot. He must express his opinion about the work as a whole and judge it on the basis of other works that deal with the same subject.

Imagine you are a reviewer for your class. From the selections listed above, choose the one you either like or dislike the most. Write a review for your classmates, telling them why they should or should not read the selection. If you are reviewing one of the short stories, concentrate on plot, characterization, tone, and theme. If you review the poem, comment on its form as well as its tone. In reviewing "Fortunata Writes a Letter," discuss the suitability of dialogue in the play. Limit your review to 300 words or less.

LESSON 30
Explanation

Based on "The Battle of Blenheim," "The Graveyard," and "A Ride Through Spain," pages 476–491.

As you read the selections in this text, you formed mental images of characters and places. You learned to recognize various tones in writing; often you found that works contained more meaning than they seemed to hold at first reading. Like you, the artists who illustrated the book formed their own interpretations of the selections assigned them. Each artist drew the sort of illustration he thought was most suitable to the material. Sometimes an artist's illustrations may have seemed exactly right to you; at other times you probably disagreed with his interpretation. What, for example, is your opinion of the illustration for "The Graveyard"?

Choose the illustration in *Projection* which you feel is best suited to the material it accompanies. In a short composition, explain why you feel this way. In writing the composition, you might explain how the illustration added to your understanding of the selection. Did it arouse your curiosity or stimulate your interest? Did it help you visualize characters and settings? Did it give you insight into

important symbols? Did the tone of the illustration reinforce the tone of the selection? If you wish, you might strengthen your explanation by referring to an illustration you do not feel is especially suitable and showing why you think it is not effective.

LESSON 31

Character Sketch

Based on "The River Merchant's Wife," "Misery," and "The Old Demon," pages 492–509.

The selections in *Projection* introduced you to many different sorts of characters: shy, sensitive Jody ("The Gift"), who loses something very dear to him; Marty ("The New Kid"), who is haunted by an intense desire to belong; Cal Crawford ("A Time of Greatness"), an old man who has outlived his usefulness; Ananse ("The Separation of God from Man"), a cruel and cunning trickster; Iona ("Misery"), a lonely sleigh-driver who can find no one to share his grief.

Of all the characters you have read about, which one would you most like to meet? In a composition of no more than 300 words, discuss the character that interests you most. Before you begin to write, consider the following questions: What would you say to the character you have chosen? Is there anything you might like to explain to him? Would you give him advice? Begin your composition by summarizing the character's traits and attitudes. Then explain why you would like to meet him.

LESSON 32

Evaluation

Based on Projection in Literature.

While assembling this anthology, the editors asked many seventh-graders throughout the country to read various selections being considered for inclusion in the text. The students in these groups were asked to answer four questions: What do you think this selection is about? What did you like about it? What did you dislike about it? Do you think it should be used in a seventh-grade anthology?

Given below are some of the answers the editors received. Each of these answers is, of course, simply one student's opinion. Choose the opinion with which you most strongly agree or disagree. Then write a composition in which you point out what you see as the faults or the strong points in the student's thinking.

1. Everything about "The Gift" was enjoyable except the way it ended. The pony should have lived.
2. "Swinger" isn't a good story because the things that happen to Hal couldn't really happen in real life.
3. I think "A Loud Sneer for Our Feathered Friends" is suitable for seventh-graders because it will teach them never to tell lies.
4. "Fortunata Writes a Letter" was a good play except that the characters should have used bigger words.
5. "Metropolitan Nightmare" condemns people for their self-centered ways.
6. "The Ugly Duckling" pokes fun at the sometimes ridiculous emphasis we place on physical beauty.
7. Although "The Battle of Blenheim" is an old poem it makes a point that is still important: war is a waste.

Glossary

The pronunciation of each word is shown just after the word, in this way: **ab bre vi-ate** (ə brē′vē āt). The letters and signs used are pronounced as in the words below. The mark ′ is placed after a syllable with primary or strong accent, as in the example above. The mark ′ after a syllable shows a secondary or lighter accent, as in **ab bre vi-a tion** (ə brē′vē ā′shən).

Some words, taken from foreign languages, are spoken with sounds that otherwise do not occur in English. Symbols for these sounds are given at the end of the table as "Foreign Sounds."

a	hat, cap	o	hot, rock		ə represents:
ā	age, face	ō	open, go		a in about
ä	father, far	ô	order, all		e in taken
		oi	oil, voice		i in pencil
b	bad, rob	ou	house, out		o in lemon
ch	child, much				u in circus
d	did, red				
		p	paper, cup		
e	let, best	r	run, try		FOREIGN SOUNDS
ē	equal, see	s	say, yes		
ėr	term, learn	sh	she, rush		Y as in French *du*. Pro-
		t	tell, it		nounce (ē) with the lips
f	fat, if	th	thin, both		rounded as for (ü).
g	go, bag	ŦH	then, smooth		
h	he, how				
		u	cup, butter		œ as in French *peu*. Pro-
i	it, pin	ù	full, put		nounce (ā) with the lips
ī	ice, five	ü	rule, move		rounded as for (ō).
j	jam, enjoy				
k	kind, seek	v	very, save		N as in French *bon*. The N is
l	land, coal	w	will, woman		not pronounced, but shows
m	me, am	y	young, yet		that the vowel before it is
n	no, in	z	zero, breeze		nasal.
ng	long, bring	zh	measure, seizure		
					H as in German *ach*. Pro-
					nounce (k) without closing
					the breath passage.

ETYMOLOGY KEY

<	from, derived from, taken from	*dial.*	dialect	*neut.*	neuter
?	possibly	*dim.*	diminutive	*pp.*	past participle
abl.	ablative	*fem.*	feminine	*ppr.*	present participle
accus.	accusative	*gen.*	genitive	*pt.*	past tense
cf.	compare	*lang.*	language	*ult.*	ultimately
		masc.	masculine	*var.*	variant

AF	Anglo-French (= Anglo-Norman, the dialect of French spoken by the Normans in England, esp. 1066–c. 1164)		Med.	Medieval
			Med.Gk.	Medieval Greek (700–1500)
			Med.L	Medieval Latin (700–1500)
			MF	Middle French (1400–1600)
Am.E.	American English (word originating in the United States)		MHG	Middle High German (1100–1450)
			MLG	Middle Low German (1100–1450)
Am.Ind.	American Indian		NL	New Latin (after 1500)
Am.Sp.	American Spanish		O	Old
E	English		OE	Old English (before 1100)
F	French		OF	Old French (before 1400)
G	German		OHG	Old High German (before 1100)
Gk.	Greek (from Homer to 300 A.D.)		Pg.	Portuguese
Gmc.	Germanic (parent language of Gothic, Scandinavian, English, Dutch, German)		Scand.	Scandinavian (one of the languages of Northern Europe before Middle English times; Old Norse unless otherwise specified)
HG	High German (speech of Central and Southern Germany)			
Hindu.	Hindustani (the commonest language of India)		Skt.	Sanskrit (the ancient literary language of India, from the same parent language as Persian, Greek, Latin, Germanic, Slavonic, and Celtic)
Ital.	Italian			
L	Latin (Classical Latin 200 B.C.–300 A.D.)			
LG	Low German (speech of Northern Germany)		Sp.	Spanish
			VL	Vulgar Latin (a popular form of Latin, the main source of French, Spanish, Italian, Portuguese, and Rumanian)
LGk.	Late Greek (300–700)			
LL	Late Latin (300–700)			
M	Middle			
ME	Middle English (1100–1500)			

OTHER ABBREVIATIONS

adj.	adjective	*E*	Eastern	*pron.*	pronoun
adv.	adverb	*esp.*	especially	*sing.*	singular
Anat.	anatomy	*interj.*	interjection	*SW*	Southwestern
Ant.	antonym	*n.*	noun	*Syn.*	synonym
Brit.	British	*pl.*	plural	*U.S.*	United States
conj.	conjunction	*prep.*	preposition	*v.*	verb

The pronunciation key is from the *Thorndike-Barnhart Advanced Dictionary,* copyright © 1973 by Scott, Foresman and Company.

a back (ə bak'), *adv.* 1. toward the back; backward. 2. **taken aback,** suddenly surprised; upset or confused by something unexpected. [OE *on bæc*]

ab er ra tion (ab'ə rā'shən), *n.* 1. wandering from the right path or usual course of action. 2. deviation from a standard or ordinary type; abnormal structure or development. 3. temporary mental disorder. 4. the failure of a lens or mirror to bring to a single focus the rays of light coming from one point. Aberration causes a blurred image or an image with a colored rim.

ab nor mal (ab nôr'məl), *adj.* deviating from the normal, the standard, or a type; markedly irregular; unusual: *It is abnormal for a man to be seven feet tall.* [< *ab-* from + *normal*] —**ab nor'mal ly,** *adv.*

a breast (ə brest'), *adv., adj.* 1. side by side: *The soldiers marched four abreast.* 2. **abreast of** or **abreast with,** up with; alongside of: *Keep abreast of what is going on.*

ab scond (ab skond'), *v.* go away suddenly and secretly; go off and hide: *The dishonest cashier absconded with the bank's money.* [< L *abscondere* < *ab-* away + *condere* store]

ab sent ly (ab'sənt lē), *adv.* without paying attention to what is going on around one; inattentively.

ab sorbed (ab sôrbd', ab zôrbd'), *adj.* very much interested; completely occupied.

a byss (ə bis'), *n.* 1. a bottomless or immeasurably deep space. 2. anything too deep to be measured; lowest depth. 3. the chaos before the Creation. [< L < Gk. *abyssos* < *a-* without + *byssos* bottom]

ac cel e rate (ak sel'ə rāt), *v., -rat ed, -rat ing.* 1. go or cause to go faster; increase in speed; speed up. 2. cause to happen sooner; hasten. 3. change the speed or velocity of (a moving object).

ac cess (ak'ses), *n.* 1. right to approach, enter, or use; admission: *All children have access to the library during the afternoon.* 2. condition of being easy or hard to reach; approach: *Access to mountain towns is often difficult because of poor roads.* 3. way or means of approach: *A ladder was the only access to the attic. He has access to men who can help him get work.* 4. an attack (of disease). 5. outburst.

ac com pa ni ment (ə kum'pə nē mənt), *n.* 1. anything that goes along with something else: *Destruction and suffering are accompaniments of war.* 2. in music, a part added to help or enrich the main part.

ac tion (ak'shən), *n.* 1. doing something; process of acting: *a machine in action.* 2. activity: *A soldier is a man of action.* 3. thing done; act. 4. **actions,** *pl.* conduct; behavior. 5. effect or influence of something on another: *the action of wind on a ship's sails.* 6. way of moving or working; movement: *a motor with an easy action.* 7. the working parts of a machine, instrument, etc. The keys of a piano are part of its action. 8. a minor battle. 9. combat between military forces. 10. series of events in a story or play. 11. a legal proceeding by one party against another to enforce a right or punish a wrong; lawsuit. 12. **in action, a.** active; taking part. **b.** working. 13. **take action, a.** become active. **b.** start working. **c.** start a lawsuit; sue.

ac ti vate (ak'tə vāt), *v., -vat ed, -vat ing.* 1. make active. 2. in physics, make radioactive. 3. in chemistry, make capable of reacting or of speeding up a reaction.

a cute (ə kyüt'), *adj.* 1. having a sharp point. 2. sharp and severe: *A toothache can cause acute pain.* 3. brief and severe. An acute disease like pneumonia reaches a crisis within a short time. 4. keen: *Dogs have an acute sense of smell. An acute thinker is clever and shrewd.* 5. having the

mark (/) over it. 6. less than a right angle. —**a cute'ly,** *adv.* —**a cute'ness,** *n.*

ad dle (ad'l), *v., -dled, -dling, adj.* —*v.* 1. make or become muddled. 2. make or become rotten. —*adj.* 1. muddled; confused, as in **addlebrain, addleheaded,** etc. 2. of eggs, rotten. [OE *adela* liquid filth]

ad her ent (ad hir'ənt), *n.* faithful supporter; follower. —*adj.* sticking fast; attached.

ad ja cent (ə jā'snt), *adj.* lying near or close; adjoining: *The house adjacent to ours has been sold.*

ad just (ə just'), *v.* 1. fit or adapt (one thing to another): *adjust a seat to the height of a child.* 2. regulate for use: *adjust a radio dial.* 3. arrange satisfactorily; set right; settle: *adjust a difference of opinion.* 4. accommodate oneself; get used: *He soon adjusted to army life.*

ad just ment (ə just'mənt), *n.* 1. act or process of adjusting. 2. the orderly arrangement of parts or elements. 3. means of adjusting: *Our radio has an adjustment so that we can make the tone loud or soft.* 4. settlement of a dispute, a claim, etc.

ad mon ish (ad mon'ish), *v.* 1. advise against something; warn: *The policeman admonished him not to drive too fast.* 2. reprove gently: *The teacher admonished the student for his careless work.* 3. urge strongly; advise. 4. recall to a duty overlooked or forgotten; remind. [< *admonition*] —**ad mon'ish er,** *n.* —**ad mon'ish ment,** *n.*

a do (ə dü'), *n.* stir; bustle. [ME *at do* to do]

a do be (ə dō'bē), *n.* 1. sun-dried clay or mud. 2. a brick or bricklike piece of such material, used in building. —*adj.* built or made of sun-dried bricks.

ad ren al in (ə dren'l ən), *n.* hormone secreted by the adrenal glands. It stimulates the heart and stops bleeding.

a droit (ə droit'), *adj.* expert in the use of the hands or the mind; skillful: *A good teacher is adroit in asking questions.* —**a droit'ly,** *adv.* —**a droit'ness,** *n.* Syn. clever, deft.

aer o dy nam ics (er'ō dī nam'iks), *n.* the branch of physics that deals with the forces exerted by air or other gases in motion.

af fa ble (af'ə bəl), *adj.* easy to talk to; courteous and pleasant. [< F < L *affabilis* easy to speak to < *affari* < *ad-* to + *fari* speak] —**af'fa ble ness,** *n.* —**af'fa bly,** *adv.*

af fix (*v.* ə fiks'; *n.* af'iks), *v.* 1. make firm or fix (one thing to or on another). 2. add at the end. 3. make an impression of (a seal, etc.). 4. connect with; attach: *affix blame.* —*n.* 1. thing affixed. 2. a prefix or suffix. *Un-* and *-ly* are affixes. [< Med.L *affixare,* ult. < L *ad-* to + *figere* fix]

ag gres sive (ə gres'iv), *adj.* 1. taking the first step in an attack or quarrel; attacking; quarrelsome: *An aggressive country is always ready to start a war.* 2. U.S. active; energetic: *The police are making an aggressive campaign against crime.* —**ag gres'sive ly,** *adv.*

a ghast (ə gast'), *adj.* filled with horror; frightened; terrified. [pp. of obsolete *agast* terrify < OE *on-* on + *gæstan* frighten. Related to *ghost.*]

a gog (ə gog'), *adj.* eager; curious; excited. —*adv.* with eagerness, curiosity, or excitement. [? < F *en gogues* in happy mood]

a gue (ā'gyü), *n.* 1. a malarial fever with chills and sweating that occur at regular intervals. 2. a fit of shivering; chill.

aim less (ām'lis), *adj.* without purpose. —**aim'less ly,** *adv.* —**aim'less ness,** *n.*

a kim bo (ə kim'bō), *adj., adv.* with the hand on the hip and the elbow bent outward. [ME *in kene bowe,* apparently, in keen bow, at a sharp angle]

< = from, derived from, taken from;   cf., compare;   dial., dialect;   dim., diminutive;   lang., language; pp., past participle;   ppr., present participle;   pt., past tense;   ult., ultimately;   var., variant;   ? = possibly.

a lac ri ty (ə lak′rə tē), *n.* **1.** brisk and eager action; liveliness: *Although the man was very old, he still moved with alacrity.* **2.** cheerful willingness.

ale (āl), *n.* a heavy, bitter beer.

Al ge cir as (al′jə sir′əs)

al i bi (al′ə bī), *n., pl.* **-bis,** *v.,* **-bied, -bi ing.** —*n.* **1.** plea or fact that a person accused of a certain offense was somewhere else when the offense was committed. **2.** *U.S. Informal.* an excuse. —*v. U.S. Informal.* make an excuse. [< L *alibi* elsewhere]

a lign (ə līn′), *v.* bring into line; adjust to a line.

al lure (ə lŭr′), *v.,* **-lured, -lur ing,** *n.* —*v.* **1.** fascinate; charm. **2.** tempt by the offer of some pleasure or reward. —*n.* attractiveness; fascination.

al ter ca tion (ôl′tər kā′shən, al′tər kā′shən), *n.* an angry dispute; quarrel: *The two teams had an altercation over the umpire's decision.*

al ter na tion (ôl′tər nā′shən, al′tər nā′shən), *n.* an alternating; occurring by turns, first one and then the other: *There is an alternation of red and white stripes in the flag of the United States.*

am bi tion (am bish′ən), *n.* **1.** strong desire for fame or honor; seeking after a high position or great power. **2.** thing strongly desired or sought after.

am bi tious (am bish′əs), *adj.* **1.** having or guided by ambition. **2.** arising from or showing ambition: *an ambitious plan.* **3.** desiring strongly; eager: *ambitious of power. John is ambitious to get through high school in two years.* **4.** showy; pretentious.

am ble (am′bəl), *n., v.,* **-bled, -bling.** —*n.* **1.** gait of a horse when it lifts first the two legs on one side and then the two on the other. **2.** easy, slow pace in walking. —*v.* walk in an easy, slow pace.

a mi a ble (ā′mē ə bəl), *adj.* good-natured and friendly; pleasant and agreeable. —**a′mi a bly,** *adv.*

am phib i an (am fib′ē ən), *n.* animal that lives on land and in water. —*adj.* of both land and water; able to live both on land and in water.

am phi the a ter (am′fə thē′ə tər), *n.* **1.** a circular or oval building with tiers of seats around a central open space. **2.** something resembling an amphitheater in shape. [< L < Gk. *amphitheatron* < *amphi-* on all sides + *theatron* theater]

am phi the a tre (am′fə thē′ə tər), *n. Esp. Brit.* amphitheater.

a nach ro nism (ə nak′rə niz əm), *n.* **1.** act of putting a person, thing, or event in some time where he or it does not belong: *It would be an anachronism to speak of George Washington riding in an automobile.* **2.** something placed or occurring out of its proper time. [< F < Gk. *anachronismos* < *ana-* backwards + *chronos* time]

and i ron (and′ī′ərn), *n.* one of a pair of metal supports for wood burned in a fireplace. [< OF *andier; -iron* by association with *iron*]

an ec dote (an′ik dōt), *n.* a short account of some interesting incident or event.

an es the tist (ə nes′thə tist), *n.* person who supplies ether or other substances that cause the loss of sensation in a patient during an operation.

an guish (ang′gwish), *n.* very great pain or grief; great suffering or distress: *He was in anguish until the doctor set his broken leg.*
Syn. agony, torment, woe.

an gu lar i ty (ang′gyə lar′ə tē), *n., pl.* **-ties.** condition of having sharp or prominent corners.

A ni sya (ä nē′syə)

an tag o nism (an tag′ə niz əm), *n.* active opposition; conflict; hostility.

an te room (an′ti rüm′, an′ti rům′), *n.* a small room leading to a larger one; a waiting room.

an tiq ui ty (an tik′wə tē), *n., pl.* **-ties.** **1.** oldness; great age. **2.** times long ago; early ages of history. Antiquity usually refers to the period from 5000 B.C. to 476 A.D. **3.** people of long ago.

a pex (ā′peks), *n., pl.* **a pex es** or **ap i ces.** **1.** the highest point; tip: *the apex of a triangle.* **2.** climax. [< L]

ap o gee (ap′ə jē), *n.* **1.** point farthest from the earth in the orbit of the moon or an earth satellite. **2.** furthermost point; highest point. [< F *apogée* < Gk. *apogaion* < *apo-* away from + *ge* or *gaia* earth]

Orbit of the moon around the earth showing the apogee

ap pa ri tion (ap′ə rish′ən), *n.* **1.** ghost; phantom. **2.** something strange, remarkable, or unexpected which comes into view. **3.** act of appearing; appearance. [< LL *apparitio, -onis* < L *apparere.*]

ap pease (ə pēz′), *v.,* **-peased, -peas ing.** **1.** satisfy (an appetite or desire): *A good dinner will appease your hunger.* **2.** make calm; quiet. **3.** give in to the demands of (especially those of a potential enemy): *Chamberlain appeased Hitler at Munich.* —**ap peas′er,** *n.* —**ap peas′ing ly,** *adv.*

ap pre ci a tive (ə prē′shē ā′tiv, ə prē′shə tiv), *adj.* having appreciation; showing appreciation; recognizing the value: *appreciative of the smallest kindness.* —**ap pre′ci a′tive ly,** *adv.*

ap pre hend (ap′ri hend′), *v.* **1.** look forward to with fear; fear; dread: *A guilty man apprehends danger in every sound.* **2.** arrest: *The thief was apprehended and put in jail.* **3.** understand; grasp with the mind. [< L *apprehendere* < *ad-* upon + *prehendere* seize]

ap pre hen sion (ap′ri hen′shən), *n.* **1.** expectation of evil; fear; dread. **2.** a seizing; being seized; arrest. **3.** understanding; grasp by the mind. [< L *apprehensio, -onis* < *apprehendere.* See APPREHEND.]

ap pre hen sive (ap′ri hen′siv), *adj.* **1.** afraid; anxious; worried. **2.** quick to understand; able to learn. —**ap′pre hen′sive ly,** *adv.* —**ap′pre hen′sive ness,** *n.*

ap pro ba tion (ap′rə bā′shən), *n.* **1.** approval; favorable opinion. **2.** sanction.

ap prox i mate ly (ə prok′sə mit lē), *adv.* nearly; about.

ar bo re al (är bôr′ē əl, är bōr′ē əl), *adj.* **1.** of trees; like trees. **2.** living in or among trees. A squirrel is an arboreal animal.

ar mor y (är′mər ē), *n., pl.* **-mor ies.** **1.** place where weapons are kept; arsenal. **2.** *U.S.* place where weapons are made. **3.** a building with a drill hall, etc., for militia.

ar mour y (är′mər ē), *n., pl.* **-mour ies.** *Brit.* armory.

ar ro gance (ar′ə gəns), *n.* too great pride; haughtiness.

ar ro gant (ar′ə gənt), *adj.* too proud; haughty. [< L *arrogans, -antis,* ppr. of *arrogare* < *ad-* + *rogare* ask] —**ar′ro gant ly,** *adv.*
Syn. overbearing, presumptuous. See **haughty.**

ar tic u late (*adj.* är tik′yə lit; *v.* är tik′yə lāt), *adj., v.,* **-lat ed, -lat ing.** —*adj.* **1.** uttered in distinct syllables or words: *A baby cries and gurgles, but does not use articulate speech.* **2.** able to put one's thoughts into words: *Julia is the most articulate of the sisters.* —*v.* speak distinctly: *Be careful to articulate your words so that everyone in the room can understand you.*

---

hat, āge, fär; let, bē, tèrm; it, īce; hot, gō, ôrder; oil, out; cup, pùt, rüle; ch, child; ng, long; th, thin; ᴛʜ, then; zh, measure; ə represents *a* in about, *e* in taken, *i* in pencil, *o* in lemon, *u* in circus.

ar ti fact (är/tə fakt), *n.* anything made by human skill or work; artificial product.

ash cake (ash/kāk), *n.* a cake of corn meal, often wrapped in cabbage leaves, and baked in hot ashes.

as phalt (as/fôlt), *n.* 1. a dark-colored substance, much like tar, that is found in beds in various parts of the world. It is also obtained by evaporating petroleum. 2. mixture of this substance with crushed rock, used for pavements, roofs, etc.

as si du i ty (as/ə dü/ə tē, as/ə dyü/ə tē), *n., pl.* **-ties.** careful and steady attention; diligence.

as sim i late (ə sim/ə lāt), *v.,* **-lat ed, -lat ing.** 1. absorb; digest: *The girl reads so much that she does not assimilate it all. The human body will not assimilate sawdust.* 2. make or become like (people of a nation, etc.) in customs and viewpoint: *Swedes assimilate readily in this country. We have assimilated immigrants from many lands.* [< L *assimilare* < *ad-* to + *similis* like]

as suage (ə swāj/), *v.,* **-suaged, -suag ing.** 1. make easier or milder: *assuage pain.* 2. satisfy; appease; quench: *assuage thirst.* —**as suag/er,** *n.*

as sured (ə shurd/), *adj.* 1. sure; certain. 2. confident; bold. 3. insured against loss.

a stray (ə strā/), *adj., adv.* out of the right way.

as tute (ə stüt/, ə styüt/), *adj.* shrewd; crafty; sagacious: *Many lawyers are astute.*

at ten u ate (ə ten/yü āt), *v.,* **-at ed, -at ing.** 1. make or become thin or slender. 2. weaken; reduce.

aug ment (ôg ment/), *v.* increase; enlarge.

au gust (ô gust/), *adj.* inspiring reverence and admiration; majestic; venerable.

aus tere (ô stir/), *adj.* 1. harsh; stern. 2. strict in morals. 3. severely simple.

au thor i ta tive (ə thôr/ə tā/tiv, ə thor/ə tā/tiv), *adj.* 1. having authority; officially ordered: *Authoritative orders came from the general.* 2. commanding: *In authoritative tones the policeman shouted, "Keep back."* 3. that ought to be believed or obeyed; having the authority of expert knowledge: *His book on the Civil War is generally considered authoritative.* —**au thor/i ta/tive ly,** *adv.*

a ver sion (ə vėr/zhən, ə vėr/shən), *n.* 1. a strong or fixed dislike; antipathy. 2. thing or person disliked. 3. unwillingness.

➔ **aversion.** Either *to* or *for* follows *aversion: He has an aversion to moving fast and working hard. We'll eat alone; they have an aversion for fried shrimp.*

awk ward (ôk/wərd), *adj.* 1. clumsy; not graceful or skillful: *The seal is very awkward on land, but quite at home in the water.* 2. not well-suited to use: *The handle of this pitcher has an awkward shape.* 3. not easily managed: *This is an awkward corner to turn.* 4. embarrassing: *He asked me an awkward question.* [< obs. *awk* perversely, in the wrong way (< Scand. *öfugr* turned the wrong way) + *-ward*] —**awk/ward ly,** *adv.* —**awk/ward ness,** *n.* **Syn.** 1. **Awkward, clumsy, ungainly** mean not graceful. **Awkward** means lacking grace, ease, quickness, and skill: *An awkward girl is no help in the kitchen.* **Clumsy** suggests moving heavily and stiffly: *The clumsy boy bumped into all the furniture.* **Ungainly** means awkward in moving one's body: *He is as ungainly as a newborn calf.* 4. trying, disconcerting. —**Ant.** 2. handy.

az ure (azh/ər), *n.* 1. blue; sky blue. 2. the clear blue color of the unclouded sky. —*adj.* blue; sky-blue.

baf fle (baf/əl), *v.,* **-fled, -fling.** 1. be too hard for (a

person) to understand or solve: *This puzzle baffles me.* 2. hinder; thwart. 3. struggle without success.

baf fle ment (baf/əl mənt), *n.* 1. act of baffling. 2. state of being baffled.

bag gage (bag/ij), *n.* 1. the trunks, bags, suitcases, etc., that a person takes with him when he travels. 2. equipment that an army takes with it, such as tents, blankets, ammunition, etc.

bail (bāl), *n.* 1. guarantee necessary to set a person free from arrest until he is to appear for trial. 2. amount guaranteed.

bale ful (bāl/fəl), *adj.* evil; harmful. —**bale/ful ly,** *adv.* —**bale/ful ness,** *n.*

ban dan na or **ban dan a** (ban dan/ə), *n.* a large, colored handkerchief. [probably < Hindu. *bāndhnū* tie-dyeing]

ban do leer or **ban do lier** (ban/dl ir/), *n.* 1. a broad belt worn over the shoulder and across the breast. Some bandoleers have loops for carrying cartridges; others have small cases for bullets, gunpowder, etc. 2. one of these cases. [< F *bandoulière* < Sp. *bandolera* < *banda* band[1], ult. < Gmc.]

ban dy-leg ged (ban/dē leg/id, ban/dē legd/), *adj.* having legs that curve outward; bowlegged.

ban tam (ban/təm), *n.* 1. Often, **Bantam.** a small-sized kind of fowl. 2. a small person who is fond of fighting.

ba rom e ter (bə rom/ə tər), *n.* 1. instrument for measuring the pressure of the atmosphere, and thus determining the height above sea level, or probable changes in the weather. 2. something that indicates changes: *Newspapers are often barometers of public opinion.*

base (bās), *adj.,* **bas er, bas est.** 1. morally low; mean; selfish; cowardly: *To betray a friend is a base action.* 2. fit for an inferior person or thing; menial; unworthy: *No needful service is to be looked at as base.* 3. Archaic. of humble birth or origin. 4. having little comparative value; inferior: *Iron and lead are base metals; gold and silver are precious metals.*

bay (bā), *n.* 1. the long, deep bark of a dog: *The hunters heard the distant bay of the hounds.* 2. stand made by a hunted animal to face pursuers when escape is impossible: *The stag stood at bay on the edge of the cliff.* 3. similar stand made by a person against persecution, etc. 4. position of pursuers or enemy kept off: *The stag held the hounds at bay.* 5. **bring to bay,** put in a position from which escape is impossible. —*v.* bark; bark at: *Dogs sometimes bay at the moon.*

be fall (bi fôl/), *v.,* **-fell, -fall en, -fall ing.** 1. happen to: *Be careful that no harm befalls you.* 2. happen. [OE *befeallan*] **Syn.** 2. occur.

be grudge (bi gruj/), *v.,* **-grudged, -grudg ing.** envy (somebody) the possession of; be reluctant to give (something); grudge: *She is so stingy that she begrudges her dog a bone.* —**begrudg/ing ly,** *adv.*

be held (bi held/), *v.* pt. and pp. of **behold.**

be hold (bi hōld/), *v.,* **be held, be hold ing,** *interj.* 1. see; look at. 2. look; take notice. —**be hold/er,** *n.*

bel fry (bel/frē), *n., pl.* **-fries.** 1. tower for a bell or bells. 2. room, cupola, or turret in which a bell or bells may be hung.

be lie (bi lī/), *v.,* **-lied, -ly ing.** 1. give a false idea of; misrepresent: *Her frown belied her usual good nature.* 2. show to be false; prove to be mistaken. 3. fail to come up to; disappoint.

< = from, derived from, taken from;   cf., compare;   dial., dialect;   dim., diminutive;   lang., language; pp., past participle;   ppr., present participle;   pt., past tense;   ult., ultimately;   var., variant;   ? = possibly.

be lit tle (bi lit′l), v., **-tled, -tling.** 1. cause to seem little, unimportant, or less important; speak slightingly of: *Jealous people belittled the explorer's great discoveries.* 2. make small. **—be lit′tler,** n.

be nev o lence (bə nev′ə ləns), n. 1. good will; kindly feeling. 2. act of kindness; something good that is done; generous gift.

be nign (bi nīn′), adj. 1. gentle; kindly: *a benign old lady.* 2. favorable; mild: *a benign climate.* 3. doing no harm: *A benign swelling or tumor can usually be cured.*

Ber nal, Eu fe mio (äü fā′mēō ber′näl′)

be think (bi thingk′), v., **-thought, -think ing.** 1. **bethink oneself, a.** consider; reflect. **b.** remember. 2. think about; recall. [OE *bethencan*]

be thought (bi thôt′), v. pt. and pp. of **bethink.**

be wail (bi wāl′), v. mourn; weep; weep for; complain of.

be ware (bi wer′, bi war′), v. be on one's guard against; be careful. [< phrase *be ware; ware,* OE *wær*]

bier (bir), n. a movable stand on which a coffin or dead body is placed. [OE *bēr* < *beran* bear¹]

bile (bīl), n. 1. a bitter, yellow or greenish liquid secreted by the liver and stored in the gall bladder. It aids digestion in the small intestine by neutralizing acids and emulsifying fats. 2. ill humor; anger.

bil ious (bil′yəs), adj. 1. having to do with bile. 2. suffering from or caused by some trouble with bile or the liver: *a bilious person, a bilious attack.* 3. peevish; cross; bad-tempered. [< L *biliosus* < *bilis* bile]

bil low (bil′ō), n. 1. a great wave or surge of the sea. 2. any great wave. —v. 1. rise or roll in big waves. 2. swell out; bulge. [< Scand. *bylgja*]

bi plane (bī′plān′), n. airplane having two wings, one above the other.

bi zarre (bə zär′), adj. odd; queer; fantastic; grotesque. **—bi zarre′ly,** adv. **—bi zarre′ness,** n.

bland (bland), adj. 1. smooth; mild; gentle; soothing: *A warm spring breeze is bland.* 2. agreeable; polite. **—bland′ly,** adv. **—bland′ness,** n.

bleak (blēk), adj. 1. swept by winds; bare: *bleak and rocky mountain peaks.* 2. chilly; cold: *a bleak wind.* 3. dreary; dismal: *Life was bleak for unmarried women in earlier days.* **—bleak′ly,** adv. **—bleak′ness,** n.
Syn. 1. desolate. 2. raw.

blight (blīt), n. 1. any disease that causes plants to wither or decay. 2. insect or fungus that causes such a disease. 3. anything that causes destruction or ruin. —v. 1. cause to wither or decay. 2. destroy; ruin.

blight er (blī′tər), n. Brit. Slang. 1. a contemptible fellow; rascal. 2. a fellow; chap.

bloat (blōt), v. swell up; puff up.

bloke (blōk), n. Brit. Slang. man; fellow.

bloom ers (blü′mərz), n.pl. 1. loose trousers, gathered at the knee, formerly much worn by women and girls for physical training. 2. underwear made like these. [Am.E; first referred to in magazine published by Amelia J. *Bloomer,* 1851]

blub ber (blub′ər), n. 1. fat of whales and some other sea animals. 2. noisy weeping. —v. 1. weep noisily. 2. disfigure or swell with crying: *a face all blubbered.* [probably imitative]

blue blood, aristocratic descent.

board (bôrd, bōrd), n. 1. a broad, thin piece of wood for use in building, etc. 2. a flat piece of wood used for some special purpose: *an ironing board.* 3. table to serve food on; table. 4. food served on a table. 5. meals provided for pay.

—v. 1. cover with boards. 2. provide with regular meals, or room and meals, for pay. 3. get meals, or room and meals, for pay.

bob ble (bob′əl), n. a small ball; one in a series of tiny yarn balls used as edging.

bog (bog, bôg), n. soft, wet, spongy ground; marsh; swamp.

bo gus (bō′gəs), adj. U.S. counterfeit; sham. [Am.E]

bore dom (bôr′dəm, bōr′dəm), n. a bored condition; weariness caused by dull, tiresome people or events.

bow el (bou′əl), n. 1. part of the bowels; intestine. 2. Usually, **bowels,** pl. tube in the body into which food passes from the stomach; intestines. 3. **bowels,** pl. the inner part: *Miners dig for coal in the bowels of the earth.*

brand (brand), n. 1. a certain kind, grade, or make: *a brand of coffee.* 2. trademark. 3. mark made by burning the skin with a hot iron. Cattle and horses on big ranches are marked with brands to show who owns them. 4. an iron stamp for burning a mark. 5. mark of disgrace. 6. piece of wood that is burning or partly burned.

bran dish (bran′dish), v. wave or shake threateningly; flourish. —n. a threatening shake; flourish.

bray (brā), n. 1. the loud, harsh sound made by a donkey. 2. noise like it.

bra zen (brā′zn), adj. 1. made of brass. 2. like brass in color or strength. 3. loud and harsh. 4. shameless; impudent. —v. 1. make shameless or impudent. 2. **brazen a thing out** or **through,** act as if unashamed of it. **—bra′zen ly,** adv.

breath less (breth′lis), adj. 1. out of breath: *Running very fast makes you breathless.* 2. unable to breathe freely because of fear, interest, or excitement. 3. without breath; dead. 4. without a breeze. **—breath′less ly,** adv.

bris tle (bris′əl), n., v., **-tled, -tling.** —n. 1. one of the short, stiff hairs of a hog. Bristles are used to make brushes. 2. any short, stiff hair of an animal or plant. —v. 1. provide with bristles. 2. stand up straight: *The angry dog's hair bristled.* 3. cause (hair) to stand up straight. 4. have one's hair stand up straight: *The dog bristled.* 5. show that one is aroused and ready to fight. 6. be thickly set: *Our path bristled with difficulties.*

bro chure (brō shùr′), n. pamphlet.

bro ker (brō′kər), n. person who buys and sells stocks, bonds, grain, cotton, etc., for other people.

brow beat (brou′bēt′), v., **-beat, -beat en, -beat ing.** frighten into doing something by overbearing looks or words; bully.
Syn. intimidate, domineer.

browse (brouz), v., **browsed, brows ing,** n. —v. 1. feed; graze. 2. read here and there in a book, library, etc. [< n., or < F *brouster* feed on buds and shoots] —n. the tender shoots of shrubs; green food for cattle, etc.

bruit (brüt), v. spread a report or rumor of.

brusque (brusk), adj. abrupt in manner or speech; blunt. **—brusque′ly,** adv.

buck board (buk′bôrd′, buk′bōrd′), n. an open, four-wheeled carriage having the seat fastened to a platform of long, springy boards instead of a body and springs. [Am.E]

buck skin (buk′skin′), n. 1. a strong, soft leather, yellow-ish or grayish in color, made from the skins of deer or sheep. 2. **buckskins,** pl. breeches made of buckskin.

bud (bud), n., v., **bud ded, bud ding.** —n. 1. a small swelling on a plant that will develop into a flower, leaf, or branch. 2. time or state of budding: *The pear tree is in bud.* 3. a partly opened flower. 4. anything in its beginning stage. 5. a minute, bud-shaped part or organ: *a taste bud.* 6. **nip in**

hat, āge, fär; let, bē, tèrm; it, īce; hot, gō, ôrder; oil, out; cup, pùt, rüle; ch, child; ng, long; th, thin; ŦH, then; zh, measure; ə represents *a* in about, *e* in taken, *i* in pencil, *o* in lemon, *u* in circus.

the bud, stop at the very beginning. —*v.* **1.** put forth buds: *The rosebush has budded.* **2.** graft (a bud) from one kind of plant into the stem of a different kind. **3.** begin to grow or develop. **4.** (of birds) to eat buds.

Bud dhism (bü′diz əm, bůd′iz əm), *n.* religion that originated in the sixth century B.C. in N India and spread widely over central, SE, and E Asia. It teaches that right living will enable people to attain Nirvana, the condition of a soul that does not have to live in a body and is free from all desire and pain.

Bud dhist (bü′dist, bůd′ist), *adj.* having to do with Buddha or Buddhism. —*n.* believer in Buddhism.

bulk y (bul′kē), *adj.,* **bulk i er, bulk i est. 1.** taking up much space; large: *a bulky package.* **2.** hard to handle; clumsy. —**bulk′i ly,** *adv.* —**bulk′i ness,** *n.* Syn. **1.** massive, ponderous. **2.** unwieldy. ·

bull ock (bůl′ək), *n.* ox; steer. [OE *bulluc* bull calf]

bŭmp er (bum′pər), *n.* **1.** bar or bars of metal that protect the main part of a car or truck from being damaged if the car or truck is bumped. **2.** cup or glass filled to the brim. **3.** *Informal.* something unusually large of its kind. —*adj.* unusually large: *The farmer raised a bumper crop of wheat last year.*

bump kin (bump′kən), *n.* an awkward person from the country. [< MDutch *bommekyn* little barrel]

bun ga low (bung′gə lō), *n.* a dwelling, usually of one story or a story and a half with low, sweeping lines. [< Hindu. *banglā* of Bengal]

butt[1] (but), *n.* **1.** the thicker end of a tool, weapon, ham, etc. **2.** end that is left; stub; stump.

butt[2] (but), *n.* **1.** target. **2.** object of ridicule or scorn: *That odd boy was the butt of our jokes.*

butt[3] (but), *v.* **1.** push or hit with the head: *A goat butts.* **2. butt in,** *Slang.* meddle; interfere. —*n.* push or hit with the head.

butt[4] (but), *n.* **1.** a large barrel for wine or beer. **2.** a liquid measure equal to 126 gallons.

butte (byůt), *n.* in western United States, a steep hill standing alone. [Am.E; < F]

bux om (buk′səm), *adj.* plump and good to look at; healthy and cheerful.

by-play (bī′plā′), *n.* action that is not part of the main action, especially on the stage.

ca dence (kād′ns), *n.* **1.** rhythm. **2.** measure or beat of any rhythmical movement. **3.** fall of the voice. **4.** rising and falling sound; modulation.

ca jole (kə jōl′), *v.,* **-joled, -jol ing.** persuade by pleasant words, flattery, or false promises; coax.

ca lam i ty (kə lam′ə tē), *n., pl.* **-ties. 1.** a great misfortune, such as a flood, a fire, or loss of one's sight or hearing. **2.** serious trouble; misery. [< L *calamitas*] Syn. **1.** catastrophe.

cal cu late (kal′kyə lāt), *v.,* **-lat ed, -lat ing.** *U.S. Informal.* plan; intend.

cal dron (kôl′drən), *n.* a large kettle or boiler. Also, **cauldron.** [< OF *caudron* < L *caldus* hot]

can de la brum (kan′dl ä′brəm, kan′dl ä′brəm), *n., pl.* **-bra** (brə) or **-brums.** an ornamental candlestick with several branches for candles. [< L *candelabrum* < *candela* candle]

ca nine (kā′nīn), *adj.* **1.** of a dog; like a dog. **2.** belonging to a group of meat-eating animals including dogs, foxes, and wolves. —*n.* **1.** dog. **2.** canine tooth.

ca rous al (kə rou′zəl), *n.* a noisy revel; drinking party.

ca rouse (kə rouz′), *n., v.,* **-roused, -rous ing.** —*n.* a noisy feast; drinking party. —*v.* drink heavily; take part in noisy feasts or revels. [< obsolete adv. < G *gar aus- (trinken)* (drink) all up] —**ca rous′er,** *n.*

car ou sel (kar′ə sel′, kar′ə zel′), *n.* carrousel.

car ri on (kar′ē ən), *n.* **1.** dead and decaying flesh. **2.** rottenness; filth. —*adj.* **1.** dead and decaying. **2.** feeding on dead and decaying flesh. **3.** rotten; filthy. [< OF *carogne* < VL *caronia,* ult. < L *caries* decay. Doublet of CRONE.]

car rou sel (kar′ə sel′, kar′ə zel′), *n.* merry-go-round. [< F < Ital. *carosello* < L *carrus* cart]

cast (kast), *n.* **1.** a throw; the distance a thing is thrown. **2.** thing made by casting; thing that is molded. **3.** mold used in casting; mold: *His broken arm is in a plaster cast.* **4.** actors in a play. **5.** form; look; appearance. **6.** kind; sort. **7.** a slight amount of color; tinge: *a white dress with a pink cast.* **8.** a slight squint.

cas ta net (kas′tə net′), *n.* pair, or one of a pair, of instruments of hard wood or ivory like little cymbals. Castanets are held in the hand and clicked together to beat time for dancing or music.

cat a pult (kat′ə pult), *n.* **1.** an ancient weapon for shooting stones, arrows, etc. **2.** *Brit.* slingshot. **3.** device for launching an airplane from the deck of a ship. —*v.* shoot from a catapult; throw; hurl. [< L *catapulta* < Gk. *katapeltes,* probably < *kata-* down + *pallein* hurl]

cav ern ous (kav′ər nəs), *adj.* **1.** like a cavern; large and hollow. **2.** full of caverns.

cer e mo ni al (ser′ə mō′nē əl), *adj.* **1.** formal: *She received me in a ceremonial way.* **2.** of or having to do with ceremony: *The ceremonial costumes were beautiful.* —*n.* formal actions proper to an occasion. Bowing the head and kneeling are ceremonials of religion. —**cer′e mo′ni al ly,** *adv.*

➤ **Ceremonial, ceremonious** differ in meaning and use. **Ceremonial** means having to do with ceremony, and applies to things involving or belonging to the ceremonies and formalities of the church, law, polite conduct, fraternities, etc.: *Shriners wear ceremonial costumes.* **Ceremonious** means full of ceremony and applies to things done with ceremony or showy formality or to people who pay very strict attention to the details of polite conduct: *The banquet was a ceremonious affair.*

cer e mo ni ous (ser′ə mō′nē əs), *adj.* **1.** full of ceremony. **2.** very formal; extremely polite. —**cer′e mo′ni ous ly,** *adv.* —**cer′e mo′ni ous ness,** *n.* Syn. **2.** stiff.

➤ See **ceremonial** for usage note.

cha grin (shə grin′), *n.* a feeling of disappointment, failure, or humiliation. —*v.* cause to feel chagrin. [< F *chagrin* grained leather, vexation < Turkish *çāghrī* rump of a horse; shift of meaning comes from idea of being ruffled (cf. *gooseflesh*).] Syn. *n.* mortification, vexation.

chap fall en (chap′fôl′ən, chop′fôl′ən), *adj.* dejected; discouraged; humiliated. Also, **chopfallen.** ·

chaste (chāst), *adj.* **1.** pure; virtuous. **2.** decent; modest. **3.** simple in taste or style; not too much ornamented. —**chaste′ly,** *adv.* —**chaste′ness,** *n.*

chi can er y (shi kā′nər ē), *n., pl.* **-er ies.** low trickery; unfair practice; quibbling: *Only a dishonest lawyer will use chicanery to win a lawsuit.* Syn. deception.

child ing (chil′ding), *adj. Archaic.* bearing children.

< = from, derived from, taken from;   cf., compare;   dial., dialect;   dim., diminutive;   lang., language; pp., past participle;   ppr., present participle;   pt., past tense;   ult., ultimately;   var., variant;   ? = possibly.

chop fall en (chop′fôl′ən), *adj.* chapfallen.

chor tle (chôr′tl), *v.*, **-tled, -tling,** *n.* —*v.* chuckle or snort with glee. —*n.* a gleeful chuckle or snort. [blend of *chuckle* and *snort;* coined by Lewis Carroll]

chris ten (kris′n), *v.* 1. admit to a Christian church by baptism; baptize. 2. give a first name to at baptism. 3. give a name to: *The new ship was christened before it was launched.* 4. *Informal.* make the first use of.

chron i cle (kron′ə kəl), *n., v.*, **-cled, -cling.** —*n.* record of happenings in the order in which they happened. —*v.* record in a chronicle; write the history of; tell the story of. **Syn.** *n.* history, story.

cite (sīt), *v.*, **cit ed, cit ing.** summon to appear before a law court.

clam or (klam′ər), *n.* 1. a loud noise, continual uproar; shouting. 2. a noisy demand or complaint. —*v.* 1. make a loud noise or continual uproar; shout. 2. demand or complain noisily. Also, *esp. Brit.* **clamour.** [< OF < L *clamor* < *clamare* cry out] —**clam′or er,** *n.*

clan (klan), *n.* 1. group of related families that claim to be descended from a common ancestor. 2. group of people closely joined together by some common interest. [< Scotch Gaelic *clann* family] —**clan′like′,** *adj.*

cleat (klēt), *n.* strip of wood or iron fastened across anything for support or for sure footing. A gangway has cleats to keep people from slipping.

cleave (klēv), *v.*, **cleft** or **cleaved** or **clove, cleft** or **cleaved** or **clo ven, cleav ing.** 1. split; divide. 2. pass through; pierce; penetrate: *The airplane cleaved the clouds.* 3. make by cutting: *They clove a path through the wilderness.* [OE *clēofan*] —**cleav′a ble,** *adj.*

clink er (kling′kər), *n.* 1. piece of the rough, hard mass left in a furnace or stove after coal has been burned; large, rough cinder. 2. a very hard brick. 3. mass of bricks fused together. 4. slag. [< Dutch *klinker* brick < *klinken* ring]

cod dle (kod′l), *v.*, **-dled, -dling.** 1. treat tenderly; pamper: *coddle sick children.* 2. cook in hot water without boiling: *coddle an egg.* **Syn.** 1. humor, indulge.

col lide (kə līd′), *v.*, **-lid ed, -lid ing.** 1. come violently into contact; come together with force; crash: *Two large ships collided in the harbor.* 2. clash; conflict. [< L *collidere* < *com-* together + *laedere*, originally, strike]

come ly (kum′lē), *adj.*, **-li er, -li est.** 1. having a pleasant appearance; attractive. 2. fitting; suitable; proper.

com mend (kə mend′), *v.* 1. praise. 2. mention favorably; recommend. 3. hand over for safekeeping: *She commended the child to her aunt's care.*

com men ta tive (kom′ən tā′tiv), *adj.* of or concerning comment or commentary.

com mer cial (kə mèr′shəl), *adj.* 1. having to do with commerce. 2. made to be sold. 3. supported or subsidized by an advertiser: *a commercial radio program.* —*n.* a radio or television program, or the part of a program, that advertises something. —**com mer′cial ly,** *adv.*

com mis er ate (kə miz′ə rāt′), *v.*, **-rat ed, -rat ing.** feel or express sorrow for; sympathize with; pity.

com pete (kəm pēt′), *v.*, **-pet ed, -pet ing.** 1. try hard to obtain something wanted by others; be rivals; contend. 2. take part (in a contest): *An injury kept him from competing in the final race.* [< L *competere* < *com-* together + *petere* seek]

com pe tent (kom′pə tənt), *adj.* 1. able; fit: *a competent cook.* 2. legally qualified: *Two competent witnesses testified.* **Syn.** 1. capable.

com ply (kəm plī′), *v.*, **-plied, -ply ing.** act in agreement with a request or a command: *We should comply with the doctor's request.*

com press (*v.* kəm pres′; *n.* kom′pres), *v.* squeeze together; make smaller by pressure. —*n.* 1. pad of wet cloth applied to some part of the body to create pressure or to reduce inflammation. 2. machine for compressing cotton into bales.

com pro mise (kom′prə mīz), *v.*, **-mised, -mis ing,** *n.* —*v.* 1. settle (a dispute) by agreeing that each contestant will give up a part of what he demands. 2. put under suspicion; put in danger: *You will compromise your good name if you go around with thieves and liars.* —*n.* 1. settlement of a dispute by a partial yielding on both sides. 2. result of such a settlement. 3. anything halfway between two different things.

con cave (kon kāv′, kon′kāv, kong′kāv), *adj.* hollow and curved like the inside of a circle or sphere.

con ceit (kən sēt′), *n.* 1. too high an opinion of oneself or of one's ability, importance, etc. 2. a fanciful notion; witty thought or expression, often a farfetched one.

con ceit ed (kən sē′tid), *adj.* having too high an opinion of oneself or one's ability, importance, etc.; vain. —**con ceit′ed ly,** *adv.* —**con ceit′ed ness,** *n.* **Syn.** egotistical, proud, self-satisfied.

con ceiv a ble (kən sē′və bəl), *adj.* that can be conceived or thought of; imaginable: *We take every conceivable precaution against fire.* —**con ceiv′a bly,** *adv.*

con cert ed (kən sèr′tid), *adj.* arranged by agreement; planned or made together; combined: *a concerted attack.*

con cil i ate (kən sil′ē āt), *v.*, **-at ed, -at ing.** 1. win over; soothe. 2. gain (good will, regard, favor, etc.) by friendly acts. 3. reconcile; bring into harmony.

con de scend (kon′di send′), *v.* come down willingly or graciously to the level of one's inferiors in rank: *The king condescended to eat with the beggars.*

con du cive (kən dü′siv, kən dyü′siv), *adj.* helpful; favorable: *Exercise is conducive to health.*

con fine ment (kən fīn′mənt), *n.* 1. act of confining. 2. fact or state of being confined. 3. imprisonment.

con nu bi al (kə nü′bē əl, kə nyü′bē əl), *adj.* of or having to do with marriage.

con sci en tious (kon′shē en′shəs), *adj.* 1. careful to do what one knows is right; controlled by conscience. 2. done with care to make it right: *Conscientious work is careful and exact.* —**con′sci en′tious ly,** *adv.* **Syn.** 1. upright, honorable. 2. particular, painstaking.

con so la tion (kon′sə lā′shən), *n.* 1. comfort. 2. a comforting person, thing, or event.

con ster na tion (kon′stər nā′shən), *n.* great dismay; paralyzing terror: *To our consternation the train rushed on toward the burning bridge.*

con strict (kən strikt′), *v.* draw together; contract; compress: *A rubber band constricts what it encircles.*

con tem pla tive (kon′təm plā′tiv, kən tem′plə tiv), *adj.* 1. thoughtful; meditative. 2. devoted to religious meditation and prayer.

con tempt (kən tempt′), *n.* 1. the feeling that a person, act, or thing is mean, low, or worthless; scorn; a despising: *We feel contempt for a liar.* 2. condition of being scorned or despised; disgrace: *A cowardly traitor is held in contempt.* 3. disobedience to or open disrespect for the rules or decisions of a law court, a lawmaking body, etc. A person can be put in jail for **contempt of court.** **Syn.** 1. disdain.

---

hat, āge, fär;   let, bē, tèrm;   it, īce;   hot, gō, ôrder;   oil, out;   cup, pùt, rüle;   ch, child;   ng, long;
th, thin;   ᴛH, then;   zh, measure;   ə represents *a* in about, *e* in taken, *i* in pencil, *o* in lemon, *u* in circus.

con temp tu ous (kən temp′chü əs), *adj.* showing contempt; scornful: *a contemptuous look.* **—con temp′tu ous ly,** *adv.* **—con temp′tu ous ness,** *n.*

con ti nent (kon′tə nənt), *n.* **1.** one of the seven great masses of land on the earth. The continents are North America, South America, Europe, Africa, Asia, Australia, and Antarctica. **2.** mainland. **3. the Continent,** the mainland of Europe. It does not include the British Isles.

con tort (kən tôrt′), *v.* twist or bend out of shape; distort: *The clown contorted his face.*

con tract ed (kən trak′tid), *adj.* **1.** drawn together; made narrow; shortened; made smaller; shrunken. **2.** narrow-minded.

con triv ance (kən trī′vəns), *n.* **1.** thing invented; mechanical device. **2.** act or manner of contriving. **3.** power or ability of contriving. **4.** plan; scheme.

con verge (kən vėrj′), *v.,* **-verged, -verg ing. 1.** tend to meet in a point. **2.** turn toward each other: *If you look at the end of your nose, your eyes converge.* **3.** come together; center: *The interest of all the students converged upon the celebration.* **4.** cause to converge. [< LL *convergere* < L *com-* together + *vergere* incline]

con vic tion (kən vik′shən), *n.* **1.** act of proving or declaring guilty. **2.** state of being proved or declared guilty. **3.** act of convincing (a person). **4.** being convinced. **5.** firm belief. **Syn. 5.** certainty, assurance.

con vulse (kən vuls′), *v.,* **-vulsed, -vuls ing. 1.** shake violently: *An earthquake convulsed the island.* **2.** cause violent disturbance in; disturb violently: *His face was convulsed with rage.* **3.** throw into convulsions; shake with spasms of pain: *The sick child was convulsed before the doctor came.* **4.** throw into a fit of laughter; cause to shake with laughter: *The clown convulsed the audience with his funny acts.*

con vul sive (kən vul′siv), *adj.* **1.** violently disturbing. **2.** having convulsions. **3.** producing convulsions.

core (kôr, kōr), *n., v.,* **cored, cor ing. —n. 1.** the hard, central part, containing the seeds, of fruits like apples and pears. **2.** the central or most important part: *the core of a boil, the core of an argument.* **—v.** take out the core of: *The cook cored the apples.*

cor re la tion (kôr′ə lā′shən, kor′ə lā′shən), *n.* the mutual relation of two or more things: *There is a close correlation between climate and crops.*

cor re spond ing (kôr′ə spon′ding, kor′ə spon′ding), *adj.* **1.** agreeing; in harmony. **2.** similar; matching. **3.** exchanging letters; writing letters to each other.

cor re spond ing ly (kôr′ə spon′ding lē, kor′ə spon′ding lē), *adv.* in a corresponding manner; so as to correspond.

cor rob o rate (kə rob′ə rāt), *v.,* **-rat ed, -rat ing.** make more certain; confirm. [< L *corroborare* strengthen < *com-* + *robur* oak]

coun ter part (koun′tər pärt′), *n.* **1.** copy; duplicate. **2.** person or thing closely resembling another: *This twin is her sister's counterpart.* **3.** person or thing that complements another: *Night is the counterpart of day.*

coup (kü), *n., pl.* **coups** (küz), a sudden, brilliant action; unexpected, clever move; master stroke.

cow (kou), *v.* make afraid; frighten.

cow er (kou′ər), *v.* **1.** crouch in fear or shame. **2.** draw back tremblingly from another's threats, blows, etc. [< Scand. *kūra* sit moping]

crack er-bar rel (krak′ər bar′əl), *adj.* having the plainness, rough humor, and informality of country people; unsophisticated; practical; realistic.

cramp (kramp), *n.* **1.** a metal bar bent at both ends, used for holding together blocks of stone, timbers, etc. **2.** clamp. **3.** something that confines or hinders; limitation; restriction. **—v. 1.** fasten together with a cramp. **2.** confine in a small space; limit; restrict. **3. cramp one's style,** *Slang.* keep one from showing one's skill, ability, etc. **—adj. 1.** confined; limited; restricted. **2.** hard to read; difficult to understand.

cran ny (kran′ē), *n., pl.* **-nies.** a small, narrow opening; crack; crevice.

crit i cal (krit′ə kəl), *adj.* **1.** inclined to find fault or disapprove: *a critical disposition.* **2.** skilled as a critic. **3.** coming from one who is skilled as a critic: *a critical judgment.* **4.** belonging to the work of a critic: *critical essays.* **5.** of a crisis; being important at a time of danger and difficulty: *the critical moment.* **6.** full of danger or difficulty: *His delay was critical.* **7.** of supplies, labor, or resources, necessary for some work or project but existing in inadequate supply. **—crit′i cal ly,** *adv.* **—crit′i cal ness,** *n.*

Croe sus (krē′səs), *n.* **1.** very rich king of Lydia from 560 to 546 B.C. **2.** a very rich person.

crone (krōn), *n.* a withered old woman. [< MDutch *croonje* < OF *carogne* carcass, hag. Doublet of CARRION.]

cryp tic (krip′tik), *adj.* having a hidden meaning; secret; mysterious: *a cryptic message, a cryptic reply.*

crys tal lize (kris′tl īz), *v.,* **-lized, -liz ing. 1.** form into crystals; solidify into crystals: *Water crystallizes to form snow.* **2.** form into definite shape: *His vague ideas crystallized into a clear plan.* **3.** coat with sugar.

cudg el (kuj′əl), *n., v.,* **-eled, -el ing** or *esp. Brit.* **-elled, -el ling. —n. 1.** a short, thick stick used as a weapon; club. **2. take up the cudgels for,** defend strongly. **—v. 1.** beat with a cudgel. **2. cudgel one's brains,** try very hard to think.

cue (kyü), *n.* **1.** hint or suggestion as to what to do or when to act: *Being a stranger, he took his cue from the actions of the natives.* **2.** action or speech on or behind the stage which gives the signal for an actor, singer, musician, etc., to enter or to begin. In a play the last word or words of one actor's speech are the cue for another to come on the stage, begin speaking, etc. **3.** part one is to play; course of action. **4.** frame of mind; mood.

cul prit (kul′prit), *n.* **1.** person guilty of a fault or crime; offender. **2.** prisoner in court accused of a crime.

cul ti vat ed (kul′tə vā′tid), *adj.* **1.** prepared and used to raise crops: *A field of wheat is cultivated land; a pasture is not.* **2.** produced by cultivation; not wild: *The American Beauty rose is a cultivated flower.* **3.** improved; developed. **4.** cultured; refined.

cu po la (kyü′pə lə), *n.* **1.** a rounded roof; dome. **2.** a small dome or tower on a roof.

curt sy (kėrt′sē), *n., pl.* **-sies,** *v.,* **-sied, -sy ing. —n.** bow of respect or greeting by women, made by bending the knees and lowering the body slightly. **—v.** make a curtsy. [var. of *courtesy*]

cy clone (sī′klōn), *n.* **1.** a very violent windstorm; tornado. **2.** storm moving around and toward a calm center of low pressure, which also moves. [< Gk. *kyklon*, ppr. of *kyklóein* move around in a circle]

cym bal (sim′bəl), *n.* one of a pair of brass plates, used as a musical instrument. Cymbals make a loud, ringing sound.

< = from, derived from, taken from;   cf., compare;   dial., dialect;   dim., diminutive;   lang., language; pp., past participle;   ppr., present participle;   pt., past tense;   ult., ultimately;   var., variant;   ? = possibly.

dank (dangk), *adj.* unpleasantly damp; moist; wet: *The cave was dark, dank, and chilly.*

da ta (dā′tə, dat′ə), *n. pl. of* **datum.** things known or granted; information from which conclusions can be drawn; facts.

daunt (dônt, dänt), *v.* 1. frighten. 2. discourage. [< OF *danter* < L *domitare* < *domare* tame]
Syn. 1. intimidate. 2. dismay, dishearten.

dec a dence (dek′ə dəns, di kād′ns), *n.* a falling off; decline; decay: *The decadence of morals was one of the causes of the fall of Rome.* [< F < Med.L *decadentia* < L *de-* + *cadere* fall]

de ceit ful (di sēt′fəl), *adj.* 1. ready or willing to deceive or lie. 2. deceiving; fraudulent. 3. meant to deceive. —**de ceit′ful ly,** *adv.* —**de ceit′ful ness,** *n.*

de cep tive (di sep′tiv), *adj.* 1. deceiving. 2. meant to deceive. —**de cep′tive ly,** *adv.* —**de cep′tive ness,** *n.*

de claim (di klām′), *v.* 1. recite in public; make a formal speech. 2. speak in a loud and emotional manner; speak or write for effect.

de co rum (di kôr′əm, di kōr′əm), *n.* 1. propriety of action, speech, dress, etc.: *You behave with decorum when you do what is proper.* 2. observance or requirement of polite society. [< L *decorum* (that which is) seemly]

ded i cate (ded′ə kāt), *v.,* **-cat ed, -cat ing.** 1. set apart for a sacred or solemn purpose: *The minister was dedicated to the service of God.* 2. give up wholly or earnestly to some person or purpose. 3. address (a book, poem, etc.) to a friend or patron as a mark of affection, respect, gratitude, etc.

de fi ance (di fī′əns), *n.* 1. a defying; a standing up against authority and refusing to recognize or obey it; open resistance. 2. challenge to meet in a contest, to do something, or to prove something. 3. **bid defiance to,** defy. 4. **in defiance of,** without regard for; in spite of.

de fi ant (di fī′ənt), *adj.* showing defiance; challenging; openly resisting. —**de fi′ant ly,** *adv.*

de lib e ra tion (di lib′ə rā′shən), *n.* 1. careful thought. 2. discussion of reasons for and against something; debate: *the deliberations of Congress.* 3. slowness and care: *The hunter aimed his gun with great deliberation.* 4. slowness.

del uge (del′yüj), *n., v.,* **-uged, -ug ing.** —*n.* 1. a great flood. 2. a heavy fall of rain. 3. any overwhelming rush: *Most stores have a deluge of orders just before Christmas.* —*v.* 1. flood. 2. overwhelm: *The movie star was deluged with requests for his autograph.*

delve (delv), *v.,* **delved, delv ing.** 1. search carefully for information: *The scholar delved in many libraries for facts.* 2. *Archaic* or *Dialect.* dig. [OE *delfan*]

de ment ed (di men′tid), *adj.* insane; crazy. [< L *dementare* < *demens* mad < *de-* out of + *mens* mind]

dem i god (dem′i god′), *n.* 1. god that is partly human. Hercules was a demigod. 2. a lesser god.

de pend ent (di pen′dənt), *adj.* 1. relying on another for support or help: *A child is dependent on its parents.* 2. resulting from another thing; controlled or influenced by something else: *Good crops are dependent on the right kind of weather.* —*n.* person who relies on another for support or help.

de plor a ble (di plôr′ə bəl, di plōr′ə bəl), *adj.* 1. to be deplored; regrettable; lamentable: *a deplorable accident.* 2. wretched; miserable. —**de plor′a bly,** *adv.*

de plore (di plôr′, di plōr′), *v.,* **-plored, -plor ing.** be very sorry about; regret deeply; lament. [< L *deplorare* < *de-* + *plorare* weep]

de pose (di pōz′), *v.,* **-posed, -pos ing.** 1. put out of office or a position of authority; remove from a throne: *The king was deposed by the revolution.* 2. declare under oath; testify: *He deposed that he had seen the prisoner on the day of the murder.* [< OF *deposer* < *de-* down (< L) + *poser* put]

de prav i ty (di prav′ə tē), *n., pl.* **-ties.** 1. wickedness; corruption. 2. a corrupt act; bad practice.

dep re cate (dep′rə kāt), *v.,* **-cat ed, -cat ing.** express strong disapproval of; plead against; protest against: *Lovers of peace deprecate war.* —**dep′re cat′ing ly,** *adv.* —**dep′re ca′tor,** *n.*

de pres sion (di presh′ən), *n.* 1. act of pressing down; a sinking; a lowering: *A rapid depression of the mercury in a barometer usually indicates a storm.* 2. depressed condition. 3. a low place; hollow: *The roads were dry, but water still filled depressions in the ground.* 4. sadness; gloominess; low spirits: *In a fit of depression the invalid killed himself.* 5. reduction of activity; dullness of trade: *Many men lose their jobs during times of business depression.*
Syn. 4. dejection, melancholy.

de ri sive (di rī′siv), *adj.* mocking; ridiculing. —**de ri′sive ly,** *adv.* —**de ri′sive ness,** *n.*

de scry (di skrī′), *v.* **-scried, -scry ing.** catch sight of; be able to see; make out.

de sist (di zist′), *v.* stop; cease.

de spair (di sper′, di spar′), *n.* 1. loss of hope; state of being without hope; hopelessness; a feeling that nothing good can happen. 2. person or thing that causes despair. —*v.* lose hope; be without hope: *The doctors despaired of saving the sick man's life.*
Syn. *n.* 1. **Despair, desperation** mean hopelessness. **Despair** emphasizes loss of hope and usually suggests sinking into a state of discouragement: *In his despair over losing his job he fell in with bad companions.* **Desperation** suggests a recklessness that is caused by despair and is expressed in rash or frantic action as a last resort: *He had no job and no money, and in desperation robbed a bank.*

des per a tion (des′pə rā′shən), *n.* recklessness caused by despair; willingness to run any risk: *In desperation he jumped out of the window when he saw that the stairs were on fire.*
Syn. See **despair.**

des pi ca ble (des′pi kə bəl, des pik′ə bəl), *adj.* to be despised; contemptible: *Cowards and liars are despicable.*

de spise (di spīz′), *v.,* **-spised, -spis ing.** look down on; feel contempt for; scorn.

des pot ism (des′pə tiz′əm), *n.* 1. tyranny; oppression. 2. government by a monarch having unlimited power.

de tached (di tacht′), *adj.* 1. separate from others; isolated: *A detached house is not in a solid row with others.* 2. not influenced by others or by one's own interests and prejudices; impartial.

di a bo lo (dī ab′ə lō), *n., pl.* **-los.** game in which an hourglass-shaped piece of wood is whirled and spun on a string tied to two sticks held one in each hand.

dic tion (dik′shən), *n.* 1. manner of expressing ideas in words; style of speaking or writing. Good diction implies grammatical correctness, a wide vocabulary, and skill in the choice and arrangement of words. 2. manner of using the voice in speaking; the utterance or enunciation of words.

dig it (dij′it), *n.* 1. finger or toe. 2. any of the figures 0, 1, 2, 3, 4, 5, 6, 7, 8, 9. Sometimes 0 is not called a digit. [< L *digitus* finger]

di late (dī lāt′, də lāt′), *v.,* **-lat ed, -lat ing.** 1. make or become larger or wider. 2. speak or write in a very complete

---

hat, āge, fär;   let, bē, tėrm;   it, īce;   hot, gō, ôrder;   oil, out;   cup, pùt, rüle;   ch, child;   ng, long; th, thin;   ᴛʜ, then;   zh, measure;   ə represents *a* in about, *e* in taken, *i* in pencil, *o* in lemon, *u* in circus.

or detailed manner. [< L *dilatare* < *dis-* apart + *latus* wide]

dil et tan te (dil/ə tänt/, dil/ə tan/tē), *n., pl.* **-tes, -ti.**
1. lover of the fine arts. 2. person who follows some art or science as an amusement or in a trifling way. 3. trifler. [< Ital. *dilettante* < *dilettare* < L *delectare*.]

dil et tant ism (dil/ə tän/tiz əm, dil/ə tan/tiz əm), *n.* quality or practice of a dilettante.

din (din), *n., v.,* **dinned, din ning.** —*n.* a loud, confused noise that lasts. —*v.* 1. make a din. 2. strike with a din. 3. say over and over: *He was always dinning into our ears the importance of hard work.* [OE *dynn*]

dirge (dèrj), *n.* a funeral song or tune. [contraction of L *dirige* direct (imperative of *dirigere*), first word in office for the dead]

dis card (*v.* dis kärd/; *n.* dis/kärd), *v.* 1. give up as useless or worn out; throw aside. 2. get rid of (useless or unwanted playing cards) by throwing them aside or playing them. 3. throw out an unwanted card. —*n.* 1. act of throwing aside as useless. 2. thing or things thrown aside as useless or not wanted: *The scientists's discovery threw old theories into the discard.* 3. the unwanted cards thrown aside; card played as useless.

dis cern (də zèrn/, də sèrn/), *v.* perceive; see clearly; distinguish; recognize.

dis ci pli nar i an (dis/ə plə ner/ē ən), *n.* person who enforces discipline or who believes in strict discipline. —*adj.* disciplinary.

dis ci pli nar y (dis/ə plə ner/ē), *adj.* 1. having to do with discipline. 2. for discipline.

dis close (dis klōz/), *v.,* **-closed, -clos ing.** 1. open to view; uncover. 2. make known; reveal.

dis con cert (dis/kən sèrt/), *v.* 1. disturb the self-possession of; embarrass greatly; confuse: *His arrest of the wrong man disconcerted the policeman.* 2. upset; disorder: *The chairman's plans were disconcerted by the late arrival of the speaker.*

dis cord ant (dis kôrd/nt), *adj.* 1. not in harmony: *a discordant note in music.* 2. not in agreement; not fitting together: *Many discordant views were expressed.* 3. harsh; clashing: *Many automobile horns are discordant.* —**dis cord/ant ly,** *adv.*

dis creet (dis krēt/), *adj.* careful and sensible in speech and action; wisely cautious; showing good sense.

dis dain (dis dān/), *v.* look down on; consider beneath oneself; scorn: *The honest official disdained the offer of a bribe.* —*n.* act of disdaining; feeling of scorn.

di shev eled or **di shev elled** (də shev/əld), *adj.* 1. rumpled; mussed; disordered; untidy. 2. hanging loosely or in disorder: *disheveled hair.*

dis il lu sion (dis/i lü/zhən), *v.* free from illusion: *People are apt to become disillusioned as they grow old.* —*n.* a freeing or being freed from illusion.

dis in clined (dis/in klīnd/), *adj.* unwilling.

dis lo cate (dis/lō kāt), *v.,* **-cat ed, -cat ing.** put out of joint.

dis lodge (dis loj/), *v.,* **-lodged, -lodg ing.** drive or force out of a place, position, etc.: *The workman used a crowbar to dislodge a heavy stone from the wall. Heavy gunfire dislodged the enemy from the fort.*

dis mem ber (dis mem/bər), *v.* 1. pull apart; cut to pieces; separate or divide into parts: *The defeated country was dismembered.* 2. cut or tear the limbs from.

dis o be di ence (dis/ə bē/dē əns), *n.* refusal to obey; failure to obey.

dis or der (dis ôr/dər), *n.* 1. lack of order; confusion. 2. a

public disturbance; riot. 3. sickness; disease: *a disorder of the stomach.* —*v.* 1. destroy the order of; throw into confusion. 2. cause sickness in: *The bad food disordered my stomach.*
Syn. *n.* 1. jumble. 2. commotion, tumult.

dis pel (dis pel/), *v.,* **-pelled, -pel ling.** drive away and scatter; disperse: *The captain's cheerful laugh dispelled our fears.*

dis pir it (dis pir/it), *v.* depress; discourage; dishearten. —**dis pir/it ed ly,** *adv.*

dis port (dis pôrt/, dis pōrt/), *v.* amuse (oneself); sport; play: *People laughed at the clumsy bears disporting themselves in the water.*

dis po si tion (dis/pə zish/ən), *n.* 1. habitual ways of acting toward others or of thinking about things; nature: *a cheerful disposition.* 2. tendency; inclination: *a disposition to argue.* 3. act of putting in order or position; arrangement: *the disposition of soldiers in battle.* 4. management; settlement: *the satisfactory disposition of a difficult problem.* 5. disposal.

dis pu ta tious (dis/pyə tā/shəs), *adj.* fond of disputing; inclined to argue.
Syn. quarrelsome.

dis re gard (dis/ri gärd/), *v.* 1. pay no attention to; take no notice of: *Disregarding the child's screams, the doctor cleaned and bandaged the cut.* 2. treat without proper regard or respect; slight.

dis sent (di sent/), *v.* 1. differ in opinion; disagree. 2. refuse to conform to the rules and beliefs of an established church. —*n.* 1. difference of opinion; disagreement. 2. refusal to conform to the rules and beliefs of an established church. [< L *dissentire* < *dis-* differently + *sentire* think, feel]

dis sen tient (di sen/shənt), *adj.* dissenting, especially from the opinion of the majority. —*n.* person who dissents.

dis suade (di swād/), *v.,* **-suad ed, -suad ing.** persuade not to do something: *The father dissuaded his son from leaving school.* [< L *dissuadere* < *dis-* against + *suadere* to urge]

dis taste (dis tāst/), *n.* dislike.

dis trac tion (dis trak/shən), *n.* 1. act of drawing away the attention, mind, etc. 2. thing that draws away the attention, mind, etc. 3. confusion of mind; disturbance of thought: *The mother of the lost children scarcely knew what she was doing in her distraction.* 4. insanity; madness. 5. confusion; perplexity; dissension. 6. relief from continued thought, grief, or effort; amusement.

di van (dī/van, də van/), *n.* 1. a long, low, soft couch or sofa. 2. a Turkish court or council. 3. room where such a court or council meets. 4. a smoking room. [< Turkish *divān* < Persian *dēvān*]

di ver sion (də vèr/zhən, dī vèr/zhən), *n.* 1. a turning aside: *High tariffs often cause a diversion of trade from one country to another.* 2. amusement; entertainment; pastime: *Golf is my father's favorite diversion.*

di vert (də vèrt/, dī vèrt/), *v.* 1. turn aside: *A ditch diverted water from the stream into the fields.* 2. amuse; entertain: *Music diverted him after a hard day's work.*

di vin i ty (də vin/ə tē), *n., pl.* **-ties.** 1. a divine being; a god. 2. **the Divinity,** God. 3. divine nature or quality.

dod der (dod/ər), *v.* shake; tremble; totter: *The man dodders about as if he were ninety years old.*

doff (dof, dôf), *v.* 1. take off; remove: *He doffed his hat as the flag passed by.* 2. get rid of; throw aside. [contraction of *do off*]

< = from, derived from, taken from;   cf., compare;   dial., dialect;   dim., diminutive;   lang., language; pp., past participle;   ppr., present participle;   pt., past tense;   ult., ultimately;   var., variant;   ? = possibly.

dog ged (dô′gid, dog′id), *adj.* stubborn; persistent; not giving up: *In spite of failures he kept on with dogged determination to succeed.* [< *dog*] —**dog′ged ly**, *adv.* —**dog′ged ness**, *n.*
Syn. obstinate, headstrong.

dole (dōl), *v.*, **doled, dol ing.** 1. deal out in portions to the poor. 2. give in small portions.

dole ful (dōl′fəl), *adj.* sad; mournful; dreary; dismal.
Syn. sorrowful, woeful, plaintive.

dolt (dōlt), *n.* a dull, stupid person.

do mes tic (də mes′tik), *n.* servant in a household.

dom i cile (dom′ə sil, dom′ə səl), *n.* house; home; residence.

dom i nate (dom′ə nāt), *v.*, **-nat ed, -nat ing.** 1. control or rule by strength or power: *A man of strong will often dominates others.* 2. rise high above; hold a commanding position over: *The mountain dominates the harbor.* [< L *dominari* < *dominus* lord, master]

dote (dōt), *v.*, **dot ed, dot ing.** 1. be weak-minded and childish because of old age. 2. **dote on** or **upon,** be foolishly fond of; be too fond of.

dou blet (dub′lit), *n.* 1. a man's close-fitting jacket. Men in Europe wore doublets in the 15th, 16th, and 17th centuries. 2. pair of two similar or equal things. 3. one of a pair. 4. one of two or more words in a language, derived from the same original but coming by different routes. *Example: pallid* and *pale.*

dour (dúr, dour), *adj.* 1. gloomy; sullen. 2. *Scottish.* stern; severe. 3. *Scottish.* stubborn.

down cast (doun′kast′), *adj.* 1. directed downward: *Ashamed of his mistake, he stood with downcast eyes.* 2. dejected; sad; discouraged: *A life of failure had made her downcast.* —*n.* 1. a downcast look. 2. a casting down; overthrow.

driz zle (driz′əl), *v.*, **-zled, -zling.** *n.* —*v.* rain in very small drops like mist.

drone (drōn), *v.*, **droned, dron ing**, *n.* 1. make a deep, continuous, humming sound: *Bees droned among the flowers.* 2. talk or say in a monotonous voice: *The weary beggar droned a prayer.* —*n.* a deep, continuous, humming sound: *the drone of airplane motors.*

drow sy (drou′zē), *adj.*, **-si er, -si est.** 1. half asleep; sleepy. 2. causing sleepiness or half sleep; lulling. 3. caused by sleepiness. —**drow′si ly**, *adv.*

dub (dub), *v.*, **dubbed, dub bing.** 1. make (a man) a knight by striking his shoulder lightly with a sword. 2. give a title to; call; name.

Duk ma sov (dük mä′səv)

dull (dul), *adj.* 1. not sharp or pointed: *a dull knife.* 2. not bright or clear: *dull eyes, a dull day.* 3. slow in understanding; stupid: *a dull mind.* 4. having little feeling; insensitive. 5. not interesting; tiresome; boring: *a dull book.* 6. having little life, energy, or spirit; not active: *The coal business is dull this summer.* 7. not felt sharply: *a dull pain.* —*v.* 1. make dull. 2. become dull. [ME *dul*] —**dull′ness, dul′ness**, *n.*

du ly (dü′lē, dyü′lē), *adv.* 1. according to what is due; as due; properly; suitably; rightfully: *The documents were duly signed before a lawyer.* 2. as much as is needed; enough. 3. when due; at the proper time.

dumb found (dum′found′), *v.* dumfound.

dum found (dum′found′), *v.* amaze and make unable to speak; bewilder; confuse.

dune (dün, dyün), *n.* mound or ridge of sand heaped up by the wind.

du plic i ty (dü plis′ə tē, dyü plis′ə tē), *n., pl.* **-ties.** deceitfulness; treachery; secretly acting one way and publicly acting another in order to deceive.

du ti ful (dü′tə fəl, dyü′tə fəl), *adj.* 1. performing the duties one owes; obedient: *a dutiful daughter.* 2. required by duty; proceeding from or expressing a sense of duty: *dutiful words.* —**du′ti ful ly**, *adv.*

earth en ware (ėr′thən wer′, ėr′thən war′), *n.* 1. coarser kinds of dishes, containers, etc., made of baked clay; pottery or crockery. 2. baked clay. —*adj.* made of earthenware.

eaves drop (ēvz′drop′), *v.*, **-dropped, -drop ping.** listen to what one is not supposed to hear; listen secretly to private conversation. [probably < *eavesdropper* < *eavesdrop*, n. (influenced by *drop*), earlier (unrecorded) *eavesdrip*, OE *yfesdrype* the dripping of water from the eaves] —**eaves′drop′per**, *n.*

ec cen tric i ty (ek′sen tris′ə tē), *n., pl.* **-ties.** something queer or out of the ordinary; oddity; peculiarity.

ed dy (ed′ē), *n., pl.* **-dies**, *v.*, **-died, -dy ing.** —*n.* water, air, etc., moving against the main current, especially when having a whirling motion; small whirlpool or whirlwind. —*v.* 1. move against the main current in a whirling motion; whirl. 2. move in circles. [? < OE *ed-* turning + *ēa* stream]

ee rie (ir′ē), *adj.*, **-ri er, -ri est.** 1. causing fear; strange; weird. 2. timid because of superstition.

e lat ed (i lāt′id), *adj.* in high spirits; joyful; proud.

e lec tri fy (i lek′trə fī), *v.*, **-fied, -fy ing.** 1. charge with electricity. 2. equip to use electricity: *Some railroads once run by steam are now electrified.* 3. give an electric shock to. 4. excite; thrill.

el o cu tion (el′ə kyü′shən), *n.* 1. art of speaking or reading clearly and effectively in public; art of public speaking, including the correct use of the voice, gestures, etc. 2. manner of speaking or reading in public.

el o cu tion ar y (el′ə kyü′shə ner′ē), *adj.* of or having to do with elocution.

el o quence (el′ə kwəns), *n.* 1. flow of speech that has grace and force: *The eloquence of the President moved all hearts.* 2. power to win by speaking; the art of speaking so as to stir the feelings.
Syn. 2. elocution, oratory, rhetoric.

el o quent (el′ə kwənt), *adj.* 1. having eloquence. 2. very expressive. —**el′o quent ly**, *adv.*

e lude (i lüd′), *v.*, **e lud ed, e lud ing.** 1. slip away from; avoid or escape by cleverness, quickness, etc.: *The sly fox eluded the dogs.* 2. escape discovery by; baffle: *The cause of cancer has eluded all research.* —**e lud′er**, *n.*
Syn. 1. avoid, evade, shun. 2. foil.

e lu sive (i lü′siv), *adj.* 1. hard to describe or understand; baffling. 2. tending to elude: *an elusive enemy.* —**e lu′sive ly**, *adv.* —**e lu′sive ness**, *n.*

em bit ter (em bit′ər), *v.* make bitter; make more bitter: *The old man was embittered by the loss of his money.*

em bold en (em bōl′dən), *v.* make bold, encourage.

e mit (i mit′), *v.*, **e mit ted, e mit ting.** 1. give off; send out; discharge: *The sun emits light and heat. Volcanoes emit lava. The trapped lion emitted roars of rage.* 2. put into circulation; issue.

em phat ic (em fat′ik), *adj.* 1. spoken or done with force or stress; strongly expressed: *Her answer was an emphatic "No!"* 2. speaking with force or stress; expressing oneself strongly: *The emphatic speaker often pounded the table and*

---

hat, āge, fär; let, bē, tėrm; it, īce; hot, gō, ôrder; oil, out; cup, put, rüle; ch, child; ng, long; th, thin; ₣H, then; zh, measure; ə represents *a* in about, *e* in taken, *i* in pencil, *o* in lemon, *u* in circus.

shouted. **3.** attracting attention; very noticeable; striking: *The club made an emphatic success of their party.*
Syn. 1. expressive, positive, energetic, forcible.

em phat i cal ly (em fat′ik lē), *adv.* in an emphatic manner; to an emphatic degree.

em place ment (em plās′mənt), *n.* **1.** space or platform for a heavy gun or guns. **2.** an assigning to a place; locating.

en cour age (en kėr′ij), *v.,* **-aged, -ag ing. 1.** give courage to; increase the hope or confidence of; urge on: *Success encourages you to go ahead and do better.* **2.** be favorable to; help; support: *High prices for farm products encourage farming.* **—en cour′ag ing ly,** *adv.*
Syn. 1. hearten, inspirit. **2.** promote, advance.

en fold (en fōld′), *v.* infold. **—en fold′er,** *n.*

en gross (en grōs′), *v.* **1.** occupy wholly; take up all the attention of: *She was engrossed in a story.* **2.** copy or write in large letters; write a beautiful copy of. **3.** write out in formal style; express in legal form. **4.** buy all or much of (the supply of some commodity) so as to control prices.

en join (en join′), *v.* **1.** order; direct; urge: *Parents enjoin good behavior on their children.* **2.** in law, issue an authoritative command. Through an injunction a judge may enjoin a person to do (or not do) some act.
Syn. 1. prescribe, command, charge, bid.

en quire (en kwīr′), *v.,* **-quired, -quir ing.** inquire.

en sue (en sü′), *v.,* **-sued, -su ing. 1.** come after; follow: *The ensuing year means the next year.* **2.** happen as a result: *In his anger he hit the man, and a fight ensued.*
Syn. succeed, result.

en thrall or **en thral** (en thrôl′), *v.,* **-thralled, -thrall ing. 1.** captivate; fascinate; charm: *The explorer enthralled the audience with the story of his exciting adventures.* **2.** make a slave of; enslave. Also, **inthrall.**

en ti ty (en′tə tē), *n., pl.* **-ties. 1.** something that has a real and separate existence either actually or in the mind; anything real in itself: *Persons, mountains, languages, and beliefs are distinct entities.* **2.** being; existence. [< LL *entitas* < L *ens,* ppr. of *esse* be]

en trails (en′trālz, en′trəlz), *n.pl.* **1.** the inner parts of a man or animal. **2.** intestines; bowels. **3.** any inner parts.

e phem er al (i fem′ər əl), *adj.* lasting for only a day; lasting for only a very short time; very short-lived. [< Gk. *ephemeros* liable to be cut short < *epi-* subject to + *hemera* the day (of destiny)]

ep ic (ep′ik), *n.* **1.** a long poem that tells of the adventures of one or more great heroes. An epic is written in a dignified, majestic style, and often gives expression to the ideals of a nation or race. The *Iliad,* the *Aeneid,* and *Paradise Lost* are epics. **2.** any writing having the qualities of an epic. **3.** story or series of events worthy of being the subject of an epic. **—adj. 1.** of or having to do with an epic. **2.** like an epic; grand in style; heroic. [< L *epicus* < Gk. *epikos* < *epos* word, story] **—ep′i cal ly,** *adv.*

ep i thet (ep′ə thet), *n.* a descriptive expression; adjective or noun, or even a clause, expressing some quality or attribute: *In "crafty Ulysses" and "Richard the Lion-Hearted" the epithets are "crafty" and "the Lion-Hearted."*

er mine (ėr′mən), *n., pl.* **-mines** or (*esp. collectively*) **-mine. 1.** any of several kinds of weasel of northern climates which are brown in summer, but white with a black-tipped tail in winter. **2.** the soft, white fur of the winter phase, used for women's coats, trimming, etc. The official robes of English judges are trimmed with ermine as a symbol of purity and fairness. **3.** position, rank, or duties of a judge. [< OF < Gmc.]

er rat ic (ə rat′ik), *adj.* **1.** not steady; uncertain; irregular: *An erratic mind jumps from one idea to another.* **2.** queer; odd: *erratic behavior.*
Syn. 2. eccentric.

es py (e spī′), *v.,* **-pied, -py ing.** see; spy.

es ti ma tion (es′tə mā′shən), *n.* **1.** judgment; opinion: *In my estimation, your plan will not work.* **2.** esteem; respect. **3.** act or process of estimating.

e ther ize (ē′thə rīz′), *v.,* **-ized, -iz ing. 1.** make unconscious with ether fumes. **2.** change into ether.

e vade (i vād′), *v.,* **e vad ed, e vad ing. 1.** get away from by trickery; avoid by cleverness. **2.** avoid the truth by indefinite or misleading statements.
Syn. 1. elude, dodge.

e va sive (i vā′siv, i vā′ziv), *adj.* tending or trying to evade: *"Perhaps" is an evasive answer.* **—e va′sive ly,** *adv.*
Syn. shifty, misleading.

e ven tu al i ty (i ven′chü al′ə tē), *n., pl.* **-ties.** a possible occurrence or condition; possibility: *We hope for peace, but are ready for all the eventualities of war.*

e vince (i vins′), *v.,* **e vinced, e vinc ing. 1.** show clearly: *The dog evinced its dislike of strangers by growling.* **2.** show that one has (a quality, trait, etc.). [< L *evincere* < *ex-* out + *vincere* conquer]

e voke (i vōk′), *v.,* **e voked, e vok ing.** call forth; bring out: *A good joke evokes a laugh.* [< L *evocare* < *ex-* out + *vocare* call]

e volve (i volv′), *v.,* **e volved, e volv ing. 1.** develop gradually; work out: *The boys evolved a plan for earning money during their summer vacation.* **2.** develop by a process of growth and change to a more highly organized condition. **3.** release; give off; set free.

ex as pe rate (eg zas′pə rāt′), *v.,* **-rat ed, -rat ing.** irritate very much; annoy extremely; make angry: *The child's endless questions exasperated her father.*
Syn. incense, anger, nettle, vex, provoke.

ex ceed (ek sēd′), *v.* **1.** go beyond; be more or greater than; do more than; surpass: *The sum of 5 and 7 exceeds 10.* **2.** be more or greater than others. [< F < L *excedere* < *ex-* out + *cedere* go]
Syn. 2. excel.

ex cru ci at ing (ek skrü′shē ā′ting), *adj.* very painful; torturing; causing great suffering. [< *excruciate* crucify, torture < L *excruciare* < *ex-* utterly + *cruciare* torture, crucify < *crux* cross]

ex hil a rate (eg zil′ə rāt), *v.,* **-rat ed, -rat ing.** make merry or lively; put into high spirits; stimulate. [< L *exhilarare* < *ex-* thoroughly + *hilaris* merry]

ex ot ic (eg zot′ik), *adj.* foreign; strange; not native: *We saw many exotic plants at the flower show.* **—n.** anything exotic. [< L *exoticus* < Gk. *exotikos* < *exo* outside < *ex* out of] **—ex ot′i cal ly,** *adv.*

ex plic it (ek splis′it), *adj.* **1.** clearly expressed; distinctly stated; definite: *He gave such explicit directions that everyone understood them.* **2.** not reserved; frank; outspoken. [< L *explicitus,* pp. of *explicare* unfold, explain < *ex-* un- + *plicare* fold] **—ex plic′it ly,** *adv.*

ex po nent (ek spō′nənt), *n.* **1.** person or thing that explains, interprets, etc. **2.** person or thing that stands as an example, type, or symbol of something: *Lincoln is a famous exponent of self-education.* **3.** index or small number written above and to the right of an algebraic symbol or quantity to show how many times the symbol or quantity is to be used as a factor. *Examples:* $2^2 = 2 \times 2$; $a^3 = a \times a \times a$. [< L *exponens, -entis,* ppr. of *exponere.* See EXPOUND.]

< = from, derived from, taken from; cf., compare; dial., dialect; dim., diminutive; lang., language; pp., past participle; ppr., present participle; pt., past tense; ult., ultimately; var., variant; ? = possibly.

ex pound (ek spound′), v. 1. make clear; explain; interpret. 2. set forth or state in detail. [< OF *espondre* < L *exponere* < *ex-* forth + *ponere* put]

ex ter mi nate (ek stėr′mə nāt), v., **-nat ed, -nat ing.** destroy completely: *This poison will exterminate rats.* [< LL *exterminare* destroy < L *exterminare* drive out < *ex-* out of + *terminus* boundary]

ex traor di nar i ly (ek strôr′də ner′ə lē, eks′trə- ôr′də ner′ə lē), adv. in an extraordinary manner; to an extraordinary degree; most unusually.

ex traor di nar y (ek strôr′də ner′ē; *esp. for 2* ek′strə- ôr′də ner′ē), adj. 1. beyond what is ordinary; most unusual; very remarkable: *Seven feet is an extraordinary height for a person.* 2. outside of, additional to, or ranking below the regular class of officials; special. An **envoy extraordinary** is one sent on a special mission; he ranks below an ambassador. [< L *extraordinarius* < *extra ordinem* out of the (usual) order]
Syn. 1. uncommon, exceptional, singular.

ex u ber ant (eg zü′bər ənt), adj. 1. very abundant; overflowing; lavish: *exuberant health, good nature, or joy; an exuberant welcome.* 2. profuse in growth; luxuriant: *the exuberant vegetation of the jungle.*

fa çade (fə säd′), n. 1. the front part of a building. 2. any side of a building that faces a street or other open space. 3. an impressive appearance concealing something inferior. [< F *façade* < *face*]

fag got (fag′ət), n. *Esp. Brit.* fagot.

fag ot (fag′ət), n. 1. bundle of sticks or twigs tied together: *He built the fire with fagots.* 2. bundle of iron rods or pieces of iron or steel to be welded.

fain (fān), *Archaic and Poetic.* —adv. by choice; gladly. —adj. 1. willing, but not eager; forced by circumstances. 2. glad; willing. 3. eager; desirous. [OE *fægen*]

fal li ble (fal′ə bəl), adj. 1. liable to be deceived or mistaken; liable to err. 2. liable to be erroneous, inaccurate, or false.

fam ish (fam′ish), v. be or make extremely hungry; starve. [< ME *fame* famish < L *fames* hunger]

fash ion (fash′ən), n. 1. manner; way: *walk in a peculiar fashion.* 2. the prevailing style; current custom in dress, manners, speech, etc. 3. polite society; fashionable people. 4. **after** or **in a fashion,** in some way or other; not very well. —v. make; shape; form: *He fashioned a whistle out of a piece of wood.*

fas tid i ous (fa stid′ē əs), adj. hard to please; extremely refined or critical; easily disgusted. [< L *fastidiosus* < *fastidium* loathing] —**fas tid′i ous ly,** adv. —**fas tid′i- ous ness,** n.

fat ed (fā′tid), adj. 1. controlled by fate. 2. destined; predestined.

fath om (fa*FH*′əm), n., pl. **fath oms** or (*esp. collectively*) **fath om,** v. —n. a unit of measure equal to 6 feet, used mostly in measuring the depth of water and the length of ships' ropes, cables, etc. —v. 1. measure the depth of. 2. get to the bottom of; understand fully. [OE *fæthm* width of the outstretched arms]

fa tu i ty (fə tü′ə tē, fə tyü′ə tē), n., pl. **-ties.** self-satisfied stupidity; folly; silliness.

fat u ous (fach′ü əs), adj. stupid but self-satisfied; foolish; silly. [< L *fatuus* foolish] —**fat′u ous ly,** adv.

fe line (fē′līn), adj. 1. of or belonging to the cat family. 2. catlike; stealthy; sly: *The Indian stalked the deer with noiseless, feline movements.* —n. any animal belonging to the cat family. Lions, tigers, leopards, and panthers are felines. [< L *feles* cat]

fe roc i ty (fə ros′ə tē), n., pl. **-ties.** savage cruelty; fierceness. [< L *ferocitas* < *ferox* fierce]

fidg et y (fij′ə tē), adj. restless; uneasy.

fiend (fēnd), n. 1. an evil spirit; devil. 2. a very wicked or cruel person. —**fiend′like′,** adj.

fi es ta (fē es′tə), n. 1. a religious festival; saint's day. 2. holiday; festivity. [< Sp. *fiesta* feast]

flag on (flag′ən), n. 1. container for liquids, usually having a handle and a spout, and often a cover. 2. a large bottle, holding about two quarts. 3. contents of a flagon. [< OF *flascon.* Akin to *flask.*]

flan nel (flan′l), n. 1. a soft, warm woolen cloth. 2. flannelette. 3. **flannels,** pl. **a.** clothes made of flannel. **b.** woolen underwear. —adj. made of flannel.

flat (flat), n. apartment or set of rooms on one floor.

flaw (flô), n. 1. a defective place; crack. 2. fault; defect. —v. make or become defective; crack.
Syn. n. 1. chink, rent, breach. 2. imperfection, blemish.

flay (flā), v. 1. strip off the skin or outer covering of, as by whipping. 2. scold severely; criticize without pity or mercy.

fledg ling or **fledge ling** (flej′ling), n. 1. a young bird just able to fly. 2. a young, inexperienced person.

flex (fleks), v. bend: *He flexed his stiff arm slowly.*

flint (flint), n. 1. a very hard, gray or brown stone that makes a spark when struck against steel. It is a kind of quartz. 2. piece of this used with steel to light fires, explode gunpowder, etc. 3. anything very hard or unyielding. [OE]

flog (flog, flôg), v., **flogged, flog ging.** whip very hard; beat with a whip, stick, etc. [? English school slang for L *flagellare* whip] —**flog′ger,** n.

fluc tu ate (fluk′chü āt), v., **-at ed, -at ing.** 1. rise and fall; change continually; vary irregularly: *The temperature fluctuates from day to day.* 2. move in waves. [< L *fluctuare* < *fluctus* wave]

for ceps (fôr′seps, fôr′səps), n., pl. **-ceps.** small pincers or tongs used by surgeons, dentists, etc., for seizing, holding, and pulling.

fore doom (fôr düm′, fōr düm′), v. doom beforehand.

fore fa ther (fôr′fä′*FH*ər, fōr′fä′*FH*ər), n. ancestor.

fore noon (fôr′nün′, fōr′nün′), n. time between early morning and noon. —adj. between early morning and noon.

forge (fôrj, fōrj), n. place with fire where metal is heated very hot and then hammered into shape. A blacksmith uses a forge.

for mal i ty (fôr mal′ə tē), n., pl. **-ties.** 1. procedure required by custom or rule; outward form; ceremony. 2. attention to forms and customs: *Visitors at the court of a king are received with formality.* 3. stiffness of manner, behavior, or arrangement.

fowling piece, a light gun for shooting wild birds.

frail ty (frāl′tē), n., pl. **-ties.** 1. physical weakness. 2. moral weakness; liability to yield to temptation. 3. fault or sin caused by moral weakness.

fren zied (fren′zēd), adj. greatly excited; frantic.

frowz y (frou′zē), adj., **-zi er, -zi est.** 1. slovenly; dirty; untidy. 2. smelling bad.

frus trate (frus′trāt), v., **-trat ed, -trat ing.** 1. bring to nothing; make useless or worthless; foil; defeat. 2. thwart; oppose.

frus tra tion (fru strā′shən), n. a frustrating or being frustrated.

fry (frī), n., pl. **fry.** 1. the young of fish. 2. small adult fish

hat, āge, fär; let, bē, tėrm; it, īce; hot, gō, ôrder; oil, out; cup, pùt, rüle; ch, child; ng, long; th, thin; *FH*, then; zh, measure; ə represents *a* in about, *e* in taken, *i* in pencil, *o* in lemon, *u* in circus.

living together in large groups. 3. young creatures; off-spring; children. 4. **small fry, a.** children. **b.** people or things having little importance.

ful fill ment or **ful fil ment** (fùl fil/mənt), *n.* a fulfilling; completion; performance; accomplishment.

fur row (fėr/ō), *n.* 1. a long, narrow groove or track cut in the ground by a plow. 2. any long, narrow groove or track: *Heavy trucks made deep furrows in the muddy road.* 3. wrinkle.

fur tive (fėr/tiv), *adj.* 1. done stealthily; secret: *a furtive glance into the forbidden room.* 2. sly; stealthy; shifty: *The thief had a furtive manner.*

ga ble (gā/bəl), *n.* 1. end of a ridged roof, with the three-cornered piece of wall that it covers. 2. an end wall with a gable. 3. a triangular ornament or canopy over a door, window, etc. [< OF *gable* < Scand. *gafl*]

ga bled (gā/bəld), *adj.* built with a gable or gables; having or forming gables.

gal ley (gal/ē), *n., pl.* **-leys.** 1. a long, narrow ship of former times having oars and sails. 2. a large rowboat. 3. kitchen of a ship.

ga losh (gə losh/), *n.* Usually, **galoshes,** *pl.* a rubber overshoe covering the ankle, worn in wet or snowy weather. Also, **golosh.** [< F *galoche*]

gam bol (gam/bəl), *n., v.,* **-boled, -bol ing** or *esp. Brit.* **-bolled, -bol ling.** —*n.* a running and jumping about in play; caper; frolic. —*v.* frisk about; run and jump about in play: *Lambs gamboled in the meadow.* [< F *gambade* < Ital. *gambata* < *gamba* leg]

gan grene (gang/grēn, gang grēn/), *n.* decay of a part of a living person or animal when the blood supply is interfered with by injury, infection, freezing, etc.

gan gre nous (gang/grə nəs), *adj.* of or having gangrene; decaying.

gar ble (gär/bəl), *v.,* **-bled, -bling.** make unfair or mis-leading selections from (facts, statements, writings, etc.); omit parts of, often in order to misrepresent: *Foreign newspapers gave a garbled account of the President's speech.* [< Ital. *garbellare* < Arabic *gharbala* sift, probably < LL *cribellare,* ult. < *cribrum* sieve] —**gar/bler,** *n.*
Syn. distort, misquote.

gar ish (gār/ish, gar/ish), *adj.* unpleasantly bright; glaring; showy; gaudy. —**gar/ish ly,** *adv.* —**gar/ish ness,** *n.*

gar ter (gär/tər), *n.* band or strap to hold up a stocking or sock. It is usually elastic.

gaunt (gônt, gänt), *adj.* 1. very thin and bony; with hollow eyes and a starved look: *Hunger and suffering make people gaunt.* 2. looking bare and gloomy; desolate; forbidding; grim. [origin uncertain] —**gaunt/ly,** *adv.*
Syn. 1. lean, spare, lank.

gauze (gôz), *n.* 1. a very thin, light cloth, easily seen through. 2. a thin haze.

gear (gir), *n.* 1. wheel having teeth that fit into the teeth of another wheel of the same kind. If the wheels are of different sizes, they will turn at different speeds. 2. arrangement of fixed and moving parts for transmitting or changing motion; mechanism; machinery: *The car ran off the road when the steering gear broke.* 3. working order; adjustment: *His watch got out of gear and would not run.* 4. equipment needed for some purpose. Harness, clothes, household goods, tools, tackle, and rigging are various kinds of gear.

gen e sis (jen/ə sis), *n., pl.* **-ses** (sēz). origin; creation; coming into being. [< L < Gk.]

gen til i ty (jen til/ə tē), *n., pl.* **-ties.** 1. gentle birth; membership in the aristocracy or upper class. 2. good manners. 3. refinement.

ges tic u la tion (je stik/yə lā/shən), *n.* gesture.

gib bet (jib/it), *n., v.,* **-bet ed, -bet ing.** —*n.* 1. an upright post with a projecting arm at the top, from which the bodies of criminals were hung after execution. 2. gallows. —*v.* 1. hang on a gibbet. 2. hold up to public scorn or ridicule. 3. put to death by hanging. [< OF *gibet,* dim. of *gibe* club]

gid dy (gid/ē), *adj.,* **-di er, -di est.** 1. having a confused, whirling feeling in one's head; dizzy. 2. likely to make dizzy; causing dizziness: *The couples whirled and whirled in their giddy dance.* 3. rarely or never serious; flighty; heedless: *Nobody can tell what that giddy girl will do next.* [OE *gydig* mad, possessed (by an evil spirit) < *god* a god] —**gid/di ly,** *adv.* —**gid/di ness,** *n.*
Syn. *adj.* 1. light-headed. 3. frivolous, fickle.

gim let (gim/lit) *n.* a small tool with a screw point for boring holes. [< OF *guimbelet*]

gin ger (jin/jər), *n.* 1. spice made from the root of a tropical plant, used for flavoring and in medicine. 2. the root, often preserved in syrup or candied. 3. the plant. 4. *Informal.* liveliness; energy. 5. a light reddish or brownish yellow. —*adj.* light reddish- or brownish-yellow.

gin ger ly (jin/jər lē), *adv., adj.* with extreme care or caution. —**gin/ger li ness,** *n.*

gir dle (gėr/dl), *n., v.,* **-dled, -dling.** —*n.* 1. belt, sash, cord, etc., worn around the waist. 2. anything that surrounds or encloses: *a girdle of trees around the pond.* 3. support like a corset worn about the hips or waist. —*v.* 1. form a girdle around; encircle: *Wide roads girdle the city.* 2. cut away the bark so as to make a ring around (a tree, branch, etc.). 3. put a girdle on or around. [OE *gyrdel* < *gyrdan* gird]

glaze (glāz), *v.,* **glazed, glaz ing,** *n.* —*v.* 1. put glass in; cover with glass. Pieces of glass cut to the right size are used to glaze windows and picture frames. 2. make a smooth, glassy surface or glossy coating on (china, food, etc.). 3. become smooth, glassy, or glossy. —*n.* 1. a smooth, glassy surface or glossy coating: *the glaze on a china cup, a glaze of ice.* 2. substance used to make such a surface or coating on things. [ME *glase* (*n*) < *glas* glass, OE *glæs*]

glen (glen), *n.* a small, narrow valley.

glo ry (glôr/ē, glōr/ē), *n., pl.* **-ries,** *v.,* **-ried, -ry ing.** —*n.* 1. great praise and honor; fame; renown. 2. that which brings praise and honor; source of pride and joy. 3. adoring praise and thanksgiving. 4. radiant beauty; brightness; magnificence; splendor. 5. condition of magnificence, splendor, or greatest prosperity. 6. splendor and bliss of heaven; heaven. 7. halo. 8. **go to glory,** die. —*v.* be proud; rejoice. [< OF *glorie* < L *gloria*]

gnarled (närld), *adj.* covered with knots or hard, rough lumps; knotted; twisted; rugged.

gnaw (nô), *v.,* **gnawed, gnawed** or **gnawn, gnaw ing.** 1. bite at and wear away. 2. make by biting: *A rat can gnaw a hole through wood.* 3. wear away; consume; corrode. 4. torment.

goad (gōd), *n.* 1. a sharp-pointed stick for driving cattle, etc.; gad. 2. anything that drives or urges one on. —*v.* drive or urge on; act as a goad to: *Hunger goaded him to steal a loaf of bread.* [OE *gād*]
Syn. *v.* stimulate, spur, impel.

gos sa mer (gos/ə mər), *adj.* very light and thin; filmy.

< = from, derived from, taken from;   cf., compare;   dial., dialect;   dim., diminutive;   lang., language;   pp., past participle;   ppr., present participle;   pt., past tense;   ult., ultimately;   var., variant;   ? = possibly.

graph ic (graf′ik), *adj.* lifelike; vivid.

grat i tude (grat′ə tüd, grat′ə tyüd), *n.* kindly feeling because of a favor received; desire to do a favor in return; thankfulness.

gri mace (grə mās′, grim′is), *n.*, *v.*, **-maced, -mac ing.** —*n.* a twisting of the face; ugly or funny smile. —*v.* make grimaces. [< F < Sp. *grimazo* panic] —**gri mac′er,** *n.*

grits (grits), *n.pl.* 1. coarsely ground corn, oats, etc., with the husks removed. 2. *U.S.* coarse hominy. [OE *gryttan,* pl.]

grouse (grous), *n.*, *pl.* **grouse.** a game bird with feathered legs. The prairie chicken, sage hen, and ruffed grouse of the United States are different kinds.

grue some (grü′səm), *adj.* horrible; frightful: revolting. Also, **grewsome.** [< *grue* to shudder. Cf. MDutch, MLG *gruwen.*] —**grue′some ly,** *adv.*

guard ed ly (gär′did lē), *adv.* in a guarded manner.

gut ter (gut′ər), *n.* 1. channel or ditch along the side of a street or road to carry off water; low part of a street beside the sidewalk. 2. channel or trough along the lower edge of a roof to carry off rainwater. 3. channel; groove. 4. a low, poor, or wretched place.

gut tur al (gut′ər əl), *adj.* 1. of the throat. 2. formed in the throat; harsh: *The man spoke in a guttural voice.* 3. in phonetics, formed between the back of the tongue and the soft palate. The *g* in *go* is a guttural sound. —*n.* sound formed between the back of the tongue and the soft palate. [< NL *gutturalis* < L *guttur* throat] —**gut′tur al ly,** *adv.*

gy ro scope (jī′rə skōp), *n.* a heavy wheel or disk mounted so that its axis can turn freely in one or more directions. A spinning gyroscope tends to resist change in the direction of its axis. It is used to keep ships and airplanes balanced.

Gyroscope

ha bit u al (hə bich′ü əl), *adj.* 1. done by habit; caused by habit: *a habitual smile, habitual courtesy.* 2. being or doing something by habit: *A habitual reader reads a great deal.* 3. often done, seen, or used; usual; customary: *Ice and snow are a habitual sight in arctic regions.* —**ha bit′u al ly,** *adv.* **Syn.** 2. chronic, inveterate. 3. accustomed.

hag gard (hag′ərd), *adj.* looking worn from pain, fatigue, worry, hunger, etc.; gaunt; careworn.

half pen ny (hā′pə nē, hāp′nē), *n.*, *pl.* **half pen nies** (hā′pə niz, hāp′niz) or **half pence,** *adj.* —*n.* a British bronze coin worth half a penny. It is worth about half a cent in United States money. —*adj.* 1. worth only a halfpenny. 2. having little value; trifling.

hal ter (hôl′tər), *n.* 1. rope, strap, etc., for leading or tying an animal. 2. rope for hanging a person; noose. 3. death by hanging. 4. an abbreviated shirt for women which fastens behind the neck and across the back. —*v.* put a halter on; tie with a halter.

hang dog (hang′dôg′, hang′dog′), *adj.* ashamed; sneaking; degraded.

ha rangue (hə rang′), *n.*, *v.*, **-rangued, -rangu ing.** —*n.* 1. a noisy speech. 2. a long, pompous speech. —*v.* 1. address in a harangue. 2. deliver a harangue.

haugh ty (hô′tē), *adj.*, **-ti er, -ti est.** 1. too proud of oneself and too scornful of others. 2. showing too great pride of oneself and scorn for others: *a haughty smile.* —**haugh′ti ly,** *adv.*

Syn. 1. **Haughty, arrogant** mean too proud. **Haughty** means feeling oneself superior to others and showing it by treating them with cold indifference and scorn: *A haughty girl is always unpopular at school.* **Arrogant** means thinking oneself more important than one is and showing it by treating others in a domineering and insulting way: *He was so arrogant that he lost his job.*

haunch (hônch, hänch), *n.* 1. part of the body around the hip; the hip. 2. a hind quarter of an animal: *A dog sits on his haunches.* 3. leg and loin of a deer, sheep, etc., used for food. [< OF *hanche* < Gmc.]

haw ser (hô′zər, hô′sər), *n.* a large rope or small cable. Hawsers are used for mooring or towing ships. [apparently < OF *haucier* hoist, ult. < L *altus* high]

haze¹ (hāz), *n.* 1. a small amount of mist, smoke, dust, etc., in the air: *A thin haze veiled the hills.* 2. vagueness of the mind; slight confusion. [origin uncertain; cf. E dialectal *haze* to drizzle, be foggy]

haze² (hāz), *v.*, **hazed, haz ing.** in schools, universities, etc., force to do unnecessary or ridiculous tasks; bully: *The freshmen resented being hazed by the sophomores.* [Am.E; < OF *haser* irritate, annoy] —**haz′er,** *n.*

hear say (hir′sā′), *n.* common talk; gossip.

heart i ly (här′tl ē), *adv.* 1. sincerely; genuinely; in a warm, friendly way. 2. with enthusiasm; with a good will; vigorously.

hea then (hē′FHən), *n.*, *pl.* **-thens** or **-then,** *adj.* —*n.* 1. person who does not believe in the God of the Bible; person who is not a Christian, Jew, or Moslem. 2. people who are heathen. 3. an irreligious, uninformed, or unenlightened person. —*adj.* 1. of or having to do with heathens. 2. irreligious; unenlightened; uninformed.

he mo stat (hē′mə stat, hem′ə stat), *n.* clamp that compresses the ends of small blood vessels, used to stop bleeding.

herb age (ėr′bij, hėr′bij), *n.* 1. herbs collectively. 2. grass. 3. the green leaves and soft stems of plants.

high light (hī′līt′), *v.*, **-light ed, -light ing.** 1. cast a bright light on. 2. make prominent.

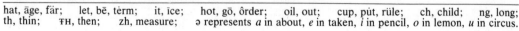

hilt (hilt), *n.* 1. handle of a sword, dagger, etc. 2. **up to the hilt,** thoroughly; completely.

hom age (hom′ij, om′ij), *n.* 1. respect; reverence; honor: *Everyone paid homage to the great leader.* 2. a formal acknowledgment that a vassal that he owed loyalty and service to his lord. 3. thing done or given to show such acknowledgment. [OF *homage* < *hom* man, vassal < L *homo*]

horde (hôrd, hōrd), *n.* 1. crowd; swarm. 2. a wandering tribe or troop: *Hordes of Mongols and Turks invaded Europe in the Middle Ages.* [< F < G < Polish < Turkish *urdū* camp]

hos tile (hos′tl; *sometimes* hos′tīl), *adj.* 1. of an enemy or enemies. 2. opposed; unfriendly; unfavorable. [< L *hostilis* < *hostis* enemy] —**hos′tile ly,** *adv.*

hos til i ty (ho stil′ə tē), *n.*, *pl.* **-ties.** 1. feeling as an enemy does; being an enemy; unfriendliness. 2. state of being at war. 3. opposition; resistance. 4. **hostilities,** *pl.* acts of war; warfare; fighting.

hue (hyü), *n.* color; shade; tint: *All the hues of the rainbow.*

hulk ing (hul′king), *adj.* big and clumsy.

hul la ba loo (hul′ə bə lü′), *n.* a loud noise or disturbance; uproar.

---

hat, āge, fär;   let, bē, tėrm;   it, īce;   hot, gō, ôrder;   oil, out;   cup, pút, rüle;   ch, child;   ng, long; th, thin;   ᵺ, then;   zh, measure;   ə represents *a* in about, *e* in taken, *i* in pencil, *o* in lemon, *u* in circus.

hu mil i ate (hyü mil′ē āt), v., **-at ed, -at ing.** lower the pride, dignity, or self-respect of. **—hu mil′i at′ing ly,** adv.
Syn. humble, mortify, chagrin, disgrace, shame.

hu mor (hyü′mər, yü′mər), n. **1.** funny or amusing quality: I see no humor in your tricks. **2.** ability to see or show the funny or amusing side of things. **3.** speech, writing, etc., showing this ability. **4.** state of mind; mood; disposition: Success puts you in good humor. **5.** fancy; whim. **6.** any of various body fluids formerly supposed to determine a person's health and disposition. The four humors were blood, phlegm, choler (yellow bile), and melancholy (black bile). **7. out of humor,** angry; displeased; in a bad mood. —v. **1.** give in to the fancies or whims of (a person); indulge. **2.** adapt oneself to; act so as to agree with. [< AF < L umor fluid] **—hu′mor less,** adj.

hys ter i cal (hi ster′ə kl), adj. **1.** unnaturally excited. **2.** showing an unnatural lack of control; unable to stop laughing, crying, etc.; suffering from hysteria.

hys ter ics (hi ster′iks), n.pl. fit of hysterical laughing and crying.

id i o syn cra sy (id′ē ō sing′krə sē), n., pl. **-sies.** a personal peculiarity. [< Gk. idiosynkrasia < idios one's own + synkrasis temperament < syn together + kerannynai mix]

ig no ra mus (ig′nə rā′məs, ig′nə ram′əs), n., pl. **-mus es.** an ignorant person.

ig no rant (ig′nər ənt), adj. **1.** knowing little or nothing; without knowledge. A person who has not had much chance to learn may be ignorant but not stupid. **2.** caused by lack of knowledge. **3.** showing lack of knowledge: an ignorant remark. **4.** uninformed; unaware: He was ignorant of the fact that the town had been destroyed. [< L ignorans, -antis, ppr. of ignorare not known] **—ig′nor ant ly,** adv.

ig nore (ig nôr′, ig nōr′), v., **-nored, -nor ing.** pay no attention to; disregard. [< L ignorare not know < ignarus unaware < in- not + OL gnarus aware; form influenced by ignotus unknown]
Syn. overlook, neglect.

ilk (ilk), adj. Archaic. same. —n. **1.** Informal. family; kind; sort. **2. of that ilk,** Informal. **a.** of the same place or name. **b.** of that kind or sort.

il log i cal (i loj′ə kəl), adj. **1.** not logical. **2.** not reasonable. **—il log′i cal ly,** adv. **—il log′i cal ness,** n.
Syn. 1. unsound, fallacious.

il lu sion (i lü′zhən), n. **1.** appearance which is not real; misleading appearance. **2.** a false impression or perception. **3.** a false idea, notion, or belief.

il lus tri ous (i lus′trē əs), adj. very famous; great; outstanding: Washington and Lincoln are illustrious Americans. [< L illustris lighted up, bright] **—il lus′tri ous ly,** adv. **—il lus′tri ous ness,** n.
Syn. distinguished, renowned.

im mense ly (i mens′lē), adv. very greatly.

im pair ment (im per′mənt, im par′mənt), n. injury; damage.

im pa la (im pä′lə), n. a South African antelope of medium size, usually yellow-brown in color.

im pa tience (im pā′shəns), n. **1.** lack of patience; being impatient. **2.** uneasiness and eagerness.

im pend ing (im pen′ding), adj. **1.** likely to happen soon; threatening; about to occur. **2.** overhanging.

im pen e tra ble (im pen′ə trə bəl), adj. **1.** that cannot be entered, pierced, or passed: A thick sheet of steel is impenetrable by an ordinary bullet. **2.** not open to ideas, influences, etc. **3.** impossible for the mind to understand; inscrutable. **—im pen′e tra bly,** adv.

im pe ri ous (im pir′ē əs), adj. **1.** haughty; arrogant; domineering; overbearing. **2.** imperative; necessary; urgent. [< L imperiosus commanding] **—im pe′ri ous ly,** adv.
Syn. 1. dictatorial.

im per son al (im pėr′sə nəl), adj. **1.** referring to all or any persons, not to any special one: "First come, first served" is an impersonal remark. **2.** having no existence as a person: Electricity is an impersonal force. **3.** in grammar, of a verb, having nothing but an indefinite it for a subject. Example: rained in "It rained yesterday."

im pet u ous (im pech′ü əs), adj. **1.** moving with great force or speed: the impetuous rush of water over Niagara Falls. **2.** acting hastily, rashly, or with sudden feeling: Boys are more impetuous than old men.

im pli ca tion (im′plə kā′shən), n. **1.** an implying or being implied. **2.** something implied; indirect suggestion; hint: There was no implication of dishonesty in his failure in business.

im plic it (im plis′it), adj. **1.** without doubting, hesitating, or asking questions; absolute: A soldier must give implicit obedience to his officers. **2.** meant, but not clearly expressed or distinctly stated; implied: Her silence gave implicit consent. **3.** involved as a necessary part or condition.
Syn. 1. unquestioning, unreserved. **2.** tacit.

im pound (im pound′), v. **1.** shut up in a pen or pound: impound stray animals. **2.** shut up; enclose; confine: A dam impounds water. **3.** put in the custody of a law court: The court impounded the documents to use as evidence. **—im pound′er,** n.

im preg na ble (im preg′nə bəl), adj. that cannot be overthrown by force; able to resist attack: an impregnable fortress, an impregnable argument.

im prob a ble (im prob′ə bəl), adj. not probable; not likely to happen; not likely to be true.

im pro vise (im′prə vīz), v., **-vised, -vis ing. 1.** compose or utter (verse, music, etc.) without preparation. **2.** prepare or provide offhand; extemporize: The boys improvised a tent out of two blankets and some long poles. [< F < Ital. improvvisare, ult. < L in- not + pro- beforehand + videre see] **—im′pro vis′er,** n.

im pu dent (im′pyə dənt), adj. without shame or modesty; forward; rudely bold. [< L impudens, -entis, ult. < in- not + pudere be modest] **—im′pu dent ly,** adv.
Syn. presumptuous.

im pul sive (im pul′siv), adj. **1.** acting upon impulse; easily moved: The impulsive child gave all his money to the beggar. **2.** driving onward; impelling. **—im pul′sive ly,** adv.
Syn. 1. rash, hasty, impetuous.

im pu ni ty (im pyü′nə tē), n. freedom from punishment, injury, or other bad consequences: If laws are not enforced, crimes are committed with impunity.

in ar tic u late (in′är tik′yə lit), adj. **1.** not distinct; not like regular speech: an inarticulate mutter or groan. **2.** unable to speak in words; unable to say what one thinks; dumb: Cats and dogs are inarticulate. **3.** not jointed: A jellyfish's body is inarticulate. [< LL inarticulatus] **—in′ar tic′u late ly,** adv. **—in′ar tic′u late ness,** n.

in cal cu la ble (in kal′kyə bəl), adj. **1.** too great in number to be counted; numerous: The sands of the beach are incalculable. **2.** not to be reckoned beforehand: A flood in the valley would cause incalculable losses. **3.** not to be relied on; uncertain. **—in cal′cu la bly,** adv.

< = from, derived from, taken from;　cf., compare;　dial., dialect;　dim., diminutive;　lang., language; pp., past participle;　ppr., present participle;　pt., past tense;　ult., ultimately;　var., variant;　? = possibly.

in cense (in sens′), v., -censed, -cens ing. make very angry; fill with rage.
  Syn. enrage, madden, provoke.

in cen tive (in sen′tiv), n. thing that urges a person on; cause of action or effort; motive; stimulus.

in ces sant (in ses′nt), adj. never stopping; continued or repeated without interruption. [< LL incessans, -antis < L in-not + cessare cease] —**in ces′sant ly,** adv.
  Syn. ceaseless, continual.

in cip i ent (in sip′ē ənt), adj. just beginning; in an early stage. —**in cip′i ent ly,** adv.

in ci sive (in sī′siv), adj. sharp; penetrating; piercing; keen: an incisive criticism. —**in ci′sive ly,** adv.

in com pa ra ble (in kom′pər ə bəl, in kom′prə bəl), adj. 1. without equal; matchless: Helen of Troy had incomparable beauty. 2. not to be compared; unsuitable for comparison. —**in com′par a bly,** adv.
  Syn. 1. peerless, unequaled.

in com pre hen si ble (in′kom pri hen′sə bəl), adj. impossible to understand.

in cred u lous (in krej′ə ləs), adj. 1. not ready to believe; not credulous; doubting: People nowadays are incredulous about ghosts and witches. 2. showing a lack of belief. —**in cred′u lous ly,** adv.

in crim i nate (in krim′ə nāt), v., -nat ed, -nat ing. accuse of a crime; show to be guilty: In his confession the thief incriminated two others who helped him steal. [< LL incriminare < L in- against + crimen charge] —**in crim′i na′tion,** n.

in cur (in kėr′), v., -curred, -cur ring. run or fall into (something unpleasant); bring (blame, danger, etc.) on oneself: The hunter incurred great danger in killing the tiger.

in dig nant (in dig′nənt), adj. angry at something unworthy, unjust, or mean. —**in dig′nant ly,** adv.
  Syn. incensed, provoked, displeased.

in dis tinct (in′dis tingkt′), adj. not distinct; not clear to the eye, ear, or mind; confused. —**in′dis tinct′ly,** adv.
  Syn. undefined, vague.

in dom i ta ble (in dom′ə tə bəl), adj. unconquerable; unyielding. —**in dom′i ta bly,** adv.

in duce (in düs′, in dyüs′), v., -duced, -duc ing. 1. lead on; influence; persuade: Advertising induces people to buy. 2. cause; bring about: Some drugs induce sleep. 3. produce (an electric current, electric charge, or magnetic change) without direct contact. 4. infer by reasoning from particular facts to a general rule or principle.
  Syn. 1. incite, impel.

in duct (in dukt′), v. 1. bring in; introduce (into a place, seat, position, office, etc.). 2. put formally in possession (of an office, etc.): Mr. Gage was inducted into the office of governor. 3. U.S. enroll in military service. 4. initiate. [< L inductus, pp. of inducere.]

in dulge (in dulj′), v., -dulged, -dulg ing. 1. yield to the wishes of; humor: We often indulge a sick person. 2. give way to: We do not indulge all our desires. 3. give way to one's pleasures; give oneself up to; allow oneself something desired: He indulges in tobacco. [< L indulgere]
  Syn. 1. gratify.

in dul gence (in dul′jəns), n. 1. an indulging. 2. thing indulged in. 3. favor; privilege. 4. in the Roman Catholic Church, remission of the punishment still due to sin after the guilt has been forgiven.

in ef fec tu al (in′ə fek′chü əl), adj. 1. without effect; useless. 2. not able to produce the effect wanted.
  Syn. ineffective, futile, vain.

in e luc ta ble (in i luk′tə bəl), adj. that cannot be escaped or avoided. [< L ineluctabilis in- not + eluctabilis escapable < eluctari to escape < ex- out + luctari to struggle, wrestle] —**in′e luc′ta bly,** adv.

in ert (in ėrt′), adj. 1. having no power to move or act; lifeless: A stone is an inert mass of matter. 2. inactive; slow; sluggish. 3. with few or no active properties: Helium and neon are inert gases. [< L iners, inertis idle, unskilled < in- without + ars art, skill] —**in ert′ly,** adv. —**in ert′ness,** n.

in ev i ta ble (in ev′ə tə bəl), adj. not avoidable; sure to happen; certain to come: Death is inevitable. [< L inevitabilis < in- not + evitabilis avoidable < evitare avoid < ex- + vitare avoid] —**in ev′i ta bly,** adv.

in ex pli ca ble (in′ik splik′ə bəl, in ek′splə kə bəl), adj. impossible to explain or understand; mysterious. [< L inexplicabilis] —**in′ex plic′a bly,** adv.

in fer nal (in fėr′nl), adj. 1. of hell; having to do with the lower world. 2. hellish; diabolical. 3. Informal. abominable; outrageous.

in fi nite (in′fə nit), adj. 1. without limits or bounds; endless. 2. extremely great: Teaching little children takes infinite patience. —n. 1. that which is infinite. 2. the Infinite, God. —**in′fi nite ness,** n.
  Syn. adj. 1. boundless, unlimited. 2. immeasurable, immense.

in fi nite ly (in′fə nit lē), adv. to an infinite degree.

in fin i ty (in fin′ə tē), n., pl. -ties. 1. state of being infinite. 2. an infinite distance, space, time, or quantity. 3. an infinite extent, amount, or number: the infinity of God's mercy. 4. to infinity, without limits or bounds; endlessly. [< L infinitas]

in flec tion (in flek′shən), n. 1. change in the tone or pitch of the voice: We usually end questions with a rising inflection. 2. in grammar, a variation in the form of a word to show case, number, gender, person, tense, mood, or comparison. 3. bending; curving. 4. bend; curve.

in fold (in fōld′), v. 1. fold in; wrap up: The old lady was infolded in a shawl. 2. embrace; clasp: The mother infolded her baby in her arms. Also, **enfold.**

in fringe ment (in frinj′mənt), n. 1. violation. 2. a trespassing.

in laid (in′lād′), adj. 1. set in the surface as a decoration or design: The desk had an inlaid design of light wood in dark. 2. decorated with a design or material set in the surface: The box had an inlaid cover.

Design made by inlaying black in white

in quire (in kwīr′), v., -quired, -quir ing. 1. try to find out by questions; ask. 2. make a search for information, knowledge, or truth; make an examination of facts or principles. Also, **enquire.** [< L inquirere < in- into + quaerere ask]

in quis i tive (in kwiz′ə tiv), adj. 1. curious; asking many questions. 2. too curious; prying into other people's affairs. —**in quis′i tive ly,** adv.

in sig nif i cant (in′sig nif′ə kənt), adj. 1. having little use or importance. 2. meaningless. —**in′sig nif′i cant ly,** adv.
  Syn. 1. petty, trifling.

in sist ent (in sis′tənt), adj. 1. insisting; continuing to make a strong, firm demand or statement: In spite of the rain he was insistent on going out. 2. compelling attention or notice; pressing; urgent.

in still or **in stil** (in stil′), v., -stilled, -still ing. 1. put in little by little; impart gradually: Reading good books instills a love for really fine literature. 2. put in drop by drop. [< L instillare < in- + stilla a drop]

hat, āge, fär;   let, bē, tėrm;   it, īce;   hot, gō, ôrder;   oil, out;   cup, pút, rüle;   ch, child;   ng, long;
th, thin;   ŦH, then;   zh, measure;   ə represents a in about, e in taken, i in pencil, o in lemon, u in circus.

in suf fer a ble (in suf′ər ə bəl), *adj.* intolerable; unbearable: *insufferable insolence.*

in su per a ble (in sü′pər ə bəl), *adj.* that cannot be passed over or overcome: *an insuperable barrier.*
Syn. insurmountable, impassable.

in te gral (in′tə grəl), *adj.* 1. necessary to the completeness of the whole; essential: *Steel is an integral part of a modern skyscraper.* 2. entire; complete.

in tel li gi ble (in tel′ə jə bəl), *adj.* capable of being understood; comprehensible. —**in tel′li gi bly,** *adv.*
Syn. understandable, plain, clear.

in tent (in tent′), *adj.* 1. very attentive; having the eyes or thoughts earnestly fixed on something; earnest: *an intent look.* 2. earnestly engaged; much interested: *He is intent on making money.* —**in tent′ly,** *adv.*

in ter cept (in′tər sept′), *v.* 1. take or seize on the way from one place to another: *intercept a letter or a messenger.* 2. cut off (light, water, etc.). 3. check; stop: *intercept the flight of a criminal.*

in ter change a ble (in′tər chān′jə bəl), *adj.* 1. capable of being used in place of each other. 2. able to change places. —**in′ter change′a bly,** *adv.*

in ter est (in′tər ist), *n.* 1. a feeling of wanting to know, see, do, own, share in, or take part in: *Boys usually have an interest in sports.* 2. power of arousing such a feeling: *A dull book lacks interest.* 3. share; part: *He bought a half interest in the farm.* 4. thing in which a person has an interest, share, or part. Any business, activity, or pastime can be an interest. 5. group of people having the same business, activity, etc. 6. advantage; benefit: *Each person should look after his own interest.* 7. **in the interest of,** for; to help. 8. money paid for the use of money. If you borrow money from a bank, you must pay interest on the loan. 9. something extra given in return: *She returned our favor with interest.* —*v.* 1. arouse the attention, curiosity, etc., of: *An exciting story interests you.* 2. cause (a person) to take a share or interest in something: *The agent tried to interest us in buying a car.*
Syn. *v.* 1. engage, occupy, entertain.

in ter ject (in′tər jekt′), *v.* throw in between other things; insert abruptly: *Every now and then the speaker interjected some witty remark.* [< L *interjectus,* pp. of *interjicere* < *inter-* between + *jacere* throw]

in ter mi na ble (in tèr′mə nə bəl), *adj.* endless; so long as to seem endless.
Syn. unending, limitless.

in tern (in′tèrn), *n.* doctor acting as a resident assistant in a hospital; interne. —*v.* act as an intern.

in ter sperse (in′tər spèrs′), *v.,* -spersed, -spers ing. 1. vary with something put here and there: *The grass was interspersed with beds of flowers.* 2. scatter here and there among other things: *Bushes were interspersed among trees.*

in ter ur ban (in′tər èr′bən), *adj.* between cities or towns. [Am.E]

in ti ma cy (in′tə mə sē), *n., pl.* -cies. 1. a being intimate; close acquaintance. 2. a familiar or intimate act.

in tim i date (in tim′ə dāt), *v.,* -dat ed, -dat ing. 1. frighten; make afraid. 2. influence or force by fear.

in tol er a ble (in tol′ər ə bəl), *adj.* unbearable; too much, too painful, etc., to be endured.

in tox i cat ed (in tok′sə kā′tid), *adj.* 1. drunk. 2. excited beyond self-control.

in trude (in trüd′), *v.,* -trud ed, -trud ing. 1. thrust oneself in; come unasked and unwanted. 2. thrust in; force in: *Do not intrude your opinions upon others.* [< L *intrudere* < *in-* in + *trudere* thrust]

in var i a ble (in ver′ē ə bəl, in var′ē ə bəl), *adj.* always the same; unchangeable; unchanging.
Syn. uniform, constant.

in vert (in vèrt′), *v.* 1. turn upside down: *invert a glass.* 2. turn around or reverse in position, direction, order, etc.: *If you invert "I can," you have "Can I?"*

in vig o rate (in vig′ə rāt′), *v.,* -rat ed, -rat ing. give vigor to; fill with life and energy. [< *in-* in + *vigor*] —**in vig′o rat′ing ly,** *adv.*
Syn. brace, refresh, stimulate, animate.

in volve (in volv′), *v.,* -volved, -volv ing. 1. have as a necessary part, condition, or result; take in; include: *House-keeping involves cooking, washing dishes, sweeping, and cleaning.* 2. have an effect on; affect: *These changes in the business involve the interests of all the owners.* 3. cause to be unpleasantly concerned; bring (into difficulty, danger, etc.): *One foolish mistake can involve you in a good deal of trouble.* 4. entangle; complicate: *A sentence that is involved is often hard to understand.* 5. take up the attention of; occupy: *She was involved in working out a puzzle.*

Io nich, Kuz ma (kəz nich′)

i rate (ī′rāt, ī rāt′), *adj.* angry. —**i′rate ly,** *adv.*

ir res o lute (i rez′ə lüt), *adj.* not resolute; unable to make up one's mind; not sure of what one wants; hesitating: *Irresolute persons make poor leaders.* —**ir res′o lute ly,** *adv.* —**ir res′o lute ness,** *adv.*
Syn. doubtful.

ir ri ta bil i ty (ir′ə tə bil′ə tē), *n., pl.* -ties. 1. a being irritable; impatience. 2. an unnatural sensitiveness (of an organ or part of the body).

---

jar (jär), *v.,* jarred, jar ring, *n.* —*v.* 1. shake; rattle: *Your heavy footsteps jar my table.* 2. make a harsh, grating noise. 3. have a harsh, unpleasant effect on; shock: *The children's screams jar my nerves.* 4. clash; quarrel: *Our opinions jar.* —*n.* 1. a shake; rattle. 2. a harsh, grating noise. 3. a harsh, unpleasant effect; shock. 4. a clash; quarrel. [probably imitative]
Syn. *v.* 2. scrape, grate.

jaun ty (jôn′tē, jän′tē), *adj.,* -ti er, -ti est. 1. easy and lively; sprightly; carefree: *The happy boy walked with jaunty steps.* 2. smart; stylish. —**jaun′ti ly,** *adv.*
Syn. 1. airy, gay.

jeer (jir), *v.* make fun rudely or unkindly; mock; scoff. —*n.* a jeering remark; rude, sarcastic comment.

jeop ard ize (jep′ər dīz), *v.,* -ized, -iz ing. risk; endanger; imperil: *Soldiers jeopardize their lives in war.*

jer kin (jèr′kən), *n.* a short coat or jacket, with or without sleeves. Men wore tight leather jerkins in the 16th and 17th centuries. [origin uncertain]

jest¹ (jest), *n.* 1. joke. 2. act of poking fun; mockery.

jet¹ (jet), *n.* 1. a stream of water, steam, gas, or any liquid, sent with force, especially from a small opening: *A fountain sends up a jet of water.* 2. a spout or nozzle for sending out a jet. 3. a jet plane.

jet² (jet), *n.* 1. a hard black mineral, glossy when polished, used for making beads, buttons, etc.

job printing (job prin′ting), *n.* small jobs such as the printing of business cards, letterheads, circulars.

jo cose (jō kōs′), *adj.* jesting; humorous; playful. [< L *jocosus* < *jocus* jest] —**jo cose′ly,** *adv.*

jounce (jouns), *v.,* jounced, jounc ing, *n.* bounce; bump; jolt. [origin uncertain]

< = from, derived from, taken from;   cf., compare;   dial., dialect;   dim., diminutive;   lang., language; pp., past participle;   ppr., present participle;   pt., past tense;   ult., ultimately;   var., variant;   ? = possibly.

jo vi al (jō′vē əl), *adj.* good-hearted and full of fun; good-humored and merry. [< L *Jovialis* pertaining to Jupiter (those born under the planet's sign being supposedly cheerful)] —**jo′vi al ly,** *adv.*

ju di cious (jü dish′əs), *adj.* having, using, or showing good judgment; wise; sensible: *A judicious historian selects and considers facts carefully and critically.* [< F *judicieux* < L *judicium* judgment < *judex* judge] —**ju di′cious ly,** *adv.* **Syn.** prudent, astute.

jun to (jun′tō), *n., pl.* **-tos.** a political faction; group of plotters or partisans.

ka ty did (kā′tē did), *n.* a large green insect somewhat like a grasshopper. The male makes a shrill noise sounding like "Katy did, Katy didn't."

keen (kēn), *adj.* 1. so shaped as to cut well: *a keen blade.* 2. sharp; piercing; cutting: *keen wind, keen hunger, keen wit, keen pain.* 3. strong; vivid: *keen competition.* 4. able to do its work quickly and accurately: *a keen mind, a keen sense of smell.* 5. *Informal.* full of enthusiasm; eager: *Tom is keen about sailing.* [OE *cēne*] —**keen′ly,** *adv.*

ker chief (kėr′chif), *n.* 1. piece of cloth worn over the head or around the neck. 2. handkerchief.

ker o sene or **ker o sine** (ker′ə sēn, ker′ə sēn′), *n.* a thin oil, a mixture of hydrocarbons, usually produced by distilling petroleum; coal oil. It is used in lamps and stoves.

kin (kin), *n.* 1. family or relatives; kindred. 2. family relationship; connection by birth or marriage: *What kin is she to you?* 3. **near of kin,** closely related. 4. **of kin,** related. —*adj.* related. [OE *cynn*] —**kin′less,** *adj.*

knave (nāv), *n.* 1. a tricky, dishonest person; rogue; rascal. 2. the jack, a playing card with a picture of a servant or soldier on it. 3. *Archaic.* a male servant; man of humble birth or position.
Syn. 1. scoundrel.

knav er y (nā′vər ē), *n., pl.* **-er ies.** 1. behavior characteristic of a knave. 2. a tricky, dishonest act.

Ky ri a kos (kē′rē ä′kôs)

lac quer (lak′ər), *n.* 1. varnish consisting of shellac dissolved in alcohol, used for coating brass. 2. varnish made from the resin of a sumac tree of SE Asia. It gives a very high polish on wood. 3. wooden articles coated with such varnish. —*v.* coat with lacquer.

lag (lag), *v.,* **lagged, lag ging.** move too slowly; fall behind.

la ment (lə ment′), *v.* 1. express grief for; mourn for: *lament the dead.* 2. express grief; mourn; weep: *Why does she lament?* 3. regret: *We lamented his absence.* —*n.* 1. expression of grief; wail. 2. poem, song, or tune that expresses grief. 3. a regret. [< L *lamentari* < *lamentum* a wailing]

lank (langk), *adj.* 1. long and thin; slender; lean: *a lank boy.* 2. straight and flat; not curly or wavy: *lank hair.* —**lank′ly,** *adv.* —**lank′ness,** *n.*

lap is laz u li (lap′is laz′yə lī, lap′is laz′yə lē), 1. a deep blue, opaque semiprecious stone used for an ornament. 2. deep blue. [< Med.L < L *lapis* stone + Med.L *lazuli,* gen. of *lazulum* lapis lazuli < Arabic < Persian *lajward.* Cf. *azure.*]

lar der (lär′dər), *n.* 1. pantry; place where food is kept. 2. stock of food.

la tent (lāt′nt), *adj.* present but not active; hidden; con-cealed: *latent germs of disease, latent powers, latent ability.* [< L *latens, -entis,* ppr. of *latere* lie hidden]

lat tice (lat′is), *n., v.,* **-ticed, -tic ing.** —*n.* 1. structure of crossed wooden or metal strips with open spaces between them. 2. window, gate, etc., having a lattice. —*v.* 1. form into a lattice; make like a lattice. 2. furnish with a lattice.

lea (lē), *n.* a grassy field; meadow; pasture.

learn ed (lėr′nid), *adj.* having, showing, or requiring much knowledge; scholarly. —**learn′ed ly,** *adv.* **Syn.** educated, erudite.

Le ta ba Riv er (le tä′bə riv′ər)

lib er ate (lib′ə rāt′), *v.,* **-rat ed, -rat ing.** set free. **Syn.** emancipate, release.

li chen (lī′kən), *n.* plant that looks somewhat like moss and grows in patches on trees, rocks, etc.

lieu (lü), *n.* 1. place; stead. 2. **in lieu of,** in place of; instead of. [< F < L *locus*]

li lac (lī′lək, lī′lak), *n.* 1. shrub with clusters of tiny fragrant flowers. 2. the cluster of flowers. Most lilacs are pale pinkish-purple or white. 3. a pale pinkish purple. —*adj.* pale pinkish-purple. [< F < Sp. < Arabic < Persian *līlak* < *nīl* indigo < Skt. *nīla*]

limn (lim), *v.* 1. paint (a picture). 2. portray in words.

list less (list′lis), *adj.* seeming too tired to care about anything; not interested in things; not caring to be active. —**list′less ly,** *adv.* —**list′less ness,** *n.*
Syn. indifferent, languid.

lit er al ly (lit′ər əl ē), *adv.* word for word; without exaggeration or imagination.

lit ur gy (lit′ər jē), *n., pl.* **-gies.** form of public worship. Different churches use different liturgies. [< LL *liturgia* < Gk. *leitourgia* < (unrecorded) *leitos* public + *ergon* work]

loath some (lōᴛʜ′səm), *adj.* disgusting; sickening: *a loathsome odor.* —**loath′some ly,** *adv.*

log ic (loj′ik), *n.* 1. science of proof. 2. science of reasoning. 3. book on logic. 4. reasoning; use of argument. 5. reason; sound sense. [< LL < Gk. *logike* (*techne*) reasoning (art) < *logos* word]

lore (lôr, lōr), *n.* 1. facts and stories about a certain subject. 2. learning; knowledge. [OE *lār.* Related to *learn.*]

lounge (lounj), *v.,* **lounged, loung ing,** *n.* —*v.* stand, stroll, sit, or lie at ease and lazily. —*n.* 1. act or state of lounging. 2. a comfortable and informal room in which one can lounge, smoke, and be at ease. 3. couch; sofa. [origin uncertain] —**loung′er,** *n.*

low[1] (lō), *adj.* 1. not high or tall: *low walls.* 2. of less than ordinary height, depth, or quantity: *The well is getting low.* 3. near the ground, floor, or base: *a low shelf.* 4. lying or being below the general level: *low ground.* 5. small in amount, degree, force, value, etc.: *a low price.* 6. not loud; soft: *a low whisper.* 7. unfavorable; poor: *I have a low opinion of his abilities.* 8. depressed or dejected: *low spirits.* 9. mean or base; coarse; vulgar; degraded: *low company.* —*adv.* 1. near the ground, floor, or base: *fly low.* 2. in, at, or to a low portion, point, degree, condition, price, etc.: *The sun sank low. Supplies are running low.* 3. at low pitch; softly: *speak low.* —*n.* 1. that which is low. 2. arrangement of the gears used for the lowest speed in an automobile and similar machines. —**low′ness,** *n.*
Syn. *adj.* 5. moderate. 9. See **base.**

low[2] (lō), *v.* make the sound of a cow; moo. —*n.* sound a cow makes; mooing.

lu cent (lü′snt), *adj.* 1. shining; luminous. 2. letting the light through; clear. [< L *lucens, -entis,* ppr. of *lucere* shine] —**lu′cent ly,** *adv.*

---

hat, āge, fär;   let, bē, tėrm;   it, īce;   hot, gō, ôrder;   oil, out;   cup, put, rüle;   ch, child;   ng, long; th, thin;   ᴛʜ, then;   zh, measure;   ə represents *a* in about, *e* in taken, *i* in pencil, *o* in lemon, *u* in circus.

lu di crous (lü′də krəs), *adj.* amusingly absurd; ridiculous. **—lu′di crous ly,** *adv.*
Syn. laughable, comical.

lus cious (lush′əs), *adj.* 1. delicious; richly sweet: *a luscious peach.* 2. very pleasing to taste, smell, hear, see, or feel. **—lus′cious ly,** *adv.* **—lus′cious ness,** *n.*
Syn. 2. savory.

lus ter (lus′tər), *n.* 1. bright shine on the surface: *the luster of pearls.* 2. brightness: *Her eyes lost their luster.* 3. fame; glory; brilliance. 4. kind of china that has a lustrous surface. 5. a thin fabric of cotton and wool that has a lustrous surface. [< F < Ital. *lustro* < *lustrare* < L *lustrare* illuminate]
Syn. 1. sheen, gloss.

lux u ri ant (lug zhūr′ē ənt, luk shūr′ē ənt), *adj.* 1. growing thick and green. 2. producing abundantly. 3. rich in ornament. **—lux u′ri ant ly,** *adv.*

mal con tent (mal′kən tent′), *adj.* discontented; rebellious. **—n.** a discontented person; rebellious person.

mal ice (mal′is), *n.* active ill will; wish to hurt others; spite. [< OF < L *malitia* < *malus* evil]
Syn. spitefulness, grudge, rancor.

ma li cious (mə lish′əs), *adj.* showing active ill will; wishing to hurt others; spiteful. **—ma li′cious ly,** *adv.*

ma lign (mə līn′), *v.* speak evil of; slander: *You malign a generous person when you call him stingy.* [< OF < L *malignus* < *malus* evil + *gen-* birth, nature]

mal le a ble (mal′ē ə bəl), *adj.* 1. capable of being hammered or pressed into various shapes without being broken. Gold, silver, copper, and tin are malleable; they can be beaten into thin sheets. 2. adaptable; yielding. [< OF < L *malleare* hammer, v. < *malleus,* n.]

man gle (mang′gəl), *v.,* **-gled, -gling.** 1. cut or tear (the flesh) roughly. 2. spoil; ruin. [< AF *mangler,* ? < OF *mahaignier* < *mahaigne* injury]
Syn. 1. lacerate, mutilate.

Ma no lis (mä nô′lēs)

mar tial (mär′shəl), *adj.* 1. of war; suitable for war: *martial music.* 2. fond of fighting; warlike; brave: *a boy of martial spirit.* **—mar′tial ly,** *adv.*

ma son ry (mā′sn rē), *n., pl.* **-ries.** work built by a mason; stonework; brickwork.

ma te ri al ize (mə tir′ē ə līz), *v.,* **-ized, -iz ing.** 1. become an actual fact; be realized: *Our plans were good, but they did not materialize.* 2. give material form to: *An inventor materializes his ideas by building a model.* 3. appear in bodily form: *A spirit materialized from the smoke of the magician's fire.* 4. cause to appear in bodily form. **—ma te′ri al i za′tion,** *n.*

mea ger or **mea gre** (mē′gər), *adj.* poor; scanty.

med i tate (med′ə tāt), *v.,* **-tat ed, -tat ing.** 1. think; reflect: *Monks and nuns meditate on holy things for hours at a time.* 2. think about; consider; plan; intend.
Syn. 1. ponder.

med i ta tive (med′ə tā′tiv), *adj.* 1. fond of meditating. 2. expressing meditation. **—med′i ta′tive ly,** *adv.*

meek (mēk), *adj.* 1. patient; not easily angered; mild. 2. submitting tamely when ordered about or injured by others: *The boy was meek as a lamb when he was reproved.* [< Scand. *mjūkr* soft] **—meek′ly,** *adv.* **—meek′ness,** *n.*
Syn. 1. forbearing. 2. submissive, yielding, docile.
Ant. 1. arrogant.

meg a phone (meg′ə fōn), *n.* a large funnel-shaped horn used to increase the loudness of the voice or the distance at which it can be heard. [Am.E; < Gk. *megas* great + *phone* sound]

mel an cho li a (mel′ən kō′lē ə), *n.* a mental disorder characterized by great depression of spirits and gloomy fears. [< LL < Gk. *melancholia* < *melas* black + *chole* bile]

mel an chol y (mel′ən kol′ē), *n., pl.* **-chol ies,** *adj.* **—n.** 1. sadness; low spirits; tendency to be sad. 2. sober thoughtfulness; pensiveness. **—adj.** 1. sad; gloomy. 2. causing sadness; depressing: *a melancholy scene.* 3. soberly thoughtful; pensive.
Syn. *n.* 1. depression, dejection. **—adj.** 1. depressed, despondent, downcast.

mel o dra ma (mel′ə drä′mə, mel′ə dram′ə), *n.* a sensational drama with exaggerated appeal to the emotions and, usually, a happy ending.

met al (met′l), *n.* 1. substance such as iron, gold, silver, copper, lead, tin, aluminum, steel, bronze, and brass. 2. any chemical element whose atoms tend to lend electrons, or any mixture of such elements. 3. broken stone, cinders, etc., used for roads and roadbeds. 4. the melted material that becomes glass or pottery. 5. material; substance: *Cowards are not made of the same metal as heroes.* **—adj.** made of metal. [< OF < L < Gk. *metallon,* originally, mine]

met a mor phose (met′ə môr′fōz), *v.,* **-phosed, -phos ing.** change in form; transform: *The witch metamorphosed people into animals.*

met a mor pho sis (met′ə môr′fə sis), *n., pl.* **-ses** (-sēz). 1. change of form. Tadpoles become frogs by metamorphosis; they lose their tails and grow legs. 2. the changed form. 3. a noticeable or complete change of character, appearance, or condition. [< L < Gk. *metamorphosis,* ult. < *meta-* over + *morphe* form]

me te or (mē′tē ər), *n.* mass of stone or metal that comes toward the earth from outer space with enormous speed; shooting star. [< L < Gk. *meteoron* (thing) in the air < *meta-* up + *-aoros* lifted < *aeirein* lift]

mid dy (mid′ē), *n., pl.* **-dies.** 1. *Informal.* midshipman. 2. middy blouse.

middy blouse, a loose blouse like a sailor's.

mis-, *prefix.* 1. bad, as in *misformation, misgovernment.* 2. badly, as in *misform, mismade, mismake.*. 3. wrong, as in *mispronunciation, misvaluation.* 4. wrongly, as in *misclassify, mislabel.* [OE *mis(s)-,* or in borrowed words < OF *mes-* < OHG *missi-, missa-*]

mis shape (mis shāp′), *v.,* **-shaped, -shaped** or **-shap en, -shap ing.** shape badly; deform; make in the wrong shape.

mis shap en (mis shā′pən), *adj.* badly shaped; deformed. **—v.** a pp. of **misshape.**

mit i gate (mit′ə gāt), *v.,* **-gat ed, -gat ing.** make or become mild; make or become milder; soften. Anger, grief, pain, punishments, heat, cold, and many other conditions may be mitigated.

mo lest (mə lest′), *v.* meddle with and injure; interfere with and trouble; disturb. [OF < L *molestare* < *molestus* troublesome < *moles* burden] **—mo lest′er,** *n.*
Syn. harass, harry.

molt (mōlt), *v.* shed the feathers, skin, etc., before a new growth. **—n.** act or time of molting. Also, *esp. Brit.* **moult.** [ME *mout* < OE *mūtian* (as in *bemūtian* exchange for) < L *mutare* change]

mon e tar y (mon′ə ter′ē, mun′ə ter′ē), *adj.* of money: *a monetary reward.*

< = from, derived from, taken from;   cf., compare;   dial., dialect;   dim., diminutive;   lang., language; pp., past participle;   ppr., present participle;   pt., past tense;   ult., ultimately;   var., variant;   ? = possibly.

mon ger (mung′gər, mong′gər), *n.* *Brit.* dealer in some article.

mo not o ny (mə not′n ē), *n.* 1. sameness of tone or pitch. 2. lack of variety. 3. wearisome sameness. [< Gk. *monotonia*, ult. < *monos* single + *tonos* tone]

mope (mōp), *v.*, **moped, mop ing**, *n.* —*v.* be indifferent and silent; be gloomy and sad. —*n.* person who mopes. —**mop′er**, *n.*

mo rale (mə ral′), *n.* moral or mental condition as regards courage, confidence, enthusiasm, etc.

mo rass (mə ras′), *n.* 1. piece of low, soft, wet ground; swamp. 2. a difficult situation; puzzling mess.

mo rose (mə rōs′), *adj.* gloomy; sullen; ill-humored. —**mo rose′ly**, *adv.*
Syn. moody, surly, gruff.

mor sel (môr′səl), *n.* 1. a small bite; mouthful. 2. piece; fragment.

mor tar (môr′tər), *n.* mixture of lime, sand, and water, or of cement, sand, and water, for holding bricks or stones together.

mo sey (mō′zē), *v.*, **-seyed, -sey ing**. *U.S. Slang.* 1. shuffle along. 2. saunter; amble. [Am.E; origin uncertain]

muff (muf), *n.* 1. a covering of fur or other material for keeping both hands warm. One hand is put in at each end. 2. a clumsy failure to catch a ball that comes into one's hands. 3. awkward handling; bungling. —*v.* 1. fail to catch (a ball) when it comes into one's hands. 2. handle awkwardly; bungle. [< Dutch *mof* < F *moufle* mitten < OF *moufle* thick glove (cf. Med.L *muffula*), probably < Gmc. Related to *muffle*.]

muf fle (muf′əl), *v.*, **-fled, -fling**, *n.* —*v.* 1. wrap or cover up in order to keep warm and dry. 2. wrap oneself in garments, etc. 3. wrap up the head of (a person) in order to keep him from speaking. 4. wrap in something in order to soften or stop the sound. 5. dull or deaden (a sound). —*n.* 1. a muffled sound. 2. thing that muffles. [< OF *mofler* to stuff (cf. OF *enmouflé*, pp., wrapped up) < *moufle* thick glove. Related to *muff*.]

mu le teer (myü′lə tir′), *n.* driver of mules.

musk (musk), *n.* 1. substance with a strong and lasting odor, used in making perfumes. 2. the odor of musk.

musk y (mus′kē), *adj.*, **musk i er, musk i est.** of musk; like musk; like that of musk: *a musky odor.*

mu tin ous (myüt′n əs), *adj.* rebellious.

na sal (nā′zəl), *adj.* 1. of, in, or from the nose: *a nasal discharge.* 2. in phonetics, requiring the nose passage to be open; spoken through the nose. *M, n,* and *ng* represent nasal sounds. —*n.* in phonetics, a nasal sound. —**na′sal ly**, *adv.*

neb u la (neb′yə lə), *n.*, *pl.* **-lae** (-lē) or **-las.** a bright spot like a small, bright cloud, visible in the sky at night. A nebula may be either a mass of luminous gas or a cluster of stars very far away from our sun and its planets. [< L *nebula* mist]

nine pins (nīn′pinz′), *n.* game in which nine large wooden pins are set up to be bowled down with a ball.

non cha lant (non′shə lənt, non′shə länt′), *adj.* without enthusiasm; cooly unconcerned; indifferent. [< F *nonchalant* < *non-* not (< L) + *chaloir* be warm < L *calere*] —**non′cha lant ly**, *adv.*

Ninepins

non com bat ant (non′kəm bat′nt, non kom′bə tənt), *n.* person who is not a fighter in the army or navy in time of war; civilian. Surgeons, nurses, chaplains, etc., are noncombatants even though with the army. —*adj.* not fighting; having civilian status in wartime.

non com mit tal (non′kə mit′l), *adj.* not committing oneself; not saying yes or no: *"I will think it over" is a noncommittal answer.* —**non′com mit′tal ly**, *adv.*

nur ture (nėr′chər), *v.*, **-tured, -tur ing** 1. rear; bring up; care for; foster; train: *She nurtured the child as if he had been her own.* 2. nourish.

o a sis (ō ā′sis, ō′ə sis), *n.*, *pl.* **-ses.** a fertile spot in the desert where there is water. [< L < Gk. *oasis*, apparently < Egyptian]

o blique (ə blēk′; *military* ə blīk′), *adj.*, *v.*, **-bliqued, -bliqu ing.** —*adj.* 1. not straight up and down; not straight across; slanting. 2. not straightforward; indirect: *She made an oblique reference to her illness, but did not mention it directly.* —*v.* advance in an oblique manner; slant. [< L *obliquus*]

o bliv i ous (ə bliv′ē əs), *adj.* 1. forgetful; not mindful: *The book was so interesting that I was oblivious of my surroundings.* 2. bringing or causing forgetfulness.
Syn. 1. unmindful, heedless.

ob scure (əb skyùr′), *adj.*, **-scur er, -scur est,** *v.*, **-scured, -scur ing.** —*adj.* 1. not clearly expressed: *an obscure passage in a book.* 2. not expressing meaning clearly: *an obscure style of writing.* 3. not well known; attracting no notice: *an obscure little village, an obscure poet, an obscure position in the government.* 4. not easily discovered; hidden: *an obscure path, an obscure meaning.* 5. not distinct; not clear: *an obscure form, obscure sounds, an obscure view.* 6. dark; dim: *an obscure corner.* 7. indefinite: *an obscure brown, an obscure vowel.* —*v.* hide from view; make obscure; dim; darken: *Clouds obscure the sun.* [< OF < L *obscurus* < *ob-* over + *scur-* cover] —**ob scure′ly**, *adv.* —**ob scure′ness**, *n.*

ob se qui ous (əb sē′kwē əs), *adj.* polite or obedient from hope of gain or from fear; servile; fawning. —**ob se′qui ous ly**, *adv.*
Syn. slavish.

O cam po (ō′käm′pō)

oc cu pan cy (ok′yə pən sē), *n.* act or fact of occupying; holding (land, houses, a pew, etc.) by being in possession.

oil cloth (oil′klôth′, oil′kloth′), *n.* 1. cloth made waterproof by coating it with paint or oil. 2. cloth made waterproof by treating it with oil; oilskin.

om i nous (om′ə nəs), *adj.* of bad omen; unfavorable; threatening: *Those clouds look ominous for our picnic.* —**om′i nous ly**, *adv.*
Syn. inauspicious, foreboding.

o paque (ō pāk′), *adj.* 1. not letting light through; not transparent. 2. not shining; dark; dull. 3. obscure; hard to understand. 4. stupid. —*n.* something opaque. [< L *opacus* dark, shady] —**o paque′ness**, *n.*

op pres sive (ə pres′iv), *adj.* 1. harsh; severe; unjust. 2. hard to bear; burdensome. —**op pres′sive ly**, *adv.*

op ti mism (op′tə miz əm), *n.* 1. tendency to look on the bright side of things. 2. belief that everything will turn out for the best. 3. doctrine that the existing world is the best of all possible worlds. [< NL *optimismus* < L *optimus* best]

hat, āge, fär;   let, bē, tėrm;   it, īce;   hot, gō, ôrder;   oil, out;   cup, pùt, rüle;   ch, child;   ng, long;
th, thin;   ᴛʜ, then;   zh, measure;   ə represents *a* in about, *e* in taken, *i* in pencil, *o* in lemon, *u* in circus.

op tion (op′shən), *n.* 1. right or freedom of choice. 2. a choosing; choice. 3. right to buy something at a certain price within a certain time: *The man paid $500 for an option on the land.*
Syn. 2. preference.

op tion al (op′shə nəl), *adj.* left to one's choice; not required. —**op′tion al ly,** *adv.*

or a tor i cal (ôr′ə tôr′ə kəl, or′ə tor′ə kəl), *adj.* 1. of oratory; having to do with orators or oratory: *an oratorical contest.* 2. characteristic of orators or oratory: *an oratorical manner.* —**or′a tor′i cal ly,** *adv.*

or a to ry (ôr′ə tôr′ē, ôr′ə tōr′ē, or′ə tôr′ē, or′ə tōr′ē), *n.* 1. skill in public speaking; fine speaking. 2. art of public speaking.
Syn. 1. eloquence.

or deal (ôr dēl′, ôr′dēl), *n.* 1. a severe test or experience. 2. in early times, an effort to decide the guilt or innocence of an accused person by making him do something dangerous like holding fire or taking poison. It was supposed that an innocent person would not be harmed by such danger.
Syn. 1. trial.

or nate (ôr nāt′), *adj.* much adorned; much ornamented.
Syn. elaborate, showy.

out land ish (out lan′dish), *adj.* not familiar; queer; strange or ridiculous.
Syn. odd, bizarre.

o ver lap (ō′vər lap′), *v.,* **-lapped, -lap ping.** lap over; cover and extend beyond: *Shingles are laid to overlap each other.*

Pa dil la, Fran cis co (frän′sēs′kō pä ᴛᴀ̄′yä)

pale¹ (pāl), *adj.,* **pal er, pal est,** *v.,* **paled, pal ing.** —*adj.* 1. without much color; whitish. 2. not bright; dim. —*v.* turn pale. [< OF < L *pallidus* < *pallere* be pale. Doublet of PALLID.] —**pale′ly,** *adv.* —**pale′ness,** *n.*
Syn. *adj.* 1. **Pale, pallid, wan** mean with little or no color. **Pale,** describing the face of a person, means without much natural or healthy color, and describing things, without much brilliance or depth: *She is pale and tired-looking. The walls are pale green.* **Pallid,** chiefly describing the face, suggests having all color drained away, as by sickness or weakness: *Her pallid face shows her suffering.* **Wan** emphasizes the idea of a faintness and whiteness coming from a weakened or unhealthy condition: *The starved refugees were wan.* 2. faint, indistinct.

pale² (pāl), *n., v.,* **paled, pal ing.** —*n.* 1. a long, narrow board, pointed on top, used for fences. 2. boundary: *outside the pale of civilized society.* 3. a broad vertical stripe in the middle of a coat of arms. —*v.* enclose with pales.

Fence made of pales

pal ing (pāl′ing), *n.* 1. fence of pales. 2. pale in a fence.

pal let (pal′it), *n.* bed of straw; poor bed.

pal lid (pal′id), *adj.* lacking color; pale: *a pallid complexion.* [< L *pallidus.* Doublet of PALE¹.]
Syn. See **pale.**

pan de mo ni um (pan′də mō′nē əm), *n.* 1. abode of all the demons. 2. place of wild disorder or lawless confusion. 3. wild uproar or lawlessness.

pang (pang), *n.* a sudden, short, sharp pain or feeling.

pa pa ya (pə pä′yə), *n.* 1. a tropical American tree having a straight, palmlike trunk with a tuft of large leaves at the top and edible, melonlike fruit with yellowish pulp. 2. the fruit. [< Sp. *papaya* (def. 2) < *papayo* (def. 1) < Carib]

par af fin (par′ə fin), *n.* a white, tasteless substance like wax, used for making candles, for sealing jars, etc. It is obtained chiefly from crude petroleum.

par a sol (par′ə sôl, par′ə sol), *n.* umbrella used as a protection from the sun. [< F < Ital. *parasole* < *para* ward off + *sole* sun]

parch (pärch), *v.* 1. dry by heating; roast slightly: *Corn is sometimes parched.* 2. make hot and dry or thirsty. 3. become dry, hot, or thirsty.
Syn. 1. scorch, sear, singe, char.

par chee si or **par che si** (pär chē′zē), *n.* game somewhat like backgammon, played by moving pieces according to throws of dice. [< Hindu. *pachīsī* < *pachīs* twenty-five (highest throw) < Skt. *pañca* five + *viñçati* twenty]

pat i o (pat′ē ō), *n., pl.* **-i os.** 1. an inner court or yard open to the sky. 2. *U.S.* a terrace for outdoor eating, lounging, etc. [Am.E; < Sp.]

pa tri arch (pā′trē ärk), *n.* 1. father and ruler of a family or tribe. In the Bible, Abraham, Isaac, and Jacob were patriarchs. 2. person thought of as the father or founder of something. 3. a venerable old man. 4. bishop of the highest rank in the early Christian Church or in the Greek Church. [< L < Gk. *patriarches* < *patria* family + *archos* leader]

pat ri mo ni al (pat′rə mō′nē əl), *adj.* relating to property inherited from one's father or ancestors.

pau per (pô′pər), *n.* a very poor person; person supported by charity. [< L *pauper* poor]

peer (pir), *n.* 1. person of the same rank, ability, etc., as another; equal. 2. man who has a title; man who is high and great by birth or rank. A duke, marquis, earl, count, viscount, or baron is a peer. [< OF *per* < L *par* equal]

pen sive (pen′siv), *adj.* 1. thoughtful in a serious or sad way. 2. melancholy. [< OF *pensif* < *penser* think < L *pensare* weigh, ponder < *pendere* weigh] —**pen′sive ly,** *adv.* —**pen′sive ness,** *n.*
Syn. 1. meditative, reflective. 2. sober, grave, sad.

per emp to ry (pər emp′tə rē, per′əmp tô′rē, per′əmp-tō′rē), *adj.* 1. imperious; positive: *a peremptory teacher.* 2. allowing no denial or refusal: *a peremptory command.* 3. leaving no choice; decisive; final; absolute: *a peremptory decree.* —**per emp′to ri ly,** *adv.*

per func to ry (pər fungk′tə rē), *adj.* 1. done merely for the sake of getting rid of the duty; mechanical; indifferent: *The little boy gave his face a perfunctory washing.* 2. acting in a perfunctory way: *The new nurse was perfunctory; she did not really care about her work.* —**per func′to ri ly,** *adv.*
Syn. 1. careless, superficial.

per plex (pər pleks′), *v.* 1. trouble with doubt; puzzle; bewilder. 2. make difficult to understand or settle; confuse. —**per plex′ing ly,** *adv.*
Syn. 1. mystify, nonplus.

per plex i ty (pər plek′sə tē), *n., pl.* **-ties.** 1. perplexed condition; confusion; being puzzled; not knowing what to do or how to act. 2. something that perplexes.
Syn. 1. bewilderment.

per se cute (pėr′sə kyüt), *v.,* **-cut ed, -cut ing.** 1. treat badly; do harm to again and again; oppress. 2. punish for religious reasons. 3. annoy. —**per′se cu′tor,** *n.*
Syn. 1. wrong, torment. 3. harrass, worry.

per sist ent (pər sis′tənt, pər zis′tənt), *adj.* 1. persisting;

< = from, derived from, taken from;   cf., compare;   dial., dialect;   dim., diminutive;   lang., language; pp., past participle;   ppr., present participle;   pt., past tense;   ult., ultimately;   var., variant;   ? = possibly.

having lasting qualities, especially in the face of dislike, disapproval, or difficulties: *a persistent worker, a persistent beggar.* 2. lasting; going on; continuing: *a persistent headache that lasted for three days.* —**per sist′ent ly,** *adv.*
Syn. 1. persevering, untiring, insistent.

per vade (pər vād′), *v.,* **-vad ed, -vad ing.** go or spread throughout; be throughout: *The odor of pines pervades the air.*

per verse (pər vėrs′), *adj.* 1. contrary and willful; stubborn: *The perverse child did just what we told him not to do.* 2. persistent in wrong. 3. wicked. 4. not correct; wrong: *Perverse reasoning.* —**per verse′ly,** *adv.* —**per verse′ness,** *n.*
Syn. 1. obstinate, wayward.

pes ti lent (pes′tl ənt), *adj.* 1. often causing death: *a pestilent disease.* 2. harmful to morals; destroying peace: *a pestilent den of vice, the pestilent effects of war.* 3. troublesome; annoying.

pes tle (pes′əl, pes′tl), *n., v.,* **-tled, -tling.** —*n.* tool for pounding or crushing substances into a powder. —*v.* pound or crush with a pestle. [< OF *pestel* < L *pistillum* < *pinsere* to pound]

Pe tro vna, Na dye zhda (nə dē′zhdə pē trō′fnə)

pet ti coat (pet′ē kōt), *n.* 1. skirt that hangs from the waist or from the shoulders, worn beneath the dress by women, girls, and babies. 2. skirt.

pet tish (pet′ish), *adj.* cross. —**pet′tish ly,** *adv.*

pet u lant (pech′ə lənt), *adj.* subject to little fits of bad temper; irritable over trifles. —**pet′u lant ly,** *adv.*

phlegm (flem), *n.* 1. the thick discharge from the nose or throat that accompanies a cold. 2. sluggish disposition or temperament; indifference. 3. coolness; calmness. [< OF < LL < Gk. *phlegma* clammy humor (resulting from heat) < *phlegein* burn]

pi as ter or **pi as tre** (pē as′tər), *n.* 1. coin worth from about ¹/₂ cent to about 3 cents (1964), used in Turkey, Egypt, Lebanon, Syria, etc. 2. a former Spanish silver coin worth about a dollar. [< F *piastre* < Ital. < L *emplastrum* plaster]

pick et (pik′it), *n.* 1. a pointed stake or peg driven into the ground to make a fence, to tie a horse to, etc. 2. a small body of troops, or a single man, posted at some place to watch for the enemy and guard against surprise. 3. person stationed by a labor union near a factory, store, etc., where there is a strike. Pickets try to prevent employees from working or customers from buying.

pil lage (pil′ij), *v.,* **-laged, -lag ing,** *n.* —*v.* rob with violence; plunder: *Pirates pillaged the towns along the coast.* —*n.* plunder; robbery. [< OF *pillage* < *piller* plunder < VL *pileare* flay] —**pil′lag er,** *n.*
Syn. *v.* sack, strip.

pin a fore (pin′ə fôr′, pin′ə fōt′), *n.* 1. a child's apron that covers most of the dress. 2. a light dress without sleeves. [< *pin,* v. + *afore*]

pin ion (pin′yən), *n.* 1. the last joint of a bird's wing. 2. wing. 3. any one of the stiff flying feathers of the wing.

plac id (plas′id), *adj.* calm; peaceful; quiet: *a placid lake.* —**plac′id ly,** *adv.* —**plac′id ness,** *n.*

plain tive (plān′tiv), *adj.* mournful; sad. —**plain′tive ly,** *adv.*
Syn. doleful, sorrowful.

pli ant (plī′ənt), *adj.* 1. bending easily; flexible; supple. 2. easily influenced; yielding. —**pli′ant ly,** *adv.*

plun der (plun′dər), *v.* rob by force; rob. —*n.* 1. things taken in plundering; booty; loot: *They carried off the plunder*

in *their ships.* 2. act of robbing by force. [< G *plündern* < *Plunder* household goods]

plush (plush), *n.* fabric like velvet but thicker and softer. [< F *pluche,* ult. < L *pilus* hair]

poign an cy (poi′nyən sē), *n.* sharpness; piercing quality.

po man der (pə man′dər, pō′man dər), *n.* ball of mixed aromatic substances formerly carried for perfume or as a guard against infection.

pome gran ate (pom′gran′it, pom gran′it, pum′gran′it), *n.* 1. a reddish-yellow fruit with a thick skin, red pulp, and many seeds. 2. tree it grows on.

pom pa dour (pom′pə dôr, pom′pə dōr), *n.* 1. arrangement of a woman's hair in which it is puffed high over the forehead. 2. arrangement of a man's hair in which it is brushed straight up and back from the forehead. [named after the Marquise de *Pompadour*]

pop u lous (pop′yə ləs), *adj.* full of people; having many people per square mile.

por tal (pôr′tl, pōr′tl), *n.* door, gate, or entrance, usually an imposing one.

port man teau (pôrt man′tō, pōrt man′tō), *n., pl.* **-teaus** or **-teaux** (-tōz). *Esp. Brit.* a stiff, oblong traveling bag with two compartments opening like a book. [< F *pormanteau* < *porter* carry + *manteau* mantle]

pos er (pō′zər), *n.* a very puzzling problem. [< *pose*]

pos ter i ty (po ster′ə tē), *n.* 1. generations of the future. 2. all of a person's descendants.

post pone ment (pōst pōn′mənt), *n.* putting off till later; delay: *the postponement of a ball game.*

Pot a pov, Io na (ē ō′nə pat ä′pəf)

pot ter (pot′ər), *n.* person who makes pots, dishes, vases, etc., out of clay.

prec i pice (pres′ə pis), *n.* a very steep cliff; almost vertical slope. [< F < L *praecipitium* < *praeceps* steep, literally, headlong < *prae-* first + *caput* head]

pre cip i ta tion (pri sip′ə tā′shən), *n.* 1. act or state of precipitating; throwing down or falling headlong. 2. a hastening or hurrying. 3. a sudden bringing on: *the precipitation of a war without warning.* 4. unwise or rash rapidity; sudden haste. 5. the separating out of a substance from a solution as a solid. **b.** substance separated out from a solution as a solid. 6. **a.** the depositing of moisture in the form of rain, dew, or snow. **b.** something that is precipitated, such as rain, dew, or snow. **c.** amount that is precipitated.

pre ci sion (pri sizh′ən), *n.* accuracy; exactness.

pre co cious (pri kō′shəs), *adj.* 1. developed earlier than usual: *This very precocious child could read well at the age of four.* 2. developed too early. [< L *praecox, -ocis,* ult. < *prae-* before (its time) + *coquere* ripen] —**pre co′cious ly,** *adv.* —**pre co′cious ness,** *n.*

pred e ces sor (pred′ə ses′ər), *n.* 1. person holding a position or office before another: *John Adams was Jefferson's predecessor as President.* 2. thing that came before another. 3. ancestor; forefather.

pre dic a ment (pri dik′ə mənt), *n.* 1. an unpleasant, difficult, or dangerous situation. 2. any condition, state, or situation.

prej u dice (prej′ə dis), *n., v.,* **-diced, -dic ing.** —*n.* 1. opinion formed without taking time and care to judge fairly: *a prejudice against doctors.* 2. harm; injury: *I will do nothing to the prejudice of my cousin in this matter.* —*v.* 1. cause a prejudice in; fill with prejudice: *One unfortunate experience prejudiced him against all lawyers.* 2. damage; harm; injure. [< F < L *praejudicium* < *prae-* before + *judicium* judgment]

---

hat, āge, fär;   let, bē, tėrm;   it, īce;   hot, gō, ôrder;   oil, out;   cup, půt, rüle;   ch, child;   ng, long;
th, thin;   ƒH, then;   zh, measure;   ə represents *a* in about, *e* in taken, *i* in pencil, *o* in lemon, *u* in circus.

pre sump tion (pri zump′shən), *n.* 1. act of presuming. 2. thing taken for granted: *Since he had the stolen jewels, the presumption was that he was the thief.* 3. cause or reason for presuming; probability. 4. unpleasant boldness: *It is presumption to go to a party when one has not been invited.* **Syn.** 4. forwardness.

pri me val (prī mē′vl), *adj.* 1. of or having to do with the first age or ages, especially of the world: *In its primeval state the earth was a fiery glowing ball.* 2. ancient; *primeval forests untouched by the ax.* [< L *primaevus* early in life < *primus* first + *aevum* age]

pro ceed ing (prə sē′ding), *n.* 1. action; conduct; what is done. 2. **proceedings,** *pl.* **a.** action in a case in a law court. **b.** record of what was done at the meetings of a society, club, etc. **Syn.** 1. performance.

proc la ma tion (prok′lə mā′shən), *n.* an official announcement; public declaration: *the President's annual Thanksgiving proclamation.*

pro fane (prə fān′), *adj.* 1. not sacred; worldly: *profane literature.* 2. with contempt or disregard for God or holy things: *profane language.*

pro fuse (prə fyüs′), *adj.* 1. very abundant: *profuse thanks.* 2. spending or giving freely; lavish; extravagant: *He was so profuse with his money that he is now poor.* [< L *profusus* poured forth, pp. of *profundere* < *pro-* forth + *fundere* pour] **—pro fuse′ly,** *adv.*

pro fu sion (prə fyü′zhən), *n.* 1. great abundance. 2. extravagance; lavishness.

prom e nade (prom′ə nād′, prom′ə näd′), *n., v.,* **-nad ed, -nad ing.** **—n.** 1. walk for pleasure or display: *The Easter promenade is well known as a fashion show.* 2. a public place for such a walk. 3. dance; ball. 4. march of all the guests at the opening of a formal dance. **—v.** 1. walk about or up and down for pleasure or for display: *He promenaded back and forth on the ship's deck.* 2. walk through. 3. take on a promenade. [< F *promenade* < *promener* take for a walk] **—prom′e nad′er,** *n.*

prom on to ry (prom′ən tô′rē, prom′ən tō′rē), *n., pl.* **-ries.** a high point of land extending from the coast into the water; headland.

pro mo tion (prə mō′shən), *n.* 1. advance in rank or importance: *The clerk was given a promotion and an increase in salary.* 2. helping to grow or develop; helping along to success: *The doctors were busy in the promotion of a health campaign.* 3. helping to organize; starting: *It took much time and money for the promotion of the new company.*

pro nounced (prə nounst′), *adj.* strongly marked; decided: *She held pronounced opinions on gambling.*

pro nounc ed ly (prə noun′sid lē), *adv.* in a pronounced manner; to a pronounced degree.

pro phet ic (prə fet′ik), *adj.* 1. belonging to a prophet; such as a prophet has: *prophetic power.* 2. containing prophecy: *a prophetic saying.* 3. giving warning of what is to happen; foretelling.

pro pound (prə pound′), *v.* put forward; propose: *propound a theory, a question, or a riddle.*

pros e cute (pros′ə kyüt), *v.,* **-cut ed, -cut ing.** 1. bring before a court of law: *Reckless drivers will be prosecuted.* 2. bring a case before a law court. 3. carry out; follow up: *He prosecuted an inquiry into reasons for the company's failure.* 4. carry on (a business or occupation). [< L *prosecutus,* pp. of *prosequi* pursue < *pro-* forth + *sequi* follow]

prov i dence (prov′ə dəns), *n.* 1. God's care and help. 2. instance of God's care and help. 3. care for the future; good management. 4. **Providence,** God.

pro voc a tive (prə vok′ə tiv), *adj.* 1. irritating; vexing. 2. tending or serving to call forth action, thought, laughter, anger, etc.: *a remark provocative of mirth.* **—n.** something that rouses or irritates. **—pro voc′a tive ly,** *adv.* **—pro voc′a tive ness,** *n.*

pro voke (prə vōk′), *v.,* **-voked, -vok ing.** 1. make angry; vex. 2. stir up; excite: *An insult provokes a person to anger.* 3. call forth; bring about; start into action; cause. **Syn.** 1. exasperate. 2. rouse, kindle.

prox im i ty (prok sim′ə tē), *n.* nearness; closeness.

pru dent (prüd′nt), *adj.* planning carefully ahead of time; sensible; discreet: *A prudent man saves part of his wages.* **—pru′dent ly,** *adv.* **Syn.** judicious, wise.

prud er y (prü′dər ē), *n., pl.* **-er ies.** 1. extreme modesty or propriety, especially when not genuine. 2. a prudish act or remark.

pub li cize (pub′lə sīz), *v.,* **-cized, -ciz ing.** give publicity to.

puce (pyüs), *n.* a purplish brown. **—adj.** purplish-brown.

punk (pungk), *n.* 1. a preparation that burns very slowly. A stick of punk is used to light fireworks. 2. decayed wood used as tinder. **—adj.** *U.S. Slang.* poor or bad in quality. [Am.E; ? < Am.Ind.]

pur chase (pėr′chəs), *n.* 1. act of buying. 2. thing bought. 3. a firm hold to help move something or to keep from slipping: *Wind the rope twice around the tree to get a better purchase.* 4. device for obtaining such a hold.

pur ga to ry (pėr′gə tô′rē, pėr′gə tō′rē), *n., pl.* **-ries.** 1. in some religious beliefs, a temporary condition or place in which the souls of those who have died in grace are purified from sin by punishment. 2. any condition or place of temporary suffering or punishment.

pur loin (pər loin′), *v.* steal.

pu sil lan i mous (pyü′sə lan′ə məs), *adj.* cowardly; mean-spirited; faint-hearted. **—pu′sil lan′i mous ly,** *adv.* **Syn.** timorous, spiritless.

pu tre fy (pyü′trə fī), *v.,* **-fied, -fy ing.** rot; decay.

put ter (put′ər), *v.* keep busy in a rather useless way. Also, *esp. Brit.* **potter. —put′ter er,** *n.*

quad rant (kwod′rənt), *n.* 1. quarter of a circle or of its circumference. 2. instrument used in astronomy, navigation, etc., for measuring altitudes.

quaff (kwäf, kwaf, kwôf), *v.* drink in large draughts; drink freely. **—n.** a quaffing. [origin uncertain]

quaint (kwānt), *adj.* strange or odd in an interesting, pleasing, or amusing way: *Old photographs seem quaint to us today.* [< OF *cointe* pretty < L *cognitus* known] **—quaint′ly,** *adv.* **—quaint′ness,** *n.*

quea sy (kwē′zē), *adj.,* **-si er, -si est.** 1. inclined to nausea; easily upset. 2. tending to unsettle the stomach. 3. uneasy; uncomfortable. 4. squeamish; fastidious. **—quea′si ly,** *adv.* **—quea′si ness,** *n.*

ra di ate (rā′dē āt; *adj. also* rā′dē it), *v.,* **-at ed, -at ing.** *adj.* **—v.** 1. give out rays of: *The sun radiates light and heat.* 2. give out rays; shine. 3. issue in rays: *Heat radiates from those hot steam pipes.* 4. give out; send forth: *Her face radiates joy.* 5. spread out from a center: *Roads radiate from the city in every direction.* **—adj.** 1. having rays: *A*

< = from, derived from, taken from;　　cf., compare;　　dial., dialect;　　dim., diminutive;　　lang., language; pp., past participle;　　ppr., present participle;　　pt., past tense;　　ult., ultimately;　　var., variant;　　? = possibly.

daisy is a radiate flower. 2. radiating from a center. [< L *radiare*]

ram bunc tious (ram bungk′shəs), *adj.* *U.S. Slang.* 1. wild and uncontrollable; unruly. 2. noisy and violent; boisterous.

rank (rangk), *adj.* strongly marked; extreme.

rant (rant), *v.* speak wildly, extravagantly, violently, or noisily. —*n.* extravagant, violent, or noisy speech.

rapt (rapt), *adj.* 1. lost in delight. 2. so busy thinking of or enjoying one thing that one does not know what else is happening. 3. carried away in body or spirit from earth, life, or ordinary affairs. 4. showing a rapt condition; caused by a rapt condition: *a rapt smile.* —**rapt′ly,** *adv.* **Syn.** 1. enraptured, ecstatic. 2. engrossed, spellbound. 3. transported.

rar i ty (rer′ə tē, rar′ə tē), *n., pl.* **-ties.** 1. something rare: *A man over a hundred years old is a rarity.* 2. fewness; scarcity. 3. lack of density; thinness: *The rarity of the air in the mountains is bad for people with weak hearts.*

rash¹ (rash), *adj.* too hasty; careless; reckless; taking too much risk. —**rash′ly,** *adv.*

rash² (rash), *n.* a breaking out with many small red spots on the skin. Scarlet fever causes a rash.

re as sur ance (rē′ə shùr′əns), *n.* 1. new or fresh assurance. 2. restoration of courage or confidence.

re cip ro cate (ri sip′rə kāt), *v.,* **-cat ed, -cat ing.** 1. give, do, feel, or show in return: *She likes me, and I reciprocate her liking.* 2. move or cause to move with an alternating backward and forward motion.

re cit al (ri sī′tl), *n.* 1. act of reciting; telling facts in detail: *Her recital of her experiences in the hospital bored her hearers.* 2. story; account. 3. a musical entertainment, given usually by a single performer. **Syn.** 2. narration.

re com mence (rē′kə mens′), *v.,* **-menced, -menc ing.** begin again.

rec on cile (rek′ən sīl), *v.,* **-ciled, -cil ing.** 1. make friends again. 2. settle (a quarrel, disagreement, etc.). 3. make agree; bring into harmony: *It is impossible to reconcile his story with the facts.* 4. make satisfied; make no longer opposed: *It is hard to reconcile oneself to being sick a long time.* [< L *reconciliare*, ult. < *re-* back + *concilium* bond of union] —**rec′on cil′a ble,** *adj.* —**rec′on cil′er,** *n.*

re count (ri kount′), *v.* tell in detail; give an account of: *He recounted all the happenings of the day.*

re crim i na tion (ri krim′ə nā′shən), *n.* accusing in return; counter accusation.

re es tab lish or **re-es tab lish** (rē′ə stab′lish), *v.* establish again; restore.

re it e rate (rē it′ə rāt′), *v.,* **-rat ed, -rat ing.** say or do several times; repeat (an àction, demand, etc.) again and again: *The boy did not move though the teacher reiterated her command.* [< L *reiterare*, ult. < *re-* again + *iterum* again] —**re it′e ra′tion,** *n.*

re join (ri join′), *v.* answer; reply.

re lent (ri lent′), *v.* become less harsh or cruel; be more tender and merciful.

re luc tance (ri luk′təns), *n.* 1. a reluctant feeling or action; unwillingness. 2. slowness in action because of unwillingness.

re luc tant (ri luk′tənt), *adj.* 1. unwilling; showing unwillingness. 2. slow to act because unwilling: *He was very reluctant to give his money away.* [< L *reluctans, -antis* struggling against, ppr. of *reluctari*, ult. < *re-* back + *lucta* wrestling] —**re luc′tant ly,** *adv.*

re ly (ri lī′), *v.,* **-lied, -ly ing.** depend; trust: *Rely on your own efforts.* [< OF *relier* < L *religare* bind fast < *re-* back + *ligare* bind]

re morse (ri môrs′), *n.* deep, painful regret for having done wrong: *The thief felt remorse for his crime and confessed.* [< L *remorsus* tormented, ult. < *re-* back + *mordere* to bite] **Syn.** compunction, contrition.

rend (rend), *v.,* **rent, rend ing.** 1. pull apart violently; tear: *Wolves will rend a lamb.* 2. split: *Lightning rent the tree.* 3. disturb violently: *His mind was rent by doubt.* 4. remove with force or violence. [OE *rendan*] **Syn.** 1. rip.

ren der (ren′dər), *v.* 1. cause to become; make: *An accident has rendered him helpless.* 2. give; do: *She rendered us a great service by her help.* 3. offer for consideration, approval, payment, etc.; hand in; report: *The treasurer rendered an account of all the money spent.* 4. give in return: *Render thanks for your blessings.* 5. pay as due: *The conquered rendered tribute to the conqueror.* 6. bring out the meaning of; represent: *The actor rendered the part of Hamlet well.* 7. play or sing (music). 8. change from one language to another; translate. 9. give up; surrender. 10. melt (fat, etc.); clarify or extract by melting. Fat from hogs is rendered for lard.

rent (rent), *n.* a torn place; tear; split. —*adj.* torn; split. —*v.* pt. and pp. of **rend.** [originally v., var. of *rend*]

re pel (ri pel′), *v.,* **-pelled, -pel ling.** 1. force back; drive back; drive away: *They repelled the enemy.* 2. force apart or away by some inherent force. Particles with similar electric charges repel each other. 3. be displeasing to; cause disgust in. 4. cause dislike; displease. 5. reject. [< L *repellere* < *re-* back + *pellere* to drive]

rep er toire (rep′ər twär, rep′ər twôr), *n.* the list of plays, operas, parts, pieces, etc., that a company, an actor, a musician, or a singer is prepared to perform.

rep e ti tion (rep′ə tish′ən), *n.* 1. a repeating; doing again; saying again. 2. thing repeated.

re pet i tive (ri pet′ə tiv), *adj.* of or characterized by repetition.

re proach (ri prōch′), *n.* 1. blame. 2. disgrace. 3. object of blame, censure, or disapproval. 4. expression of blame, censure, or disapproval. —*v.* 1. blame. 2. disgrace. **Syn.** *n.* 1. censure. 2. discredit. —*v.* 1. upbraid.

re proach ful (ri prōch′fəl), *adj.* full of reproach; expressing reproach. —**re proach′ful ly,** *adv.*

re prove (ri prüv′), *v.,* **-proved, -prov ing.** find fault with; blame: *Reprove the boy for teasing the cat.*

re pug nance (ri pug′nəns), *n.* strong dislike, distaste, or aversion.

Req ui em or **req ui em** (rek′wē əm, rē′kwē əm), *n.* 1. Mass for the dead; musical church service for the dead. 2. music for it. [< L *requiem*, accus. of *requies* rest; the first word of the Mass for the dead]

res ig na tion (rez′ig nā′shən), *n.* 1. act of resigning. 2. a written statement giving notice that one resigns. 3. patient acceptance; quiet submission: *She bore the pain with resignation.* **Syn.** 3. meekness.

res o lute (rez′ə lüt), *adj.* determined; firm; bold: *He was resolute in his attempt to climb to the top of the mountain. A soldier must be resolute in battle.* [< L *resolutus,* pp. of *resolvere* resolve] —**res′o lute ly,** *adv.*

re splend ent (ri splen′dənt), *adj.* very bright; shining; splendid: *The queen was resplendent with jewels.*

---

hat, āge, fär;   let, bē, tėrm;   it, īce;   hot, gō, ôrder;   oil, out;   cup, pùt, rüle;   ch, child;   ng, long;
th, thin;   ᴛʜ, then;   zh, measure;   ə represents *a* in about, *e* in taken, *i* in pencil, *o* in lemon, *u* in circus.

res ur rect (rez′ə rekt′), v. 1. raise from the dead; bring back to life. 2. bring back to sight, use, etc.: *resurrect an old custom.* [< *resurrection*]

re sus ci tate (ri sus′ə tāt), v., **-tat ed, -tat ing.** bring or come back to life or consciousness; revive. [< L *resuscitare*, ult. < *re-* again + *sub-* up + *citare* rouse < *ciere* stir up] **—re sus′ci ta′tion,** n.

re tal i ate (ri tal′ē āt), v., **-at ed, -at ing.** pay back wrong, injury, etc.; return like for like, usually to return evil for evil. [< L *retaliare* < *re-* in return + *tal-* pay; influenced by *talis* such]

re trac tor (ri trak′tər), n. 1. person or thing that draws back something. 2. muscle that retracts an organ, protruded part, etc. 3. a surgical instrument or appliance for drawing back an organ or part.

rev el (rev′əl), v., **-eled, -el ing** or *esp. Brit.* **-elled, -el ling,** n. —v. 1. take great pleasure (*in*): *The children revel in country life.* 2. make merry. —n. a noisy good time; merrymaking. [< OF *reveler* be disorderly, make merry < L *rebellare*] **—rev′el er,** *esp. Brit.* **rev′el ler,** n.

rev e la tion (rev′ə lā′shən), n. 1. act of making known: *The revelation of the thieves' hiding place by one of their own number caused their capture.* 2. the thing made known: *Her true nature was a revelation to me.*

re ver be ra tion (ri vėr′bə rā′shən), n. 1. echoing back of sound; echo. 2. reflection of light or heat.

rev er ence (rev′ər əns), n., v., **-enced, -enc ing.** —n. 1. a feeling of deep respect, mixed with wonder, awe, and love. 2. a deep bow. 3. **Reverence,** title used in speaking of or to a clergyman. —v. regard with reverence; revere. [< L *reverentia* < *reverens*] **Syn.** n. 1. veneration, adoration.

re vive (ri vīv′), v., **-vived, -viv ing.** 1. bring back or come back to life or consciousness: *revive a half-drowned person.* 2. bring or come back to a fresh, lively condition: *Flowers revive in water.* 3. make or become fresh; restore: *Hot coffee revived the cold, tired man.* 4. bring back or come back to notice, use, fashion, memory, activity, etc.: *An old play is sometimes revived on the stage.* [< L *revivere* < *re-* again + *vivere* live] **—re viv′er,** n. **Syn.** 3. refresh.

rib ald (rib′əld), adj. offensive in speech; coarsely mocking; irreverent; indecent; obscene.

rife (rīf), adj. 1. happening often; common; numerous; widespread. 2. full; abounding: *The land was rife with rumors of war.* [OE *rīfe*]

rill (ril), n. a tiny stream; little brook.

riv et (riv′it), n. a metal bolt with each end hammered into a head. Rivets fasten heavy steel beams together. —v. 1. fasten with a rivet or rivets. 2. flatten (the end of a bolt) so as to form a head. 3. fasten firmly; fix firmly: *Their eyes were riveted on the speaker.*

roach (rōch), n., pl. **roach es** or (*esp. collectively*) **roach.** 1. a European fresh-water fish related to the carp. 2. any of various similar fishes, such as the American sunfish.

roe (rō), n., pl. **roes** or (*esp. collectively*) **roe.** a small deer of Europe and Asia, with forked antlers.

rout (rout), n. 1. flight of a defeated army in disorder. 2. a complete defeat. —v. 1. put to flight: *Our soldiers routed the enemy.* 2. defeat completely.

row el (rou′əl), n., v., **-eled, -el ing** or *esp. Brit.* **-elled, -el ling.** —n. a small wheel with sharp points, attached to the end of a spur. —v. use a rowel on.

ru bi cund (rü′bə kund), adj. reddish; ruddy.

ru di men ta ry (rü′də men′tər ē), adj. 1. to be learned

or studied first; elementary. 2. in an early stage of development; undeveloped.

rue ful (rü′fəl), adj. 1. sorrowful; unhappy; mournful: *a rueful expression.* 2. causing sorrow or pity: *a rueful sight.* **—rue′ful ly,** adv. **—rue′ful ness,** n. **Syn.** 1. doleful, woeful, lugubrious, melancholy.

ru mi nate (rü′mə nāt), v., **-nat ed, -nat ing.** 1. chew the cud. 2. chew again: *A cow ruminates its food.* 3. ponder; meditate: *He ruminated on the strange events of the past week.* [< L *ruminare* chew a cud < *rumen* gullet]

ru mi na tive (rü′mə nā′tiv), adj. meditative; inclined to ruminate.

ruse (rüz, rüs), n. trick; stratagem. [< F *ruse* < *ruser* dodge] **Syn.** artifice, dodge, wile.

rus tic (rus′tik), adj. 1. belonging to the country; rural; suitable for the country. 2. simple; plain: *His rustic speech and ways made him uncomfortable in the city school.* 3. rough; awkward. 4. made of branches with the bark still on them. —n. a country person.

sa chet (sa shā′, sash′ā), n. 1. a small bag or pad containing perfumed powder. 2. perfumed powder. [< F *sachet*, dim. of *sac* sack]

sac ri lege (sak′rə lij), n. an intentional injury to anything sacred; disrespectful treatment of anyone or anything sacred: *Robbing the church was a sacrilege.* [< OF < L *sacrilegium* temple robbery < *sacrum* sacred object + *legere* pick up] **Syn.** profanation.

sage (sāj), n. 1. plant whose leaves are used as seasoning and in medicine. 2. its dried leaves. 3. sagebrush.

sar casm (sär′kaz əm), n. 1. a sneering or cutting remark; ironical taunt. 2. act of making fun of a person to hurt his feelings; bitter irony: *"How unselfish you are!" said Ellen in sarcasm as Mary took the biggest piece of cake.*

sar cas tic (sär kas′tik), adj. using sarcasm; sneering; cutting: *"Don't hurry!" was his sarcastic comment as I began to dress at my usual slow rate.* **—sar cas′ti cal ly,** adv. **Syn.** ironical, satirical, taunting, caustic.

sar don ic (sär don′ik), adj. bitter; sarcastic; scornful; mocking: *a fiend's sardonic laugh.* [< F < L < Gk. *Sardonios,* a supposed Sardinian plant that produced hysterical convulsions] **—sar don′i cal ly,** adv.

saun ter (sôn′tər, sän′tər), v. walk along slowly and happily; stroll: *saunter through the park.* —n. 1. a leisurely or careless gait. 2. a stroll. **—saun′ter er,** n.

sa vor (sā′vər), n. 1. taste or smell; flavor: *The soup has a savor of onion.* 2. a distinctive quality; noticeable trace: *There is a savor of conceit in everything he says.* —v. 1. taste or smell (*of*): *That sauce savors of lemon.* 2. enjoy the savor of; perceive or appreciate by taste or smell: *He savored the soup with pleasure.* 3. give flavor to; season. 4. have the quality or nature (*of*): *a request that savors of a command.* 5. show traces of the presence or influence of: *Bad manners savor a bad education.* **—sa′vor er,** n. **—sa′vor less,** adj.

scab bard (skab′ərd), n. sheath or case for the blade of a sword, dagger, etc. See **hilt** for picture.

scape goat (skāp′gōt′), n. person or thing made to bear the blame for the mistakes or sins of others. The ancient Jewish high priests used to lay the sins of the people upon a goat (called the scapegoat) which was then driven out into the wilderness. [< *scape,* var. of *escape* + *goat*]

< = from, derived from, taken from;   cf., compare;   dial., dialect;   dim., diminutive;   lang., language; pp., past participle;   ppr., present participle;   pt., past tense;   ult., ultimately;   var., variant;   ? = possibly.

scep ter (sep′tər), *n.* **1.** the rod or staff carried by a ruler as a symbol of royal power or authority. **2.** royal or imperial power or authority.

scep tre (sep′tər), *n. esp. Brit.* scepter.

scope (skōp), *n.* **1.** distance the mind can reach; extent of view: *Very hard words are not within the scope of a child's understanding.* **2.** space; opportunity: *Football gives scope for courage and quick thinking.*

scorch (skôrch), *v.* **1.** burn slightly; burn on the outside: *The cake tastes scorched. The maid scorched the shirt in ironing it.* **2.** dry up; wither: *grass scorched by the sun.* **3.** criticize with burning words. **4.** *Informal.* ride very fast. —*n.* a slight burn. [origin uncertain]

score (skôr, skōr), *n., v.,* **scored, scor ing.** —*n.* **1.** record of points made in a game, contest, test, etc.: *The score was 9 to 2 in our favor.* **2.** amount owed; debt; account: *He paid his score at the inn.* **3.** group or set of twenty; twenty. **4. scores,** *pl.* a large number: *Scores died in the epidemic.* **5.** a written or printed piece of music arranged for different instruments or voices: *the score of a musical comedy.* **6.** a cut; scratch; stroke; mark; line: *The slave's back showed scores made by the whip.* **7. on the score of,** because of; on account of. **8. pay off** or **settle a score,** get even for an injury or wrong. —*v.* **1.** make as points in a game, contest, test, etc. **2.** make points; succeed. **3.** keep a record of (the number of points made in a game, contest, etc.). **4.** make an addition to the score; gain; win: *He scored five runs for our team.* **5.** keep a record of as an amount owed; mark; set down: *The innkeeper scored on a slate the number of meals each person had.* **6.** arrange (a piece of music) for different instruments or voices. **7.** cut; scratch; mark; line: *Mistakes are scored in red ink.* **8.** *U.S. Informal.* blame or scold severely. [< Scand. *skor* notch] —**score′less,** *adj.* —**scor′er,** *n.*

scorn ful (skôrn′fəl), *adj.* showing contempt; mocking; full of scorn. —**scorn′ful ly,** *adv.* —**scorn′ful ness,** *n.* **Syn.** contemptuous, disdainful, derisive.

screen (skrēn), *n.* **1.** a covered frame that hides, protects, or separates. **2.** wire woven together with small openings in between: *We have screens at our windows to keep out flies.* **3.** an ornamental partition. **4.** anything like a screen: *A screen of trees hides our house from the road.* **5.** surface on which motion pictures, etc., are shown. **6.** motion pictures; films. **7.** sieve for sifting sand, gravel, coal, seed, etc. —*v.* **1.** shelter, protect, or hide with, or as with, a screen: *She screened her face from the fire with a fan. The mother tried to screen her guilty son.* **2.** show (a motion picture) on a screen. **3.** photograph with a motion-picture camera. **4.** adapt (a story, etc.) for reproduction as a motion picture. **5.** be suitable for reproducing on a motion-picture screen. **6.** sift with a screen. [< OF *escren* < Gmc.] —**screen′a ble,** *adj.* —**screen′er,** *n.* —**screen′like′,** *adj.* **Syn.** *n.* **1.** shield, protection, fender. —*v.* **1.** shield.

scru ti nize (skrüt′n īz), *v.,* **-nized, -niz ing.** examine closely; inspect carefully: *The jeweler scrutinized the diamond for flaws.* —**scru′ti niz′ing ly,** *adv.*

scut tle (skut′l), *v.,* **-tled, -tling,** *n.* scamper; scurry.

sear (sir), *v.* **1.** burn or char the surface of: *The hot iron seared his flesh.* **2.** make hard or unfeeling: *That cruel man must have a seared conscience.* **3.** dry up; wither. **4.** become dry, burned, or hard.

sea son (sē′zn), *n.* **1.** one of the four periods of the year; spring, summer, autumn, or winter. **2.** any period of time marked by something special: *the Christmas season, the harvest season.* **3.** time when something is occurring, active,

at its best, or in fashion: *the baseball season.* **4.** a period of time: *a season of rest.* **5.** period of the year when a place is most frequented or active: *the London season.* **6.** a suitable or fit time. **7. for a season,** for a time. **8. in good season,** early enough. **9. in season, a.** at the right or proper time. **b.** in the time or condition for eating, hunting, etc. **c.** early enough. **10. in season and out of season,** at all times. —*v.* **1.** improve the flavor of: *season soup with salt.* **2.** give interest or character to: *season conversation with wit.* **3.** make fit for use by a period of keeping or treatment: *Wood is seasoned for building by drying and hardening it.* **4.** become fit for use. **5.** accustom; make used: *Soldiers are seasoned to battle by experience in war.* **6.** make less severe; soften: *Season justice with mercy.* —**sea′son er,** *n.*

se clud ed (si klü′did), *adj.* shut off from others; undisturbed. **Syn.** withdrawn, isolated.

se date (si dāt′), *adj.* quiet; calm; serious: *She is very sedate for a child and would rather read or sew than play.* [< L *sedatus,* pp. of *sedare* calm] —**se date′ly,** *adv.*

seed y (sē′dē), *adj.,* **seed i er, seed i est. 1.** full of seed. **2.** gone to seed. **3.** *Informal.* shabby; no longer fresh or new: *seedy clothes.* —**seed′i ly,** *adv.*

seethe (sēᴛн), *v.,* **seethed, seeth ing. 1.** be excited; be disturbed: *The pirate crew was seething with discontent and ready for open rebellion.* **2.** bubble and foam: *Water seethed under the falls.* **3.** soak; steep. **4.** boil.

self-con fi dent (self′kon′fə dənt), *adj.* believing in one's own ability, power, judgment, etc.

se man tics (sə man′tiks), *n.* the scientific study of the meanings, and the development of meanings, of words. [< LL *semanticus* < Gk. *semantikos* having meaning, ult. < *sema* sign]

sem blance (sem′bləns), *n.* **1.** outward appearance: *His story had the semblance of truth but was really false.* **2.** likeness: *These clouds have the semblance of a huge head.* [< OF *semblance* < *sembler* seem, ult. < L *similis* similar]

sen si tive (sen′sə tiv), *adj.* **1.** receiving impressions readily: *The eye is sensitive to light.* **2.** easily affected or influenced: *The mercury in the thermometer is sensitive to changes in temperature.* **3.** easily hurt or offended. **4.** of or connected with the senses or sensation.

sen su al (sen′shü əl), *adj.* **1.** having to do with the bodily senses rather than with the mind or soul: *sensual pleasures.* **2.** caring too much for the pleasures of the senses. **3.** lustful; lewd. **4.** of or having to do with the senses or sensation. [< LL *sensualis* < L *sensus.* See SENSE.] —**sen′su al ly,** *adv.*

Syn. **1, 2. Sensual, sensuous** mean of or concerned with the senses. **Sensual** describes things that give pleasurable satisfaction to the bodily senses and appetites and people who indulge their desires and feelings for pure physical pleasure, and almost always suggests baseness or excess: *A glutton derives sensual pleasure from eating.* **Sensuous,** always favorable, describes people highly sensitive to beauty and the pleasure of the senses and feelings, but never of appetite, and things that give pleasure through the senses: *She derives sensuous delight from old church music.* **3.** wanton, lecherous.

Ant. 3. continent, chaste.

sen su ous (sen′shü əs), *adj.* **1.** of or derived from the senses; having an effect on the senses; perceived by the senses: *the sensuous thrill of a warm bath, a sensuous love of color.* **2.** enjoying the pleasures of the senses. —**sen′su ous ly,** *adv.* —**sen′su ous ness,** *n.*

---

hat, āge, fär;   let, bē, tėrm;   it, īce;   hot, gō, ôrder;   oil, out;   cup, pùt, rüle;   ch, child;   ng, long;
th, thin;   ᴛн, then;   zh, measure;   ə represents *a* in about, *e* in taken, *i* in pencil, *o* in lemon, *u* in circus.

se rene (sə rēn′), *adj.* 1. peaceful; calm: *a serene smile.* 2. clear; bright; not cloudy: *a serene sky.* [< L *serenus*] —**se rene′ly,** *adv.*
Syn. 1. tranquil, placid.

se ren i ty (sə ren′ə tē), *n., pl.* **-ties.** 1. quiet peace; calmness. 2. clearness; brightness.

serge (sèrj), *n.* kind of cloth having slanting lines or ridges on its surface. [< F *serge,* ult. < L *serica* (*vestis*) silken (garment) < Gk. *serike* < *Seres* the Chinese]

shab by (shab′ē), *adj.,* **-bi er, -bi est.** 1. much worn: *His old suit looks shabby.* 2. wearing old or much worn clothes. 3. not generous; mean; unfair: *It is shabby not to speak to an old friend because he is poor.* —**shab′bi ly,** *adv.* —**shab′bi ness,** *n.*

shift less (shift′lis), *adj.* lazy; inefficient. —**shift′less ly,** *adv.* —**shift′less ness,** *n.*

shim my (shim′ē), *n., pl.* **-mies,** *v.,* **-mied, -my ing.** —*n.* 1. *Slang.* a jazz dance with much shaking of the body. 2. an unusual shaking or vibration. —*v.* 1. dance the shimmy. 2. shake; vibrate.

ship shape (ship′shāp′), *adj.* in good order; trim. —*adv.* in a trim, neat manner.

shoot (shüt), *v.,* **shot, shoot ing,** *n.* —*v.* 1. hit, wound, or kill with a bullet, arrow, etc.: *shoot a rabbit.* 2. send swiftly: *He shot question after question at us.* 3. fire or use (a gun, etc.). 4. of a gun, etc., send a bullet: *This gun shoots straight.* 5. kill game in or on: *shoot a farm.* 6. move suddenly and swiftly: *A car shot by us. Flames shot up from the burning house. Pain shot up his arm. He shot back the bolt.* 7. pass quickly along, through, over, or under: *shoot Niagara Falls in a barrel.* 8. hurt sharply from time to time. 9. come forth from the ground; grow; grow rapidly: *Buds shoot forth in the spring. The corn is shooting up in the warm weather.* 10. take (a picture) with a camera; photograph. 11. project sharply: *a cape that shoots out into the sea.* 12. dump; empty out. 13. vary with some different color, etc.: *Her dress was shot with threads of gold.* 14. measure the altitude of: *shoot the sun.* 15. send (a ball, etc.) toward the goal, pocket, etc. —*n.* 1. shooting practice. 2. trip, party, or contest for shooting. 3. a new part growing out; young bud or stem. 4. a sloping trough for conveying coal, grain, water, etc., to a lower level; chute. [OE *scēotan*] —**shoot′er,** *n.*
Syn. *v.* 11. jut, extend.

shrew (shrü), *n.* 1. a bad-tempered, quarrelsome woman. 2. a mouselike mammal with a long snout and brownish fur, that eats insects and worms.

shrewd (shrüd), *adj.* 1. having a sharp mind; showing a keen wit; clever. 2. keen; sharp. 3. **shrewd turn,** a mean trick; mischievous act. [earlier *shrewed,* < *shrew,* v. in sense of "scold"] —**shrewd′ly,** *adv.* —**shrewd′ness,** *n.*

shriv el (shriv′əl), *v.,* **-eled, -el ing** or *esp. Brit.* **-elled, -el ling.** 1. dry up; wither; shrink and wrinkle: *The hot sunshine shriveled the grass.* 2. waste away; become useless. 3. make helpless or useless. [origin unknown]

shroud (shroud), *n.* 1. cloth or garment in which a dead person is wrapped for burial. 2. something that covers, conceals, or veils: *The fog was a shroud over the city.* 3. Usually, **shrouds,** *pl.* rope from a mast to the side of a ship. Shrouds help support the mast. —*v.* 1. wrap for burial. 2. cover; conceal; veil: *The earth is shrouded in darkness.*

si dle (sī′dl), *v.,* **-dled, -dling,** *n.* —*v.* 1. move sideways. 2. move sideways slowly so as not to attract attention: *The little boy shyly sidled up to the visitor.* —*n.* movement sideways. [< *sideling* sidelong]

si es ta (sē es′tə), *n.* a nap or rest taken at noon or in the afternoon. [< Sp. < L *sexta* (*hora*) sixth (hour), noon]

sig nif i cant (sig nif′ə kənt), *adj.* 1. full of meaning; important; of consequence: *July 4, 1776, is a significant date for Americans.* 2. having a meaning; expressive: *Smiles are significant of pleasure.* 3. having or expressing a hidden meaning: *A significant nod from his friend warned him to stop talking.* —**sig nif′i cant ly,** *adv.*

sil hou ette (sil′ü et′), *n., v.,* **-et ted, -et ting.** —*n.* 1. an outline portrait cut out of a black paper or filled in with some single color. 2. a dark image outlined against a lighter background. 3. **in silhouette,** shown in outline, or in black against a white background. —*v.* show in outline: *The mountain was silhouetted against the sky.* [named after E. de Silhouette (1709-67), French politician]

sil ver-tongued (sil′vər tungd′), *adj.* eloquent.

sim ple ton (sim′pəl tən), *n.* a silly person; fool.

si mul ta ne ous ly (sī′məl tā′nē əs lē, sim′əl tā′nē əs-lē), *adv.* at once; at the same time; together.

sin ew (sin′yü), *n.* 1. a tough, strong band or cord that joins muscle to bone; tendon: *You can see the sinews in a cooked chicken leg.* 2. strength; energy. 3. means of strength; source of power: *Men and money are the sinews of war.* —*v.* furnish with sinews. [OE *sinonu*]

sin gu lar i ty (sing′gyə lar′ə tē), *n., pl.* **-ties.** 1. peculiarity; oddness; strangeness; unusualness: *The singularity of the dwarf's appearance attracted much attention.* 2. something singular; peculiarity; oddity: *One of the giraffe's singularities is the length of its neck.*

Skam ni a (skäm′nē ä)

skein (skān), *n.* 1. a small, coiled bundle of yarn or thread. There are 120 yards in a skein of cotton yarn. 2. a confused tangle. [< OF *escaigne*]

skull cap (skul′kap′), *n.* a close-fitting cap without a brim.

slap stick (slap′stik′), *n.* 1. two long, narrow sticks fastened so as to slap together loudly when a clown, actor, etc., hits somebody with it. 2. comedy full of rough play. —*adj.* full of rough play. In slapstick comedy, the actors knock each other around to make people laugh. [Am.E]

sloth ful (slōth′fəl, slôth′fəl), *adj.* unwilling to work or exert oneself; lazy; idle. —**sloth′ful ly,** *adv.* —**sloth′ful ness,** *n.*
Syn. sluggish.

slough (slou *for 1 and 3;* slü *for 2*), *n.* 1. a soft, deep, muddy place; mud hole. 2. *U.S.* and *Canada.* swamp. 3. hopeless discouragement; degradation.

sluice (slüs), *n., v.,* **sluiced, sluic ing.** —*n.* 1. structure with a gate for holding back or controlling the water of a canal, river, or lake. 2. gate that holds back or controls the flow of water. When the water behind a dam gets too high, the sluices are opened. 3. water held back or controlled by such a gate. 4. thing that controls the flow or passage of anything: *War opens the sluices of hatred and bloodshed.* 5. a long, sloping trough through which water flows, used to wash gold from sand, dirt, or gravel. 6. channel for carrying off water. —*v.* 1. let out or draw off (water) by opening a sluice. 2. flow or pour in a stream; rush: *Water sluiced down the channel.* 3. flush or cleanse with a rush of water; pour or throw water over. 4. wash (gold) from sand, dirt, or gravel in a sluice. 5. send (logs, etc.) along a channel of water. [OF *escluse,* ult. < L *ex-* out + *claudere* shut]

smug (smug), *adj.* too pleased with one's own goodness, cleverness, respectability, etc.; self-satisfied; complacent.

snig ger (snig′ər), *n., v.* snicker.

so journ (*v.* sō jèrn′, sō′jèrn; *n.* sō′jèrn), *v.* stay for a

< = from, derived from, taken from;   cf., compare;   dial., dialect;   dim., diminutive;   lang., language; pp., past participle;   ppr., present participle;   pt., past tense;   ult., ultimately;   var., variant;   ? = possibly.

time: *The Israelites sojourned in the land of Egypt.* —*n.* a brief stay. [< OF *sojorner*, ult. < L *sub-* under + *diurnus* of the day] —**so journ′er,** *n.*

sol emn (sol′əm), *adj.* 1. serious; grave; earnest: *a solemn face.* 2. causing serious or grave thoughts: *The organ played solemn music.* 3. done with form and ceremony. 4. connected with religion; sacred. —**sol′emn ly,** *adv.* —**sol′emn ness,** *n.*

Syn. 2. impressive.

so lic i tous (sə lis′ə təs), *adj.* 1. showing care or concern; anxious; concerned: *Parents are solicitous for their children's progress.* 2. desirous; eager: *solicitous to please.* [< L *sollicitus* < OL *sollus* all + *citus* stirred up, pp. of *ciere* arouse] —**so lic′it ous ly,** *adv.*

som ber (som′bər), *adj.* 1. dark; gloomy: *A cloudy winter day is somber.* 2. melancholy; dismal: *His losses made him very somber.* —**som′ber ly,** *adv.*

Syn. 1. cloudy, murky. 2. depressing, sad.

som brer o (som brer′ō), *n., pl.* **-brer os.** a broad-brimmed hat worn in the SW United States, Mexico, etc. [Am.E; < Sp. *sombrero*, ult. < L *sub-* under + *umbra* shade]

som no lent (som′nə lənt), *adj.* sleepy; drowsy.

so na ta (sə nä′tə), *n.* piece of music, usually for the piano, having three or four movements in contrasted rhythms but related keys. [< Ital. *sonata*, literally, sounded (on an instrument, as distinguished from sung)]

sough (suf, sou), *v.* make a rustling or murmuring sound: *The pines soughed when the wind blew.* —*n.* a rustling or murmuring sound.

span (span), *n., v.,* **spanned, span ning.** —*n.* 1. the distance between the tip of a man's thumb and the tip of his little finger when the hand is spread out; about 9 inches. 2. distance between two supports: *The arch had a fifty-foot span.* 3. part between two supports: *The bridge crossed the river in three spans.* 4. a short space of time: *"A life's but a span."* 5. the full extent: *the span of a bridge, the span of memory.* —*v.* 1. measure by the hand spread out: *This post can be spanned by one's two hands.* 2. extend over: *A bridge spanned the river.* [OE *spann*]

spat[1] (spat), *n., v.,* **spat ted, spat ting.** —*n.* 1. a slight quarrel. 2. a light blow; slap. —*v.* 1. *Informal.* quarrel slightly. 2. slap lightly. [? imitative]

spat[2] (spat), *v.* a pt. and a pp. of **spit.**

spat[3] (spat), *n.* Usually, **spats,** *pl.* a short gaiter covering the ankle. [short for *spatterdash*]

spat[4] (spat), *n., v.,* **spat ted, spat ting.** —*n.* the spawn of oysters; young oysters. —*v.* of oysters, spawn. [origin uncertain]

Spats

spig ot (spig′ət, spik′it), *n.* 1. valve for controlling the flow of water or other liquid from a pipe, tank, barrel, etc. 2. *U.S.* faucet. 3. peg or plug used to stop the small hole of a cask, barrel, etc.; bung. [ME; origin uncertain]

spir it ed (spir′ə tid), *adj.* lively; dashing: *a spirited race horse.* —**spir′it ed ly,** *adv.* —**spir′it ed ness,** *n.*

splay (splā), *v.* 1. spread out. 2. spread; flare. 3. make slanting. —*adj.* 1. wide and flat. 2. awkward; clumsy. —*n.* 1. a spread; flare. 2. a slanting surface; surface which makes an oblique angle with another. [< *display*]

sport (spôrt, spōrt), *v.* 1. amuse oneself; play: *Lambs sport in the fields.* 2. jest. 3. *Informal.* display: *sport a new hat.* 4. become or produce a sport. —*adj.* of sports; suitable for sports. [ult. short for *disport*]

spur i ous (spyùr′ē əs), *adj.* 1. not coming from the right

source; not genuine; false; sham: *a spurious document.* 2. illegitimate. —**spur′i ous ly,** *adv.*

squall[1] (skwôl), *n.* 1. a sudden, violent gust of wind, often with rain, snow, or sleet. 2. *Informal.* trouble. [cf. Swedish *skval-regn* sudden downpour of rain]

squall[2] (skwôl), *v.* cry out loudly; scream violently: *The baby squalled.* —*n.* a loud, harsh cry: *The parrot's squall was heard all over the house.* [< Scand. *skvala* cry out] —**squall′er,** *n.*

stac ca to (stə kä′tō), in music: —*adj.* with breaks between the successive tones; disconnected; abrupt. —*adv.* in a staccato manner. [< Ital. *staccato*, literally, detached]

staid (stād), *adj.* having a settled, quiet character; sober; sedate. —*v. Archaic.* a pt. and a pp. of **stay**[1]. [originally pp. of *stay*[1] in sense of "restrain"] —**staid′ly,** *adv.* —**staid′ness,** *n.*

Syn. *adj.* grave, serious, steady.

stanch (stänch, stanch), *adj.* 1. firm; strong: *stanch walls, a stanch defense.* 2. loyal; steadfast: *a stanch friend, a stanch supporter of the law.* 3. watertight: *a stanch boat.* Also, **staunch.** —**stanch′ly,** *adv.* —**stanch′ness,** *n.*

Syn. 2. constant, true, faithful, steady, unswerving.

sta ple (stā′pəl), *adj.* 1. most important; principal: *The weather was their staple subject of conversation.* 2. established in commerce: *a staple trade.* 3. regularly produced in large quantities for the market.

stark (stärk), *adj.* 1. downright; complete: *That fool is talking stark nonsense.* 2. stiff: *The dog lay stark in death.* 3. harsh; stern. 4. *Archaic.* strong; sturdy. —*adv.* 1. entirely; completely. 2. in a stark manner. [OE *stearc* stiff, strong] —**stark′ly,** *adv.*

staunch (stônch, stänch), *v., adj.* stanch. —**staunch′ly,** *adv.* —**staunch′ness,** *n.*

steep (stēp), *v.* 1. soak: *Let the tea steep in boiling water for five minutes. His sword was steeped in blood.* 2. immerse; imbue: *ruins steeped in gloom.* 3. **steeped in,** filled with; permeated by. —*n.* 1. a soaking. 2. liquid in which something is soaked. [probably < OE *steap* bowl] —**steep′er,** *n.*

sti fle (stī′fəl), *v., -fled, -fling.* 1. stop the breath of; smother: *The smoke stifled the firemen.* 2. be unable to breathe freely: *I am stifling in this close room.* 3. keep back; suppress; stop: *stifle a cry, stifle a yawn, stifle business activity, stifle a rebellion.* [ME *stuffle(n), stiffle(n)* < *stuffe(n)* stuff, stifle; influenced by Scand. *stīfla* dam up]

Syn. 1, 2. choke, strangle. 3. extinguish, repress.

stip u late (stip′yə lāt), *v., -lat ed, -lat ing.* arrange definitely; demand as a condition of agreement: *He stipulated that he should receive a month's vacation every year if he took the job.*

stoop (stüp), *n. U.S.* porch or platform at the entrance of a house.

stra te gic (strə tē′jik), *adj.* 1. of strategy; based on strategy; useful in strategy. 2. important in strategy: *The Panama Canal is a strategic link in our national defense.* 3. having to do with raw material necessary for warfare which must be obtained, at least partially, from an outside country. 4. of an air force or bombing, specially made or trained for destroying enemy bases, industry, or communications behind the lines of battle. —**stra te′gi cal ly,** *adv.*

stren u ous (stren′yü əs), *adj.* 1. very active: *We had a strenuous day moving into our new house.* 2. full of energy: *a strenuous worker.* [< L *strenuus*] —**stren′u ous ly,** *adv.* —**stren′u ous ness,** *n.*

stri dent (strīd′nt), *adj.* making or having a harsh sound;

hat, āge, fär;   let, bē, tèrm;   it, īce;   hot, gō, ôrder;   oil, out;   cup, pùt, rüle;   ch, child;   ng, long; th, thin;   ᴛʜ, then;   zh, measure;   ə represents *a* in about, *e* in taken, *i* in pencil, *o* in lemon, *u* in circus.

585

grating; shrill. [< *stridens, -entis*, ppr. of *stridere* sound harshly] **—stri′dent ly,** *adv.*

stu pe fy (stü′pə fī, styü′pə fī), *v.*, **-fied, -fy ing. 1.** make stupid, dull, or senseless. **2.** overwhelm with amazement; astound: *They were stupefied by the calamity.* **—stu′pe-fi′er,** *n.*
Syn. 1. deaden, stun.

styl ize (stī′līz), *v.*, **-ized, -iz ing.** conform to a particular or to a conventional style.

sua vi ty (swä′və tē, swav′ə tē), *n., pl.* **-ties.** smoothly agreeable quality of behavior; blandness; smooth politeness.

sub stan tial (səb stan′shəl), *adj.* **1.** real; actual: *People and things are substantial; dreams and ghosts are not.* **2.** large; important; ample: *John has made a substantial improvement in health.* **3.** strong; firm; solid: *The house is substantial enough to last a hundred years.* **4.** in the main; in essentials: *The stories told by the two boys were in substantial agreement.* **5.** well-to-do; wealthy.

sub tle (sut′l), *adj.* **1.** delicate; thin; fine: *a subtle odor of perfume.* **2.** faint; mysterious: *a subtle smile.* **3.** having a keen, quick mind; discerning; acute: *She is a subtle observer of slight differences in things.* **4.** sly; crafty; tricky: *a subtle scheme to get some money.* **5.** skillful; clever; expert. **—sub′tle ness,** *n.*
Syn. 1. tenuous, rare. **3.** discriminating. **4.** artful, cunning, insidious.

suf fo cate (suf′ə kāt), *v.*, **-cat ed, -cat ing. 1.** kill by stopping the breath. **2.** keep from breathing; hinder in breathing. **3.** choke; gasp for breath. **4.** die for lack of air. **5.** smother; suppress.

sul fa nil a mide (sul′fə nil′ə mīd, sul′fə nil′ə mid), *n.* a white, crystalline substance, derived from coal tar and used in treating various infections. Sulfanilamide was the first sulfa drug to be widely used.

sul try (sul′trē), *adj.*, **-tri er, -tri est. 1.** hot, close, and moist: *We expect sultry weather during July.* **2.** hot. [< obsolete *sulter, v.*; akin to *swelter*] **—sul′tri ness,** *n.*

sup ple (sup′əl), *adj.*, **-pler, -plest,** *v.*, **-pled, -pling.** **—***adj.* **1.** bending easily: *a supple birch tree, supple leather.* **2.** readily adaptable to different ideas, circumstances, people, etc.; yielding: *a supple mind.* **—***v.* make or grow supple. [< OF < L *supplex* submissive < *supplicare*] **—sup′ple ly,** *adv.* **—sup′ple ness,** *n.*
Syn. adj. 1. pliant, pliable, flexible.

sur mount (sər mount′), *v.* **1.** rise above. **2.** be above or on top of: *The peak surmounts the valley.* **3.** go up and across: *surmount a hill.* **4.** overcome: *surmount difficulties.* [< OF *surmonter* < *sur-* over (< L *super-*) + *monter* mount < L *mons* mountain] **—sur moun′ta ble,** *adj.*

sur rep ti tious (sėr′əp tish′əs), *adj.* **1.** stealthy; secret. **2.** secret and unauthorized. [< L *surrepticius*, ult. < *sub-* secretly + *rapere* snatch] **—sur′rep ti′tious ly,** *adv.*

su sur rus (sü sėr′əs), *n.* a soft, low whispering sound; whisper.

su ture (sü′chər), *n., v.*, **-tured, -tur ing.** **—***n.* **1.** seam formed in sewing up a wound. **2.** method of doing this. **3.** one of the stitches or fastenings used. **4.** a sewing together or a joining as if by sewing. **5.** line where two bones, especially of the skull, join. **6.** line between adjoining parts in a plant or animal such as that along which clamshells join or pea pods split. **—***v.* unite by suture or as if by a suture.

switch (swich), *n.* **1.** a slender stick used in whipping. **2.** a stroke; lash: *The big dog knocked a vase off the table with a switch of his tail.* **3.** bunch of long hair worn by a woman in

addition to her own hair. **4.** device for changing the direction of something or for making or breaking a connection. A railroad switch shifts a train from one track to another. An electric switch turns the current off or on. **5.** a turn; change; shift: *a switch of votes to another candidate.* **—***v.* **1.** whip; strike: *He switched the boys with a birch stick.* **2.** move or swing like a switch: *The horse switched his tail to drive off the flies.* **3.** change, turn, or shift by using a switch. [probably < var. of LG *swutsche*] **—switch′er,** *n.*

swoon (swün), *v.* **1.** faint: *She swoons at the sight of blood.* **2.** fade or die away gradually. **—***n.* a faint. [ūñʀ. < OE *geswōgen* in a swoon]

sym pho ny (sim′fə nē), *n., pl.* **-nies. 1.** an elaborate musical composition for an orchestra. It usually has three or more movements in different rhythms but related keys. **2.** harmony of sounds. **3.** harmony of colors: *In autumn the woods are a symphony in red, brown, and yellow.* [< L < Gk. *symphonia* harmony, concert, band < *syn-* together + *phone* voice, sound]

tact (takt), *n.* ability to say and do the right things; skill in dealing with people or handling difficult situations. [< L *tactus* sense of feeling < *tangere* touch]

tact ful (takt′fəl), *adj.* **1.** having tact. **2.** showing tact. **—tact′ful ly,** *adv.* **—tact′ful ness,** *n.*

Tah quitz *tä′kēts′)

tai lor (tā′lər), *n.* man whose business is making or repairing clothes. **—***v.* **1.** make by tailor's work: *The suit was well tailored.* **2.** fit or furnish with clothes made by a tailor. [< AF *taillour*, ult. < LL *taliare* cut < L *talea* rod, cutting]

tart[1] (tärt), *adj.* **1.** having a sharp taste; sour. **2.** sharp: *a tart reply.* [OE *teart*] **—tart′ly,** *adv.* **—tart′ness,** *n.*

tart[2] (tärt), *n.* pastry filled with cooked fruit, jam, etc. In the United States, a tart is small and the fruit shows; in England, any fruit pie is a tart.

tat ter (tat′ər), *n.* **1.** a torn piece; rag: *After the storm the flag hung in tatters upon the mast.* **2. tatters,** *pl.* torn or ragged clothing. **—***v.* tear or wear to pieces; make ragged. [ult. < Scand. var. of *tötturr* rag]

taunt (tônt, tänt), *v.* **1.** jeer at; mock; reproach. **2.** get or drive by taunts: *They taunted him into taking the dare.* **—***n.* a bitter or insulting remark; mocking; jeering.
Syn. v. 1. deride, ridicule, gibe, flout.

taut (tôt), *adj.* **1.** tightly drawn; tense. **2.** in neat condition; tidy. **—taut′ly,** *adv.* **—taut′ness,** *n.*

tech ni cian (tek nish′ən), *n.* **1.** person experienced in the technicalities of a subject. **2.** person skilled in the technique of an art.

tel e cast (tel′ə kast′), *v.*, **-cast** or **-cast ed, -cast ing,** *n.* **—***v.* broadcast by television. **—***n.* a television program. [< *tele(vision)* + *(broad)-cast*] **—tel′e cast′er,** *n.*

tem po (tem′pō), *n., pl.* **-pos, -pi** (-pē). **1.** in music, the time or rate of movement; proper or characteristic speed of movement. **2.** rhythm; characteristic rhythm: *the fast tempo of modern life.* [< Ital. *tempo* time < L *tempus*]

ten dril (ten′drəl), *n.* **1.** a threadlike part of a climbing plant that attaches itself to something and helps support the plant. **2.** something similar: *tendrils of hair curling about a child's face.*

ten si ty (ten′sə tē), *n.* tense quality or state.

ten ta tive (ten′tə tiv), *adj.* done as a trial or experiment; experimental: *a tentative plan.* [< Med.L *tentativus* < L *tentare* try out, intensive of *tendere* stretch, aim; associated

---

< = from, derived from, taken from;   cf., compare;   dial., dialect;   dim., diminutive;   lang., language; pp., past participle;   ppr., present participle;   pt., past tense;   ult., ultimately;   var., variant;   ? = possibly.

in L with *temptare* feel out] **—ten′ta tive ly,** *adv.*
—ten′ta tive ness, *n.*

ten u ous (ten′yü əs), *adj.* 1. thin; slender. 2. not dense:
Air ten miles above the earth is very tenuous. 3. having slight
importance; not substantial. [< L *tenuis* thin] **—ten′u ous-**
ly, *adv.* **—ten′u ous ness,** *n.*

te qui la (tə kē′lə), *n.* 1. a Mexican century plant. 2. an
alcoholic liquor distilled from the juices of the stem of this
plant.

ter ma gant (tėr′mə gənt), *n.* a violent, quarreling, scolding woman. —*adj.* violent; quarreling; scolding. [ult. < OF
Tervagan, fictitious Moslem deity]

teth er (teᴛʜ′ər), *n.* 1. rope or chain for fastening an animal
so that it can graze only within certain limits. 2. **at the end**
of one's tether, at the end of one's resources or endurance.
—*v.* fasten with a tether.

The o phá nis (thā ō fä′nēs)
Tho do ros (thō ᴛʜô′rōs)

thresh old (thresh′ōld, thresh′hōld), *n.* 1. piece of wood
or stone under a door. 2. doorway. 3. point of entering;
beginning point: *The scientist was on the threshold of an*
important discovery. [OE thresc(w)old]

tim or ous (tim′ər əs), *adj.* easily frightened; timid.
[< Med.L *timorosus* < L *timor* fear] **—tim′or ous ly,** *adv.*
—tim′or ous ness, *n.*

tink er (ting′kər), *n.* 1. man who mends pots, pans, etc.
2. unskilled or clumsy work; activity that is rather useless.
3. person who does such work. —*v.* 1. mend; patch.
2. work or repair in an unskilled or clumsy way. 3. work or
keep busy in a rather useless way. [? ult. < *tin*]

tit il late (tit′l āt), *v.,* **-lat ed, -lat ing.** 1. excite pleasantly;
stimulate agreeably. 2. tickle.

tor pid (tôr′pid), *adj.* 1. dull; inactive; sluggish. 2. not
moving or feeling. Animals that hibernate become torpid in
winter. 3. numb. [< L *torpidus* < *torpere* be numb]
—tor′pid ly, *adv.* **—tor′pid ness,** *n.*
Syn. 1. lethargic, apathetic.

tor por (tôr′pər), *n.* torpid condition.

tote (tōt), *v.,* **tot ed, tot ing.** *U.S. Informal.* carry.

tran quil (trang′kwəl), *adj.,* **-quil er, -quil est** or *esp.*
Brit. **-quil ler, -quil lest.** calm; peaceful; quiet.
—tran′quil ly, *adv.*
Syn. placid, serene, undistrubed.

trans fix (tran sfiks′), *v.* 1. pierce through: *The hunter*
transfixed the lion with a spear. 2. fasten by piercing through
with something pointed. 3. make motionless (with amazement, terror, etc.). [< L *transfixus,* pp. of *transfigere* <
trans- through + *figere* fix]

tran sient (tran′shənt), *adj.* 1. passing soon; fleeting; not
lasting. 2. passing through and not staying long: *a transient*
guest in a hotel. —*n.* visitor or boarder who stays for a short
time. [< L *transiens, -entis,* ppr. of *transire* pass through <
trans- through + *ire* go] **—tran′sient ly,** *adv.*
Syn. *adj.* 1. momentary.

trans lu cent (tran slü′snt, tranz lü′snt), *adj.* letting light
through without being transparent: *Frosted glass is trans-*
lucent. [< L *translucens, -entis,* ppr. of *translucere* < *trans-*
through + *lucere* shine] **—trans lu-cent ly,** *adv.*

trans mute (tran smyüt′, tranz myüt′), *v.,* **-mut ed,**
-mut ing. change from one nature, substance, or form into
another: *We can transmute water power into electrical*
power. [< L *transmutare* < *trans-* thoroughly + *mutare*
change] **—trans mut′er,** *n.*

treach er ous (trech′ər əs), *adj.* 1. not to be trusted; not

faithful; disloyal: *The treacherous soldier carried reports to*
the enemy. 2. having a false appearance of strength, security, etc.; not reliable; deceiving: *Thin ice is treacherous.*
—treach′er ous ly, *adv.* **—treach′er ous ness,** *n.*

trel lis (trel′is), *n.* frame of light strips
of wood or metal crossing one another
with open spaces in between; lattice,
especially one supporting growing vines.
—*v.* 1. furnish with a trellis. 2. support
on a trellis. 3. cross as in a trellis. [< OF
trelis, ult. < L *trilix* tripletwilled < *tri-*
three + *licium* thread]

Trellis

trem u lous (trem′yə ləs), *adj.*
1. trembling; quivering. 2. timid; fearful.

trib u la tion (trib′yə lā′shən), *n.*
great trouble; severe trial; affliction.

trice¹ (trīs), *v.,* **triced, tric ing.** haul up and fasten with a
rope: *trice up a sail.* [< MDutch *trisen* hoist < *trise* pulley]

trice² (trīs), *n.* a very short time; moment; instant. [ab-
stracted from phrase *at a trice* at a pull. Cf. *trice¹*]

troupe (trüp), *n.* troop; band; company; especially, a group
of actors, singers, or acrobats. [Am.E; < F]

truc u lent (truk′yə lənt, trü′kyə lənt), *adj.* savagely
threatening or bullying; belligerent. **—truc′u lent ly,** *adv.*

trudge (truj), *v.,* **trudged, trudg ing,** *n.* —*v.* 1. walk.
2. walk wearily or with effort. —*n.* a hard or weary walk: *It*
was a long trudge up the hill. [origin uncertain]

tweed (twēd), *n.* 1. a woolen cloth with a rough surface,
usually woven of yarns of two or more colors. 2. suit, etc.,
made of this cloth. 3. **tweeds,** *pl.* clothes made of tweed.
[said to be misreading of *tweel,* var. of *twill*]

tyr an ny (tir′ə nē), *n.* cruel or unjust use of power.

un as sum ing (un′ə sü′ming), *adj.* modest; not putting
on airs. **—un′as sum′ing ly,** *adv.* **—un′as sum′ing-**
ness, *n.*

un bear a ble (un ber′ə bəl), *adj.* that cannot be endured. **—un bear′a ble ness,** *n.* **—un bear′a bly,** *adv.*
Syn. intolerable, insufferable.

un con cern ed ly (un′kən sėr′nid lē), *adv.* in an unconcerned manner; without concern or anxiety.

un con ven tion al (un′kən ven′shə nəl), *adj.* not
bound by or conforming to convention, rule, or precedent;
free from conventionality. **—un′con ven′tion al ly,** *adv.*

un couth (un küth′), *adj.* 1. awkward; clumsy; crude:
uncouth manners. 2. unusual and unpleasant; strange: *The*
poor idiot made uncouth noises.

un de cid ed (un′di sī′did), *adj.* 1. not decided or settled.
2. not having one's mind made up. **—un′de cid′ed ly,** *adv.*
—un′de cid′ed ness, *n.*
Syn. 2. irresolute, wavering.

un der mine (un′dər min′, un′dər mīn′), *v.,* **-mined,**
-min ing. 1. make a passage or hole under; dig under: *The*
soldiers undermined the wall. 2. wear away the foundations
of: *The cliff was undermined by the waves.* 3. weaken by
secret or unfair means: *undermine a man's reputation by*
scandal. 4. weaken or destroy gradually: *Many severe colds*
had undermined her health. **—un′der min′er,** *n.*

un du late (*v.* un′jə lāt, un′dyə lāt; *adj.* un′jə lit, un′jə lāt,
un′dyə lit, un′dyə lāt), *v.,* **-lat ed, -lat ing,** *adj.* —*v.*
1. move in waves: *undulating water.* 2. have a wavy form or
surface: *undulating hair.* 3. cause to move in waves. 4. give
a wavy form or surface to. —*adj.* wavy.

---

hat, āge, fär;   let, bē, tėrm;   it, īce;   hot, gō, ôrder;   oil, out;   cup, pút, rüle;   ch, child;   ng, long;
th, thin;   ᴛʜ, then;   zh, measure;   ə represents *a* in about, *e* in taken, *i* in pencil, *o* in lemon, *u* in circus.

un du ly (un dü′lē, un dyü′lē), *adv.* 1. improperly. 2. excessively.

un earth (un ėrth′), *v.* dig up.

un en ter pris ing (un en′tər prīz ing), *adj.* not enterprising; not bold or adventuresome.

un err ing (un ėr′ing, un er′ing), *adj.* making no mistakes; exactly right. —**un err′ing ly,** *adv.* —**un err′ing ness,** *n.* Syn. infallible, sure.

un fre quent ed (un′frē kwent′tid), *adj.* not frequented; seldom visited; rarely used.

un gain ly (un gān′lē), *adj.* awkward; clumsy. [ME *ungaynly* < *un-* not + *gaynly* agile] —**un gain′li ness,** *n.* Syn. uncouth, ungraceful.

un hal lowed (un hal′ōd), *adj.* 1. not made holy; not sacred. 2. wicked.

u nique (yü nēk′), *adj.* 1. having no like or equal; being the only one of its kind. 2. *Informal.* rare; unusual. —**u nique′ly,** *adv.* —**u nique′ness,** *n.* Syn. 1. unmatched, sole.

un kempt (un kempt′), *adj.* 1. not combed. 2. neglected; untidy.

un nerve (un nėrv′), *v.,* **-nerved, -nerv ing.** deprive of nerve, firmness, or self-control.

un ob jec tion a ble (un′əb jek′shə nə bəl), *adj.* not objectionable; acceptable.

un prec e dent ed (un pres′ə den′tid), *adj.* having no precedent; never done before; never known before. Syn. unexampled, new.

un re spon sive (un′ri spon′siv), *adj.* not responsive or inclined to respond; not reacting.

un stead y (un sted′ē), *adj.* 1. not steady; shaky. 2. likely to change; not reliable. 3. not regular in habits. —**un stead′i ly,** *adv.* —**un stead′i ness,** *n.*

un world ly (un wėrld′lē), *adj.* not caring much for the things of this world, such as money, pleasure, and power. —**un world′li ness,** *n.*

up surge (up′sėrj′), *v.,* **-surged, -surg ing.** *n.* —*v.* to surge up; rise; increase. —*n.* a rapid increase; a sudden rise.

ur chin (ėr′chən), *n.* 1. a small boy. 2. a mischievous boy. 3. a poor, ragged child. 4. *Archaic* or *Dialect.* hedgehog. 5. sea urchin. 6. *Archaic.* elf. [< OF *irechon* < L *ericius* hedgehog < *er* hedgehog]

ur gent (ėr′jənt), *adj.* 1. demanding immediate action or attention; pressing; important. 2. insistent. —**ur′gent ly,** *adv.* Syn. 1. imperative, necessary.

vague (vāg), *adj.,* **va guer, va guest.** not definite; not clear; not distinct: *In a fog everything looks vague. Nobody can be sure just what a vague statement means.* [< OF < L *vagus* wandering] —**vague–ly,** *adv.* —**vague–ness,** *n.* Syn. ambiguous, hazy.

val iant (val′yənt), *adj.* brave; courageous: *a valiant soldier, a valiant deed.* [< OF *vaillant,* ppr. of *valoir* be strong < L *valere*] —**val′iant ly,** *adv.* —**val′iant ness,** *n.*

va lid i ty (və lid′ə tē), *n., pl.* **-ties.** 1. truth; soundness: *the validity of an argument.* 2. legal soundness or force; being legally binding. 3. effectiveness.

Va ska (vä′skə)

ve he ment (vē′ə mənt), *adj.* 1. having or showing strong feeling; caused by strong feeling; eager; passionate. 2. forceful; violent. [< L *vehemens, -entis* < *vehere* carry] —**ve′he ment ly,** *adv.* Syn. 1. ardent, fervid.

vent (vent), *n.* 1. hole; opening, especially one serving as an outlet. 2. outlet; way out: *His great energy found vent in hard work.* 3. expression: *She gave vent to her grief in tears.* —*v.* 1. let out; express freely: *He vented his anger on the dog.* 2. make a vent in. [partly < MF *vent* wind < L *ventus;* partly < MF *event* vent, blowhole, ult. < L *ex-* out + *ventus* wind]

ve ran da or **ve ran dah** (və ran′də), *n.* a large porch along one or more sides of a house. [< Hindu. and other Indian langs. < Pg. *varanda* railing]

ver ba tim (vər bā′tim), *adv., adj.* word for word; in exactly the same words: *His speech was printed verbatim in the newspaper.*

ver i ly (ver′ə lē), *adv.* in truth; truly; really.

versed (vėrst), *adj.* experienced; practiced; skilled: *A doctor should be well versed in medical theory.* Syn. proficient, acquainted.

ver ti go (vėr′tə gō), *n., pl.* **ver ti goes, ver tig i nes** (vər tij′ə nēz). dizziness; giddiness. [< L *vertigo* < *vertere* turn]

ves tige (ves′tij), *n.* 1. a slight remnant; trace: *Ghost stories are vestiges of a former widespread belief in ghosts.* 2. in biology, a part, organ, etc., that is no longer fully developed or useful. 3. *Rare.* footprint. [< F < L *vestigium* footprint]

vex (veks), *v.* 1. anger by trifles; annoy; provoke. 2. disturb; trouble. [< L *vexare*]

vex a tion (vek sā′shən), *n.* 1. a vexing; being vexed: *His face showed his vexation.* 2. thing that vexes. Syn. 1. irritation, exasperation, annoyance, chagrin.

vie (vī), *v.,* **vied, vy ing.** strive for superiority; contend in rivalry; compete. [< F *envier* challenge < L *invitare* invite]

vig il (vij′əl), *n.* 1. a staying awake for some purpose; a watching; watch: *All night the mother kept vigil over the sick child.* 2. a night spent in prayer. 3. the day and night before a solemn church festival. 4. Often, **vigils,** *pl.* devotions, prayers, services, etc., on the night before a religious festival. [< OF < L *vigilia* < *vigil* watchful]

vig or ous (vig′ər əs), *adj.* full of vigor; strong and active; energetic; forceful: *wage a vigorous war against disease.* —**vig′or ous ly,** *adv.*

vim (vim), *n.* force; energy; vigor. [Am.E; < L *vim,* accus. of *vis* force]

vi ra go (və rā′gō, və rä′gō), *n., pl.* **-goes** or **-gos.** a violent, bad-tempered, or scolding woman.

vi ril i ty (və ril′ə tē), *n., pl.* **-ties.** 1. manly strength; masculine vigor. 2. manhood. 3. vigor; forcefulness.

vir tu o so (vėr′chü ō′sō), *n., pl.* **-sos, -si** (-sē). 1. person skilled in the methods of an art, especially in playing a musical instrument. 2. person who has a cultivated appreciation of artistic excellence. 3. student or collector of objects of art, curios, antiquities, etc. [< Ital. *virtuoso* learned]

vis age (viz′ij), *n.* 1. face. 2. appearance. [< OF *visage* < *vis* face < L *visus* a look < *videre* see]

vol ley (vol′ē), *n., pl.* **-leys,** *v.,* **-leyed, -ley ing.** —*n.* 1. shower of stones, bullets, arrows, words, oaths, etc. 2. the discharge of a number of guns at once. 3. the hitting or return of a tennis ball, etc., before it touches the ground. —*v.* 1. discharge or be discharged in a volley: *Cannon volleyed on all sides.* 2. hit or return (a tennis ball, etc.) before it touches the ground. [< F *volée* flight < *voler* fly < L *volare*]

vo lu mi nous (və lü′mə nəs), *adj.* of great size; very bulky; large.

< = from, derived from, taken from;   cf., compare;   dial., dialect;   dim., diminutive;   lang., language; pp., past participle;   ppr., present participle;   pt., past tense;   ult., ultimately;   var., variant;   ? = possibly.

vo lup tu ous (və lup′chü əs), *adj.* 1. caring much for the pleasures of the senses. 2. giving pleasure to the senses: *voluptuous music or beauty.* [< L *voluptuosus* < *voluptas* pleasure < *volup (e)*, neut., agreeable] —**vo lup′tu ous ly,** *adv.* —**vo lup′tu ous ness,** *n.*

Vy borg ska ya (vi′bərk skə yə)

waft (waft), *v.* 1. carry over water or through air: *The waves wafted the boat to shore.* 2. float. —*n.* 1. a breath or puff of air, wind, etc. 2. a waving movement. [< earlier *wafter* convoy ship < Dutch and LG *wachter* guard]

wa ger (wā′jər), *n.* 1. something staked on an uncertain event. 2. act of betting; bet. —*v.* bet; gamble. [< AF *wageure* < OF *wage* pledge < Gmc.]

wail (wāl), *v.* 1. cry loud and long because of grief or pain. 2.**make a mournful sound:** *The wind wailed around the old house.* 3. lament; mourn. —*n.* 1. a long cry of grief or pain. 2. a sound like such a cry. [< Scand. *vǽla*] —**wail′er,** *n.*

waist coat (wāst′kōt′, wes′kət), *n. Esp. Brit.* a man's vest.

wam pum (wom′pəm, wôm′pəm), *n.* 1. beads made from shells, formerly used by American Indians as money and ornament. 2. *Slang.* money. [Am.E; < Algonquian]

war (wôr), *n., v.,* **warred, war ring,** *adj.* —*n.* 1. a fight carried on by armed force between nations or parts of a nation. 2. fighting; strife; conflict: *Doctors carry on war against disease.* 3. the occupation or art of fighting with weapons; military science: *Soldiers are trained for war.* 4. **at war,** taking part in a war. 5. **go to war, a.** start a war. **b.** go as a soldier. —*v.* fight; make war. —*adj.* used in war; having to do with war; caused by war. [< OF *werre,* var. of *guerre* < Gmc.*fl* —**war′less,** *adj.*

Syn. *n.* 1. warfare, hostilities.

ward room (wôrd′rüm′, wôrd′rum′), *n.* the living and eating quarters for all the commissioned officers on a warship except the commanding officer.

ware[1] (wer, war), *n.* 1. Usually, **wares,** *pl.* a manufactured thing; article for sale: *The peddler sold his wares cheap.* 2. kind of manufactured thing or article for sale; goods (now chiefly in compounds): *silverware and tinware.* 3. pottery: *Delft is a blue-and-white ware.* [OE *waru*]

ware[2] (wer, war), *adj., v.,* **wared, war ing.** —*adj.* Archaic. aware. —*v.* Arachaic. look out (for); beware (of). [OE *wær*]

war horse, 1. horse used in war. 2. *Informal.* person who has taken part in many battles, struggles, etc. 3. a much overused musical composition, play, etc.

warp (wôrp), *v.* 1. bend or twist out of shape: *This floor has warped so that it is not level.* 2. bend: *The aviator warped a wing tip to regain balance.* 3. mislead; pervert: *Prejudice warps our judgment.* 4. move (a ship, etc.) by ropes fastened to something fixed. —*n.* 1. a bend or twist; distortion. 2. rope used in moving a ship. 3. the threads running lengthwise in a fabric. The warp is crossed by the woof. [OE *weorpan* throw]

war y (wer′ē, war′ē), *adj.,* **war i er, war i est.** 1. on one's guard against danger, deception, etc.: *a wary fox.* 2. cautious; careful: *He gave wary answers to all of the stranger's questions.* 3. **wary of,** cautious about; careful about. [< *ware*[2]]

Syn. 1. alert, guarded, vigilant, watchful. 2. circumspect, prudent.

wa ter buck (wô′tər buk′, wot′ər buk′), *n.* any of vari-

ous African antelopes that frequent rivers, marshes, etc. [< Dutch *waterbok*]

way ward (wā′wərd), *adj.* 1. turning from the right way; disobedient; willful. 2. irregular; unsteady.

weal[1] (wēl), *n. Archaic.* well-being; prosperity; happiness: *Good citizens act for the public weal.* [OE *wela*]

weal[2] (wēl), *n.* streak or ridge on the skin made by a stick or whip; welt.

Waterbuck (about 3 ft. high at the shoulder)

weath er (weᴛʜ′ər), *n.* 1. condition of the atmosphere with respect to temperature, moisture, cloudiness, etc.: *hot weather, windy weather.* 2. windy or stormy weather. 3. **keep one's weather eye open,** be on the lookout for possible danger or trouble. 4. **under the weather,** *Informal.* sick; ailing. —*v.* 1. expose to the weather; dry; season; wear by sun, rain, frost, etc.; discolor thus: *Wood turns gray if weathered for a long time.* 2. become discolored or worn by air, rain, sun, frost, etc. 3. go or come through safely: *The ship weathered the storm.* 4. sail to the windward of: *The ship weathered the cape.* 5. make (boards, tiles, etc.) slope so as to shed water. —*adj.* toward the wind; windward; of the side exposed to the wind: *It was very cold on the weather side of the ship.* [OE *weder*]

well-ground ed (wel′groun′did), *adj.* 1. based on good reasons. 2. thoroughly instructed in the fundamental principles of a subject.

wend (wend), *v.* **wend ed** or (*Archaic*) **went, wend ing.** 1. direct (one's way): *We wended our way home.* 2. go.

were wolf (wir′wulf′, wėr′wulf′), *n., pl.* **-wolves** (wülvz′). in folklore, a person changed into a wolf; person who can change himself into a wolf, while retaining human intelligence. [OE *werwulf* < *wer* man < *wulf* wolf]

whee dle (hwē′dl), *v.,* **-dled, -dling.** 1. persuade by flattery, smooth words, caresses, etc.; coax: *The children wheedled their mother into letting them go to the picnic.* 2. get by wheedling: *They finally wheedled the secret out of him.* [OE *wǣdlian* beg] —**whee′dler,** *n.* —**whee′dling ly,** *adv.*

Syn. 1. cajole, blandish.

whet (hwet), *v.,* **whet ted, whet ting,** *n.* —*v.* 1. sharpen by rubbing: *whet a knife.* 2. make keen or eager; stimulate: *The smell of food whetted my appetite.* —*n.* 1. act of whetting. 2. something that whets. 3. appetizer.

whim si cal (hwim′zə kəl), *adj.* 1. having many odd notions or fancies; fanciful; odd. 2. full of whims. —**whim′si cal ly,** *adv.*

Syn. 1. capricious, notional.

whit (hwit), *n.* a very small bit: *The sick man is not a whit better.* [var. of OE *wiht* thing, wight]

wick er (wik′ər), *n.* 1. a slender, easily bent branch or twig. 2. twigs or branches woven together. Wicker is used in making baskets and furniture. —*adj.* 1. made of wicker. 2. covered with wicker.

wide-a wake (wīd′ə wāk′), *adj.* 1. with the eyes wide open; fully awake. 2. alert; keen; knowing. —*n.* an obsolete kind of soft felt hat with a broad brim.

wil ful (wil′fəl), *adj.* willful. —**wil′ful ness,** *n.*

wile (wīl), *n., v.,* **wiled, wil ing.** —*n.* 1. a trick to deceive; cunning way: *The serpent by his wiles persuaded Eve to eat the apple.* 2. subtle trickery; slyness; craftiness. —*v.*

hat, āge, fär; let, bē, tėrm; it, īce; hot, gō, ôrder; oil, out; cup, pùt, rüle; ch, child; ng, long; th, thin; ᴛʜ, then; zh, measure; ə represents *a* in about, *e* in taken, *i* in pencil, *o* in lemon, *u* in circus.

1. coax; lure; entice: *The sunshine wiled me from work.* **2. wile away,** while away; pass easily or pleasantly. [OE *wīgle* magic]

Syn. *n.* **1.** artifice, stratagem, ruse.

will ful (wil′fəl), *adj.* **1.** wanting or taking one's own way; stubborn. **2.** done on purpose; intended: *willful murder, willful waste.* Also, **wilful.** **—will′ful ness,** *n.*

Syn. **1.** obstinate, headstrong, perverse. **2.** deliberate, intentional.

wince (wins), *v.,* **winced, winc ing,** *n.* **—***v.* draw back suddenly; flinch slightly: *The boy winced at the sight of the dentist's drill.* **—***n.* act of wincing.

Syn. *v.* shrink, recoil.

win now (win′ō), *v.* **1.** blow off the chaff from (grain); drive or blow away (chaff). **2.** blow chaff from grain. **3.** sort out; separate; sift: *winnow truth from falsehood.* **4.** fan (with wings); flap (wings). [OE *windwian* < *wind* wind[1]]

wit (wit), *n.* **1.** the power to perceive quickly and express cleverly ideas that are unusual, striking, and amusing. **2.** person with such power. **3.** understanding; mind; sense: *People with quick wits learn easily. The child was out of his wits with fright. That poor man hasn't wit enough to earn a living.* **4. at one's wit's end,** not knowing what to do or say. **5. have** or **keep one's wits about one,** be alert. [OE *witt*]

Syn. **1. Wit, humor** mean power to see and express what is amusing or causes laughter. **Wit** means a mental sharpness and quickness in perceiving what is striking, unusual, inconsistent, or out of keeping and in expressing it in cleverly surprising and amusing sayings: *Bernard Shaw was famous for his wit.* **Humor** means a power to see and show with warm sympathy and kindness the things in life and human nature that are funny or absurdly out of keeping: *Her sense of humor eased her trouble.* **3.** intelligence.

with ers (wiᴛʜ′ərz), *n. pl.* the highest part of a horse's or other animal's back, behind the neck.

wolf (wŭlf), *n., pl.* **wolves,** *v.* **—***n.* **1.** either of two species of carnivorous wild mammals of the dog family, with a long muzzle, high, pointed ears, and a bushy tail. Wolves usually hunt in packs and are sometimes destructive to livestock. **2.** any of several similar mammals. **3.** a cruel, greedy person. **—***v.t.* eat greedily: *The starving man wolfed down the food.* [OE *wulf*] **—wolf′like′,** *adj.*

won der ment (wun′dər mənt), *n.* wonder; surprise.

won drous (wun′drəs), *adj.* wonderful. **—***adv.* wonderfully. **—won′drous ly,** *adv.* **—won′drous ness,** *n.*

wraith (rāth), *n.* **1.** ghost of a person seen before or soon after his death. **2.** specter; ghost.

wrap per (rap′ər), *n.* **1.** person or thing that wraps. **2.** thing in which something is wrapped; covering or cover: *Some magazines are mailed in paper wrappers.* **3.** a woman's long, loose garment to wear in the house. **4.** leaf or leaves forming the outside layer of tobacco in a cigar.

wrath (rath), *n.* very great anger; rage.

wrath ful (rath′fəl, räth′fəl), *adj.* feeling or showing wrath. **—wrath′ful ly,** *adv.* **—wrath′ful ness,** *n.*

wrench (rench), *n.* **1.** a violent twist or twisting pull: *The knob broke off when he gave it a sudden wrench.* **2.** injury caused by twisting. **3.** grief; pain: *It was a wrench to leave the old home.* **4.** distortion of the original or proper meaning, interpretation, etc. **5.** tool for turning nuts, bolts, etc.**—***v.t.* **1.** twist or pull violently: *The policeman wrenched the gun out of the man's hand.* **2.** injure by twisting: *She wrenched her back in falling from the horse.*

wretch ed (rech′id), *adj.* **1.** very unfortunate or unhappy. **2.** very unsatisfactory; miserable: *a wretched hut.* **3.** very bad: *a wretched traitor.* **—wretch′ed ly,** *adv.* **—wretch′ed ness,** *n.*

writhe (rīᴛʜ), *v.,* **writhed, writhed** or (*Obs. except Poetic*) **with en** (riᴛʜ′ən), **with ing.** **1.** twist and turn; twist: *The snake writhed along the branch. The wounded man writhed in agony.* **2.** suffer mentally; be very uncomfortable.

yon der (yon′dər), *adv.* within sight, but not near; over there: *Look yonder.* **—***adj.* **1.** situated over there; being within sight, but not near: *He lives in yonder cottage.* **2.** farther; more distant; other: *There is snow on the yonder side of the mountains.* [ME]

yore (yôr, yōr), *adv.* **1. of yore,** of long ago; formerly; in the past. **2.** *Obsolete.* long ago; years ago. [OE *geāra,* gen. pl. of *gēar* year]

zeal (zēl), *n.* eager desire; earnest enthusiasm.

zest (zest), *n.* **1.** keen enjoyment; relish: *The hungry man ate with zest.* **2.** a pleasant or exciting quality, flavor, etc.: *Wit gives zest to conversation.* **—***v.* give a zest to.

< = from, derived from, taken from;   cf., compare;   dial., dialect;   dim., diminutive;   lang., language; pp., past participle;   ppr., present participle;   pt., past tense;   ult., ultimately;   var., variant;   ? = possibly.

INDEX OF LITERARY TYPES

BIOGRAPHY AND AUTOBIOGRAPHY
from *Harriet Tubman*, 129; *Hunger*, 275;
from *The Boy Shelley*, 514

DRAMA
The Pharmacist's Mate, 138; *The Monsters Are Due on Maple Street*, 284; *The Ugly Duckling*, 336; *Fortunata Writes a Letter*, 464

ESSAYS
Emergency at Sea, 164; *The Campers at Kitty Hawk*, 180; *A Loud Sneer for Our Feathered Friends*, 265; *A Ride Through Spain*, 487

FOLK TALES
How the Animals Got Their Color, 411; *How the Animals Got Their Tails*, 411; *Why There Are Cracks in Tortoise's Shell*, 412; *Why the Woodpecker Has a Long Beak*, 414; *The Dog, the Snake, and the Cure of Headache*, 415; *Why the Stork Has No Tail*, 416; *The Leftover Eye*, 419; *The Two Strangers*, 420; *A Tug-of-War*, 421; *The Separation of God from Man*, 425; *The Flying Ship*, 431; *Fish in the Forest*, 438; *The Dog's Wisdom*, 440

INTERVIEWS
Questions Put to a Poet (Richard Eberhart), 55; *Questions Put to a Playwright (Rod Serling)*, 298

MYTHS
The Storytelling Stone, 388; *The Blackfoot Genesis*, 394; *How the Lame Boy Brought Fire from Heaven*, 400; *How Raven Helped the Ancient People*, 402; *Man Chooses Death*, 403; *The Origin of Death*, 403; *Why the Sun and the Moon Live in the Sky*, 404; *The Man Who Acted As the Sun*, 405

NOVEL EXCERPT
The Dubbing of General Garbage, 4

POETRY
Speed Adjustments, 16; *Death by Drowning*, 54; *Old Age Sticks*, 68; *Speaking: The Hero*, 106; *The Companion*, 116; *Advice to a Knight*, 178; *Simultaneously*, 190; *The Demon of the Gibbet*, 192; *Rain*, 194; *One A.M.*, 195; *Apparently With No Surprise*, 196; *The Pasture*, 197; *Good-by and Keep Cold*, 198; *Of Robert Frost*, 199; *The Circus; Or One View of It*, 200; *The Contraption*, 203; *Crystal Moment*, 205; *I'm Nobody*, 241; *The Boy Who Laughed at Santa Claus*, 271; *The Skunk*, 274; *Macavity: The Mystery Cat*, 312; *Jabberwocky*, 320; *Metropolitan Nightmare*, 358; *The Builders*, 364; *The Fox and the Grapes*, 365; *Requiem for a Modern Croesus*, 366; *To a Dead Goldfish*, 367; *Artifact*, 368; *Visits*, 371; *Time Out*, 372; *Who Knows If the Moon's*, 374; *At the Aquarium*, 376; *Thoughts in a Zoo*, 377; *Street Window*, 378; *Primer Lesson*, 379; *The Forecast*, 380; *Held Back*, 381; *Mama Is a Sunrise*, 452; *On Hearing French Children Speak French*, 463; *The Battle of Blenheim*, 476; *The River Merchant's Wife: A Letter*, 492; *Caribbean*, 524; *Hawk*, 526; *Two Blind Mice*, 532; *Fable*, 536; from *To a Small Boy Standing on My Shoes While I Am Wearing Them*, 537

SHORT STORIES
Thanksgiving Hunter, 18; *Strawberry Ice Cream Soda*, 24; *Beauty Is Truth*, 34; *The Lesson*, 42; *The Pheasant Hunter*, 56; *The Gift*, 70; *Swinger*, 96; *The Rescue*, 108; *The Two Hoaxers*, 119; *A Time of Greatness*, 165; *First Principal*, 208; *The New Kid*, 216; *Nancy*, 228; *Win or Lose*, 242; *Sled*, 249; *The Baroque Marble*, 256; *Rikki-tikki-tavi*, 299; *The Storyteller*, 314; *Rip Van Winkle*, 322; *Virtuoso*, 352; *My Father and the Hippopotamus*, 444; *The Jar*, 454; *The Graveyard*, 478; *Misery*, 494; *The Old Demon*, 500

INDEX OF AUTHORS AND TITLES

ABRAMS, LAURIE; *Held Back*, 381; *Hawk*, 526

ADAMS, THOMAS, 255; *Sled*, 249

Advice to a Knight, 178

Apparently With No Surprise, 196

APSTEIN, THEODORE, 475, *Fortunata Writes a Letter*, 464

Artifact, 368

At the Aquarium, 376

Baroque Marble, The, 256

Battle of Blenheim, The, 476

Beauty Is Truth, 34

BENÉT, LAURA; from *The Boy Shelley*, 514

BENÉT, STEPHEN VINCENT, 360; *Metropolitan Nightmare*, 358

Blackfoot Genesis, The 394

BOLES, PAUL DARCY, 105; *Swinger*, 96

Boy Shelley, from *The*, 514

Boy Who Laughed at Santa Claus, The, 271

BROOKS, GWENDOLYN; *Of Robert Frost*, 199

BUCK, PEARL S., 509; *The Old Demon*, 500

Builders, The, 364

Campers at Kitty Hawk, The, 180

CAPOTE, TRUMAN, 491; *A Ride Through Spain*, 487

Caribbean, 524

CARROLL, LEWIS (Charles Lutwidge Dodgson), 321; *Jabberwocky*, 320

CHEKHOV, ANTON, 499; *Misery*, 494

CIARDI, JOHN, 17; *Speed Adjustments*, 16

Circus; Or One View of It, The, 200

COFFIN, ROBERT P. TRISTRAM, 274; *Crystal Moment*, 205; *The Skunk*, 274

Companion, The, 116

Contraption, The, 203

Crystal Moment, 205

CULLEN, COUNTEE, 377; *Thoughts in a Zoo*, 377

CUMMINGS, E. E., 69; *Old Age Sticks*, 68; *Who Knows If the Moon's*, 374

Death by Drowning, 54

DEHN, PAUL; *Two Blind Mice*, 532

Demon of the Gibbet, The, 192

DICKINSON, EMILY, 241; *Apparently With No Surprise*, 196; *I'm Nobody*, 241

DODGSON, CHARLES LUTWIDGE, 321; *Jabberwocky*, 320

Dog, The Snake, and the Cure of Headache, The, 415

Dog's Wisdom, The, 440

DOS PASSOS, JOHN, 186; *The Campers at Kitty Hawk*, 180

Dubbing of General Garbage, The, 4

EASTMAN, MAX, 376; *At the Aquarium*, 376

EBERHART, RICHARD; *Death by Drowning*, 54; *Questions Put to a Poet*, 55

EDMAN, IRWIN, 463; *On Hearing French Children Speak French*, 463

ELIOT, T. S., 313; *Macavity: The Mystery Cat*, 312

Emergency at Sea, 164

EMERSON, RALPH WALDO; *Fable*, 536

ENRIGHT, ELIZABETH, 240; *Nancy*, 228

Fable, 536

First Principal, 208

Fish in the Forest, 438

Flying Ship, The, 431

Forecast, The, 380

Fortunata Writes a Letter, 464

Fox and the Grapes, The, 365

FROST, ROBERT, 199; *The Pasture*, 197; *Good-by and Keep Cold*, 198

Gift, The, 70

GLANVILLE, BRIAN, 248; *Win or Lose*, 242

GOLDSTONE, HERBERT, 357; *Virtuoso*, 352

Good-by and Keep Cold, 198

Graveyard, The, 478

GUEST, ANNA; *Beauty Is Truth*, 34

GUTHRIE, A.B., 217; *First Principal*, 208

HALL, DONALD; *Caribbean*, 524

HARDISON, O. B. JR.; *To a Dead Goldfish*, 367

Harriet Tubman, from, 129

Hawk, 526

HAY, SARA HENDERSON; *The Builders*, 364

Held Back, 381

HEYERT, MURRAY, 227; *The New Kid*, 216

How the Animals Got Their Color, 411

How the Animals Got Their Tails, 411

How the Lame Boy Brought Fire from Heaven, 400

How Raven Helped the Ancient People, 402

HUGO, LEON, 451; *My Father and the Hippopotamus*, 444

Hunger, 275

HUNT, EVELYN TOOLEY, 453; *Mama Is a Sunrise*, 452

IGNATOW, DAVID, 191; *Simultaneously*, 190

I'm Nobody, 241

In the Beginning . . ., Introduction to, 382

IRVING, WASHINGTON, 335; *Rip Van Winkle*, 322

Jabberwocky, 320

JAFEE, DAN; *The Forecast*, 380
Jar, The, 454
JOHNSON, DOROTHY, 177; *A Time of Greatness*, 165
JONES, T. H., 179; *Advice to a Knight*, 178
KEMP, LYSANDER, 486; *The Graveyard*, 478
KENNEDY, X.J., 195; *One A.M.*, 195
KIPLING, RUDYARD, 311; *Rikki-tikki-tavi*, 299
Leftover Eye, The, 419
Lesson, The, 42
LI T'AI-PO, 493; *The River Merchant's Wife: A Letter*, 492
Loud Sneer for Our Feathered Friends, A, 265
Macavity: The Mystery Cat, 312
Mama Is a Sunrise, 452
Man Chooses Death, 403
Man Who Acted As the Sun, The, 405
MCKENNEY, RUTH, 270; *A Loud Sneer for Our Feathered Friends*, 265
Metropolitan Nightmare, 358
MILNE, A. A., 351; *The Ugly Duckling*, 336
Misery, 494
Monsters Are Due on Maple Street, The, 284
MONTAGUE, JOHN, 373; *Time Out*, 372
MOORE, MARIANNE, 365; *The Fox and the Grapes*, 365
MUNRO, H. H., 319; *The Storyteller*, 314
My Father and the Hippopotamus, 444
MYRIVILIS, STRATIS, 128; *The Two Hoaxers*, 119
Nancy, 228
NASH, OGDEN, 273; *The Boy Who Laughed at Santa Claus*, 271; from *To a Small Boy Standing on My Shoes While I Am Wearing Them*, 537
New Kid, The, 216
O'BRIEN, FITZ-JAMES, 193; *The Demon of the Gibbet*, 192
Of Robert Frost, 199
Old Age Sticks, 68
Old Demon, The, 500
On Hearing French Children Speak French, 463
One A.M., 195
Origin of Death, The, 403
PARMENTER, ROSS, 194; *Rain*, 194
Pasture, The, 197
PETRY, ANN, 137; from *Harriet Tubman*, 129
Pharmacist's Mate, The, 138
Pheasant Hunter, The, 56
PIRANDELLO, LUIGI, 462; *The Jar*, 454

POLLAK, FELIX, 107; *Speaking: The Hero*, 106
POUND, EZRA (translator); *The River Merchant's Wife; A Letter*, 492
Primer Lesson, 379
PRITCHARD, SHEILA, 369; *Artifact*, 368
PROULX, E. A., 264; *The Baroque Marble*, 256
Questions Put to a Playwright, 298
Questions Put to a Poet, 55
Rain, 194
Requiem for a Modern Croesus, 366
Rescue, The, 108
Ride Through Spain, A, 487
Rip Van Winkle, 322
River Merchant's Wife: A Letter, The, 492
RUTSALA, VERN; *Visits*, 371
SAKI (H. H. Munro), 319; *The Storyteller*, 314
SANDBURG, CARL, 379; *Street Window*, 378; *Primer Lesson*, 379
SARETT, LEW, 366; *Requiem for a Modern Croesus*, 366
SAROYAN, WILLIAM, 67; *The Pheasant Hunter*, 56
SCHULBERG, BUDD, 163; *The Pharmacist's Mate*, 138
Separation of God from Man, The, 425
SERLING, ROD; *The Monsters Are Due on Maple Street*, 284; *Questions Put to a Playwright*, 298
SHAW, IRWIN, 33; *Strawberry Ice Cream Soda*, 24
Simultaneously, 190
Skunk, The, 274
Sled, 249
SOUTHEY, ROBERT, 477; *The Battle of Blenheim*, 476
Speaking: The Hero, 106
Speed Adjustments, 16
SPENCER, THEODORE, 202; *The Circus; Or One View of It*, 200
STEELE, MAX, 115; *The Rescue*, 108
STEINBECK, JOHN, 92; *The Gift*, 70
Storyteller, The, 314
Storytelling Stone, The, 388
Strawberry Ice Cream Soda, 24
Street Window, 378
STUART, JESSE, 23; *Thanksgiving Hunter*, 18
SWENSON, MAY, 204; *The Contraption*, 203
Swinger, 96
TAUBES, SUSAN, *Introduction to In the Beginning . . .*, 382

Thanksgiving Hunter, 18
Thoughts in a Zoo, 377
Time of Greatness, A, 165
Time Out, 372
To a Dead Goldfish, 367
To a Small Boy Standing on My Shoes While I Am Wearing Them, from, 537
Tug-of-War, A, 421
Two Blind Mice, 532
Two Hoaxers, The, 119
Two Strangers, The, 420
Ugly Duckling, The, 336
UNTERMEYER, LOUIS (translator); *A Meeting,* 190
Virtuoso, 352
Visits, 371

WELLER, GEORGE; *Emergency at Sea,* 164
WEST, JESSAMYN, 53; *The Lesson,* 42
Who Knows If the Moon's, 374
Why the Stork Has No Tail, 416
Why the Sun and the Moon Live in the Sky, 404
Why the Woodpecker Has a Long Beak, 414
Why There Are Cracks in Tortoise's Shell, 412
Win or Lose, 242
WRIGHT, RICHARD, 279; *Hunger,* 275
WOUK, HERMAN, 15; *The Dubbing of General Garbage,* 4
YEVTUSHENKO, YEVGENY, 118; *The Companion,* 116

INDEX OF SKILLS

Interpretative Skills

BIOGRAPHY. Handbook: 514. *Application:* 136, 186, 187.

CHARACTERIZATION I. METHODS OF. Handbook: 516. *Application:* 53, 163, 256, 264, 311, 475, 499, 509.

CHARACTERIZATION II. MOTIVATION. Handbook: 516. *Application:* 91, 105, 227, 256, 279, 509.

CONFLICT. Handbook: 518. *Application:* 23, 32, 41, 52, 67, 92, 162, 176, 240, 297.

CONTRAST. Handbook: 519. *Application:* 240, 367, 453, 491.

ENDINGS. Handbook: 520. *Application:* 177, 187, 217, 297, 475, 499.

FANTASY. Handbook: 521. *Application:* 297, 335, 351, 357, 360, 361.

FIGURATIVE LANGUAGE. Handbook: 522. *Application:* 366, 367, 376, 377, 379, 491.

IMAGERY. Handbook: 524. *Application:* 194, 202, 204, 205, 240, 274, 311, 335, 365, 373, 375, 376, 499.

INFERENCES. Handbook: 526. *Application:* 193, 247, 369, 486, 493.

IRONY I. IRONY OF SITUATION. Handbook: 528. *Application:* 462, 510.

IRONY II. IRONIC TONE. Handbook: 528. *Application:* 477.

NARRATOR. Handbook: 529. *Application:* 256, 264, 335, 451, 486.

PLOT. Handbook: 531. *Application:* 128, 162, 187.

SATIRE. Handbook: 532. *Application:* 319, 335, 351, 361.

SETTING. Handbook: 533. *Application:* 41, 67, 92, 105, 177, 191, 193, 195, 215, 264, 297, 335, 475, 486, 491, 499.

SUSPENSE. Handbook: 534. *Application:* 163, 187, 310, 475.

SYMBOL. Handbook: 534. *Application:* 247, 256, 264, 335.

THEME. Handbook: 536. *Application:* 215, 227, 240, 264, 297, 357, 360, 366, 367, 377, 486, 499.

TONE. Handbook: 537. *Application:* 270, 273, 274, 279, 311, 319, 335, 351, 361, 365, 367, 381, 404, 451, 477, 499.

Vocabulary Skills

AFFIXES. 41, 270, 509.

CONTEXT. 32, 91, 137, 215, 257, 335, 351, 462.

DICTIONARY. 53, 91, 177, 257, 335, 357, 462.

ETYMOLOGY. 128, 202, 270, 311, 357, 475, 499, 509.

HOMOGRAPHS. 215.

IDIOMS. 399, 418, 430.

SPECIFIC VERBS. 451.

STRUCTURE. 41, 91, 202, 270, 393, 462, 509.

SYNONYMS. 257, 351.